Chinese-Language Film

Chinese-Language Film

Historiography, Poetics, Politics

EDITED BY SHELDON H. LU
AND EMILIE YUEH-YU YEH

 University of Hawai'i Press
Honolulu

Library of Congress Cataloging-in-Publication Data

Chinese-language film : historiography, poetics, politics /
edited by Sheldon H. Lu and Emilie Yueh-yu Yeh.

   p. cm.

Filmography: p.

Includes bibliographical references and index.

ISBN 0-8248-2813-5 (alk. paper)

ISBN 0-8248-2869-0 (pbk. : alk. paper)

1. Motion pictures—China.   2. Motion pictures—Taiwan.
I. Lu, Sheldon H.   II. Yeh, Emilie Yueh-yu.

PN1993.5.C4C463 2005

791.43'0951—dc22   2004012413

Designed by April Leidig-Higgins

Printed by The Maple-Vail Book Manufacturing Group

Contents

Acknowledgments

We wish to express our gratitude to Gerald Duchovnay, editor of *Post Script: Essays in Film and the Humanities,* for helping us edit a special double issue on Chinese cinema in *Post Script*—vol. 20, nos. 2 and 3 (winter/spring and summer 2001)—and for granting us permission to reprint the early material. The journal provided in part the impetus for this collection. Portions and early versions of many essays in this anthology first appeared in that special issue of *Post Script*. These essays are written by the following authors: Mary Farquhar and Chris Berry, Zhang Zhen, Shuqin Cui, David Bordwell, Darrell Davis, Shiao-ying Shen, David Desser, Chu Yiu Wai, Emilie Yeh, and Sheldon Lu. The pieces have been later revised for inclusion in the anthology.

An early version of chapter 5, "Chinese Film Culture at the End of the Twentieth Century: The Case of *Not One Less* by Zhang Yimou," first appeared in the *Journal of Modern Literature in Chinese* 4.2 (January 2001): 125–144. We thank the journal for allowing us to reprint the essay here.

We thank Patricia Crosby, executive editor of the University of Hawai'i Press, for her warm support and graceful handling of the book project. We greatly appreciate the efficient and careful work of Cheri Dunn, managing editor, and Joseph Parsons, copy editor. The two readers of the University of Hawai'i Press made many helpful comments for revision, and we thank them for their suggestions and endorsement. Finally, we acknowledge the kind support from the David C. Lam Institute for East-West Studies at Hong Kong Baptist University.

Sheldon Lu, Davis, California
Emilie Yeh, Hong Kong

Note on Romanization

The book uses a combination of pinyin, Wade-Giles, and specific manners of romanization that have been used historically in regard to certain names in some regions. Although we try to adopt pinyin in most cases in order to create consistency and unity in this anthology, we sometimes keep the ways certain terms have been transliterated by convention, custom, or choice in Hong Kong, Taiwan, and the Chinese diaspora.

Chinese-Language Film

SHELDON H. LU AND

EMILIE YUEH-YU YEH

Introduction

Mapping the Field of Chinese-Language Cinema

Language and Film

This collection of essays covers the cinematic traditions of mainland China, Taiwan, Hong Kong, and the Chinese diaspora from the beginning of Chinese film history to the present moment. In compiling a highly selective "film historiography," as it were, we editors face once again the dilemma of choice and inclusion—namely, what constitutes "Chinese cinema" or "Chinese-language cinema." As we attempt to come to terms with an ever-evolving phenomenon and a developing subject of investigation, we provisionally define Chinese-language films as films that use predominantly Chinese dialects and are made in mainland China, Taiwan, Hong Kong, and the Chinese diaspora, as well as those produced through transnational collaborations with other film industries.

Sometimes Chinese-language cinema is synonymous with Chinese cinema if national boundary and language coincide, for instance, in the case of a Mandarin-language film made and released in the People's Republic of China (PRC). Yet, at other times, Chinese-language cinema is not equivalent to Chinese cinema if the Chinese-language film is made outside the sovereign Chinese nation-state —for example, in Hollywood, Singapore, or elsewhere. Here language spills over the territorial fixity of the nation-state, and such a situation casts doubt on neat and easy assumptions about the isomorphism of geography, culture, nation, identity, and citizenship. There are also transnational Chinese-language films that are not made in and by the Chinese state. Rather, they are funded by a variety of external sources and mainly circulate in international film markets. Thus, Chinese-language cinema is a more comprehensive term that covers all the local, national, regional, transnational, diasporic, and global cinemas relating to the Chinese language. The nonequivalence and asymmetry between language and nation bespeaks continuity and unity as well as rupture and fragmentation in the body politic and cultural affiliations among ethnic Chinese in the modern world.

At this juncture, it is helpful to revisit Benedict Anderson's seminal formulation of the idea of nationhood as an "imagined community." Anderson emphasizes the importance of language in the origin and spread of nationalism. For him, "print-languages laid the bases for national consciousness."[1] If print-languages played a crucial role in the formative period of nationalism historically, the importance of the cinema in the maintenance and reinvention of nationhood cannot be underestimated since the beginning of the twentieth century. Nationhood/nationalism must be perpetually reinvented as time goes by long after its original historical formation. Although the modern nation-state is territorially fixed, the "element of artifact, invention and social engineering" is of paramount importance in nation-building.[2] Cinema has increasingly participated in the "birth of a nation."

The historical formation of nation-states in Western Europe predates the appearance of the cinema at the turn of the twentieth century. Hence the importance of print-languages (novels, newspapers) in the eighteenth and nineteenth centuries. In many other parts of the world, however, the establishment of the modern nation-state is roughly concurrent with the development of cinema—for example, in the case of the founding of the Republic of China, in 1912. And numerous nations in Africa and Asia gained independence many decades after the appearance of the cinema. For Ousmane Sembene, his film is a "night school" (école du soir) to educate the illiterate masses in Africa. In the socialist Mao era, the Chinese state regularly dispatches projectionists to screen films in remote villages where movie theaters do not exist. In such a fashion, film culture is spread far beyond the boundaries of metropolises such as Shanghai, and is effectively used to both entertain and educate the masses in the socialist nation-building project. In the present age of global media, people watch films and television as much as, if not more than, they read novels and newspapers.

The questions of both film as language and language(s) in film must be reviewed more carefully. First, film itself is a special symbolic language, a semiotic system, a vehicle of representation, and an audiovisual technology.[3] As such, film preserves, renews, and creates a sense of nationhood as an imaginary unity through an artful combination of images, symbols, sound, and performance. The nation-state is thus performed, staged, represented, and narrated afresh in a film each time.

Second, the issue of language or languages in film is particularly significant. Chinese-language users, along with Chinese-language films, cover vast networks, stretching from mainland China to Taiwan, which wavers between a nation-state and a "renegade province," to the special administrative regions (SARs) of postcolonial Hong Kong and Macau, the independent city-state Singapore, large Chinese populations in Southeast Asia (Malaysia and so forth), Asian-American communities in the United States, and Chinese immigrants throughout the entire world.

If language is in part what lends unity to the Chinese nation-state and more broadly to a sense of Chineseness among the diasporic populations, it is also a force fraught with tension and contention. As we know, Mandarin, the Beijing dialect (*guoyu*, or *putonghua*), has been designated as the official language and dialect by the state (both the Republic of China and the People's Republic of China), but numerous Chinese dialects are spoken by Chinese nationals inside China as well as by immigrants outside China. The different dialects constitute distinct speech genres, as it were, and exist in a state of polyglossia. Sometimes they engage in Bakhtinian dialogic exchanges in a lively, noisy, and yet peaceful atmosphere;[4] but oftentimes they fail to achieve the desired effect of rational, intersubjective, communicative speech acts in a Habermasian fashion.[5] Both past history and contemporary cultural production have continuously testified to the linguistic hierarchy and social discrimination embedded in Chinese cinema and society. Remember the banning of Cantonese-language films under the Nationalist Party (Guomindang) in the Republican era for the sake of national and linguistic unity. Or recall the depiction of reverse discrimination in recent Hong Kong films, for instance, *Comrades, Almost a Love Story* (*Tian mimi,* 1997) by Peter Chan, where Mandarin speakers are stigmatized in Hong Kong society. Or in Wong Kar-wai's *In the Mood for Love* (*Huayang nianhua,* 2000), the Shanghainese dialect evokes a warm nostalgia for a close-knit linguistic community consisting of émigrés living in Hong Kong in a bygone era. The use of local dialects (Sichuanese, northern Shaanxi dialect, and so forth) in numerous mainland films, especially the country films, aims at achieving multiple ends: comedic effects of defamiliarization and refamiliarization, regional flavor, and, no less important, the ever-expanding and changing definition of China and the Chinese people. Dialects and accents create both intimacy and distance on-screen for the characters in the film as well as offscreen among the audience. In such a manner, filmic discourse attempts to articulate again and again a national self-definition in relation to the linguistic, dialectal, ethnic, and religious others. The adoption of particular languages, dialects, and idiolects in film belongs to

Lizhen (Maggie Cheung) and Mr. Zhou (Tony Leung Chiu-wai), both modern yet old-fashioned, communicate in *In the Mood for Love* (Wong Kar-wai, Hong Kong, 2000).

the procedures of inclusion and exclusion in the imagining of a national community. Hence, Chinese language is at once a centrifugal and centripetal force in the nation-building process. In the least, language helps forge a fluid, deterritorialized, pan-Chinese identity among Chinese speakers across national boundaries.

Chinese-language film, or "Sinophone film," is yet to be distinguished from varieties of postcolonial cinemas—for instance, Francophone cinema, or Anglophone cinema. The scattering of Chinese-language speakers around the globe is by and large not the result of the historical colonization of indigenous peoples of the Southern hemisphere and the consequent imposition of colonizers' languages on them, as in the case of the former colonies of France.[6] Nor is the Chinese language in the position of a hegemonic language, the lingua franca of international business, world politics, tourism, as in the case of English in contemporary time. To a great extent, Chinese-language cinema is the result of the migration of Chinese-dialect speakers around the world. This is not to say that China was historically exempt from imperialism and colonialism and is currently free from their aftereffects. Part of China proper, Taiwan, Hong Kong, and Macau were indeed embroiled in those merciless processes. English, Portuguese, and Japanese were instituted as official languages at the geographic peripheries of China—in the islands of Hong Kong, Macau, and Taiwan, respectively, in various historical periods. The point to be made here is that speakers of Chinese dialects around the world have been mostly ethnic Chinese rather than indigenous peoples who were forced or inculcated to speak the language of external colonizers. Fissures and dissent often stem from situations related to inter-Chinese linguistic and dialectal priority and hierarchy. Communication frequently breaks down and speech acts turn quarrelsome between different dialectal regions from within mainland China, and, despite a common "mother tongue," one often hears a profusion of sound and fury from the noisy isles of Taiwan and Hong Kong as their citizens strive to maintain a distinct sense of community vis à vis the traditional political hegemony of the mainland.

It appears that the function of language in relation to the nation-state and identity-formation in Sinophone cinema has been manifested in several important ways. In the first type, language, dialects, and accents are coterminous with the realm of the nation-state. They may serve the interests of the nation or be used as critiques of the nation. In either case, the national is the ultimate referent and horizon of meaning. An obvious example would be any Mandarin-language film made in China. Even when Mandarin is not spoken, local dialects are subordinated to an overarching discourse of the nation-state. Dialects and accents serve as a backdrop to show a lively diversity within a grand national unity. For instance, *Rounding up Draftees* (*Zhua zhuangding,* 1963) is an entirely Sichuanese-dialect film made in the People's Republic of China. Set in the period of the War of Resistance against Japan (1937–1945), the film is a satire of the corruption and cruelty of the Guomindang (the ruling Nationalist Party). The film depicts how local Guomindang officers economically exploited poor peasants and coerced them to join the army. The local dialect is meant to expose the provincialism of the Guomindang and ultimately points to the necessity of rebellion and revolution against the existing order. Here the Sichuanese dialect is utilized to support a specific political vision of China.

We may take a recent film in western Hunan (*Xiangxi*) dialect as another example. Dai Sijie's film *The Little Chinese Seamstress* (*Xiao caifeng,* 2003) is an international coproduction and "transnational film" and seems to be at the opposite end of the ideology of a Mao-era film such as *Rounding up Draftees.* This Franco-Chinese coproduction, however, also narrowly refers to the nation-state of China as a political object. Except for the ending, which takes place in present-day Shanghai, the setting of the film is a mountainous region in western Hunan province, near the hometown of the great writer Shen Congwen, reminiscent of his masterpiece *Border Town (Bian cheng).* Although beautiful and idyllic, the locale is scarred by poverty and political turmoil. The film covers the Cultural Revolution period, and remains another work of the "Cultural Revolution genre" denouncing the political oppression and cultural deprivation that the Chinese people suffered in those years. A transnational, diasporic film ends up being a specifically politicized, humanist film. At the same time, the local dialect augments the regional flavor of the setting, serves as a stylistic ornamentation, and builds a sense of rural innocence in a Chinese province.

The second type of films refers to those films in which the use of dialects reaches below and beneath the level of the national, fortifies a strong feeling of regionalism, and articulates an ambivalent relationship with the discourse of the nation-state. Fukienese and Cantonese films and television dramas in Taiwan and Hong Kong often assert a distinct regional identity versus the historical and present domination of Mandarin and the mainland. In the case of Taiwanese-language films, there has been a historical resentment against the past oppression of the Mandarin-speaking Guomindang, and currently there is the fear of a mainland Chinese takeover. In the case of Hong Kong, the century-long British colonial rule coupled with the Cantonese dialect has created a culture that is distinct from the motherland.

City of Sadness is a supreme example of regionalism and multiple languages in Sinophone cinema. There is a plethora of dialects in the film—Mandarin, Fukienese, Hakka, Shanghainese, and Japanese—each coming out the life-world of specific communities and expressing different cultural identities and political convictions. Most extraordinary of all is Lin Wen-ch'ing (Tony Leung Chiu-wai), the deaf-mute photographer. His inability to speak means his refusal to accept any definitive word and official verdict on a series of events in Taiwanese history—Japanese occupation, the Guomindang takeover, the February 28 Incident, and the White Terror that persisted in the following decades. As a photographer, he documents history in his own quietly perceptive manner with the camera's eye.

A third function of language and dialects in cinema is that filmic discourse expands above and beyond the level of the national to create a fluid, deterritorialized, global, pan-Chinese identity. Although the setting may be somewhere in China, the film itself does not engage specifically geopolitical considerations. This is especially true of certain film genres, such as martial arts and action. These films tend to project a generalized abstract sense of Chineseness and make China into a cultural marker that manifests itself in martial arts, swordplay, kung-fu, cuisine, oriental philosophy, and so on. The political allegory of the nation largely disappears, and the values of foreign culture, entertainment, exoticism, and world tourism are high on the silver screen, all heartened to secure a greater share of the regional, as well as global, film market.

Such examples include Ang Lee's *Crouching Tiger, Hidden Dragon* (*Wohu canglong,* 2000) and recent films of Jackie Chan. In *Crouching Tiger, Hidden Dragon,* the lead actors Chow Yun-fat and Michelle Yeoh speak Mandarin with heavy Cantonese accents. Their accented speech violates the rule of verisimilitude, because they are supposed to portray characters from a particular region of China. Although this appears laughable and improbable for audiences in mainland China and Taiwan, it does not matter for international audiences who watch the film through subtitles. The non-Chinese viewers could enjoy the spectacular scenery, incredible action choreography, and marvelous legends as they spend time learning about a depoliticized "cultural China" set in the past.

The three functions of languages and dialects as outlined above are heuristic guides rather than absolute categories. Sometimes the dominant dialectal function in a given Chinese-language film may change from viewer to viewer, or more than one function may coexist in a viewing experience. For instance, a film such as Wong Kar-wai's *In the Mood for Love* could mean different things for different viewers in a rather personal way. Hong Kong residents, Shanghainese immigrants, Chinese citizens, and international audiences could relate to the themes and experiences of immigration, love, memory, nostalgia, and cultural identity in their own meaningful manners.

Stylistically, the predominant use of local dialects in contemporary Chinese art cinema has helped create an immediacy and a raw quality in the texture of the films. Here are some examples that have gained visibility and critical acclaim in international arthouse film circuits in recent years: a Shaanxi dialect is used in *The Story of Qiu Ju* (*Qiu Ju da guansi*, Zhang Yimou, 1993); a Hebei dialect is used in *Ermo* (*Ermo*, Zhou Xiaowen, 1994); Henan dialects are used in *Orphan of Anyang* (*Angyang ying'er*, Wang Chao, 2001) and *Blind Shaft* (*Mang jing*, Li Yang, 2003); and Jia Zhangke uses the Shanxi dialects of Fenyang and Datong in his films *Xiao Wu* (*Xiao Wu*, 1997), *Platform* (*Zhantai*, 2000), and *Unknown Pleasures* (*Ren xiaoyao*, 2002). The consistent and pervasive employment of these various northern Chinese dialects effectively builds the realism of characters, ambiance, locale, and atmosphere. Here we may speak of "Chinese-dialect film" as a subgenre of Chinese-language film.

In contemporary Chinese mainstream popular cinema, however, local dialects are deployed to elicit the appropriate effects of comedy, humor, and satire. For instance, if particular characters speak dialects rather than Mandarin, it shows the lovely, down-to-earth, provincial quality of the individuals, who may have difficulty adjusting to the fast-paced life in a big city like Beijing. The quaint, unfamiliar accents are intended to be funny and entertaining for the urban audience. This is precisely the dialectal strategy adopted in yet another highly successful commercial film by Feng Xiaogang, *Cell Phone* (*Shouji*, 2003). Here we have the old material and spiritual divide between the rural and the urban, the primitive and the modern. The earthbound and homely represented by the dialect users are pitted against the forces of globalization and telecommunication that gather momentum in China's metropolises. In general, the use of dialects in Chinese-language films could alternatively or simultaneously create Brechtian distancing, defamiliarizing effects as well as conveying feelings of directness and closeness.

At an even more profound level, linguistic and dialectal differences within Greater China point to the enormous uneven economic formations and the schizophrenic mentality of the nation-state at large. Fruit Chan's *Durian Durian* (*Liulian piaopiao*, 2001) is an interesting case in point. The film consists of two parts, the first set in Cantonese-speaking capitalist Hong Kong and the second in the Northeast (Dongbei) in postsocialist China, where the northeast dialect is spoken. The northeast, seen through the city of Mudanjiang, and signified by the northeast accent, is a typical postindustrial, postsocialist city in decay and ruins. The heroine, Xiao Yan, a young woman from Dongbei, leaves her native city behind and comes to Hong Kong to make money by becoming a prostitute. The film opens with Xiao Yan's voice-over narration in a distinctive and seductive northeast dialect, and the frame is filled with a shot of the scenic Victoria Harbor in Hong Kong superimposed with and turning into muddy Mudan River in the Northeast. While serving her various male customers in Hong Kong, she speaks different dialects, sometimes Cantonese and sometimes Mandarin, and lies to them about what part of China she comes from. Indeed, mainland prostitutes in Hong Kong arrive from all over China—Shanghai, Hunan, Sichuan, and so on. The first half of the film set in warm, glitzy, fast-paced, capitalist Hong Kong forms a strong contrast to the second part, set in drab, cold, dusty postsocialist Dongbei. Northeast China was one of most industrialized regions in the Mao era, but it has suffered decay and high rates of unemployment since the economic reforms. Numerous state-owned enterprises (SOEs) have gone bankrupt one after one, and millions of Dongbei residents have been laid off. As a result, Dongbei prostitutes are present everywhere in China. Thus, the Cantonese dialect in capitalist Hong Kong and the northeast dialect in the hinterland of postsocialist China, spoken by the same woman, indicate the two halves of the Chinese national psyche and dramatize the social and economic disparity within China through the mouth and body of the same prostitute. What the film reveals is the historic transition from old-style industrial production to affective labor and service industry, to the ascendancy of biopower or the biopolitical regime, in the words of Michael Hardt and Antonio Negri.[7] As a matter of fact, Xiao Yan's ex-husband and former male friends also turn to the service industry for survival in Mudanjiang. They become dancers in a local nightclub. This aspect of the film is very much like what happened in the film *The Full Monty* (1997), where former factory workers in a rundown postindustrial city choose to become male strippers in a transitional period of British history. What occurred in the West decades ago is happening in China today.

This shift from modernity to postmodernity, a process that is at times painful and other time exhilarating, is vividly described in many Chinese-dialect films. Human tragedies in dangerous coalmines, abandoned factories, and ghost towns result from antiquarian industrial modes of production in such Henan-dialect films as *Blind Shaft* and *Orphan of Anyang*. Viewers can also glimpse at ultramodern cities like Beijing and get a laugh out of the silliness of Chinese citizens equipped with new communication conveniences. In *Cell Phone*, adventurous married men cannot escape from the omnipresence of a modern telecommunication technology as they attempt to hide extramarital affairs from their spouses. The cell phone beeps, and if you do not answer, where are you? The Sichuanese-speaking character, Lao Mo (Zhang Guoli), head of a television station, clumsily makes a fool of himself as he tries unsuccessfully to have an illicit love affair. His conclusion is that a primitive agrarian society is superior to a postmodern society of instant communication. There is no place to hide these days. The magic object "cell phone" performs the function of surveillance in a postmodern disciplinary society. The classic Marxian model of successive modes of production is inadequate for an analysis of these kinds of films and must be supplemented by an examination of modes of communication, spectatorship, and consumption.

Each and every attempt to revisit film history is inevitably a matter of "reinventing film studies" from a different critical angle.[8] Anthologies on Chinese films reinterpret the objects of investigation, give them new life, and, as a result, the objects themselves change and grow. Earlier volumes in English are cognizant of the multiple formations in Chinese film history. For instance, *Perspectives on Chinese Cinema* (1991), edited by Chris Berry, includes chapters on films from China, Taiwan, and Hong Kong, although "Chinese cinema" is in the singular in the book's title.[9] In *New Chinese Cinemas: Forms, Identities, and Politics* (1994), Chinese cinemas ostensibly become a plural entity, containing PRC, Taiwan and Hong Kong. The editors of this book are acutely aware of the differences between the three cinematic practices, but still retain the umbrella term "Chinese."[10] *Transnational Chinese Cinemas: Identity, Nationhood, Gender* (1997) adds the qualifier "transnational" to account for certain problematic areas often overlooked by national cinema studies.[11] *The Oxford Guide to Film Studies* (1998) has separate entries for Chinese cinema, Taiwanese cinema, and Hong Kong cinema under the general rubric of "world cinema."[12]

These adjustments indicate the difficulties of using a single term to contain a body of work known generally in the West as "Chinese film." They also signify efforts to gain a greater understanding and knowledge about films made from the three major film production centers in the region. Therefore, just when geopolitical developments have called for adjustments to the term "China," film studies itself has also gone through a major change in the studies of "national cinema."

A similar situation occurred in the academic studies of Chinese films among scholars in the Chinese-speaking world. In the Chinese language, the term for "Chinese cinema" has been customarily *"Zhongguo dianying."* Recent historical developments in the "Greater China" area, however, have changed academic conceptions of what "China" is and even more so the potential meanings of "Chinese cinema." Film artists, critics, and scholars in China, Taiwan, and Hong Kong have begun to visit and establish contact with each other across geographic regions and political allegiances. As a result, a new phrase, "Chinese-language film" *(huayu dianying)*, has come into currency.

This term was originally introduced by scholars based in Taiwan and Hong Kong in the early 1990s.[13] As a result of a thaw in relations between Taiwan and the mainland at that time, mainland film scholars were invited to Taiwan for the first time. Consequently, *huayu dianying* was used in Taiwanese scholarship to indicate any film produced in a Chinese-speaking society, to clarify the categories formerly used to distinguish mainland films *(dalu pian)*, Hong Kong films *(gangpian)*, and Taiwanese films *(guopian)*. In other words, a linguistic description was used to unify and supersede older geographical divisions and political discriminations. Similarly, musical terms such as *huayu gequ* (Chinese-language songs) and *huayu yinyue* (Chinese-language music) are used to designate pan-Chinese popular music across the Taiwan Straits. Likewise, terms such as *huawen wenxue, huayu wenxue,* and *Zhongwen wenxue* signify Chinese-language literature written by authors globally, not just Chinese literature produced in mainland China. It is not without irony that the first "Chinese" Nobel Prize winner in literature, Gao Xingjian, lives in France but writes in Chinese. This "cultural turn" in the game of naming, the actual practices of film coproduction, and the increasing regional integration within the "Greater China economic zone" are all gestures to establish connections and linkages in the Chinese-speaking world beyond the political borderlines of the modern nation-state.

Having said this, it should also be noted that these developments in Chinese-language film scholarship are not a simple reflection of the political changes that have happened between socialist PRC, democratic Taiwan, and postcolonial Hong Kong. Certainly, these changes have made Chinese film scholarship across old national and regional borders an engaging, diverse, and unpredictable field; more important, the excitement in doing Chinese film studies is born not only of politics but also of Chinese-language film itself: its energy, resilience, and remarkable innovation in storytelling, sound, image, and design. As a result, Chinese-language cinemas, however they are defined, belong to the most dynamic contemporary cinemas in the world.

Cinema studies is a relatively young discipline in comparison to other fields such as literary studies. The study of "national cinema" has recently developed into an important branch of cinema studies. Ironically, just as film studies is defining its geographic borders and theoretical perimeters, the forces of globalization have forced film scholars to reexamine their assumptions and practices. Border crossing and transnationalism have been part of the film medium from the beginning, because film itself is a truly international technology. Nevertheless, these tendencies have intensified in the post–cold war era. The kinds of phenomena that critics of Asian film witness and describe are also evident in other cinematic traditions. Thus, a critic writes about the difficulty of establishing the national origin of a film in the context of European cinema:

> What determines the national identity of a film when funding, language, setting, topic, cast, and director are increasingly mixed? How can we classify films such as Louis Malle's 1992 film *Damage* (French director, Franco-British cast, English settings), Krzysztof Kieslowski's *Three Colours* trilogy (*Blue*, 1993; *White*, 1993; *Red*, 1994; made by a Polish director with French funds and a Franco-Polish cast), and Lars von Trier's 1996 film *Breaking the Waves* (Danish director, Norwegian-European funds, British cast, Scottish setting)?[14]

Here Ginette Vincendeau enumerates instances of pan-European production and inter European collaborations. Examples of pan-Chinese production and inter-Chinese and inter-Asian co-collaborations are no less abundant. Whether in Europe or Asia, cross-regional and transnational filmmaking has become a trend trespassing narrow national boundaries.

The essays collected in this volume explore the manifold dimensions of Chinese-language films and highlight areas that previous studies overlooked. The contributors take up issues and topics ranging from the beginnings of Chinese cinema in the early twentieth century, through various historical periods, to the turn of the twenty-first century. Their cross-cultural engagements with individual films are accomplished with an acute sense of chronology and history. Because of the broad areas covered, there is a risk of oversimplification in dividing them according to some a priori principles. For the sake of clarity and convenience, we divide the chapters into three parts. Part I deals with the diachronic issues of film history, periodization, and trends. The scholars in part I revise old models of film history as well as write new chapters on the evolving Chinese cinemas. Part II focuses on synchronic questions of poetics, aesthetics, form, and directorial style. Part III tackles the politics of filmmaking and film reception, the prominent themes of contemporary cultural studies, and issues of identity, gender, the national, the transnational, the postcolonial, and globalization. It would be wrong to assume that questions concerning film style or film history have no bearing on such themes as national and cultural identity or that abstract cultural studies can be somehow detached from the concrete analysis of film genres, forms, and directors. More often than not, these various lines of thought are intricately interlocked with each other, as many of the chapters contained here convincingly demonstrate. Although we have divided the chapters according to the three major categories represented by the parts of the volume, in fact, the individual chapters grouped in one part frequently address issues in the other part of the volume.

Part I: Historiography, Periodization, Trends

The writing of Chinese film history—namely, the project of "historiography" —is a major task in our collective enterprise. Historiography is necessarily always already revisionist as historians endeavor to look at the past with a fresh eye. "Periodization" focuses on moments in time: the "pre-" and the "post-," "early" and "late," "beginning" and "end," "contemporary" and "past," as some of the chapter titles indicate. Such temporal differentiations are intended to describe the movements and trends in China's long film history with more coherence and clarity.

The chapter jointly written by Mary Farquhar and Chris Berry proposes a new way of looking at the historical evolution of Chinese film art. Taking a cue from Tom Gunning's idea of "cinema of attractions," they look at the history and aesthetics of Chinese opera film. From "shadow play" in early twentieth century to the heyday of "revolutionary model opera" in the 1960s and 1970s, Chinese film artists are bound to a vital indigenous tradition rooted in past centuries.[15] This chapter points to the importance of a nonmimetic, expressionist tradition in Chinese film as opposed to the realist tendency based on imitation or mimesis.

Zhang Zhen's chapter guides us to an intriguing episode in early Chinese film history. Martial arts film flourished in Shanghai in the 1920s and 1930s. The Republican government, however, soon took action to ban such films in the name of modernization, nation-building, and science. Film censors saw ghosts and improbable supernatural feats as vestiges of feudalism and superstition from old China. Likewise, intellectuals regarded martial arts heroes and heroines as anachronistic and reactionary. Afterward, the martial arts genre, apparently incompatible with the ethos of modernity, flourished only at the margins of Chinese civilization beyond the reach of the Chinese nation-state—the tiny island of Hong Kong under the benign neglect of British colonial rule.[16] It is important to see that, at the same moment, for reasons of national unity the film censors of the Republican government banned the use of the Cantonese dialect in films. Only Mandarin, the official Chinese dialect, can be used. Cantonese-language films survived and flourished in the remote island of Hong Kong in the years that followed.

With the demise of martial arts film and the death of the symbolic old China, film culture was dictated by the tastes and viewing habits of the modernizing urbanites in metropolises such as Shanghai in the republican era (1911–1949). Film gave rise to a new urban culture, an alternative public sphere based on the sensory-reflexive experiences of modernity, and became a Chinese/Shanghainese version of "vernacular modernism." In the words of Miriam Hansen, "Shanghai cinema of the 1920s and 30s represents a distinct brand of vernacular modernism, one that evolved in a complex relation to American—and other foreign —models while drawing on and transforming Chinese traditions in theater, literature, graphic, and print culture, both modernist and popular. I think this case can be made at several levels: the thematic concerns of the films; their mise-en-scène and visual style; their formal strategies of narration, including modes of performance, character construction, and spectatorial identification; and the films' address to and function within a specific horizon of reception."[17]

In the face of the brutal realities of wars and revolutions, vernacular modernism, or modernism as such in literature and arts across the board, disappeared all too quickly from China's cultural landscape. Modernism was seen as decadent and individualistic, and hence incompatible with the ethos of the suffering Chinese masses and the nation at war. Realism, be it "socialist realism" on the mainland throughout the Mao era, or Hong Kong's left-wing cinema of the 1950s, or "healthy realism" in Taiwan, took hold in Chinese film culture. It was not until the emergence of "new waves" in Hong Kong, Taiwan, and China in the 1980s that the tyranny of various instrumental realisms began to recede. The "new waves," also in the name of reclaiming the real, attempted to capture the scenes, sight, and sound of reality with a renewed cinematic language. The stylistic characteristics and critical orientations of the new wavers first caught the attention of world audiences and served as a catalyst in promoting Chinese cinema studies in the West into a legitimate and growing academic field.

Meiling Wu writes a new chapter in Taiwan New Cinema—that of "post-sadness." Hou Hsiao-hsien's work, especially *City of Sadness*, remains the defining ethos of the classic Taiwan New Cinema in many ways; however, Taiwanese films have entered a new phase of development. If the affectations of previous genres and styles of Taiwanese cinema such as the nationalist government's propaganda films, sappy melodramas adapted from Qiong Yao's romances, "healthy realism" of the 1960s, and "social realism" of the late 1970s, all appear hopelessly hackneyed and out of touch with reality, the New Cinema movement led by Hou Hsiao-hisen and his like aims to restore realism and authenticity to Taiwanese film and give true expression to Taiwanese history and reality. Yet, in the eyes of a younger generation of Taiwanese directors, it is time to go beyond Hou's idiosyncrasies and mannerisms. Gone are the personal quest for and collective reconstruction of the local/national history of Taiwan, the nostalgia for the idyllic past, and anguished reflection on the fate of an entire people. Wu tackles the film art of Tsai Ming-liang and Lin Cheng-sheng as representative of a new spirit in Taiwanese cinema. Now the camera focuses on the existential absurdities of private individuals and the malaise of urban daily life in contemporary, postmodern cities of Taiwan. The rituals and routines of everyman and everywoman are depicted in painful minute details without being assimilated to some higher national pathos.

The transition between generations of filmmakers in the mainland is not so different from the situation in Taiwan. The mythic grand tales of China as spun by the giants of previous generations have given way to the emergence of new "post–fifth generation directors" *(hou diwudai daoyan)*. Likewise, the disorienting feelings and fragmentary experiences of ordinary folks in the contemporary Chinese city find expression in numerous films. Shuqin Cui tackles the politics of naming and labeling in a controversial area, that of Chinese independent directors in the 1990s. Terms such as "independent," "underground," "experimental," and "nonofficial/nonmainstream" reveal ideological perspectives from which one approaches a corpus of films and a group of directors. Urban space and city life, the personal and subjective, the artist-self, and descriptions of youthful, emerging sexuality all find their way into the work of a new generation of directors.[18] They are distinguished from the so-called fifth generation that emerged in the 1980s.

Sheldon H. Lu dissects a slice of Chinese film culture at the end of the twentieth century by examining the film *Not One Less* by Zhang Yimou, the most active and visible figure from the fifth generation. This chapter studies the sociology of the Chinese film industry—audiences, box-sales figures, and popular attitudes, as well as the international politics of film festivals. Furthermore, it points to the ways in which the old rural themes in Zhang's previous work stubbornly persist in his new films while numerous Chinese citizens are already enmeshed in the midst of messy, dizzying urban lives and are caught in the throes and exhilarations of global postmodernization.[19]

Part II: Poetics, Directors, Styles

Film is an international technology, yet each national cinematic tradition draws on its own artistic legacies for inspiration and innovation. The fruitful tension between the national and the international, between indigenous forces and Euro-American conventions, animates the growth and development of Chinese cinemas. In this section, some chapters provide lucid, synchronic, structural(ist), transhistorical accounts of the poetics and aesthetics of Chinese film as an integral part of world cinema. Still other chapters explore directorial styles in social and historical specificity.

As David Bordwell's illuminating chapter shows, the cinemas of China, Taiwan, and Hong Kong can be understood in the context of international film style. And this style, as Bordwell suggests, is rooted in three cinematic patterns—continuity editing, planimetric composition, and the long take. In this regard, Chinese filmmaking is perhaps not so different from its Western counterparts, as many Chinese scholars have claimed. Classic Hollywood continuity, as the most economical and effective way of storytelling, was adopted and refined by generations of Chinese filmmakers. This cinematic pattern is further intensified in the hands of Hong Kong filmmakers with their own kinetic variations. In appropriating Hollywood continuity, the planimetric composition of European art cinema, and the device of the long take, Chinese film artists have participated in and contributed to a transcultural poetics of cinema.

Emilie Yueh-yu Yeh's article takes us to the "treasure island" off the mainland shore to explore issues surrounding Taiwanese director Hou Hsiao-hsien. Recently called "the best narrative filmmaker alive today," Hou is a controversial director at home. In Taiwan, Hou is seen as a master without an audience. Yeh's article discusses the nagging problem of the reception gap of Chinese films in the world and at home. She argues that assessing Hou's films from a poetic standpoint releases a barrage of critical, political pronouncements that form a clashing, discordant context.

Xiaoping Lin analyzes a cycle of three films by Jia Zhangke, one of the most gifted independent directors from the so-called sixth generation in mainland China. Jia usually stages a nonprofessional cast who perform the roles of ordinary people and "antiheroes," a sharp contrast to the mythic larger-than-life figures of the fifth-generation films, which cash in on the status of bankable stars such as Gong Li. The gritty, documentary, realistic style of Jia's films closely observes and chronicles the impact of social change and globalization on small-town characters in post-Mao China, a country caught in a transition from socialism to a capitalist market economy.

Thomas Luk's article examines the aesthetics, style, and mood of *In the Mood for Love* (*Huayang nianhua*, 2000) by Wong Kai-wai, the internationally celebrated art-house director from Hong Kong. Wong sumptuously evokes nostalgia for a bygone era through the atmospherics of music, image, clothing, mise-en-scène, and milieu. Luk traces the literary inspirations for the film, a 1972 nostalgic novella *Tête-Bêche (Intersection)*, a tale by celebrated Hong Kong writer Liu Yichang and *Shinju*, a double-suicide love story by Japanese writer Komatsu Sakyo. Luk argues that the film's sharp departure from the novels indicates Wong's reinvention of memory through anxiety about the future of Hong Kong. The realm of fantasy, desire, love, and psychic repression is ultimately linked to the larger arena of geopolitics in world history as indicated in the ending of the film.

Wong Kar-wai has occupied a special place in the international arthouse film circuits. Indeed, his perpetual fascination with temporality has become his artistic trademark. If Hong Kong action and martial arts films exemplify the "movement-image" and "action-image," it may be said that Wong's film art is the quintessence of Deleuzian "time-image."[20] *Ashes of Time (Dongxie xidu, 1994), Chungking Express (Chongqing senlin, 1994), Happy Together (Chunguang zhaxie, 1997)*, and *In the Mood for Love* are musings on the structure of time itself. Thematically, Wong's films explore the existential human states of waiting, anticipation, departure, journey, memory, loss, and nostalgia. There are projections of the future *(Chungking Express)* as well as remembrances of things past *(In the Mood for Love)*. Cinematically, he distills the very images of time and allows the viewer to watch the physical passage of time—slow motion, fast forward, smudge, freeze, overlapping temporal orders, temporal fragmentation, temporal continuity and discontinuity. Transience and timelessness, motion and stillness, fullness and emptiness (both spatially and psychologically in an Ozuesque style) are the central modalities of "being and time" that his film art attempts to capture.

Sheldon Lu's chapter discusses the cultural politics of Ang Lee's commercial blockbuster *Crouching Tiger, Hidden Dragon (Wohu canglong, 2000)*, by far the most successful Chinese-language film in terms of box office sales worldwide. A "Hollywood-made" (Columbia Pictures) "Chinese-language film" is far from being an oxymoron, a categorical confusion, but is cheered by mass audiences from around the globe in the postnational, borderless world. The film is an example of transnational and global cinema par excellence. Although set in ancient China, the film has little to do with actual history. As Lee says, this film is his invention of ancient China, a world that does not exist anymore but remains an imagination in his mind. Culture, tradition, ethnicity, and "Chineseness" for that matter, are dehistoricized, decontextualized, and disembedded from deep national roots. Chinese culture, in the form of martial arts or ethnic cuisine, becomes a portable package that travels, is carried over, and is ultimately consumed effortlessly from region to region across the globe—such is the state of cultural consumption and entertainment in the age of globalization.

Part III: Politics, Nationhood, Globalization

In the development and fine-tuning of distinct film styles and poetics, imaginary representations of identity, nationality, and citizenship loom large in cinematic discourses. The interpellation, or "hailing," of individuals as subjects for the goal of nation-building and modernization is a constant endeavor among China's policy makers, the intellectual elite, and public opinion throughout the twentieth century (through censorship, state ownership of film studios, and so on). The boundaries of nationhood and citizenship can be more effectively maintained and policed within the Chinese nation-state, be it Republican China or the PRC.

But the problem of identity formation has been complicated by the historical conditions of Taiwan and Hong Kong as ex-Japanese and ex-British colonies, as outlying islands far from the geopolitical center of China, and as places inhabited by people who speak Hokkien (also known as Fukienese), Hakka, and Cantonese, dialects incomprehensible to the ears of Mandarin speakers. As a result, Taiwan's and Hong Kong's relations with China are ambivalent, involving both identification with and resistance to "Chinese" culture and the hegemony of the nation-state.

Darrell W. Davis introduces the Taiwanese film *Dou-san: A Borrowed Life* (Wu Nianzhen, 1994) as a strong case of psychological postcolonialism. He places the film in the context of the Japanese occupation, Taiwan New Cinema, Wu's other works, and the conceptual frameworks of postcolonial studies. In light of Taiwan's occupation by various outsiders, Davis offers conclusions about the role of contemporary media in the formation and political uses of modern Taiwanese identity.

The interrogation of identity and subjectivity in Chinese cinematic discourse is not a vague, abstract process, but is embodied in specific film genres in different historical periods and in response to unique social circumstances. Shiao-ying Shen's chapter asks whether a feminine inscription exists in Taiwanese cinema. She looks at two cases—a controversial Taiwanese actress Yang Huei-shan in the 1980s and the Taiwanese/Hong Kong director Sylvia Chang. Her discussions demonstrate that body, performance, and direction are ways of facilitating feminine writing.

David Desser considers the corporeality of Chinese identity, visible in male megastars such as Bruce Lee, Jackie Chan, and Jet Li. He unpacks various aspects of nationalist embodiment, from epistemology (body of knowledge) to diaspora (bodies in exile) to artistic corpus (body of work) by reviewing several decades of Hong Kong martial arts films. Whereas Shiao-ying Shen analyzes the problem and representation of female authorship and performance in Taiwanese cinema, Desser confronts issues of nationalism and masculine cultural pride in Hong Kong cinema head-on. Ultimately, the global reception of Chinese cinema cannot be understood without accounting for its emergence from under the tutelage, and condescension, of Western eyes.

The cultural politics of mainland China, Taiwan, and Hong Kong is intensified by global developments after the end of the cold war as well as the return of Hong Kong to mainland China. Large numbers of Hong Kong residents (many of whom are Chinese nationals) find themselves in the traffic of cross-national travel. Sheldon Lu examines Hong Kong diaspora film from the mid-1980s to the handover. He pinpoints a paradigm change in the representation of place, self, and nationality in this film genre. It is a shift from the pathos of the nation-state (the "China syndrome," "exile complex," "persecution complex") to a discourse of flexible citizenship and transnationality. Moreover, he analyzes the emergence of a new type of "transnational TV drama," a joint CBS–Hong Kong coproduction, *Martial Law*. Diaspora as typified by Hong Kong residents and portrayed in Hong Kong films, as well as international collaborations involving Hong Kong film artists, indicates a decentered, deterritorialized, and fluid mechanism of identity formation, a sense of being-in-mobility.

Chu Yiu Wai begins where Sheldon Lu stops, by focusing on Hong Kong films from the posthandover, postcolonial period. He explores the formation of local identity in cinematic representation. Even in those films that purport to reenact Hong Kong's local history, Chu argues that the reconstructed Hong Kong identity remains impure, "inauthentic," unstable, plural, and mixed. The local, the national, and global all meet in the dialogic space of the filmic text.

As an independent, autonomous city-state since 1965, Singapore lies outside the territorial boundary of the Chinese nation, yet the island country's population is predominantly ethnic Chinese. Although English, Mandarin, Malay/Bahasa, and Tamil are the designated official languages, Singlish (Singaporean English) and a variety of Chinese dialects are spoken by the people on a daily basis: Hokkien, Cantonese, and Shanghainese. Gina Marchetti's chapter examines the Chinese-language and hybrid-language films of the Singaporean director Eric Khoo. While Khoo's films usher in an emergent Singaporean national cinema, at the same time they partake of a nexus of transnational Chinese-language film culture. Marchetti points out a central tension in the political and cultural imaginary of Singapore. On the one hand, Singapore is a postcolonial hybrid culture, a thriving port city that functions as one of the busiest transit points in the transnational flows of ships, capital, commodity, and labor. On the other hand, it is engaged in the earnest business of nation-building and the formation of a Confucian, orderly, clean model state. Such a basic contradiction in Singapore's politics is manifested in filmic discourse.

In regard to Khoo's films, as well as Ang Lee's *Crouching Tiger, Hidden Dragon,* the existence of Chinese-language cinema outside the boundaries of the Chinese nation-state demarcates new categories of films that cannot be adequately accounted for by the old paradigm of national cinema. Therefore, it seems that transnational Chinese cinema and Chinese-language cinema are more comprehensive, productive, and useful concepts in dealing with the multifarious strands of film culture that exist in mainland China, Taiwan, Hong Kong, and the Chinese diaspora.

In tracking the historical trajectory of Chinese-language cinemas as a whole, these chapters nevertheless focus on specific areas of investigation. Beneath and beyond the general tripartite division of the book, there exist further multiple threads linking the concerns of the various authors:

- The formulation of a Chinese film *poetics,* be it universal, indigenous, or auteuristic (Bordwell, Farquhar/Berry, Yeh).
- *Directorial style* in the cases of Hou Hsiao-hsien, Zhang Yimou, Wong Kai-wai, Ang Lee, Wu Nianzhen, Tsai Ming-liang, Lin Cheng-sheng, Eric Khoo, and Jia Zhangke (Yeh, Wu, Lu, Lin, Luk, Marchetti, Davis).
- The history, evolution, and fate of individual *genres,* whether the extinction of the early martial arts film (Zhang), or the later international expansion of Hong Kong martial arts and *wuxia* (swordplay) film (Desser, Lu).
- The construction and deconstruction of *subjectivity, identity, nationality,* and *citizenship* in contemporary films from Taiwan, Hong Kong, and Singapore (Davis, Chu, Lu, Marchetti).
- Attempts at coming to terms with both *history* and *contemporaneity* among post–fifth generation mainland Chinese filmmakers (Cui) as well as postsadness Taiwanese directors (Wu, Davis).
- Gender formations, sexual performance, and sexual politics, whether female authorship or femininity in Taiwanese melodramas (Shen) or masculinity in Hong Kong martial arts films (Desser).

These are only a few of the main strands in the long history of Chinese-language films, a history that waits for further explorations.

Intimations at the Turn of the Twenty-First Century

In the last years of the twentieth century and the beginning of the twenty-first century, films from the mainland, Taiwan, Hong Kong, and the Chinese diaspora continue to capture worldwide attention. In 2000, Taiwanese director Edward Yang's film *Yi Yi* (A One and a Two) was voted the best film by the National Society of Film Critics in the United States and received the best director award at

Cannes. Hong Kong director Wong Kar-wai's film *In the Mood for Love* was voted the number one film in the *Village Voice* poll, and Tony Leung Chiu-wai, the lead actor in the film, received the best actor award at the Cannes Film Festival. As a classic example of transnational as well as global cinema, *Crouching Tiger, Hidden Dragon,* by the Taiwanese/Chinese/American director Ang Lee, was a Chinese-language film jointly produced and distributed by Sony Classics/Columbia Pictures and studios in Taiwan and China. This film was released in its original Chinese language and proved a big hit in the global film markets. It received the best director award at the Golden Globe awards in January 2001. It was also nominated for ten Oscars, and eventually won four, including the best foreign language picture, in March 2001.

Ang Lee's example prompted his friend and competitor Zhang Yimou to create his own martial arts film with hopes of similar global success. China's entry to the World Trade Organization (WTO) also caused the government and the domestic industry to seek new modes of film production to compete with the influx of foreign film exports, particularly Hollywood blockbusters. Zhang's *Yingxiong* (Hero), loosely based on the story of the attempted assassination of the First Emperor of China, employed a cast of megastars from Greater China (Jet Li, Zhang Ziyi, Maggie Cheung, Tony Leung Chiu-wai, Chen Daoming) and debuted in early 2003. Its sumptuous cinematography and spectacular choreography rivaled Lee's film; however, it did not finally capture the Oscar Zhang sought and could not compare with the success of *Crouching Tiger, Hidden Dragon* in the international market. Nevertheless, it overwhelmingly broke box-office records in mainland China, thanks to the Chinese government's preemptive strike against privacy and the introduction of computerized counting of ticket sales. As a product of transnational, trans-Chinese collaboration and as China's initial response to her entry to the WTO, *Hero* revived China's national cinema vis-à-vis the ascending hegemony of Hollywood films in China's domestic film market.

Transnational cooperation between the U.S. film industry and Asian directors and companies accelerated at the turn of the twenty-first century. Sony's Columbia Pictures formed an Asian wing—Columbia Pictures Film Production Asia —to coproduce local language films for the Asian and overseas markets. Led by Barbara Robinson, Columbia Asia produced the Taiwanese hit *Shuangtong* (Double Vision) and the mainland Chinese film *Dawan* (Big Shot's Funeral), which was directed by Feng Xiaogang. It is also remaking Hollywood films for the Asian market. (David Mamet's 1998 film *Things Change* is the first effort for the Korean market.) Another media giant, Miramax, purchased the right to distribute Zhang Yimou's *Hero* in North America for US$15 million. It also acquired Stephen Chow's *Shaolin Soccer* (2001) and released a dubbed, recut version in summer

2004. Its increasingly monopolistic worldwide control of some of Hong Kong's best-known films is changing the rules of the game in transnational cinema production, marketing, and distribution. Miramax spends large sums of money to buy remake rights to various Asian films (for example, the Korean film *Jail Breakers*). With the involvement of major U.S. film producers and distributors in the financing and marketing of Asian films, perhaps a new model of the relationship between art and commerce on a global scale is being created.[21]

Meanwhile, film festivals at various places outside the PRC such as Hong Kong, Los Angeles, New York City, and Rotterdam were busy launching and promoting a new breed of mainland Chinese film artists to international audiences. This young, urban, post–fifth generation of directors forges a new kind of film aesthetic in the representation of China, a film aesthetic that captures the angst and experiences of contemporary city life and as such remains distinct from the manners of previous generations. The cooptation and promotion of these young directors in such "art film" festivals offers an alternative venue to the Hollywood commercial route of distribution as exemplified by figures such as Ang Lee and Zhang Yimou.

In the United States, Asian film conventions and genres—especially the martial arts, action, and gangsters—have been appropriated by Hollywood filmmakers and in some way have changed the face of the American cinema. Popular films such as *Charlie's Angels* (2000), *Charlie's Angels 2: Full Throttle* (2003), the *Matrix* trilogy (1999, 2003), and *Kill Bill* (volume 1, 2003; volume 2, 2004) lavishly absorb and borrow the styles, motifs, storylines, personnel, props, settings, and just about everything else, from the classic Hong Kong action films of the Shaw Brothers to Bruce Lee to Japanese *yakuza* films. As a result, the internationalization of Chinese-language cinema from within Hollywood has contributed to the transformation of mainstream American film culture. In these examples, film has become a global melting pot where the styles of Chinese and American cinema are hybridized and become indistinguishable.

In the realm of academic studies, Chinese cinemas stand as both an alternative paradigm and a testimony to the development of film as an international art. It has become increasingly important for general historians and theorists to take into account the Chinese case as they attempt to formulate film theories with global pretensions. Chinese examples are often cited as a significant non-Hollywood tradition in support of specific brands of film theory. As a result, Chinese film studies has not only enlarged the scope of China studies as an "area studies," but also played a crucial part in the ongoing debates about international film history and theory. Along with various other local, regional, and national cinematic traditions, Chinese-language films provide prime materials and provocative cases for scholars of world cinema to rethink the crucial yet perplexed relationship between cinema and nation, to observe the imaging and imaginary formation of the nation-state, nationality, and nationalism on screen, and to re-examine the construction as well as deconstruction of national identity in filmic discourse.[22] The existence of Chinese-language cinema outside the boundaries of the Chinese nation-state once more calls into question the old paradigm of "national cinema." On a lighter note, after a full century of evolution and inno-vation, Chinese-language films have given more than enough guilty and legiti-mate pleasures to a variety of film fans from around the world. Furthermore, they have presented and will continue to present plenty of opportunities for film scholars to challenge their critical assumptions and expand their intellec-tual horizons.

Notes

1. Benedict Anderson, *Imagined Communities: Reflections on the Origin and Spread of Nationalism*, rev. ed. (London: Verso, 1991), 44.

2. E. J. Hobsbawm, *Nations and Nationalism since 1780: Programme, Myth, Reality*, 2nd ed. (Cambridge: Cambridge University Press, 1990), 10. For relevant discussion, see also Ernest Gellner, *Nations and Nationalism* (Ithaca, N.Y.: Cornell University Press, 1983).

3. For structuralist, semiological studies of the question of film language, see Christian Metz, *Language and Cinema*, trans. Donna Jean (The Hague: Mouton, 1974); Christian Metz, *Film Language: A Semiotics of the Cinema*, trans. Michael Taylor (New York: Ox-ford, 1974); and Yuri Lotman, *Semiotics of Cinema*, trans. Mark E. Suino (Ann Arbor: Michigan Slavic Contributions, 1976). Gilles Deleuze offers a critique of this approach and proposes a Peircean semiotic account of film language in his provocative study *Cin-ema II: The Time-Image*, trans. Hugh Tomlinson and Robert Galeta (Minneapolis: Uni-versity of Minnesota Press, 1989).

4. See M. M. Bakhtin, *Speech Genres and Other Late Essays*, trans. Vern W. McGee, ed. Caryl Emerson and Michael Holquist (Austin: University of Texas Press, 1986), and *The Dialogic Imagination*, ed. Michael Holquist, trans. Caryl Emerson and Michael Holquist (Austin: University of Texas Press, 1981).

5. Jürgen Habermas, *The Theory of Communicative Action*, trans. Thomas McCarthy (Boston: Beacon Press, 1985).

6. For sample studies of postcolonial Francophone cinema, see Dina Sherzer, ed., *Cin-ema, Colonialism, Postcolonialism: Perspectives from the French and Francophone World* (Austin: University of Texas Press, 1996); Lieve Spaas, *The Francophone Film: A Struggle for Identity* (Manchester: Manchester University, Press, 2000).

7. See Michael Hardt and Antonio Negri, *Empire* (Cambridge, Mass.: Harvard Univer-sity Press, 2000).

8. For such a recent attempt, see Christine Gledhill and Linda Williams, eds, *Reinvent-ing Film Studies* (London: Arnold/New York: Oxford University Press, 2000). An account of the relatively short history of film studies in the West is given by Dudley Andrew, "The

'Three Ages' of Cinema Studies and the Age to Come" *PMLA* 115.3 (May 2000): 341–351. Yingjin Zhang offers a critical overview of contemporary Chinese film studies in the United States in *Screening China: Critical Interventions, Cinematic Reconfigurations, and the Transnational Imaginary in Contemporary Chinese Cinema* (Ann Arbor: University of Michigan Center for Chinese Studies, 2002).

9. Chris Berry, ed., *Perspectives on Chinese Cinema* (London: British Film Institute, 1991).

10. Nick Browne, Paul G. Pickowicz, Vivian Sobchack, Esther Yau, eds, *New Chinese Cinemas: Forms, Identities, Politics* (Cambridge: Cambridge University Press, 1994). For a review and critique of this book, see Yeh Yueh-yu, "Defining 'Chinese,'" *Jump Cut* 42 (1998): 73–76.

11. Sheldon H. Lu, ed., *Transnational Chinese Cinemas: Identity, Nationhood, Gender* (Honolulu: University of Hawai`i Press, 1997). Gina Marchetti speaks of Chinese cinemas as "plural and transnational" in her introduction to a special section on "Chinese and Chinese Diaspora Cinema" in *Jump Cut* 42 (1998): 68–72. Chris Berry and Mary Farquhar further elaborate on the interrelations between the national and the transnational in cinema studies in their joint essay "From National Cinemas to Cinema and the National: Rethinking the National in Transnational Chinese Cinemas," *Journal of Modern Literature in Chinese* 4.2 (January 2001): 109–122. In April 2000, Hong Kong Baptist University held an international film conference called "Year 2000 and Beyond: History, Technology, and the Future of Transnational Chinese Film and Television," highlighting the significance of the transnational in cinema studies.

12. See John Hill and Pamela Church Gibson, eds., *The Oxford Guide to Film Studies* (Oxford: Oxford University Press, 1998). The section on world cinema is later reprinted as a separate volume, also edited by Hill and Gibson, titled *World Cinema: Critical Approaches* (Oxford: Oxford University Press, 2000).

13. For instance, Lee Tain-Dow organized a conference on Chinese-language films in Taipei in 1992. A similar conference on Chinese-language films was also held at Hong Kong Baptist University in fall 1996. For book-length critical studies centered on the idea of "*huayu dianying*," see Zheng Shusen (William Tay), ed., *Wenhua piping yu huayu dianying* (Cultural criticism and Chinese-language cinemas) (Taipei: Maitian, 1995); Loo Tain Dow, ed., *Dangdai huayu dianying lunshu* (Studies in contemporary Chinese-language film) (Taipei: Shibao wenhua, 1996); Yeh Yueh-yu, Cheuk Pak-tong, Ng Ho, eds., *Sandi chuanqi: huayu dianying ershi nian* (Romance of three places: twenty years of Chinese-language cinemas) (Taipei: Caituan faren guojia dianying ziliaoguan, 1999); Pu Feng and Li Zhaoxing, eds., *Jingdian liangbai: zuijia huayu dianying liangbaibu* (Two hundred classics: two hundred best Chinese-language films) (Hong Kong: Hong Kong Film Critics Society, 2002).

14. Ginette Vincendeau, "Issues in European Cinema," in John Hill and Pamela Church Gibson, eds., *World Cinema: Critical Approaches* (Oxford: Oxford University Press, 2000), 58–59.

15. For previous studies of indigenous Chinese traditions in English, see Wai-fong Loh, "From Romantic Love to Class Struggle: Reflections on the Film *Liu Sanjie*," in Bonnie McDougall, ed., *Popular Chinese Literature and Performing Arts in People's Republic of*

China, 1949–1979 (Berkeley: University of California Press, 1984), 165–176; Gina Marchetti, " *Two Stage Sisters*: The Blossoming of a Revolutionary Aesthetic," in Lu, ed., *Transnational Chinese Cinemas*, 59–80.

16. For further studies of film censorship in the name of nation-building in the Republican period, see Zhiwei Xiao, "Anti-Imperialism and Film Censorship during the Nanjing Decade, 1927–1937," in *Transnational Chinese Cinemas*, 35–57; Xiao, "Constructing a New National Culture: Film Censorship and Issues of Cantonese Dialect, Superstition, and Sex in the Nanjing Decade," in Yingjin Zhang, ed., *Cinema and Urban Culture in Shanghai: 1922–1943* (Stanford, Calif.: Stanford University Press, 1999).

17. Miriam Bratu Hansen, "Fallen Women, Rising Stars, New Horizons: Shanghai Silent Film as Vernacular Modernism," *Film Quarterly* 54.1 (2000): 13.

18. Zhang Yuan has been regarded as one of the most prominent directors from the post–fifth generation. For critical studies of his work, see Chris Berry, "Staging Gay Life in China: *East Palace, West Palace,*" *Jump Cut* 42 (1998): 84–89; Zhang Zhen, "Zhang Yuan," in Yvonne Tasker, ed., *Fifty Contemporary Filmmakers* (London and New York: Routledge, 2002), 418–429. Jenny Kwok Wah Lau offers a useful broad discussion of this new generation of filmmakers in "Globalization and Youthful Subculture: The Chinese Sixth-Generation Films at the Dawn of the New Century," in Jenny Kwok Wah Lau, ed., *Multiple Modernities: Cinemas and Popular Media in Transcultural East Asia* (Philadelphia: Temple University Press, 2002), 13–27.

19. For a comprehensive mapping of the cultural landscape of China in the late-twentieth century, as well as discussions of the interrelations of postmodernism and visual culture, see Sheldon H. Lu, *China, Transnational Visuality, Global Postmodernity* (Stanford, Calif.: Stanford University Press, 2001).

20. See Gilles Deleuze, *Cinema I: The Movement-Image,* trans. Hugh Tomlinson and Barbara Habberjam (London: Athlone Press, 1986); Deleauze, *Cinema II: The Time-Image.*

21. We owe Stanley Rosen at the University of Southern California for the information and insight expressed in this paragraph. See his unpublished essay "Hollywood, Globalization and Film Markets in Asia: Lessons for China?"

22. Some informative studies of the interrelations of film and nation from global perspectives have been published recently. See, for example, Mette Hjort and Scott MacKenzie, eds., *Cinema and Nation* (London: Routledge, 2000); Alan Williams, ed., *Film and Nationalism* (New Brunswick, N.J.: Rutgers University Press, 2002).

PART ONE

Historiography, Periodization, Trends

CHAPTER ONE

MARY FARQUHAR
AND CHRIS BERRY

Shadow Opera

Toward a New Archaeology of the Chinese Cinema

Introduction

Until the 1980s in the West, early cinema was seen as "immature babblings" within a linear approach to film history.[1] The view was that "primitive" cinema matured into "classic" cinema, exemplified worldwide by Hollywood. Scholars such as Thomas Elsaesser, Robert C. Allen, Noël Burch, André Gaudreault, Tom Gunning, and Miriam Hansen have since transformed our view of early cinema, claiming it represents an alternative, not primitive, approach to filmmaking. Elsaesser calls this "a new archaeology of the art."[2]

Within this new archaeology, Gunning's work on early American cinema is one of many areas that have been extended to other cinemas, including Chinese. Gunning rejects the realist prejudice that disparages early cinema as theatrical and, therefore, somehow not really cinematic at all. He recasts it as "a cinema of attractions" that aggressively addresses the spectator, akin to vaudeville. Gunning states, "To summarize, the cinema of attractions directly solicits spectator attention, inciting visual curiosity, and supplying pleasure through an exciting spectacle—a unique event, whether fictional or documentary, that is of interest in itself. The attraction to be displayed may also be of a cinematic nature, such as the early close-ups.... Theatrical display dominates over narrative absorption."[3]

Chinese peepshow, 1932.

Film-vaudeville coexhibition determined that viewers first saw early film as spectacle. This mode was supposedly then displaced by classic (Hollywood) cinema's "purely narrative mode" that absorbs spectators into the story as they sit isolated in dark theatres.[4] Early Chinese cinema was clearly a cinema of attractions, "a sort of hailing of the viewer" in public spaces (teahouses, markets, parks and theatres) used for a variety of traditional performances such as acrobatics, opera, peep shows (*la yangpian*), and the many performing arts known as *"quyi."*[5] Such similarities between early Western and Chinese cinemas are not surprising, in view of the fact that Western, especially American, films long dominated the Chinese market in the first half of the twentieth century. Our point is that early cinema fitted neatly into the exhibition context of China's indigenous aesthetic of attractions, including the strong tradition of curiosity/curio *(wanyi'r)* that rapidly exploited any technological innovation as novel entertainment.[6]

A Chinese cinema of attractions continued as one major mode throughout the century. Performativity, spectacle, and intertextuality are flaunted in diverse genres from opera films to martial arts movies. The crux of this cinema, even when radically transformed in the People's Republic of China (PRC), is a cultural identity that is read through China's changing tradition of the popular and performing arts, especially (but not only) opera and its transposition into film. Geremie Barmé, for example, sees opera and popular fiction as the constant influence on all twentieth-century Chinese cinema, with opera as "the backbone not only of film itself but also of the viewing habits of the public."[7] Lu Hongshi claims that the merger of opera and film produced a distinctive and dynamic cinema in China that has enriched the world.[8]

This mode, which we call "shadow opera," hails viewers first and foremost as Chinese people seeing a Chinese spectacle. Its core genre, opera film, is an example of an old, yet new, commercialized entertainment where film transformed opera into a "national infatuation," disseminating major works beyond their former regional and linguistic boundaries.[9] This transformation was part of the early Republican nation-building project in China, which included transforming local forms, such as Beijing opera, into national cultural forms. Stephen Teo sees opera film as cultural nationalism.[10] Sek Kei traces its origins to operatic displays of Han ethnic identity during the Mongol Yuan dynasty when opera first flourished. Thus, opera and opera film signal a national identity during times of crisis.[11]

Viewers, however, are not necessarily addressed as homogeneously Chinese in this cinema. They may be a particular teahouse clientele (China's first films), members of a regional culture (Cantonese language operas and martial arts), or a social class such as "the masses" of workers, peasants, and soldiers (revolutionary operas). Until the revolutionary model, the perceived problem with this cinema was its feudal content and regional diversity, the flipside of the grand narrative of an imagined modern nation. Traditional arts including shadow opera were considered popular, but feudal; early reformist arts were modern, but lacked "a common language with the Chinese working people," according to Qu Qiubai, China's first Marxist literary theorist.[12] Qu—and later Mao Zedong—advocated that popular art forms become *the* common language for revolutionary mobilization. The popular was to be popularized (*tongsuhua*) and made revolutionary in pursuit of a socialist nation-state. In practice, opera constituted a common Chinese language for conservative, entrepreneurial, and revolutionary filmmakers alike. So it was variously criticized, censored, and reformed last century, all in the name of the abstract citizen-spectator. But when flesh-and-blood spectators could choose, they flocked to this cinema that surfaced, again and again, across the Chinese world.

This chapter explores shadow opera through the concept of shadowplay, through early opera films and, finally, through revolutionary opera film in mainland China. Opera film and martial arts movies in colonial Hong Kong—which produced more of these films than China or Taiwan—have been the subject of excellent studies and film retrospectives. Our emphasis on opera film in mainland China supplements this work, recasting it as shadow opera under the rubric of a cinema of attractions.

Shadowplay and Shadow Opera: A Cinema of Attractions

Gunning's cinema of attractions fits with recent Chinese archaeological studies of their own cinema.[13] Post-Mao historians in China have been delving into film archives and rethinking early Chinese cinema outside the mandatory Marxist-Leninist framework of former years. One strand is dominated by an evolution-ary approach. In their seminal work on Chinese silent film, Li Suyuan and Hu Jubin claim, for example, that early film progressed through a number of stages: "from the making of traditional opera films to the making of documentaries and short fiction films and finally to the completion of a number of feature films."[14] Maturity arrived with the making of realist feature films from the late 1920s in Shanghai. As in the West, the rich archival studies have also led to alternative ap-proaches to early Chinese cinema, often by the same scholars. Zhong Dafeng and Chen Xihe, for example, claim a distinctive Chinese film theory called "shadow-play" (yingxi).[15] "Shadowplay," the earliest term for film, combines ying (shadow or film) and xi (play or drama or opera). Thus, many scholars claim that early film was primarily perceived as drama: yingxizhe, xi ye.[16] Over the next sixty years, theatre was so enmeshed with film that leading critics in the post-Mao period exhorted Chinese filmmakers "to throw away the walking stick of drama."[17] As in the West, theatricality has been viewed pejoratively.[18] But what sort of the-atre? Xi and its synonym, ju, more commonly mean opera or performance to or-dinary Chinese rather than the Western-style realistic theatre familiar to edu-cated, urban elites. Hence, one valid translation of yingxi is shadow opera.

Nevertheless, the earliest reading of xi is as "play" or "show." Like Gunning, Li Suyuan looks at text-spectator relations and finds that the xi in yingxi initially related to viewer perceptions of film as vaudeville or variety show. As in the West, shadowplay was a novel performance "far removed from [traditional or modern] drama."[19] At the end of the nineteenth century, according to Li, xi was a common linguistic ending in the Shanghai region where the term was first used. Thus, xi denotes variety shows, such as baxi for acrobatics (zaji), xifa for magic shows (moshu), and maxi for circuses. Yingxi specifically refers to China's ancient lantern shadowplay (dengyingxi) that used a lantern to throw shadows of pup-pets against a screen. The fuller terms for film were "electric shadowplay" (dian-guang yingxi), "Western shadowplay" (xiyang yingxi), or "moving shadowplay" (huodong yingxi), the modifiers differentiating the film show from traditional shadowplay technology. Indeed, as Li argues, the first Chinese film appreciation, published in 1897, emphasizes yingxi as marvelous spectacles (qiguan) rather than as onscreen drama. The illusory and elusive nature of American shadow-play was said to condense the world and clearly conjure up "the secrets of the universe," making life seem as "dreams and bubbles."[20] Film technology was itself part of the attraction. Later in the 1920s, when Chinese were making their own films, film was perceived by some—though not all—filmmakers as primarily drama, but even then not necessarily as the realistic Western-style "civilized plays" *(wenmingxi)* that Zhong Dafeng calls the "stepmother" of many early Chinese films.[21] According to Li, early film theory was richly diverse. So, too, was early Chinese cinema.

In fact, China's first films were opera films *(xiqupian)*. Classic operas were selected or adapted for the screen. Thus, intertextuality between film and well-known operas, in this case, was a crucial attraction of early Chinese cinema. If vernacular, civilized plays are cinema's stepmother, then opera is the mother in terms of first film productions, whether on the mainland (1905)[22] or in Hong Kong (1909).[23] Opera films were also the first productions in major regional language films, Cantonese (1933)[24] and Taiwanese (1954).[25] There is no doubt that opera film was popular, familiar, and obviously Chinese, comprising a substantial slice of the films produced in the embryonic period (1905–1921) and providing a reconstituted sense of community among new urban viewers from diverse regional backgrounds.[26] With opera excerpts as the exception, early feature films were essentially fragments, slapsticks, folktales, short features, and "magical illusions" as in the West.[27] Of these genres, Luo Yijun argues that opera films represent the earliest merger of Western cinema and Chinese aesthetics, and "they are still the favorite form of the people, especially in the villages."[28] He claims this genre (along with animation) as the most successful Chinese films. But, he writes, the aesthetics of West and East clash and they are always "incomplete."[29] As a cinema of attractions, however, opera films are not incomplete works, but a style of cinema where "narrative coherence is supplied in the act of reception rather than inherent in the film itself."[30]

Opera film (and opera in film) did not decline with the rise of classic realist cinema in the golden age of the late 1920s and the 1930s. Opera film was a staple, even though there were successive crazes for more exciting hybrid genres. Opera film was also a pioneer. In 1931, opera scenes, songs, and music delighted audiences of China's first sound film, *Sing-Song Girl Red Peony*, directed by a founding father of Chinese film, Zhang Shichuan.[31] China's first color film in 1948 was a full opera, starring China's foremost opera and film actor, Mei Lanfang, as the main attraction.[32] In the 1950s and 1960s, after World War II and the founding of the People's Republic, opera film again became "phenomenally popular" with mainland, Hong Kong, and Taiwanese audiences, so it is not surprising that the first PRC–Hong Kong coproductions in the 1950s were opera films.[33] Indeed, opera film is more than a genre; it is the core genre of a vital cinema of spectacle-attractions.

A few famous examples demonstrate this cinema's resilience, diversity and

A poster of the 1954 Taiwanese
opera, Wang Baochuan
and Xue Pinggui.

overt intertextuality. Across China—whether mainland, Hong Kong, Taiwan, or the diaspora—various film versions of the operatic romance, *Liang Shanbo and Zhu Yingtai*, began in 1935 and climaxed in the Shaw Brother's box office hit and most frequently revived movie, the Li Hanxiang and King Hu (also known as Hu Jinquan) production of 1963.[34] Film critic, Lin Nien-tung, describes such "catering to vulgar tastes" as "pernicious."[35] Nevertheless, the Li-Hu film began a fad for Anhui-style "yellow-plum-melody" *(huangmeidiao)* opera films.[36] By the mid-1960s, Hong Kong audiences tired of opera film romances, with effete heroes, and seriously turned to action heroes in sword-play martial arts films *(wuxiapian,* also colloquially called *gongfupian* or *wudapian).*[37] Yet this genre too derived as much from diverse regional operas in terms of performance as from popular stories of knight-errants. In Cantonese martial arts movies, Guan Dexing (Kwan Tak-hing)—whose role is synonymous with the hero in the famous Huang Feihong (Wong Fei-Hong) series directed by Hu Peng from 1949 onward —was a Cantonese opera star.[38] King Hu's movies in Mandarin, directed from both Hong Kong and Taiwan, are influenced by the northern-style, Beijing opera.[39] Indeed, Teo calls Hu's films "cinema opera" *(xiqu fengwei dianying)* because of their operatic style, especially in the spectacular combat scenes.[40] Meanwhile, as opera film lost audiences to martial arts movies in Taiwan and Hong Kong, the Maoists under Jiang Qing were developing revolutionary model works *(yang-banxi)*, mainly Beijing operas. Revolutionary opera films were a specialized art with special committees during the Cultural Revolution. Their famous forerunner was the Shaanxi *yangge* opera, *The White-Haired Girl*, written in Yan'an and filmed in 1950.[41] Yet these works are frequently dismissed as political propaganda in the post-Mao period. The long tradition of opera as attraction *within* films then resurfaced.[42] Chen Kaige's post-Mao film, *Farewell My Concubine,* is a recent example. It too attracted criticism, this time for exoticizing old China for foreign viewers.[43]

Despite censorship and criticism, a constantly changing cinema of attractions continued in China, where shadow opera flourished during the twentieth century. Whereas Elsaesser has speculated on a return to earlier performative model — "the show" coupled with a "pervasive narrativization"[44]—in late-twentieth-century Western media, Chinese viewers have continuously enjoyed such a cinema throughout a turbulent century.

Early Opera Film as a Commercial Cinema of Attractions

Early opera films no longer exist. Therefore, scholars are still archivists and historians as well as analysts of film texts. Indeed, when Lu investigated China's first films—made by Ren Qingtai between 1905 and 1909—he described himself as a paleontologist, reconstructing the films' look from a few skeletal remains.[45] As isolated texts, these films are usually described as documentaries. Within the framework of a cinema of attractions, however, Chinese audiences would view them as glimpses of traditional complex narratives performed onscreen. The novelty is threefold: film as technology, the Chinese story, and performances by the "King of Beijing Opera" in the first films.[46]

FIRST, FILM AS TECHNOLOGY

Li Suyuan argues that Chinese first saw film as a marvelous spectacle. But it was a *foreign* spectacle. Ren Qingtai made film a *Chinese* spectacle. A photographer and entrepreneur, he screened films at his own entertainment centers in Beijing: Dongan Market and Daguanlou. Daguanlou was a theatre built in the traditional teahouse style of horizontal rows of seating, with women (upstairs) segregated from men (downstairs). The seats were always full, offering a variety-show format that included opera and short foreign films of slapstick, magic, and Chinese and foreign scenery. This commercial exhibition mode is central to a cinema of attractions. Ren included moving pictures of opera—an extension of his business selling photos of opera stars through his photography shop—as a novel

Chinese addition to the repertoire.[47] "So China's first films were born!"[48] *Dingjun Mountain* was the earliest and apparently so popular that Ren continued to film more favorites, after first performing the stage versions at Daguanlou. He selected excerpts such as fighting and acrobatics that emphasized the spectacle of early silent film technology: visuality and movement *(shijue yundong)*.[49]

SECOND, THE STORY

By the time Ren made his opera films, narrative was a feature of foreign films exhibited in China.[50] According to Charles Musser, these films adopted three overlapping strategies for clarifying the narrative: audience familiarity (the spectator), simple but self-sufficient narratives (the film), and the lecturer/narrator (exhibition).[51] Ren adopted the first audience-centered strategy. Whereas audience foreknowledge was apparently "doomed" in the West because of the limited number of original and widely known stories,[52] China had a vast treasury of raw narrative to be reworked onscreen. Opera is merely one of the performing arts that retell long, complex, and multilayered stories from popular fiction such as *The Three Kingdoms* (history, statesmen, and heroes), *Water Margin* (heroes, outlaws, and martial arts), *Journey to the West* (monks, superwarriors, gods, and demons), and *Strange Tales of Liaozhai* (scholars, beauties, fairies, flower spirits, ghosts, demons, goblins, and foxes).[53] But much popular fiction itself originated as oral folktales and story cycles that not only continued alongside the written works but are also inscribed in their form. Thus, chapters are cycles, or *hui*. Popular performances are usually excerpts or story cycles familiar to the audience. Opera is considered the richest and most complex of these traditional performing arts. But it is also regional. Ren made his films in Beijing. He chose excerpts from the most loved operas in the most widespread but also local style, Beijing opera with its repertoire of 1,220 stories,[54] and featured China's most famous Beijing opera stars. This began the tradition of opera film as a national film form.

Dingjun Mountain, for example, is a classic opera based on the seventieth and seventy-first *hui* of *Romance of the Three Kingdoms*, China's first novel which came out of the oral storytelling tradition. It is a favorite source for opera.[55] As a film text, *Dingjun Mountain* is rudimentary narrative. As a text in a specific cultural context, the film is a novel glimpse of a rich narrative familiar to Chinese viewers. This is true for all Ren's opera films that followed.[56] If early Western cinema (and now Western cinema and television) is approached as media-intertext in the new archaeology,[57] then so too is this Chinese performative film tradition. It is difficult to talk of definitive sources for a given film but we can talk of intertextuality as a dynamic relationship between film and other art forms. Opera cinema is *not* traditional art or *just* documentary; it *devours, selects, transposes* and *transforms* traditional arts in its voracious appetite for novel displays of well known stories and these arts in turn animate Chinese film. Ren did not adapt opera for the screen; he selected bits of cycles best suited to the silent film medium.

THIRD, THE PERFORMANCE

Opera stars were China's first film stars. They were the billing attraction in these first films. *Dingjun Mountain* featured Tan Xinpei (1847–1917), one of China's foremost actors who specialized in *laosheng,* or mature male, and especially military, roles that dominated the stage from the 1830s.[58] These roles replaced the previous emphasis on *dan* (or male actor) female roles that again became prominent from the 1920s through the virtuoso performances of famous actor and film star, Mei Lanfang (1894–1961).[59] Thus, Beijing opera was not a static art and opera film extended its reach deep into the urban populace. Audience tastes in opera previously roamed among fads for civilian *(wen)* dramas of righted injustice, love, and the family to military *(wu)* dramas of war, rebellion, and heroic adventure. So, too, film fads first exploited military operas and, by the mid-1920s, developed into successive crazes for ancient costume films *(guzhuangpian,* incorporating the notion of opera, also called *guzhuangxi),* and martial arts films.[60] These stories are found in popular literature and art and performed in a variety of modes, especially opera. Ren's opera films are embryonic shadow opera.

Dingjun Mountain belonged to the military *(wu)* category of opera with battle scenes and "spectacular acrobatics."[61] It is a foretaste of the martial arts genres to come. Tan was so famous for his military, male roles *(wushengxi),* his martial arts *(wushu),* and his sword fighting *(wudao)* that the famous reformer, Liang Qichao, wrote: "his name evokes a roar like thunder everywhere in the world."[62] Acting was far from the naturalistic or realist civilized play performances. The whole point was capturing the "essence" *(xieyi)* through fluid scenes, through plasticity (a minimalist, flexible stage that was replaced by "natural" scenery in later opera films), through sculpturality (three dimensional characters onstage) and through conventionalism (an elaborate and symbolic code governing meaning). Spectators understood these conventions, such as painted faces *(lianpu)* denoting character.[63] According to Huang Zuolin, this "outer" essentialism is matched by an "inner" essentialism: typicalized life, rhythmic movement, lyrical language and minimalist décor. For Huang, operatic performance is not a question of audience-character identification but a Brechtian audience-character distance.[64] This feature of spectator-text relations is a core difference between a cinema of attractions and realist cinema. It is certainly a feature of Tan's performance in *Dingjun Mountain.* It was shot outside to music. Ren used a fixed camera, natural light and no scenery, just a plain white cloth. The film was presumably shown accompanied by a live orchestra as part of Ren's variety

Tan Xinpei, "The King of Opera,"
in *Dingjun Mountain*, 1905.

show. Audiences experienced the film as a performance: "The human figure was clear and everyone could see that it was Tan Xinpei. But once the sword was brandished, all one could see was the moving of the sword; the human figure was nowhere to be found. In another scene, the upper half of the boot was missing. Even so, people enjoyed the film very much."[65]

This early filmmaking ended when Ren's Fengtai Studio burned down in 1909. After a hiatus, mainland Chinese again began making films in 1913, and, by the 1920s, film and cinemas were established features of urban cultural landscapes. According to histories, "social, romantic and ethical" Chinese films (1922–1926) were followed by a craze for costume films and martial arts movies (1927–1931).[66] Advocates claimed costume films were popular and challenged the prevailing Westernization of Chinese cinema. But there were problems with opera film. It was said that audience and actor often brought inappropriate operatic habits (*jingjuhua*) to the film medium.[67] At the same time, film technology matured beyond anything that could be displayed onstage or in the marketplace, simultaneously sustaining and displacing the traditional performing arts. The box-office hit at this time was *The Burning of Honglian Temple*, made by Zheng Zhengqiu and Zhang Shichuan in 1928. Audiences were so excited by the intricate plot, the mysterious events, the special effects, and the filmic spectacle of "the unimaginable"—flying swords spat out of mouths, thunder produced by hands, flying swordsmen, and cartoon characters interspersed among the real—that seventeen sequels were made.[68] This began the martial arts genre and a complex and more covert intertextuality; in this case, *Honglian Temple* had its performance origins in opera (such as acrobatics and fighting), its story from a best-selling novel, and its sensation from the "unimaginable" capacities of foreign filmmaking, whether stories or techniques. The *Honglian Temple* sagas no longer exist. Reformist writers from the late 1920s criticized the entire corpus of costume films as feudal and the state eventually banned them in 1931 as unrealistic, unethical, and generally unsavory, especially in their influence on the uneducated masses.

Revolutionary Opera Film as a Proletarian Cinema of Attractions

At the very same time that costume films and martial arts movies were banned, Chinese revolutionaries were reassessing such popular arts in terms of audience, ideology and nation. Their concern is a continuation of the ethical dimensions of shadowplay aesthetics.[69] For Marxist-Leninists, the primary function of all the arts is revolutionary education of the masses, envisioned as masters *(zhuren)* of a Chinese socialist state. This cinema is produced by political elites, not the market. Yet in both theory and practice, the revolutionary line on film resonates with features of a proletarian cinema of attractions.[70]

The theory is political. From the late 1920s, revolutionaries critiqued traditional and urban commercialized entertainment in general as inimical to the revolution, which needed art to mobilize the masses against imperialism, especially Japanese invasion. Audience *(duixiang)* is fundamental. Qu Qiubai considered reformist arts of the May Fourth period to be Europeanized, a banquet for the gentry while "the laboring people were still starving."[71] The answer was "new wine in old bottles": to fill popular art forms with revolutionary content. Qu specifically advocated the use of a street vernacular in popular old and new forms—including cinema and comic books, which were accessible to the illiterate—to attract the masses. Hence, intertextuality is also crucial. This cinema exhorts the spectator to move from film viewing to revolutionary action. To save China from its enemies, Qu told artists to take revolutionary arts to the people, to "the streets, factories, slums, teahouses and bookstalls," and to infiltrate the film industry.[72] This urban strategy became rural under Mao when Qu became commissar of education in the Jiangxi soviet in 1934.[73] The definitive statement is in Mao's "Talks at the Yan'an Forum on Literature and Art" in 1942. Artists were to

A scene from the opera *The White-haired Girl*, 1945.

produce works that "awaken the masses, fire them with enthusiasm and impel them to unite and struggle to transform their environment."[74] Finally, then, this art is not self-sufficient, but one that consciously hails the spectator as a collectivity, as a class, as a country. Audience acknowledgement, intertextuality, and performativity are core elements of a proletarian cinema of attractions.

A proletarian cinema of attractions had to be Chinese. To achieve this, a Marxist-Leninist archive of "Chineseness" was formulated that inherited earlier Republican efforts. The theory and practice is still about sinicizing *(Zhongguohua)* all the arts, including cinema, but is now a subcategory of sinicizing Marxism itself. In rural Yan'an the question of national form *(minzu xingshi)* in the arts was again fiercely debated from 1938 to 1940. At its core was the old tension between Chinese and Western art forms. David Holm states that the Yan'an solution of "new wine in old bottles" led not to transformed Chinese art, but to a "patchwork," a "bricolage," a "hodge-podge."[75] The model revolutionary genres —Yan'an's new *yangge* opera, such as *The White-Haired Girl*, and the Cultural Revolution's model ballets and model operas—are, Holm rightly states, "single, hybrid model genre[s]."[76] When adapted to film, however, it is precisely this hybridity and theatricality which hail and attract the spectator.

In practice after 1949, opera film became an archetypal national film form under Mao's Yan'an line on the arts. The early classic is *The White-Haired Girl (Baimao nü)*, a textbook case of intertextuality, performativity, and spectacle. Its genre transposition mirrors traditional narrative performances and spans the evolution of revolutionary cinema in Maoist China. With some modifications, the 1950 film basically follows the classic opera version, a somewhat sanitized re-working of local *yangge* opera into hybrid form. The opera and then the film were displayed as models for class struggle during land reform. Like Ren's films, the opera was first tested on the local populace. A Yan'an dress rehearsal in which the landlord, Huang, escaped punishment evoked strong local criticism. Holm reports, "There was a cook in the kitchens who emphasized what he was saying by continuing to chop vehemently at the cabbage on his chopping block, 'The play's all right, but not to shoot that evil bastard Huang Shiren, that's just too unjust!' As Zheng Gang remarks, 'At the time [of the United Front] we still felt that basically one should work for solidarity with the landlord class. If he were to be shot, that would certainly have gone against government policy. So we didn't change it.'"[77]

The cook was right. Huang had to be shot. There was to be no compassion for class enemies. After a public performance before Mao and other Yan'an leaders, the central secretariat approved the opera and passed down the following pol-icy decision: "Huang Shiren is a character so steeped in evil that it would not be right not to have him shot [*sic*]. The broad masses will definitely not tolerate that."[78] In the fighting *yangge* of Communist Yan'an, peasant audiences could empathize with their own world, their own wounds, their own people, in their own language and stylized in their own operatic form. A 1947 observer reported that village audiences stood and shouted, "Kill, kill," like the cook, while women in particular wept.[79]

The 1950 film of *The White-Haired Girl* was a model (*dianxing*) for revolu-tionary cinema, whether opera or socialist realist.[80] The crux of this cinema is class struggle. Film scholar Li Haiyan cites *The White-Haired Girl* as an early model for the "racialization" (*zhongzuhua*) of class status in revolutionary narratives, claiming that class becomes a fixed, political and biological—rather than economic—category that is inherited through family background. She argues that the work-ing people (*laodong renmin*) are constructed as the "fictitious" moral founda-tion of the socialist nation-state.[81] These people become "masters of the screen."[82] Class struggle means class purification, a continuous war against class enemies that is exemplified in the film by the gradual writing out of the landlord's rape of the peasant girl, Xi'er, and the resulting baby: "vile spawn" (*niezhong*).[83] Thus, Xi'er is depicted in film reviews in the 1950s "not as an ordinary, victimized character but an embodiment of the unyielding, anti-feudal fighting spirit of China's laboring people."[84] It is a militant *(wu)* opera film, read as an allegory of the fight for nationhood led by the Communist Party. (For a summary of the evolution of *The White-Haired Girl*, see the appendix.)

Azalea Mountain (Dujuan shan) is an example of opera film form towards the end of the Cultural Revolution and so representative of the corpus of works filmed in this period.[85] All are militant, celebrating class struggle. Revolutionary operas continued the Republican transformation of China's best-known regional form, Beijing opera, into a national form. The filming principle was "to restore the stage and improve on the stage" *(huanyuan wutai, gaoyu wutai)* and a three-month conference in 1973 studied film adaptations of opera.[86] *Azalea Mountain* was filmed after the conference, and—while too late to be designated a model work *(yangban xi)* —was nevertheless considered not only one of the best at the time but also "a mirror" of peasant uprisings over 2,000 years of Chinese history.[87] Set in 1928, Lei Gang, who leads a local peasant guerilla group, rescues Ke Xiang from civil guards as they lead her to execution. Lei Gang is shocked to learn that this Party member is a woman. Ke Xiang brings sound Party leadership to the peasant partisans. She leads a force to rescue Lei Gang and others who have been captured because of Lei's impetuosity. The peasants under Ke and Lei finally go to Jinggang Shan to join Mao's guerillas. The opera distinguishes failed, traditional peasant rebellions from successful peasant revolution, led by the Communist Party under Mao Zedong. In this sense, it is the ongoing cinematic correction of *The Life of Wu Xun (Wu Xun zhuan)*, a historical costume film made in 1950 and much criticized for defiling revolutionary peasant struggle, the lynchpin of revolutionary history.[88] As narrative, then, *Azalea Mountain* is familiar and sprinkled with quotations from Chairman Mao.

Like all revolutionary Beijing operas, *Azalea Mountain* as a text shows appropriations from the West in linear plot, music, scenery, and costume.[89] It is therefore within the modern tradition of hybridity that began a century earlier. The work also retains many vestiges of operatic artifice, such as symbolic props (chains and bayonets, for example, that abound in revolutionary cinema), "the (painted) face denoting character," stylized movement, and a mixture of song, dialogue, dance, and martial arts.[90] Film added powerful techniques lacking in drama. Revolutionary opera films perfected a rhythmic visual movement from establishing shot to full close-up of the hero/ine. This rhythm realizes "the three prominences" *(san tuchu)*, which prescribed overwhelming focus on hero/ines, far more successfully than any other art form. The rule was "close, big and bright" *(jin, da, ming)* for hero/ines; "far, small and black" *(yuan, xiao, hei)* for villains.[91] This rule was partly realized in film by marrying the operatic *liangxiang* with the cin-

Revolutionary heroine, Ke Xiang, in *Azalea Mountain.*

ematic gaze. A *liangxiang* is a frozen, sculptural pose that visually conveys "archetypal images and emotions" onstage.[92] In film, the full *liangxiang* close-up on the character's face and especially eyes intensifies the emotional impact; we call this cinematic look the *liangxiang gaze.* The *liangxiang gaze* was already systematized in many opera and feature films during the 1950s and 1960s. In the 1970s, the camera fully exploited this convention.

The second scene in *Azalea Mountain,* when Ke Xiang first appears on her execution day, is an example of its use. This scene pulsates with dance-freeze/dance-freeze, varied by music and interspersed with song. The camera position is also frozen with Ke Xiang consistently centered high in the frame or in the center of a cowering circle of black-clad villains. They are always below her. The camera focus on Ke Xiang, however, moves back and forth within a restricted depth of field akin to a stage. The rhythm of Ke Xiang's first appearance is simplified below:

Establishing shot (still): The *yamen* next to the market square. [The enemy].

Close-up (still): The *yamen's* forbidding gates, she sings unseen.

Long shot (still): The gates open, guards run out. Ke Xiang briefly moves into the gateway.

Medium shot (still): She moves, framed in the gateway, a *liangxiang* of defiance with one arm upstretched, the other with a clenched fist, holding chains. Eyes gaze over the unseen crowd. She then moves, tossing back her hair and tossing back the chains. [The principal heroine]

Close-up of face (still): Her face fills the frame, light, young, robust. Brief *liangxiang* of dedication/defiance. Looking beyond her captors, she sings. Her eyes never flicker, her head stays still.

Close-up (forward zoom)

(face to half-body): Bayonet tips point towards her heart as she sings.

Close-up (half-body, still): An exaggerated tilt downward of her head. Unflickering eyes focus on the enemy, *liangxiang* of distilled hate.

The camera tracks back, and so do the enemies, as Ke Xiang proudly walks down the *yamen* steps, from prison to people. Musical accompaniment: "The Internationale." The scene ends when the people, under Lei Gang, fight and free Ke Xiang and the rebels are together under party leadership.

This scene illustrates screen techniques that dominated the production of revolutionary film—both realist and performative—from the 1950s to the 1970s in the People's Republic. The basis is Xia Yan's essays, the definitive working statements on the dramatic structure and techniques of film within the shadowplay tradition.[93] Ke Xiang's first appearance as the principal character fulfills the three essentials required by Xia Yan. She is previously introduced in scene 1: her character is certainly distinctive, and she is immediately involved in dramatic crisis, her own execution. Indeed, as Xia Yan insists, she "strikes a pose" and "briefs" us through action, dialogue, and song, which are emphasized, as he suggests, by close-ups and smooth, rhythmic editing, or montage.[94] The whole point is viewer identification so that emotion is aroused. This, for Xia, is national form and national style.[95]

Because the film is clearly opera, however, viewing habits would simultaneously distance and collapse the spectator-text relationship. At this time, a mass popularization movement to perform operas *(xuechang yangbanxi)* was in vogue so that people of all ages learned the arias, mimicking the filmic representation. Ordinary spectators became everyday actors in a mimetic circulation from stage, to screen, to nationwide performance in public and private spaces. Hence, a crucial point of the play is the performance. In *Azalea Mountain,* this is film form. The cinematic rhythm is a complex dance between revolutionary movement

Revolutionary heroine, Ke Xiang, in *Azalea Mountain*.

and perfect stillness, of camera, pose, and gaze. This is *xieyi*, or expressionist cinema. *Xieyi* freezes revolutionary action, and universalizes the particular. Stylized movement and stillness counterpoint each other. Luo Yijun claims that *xieyi* in traditional aesthetics is about expressing emotion *(qing)*.[96] It is also about expressing cosmic (transformed as class) energy *(qi)*. Ke Xiang's *liangxiang* gaze combines *qing* and *qi*. It says very clearly, very expressively, and very definitely — again and again — *we are* the rightful masters of new China and *we do* control our destiny. This is the success of China's revolution. This is the performance and pride that is constantly recited in China's proletarian cinema of attractions. But it lacks a crucial component — novelty — finally boring spectators with its relentless politics, limited repertoire, and black and red characters.

Conclusion

Sek Kei believes that opera film is now almost dead in Hong Kong.[97] Audience familiarity with the original form and its conventions at the beginning of last century no longer operates with the same force a century later. Nevertheless, it remains a vital genre screened on mainland television, with "golden oldies" subversively recited to a disco beat by a dissident post-Mao generation to annoy the authorities.[98] Shadow opera also continues in a dynamic merger between the realistic and performative modes. Zhang Yimou's *To Live* visually recuperates traditional puppet shadowplay as performance, spectacle, and subnarrative.[99] Chen

Kaige's *Farewell My Concubine* interweaves the operatic and the realistic in a story of Beijing opera actors during a century of revolution. And Jackie Chan, sent from Australia to study Beijing opera for ten years in Hong Kong, marries farce[100] and *gongfu* martial arts—a counterpart of swordplay—in box office hits that echo with favorite themes from the earliest Chinese cinema of attractions. More work needs to be done, especially in genres such as martial arts, where spectacle is supreme and intertextuality is complex. This genre appropriates indigenous cultural forms, but also elements from samurai swordplay and Hollywood action films, for example.

International film scholars further speculate that cinema as the classic institution for mediating film is perhaps also dead, superseded by audiovisual media where the viewer/spectator becomes the actor/participant.[101] Cinema is now an old medium. Yet it is also part of new media. Elsaesser, for instance, sees media kinships as a convergence of audiovisual media that cross both genres and species and, in the process, return to earlier filmmaking modes through overt intertextuality, special effects, and high-tech performances.[102] In the new media, then, classic cinema may well be the transitional mode.[103] Whatever the case, China produced one of the most complex and neglected cinemas of attractions in the old medium. Its performance already includes viewers as actors. The archaeology of shadow opera is part of "the archaeology of cinema's possible futures,"[104] whether in Chinese regions or around the world.

Appendix: Evolution of *The White-Haired Girl*

ORAL FOLKTALE

Supposedly a 1940 folktale about a "white-haired goddess," the story spread from northwest Hebei and reached Yan'an in 1944. In the tale, a landlord abducts Xi'er, a seventeen-year-old peasant girl, as payment for her father's debts. He rapes her, and she becomes pregnant. When the landlord attempts to kill her, she runs away and lives in a cave for nine years. During her isolation, her hair turns white, and locals believe she is a goddess. In the end, an Eighth Route army officer liberates her and the landlord is exposed.

OPERA AND FILM

Yan'an Local Opera and Beyond, 1945

The folktale is the basis for a five-act opera by He Jingzhi and Ding Yi first performed in Yan'an in April 1945. The operatic form is adapted primarily from local *yangge,* a mixture of song, dance, and ribald comic action in the Yan'an region and beyond, in accordance with the precepts of Mao's talks. From 1945 to 1949, the new opera *(xin geju)* was performed widely in liberated areas or adapted into other forms of local opera. In 1958, it was performed as a Beijing opera. It has also featured as a spoken play *(huaju)* and a comic book *(lianhuan-tuhua)* by Hua Sanchuan that followed the film, not the opera, version. The He-Ding opera is the classic text.

Feature Film, 1950

Directed by Wang Bin and Shui Hua (Northeast Film Studio), the feature film was adapted from the He-Ding opera with some revisions, particularly the down-playing of Xi'er's baby. This version is now seen as a classic work of early revolutionary cinema produced by the first communist-run film studio. When Xi'er is rescued by the Party, her hair returns to black.

BALLET AND FILM

The first ballet was produced in Japan in 1955. It was performed in Beijing in 1957. In 1964, a half-hour Chinese ballet version—by the Shanghai Dance School—was approved by Jiang Qing.

In 1965, the full revolutionary ballet of The White-Haired Girl was performed in Shanghai. It was later adopted as one of the few model dramas *(yangbanxi)* performed during the Cultural Revolution. In this version, Xi'er fights back, is not raped, and has no baby. Her hair, however, does turn white.

In 1971, a faithful filmed version of the opera was released featuring the Shanghai Dance School, revolutionary dance-dramas, *The White-Haired Girl* Troupe *(Shanghai dianying zhipianchang).*

Notes

This chapter develops an approach taken in our book on Chinese cinema, *China on Screen: Cinema and Nation* (New York: Cambridge University Press, forthcoming). Thanks to Hu Jubin and Geremie Barmé, for their expert comments on this chapter, and to Colin Mackerras, Sang Ye, and Nick Knight, for many discussions of, respectively, opera, film, and Chinese Marxist philosophy. Geremie Barmé's comments are cited as Barmé (July 2000), when they extend the argument.

1. Luo Yijun, *"Dianyingde minzu fengge chutan"* (A preliminary discussion of national style in film), in Li Pusheng, Xu Hong, and Luo Yijun, eds., *Zhongguo dianying lilun wenxuan, 20–80 niandai* (An anthology of Chinese film theory) (Beijing: Wenhua yishu chubanshe, 1989), 2: 268–269. Originally in *Dianying yishu,* 11 (1981). See also Tom Gun-

ning, "Early American Cinema," in John Hill and Pamela Church Gibson, eds., *The Oxford Guide to Film Studies* (Oxford: Oxford University Press, 1998), 255.

2. Thomas Elsaesser, "General Introduction, Early Cinema: From Linear History to Mass Media Archaeology," in Thomas Elsaesser with Adam Barker, eds., *Early Cinema: Space Frame Narrative* (London: British Film Institute, 1990), 1.

3. Gunning, "The Cinema of Attractions: Early Film, Its Spectator, and the Avant-Garde" in Elsaesser with Barker, eds., *Early Cinema,* 58–59.

4. Gunning, "Early American Cinema," 256–258.

5. Gunning, "Early American Cinema," 258; Zhen Zhang, "Teahouse, Shadowplay, Bricolage: *Laborer's Love* and the Question of Early Chinese Cinema," in Yingjin Zhang, ed., *Cinema and Urban Culture in Shanghai, 1922–1943* (Stanford, Calif.: Stanford University Press, 1999), 27–50.

6. Geremie Barmé (July 2000). For a cinematic version of this tradition, see the scenes on toy making in the film, *Little Toys (Xiao wanyi),* dir. Sun Yu, Lianhua Film Company, 1933.

7. Barmé, "Persistence de la tradition au 'royaume des ombres': Quelques notes visant à contribuer à une approche nouvelle du cinéma chinoise," *Le Cinéma Chinois* (Paris: Catalogue of Centre Georges Pompidou, Chinese Film Retrospective, 1985), 113.

8. Lu Hongshi, *"Ren Qingtai yu shoupi guochanpian kaoping"* (Evaluations of Ren Qingtai and first Chinese films), *Dianying yishu* 2 (1992): 86.

9. Sek Kei, "Thoughts on Chinese Opera and the Cantonese Opera Film," in *Yueyu xiqupian huigu* (Cantonese opera film retrospective), Eleventh International Film Festival of Hong Kong (Hong Kong: Urban Council, 1987), 16.

10. Stephen Teo, *Hong Kong Cinema, The Extra Dimensions* (London: British Film Institute: 1997), 111. Although the statements by both Teo and Sek Kei (above and below) refer to Cantonese opera film and Hong Kong martial arts, they apply more generally to twentieth-century opera cinema, as recognized in Mao Zedong's famous "Talks at the Yan'an Forum on Literature and Art" (1942), for example.

11. Sek Kei, "Thoughts on Chinese Opera and the Cantonese Opera Film," 16.

12. Paul G. Pickowicz, *Marxist Literary Thought in China: The Influence of Chú Ch'iu-pai [Qu Qiubai]* (Berkeley: University of California Press, 1981), 99.

13. Chen Xihe, "Shadowplay: Chinese Film Aesthetics and Their Philosophical and Cultural Fundamentals," in George S. Semsel, Xia Hong, and Hou Jianping, eds., *Chinese Film Theory: A Guide to a New Era.* Translated by Hou Jianping, Li Xiaohong, and Fan Yuan (New York: Praeger, 1990), 192. Chen calls for "an archaeological" comparative study of Chinese film aesthetics.

14. Li Suyuan and Hu Jubin, *Chinese Silent Film History.* Translated by Wang Rui, Huang Wei, Hu Jubin, Wang Jingjing, Zhen Zhong, Shan Wanli, and Li Xun (Beijing: China Film Press, 1997), 39.

15. Dafeng Zhong, Zhen Zhang, and Yingjin Zhang, "From *Wenmingxi* (Civilized Play) to *Yingxi* (Shadowplay): The Foundations of Shanghai Film Industry in the 1920s," *Asian Cinema* 9.1 (fall 1997): 53; Xihe, "Shadowplay: Chinese Film Aesthetics and their Philosophical and Cultural Fundamentals," 192–204.

16. Xu Zhuodai, *Yingxizhe xi ye* (Film is drama), *Minxin tekan* 4, *Sannian yihou*

zhuankan (Special edition after three years) (December 1926): n.p., cited in Li Suyuan, *Guanyu Zhongguo zaoqi dianying lilun* (About film theories in early China), *Dangdai dianying* 61. 4 (1994): 25.

17. Bai Jingshen, "Throw Away the Walking Stick of Drama," in Semsel et al., eds., *Chinese Film Theory,* 5–9.

18. As Barmé (July 2000) notes, there is an interesting temporal shift in the late 1970s that reconstitutes the premodern not only as feudal (as before), but also as Marxist-Leninist cultural praxis, manifested in such works as revolutionary opera films.

19. Li, "About Film Theories in Early China," 22. Li analyzes three categories of terms used to denote early film: the northern word "electric shadows" *(dianying)* still used today; terms emphasizing film's technological visuality, such as "moving shadow pictures" *(huodong yinghua)*; and "shadowplay."

20. Cheng Jihua, ed., *Zhongguo Dianying Fazhanshi, shang* (A history of the development of Chinese cinema, vol. 1) (Beijing: Zhongguo dianying chubanshe, 1981), 8–9, n. 4.

21. Li Suyuan, "About Film Theories in Early China," 22.

22. *Dinjun Mountain (Dingjun shan),* dir. Ren Qingtai, Fengtai Studio, Beijing, 1905.

23. *Right a Wrong with Earthernware Dish (Wa pen shen yuan)* and *Stealing a Roasted Duck (Tou shaoya),* dir. Liang Shaobo, Asia Film Company, Hong Kong, 1909.

24. The first Cantonese film was of the Cantonese opera, *White Gold Dragon (Baijinlong,* 1933), made in Shanghai. According to Teo (*Hong Kong Cinema,* 40), it broke all box-office records in Hong Kong and Guangdong.

25. *Xue Pinggui and Wang Baochuan (Xue Pinggui yu Wang Baochuan),* dir. Li Quanxi, Taipei, 1954. For a history of Taiwanese-language films, see *Guojia dianying ziliaoguan koushi dianyingshi xiaozu* (Oral Cinema History Unit, Taipei Film Archive), *Taiyupian shidai 1* (The era of Taiwanese-language films, vol. 1), Taiwan Cinema History Series no. 3 (Taipei: Guojia dianying ziliaoguan, 1994).

26. Li Suyuan and Hu Jubin, *Chinese Silent Film History,* 39; Barmé (July 2000).

27. Tom Gunning, "Early American Cinema," 258 and 263. Li Suyuan and Hu Jubin, *Chinese Silent Film History,* 59.

28. Luo Yijun, "A Preliminary Discussion of National Style in Film," 273–274.

29. Ibid., 274.

30. Tom Gunning, "Early American Cinema," 263.

31. *Genü hongmudan,* dir. Zhang Shichuan (Mingxing, 1931). Li Hongshi, 86.

32. *Remorse at Death (Shengi hen),* dir. Fei Mu (Yihua Film Company, 1948). Lu, "Evaluations of Ren Qingtai and First Chinese Films," 86. Barmé, "Persistence de la tradition au 'royaume des ombres,'" 114.

33. Hu Ke, "Hong Kong Cinema in the Chinese Mainland (1949–1979)," in *Xianggang dianying huigu zhuanti: kuajiede Xianggang dianying* (Hong Kong cinema retrospective: border crossings in Hong Kong cinema), The Twenty-Fourth Hong Kong International Film Festival (Hong Kong: Leisure and Culture Services Department, 2000) 23. Sek Kei, "Thoughts on Chinese Opera and the Cantonese Opera Film" 16.

34. *Liang Shanbo yu Zhuyingtai,* also translated as *Love Eterne,* dir. Li Hanxiang and Hu Jinquan, Shaw Brothers, 1963. See Teo, *Hong Kong Cinema* 77–78.

35. Lin Nien-tung, "Some Problems in the Study of Cantonese Films of the 1950s," in

Wushi niandai, Yueyu dianying huiguzhan (Cantonese cinema retrospective, 1950–1959), Second International Film Festival of Hong Kong (Hong Kong: Provisional Urban Council, 1978), 32.

36. For example, a third of the films produced in the People's Republic between 1960 and 1963 were regional varieties of opera films, including Beijing opera, *kunqu*, *huangmeidiao*, and Cantonese operas. Yingjin Zhang and Zhiwei Xiao, *Encyclopaedia of Chinese Film* (London: Routledge, 1999), 167.

37. Sek Kei, "Li Hanxiang," in *Hong Kong Cinema Survey (1946–1968)*, Third Hong Kong International Film Festival Catalogue (Hong Kong: Provisional Urban Council, 1979), 93. See also Lin Nien-tung, "Foreword: Some Notes on the Post-war Hong Kong Cinema Survey, 1946–1968," in *Hong Kong Cinema Survey (1946–1968)*, 4.

38. Wu Hao (Ng Ho), "The Legend and Films of Huang Fei-hong," in *Wushi niandai, Yueyu dianying huiguzhan* (Cantonese cinema retrospective, 1950–1959), Second International Film Festival of Hong Kong (Hong Kong: Provisional Urban Council, 1978), 101.

39. Teo, "Only the Valiant: King Hu and His *Cinema Opera*," in *Transcending the Times: King Hu and Eileen Chang*, Twenty-Second Hong Kong International Film Festival Catalogue (Hong Kong: Provisional Urban Council, 1998), 20.

40. Teo, "Only the Valiant," 19–24.

41. *Baimao nü*, dir. Wang Bin and Shui Hua, Northeast Film Studio, 1950. The PRC government supported this genre in the 1950s and 1960s. See Yingjin Zhang and Zhiwei Xiao, *Encyclopaedia of Chinese Film*, 167.

42. For example, *Sing-Song Girl Red Peony* (dir. Zhang Shichuan, 1930) and *Two Stage Sisters* (*Wutai jiemei*, dir. Xie Jin, Shanghai, Tianma Film, 1965).

43. *Bawang bieji*, dir. Chen Kaige, Tomson Film, 1993. See Ben Xu, "Farewell My Concubine and its Nativist Critics," *Quarterly Review of Film and Video* 16.2 (1997): 155–170.

44. Elsaesser, "General Introduction, Early Cinema," 4.

45. Lu, "Evaluations of Ren Qingtai and First Chinese Films," 82. Lu corrects many factual errors, including his misidentification as Ren Fengtai.

46. Yingjin Zhang and Zhiwei Xiao, *Encyclopaedia of Chinese Film*, 5.

47. Li Suyuan and Hu Jubin, *Chinese Silent Film History*, 40.

48. Lu, "Evaluations of Ren Qingtai and First Chinese Films," 83.

49. Ibid., 86.

50. Ibid., 85. Thus, unlike the West, the "narrative impulse" pervades the Chinese cinema from its inception. For a comparison, see Gunning, "The Cinema of Attractions," 56–57.

51. Charles Musser, "The Nickelodeon Era Begins: Establishing the Framework for Hollywood's Mode of Representation," in Elsaesser with Barker, eds., *Early Cinema*, 257.

52. Ibid., 262.

53. Lu Hsun (Lu Xun), *A Brief History of Chinese Fiction*, translated by Yang Hsien-I and Gladys Yang (Peking: Foreign Languages Press, 1976), 320. These novels, all discussed by Lu Xun, are, respectively, *Sanguozhi yanyi* (154–164), *Shuihu zhuan* (174–186), *Xiyouji* (192–107), and Pu Songling's *Liaozhai zhiyi* (254–262).

54. Colin Mackerras, *Chinese Drama: A Historical Survey* (Beijing: New World Press, 1990), 71.

55. Mackerras, *The Rise of Peking Opera, 1770–1870* (Oxford: Clarendon Press, 1972), 263.

56. The recorded films are *Chang Ban Po* (1905); *The Thugs* (*Dachushou*, 1906) from *Bright Sun Tower* (*Yanyanglou*); *Sword versus Sword* (*Duidao*, 1906) from *Green Stone Mountain* (*Qingshishan*); *Leopard* (*Jinqianbao*, 1906); *White-Water Beach* (*Baishuitan*, 1907); *Conquer Guan Sheng* (*Shou Guan Sheng*, 1907); *Spinning Cotton* (*Fang Mianhua*, 1908); and *Retribution for Killing One's Own Son* (*Shazibao*, 1908). See Li Suyuan and Hu Jubin, *Chinese Silent Film History*, 18–19, and the Chinese original, *Zhongguo wusheng dianying shi* (Beijing: Zhongguodianying chubanshe, 1996), 15–16.

57. Elsaesser, "The Institution Cinema," in Elsaesser with Barker, eds., *Early Cinema*, 160.

58. Mackerras, *Chinese Drama*, 67.

59. Wu Zuguang, Huang Zuolin, and Mei Shaowu, *Peking Opera and Mei Lanfang* (Beijing: New World Press, 1981), 8–9.

60. Hong Shi, *"Diyici langchao, Mopianqi Zhongguo shangye dianying xianxiang shuping"* ("The first tide of movie: on the phenomenon of Chinese commercial movie in the period of silent film" [*sic*]), *Dangdai Dianying* 65.2 (1995): 6.

61. Mackerras, *Chinese Drama*, 71.

62. Lu, "Evaluations of Ren Qingtai and First Chinese Films," 83.

63. Wu Zuguang, Huang Zuolin, and Mei Shaowu, *Peking Opera and Mei Lanfang*, 88–89.

64. Huang Zuolin, "Mei Lanfang, Stanislavsky, Brecht — A Study in Contrasts," Wu Zuguang, Huang Zuolin, and Mei Shaowu, *Peking Opera and Mei Lanfang*, 15–16, 29. Barmé, "Persistence de la tradition au 'royaume des ombres,'" 114. See also Gina Marchetti, *"Two Stage Sisters: The Blossoming of a Revolutionary Aesthetic,"* *Jump Cut* 34 (1989): 103, for a discussion of Brecht and Chinese opera, especially Brecht's understanding of Chinese opera as "alienating" and the actors' "awareness of being watched," core features of a cinema of attractions and Faye Chunfang Fei, *Huang Zuolin: China's Man of the Theater*, Ph.D. diss., City University of New York, 1991.

65. Li Suyuan and Hu Jubin, *Chinese Silent Film History*, 18.

66. Ibid., 85–262.

67. Chen Zhiqing, *"Duiyu shizhi guzhuang yingpianzhi yijian"* (My views on making costume films), in Zhongguo Dianying Ziliaoguan (Chinese Film Archives), ed., *Zhongguo wusheng dianying* (Chinese silent film) (Beijing: Zhongguo dianying chubanshe, 1996), 639–642. One complaint was that some onscreen female actors fell far short of the traditional onstage art of male *dan*.

68. *Huoshao hongliansi*, screenwriter Zheng Zhengqiu, dir. Zhang Shichuan, Mingxing, 1928. See Li Suyuan and Hu Jubin, *Chinese Silent Film History*, 245–249.

69. Chen Xihe, "Shadowplay," 196–197.

70. The title, a proletarian cinema of attractions, is adapted from Qu Qiubai's call for a "proletarian May Fourth." See Paul Pickowicz, *Marxist Literary Thought in China: The Influence of Ch'u Ch'iu-pai* (Los Angeles: University of California Press, 1981), 175.

71. Qu Qiubai, cited in Paul Pickowicz, *Marxist Literary Thought in China*, 109. From *Qu Qiubai wenji* (Selected literary works of Qu Qiubai), vol. 2 (Beijing: Renmin wenxue chubanshe, 1953–1954, 885.

72. Pickowicz, *Marxist Literary Thought in China,* 163–164.

73. Ibid., 201–209.

74. Mao Tse-tung (Mao Zedong), "Yenan Forum on Literature and Art," *Selected Works of Mao Tse-tung* (Peking: Foreign Languages Press, 1975), vol. 3: 82.

75. David Holm, *Art and Ideology in Revolutionary China* (Oxford: Clarendon Press, 1991), 312–313.

76. Ibid., 332.

77. Ibid., 322. Translated from Zhang Geng, *"Huiyi Yan'an wenyi zuotanhui qianhou 'luyi'de xiju huodong"* (Reminiscences of the drama movement in "Luyi" before and after the Yan'an Forum on Literature and Art), *Xijubao* 5.5 (1962): 11.

78. David Holm, *Art and Ideology in Revolutionary China,* 322. Translated from Zhang Geng, "Reminiscences," 11–12.

79. Lois Wheeler Snow, *China on Stage: An American Actress in the People's Republic* (New York: Random House, 1972), 202. Quoting Jack Belden, *China Shakes the World* (New York: Monthly Review Press, nd), 210–211.

80. Li Yiming, *" 'Shiqi Nian' Shaoshu Minzu Ticai Dianying Zhong de wenhua Shidian yu Zhuti* (The cultural perspective and themes of minority nationality films after the "Seventeen Years"), in Zhongguo dianying xiehui (Chinese Filmmakers Association), ed., *Lun Zhongguo shaoshu minzu dianying* (A discussion of Chinese minority films) (Beijing: Zhongguo dianying chubanshe, 1997), 177.

81. Li Haiyan, *"Huashuo Baimao nü: Minzu xuzhizhongde jieji yu xingbie zhengzhi"* (On *The White-Haired Girl*: class and sexual politics in the national narrative), *Ershiyi shiji* 59 (1999): 110.

82. Yuan Wenshu, "Film Tradition and Innovation," translated by Li Xiaohong, in Semsel et al., eds., *Chinese Film Theory,* 169. Yuan gives a long list of the "best" of the revolutionary films.

83. Zhou Weizhi, *"Ping Baimaonü yingpian"* (On the film *The White-Haired Girl*), in Wang Baishi and Wang Wenhe, eds., *Dangdai Zhongguo dianying pinglunxuan, shang* (Anthology of contemporary Chinese film criticism) (Beijing: Zhongguo guangbo dianshe chubanshe, 1987), vol. 1: 18.

84. Ibid., 15. Note that black and white characterization is a feature of a cinema of attractions. See Gunning, "The Cinema of Attractions," 59.

85. *Dujuan Shan,* dir. Xie Tieli, Beijing Film Studio, 1974, adapted from the opera of the same name by Wang Shuyuan.

86. Zhai Jiannong, *"Yangbanxi dianyingde xingshuai—wenge dianying: 20 shiji teshude wenhua xianxiang"* (Ups and downs of the film of *Model of Modern Beijing Opera:* the films of the Cultural Revolution period: the special cultural phenomenon. first part), *Dangdai Dianying* 65.2 (1995): 40.

87. Colin Mackerras, *The Chinese Theatre in Modern Times, from 1840 to the Present Day* (London: Thames and Hudson, 1975), 209–210, from *Peking Review,* 18.4 (January 25, 1974) 12. See also Lowell Ditmer, "Radical Ideology and Chinese Political Culture: An Analysis of the Revolutionary *yangbanxi,*" in Richard Wilson, Sidney Greenblatt, and Amy Wilson, eds. *Moral Behaviour in Chinese Society* (New York: Praeger, 1981), 126–151; and Mackerras, *Peking Opera* (Hong Kong: Oxford University Press, 1997).

88. *Wu Xun zhuan*, dir. Sun Yu, Kunlun Film, 1950. See Shao Zhou, *Sun Yu yu dianying Wu Xun Zhuan* (Sun Yu and the film, *The Life of Wu Xun*), *Dianying Yishu* 215.6 (1990) 96.

89. Richard Curt Kraus, *Pianos and Politics in China: Middle-Class Ambitions and the Struggle over Western Music* (New York: Oxford University Press, 1989), 133–139.

90. Luo Yijun, "A Preliminary Discussion of National Style in Film," 271.

91. Zhai Jiannong, "Ups and Downs of the Film of 'Model of Modern Beijing Opera,'" 41.

92. Barmé, "Persistence de la tradition au 'royaume des ombres,'" 119–120.

93. Dai Jinhua, "On Reading Xia Yan's *Problems of Screenwriting*," in Semsel et al., eds. *Film in Contemporary China*, 75–84.

94. Dai Jinhua, "On Reading Xia Yan's *Problems of Screenwriting*," 81. Cited in Xia Yan, *Problems of Screenwriting* (Beijing: China Film Press, 1959), np.

95. Dai Jinhua, "On Reading Xia Yan's *Problems of Screenwriting*," 80.

96. Luo Yijun, "A Preliminary Discussion of National Style in Film," 268–269.

97. Sek Kei, "Thoughts on Chinese Opera and the Cantonese Opera Film," 17.

98. Barmé (July 2000).

99. *Huozhe*, dir. Zhang Yimou, Era and Shanghai Film Studio, 1994.

100. Li Suyuan and Hu Jubin, *Chinese Silent Film History*, 58.

101. Siegfried Zielinski, *Audiovisions, Cinema, and Television as Entr'actes in History*, translated by Gloria Custance (Amsterdam: Amsterdam University Press, 1999), 268.

102. Elsaesser, "Cinema Futures: Convergence, Divergence, Difference," in Thomas Elsaesser and Kay Hoffman, eds., *Cinema Futures: Cain, Abel or Cable?* (Amsterdam: Amsterdam University Press, 1998), 16.

103. Elsaesser, "General Introduction," 4.

104. Ibid., 14.

CHAPTER TWO

Bodies in the Air

The Magic of Science and the Fate of the Early "Martial Arts" Film in China

Among all the film genres invented and reinvented in the twentieth century in different parts of the world, the "martial arts" film, with its foregrounded body language and spectacular visual choreography, is one of the few genres with such far-reaching popularity. It has appealed to people of different ages, genders, and cultural origins. "Martial arts" film stars such as Jackie Chan, Michelle Yeoh, and Jet Li are not only household names in Asia, but have also joined the boldfaced vocabulary of the global cinematic vernacular. The city of Hong Kong, the Hollywood in the East, where most "martial arts" films have been produced in the past few decades, has over time become almost synonymous with the genre. Many are familiar with the more recent success saga of Hong Kong cinema, the attraction of which escalated to an international frenzy with the recent "handover" of Hong Kong to China. Few critics, however, have attempted to historicize the Hong Kong phenomenon in general and the mythology of the "martial arts" film in particular. My research on early Shanghai cinema has made me realize that the hitherto much neglected cinematic legacy is in many respects the historical "preconscious" of the Hong Kong cinema. And the question of the "martial arts" film has been one of the focal points of a larger historical project.[1]

My return to the "martial arts" film of the old Shanghai cinema that flourished in the 1920s and 1930s will be a "flight" in a double sense. First, on a literal level, it was a major step to take in the early experiments to cinematically create the kinesthetic experience of flying, which in turn became a staple ingredient of the "martial arts" film. Second, "flight" as a dialectic trope is employed here in a way close to Walter Benjamin's investment in the term, in the attempt to reconnect the past with the present on a simultaneous plane. A "flight" to the past, as in Benjamin's "tiger's leap" to nineteenth-century Paris, is thus by no means an escape to a phantom golden past, but part of the archaeology of the modern experience enmeshed in the here and now, which attempts to "blast open the continuum of history."[2]

My interest in "flight" as both a cinematic and historical trope embodied by the "martial arts" film has led me to explore a cluster of issues related to the question of modernity, in particular, the role of science and its bearing on the magical new art of cinema in the Chinese context. I found that, far from being formulaic and homogeneous, the "martial arts" film stems from a promiscuous family tree that complicates any facile definition of the genre as such. In fact, the term used for the genre in the late 1920s is a compound phrase—*wuxia shenguai pian,* or the "martial arts-magic spirit" film. The genre was attacked by the cultural elite, as well as official censors, for serving as a vehicle for entrenched "feudal superstitions" that hindered the progression of nation building and modernization. It was eventually banned and cast into the "historical trash bin" in the early 1930s, which, however, did not prevent it from future resurrections. Another exciting finding is that there existed a visible subgenre that situates the female knight-errant at the center of dramatic tension and visual spectacle. This female-centered subgenre, or *nüxia pian,* I believe, is the precursor of a similar phenomenon in the later Hong Kong martial arts film. The legendary Michelle Yeoh, who recently lent some of her martial skills to James Bond in *Tomorrow Never Dies* and shone brightly in Ang Lee's *Crouching Tiger, Hidden Dragon,* is not a miracle woman with a "pair of lethal legs" born in a postmodern vacuum. Rather, she is a descendant of the pantheon of female knight-errant stars (Wu Lizhu [1910–1978], Hu Die [1908–1989], Wu Suxin [1905–?], Fan Xuepeng [1908–1974], and Xia Peizhen [1908–?], to name just a few) in a rich, if hitherto repressed, cinematic tradition. A "flight" to that buried past will, hopefully, shed some light on the fate of the "martial arts" film in China as a whole, more specifically, on the kinship between the early Shanghai cinema and Hong Kong cinema within the span of the twentieth century. Although the main story in this chapter is about how the early Shanghai film culture gave birth to the "martial arts" film, in a circular sense it is also a tale of two cities whose cosmopolitan yearnings and experience have always exceeded the narrow confines of nationalism and parochialism.

The Family of a Promiscuous Genre

The "martial arts-magic spirit" film flourished and declined at a dizzying speed in Shanghai between 1928 and 1932. The total number of silent films produced by some fifty studios during the four-year period is estimated to be 241 (approximately 60 percent of the total output of Shanghai studios at the time), of which eighty-five were released in 1929—the peak year of the craze.[3] The genre was widely popular and proved to be a commercial miracle. In essence, most "martial arts-magic spirit" films made in this period were fast and cheaply produced commodities that fed the seemingly insatiable appetite of the market. The impact of the genre's reception is equally astounding. Some spectators were so enthralled by the power and freedom embodied in the image of the knight-errant that they went to the mountains to become disciples of martial arts or Daoist masters.[4] One frequently cited story in film magazines at the time was how spectators began to burn incense inside theaters to worship the almighty spirits appearing on the screen.[5] The entire film world seemed spellbound. Producers, distributors, critics, and spectators alike became mesmerized and confused by the commercial power and social energy generated by the genre. A first-hand witness account by Shen Yanbing, a prominent May Fourth writer, recorded his ambivalent reaction to the genre at a movie house in Shanghai:

> As soon as you arrive at a movie house, you could witness the great attraction of *Huoshao Hongliansi* (Burning of the Red Lotus Temple) to the petty urban dwellers. As cheering and applauding are not prohibited in those theaters, you are from the beginning to the end surrounded by a fanatic crowd. Whenever the swordsmen in the film begin to fight with their flying swords, the mad shouting of the spectators *[kanke]* is almost warlike. They cheer at the appearance of the flying Honggu, not so much because the role is played by the female star Hu Die as because she is a swordswoman and the protagonist in the film. . . . For them, a shadowplay *[yingxi]* is really not "play," but reality![6]

The phenomenon spurred strong reactions from film critics as well as cultural bureaucrats of the Nationalist government, which had been established in 1927. They considered themselves the guardians of the growing Chinese film industry. The liberal or left-minded critics, after a brief period of excitement over its liberatory potential (politically as well as aesthetically), lashed out at the genre for its overt commercial interests, shoddy quality, and superstitious indulgence and vulgar tastes. The official censors were concerned with the anarchic tendency manifested by the genre in particular and the film industry as a whole. Beginning in 1931, the authorities sought to regulate and streamline the production of the genre, closing down many small studios that prospered from making

Burning of the Red Lotus Temple, directed by Zhang Shichuan, China.

low-budget "martial arts-magic spirit" films, and banning large number of films from release or reexhibition. Several companies continued to work sporadically with the genre after 1931, but as experimentation with sound film began and the left-wing filmmakers came to occupy a substantial place in the film scene, this mass cultural phenomenon quickly receded into the background.

What is the historical and cultural significance of the invention and reception of the "martial arts-magic spirit" film, a genre that has left lasting echoes in Hong Kong cinema and global film culture to this day? To begin with, why is this popular genre a compound phenomenon, that is, the double facets of the "martial arts" *(wuxia)* and "magic spirit" *(shenguai)*? How are conceptions of the body in traditional discourses of martial arts confronted but also transformed by cinematic technology? What is the relationship between its aesthetic of excess and a political anarchism pervading social, cultural, and cinematic discourses within the larger historical frame? To what extent is the proliferation of the *wuxia* figure suggestive of the anxiety toward strong women against the modern background and the technological power they embodied? Ultimately, these questions are bound to issues concerning the role of science, the tension between elite and popular culture, the relation of this cinema to a modern folk culture as well as the meaning of the body as it was articulated through this hybrid genre.

To study the formation of a genre, according to Rick Altman, is essentially to ask, "How did the whale become a mammal?" It is about establishing a corpus in light of a particular historical paradigm and in relation to "the strategies of the society that spawns a genre."[7] If genre can be defined essentially as the "order"

of things,[8] the "martial arts-magic spirit" film that evolved into a mass phenomenon in Shanghai in the late 1920s is emphatically a hypergenre characterized by
disorder, chaos, and cross-fertilization. Since its inception, this genre has received
mixed reactions. On the one hand, the audience and critics marveled at the
spectacular pyrotechnic display and the entertaining suspense produced by the
dramatic or supernatural elements in the films. It was hailed as a "new art" that
could bring "new knowledge, new technique, new ideal and new courage" and
was considered democratic in its address.[9] The origin of the genre can be found
in the teahouse milieu, where the storytelling of traditional tales and folklore,
on which many films were later based, catered to the taste of the layman. Stories
told in that fashion remained, however, "idealist" *(weixinde)*, or invisible, as opposed to concrete and visible. Although the reformed theater with "magic devices" could present some of the fantastic features in the vernacular tales, the layman usually could not afford this type of live show. Most small movie theaters
in the Shanghai area were near factories and thus were ideal for attracting this
type of audience to see the wonders of the "magic-spirit" film.[10]

The exaltation of the valiant spirit and physical prowess in "martial arts-
magic spirit" film was regarded as particularly empowering by a people, who had
come to internalize the image of the "sick man of the orient" *(dongya bingfu)*,
since China's defeat in the Opium Wars and subsequently the suppression of the
Boxer Rebellion by Western powers. At the same time, when the genre seemed
to multiply beyond control in quantity and thematic variations and spun the
film market into frenzied competition, attacks were launched at the outlandish
use of "superstitious" motifs, cinematic tricks, sexual promiscuity, and gender
ambiguity. Critics, who were mouthpieces for major studios such as Mingxing
and Tianyi, were especially exacerbated by the fact that dozens of small companies swarmed the market with their low-budget productions, causing frantic
competition and confusion.

The emergence of the "martial arts-magic spirit" film is filtered through layers of diachronic and synchronic cultural strata. It is a commonplace that China
has a long tradition of martial arts practice and literature. The central ethos of
the martial arts *(wuxia)* is the idea of *xia*, for which the approximate, but hardly
adequate, equivalent in English will be "knight-errantry." As a social and moral
trope, the origin of *xia* is commonly traced to the Warring States (approximately
403–221 B.C.), when political chaos and feudal power divisions gave rise to a distinct group of independent warriors, who dispensed justice and offered protection
to the weak and the dispossessed. Over time, the historical facticity associated with
early knightly figures *(xiake)* gave way to more mythic representations, branch-
ing into vernacular literature, popular iconography, and folklore.

In the 1920s, "martial arts" literature experienced a huge boom, largely made possible by the spread of vernacular literacy and modern print technology. Numerous newspapers and magazines serialized popular "martial arts" works, among which Pingjiang Buxiaoshen's (original name Xiang Kairan, 1890–1957) *Jianghu qixia zhuan* (Tales of Strange Knights-Errant in the Wilderness) is often seen as the pioneering text that "raised the curtain" of the surge of martial arts fiction in the Republican period.[11] Part of the novel was adapted to screen by the Mingxing Company in 1928. The *Burning of the Red Lotus Temple,* a result of the adaptation, became an instant hit, which led to three sequels in the same year, and another fourteen in the following three years. Comic strips based on the film(s) quickly appeared on sale at street corners, satisfying the craving of children and the poor who could not afford to attend the cinema. The whole city was aflame with a burning passion for the saga of the "Red Lotus Temple." In the film industry alone, the "fire" quickly spread to other studios, which tried to repeat Mingxing's success. A host of films that had titles containing the word "burning" *(huoshao)* filled the silver screen. Although no other studio was as ambitious and affluent as Mingxing, which produced eighteen series, many attempted several series or at least one sequel.

The birth of a genre is more about the production of form than content. Yet form as such is never instantly complete and self-sufficient. This process can moreover appear in the form of voracious appropriation of foreign resources. Modeled on a French serial film, (likely Feuillade's *Les Vampires* of 1915), *Hongfen kulou* (Red Skeleton, 1921) features a heroine who disguises herself to rescue her lover out of the villains' den. The film, shot mostly in the exterior, is replete with elements of "the detective, adventure, martial arts, romance, and comedy."[12] Coming from the theater background, its director Guan Haifeng introduced several mechanical devices into the film to produce sensations of thrill, horror, and mystery. In this sense, *Red Skeleton* may be seen as a forerunner in combining elements of both the "martial arts" and "magic spirit," as well as in portraying women as knightly subjects on the screen.

The boom of the so called "unofficial historical" film and the "classical costume drama" between 1925 and 1927 installed an ambiguous "archaic" look to the Shanghai commercial cinema. The Tianyi Company, established in 1925 by the Shaw brothers (who were to become the major movie tycoons in Hong Kong and the Chinese diaspora), set the trend. The materials that attracted producers most were from the vast reservoir of folklore, traditional literature, and unofficial history. The aesthetic emphasis of these cinematic adaptations was placed on the "strange machination" or the "wondrous coincidence" *(xuanji),* because these elements allowed cinematic embodiment of spectacle and metamorphosis in dramatic spatial and temporal transition. In spite of Tianyi's original aim of "focusing on old morals and ethics" *(zhuzhong jiu daode, jiu lunli),* many "classical costume drama" films often appear ultramodern, replete with contemporary fashion, expressionist sets, and even seminude scenes. *Pansi dong* (The Cave of the Spider Spirit, 1927), adapted from an episode in the classical novel *Xi you ji* (Journey to the West), is a spectacular "classical costume drama" par excellence. The cave in which the spider queen reigns is designed in both "realistic and magnificent" ways so as to evoke an animate yet ghostly ambience. The biggest attraction of the film seems to be the scene of swimming spider-beauties shot through an underwater camera—allegedly the first of its kind in China. An adaptation from the classical romantic novel, *Honglou meng* (Dream of the Red Chamber), by the Fudan Company (affiliated with Fudan University) in 1927 simply had the cast appear in modern fashion. The female protagonist Lin Daiyu wears a flowing long robe and high heels, her hair adorned with white ribbons. The color cover of the special issue for the film published by the company is rendered in art nouveau style featuring a scantily clad romantic couple ascending to the sky amid clouds.

The provocative, and often erotic, appeal of the "classical costume drama" created a phantasmagoria of overlaid temporality; the alternative versions of "history" when rendered cinematic became the place where magic and technology, archaic fantasy and modern desire, fused into a feast of visual display. These bold experiments with the "magic spirit" of the cinema also paved the way for the emergence of the composite genre, the "martial arts-magic spirit" film, a new formula for presenting both visual attraction and narrative suspense, physical action and psychic power, natural wonder and supernatural forces. The supple and cunning female figures in *The Cave of the Spider Spirit*, though portrayed as negative forces in the film, may be seen as the prototype of the breed of *nüxia* who were to crowd the screen in less than a year.

Body in the Air: Science or Magic?

The emergence of the "martial arts-magic spirit" film marked a turning point in the presentation and perception of the body in early Chinese cinema. Until this time, the narrative and performing style of the "socioethical" film, romance film, and most "classical costume drama" is generally characterized by *wen* (which has a polysemous meaning of being literary, restrained, and elegant) and its tie to the literati culture. The "martial arts" film, on the other hand, embodies the spirit of *wu*—which means the state of being virile and military—and its patent presentational paraphernalia, for example, martial arts and related instruments, the physical landscape, and in instances of the modern costume martial arts film, skills such as driving a car. In other words, the body in motion, in di-

rect contact with the physical world and basic elements, is the distinct trademark of the genre. The emphasis is clearly on the body's kinetic experience and
its transformative power. The martial body, however, does not roam about entirely in the physical landscape. In fact, it constantly moves in the unstable zone
between nature and culture. The physiological character of the body is thus inscribed in the social landscape at large. The abundance of visual delight and
magical effect so crucial to the "martial arts-magic spirit" film serves another
purpose as well; it contributes to the redemption of *xia* (knight-errantry) as a
kind of embodied aura in a modernizing society. For this reason, the genre was
seen by one critic as a "stimulant" *(xingfen ji)*, which could "lift [one's] aspira-
tion for the martial spirit: "The martial spirit is something everyone ought to
possess. Yet, if there is nothing to awaken it, it will always be shrouded and will
never attain exciting expressions. As a result, one will look like a weakling. . . .
Those stirring and extraordinary martial arts films, however, demonstrate all
kinds of shocking yet most gratifying action [*dongzuo*], as well as events that
can solicit everybody's sympathy . . . These are really the special merits of the
martial arts film."[13] The preeminence of physicality is thus fraught with moral
and cultural significance. Most of the *wuxia* films unfailingly convey the message of "eradicating villains and wiping out despots, saving the good and aiding
the poor" *(chujian chubao, jiuliang jiping)*.[14] The sense of wonder evoked by the
"shocking and most gratifying action" in the "martial arts" film on the one hand,
and the critics' desire to rationalize the genre as a social remedy, on the other,
speak to a contradictory conception of the relationship between aesthetics and
politics, magic and science, which constitutes the ambiguous foundation of the
genre. Conflicting meanings were invested in the martial body. The critical focus
was put on both the sensual quality of physicality and the socioethical power it
embodied. This conflict was further complicated, or amplified, by the contemporary discourse on machinery, in particular the flying machine, and with it,
the power of modern technology.

One of the modern-style "martial arts" films produced by the Huaju Company, *Hangkong daxia* (The Great Knight-Errant of Aviation, 1928), is a case in
point. The film was based on a real-life modern hero, Zhang Huizhang, the first
pilot to complete successfully a long-distance flight in China.[15] Zhang Huimin,
a cofounder of the company and an expert on martial arts, played the pilot-
cum–knight-errant, who "practiced righteousness and observed loyalty" *(renxia haoyi)*. One day, riding the train after completing a "knightly mission" *(xingxia)*, the pilot caught the sight of a bandit nicknamed the "Flying Tiger" coercing
a young woman (played by Zhang's partner Wu Suxin). He rescues the beauty
and rides away with her on horseback. As it turns out, the woman he rescued is

actually his future wife betrothed to him by their parents when they were still children. Against a beautiful sky, the reunited lovers spend their honeymoon cruising in the open space. The traditional practice of arranged marriage is thus reconciled with free love, emblematized by the flying machine.

Ostensibly parading as a "martial arts" film, *The Great Knight-Errant of Aviation*, contains, however, neither traditional swordplay nor classical costumes.[16] The film is in fact a virtuoso display of the wonder of the flying machine and the fantasy about modern science. Yet, the blending of chivalric routines of the knight-errant and the shop-worn motif of the horse as the extension of the martial hero's prowess and speed with modern transportation vehicles, such as the train and the airplane, create a sensational effect of transmutation. To borrow Gaston Bachelard's central idea in conceiving the mode of change in scientific knowledge, such cinematic transmediation of existing stock elements of the martial arts practice on the silver screen, in the form of visual spectacle, may be seen as a particular procedure of *réfonte*, or recasting. It refers to a procedure by which new sciences, new forms of knowledge are born through breakages and leaps rather than through homogeneous evolution and accumulation.[17] These "breakages" and "leaps," in the realm of cinema, are achieved through techniques such as editing, trick shot, and superimposition that make possible not only the transfer and combination between different forms of knowledge, representation, and genre, but also materialize these processes in the form of moving images. The instant spatiotemporal transition from the scene when the hero rides away with the beauty on a horse is literally "sprung" into the next shot of the airplane in the sky. The attraction here rests not so much in any logical narrative progression, as in the compressed spectacle of speed and metamorphosis from an organic version of the "martial arts" carried by the symbol of the horse to that of the mechanical incarnation, the plane.

The "flight" toward the mechanical stage in *The Great Knight-Errant of Aviation* is not rationalized as a painful transition from nature to culture, or from the premodern to the modern, but rather as a "natural" and delightful crossing of contiguous realms of experience. Just as the hero effortlessly inhabits the double identity of the archetypal knight-errant and the pilot in his modern armor, the airplane and the horse are not necessarily antithetical icons for different temporalities and consciousness, either. The airplane may be seen as a winged horse, a mechanized creature that gives the "martial arts" plot a touch of the "magic spirit." In light of the fact that the airplane was still a rare object at the time, the flying machine in the film is not simply a realistic mise-en-scène prop subordinated to the diegesis. Rather, its traceless appearance and disappearance are perceived as "natural" precisely because of its mythical aura. According to a contemporary description of the film, "when weak and oppressed people hear the engine of the plane from afar, their faces are lit up as though in a shadow-play; their sad, distressful expressions are replaced by joy and relief."[18]

The reception of such cinematic "recasting" of tradition was never uniform, however, and some critics regarded it with shock and disdain. The example one critic cited was Tang Sanzang (the monk in the classical novel *Journey to the West*) riding a motorbike, instead of a white horse. The critic accuses the studio of blindly catering to the "curiosity" *(xinqi)* of the audience in order to make quick cash.[19] The question to be asked, however, is why the audience was so enthralled by "curiosities" that were considered "neither horse nor donkey" *(feilü feima)*.[20] What was really disconcerting to people like this critic is perhaps the extent to which the irreverent cross-fertilization of the past and the present, the body and the machine, literary canons and cinematic technology, effected a temporal collapse, a disintegration of a certain order of things. The cartoon-like image of the legendary monk riding a motorbike is outrageous because it redefines the sacrosanct body of the pious monk by aligning it with the machine age. Whereas the classical figure is associated with rugged natural landscape on his journey to India to fetch scriptures, the motorbike takes him directly into the urban jungle.[21]

The classical opposition between the organic folk world and the mechanical world or, for that matter, the premodern and the modern held by traditional folklore studies encounters a challenge here. Just as the plane was to the pilot, the motorcycle to the monk becomes an "extension of his bodily scheme." The apparati at their disposal is not presented as something ontologically transcending, but rather intimately related to the operating agents and their awareness of its (practical) function.[22] It is thus hard to distinguish the "objectification" of the body by technology from the domestication of the machine in this fusion of fantasy and reality. As Hermann Bausinger points out, inventors and technicians often treat their work as something beyond the realm of science. When a new gadget or machine is first tested, the experimental impulse and anxiety are evoked more as an "experience," often tinged with "demonic power."[23] In this experiential dimension the boundary between the rational and irrational becomes quite irrelevant as the body and the machine constitute a new assemblage of reality through kinesthetic sensation.

The negative reaction against such voracious mixing of premodern tropes and modern technology, canonical literature and commodity culture, is part and parcel of a larger anxiety toward modernity in early twentieth century China. The connection, or interpenetration, between the human body and machines had captured the Chinese imagination already in the late Qing period. The popular illustrated newspaper *Dianshizhai huabao* carried numerous reports and illustrations of how various new apparatus and instruments dramatically altered people's perception of the body in time and space. The machines that appear most frequently are the x-ray, the camera, the train, and the airplane. Airplanes are seen as mythic flying ships, with wings attached on the sides, cruising over exotic landscapes.

After the fall of the Qing dynasty in 1911, the clamor for more radical changes in social infrastructure and consciousness ultimately culminated in the radical May Fourth movement. The humiliating outcome of the Versailles conference in 1919 convinced the intellectuals that the reasons for China's inferiority had to do with its slowness in embracing Mr. De (democracy) and Mr. Sai (science). For the same reason, any residual feudal beliefs and Confucian doctrines should be cast into the historical trash bin. The cult of science went hand in hand with the iconoclastic antireligious movement and an extensive effort to reevaluate and reorder traditional heritage. Antiquity is cast in light of scientific methods that had been introduced to China since the late nineteenth century and especially in the wake of the visits of John Dewey, Bertrand Russell, and other Western thinkers in the early 1920s. The supreme status given to modern science and civilization was seriously challenged in 1923–1924, in an intellectual debate on "science and metaphysics." The debate intensified the split among the intellectuals with regard to the place of science and Western philosophy in the Chinese project of modernity.[24] The impact of the debate was far reaching. Extending over one and a half years, it involved leading intellectuals of diverse persuasions and ideologies, who produced more than forty polemic essays, which were published in influential magazines in major urban centers. Some of the basic issues coming out of the debate were echoed by the conflicting discourses on the "martial arts-magic spirit" film a few years later. Toward the end of the 1920s, after the establishment of the Nationalist government in Nanjing in 1927 and in the midst of the "martial arts-magic spirit" film boom, a number of publications on the subject appeared, in an effort to evaluate and conclude the earlier debate.[25]

Popular cinema, largely operating on the margins of these intellectual movements yet occupying a substantial space in the vernacular culture at large, engages with the contemporary controversy and its aftershocks in an indirect but complex way. The plots of most "martial arts" films were largely derived from traditional sources, and the adaptations often privileged strange, magical, and improbable elements to enhance narrative suspense and visual effect; however, the cinematic recreation, or visual realization, of the fantastic and mythical world, indispensable from techniques of editing, multiple camera set-ups, superimposition, and so on, render what is impossible in real life or on a theater stage possible and even believable.

The *Burning of the Red Lotus Temple* is the first large-scale production to combine the "martial arts" with "magic-spirit" and experiment with film tech-

Burning of the Red Lotus Temple, directed by Zhang Shichuan, China.

nology to create special effects and a mystical ambience. Dong Keyi (1906–1978), the cameraman, found an ingenious way to solve the problem of spatial contiguity by aligning the temple roof painted on the glass with the roofless life-size backdrop, creating a "magnificent" piece of virtual architecture.[26] His most important invention, partly borrowed from a description in an American magazine, is the "flying knight-errant" *(feixia)*, which quickly became a ubiquitous trademark of the genre.[27] The head turban of the heroine was dyed red, highlighting the prominence and androgynous look of the female knight-errant.[28] These techniques not only brought to state of the art level the production of "martial arts-magic spirit" film, but also helped modernize the Chinese film industry as a whole. It is through the innovative play between science and magic, film technology and folklore, avant-garde aesthetics, and popular tastes, that the martial arts film came to embody the multiple "faces" of modernity.[29]

These interwoven "faces" created a new perception and knowledge about the body that is at once corporeal and "metaphysical," visible and invisible, material and magical, human and mechanical. If the "body is man's first and most natural instrument," as Marcel Mauss has remarked, the "techniques of the body" in the "martial arts-magic spirit" film constitutes a particular "habitus" in which the body is both the medium (instrument) and a new focus of a cultural practice.[30] In the historical context of the early twentieth-century China, this "habitus" may be located in the composite space of traditional folklore and an emergent urban–based modern folk culture. The "martial arts-magic spirit" film, stemming from a promiscuous body of cultural forms and sensibilities, articulates this space cinematically.

The flying body of the knight-errant may be seen as the quintessential embodiment of this mosaic space. Suspended by invisible devices in the air, the ability of this mobile body to traverse geographical distance in lightening speed produces a visual and kinesthetic experience that materializes the legendary tricks that previously only existed in oral tales, literature, theater, and—to a limited extent—pictorial forms. The hero's bodily form and spiritual aura are fused together in this virtual and liminal space. Such an extraordinary skill was certainly practiced and realized to varying degrees in the past; however, the technique had been largely considered superhuman and possessed by a few esoteric masters, not by the layman in everyday life. When the film actors who are neither real masters of martial arts nor Daoist hermits are able to perform these skills "effortlessly" and repeatedly on the silver screen, the flying body becomes the site of mass attraction and identification. It is partly this frenzy of identification and emulation that led the cultural elite and authorities to denounce the genre for corrupting the young and the innocent, and to take measures to curb the production and consumption fever surrounding the genre.

The Subgenre with Martial Heroines

Now I shall turn to the female subgenre of the "martial arts" film to highlight the gender dimension of the phenomenon. Traditionally associated with male prowess and moral superiority, the genre was also seen, at least at the initial stage, as a revival of the martial spirit much needed in a time of political instability and cultural fragmentation. It served as a compensation for the image of China as the "sick man of the Orient" since the Opium Wars. The martial hero, such as the pilot in *The Great Knight-errant of Aviation,* became an icon for a different masculinity in modern times. His superman-like image and his pilot gear as modern armor create an aura charged with mobility and velocity that epitomizes the new epoch.

Nevertheless, the martial aura and "magic spirit" were not reserved for men alone in the "martial arts-magic spirit" film. Although the male martial hero is a more familiar, culturally received archetype, what gave the genre a distinctive marker and increased its popularity is the proliferation of the image of the female knight-errant. This no doubt corresponded to the proliferation of swordswoman characters in traditional as well as contemporary martial arts fiction, which provided raw material for screen adaptations. Although very few films of this subgenre have survived, the film titles alone, with the character *nü* (female) and *xia* (knight-errant) appearing ubiquitously, testifies to the popularity of the subgenre with martial heroines:

- *Nüxia Li Feifei* (The Female Knight-Errant Li Feifei, Tianyi, 1925)
- *Ernü yingxiong* (Hero and Heroine; Youlian, four series, 1927–1930)
- *Xianü jiu furen* (The Female Knight-Errant Rescues the Lady; Mingxing, 1928)
- *Wunü fuchou* (Five Vengeful Girls; Minxin, 1928)
- *Mulan congjun* (Mulan Joins the Army; Tianyi, 1927)
- *Jianghu qingxia* (He and She; Youlian, 1928)
- *Feixia Lü Sanniang* (The Flying Knight-Errant Lü Sanniang; Da zhonghua beihe, 1928)
- *Wu dalishi* (The Great Woman; Da zhonghua beihe, 1929)
- *Wuxia bai meigui* (The Valiant Girl White Rose; Huaju, 1929)
- *Hong xia* (Red Heroine; Youlian, 1929)
- *Langman nü yingxiong* (A Romantic Heroine; Xintian, 1929)
- *Wu haidao* (The Female Pirate; Da zhonghua baihe, 1929)
- *Huangjiang nüxia* (Swordswoman from the Huangjiang River; Youlian, thirteen series, 1929–1932)
- *Lan guniang* (A Girl Bandit; Huaju, 1930)
- *Nü biaoshi* (also known as *Guandong nüxia*; A Woman Bodyguard; Yueming, four series, 1931)
- *Nüxia Heimudan* (The Female Knight-Errant Black Peony; Yueming, 1931)

The Youlian Company, like the Huaju Company, was most prolific in producing the *nüxia* film. Its *Red Heroine* is the most complete out of the few extant films (or fragments) of the genre. In many respects, *Red Heroine* is an exemplary film that illustrates the diverse yet overlapping faces of the genre. The most striking feature in the film is the alliance between the heroine Yungu and an old Daoist master called (and resembling) the White Monkey who not only rescues her, but also teaches her martial arts and the magic of flying. The force of evil is represented by a decadent bandit, surrounded by a bevy of half-nude girls and minions (including one with protruding wolf teeth); all of them reside in a sumptuous palace in the wilderness. The orphaned heroine, abducted by the bandit in the beginning of the film, accomplishes her mission of avenging her grandmother's death and rescues another maiden from the claws of the bandit with her martial arts and magical powers. Her abilities include such feats as instantly "transporting" her body in a puff of smoke.

The first episode, *Danao Baolin si* (Uproar at the Baolin Temple), of the thirteen-series *Swordswoman from the Huangjiang River*, features a heroine (played by Xu Qinfang, 1909–1985) who roams the rugged landscape of northern China and

Red Heroine, directed by Yao Shiquan and Wen Yimin, China, 1929.

saves villagers from terrorization by monstrous birds. Another mission in the episode involves a visit, in which she masquerades as an old woman, to a martial heroine in a neighboring village. After a sisterly swordplay competition, the two join hands to raid the den of a bandit to avenge the death of the younger heroine's father.

In the *nüxia* subgenre as a whole, the heroine is usually pushed onto "stage" by default, because of either the absence or enfeebled condition of a male heir in the family. Having assumed the role of avenger for an unjust death in the family and of the guardian of a community under external threat, the heroine takes up the responsibility and renounces or postpones her sexual desire. Her transformation is usually signaled by visible changes in her iconography and body language and by her newly acquired martial skills. Her obligatory departure from her home community for a specific quest in a far away place also propels the narrative to enter, quite literally, an otherworldly dimension.

These films typically open with a narration of an emergency situation in an ordinary community. *Red Heroine,* for example, literally "opens" in the mouth of a villager who announces to the camera (and the spectator) the imminent arrival of the bandits. This "oral" expression attracts the audience through a sensory organ and demonstrates the embodied nature of cinematic storytelling. Against the backdrop of emergency, the narration gradually gravitates toward a more fantastic representation of reality with the transformation of the heroine from a country lass into a woman warrior. From that point on, the unfolding of the film tends to operate on two parallel planes—often in the form of crosscutting. One continues with the realist presentation of the distressful situation at home involving the people who are related to the heroine; the other follows the heroine's trajectory of transformation, mediated by magical powers that complicate or intervene in the unfolding of the plot proper. The resolution of these films largely falls within the "happy-ending" paradigm, often culminating in marriage or family reunion. Such an ending does, however, not always return the heroine back to her original maiden form and often surprises the audience with disconcerting developments.

Unfailingly, the heroine is endowed with extraordinary body techniques that mark her as a cyborg-like creature. One such technique is the ability to effortlessly move the body either horizontally or vertically, such as flying in the sky or leaping over a tall wall. In other words, what makes possible the instant bodily transportation from one location to another hinges upon the capability of losing one's gravity in space and overcoming the restraint of time. It is thus only natural that the name of the female knight-errant in *Red Heroine* is Yungu, "maiden of the clouds."[31] Her name is figuratively spelled out in the sky when after three years of training in the holy Ermei Mountain, Yungu returns walking on the clouds in a patent *nüxia* outfit. A head turban covers her hair as well as her maiden identity, and the unisex "martial arts" dress is completed with a pair of black boots. Diagonally flying down from the upper right corner of the frame toward the audience, her appearance is a shocking contrast to her image as a victim "three years" ago. The itinerary of her missions cannot be traced or charted, because she appears and vanishes only in a puff of smoke. At the end of the film, after she fulfills her role as the matchmaker between the maiden and the scholar, she disappears in the smoke rising from the ground. In the next shot, through the point of view of the young couple, we see her in the sky, brandishing her sword, moving rapidly away. Her mobile image ultimately exceeds the screen, which can no longer contain the velocity and energy of the androgynous "body in the air."

Similarly, Fang Yuqin, the heroine in *Swordswoman* is also capable of defying gravity, if not precisely flying across vast distances. After she enters a cave to rescue a boy kidnapped by the monstrous "Golden-Eyed Bird," she holds the boy in her arms and jumps over a precipitous chasm. This spectacle in silhouette is accomplished in a long shot, with the aid of animation technique. In a later sequence, at a temple where Fang meets her nemesis (who killed her father), she performs an effortless jump over a tall wall into the courtyard. Likewise, Nian, a girl from another village who has invited Fang to assist avenging her own father's death, also has a strong and supple body. In one remarkable scene, Nian jumps onto a wall carrying a huge pair of grinding stones (passing for weights). The backlit lighting makes Nian's image atop the wall extremely imposing, echoing yet amplifying the earlier image of Fang jumping over the chasm. This performance is presented as a public spectacle in front of the villagers. Fang, disguised as an old beggar with her sword hidden in her luggage, arrives in time to witness the show. Through this repetition, as well as identification, the two forge their sisterhood in the world of martial arts.

The device of masquerade and identity change is important for the latent theme of female bonding or even love in these films. In *Red Heroine,* Yungu, after her return as an androgynous knight-errant, rescues another girl who is trapped in her former situation. Unlike the heroines in other films who enter the world of martial arts to avenge or aid their fathers, Yungu's mission is to avenge her grandmother's death and, with the development of the plot, to rescue the neighbor's daughter who is forced to repeat Yungu's plight. Her role as a surrogate parent to the girl becomes apparent at the end of the film when she presides over the engagement between the girl and her scholar cousin. She then vanishes into the sky. In a similar way, Fang Yuqin, the heroine in *Swordswoman,* disguised as an elderly woman, encounters the younger heroine who has solicited her help to avenge her father's death. Their duel in the courtyard, with each gazing into the other's eyes, is not so much a competition as a ritual of bonding— a practice that is common in the world of martial arts, especially among men. After the competition, in which the more experienced Fang wins, the two heroines drink wine to cement their bonding as sworn sisters.

The flying female knight, as typified by Yungu, may be considered a protocyborg. The constitution of this flexible female subject defies anthropocentric reproductive laws and social hierarchies.[32] In making the phantom leap into the sky, Yungu literally approximates the ideal of the "Unification of Heaven and [Wo]man," which the traditional literati strives for. The leap into a new dimension, or a cinematic space, accentuated by the martial arts outfit that endows her with the sartorial attributes of an androgynous angel, also considerably alters her social and gender identity. She is no longer bound by social norms regulating marriage and family. This change, however, does not necessarily entail an escapist transcendence. Instead, Yungu's expanded physical capacity and supernatural power enable her, if at a "remove," to serve her native community in an effective way. It is this combination of being at once a supernatural creature, a social subject, and a technological hybrid that makes her a protocyborg—"a condensed image of both imagination and material reality."[33] Through this condensation, fantasy becomes a lived experience, magic an embodied reality.

The Fate of the Martial Arts Film

The proliferating and profitable "martial arts-magic spirit" film came to an abrupt halt in 1931, when the newly established National Film Censorship Committee (NFCC) of the Nationalist government officially banned the showing of a large number of films, chief among them the sensationally successful *Burning*.[34] Within three years, more than sixty films in the genre were exiled from the silver screen, some of which had never been publicly shown. This massive onslaught against the genre was part of the Nationalists' antisuperstition campaign,[35] as well as a response to the outcry of the cultural elite in and outside the film world. The genre was considered a dangerous vehicle for feudal ideology and a threat to the "health" of a modernizing society and the film industry. In other words, the Nationalists were concerned with disciplining the film culture as a whole as part of its program to create order and inculcate citizens with its party ideology and modern values.[36] The censorship of the "martial arts-magic spirit" film, with the aim of promoting moral and physical health of the national culture, thus inadvertently paved the way for the New Life movement with similar but more rigorously defined goals, which was launched in 1934. The censorship quickly extended to martial arts fiction as well, which had given rise to the film genre. *Tales of the Strange Knights-Errant*, the novel which inspired the making of *Burning*, was deemed "absurd in content" and ideologically "countering the Party doctrines." The ministries of education and internal affairs joined the censors in issuing orders prohibiting the publication and adaptation of such fiction.[37] It was obviously the anarchic spirit and mass appeal of the genre, both on and off the screen, that caused the paranoid reaction of the fledgling regime.

Official censorship notwithstanding, the May Fourth writers and ideologues had also been raging a war against Butterfly literature from whose fertile ground the "martial arts-magic spirit" film launched its commercial success. Their attack against this literature had begun in the late 1910s and the early 1920s when the May Fourth movement was in full force. The writers who spearheaded the attack include Lu Xun, Mao Dun (Shen Yanbing), Qu Qiubai, and Zheng Zhenduo. In 1919, in *New Youth*, the flagship journal of the New Culture movement, Lu Xun voiced his distaste for fiction about knight-errantry and scholar-beauty romance as a whole.[38] In another newspaper article titled *"Mingzi"* (Names) published in 1921, Lu Xun listed four kinds of pen names of popular writers whose works he would not bother to read. The first category contains names such as *Xianhun* (A Knightly Soul) and *Guaixia* (A Strange Knight-Errant).[39] Despite his overall sensitivity to popular culture, Lu Xun's view of the martial arts fiction and the cinema derived from it remained negative and dismissive.

In spite of their opposing political and ideological interests, the official censors and the May Fourth writers were united in their denunciation of the genre (from fiction to film to comic books) as essentially "unscientific" *(fei kexuede)* and "feudal." The left-wing writers were eager to exorcise the demon of the "martial arts" fiction in particular and Butterfly literature in general from the literary scene in order to make room for May Fourth literature, especially realist fiction which was deemed to be capable of bringing social change. The Nationalist government, on the other hand, was primarily concerned with establishing a social order in which the culture industry should be at its service rather than causing unrest. For both the Left and the Right, the impact of the genre, aggravated by the cinema and other media, generated a surplus and "misdirected" social energy harmful to the project of Enlightenment and modernization.

Ironically, both parties choose to overlook the modernity of the genre, especially how it was borne out in its cinematic form and how its reception produced a public that, though "low" in social status, was powerful in number and social impact. As Shen's rather paranoid account of the spectatorial sensation in the theater suggests, it is neither the film *Burning* per se nor the original "martial arts" fiction on which the film is based that upset the status quo or the leftist critic. What is at stake is the emergence of a sociophysiological sensorium inside and outside the auditorium space that seems to have exceeded the political imagination of both the Right and the Left. The eruption of the "magical power" on the screen is echoed by the kinesthetic energy of the audience, creating a near-anarchic experience that is predicated on mobility, sensation, intensity of enjoyment, and identification rather than passivity, stability, and conformism. The immense size of the audience that ceaselessly grows beyond the bounds of the urban setting and even the nation is matched by its demographic complexity. In fact, the biggest market for the "martial arts-magic spirit" film is the Chinese diaspora in Southeast Asia, or Nanyang. The combination of their cultural proximity and geographical distance creates a certain degree of (self)-exoticism in the reception of the genre, which has the mosaic look of both the familiar and the strange, the archaic and the modern. *The Spider's Cave, Swordswoman, Journey to the West,* and *Burning* were allegedly among the best-selling films among the Nanyang distributors and theater owners.[40] In fact, because their representatives stationed in Shanghai were always inclined to pay more for prints than local exhibitors, the Nanyang distributors had a direct influence on what kind of films were made. The "martial arts-magic-spirit" film, which captured the imagination of the diaspora Chinese communities in Southeast Asia, thus became a staple product in this lucrative market for a long time to come.

What this overseas saga of the reception of the genre tells us is how its attraction literally crosses the national boundary and markets an image of China that is at odds with the blueprint of the modernizers at home. And this transnational branch of the family tree of the "martial arts" film appropriately directs my "flight" to the film world in the old Shanghai back to where I started this chapter, namely, Hong Kong.

The Shaw Brothers, who founded the Tianyi Company in 1925, were instrumental in transplanting the "martial arts" film to the vast overseas market. After the Japanese bombing of Shanghai in February 1932, as well as the ascendance of sound and left-wing cinema, Tianyi decided to transfer part of its equipment and personnel to Hong Kong in 1934, establishing the Tianyi Hong Kong Branch, which specialized in making Cantonese-speaking films. In 1937, to avoid wartime destruction and to be closer to its expanding Nanyang market, Tianyi moved all its assets and equipment to Hong Kong, changing the company name, quite appropriately, to Nanyang Film Company. With this move, Tianyi left behind its Shanghai identity and embraced the Cantonese- (and other languages) speaking world in Southeast Asia and, gradually, extending to the vast diaspora communities in other parts of the world. The new-style swordplay and martial arts films developed in the 1950s and the 1960s were key to its success in the international market, while the "classical costume drama" that Tianyi invented decades earlier continued to arouse sensations in the Chinese-speaking world, except for the insulated Mainland.

With the decline of the Shaw Empire in the early 1980s, however, the "martial arts" film took on a new life. The Golden Harvest studio, which was responsible for discovering Bruce Lee and Jackie Chan, overtook the Shaw enterprise in producing the "martial arts" film. A new generation of filmmakers who were trained abroad and had spent their apprenticeship in television also began to infuse the old genre with new vitality and techniques. It is noteworthy that the new surge of the martial arts film in the 1980s took place in Hong Kong and the Mainland concomitantly. With the open-door policy and the increasing demand for entertainment film, the "martial arts" film in the Mainland was revived, partly under the impact of the Hong Kong cinema and capital, which were eager to knock open the door of the enormous market in China. *Shaolin si* (The Shaolin Temple, 1982), in which Jet Li made his debut, was produced by a Hong Kong studio but was shot on location and widely shown in China. Its place as a landmark in the recent chapter of the "martial arts" film in China is comparable to that of *Burning* several decades ago. The Mainland-born Jet Li, considered more handsome and sexier than the veteran Jackie Chan, has since become smoothly groomed into the latest icon for the "martial arts" film. His mixed identity, being claimed by both the Mainland and Hong Kong fans, may be dissolving into an even more ambiguous collage now that Hong Kong has "returned" to China. But is Hong Kong cinema, the "martial arts" film in particular, as an orphan that had grown big and globally oriented, making a comfortable homecoming? The fate of the "martial arts" film seems precarious again at this moment, a moment at which the future of the genre as well as Hong Kong and Chinese cinema, however, may also be imagined and created.

Notes

A Chicago Humanities Institute Fellowship in 1997–1998 enabled the writing of the first draft of this essay. I would like to thank my teachers (particularly Miriam Hansen, Tom Gunning, Harry Harootunian, and Judith Zeitlin) for their encouragement. I am also indebted to Juliette Chung, Magnus Fiskesjö, Helen Koh, Sheldon Lu, James St. André, and my colleagues at the Department of Cinema Studies at New York University for their valuable comments.

1. See my article, "The 'Shanghai Factor' in Hong Kong Cinema: A Tale of Two Cities in Historical Perspectives," *Asian Cinema* 10.1 (fall 1998): 146–159, and my dissertation, "An Amorous History of the Silver Screen: Film Culture, Urban Modernity, and the Vernacular Experience in China, 1896–1937," University of Chicago, 1998.

2. Walter Benjamin, "Theses on the Philosophy of History," in Hannah Arendt, ed., *Illuminations* (New York: Harcourt, Brace & World, 1968), 261–262.

3. Li Suyuan and Hu Jubing, *Zhongguo wushen dianyin shi* (A history of Chinese silent film) (Beijing: Zhongguo dianying chubanshe, 1996), 239. The original source is from *Zhongguo dianying zongmulu* (A comprehensive catalogue of Chinese films) (Beijing: Zhongguo dianying ziliaoguan, 1960).

4. See for instances, Tong Gong, "*Wuhu huoshao*" (Apropos burning) and Li Changjian, "*Shengguaipian zhen hairen*" (The magic-spirit film is really harmful), both in *Yingxi shenghuo* (Movie weekly) 1.7 (1931). The Emei Mountain in Sichuan province is a famous Daoist pilgrimage site and one of the favorite destinations for these escapades.

5. For instance, some viewers would start burning incense and bowing to the image of Ne Zha (a mythic child hero in the classical work *Fengshen bang*) appearing on the screen. Huang Yicuo, "*Guochan yingpiande fuxin wenti*" (The problem of reviving the domestic cinema), *Yingxi zazhi* (Movie magazine) 1:7/8 (June 1930): 24. The specific film referred to here is *The Birth of Ne Zha (Ne Zha chushi)* (Changcheng, 1928).

6. Shen Yanbing. "*Fengjiande xiaoshimin wenyi*" (The feudal arts of the petty urban dwellers), in Wei Shaochang, ed., *Yuanyang hudie pai yanjiu ziliao* (Research material on the Mandarin ducks and butterflies literature) (Shanghai: Wenyi chubanshe, 1984), vol. 1: 47–52.

7. Rick Altman, "An Introduction to the Theory of Genre Analysis," *American Film Musical* (Bloomington: Indiana University Press, 1987), 1–9.

8. Stuart Kaminsky and Jeffrey Mahan, *American Television Genres* (Chicago: Nelson-Hall, 1986), 17.

9. Ying Dou, "*Shenguai ju zhi wo jian*" (My opinion on the magic-spirit film) [1927], in *Zhongguo wusheng dianying* (Chinese silent film) (Beijing: Zhongguo dianying chubanshe, 1996), 662–663.

10. See Jin Taipu, *"Shenguaipian chajin hou: jinhou de dianyingjie xiang nali zou?"* (After the censoring of the magic-spirit film: where is the film world heading?), *Yingxi shenghuo* 1.32 (1931): 1–4.

11. Jia Leilei, *"Zhongguo wuxia dianying yuanliu lun"* (On the origin of the Chinese martial arts film), *Yingshi wenhua* 5 (1992): 213. The novel was serialized in the Butterfly magazine *Hong* (Red), whose name was later changed to *Hong meigui* (Red rose), in 1923–1927. Xiang Kairan was inspired by folk tales in the Hunan region, where the novel was set. See Zhang Gansheng, *Minguo tongsu xiaoshuo lungao* (Studies on popular fiction of the Republican period) (Chongqing: Chongqing chubanshe, 1991), 111–124. Before becoming a popular writer, Xiang had been involved in the anti–Yuan Shikai revolution and subsequently studied in Japan. He was said to be the only martial arts fiction writer who mastered the arts he wrote about.

12. Xinya's advertisement, as quoted in Li Suyuan and Hu Jubing, *Zhongguo wusheng dianyingshi,* 77.

13. Yao Gengchen, *"Tan wuxia pian"* (On the martial arts film) [1927], in Li Suyuan and Hu Jubing, *Zhongguo wusheng dianying,* 670.

14. Ibid.

15. Because the film is not extant, the discussion is based on the synopsis and still photos published in *Dianying yuebao* (Movie monthly) 7 (October 1928). Zhang Huimin has a strong interest in aviation as well. The first Chinese encounter with the flying machine took place in 1911, when the French pilot René Vallon came to Shanghai and entertained the urban crowd with his flight skills. He was, however, killed in a flying accident in the same year. See Betty Peh-T'i Wei, *Crucible of Modern China* (Hong Kong: Oxford University Press, 1987), 195.

16. Flying as a motif of the modern fairy tale had appeared in *Feixing xie* (The Flying Shoes) (Minxin, 1928) one year earlier. The film was allegedly based on a German folktale. Another contemporary film, *Feixing dadao* (The Great Flying Bandit, also known as Little Sister, I Love You) (1929), also rests its attraction on flying.

17. Quoted in Roy Bhaskar, *Reclaiming Reality: A Critical Introduction to Contemporary Philosophy* (London: Verso, 1989), 42.

18. Juanhong, *"Hangkong daxia"* (The great knight-errant of aviation), *Dianying yuebao,* 7 (October 1928).

19. Sun Shiyi, *"Dianyingjie de guju fengkuangzheng"* (The craze for the old drama in the film world) [1926]. In *Zhongguo wusheng dianying,* 643–645.

20. E Chang, *"Guzhuangpian zhong zhi yin zhuyi zhe"* (Things to consider in the classical costume drama) [1927]. In *Zhongguo wusheng dianying,* 654.

21. It is unclear which film the critic was referring to. In 1927, one of the numerous "classical costume" films based on *Journey to the West* is called *Zhubajie you Shanghai* (The Pig Bajie Tours Shanghai). The three-reel comedy is clearly in the tradition of early Mingxing comedies such as *Huaji dawang you hu ji* (The King of Comedy Tours Shanghai) and *Laogong zhi aiqing* (Laborer's Love). Such modern remaking of the classical novel culminated in Mingxing's *Xin Xinyouji* (New Journey to the West), of 1929, sporting a female lead with the name of Miss K. and urban venues such as the dance hall.

22. Friedrich G. Jünger, as quoted in Hermann Bausinger, *Folk Culture in a World of Technology.* Translated by Elke Dettmer (Bloomington: Indiana University Press, 1990), 10.

23. Ibid., 16–17.

24. For a concise review of the debate as a whole, see Fan Dainian, *"Dui 'Wusi' Xinwen-hua yundongde zhexue fansi: ji ershi niandai chu de kexue yu renshenguan da lunzhan"* (A philosophical reflection on the May Fourth New Culture movement: on the great debate on science and the view of life in early twentieth century), in Fang Lizhi ed., *Kexue shi lunji* (An anthology on the history of science) (Hefei: Zhongguo kexue jishu daxue chubanshe, 1987), 255–276.

25. These are Luo Zhixi, *Kexue yu xuanxue* (Science and metaphysics) (Shanghai: Commercial Press, [1927] 1930); Peng Kang, *"Kexue yu renshenguan: jin jinain lai Zhong-guo sixiangjie de zong jiesuan"* (Science and the view of life: a summary of Chinese think-ing in recent years), *Wenhua pipan* (Cultural critique) 3 (1928); Wang Gangshen, *Kexue lun ABC* (The ABC of science studies) (Shanghai: Shanghai shuju, 1928).

26. The technique is called *jieding,* meaning "connecting the roofs." Dong entered the Mingxing company as an apprentice and quickly became its chief cinematographer. In his later years, he served as the technical consultant for the Shaw Brothers Co. in Hong Kong.

27. He Xiujun, *"Zhang Shichuan he Mingxing yingpian gongsi"* (Zhang Shichuan and the Mingxing film company), *Wenshi ziliao xuanji* (An anthology of research material on cultural history) 67 [Beijing: Zhonghua shuju, 1980]. In *Zhongguo wusheng dinaying,* 1528. The author is Zhang's widow, who wrote the memoir in 1965. According to He, the article in the American magazine contained no more than a few foreign terms, so Dong had to resort to his homespun methods to achieve the intended special effect.

28. In Chinese folklore and as a literary trope, female warriors were often called *jin-guo yingxiong* (heroes with headscarf). Invariably, the female knight-errant in the "mar-tial arts" film wears a head turban that covers her long hair. Fan Xuepeng, who starred in *Red Heroine,* recalls that she had the idea of dying footage of her character with "red ink" to make her authentically "red." Because of that, the film was more popular with the Nanyang audience and, as a result, the company made a big profit. She claims that Mingxing partly borrowed this idea in portraying Honggu (Red Maiden) in *Burning.* Fan Xuepeng, *"Wo de yinmu shenghuo de huiyi"* (Remembering my life on the silver screen) [1956]. In *Zhongguo wusheng dianying,* 1480.

29. The term is derived from Matei Calinescu, *Five Faces of Modernity: Modernism, Avant-Garde, Decadence, Kitsch, Postmodernism* (Durham, N.C.: Duke University Press, 1987). Calinescu identifies these "faces" as distinctive aesthetic categories of modernity. The "martial arts-magic spirit" film, I think, blend these categories in a way that dissolves the boundary between the "high" and "low." The proliferation of the genre in recent Hong Kong cinema may be indicative of the genre's postmodern "face."

30. Marcel Mauss, "Techniques of the Body," *Economy and Society* 2.1 (February 1973): 73–75.

31. The Chinese character for Yun in her name has the "grass" radical on top of "cloud." But both characters (with or without the radical) are pronounced the same.

32. See Donna Haraway, "A Cyborg Manifesto: Science, Technology, and Socialist-Feminism in the Late Twentieth Century," in her *Simians, Cyborgs, and Women: The Rein-vention of Nature* (London: Free Association Books, 1991), 149–182. Haraway defines a cy-borg as "a cybernetic organism, a hybrid of machine and organism, a creature of social

reality as well as a creature of fiction" (149). Although Haraway addresses primarily the prevalent phenomenon of the "odd techno-organic, humanoid hybrids" in recent science fiction, I found the concept also applicable to earlier science fiction movements in which the figure of the modern woman was crucially shaped by the interaction with machines, if not yet incorporated with them.

33. Ibid., 150.

34. Wang Zhaoguang, *"Sanshi niandai chuqi de Guomingdang dianying jiancha zhidu"* (The film censorship system of the Nationalist Party in the early 1930s), *Dianying yishu* (Film art) 3 (1997): 63. After its establishment in November 1930, the NFCC systematically began to issue licenses to films. *Burning* received a license on June 27, but it was soon revoked, on July 21.

35. See Duara Prasenjit, "Knowledge and Power in the Discourse of Modernity: The Campaign against Popular Religion in Early Twentieth-Century China," *Journal of Asian Studies* 50.1 (February 1991): 67–83.

36. *Zhongguo dianying nianjian* (Yearbook of China cinema) of 1934, edited by the official China Educational Film Association and prefaced by the minister of propaganda, Chen Lifu, is a publication that demonstrates the Nationalists' systematic effort to control the film industry for the purpose of nation building. The central theme of the book is "education" through cinema. A whole section is devoted to introducing foreign practices of film censorship. The following section is on "Chinese film administration," which offers detailed description of the establishment of the NFCC and a list of censored domestic and imported films.

37. Quoted in Wang Zhaoguang, "The film censorship system of the Nationalist Party in the early 1930s," 63. The original source of this information is NFCC, ed., *"Dianying jiancha gongzuo zong baogao"* (A general report on the work on film censorship), and Luo Gang, *"Zhongyang dianjianhui gongzuo gaikuang"* (An overview of the work of the NFCC), both in *Zhongguo dianying nianjian* (1934).

38. Lu Xun, *"Youwu xiangtong"* (Each supplies what the other needs), *Xin qingnian* 6.6 (November 1919), in *Lu Xun quanji* (Collected works of Lu Xun) (Beijing: Renmin wenxue chubanshe, 1982), vol. 1: 364–365. In the essay, Lu Xun attributes the "knightly" or martial style to the northern writers and the sentimental style to the southern writers.

39. Lu Xun, *"Mingzi"* (Names), in *Lu Xun quanji*, vol. 8, 99–100.

40. Wu Xiwen. *"Guochan yingpian yu nanyang wenhua"* (Chinese film and Nanyang culture). *Zhongnan qingbao* (Bulletin of information on the Zhongnan region) 2 (March 1935): 20–22.

CHAPTER THREE

Postsadness Taiwan New Cinema

Eat, Drink, Everyman, Everywoman

The ethos of *sadness* has been a crucial concept in making Taiwan New Cinema distinctive from other Chinese-language cinemas. Aiming to address the estranged political groups and to recreate a sense of social unity in Taiwan, the assertion of "walking out of sadness" *(zouchu beiqing)* has become one of the central issues in political campaigns of different political parties for the affluent, highly urbanized, contemporary communities in Taiwan. Because Taiwan has rapidly developed into a democratic society since the lifting of the emergency decree that ended martial law in 1987, it is difficult to conceive why such an assertion should be necessary. The positive changes, including Taiwan's economic growth that has lead to a spectacular increase in living standards, mask the negative social consequences of the rush to become a modern and highly industrial nation. Although people in Taiwan still undergo the aftereffect of political oppression and cultural repression of the martial law era (1949–1987), sadness has become a metaphorical shadow that had been cast upon and still exists in every healthy, progressive, optimistic image of Taiwan.

The Taiwan New Cinema filmmakers of the current wave, who had enough of historical exposés and personal grief, attempted to make breaks with the concept of representing the sadness of the past. Therefore, a new trend of representation, which rejects the nostalgic, historical approach, shifts their focuses to explore the pain, transgression, and absurdities of contemporary life in Taiwan. The current wave of Taiwan New Cinema not only reexamines the ethos of sadness, but also tries hard to present the spatial and temporal contiguity of the postsadness era in different lights. Therefore, the portrayal of ordinary Taiwanese people in the postsadness era has become one of the key aspects of the new trend of Taiwan New Cinema filmmakers.

The Ethos of Sadness

Taiwanese cinema has a long tradition in association with realism. From the Taiwanese-language films that were ever popular between 1955–1974 to the governmental promotion of Mandarin-language films in Taiwan (1964–1980s) and to the emergence of Taiwan New Cinema (1982 to present), realistic portrayal of Taiwanese life and experience has been the most popular motif that attracts the film audiences' attention.[1] Taiwan New Cinema, which has been compared stylistically to Italian neorealism,[2] was initially inspired by Taiwan's nativist literature of the 1960s and 1970s. The neorealistic New Cinema movement struggles to depart from both the entertainment-orientated cinema, dominated by grade-B kung-fu movies and sugarcoated romances, and propaganda-oriented genres, Healthy Realism[3] films of the 1960s, and Social Realism[4] films of the 1970s.

The Healthy Realism promoted by the post 1949 ruling Kuomintang government overlooks the negative aspects of Taiwanese experience. Such neglect creates a void in writing Taiwanese history because Healthy Realistic cinema emphasizes promoting Taiwan's positive image and reinforcing morals. Until martial law was lifted in 1987, the Central Motion Picture Corporation supported talented young directors who were willing to provide a different kind of cinema to represent Taiwan in realistic and sympathetic lights. These pioneering Taiwan New Cinema filmmakers belong to the postwar generation and grew up with Taiwan's socioeconomic restructuring from an agricultural to an industrialized and capitalist society. In their semidocumentary, semibiographical style of representation, Taiwan New Cinema filmmakers applied their life experiences in filmmaking to break away from genres such as martial arts, melodramatic romances, and historical epics. By taking new approaches in making films, the New Cinema filmmakers reconstructed a personal, socially conscious, and nostalgic history, a history of sadness. Their neorealistic style attempts to recover the issues of historiography, language, and gender concerns, which had been overlooked by other post-1949 directors of propaganda or popular genres.

Taiwan New Cinema directors, such as Hou Hsiao-hsien, Edward Yang, Wang Tung, and others, adopt literary works with a strong Taiwanese flavor, integrate with their personal experiences, take on a realistic and sympathetic approach to

reconstruct the missing history of Taiwan. Their attempt at historical reconstruction of neglected, erased, or taboo postwar history of Taiwan generated the
ethos of sadness in cinematic representations. Particularly in evidence is Hou
Hsiao-hsien's film *Beiqing chengshi* (City of Sadness,1989),[5] which initiated this
cinematic trend of sadness. Hou's *City of Sadness* reveals one of the most traumatic events in modern history in Taiwan, the February 28 Incident. The political violence of the February 28 Incident and the subsequent sociopolitical repression not only silenced Taiwanese people, it also planted the ethos of sadness
into the unconscious of people in Taiwan. Such ethos of sadness never finds a
channel to express until the emergence of Taiwan New Cinema.

In the mid 1990s, a number of talented filmmakers started to generate a second wave or a third wave of New Cinema movement. They attempted to depart
from the ethos of sadness. These new directors' movies explore a wider variety
of contents and styles while still placing the subjects in a unique Taiwanese milieu. The current wave of filmmakers also rejected nostalgic, historical, and *sad*
approaches of the earlier wave. Instead, they moved their lens to explore into the
private scopes of painful, ambivalent, and absurd contemporary life. Taiwanese
postsadness cinema as presented in these directors' works portrays characters as
trapped in the new disoriented urbanism.[6] Moved beyond the introspective approach in examining the history of sadness, this new trend shifts its focus to the
present and the private. In this chapter, I will discuss how Tsai Ming-liang and
Lin Cheng-sheng, two prominent filmmakers of this latest wave of Taiwan New
Cinema, employ their cinematic talents to portray contemporary postsadness
Taiwan. The discussion of postsadness Taiwan New Cinema will focus on how
these directors depict Taiwan from novel perspectives and how they portray ordinary people in reaction to everyday life to demonstrate how the current wave
of the New Cinema movement moves beyond the ethos of sadness.

Tsai Ming-liang's films depict accidental gender and family relationships em-
ploying the concept of desire displacement. Unlike the filmmakers of earlier
trends, in which individuals are always situated in families and inevitably ma-
nipulated by historical forces, Tsai places his characters in isolated, or even absurd, circumstances. Tsai subverts Confucian family-oriented relationships and
conceptualizes postsadness relationships among men and women as the byprod-
ucts of accidental encounters in both films *Aiqing wansui* (Vive L'Amore, 1994)
and *Dong* (The Hole, 1998). The dysfunctional family relationships in *Heliu* (The
River, 1997) and its sequel, *Ni neibian jidan* (What Time Is It There? [2001]), bring
forward Tsai's perception of domestic role displacement in ordinary Taiwanese
family. The concept of displacement moves beyond the ethos of sadness, which
focuses mostly on tragic, work-burdened, and politically victimized representation of Taiwanese family. Instead, Tsai Ming-liang envisions relationships among

men and women in postsadness Taiwan as accidental and replaceable. Evidently, ethos of sadness is no longer an attractive subject to the current wave directors such as Tsai Ming-liang and Lin Cheng-sheng.

The discussion of Lin Cheng-sheng's films, *Fanglang* (Sweet Degeneration, 1997), *Meili zai changge* (Murmur of Youth, 1997), and *Ai ni ai wo* (Betelnut Beauty, 2001) also touches on the issues of family dysfunction, yet the focus will be on Lin's concept of forbidden crossing. Whereas all three films touch on taboo relationships—incest, homosexuality, and prostitution—the forbidden crossing suggests not only rebellious attempts, but also attempts to reach the unknown. The danger of crossings exposes the fact that postsadness Taiwanese identity is situated on fragile ground; such identity is constantly facing crisis and may result in an ultimate displacement. Unlike the earlier wave that constructed cinematic chronicle of the *history of* sadness, the current wave takes on accidental, forbidden, and destructive approaches in presenting the postsadness era. Whereas eat, drink, man and woman are dominant themes in both directors' films, the connection between ordinary man and woman no longer revolves around the infrastructure of existing or prospective family values. Through constant searching, finding, exchanging, and losing, the ever-changing relationships between man and woman reveal how postsadness Taiwanese are trapped in the process of endless attempts of replacement and displacement.

Tsai Ming-liang

Tsai Ming-liang's films portray life and absurdities in today's Taiwanese affluent society where cultural norms are no longer clear. Tsai's films, marked by nihilism and an overwhelming despair of self-imposed isolation, are characterized by an inability to communicate. Unlike the representation of sadness of the earlier trend, Tsai's presentation of the absence of communication does not relate to an identifiable political repression, but to unconscious and instinctive desire. The setting of *Vive L'Amour* presents urban Taiwan as a luxurious place in which people dress nicely and houses are lavishly decorated. The film takes an existential approach to the plight of the urban Taiwanese man and woman who are active participants yet at the same time on the margins of the contemporary affluent society.

In this story about urban alienation, all three characters accidentally share a living space (an expensive apartment for sale), yet they barely interact or develop attachments to each other. Because their tenuous relationship was triggered accidentally, it ends abruptly without affecting engagement. Coincidence and crisscross encounters among the three characters subvert the sexually predetermined gender roles. Their instinctive desire for sex and unconscious desire for love

Betelnut Beauty (*Ai ni ai wo*), directed by Lin Cheng-sheng, Taiwan, 2001.

awakens the individual's ignorance of his or her solitude, rejection, and alienation. Therefore, the title, "ironically, means 'long live love' and in this case it's more of a prayer than a vindication."[7] The accidental relationship fulfills no longing for love and its byproduct, casual sex, generates more needs for desire replacements.

There are only three characters in the film, May, Ah-Jong, and Little Kang. Throughout the film, none of these characters care to be identified with family names. Identifying the characters only by nicknames in Tsai's films suggests that the bequeathed family identity and the rootedness of the Confucian family-state have been defied in the postsadness era. Consequently, without the privilege of preestablished family association, the semianonymous man and woman are incapable of initiating a connection with other people in this urban environment. Tsai's concept of displacement in the postsadness society first appears in *Vive L'Amour*, when Ah-Jong serves as both May's and Little Kang's desire replacement. In addition to the street vendor Ah-Jong, the real estate agent May and the columbarium salesman Little Kang stand as Tsai's typical characters—depressed, alienated, and apathetic urbanites. The final discovery of the love triangle provides a surprising twist to this accidental relationship. For man and woman of the postsadness Taiwan, the replacement of alienation and depression brings forth nothing but another alienation and depression. The sense of desire replacement reminds ordinary man and woman of what is lacking in his or her life. This lack, a hole in his or her heart, has been unconscious yet now visible. Not until another accidental encounter takes place and a metaphorical hole becomes visible is a path to possible salvation paved.

Tsai Ming-liang's *The Hole* is set seven days before the turn of the twenty-first century and is called "a love story for the millennium." While the title, *Vive L'Amour*, implies an ironic aspect in the celebration of love in postsadness Taiwan, the film's subtitle suggests it is a story about the apocalypse of love. This film envisions the lives of a man and a woman with no name or identity. All they have in common is that they live in the same apartment building. Like the semi-anonymous real estate agent May and the columbarium salesman Little Kang in *Vive L'Amour*, this downstairs woman and the upstairs man exist in almost unremitting loneliness and alienation. The metaphorical hole, created by yet another irresponsible work, becomes an accidental path that opens up both solitary ends, upstairs and downstairs. But through this hole, bereft of human connection or meaningful action, Tsai once again envisions enigmatic situations.

In contrast to the gleaming metropolitan setting of *Vive L'Amour*, Tsai's portrayal of urbanity in *The Hole* is dystopian. The synopsis of *The Hole* at the beginning of the film reads like an apocalypse: "Somewhere in Taiwan, the rain doesn't let up. A mysterious disease reaches epidemic proportions. The government demands a massive transfer out of the quarantine zone. Officials warn those residents who refuse to move that the garbage will go uncollected and the water supply will be gone soon. Despite all of this, some residents still refuse to move away."[8]

In this film, the decaying architecture and decrepit buildings are Tsai's visual representation of urban dystopian; inside the building, there are grimy walls, peeling wallpaper, signs of water damage and unattended garbage. The strong contrast between the chic appeal of the downstairs woman and her desperate surroundings reflects an uncanny sense of absurdity, and her unconscious craving for desire replacement.

The Hole is regularly interrupted by surreal cabaret sequences, fantasies of romance, or seductive musical displays set to Tsai's favorite Grace Chang songs. The fantasies of the anonymous woman are bright, lively, and seductive, which act as the sharp contrast to her disastrous reality. Tsai's careful framing of all her fantasies in elevators, staircases, or open corridors suggests that she desires and fantasizes escape from her desperate living conditions. Her transfiguration fantasy is a liberating act, which reveals her inner frustration cannot be ascertained from her quiet and passive acceptance of her surroundings. Like the anonymous woman's fantasy that helps her to escape from her disastrous reality, the self-induced image of an affluent, highly urbanized, and gleaming Taipei is only an appearance wearing colorful, progressive, and cheerful cosmetics. Under heavy

The Hole (Dong), directed by Tsai Ming-liang, Taiwan, 1998.

makeup, anxiety, insecurity, and despair continuously accumulate in people's unconsciousness and, consequently, the approaching apocalypse will destroy everything.

Tsai Ming-liang's metaphor of pouring rain functions as revelation prior to the apocalypse. In his production notes to *The Hole*, he explains: "It's always raining, which makes my characters somewhat aloof from their environment. . . . They are romantic but the environment is out of key with this romanticism. They believe they can hide themselves in a safe world behind the door and put the garbage outside which they don't see. But the world isn't so safe inside. Danger creeps in all the same, like the unending rain, the strange diseases etc."[9]

The never-ending rain evokes the deeper sense of antipathy and familiarities that people in urban and industrialized Taiwan are forced to cope with in their environment. The rundown sets in the film suggest the dilapidated and corrupt environment of the postsadness Taiwan is the unnatural consequence of irresponsible human errors. In this film, both protagonists are so apathetic to their environments that the bodily functions have been reduced to an insect-like state of eating, drinking, defecating, and having sex. The nonstop rain not only deprives people of their mobility but also reduces people's access to telecommunications. Such a nonphysical and predetermined state of existence evokes the viewers a sense of imprisonment.

The metaphor of pouring rain can also be seen in Tsai's film *The River*. In an interview, Tsai Ming-Liang explained his motivation in making his films: "I have

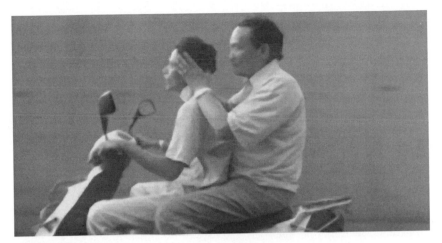

The River (He liu), directed by Tsai Ming-liang, Taiwan, 1997.

always wanted to probe deeper into the roots of humanity. While shooting *The River*, I kept reminding myself to probe into the deeper, darker half of ourselves. We don't always live happily ever after. Materialism boosts human greed to an inglorious height. We have everything we have ever wanted, yet there is something lurking in the dark to keep us from being really happy."[10]

Though clearly not portraying life in an urban environment as a happy state, all Tsai's characters are estranged and apathetic in *Vive L'Amour, The Hole*, and *The River*. Traveling deeper down Tsai's metaphorical river, the stream of unconsciousness, Tsai envisions an increasing force of the postsadness era that disintegrates family relationships. The symbolic collapse of the house by the pouring rain suggests the destruction of traditional family value. Unlike the earlier New Cinema filmmakers who commonly employ the revived family structure to carry on the notion of nation-state unity and Confucian values, Tsai's portrayal of the family in *The River* appears ultimately dysfunctional and treacherous.

A father, a mother and a child make a typical nuclear family in postsadness Taiwan, yet none of the family members communicates with each other or serves his or her conventional role in the domestic environment. This film provides another set of estranged and anonymous characters, whom again suffer from inability to communicate. "Living with his retired father and working mother, the three pass through their apartment like ships in the night, barely acknowledging one another, eating their fast-food takeout meals in silence."[11] It is a family that not only subverts Confucian pyramidal family-state structure, but also subverts Freudian and Lacanian notions of the formation of subjectivity.[12] The child's double denial of the mother and the father prohibits him from entering the realm of language, the Symbolic Order. Thus, this noncommunicative state causes not only the family dysfunction but also the rebellion against the Symbolic Order, until the child, Little Kang, develops a mysterious pain in the neck and the family members are called to function.

Family functionality is immediately under challenge while the three of them coexist in the same space, the dilapidated home. The incestuous implications in the film are revealed through Little Kang's interaction with his parents. Tsai applies a crosscut to convey these implications. After the mother offers Little Kang her vibrator to massage his warped neck, she returns alone to her room to watch pornography. Simultaneously when Little Kang is massaging his neck, the mother allows her sexual fantasies to swim through the flow of the sound of the vibrator humming. The same incestuous implication also appears in the ending scene when the father unknowingly masturbates the son in the dark gay sauna. The incestuous encounter between Little Kang and the father in a gay spa exposes the danger of the disintegration of traditional ethical/moral values, of the Confucian family-state infrastructure, and of the Symbolic Order in one moment.

In the final scene, Tsai crosscuts between the mother climbing to the source of a leak problem vis-à-vis the father and the son transgressing both the incest and homosexual taboos. The image of flooding rain symbolizes the revelation of the family secret. Until the homosexual father and bisexual son confront each other, the law of the father, though under dual challenge, is finally visible. Through their incestuous encounter, they face the source of pain caused from their previous denials. A mutual relationship thus may possibly develop between the two transgressors. In the world of Tsai's films, forming new relationships in post-sadness Taiwan overrides the Symbolic Order and rewrites morality. The family's dysfunction also becomes apparent through each character's search for a love/sex replacement (such as the father's frequent visits to the gay sauna, the mother's seductive devotion to her boyfriend who duplicates pornographic films, and the son's casual sex in response to any invitation of both genders). Searching for a desire replacement acts to kill the unidentified pain and to fill the void; it is just like the pilgrimage for an alterative cure for the son's pain on the warped neck. The torturous treatments of Little Kang's pain reinforce the message of displacement—there may be a cure for the pain, yet this cure may itself become a different kind of suffering. The displaced pain always finds its replacement and eventually consumes life unless the pain's origin has been discovered.

Yet, the pain in life may never be identified or the lack in life may never find its replacement. As in *What Time Is It There?* the father's sudden death abruptly ends the possibility to resume the Symbolic Order or to form a new relationship. As for the mother and the child, Little Kang, the abrupt death of the father evokes their long buried unconsciousness of lack. Thus, lacking a love/desire object to anguish over, the mother and the child are not able to grieve. The emotionally devastated mother puts in endless efforts to connect with the dead father through the guidance of the Taoist priest. Unable to identify her emotional void, her attempt to objectify grief is to believe that the father may reincarnate into an enormous white fish in a small tank. Whereas death acts as the ultimate displacement, the postsadness family in Taiwan is reduced to the apathetic stares of the mother at timeless void, a lifeless fish, and the dead father.

As for the child who lost the father, Little Kang suffers from a severe sense of dislocation. He, along with the mother, is excluded from the Symbolic Order and thus unable to express grief. Like the anonymous woman in *The Hole* who escapes seedy reality to her bright, lively, and seductive fantasies, Little Kang in *What Time Is It There?* fantasizes a different life in different time, at different place, of different person/gender in order to escape his indescribable void. The accidental encounter between watch vendor Little Kang and repulsive Paris-to-go woman evokes his awareness of the other, no matter how tenuous the relationship is. Tsai's carefully framing of all Little Kang's obsessions in adjusting every timepiece in Taipei he can find (including an extremely large clock on top of a tall building) to Paris time suggests that he desires to escape from his unexpressive state of void. Such void, due to the death of the symbolic father, is the ultimate displacement that every man and woman finds no way to avoid facing. For Tsai, such alienation is inescapable. In an interview, Tsai explains, "I thought that by moving to a new city full of strangers, I might feel more relaxed and discover a new self that I did not know before. But that didn't happen."[13] Little Kang's replacement, woman in Paris, does not stand as a new other self but suffers from another inexpressible depression and void. The tenuous relationship across space and time creates no salvation or remedy for individual alienation, even to the end, when Kang's other self, the woman in Paris, arrives at her ultimate end and meets Kang's ultimate displacement.

In his production notes to *The Hole*, Tsai explains his metaphor of a hole as "modern man does not know how to communicate, indeed, he doesn't know how to learn how to communicate."[14] His technique of using no musical soundtrack and keeping large portions of all his films virtually silent except for ambient noise evokes the awareness of noncommunication in postsadness Taiwan. In his films, however, it is not language diversity that causes the miscommunication (i.e., Little Kang's father speaks Mandarin, his mother speaks Taiwanese, and the child and his friends are bilingual), but it is the self-induced alienation and apathy that restrain people from expressing their feelings to each other. The limited dialogue in all films continues Tsai's attempts of showing noncommunication.

Each of Tsai's limited dialogue films falls into a pattern of eating, sleeping, defecating, and having sex. The lives of the characters are banal and voyeuristic —dominated by basic bodily functions[15]—the need to eat, the need to drink, the need for sex, and the need to release bodily waste. Although there is ordinariness in all the details of daily life, presented in Tsai's unique style, they "add up to a painfully incisive portrait of the contemporary human condition."[16] Particularly in evidence is that even the most everyday routines are plagued with difficulties; dangers of all kinds creep into people's lives just like the unidentifiable leak of the house [in *What Time Is it There?*]. Through the lens of Tsai's camera, the audience becomes a "complicit voyeur who watches the goings-on of the people in the movie who are unaware that we are watching them. It is from this position that the viewers derive pleasure in voyeurism."[17] As Tsai's camera captures the characters in odd positions when they are alone, however, the repetition of daily routines does not evoke in the spectators the sadomasochistic pleasure of dominance. Instead, the foregrounding of the daily routines creates a sense of immediacy in reality that actually induces the viewer's repulsive feelings.

In all Tsai Ming-liang's films, man and woman seek to satisfy his or her instinctive needs and to fill the void/hole of his or her life. Yet even when his or her desire is attained, it does nothing to remedy his or her extreme existential alienation. This temporary release or fulfillment of desires leads to a perpetual repetition of finding replacement, yet the lack eventually creeps into the unconscious dimension and deepens the sense of insecurity, despair, and absurdity. The repressed feelings of frustration and of self-alienation are buried inside the unconscious void, yet the unconscious will not remain perpetually buried; it may surface in dreams or through projection. Therefore, the fear of emergent unconsciousness of the void causes anxiety. And more, the anxiety of frustration in finding replacement and confronting the ultimate displacement reduces man and woman to a long enigmatic sob. Tsai Ming-liang's films *Vive L'Amour, The Hole,* and *What Is It There?* all end with the enigmatic sob of the anonymous woman weeping alone. "Tsai brings his films to a halt to let us in"[18] and forces his audiences to experience the same alienation, despair, and absurdity as his characters are experiencing. The arriving apocalypse in the postsadness Taiwan that Tsai Ming-liang attempts to convey in his films is presented beyond language.

Lin Cheng-sheng

Similar to Tsai Ming-liang's conceptualization of ordinary man and woman in postsadness Taiwan, Lin Cheng-sheng's films, *Murmur of Youth, Sweet Degeneration,* and *Betelnut Beauty,* depict the aimless, uncertain, and degenerate sense of Taiwanese urbanity in postsadness Taiwan. In his films, Lin enthuses about the same favorite subjects of the current wave directors—the problems of life in a rapidly changing Taiwanese society. Lin maps the absence of love and of family bonds onto a semirural setting. In this locale, rural equals lifeless, passé, and desolate, which counters the previous wave's representation of nostalgic, rooted, and culturally authentic rural life. Lin's urban setting, on the other hand, corresponds to vitality yet degeneration. The sudden shift between the premodern rural locality and the postmodern urbanized context reflects the characters' sense of disorientation, loss, and alienation. Ironically, the semirural locale is identified as on the outskirts of metropolitan Taipei. The image of small suburban trains, which have been a "Taiwanese new wave logo"[19] and employed to evoke the nostalgic sentiment, become a vehicle of alienation. The trains bring semirural locals to the urban environment while at the same time reflect the ambivalence between the two ends.

The realistic portrayals of ordinary people in Lin's films are similar to those in Tsai Ming-liang's works; however, Lin shifts his focus away from the rootless, accidental individuals and concentrates instead on the bilingual, family-bound, nonintellectual individuals living on the margins of society. He retains a neorealistic approach by utilizing semiprofessional actors, having the characters speak in Taiwanese rather than in Mandarin for a large part of the film, and spends a great deal of time filming daily routines. His style is like that of a documentary. Actually, before Lin Cheng-sheng became a feature filmmaker, he directed several documentaries. His documentary-like style appears most clearly in *Murmur of Youth*, which is a revision of a documentary with the same name that he made in 1991. This stylistic influence also becomes evident in the relationship between the names of his film characters and the names of the subjects of his prior directed documentaries. The name Ah-Hai in *Sweet Degeneration* is borrowed from his 1990 documentary, *Chow, Wong, Ah-Hai and his Four Workers*, and Little Feng in *Betelnut Beauty* shares the nickname with the documentary film, *Ah-Feng and Ah-Ying* made in 1992.

Inspired by his documentaries, Lin's films focus on the everyday lives of ordinary men and women. His intimate observation of the ordinary people also has a poetic, surreal quality that is demonstrated in the way he frames his images of affluent, progressive Taiwan and juxtaposes images of lifeless, trapped, ordinary individuals. Lin Cheng-sheng's view of postsadness Taiwanese youth is apathetic, selfish, and alienated, and the elders are tired, resigned, and powerless.

Lin Cheng-sheng's ultimate inspiration for portraying the typical Taiwanese woman of here and now is certainly Mei-li from one of his documentary projects: "Five years ago, I made a documentary by the same title. It was about a girl named Mei-li. I wanted to document her in her youthful innocence: the way she always fell in love and fantasized her affairs. . . . She had bizarre ideas about love and desire. As you get old, youth becomes a distant, sentimental memory. . . . This film is as 'an ode to youth.'"[20] Therefore, in Lin's *Murmur of Youth* he names both leading characters Mei-li (meaning beautiful in Chinese). As their lives cross, they are the embodiments of the ordinary. Like Tsai Ming-liang who applies this crisscrossing technique to imply tenuous connections among people, Lin uses coincidence and overlapping paths to reveal an underlying logic and pattern to ordinary lives. The juxtaposition of similarities in the two Mei-li's lives not only increases the viewers' curiosity, particularly when they pass one another without much regard, it also suggests a possibility of taking another identity, existing in another time, and appearing at another place.

Both Mei-li are apathetic about the declining patriarchal society in which the passive fathers hardly maintain the power of words. Both Mei-li have long struggled to please their fathers: one Mei-li fails to live up to her father's expectations and drops out of college; the other fantasizes about buying her father a woman to stimulate his sexless life, ignoring the fact that her mother has long suffered an exhausting married life. For them, the law of the father or the Symbolic Order is a failing boundary for resistance. Friendship gradually evolves from the two Mei-li's sexual frustrations: one Mei-li constantly falls in love with imaginary lovers, hoping that these fantasies will liberate her from her dull and frustrated reality; the other Mei-li, who experiences various sorts of sexual harassment in life, finds pleasure in listening to her counterpart's fantasies. The unconscious repression of their desires helps them to conform to societal expectations at first. When they start to converse, however, the more they share about each other's secrets and fantasies, the more they are conscious of their unfulfilled desires.

Fantasy comes into play in Lin's film *Murmur of Youth* when one Mei-li tells the other Mei-li about her fantasy lover. The descriptive love fantasies of Mei-li stand in opposition to her loveless reality. Lin's motionless camera captures the intimacy developed from their unvoiced feelings, secret aspirations, and expectations, and it also records Mei-li's testimonial verbal accounts of family, love, and sexual desires. Mei-li's fantasy and narration are the expressions of the unconscious; they are inextricably linked with desire. According to psychoanalytical theories, such desire is located in the imaginary.[21] Through language (her entry into the Symbolic Order) her fantasy-desire is brought to life. Addressing her fantasy to her counterpart, another Mei-li, is a way of dealing with her lack in life. Consequently, by entering the realm of language, she reconstructs her subjectivity. In other words, although her fantasy signifies a lack, describing her desire allows her to enter the linguistic realm of the symbolic. Entry into language means entry into to the social order, but it also means experiencing lack even further because desire can never be fully satisfied.[22]

Mei-li's development of subjectivity is short lived, because unexpected circumstances bring her and her fantasy lover face to face. This forces her to confront her fantasy or lack. Such confrontation propels her into disorientation and deep despair when she realizes that her fantasy about the lack is not a replacement but, rather, results in a displacement. This discovery brings her to the realization that she does not exist in her own fantasy or in reality. She has no existence in the imaginary or the symbolic. This becomes clear after the confrontation when Mei-li murmurs, "I never exist in his thought." Her ultimate despair leads to the consequent forbidden crossing.

The homosexual encounter suggests the narcissistic every woman, Mei-li, who loses her grip to reality by isolating herself (hiding in the box office) and by letting go of her love object. Through the metaphorical unification with her counterpart, the other Mei-li, she attempts to reassert her subjectivity and her identity by integrating her ego with her libidinal objects. Her desire is no longer sacrificed in conforming to societal expectations, but directly challenges the Symbolic Order, which ever denies and displaces her existence. Like the incestuous transgression of the Symbolic Order in *The River* that implies a dangerous breakthrough to the true subjectivity, the lesbian sexual encounter in *Murmur of Youth* foreshadows a danger of crossing. Once she transgresses the law of the symbolic, she risks reducing her subjectivity into an object of desire. Unless she is able to separate herself from her mirror image and find her entry to the symbolic, the ordinary woman of the postsadness Taiwan will continue to be displaced.

The death of the mother and the absent father in *Sweet Degeneration* suggests a double displacement to the child's subject formation. It is a Freudian twist when neither of the parents exists yet a motherly replacement, sister Ah-fen (Lin Ru-fen), plays the double role as nurturer and seducer. Incestuous love/sex drives the child into disorientation and absurdity. For Lacan, it is not the lack of the mother (being separated from the mother) that interferes with the development of subjectivity, but the displacement of the lack (in this case, the elder sister) that prevents the child from entering into language, the social, and the Symbolic Order. The incestuous relationship between the sister and the brother actually implies a Freudian incestuous mother and child. Ah-fen is the mother replacement, who is expected, under the patriarchal expectation, to bring up her younger brother. Her short-lived existence as a sister or as a woman is when she is in love. When her plan to elope fails, and her motherly role is restored in the father's house, she starts to suffer from disorientation. Mourning her lost identity propels her to make a shocking attempt, the crossing.

A recurrent theme in *Sweet Degeneration* is Lin's concept of desire displacement. In the first layer, Ah-fen is the replacement for her dead mother and her anonymous husband is the love replacement for her first love, Ah-hai (ocean). The prostitute Mei-li is also the sexual replacement for Ah-fen's anonymous husband of the second layer. Finally, the third layer conceals an incestuous relationship between Ah-fen and Ah-sheng (Chun-sheng) in which Ah-fen is the mother replacement and Ah-sheng acts a replacement for the lost lover. When the crisscrossed encounter unexpectedly finds Mei-li and Ah-sheng in love, this love affair immediately displaces all the replacements for the lack. The marriage proposal between Mei-li and Ah-sheng also represents the annulment of the incestuous displacement between sister and brother. As Ah-sheng confides his incestuous experience to Mei-li, it is suggested that it is Mei-li (the replaced love object) instead of Ah-fen (the replaced mother) who moves the child (Ah-sheng) into language. This transfiguration from replacement mother to displacement lover reflects the nonexistence of Ah-fen's subjectivity in the family as well as in the Symbolic Order. The director again shows her sense of displacement as she loses the capacity for communication. Thus, in Ah-fen's last phone call to Mei-li, there is only silence.

Lin Cheng-sheng's *Murmur of Youth* and *Sweet Degeneration* have ambiguous endings, with characters searching for the displacement woman. Lin's open ending suggests a possibility of a new relationship blooming, while the conventional interpersonal relationship has been severed, replaced, and detached. It may also suggest, however, an ultimate return to the Symbolic Order. This becomes evident in *Sweet Degeneration,* when Ah-fen's inactive husband suddenly springs to action and tries to restore her to the house of the father.

Restoring the family members to the house of the father, the Symbolic Order, is a recurrent theme in Lin's films. In *Betelnut Beauty,* Fei-Fei embodies the typical apathetic, selfish, and self-alienated youth of the postsadness urbanity. Escaping from home, in which the father of the house is replaced by a phallic mother, Fei-Fei teams up with her friend Yili to become betelnut beauties. A "betelnut beauty" refers to a girl who wears a sexy costume and sells betelnut in a glass booth. As Lin Cheng-sheng explained in an interview,[23] the betelnut beauties are the stimulators that satisfy the voyeuristic desires of society and lure lower or working-class men into consumption. Being a betelnut beauty, with heavy makeup and very little clothes, Fei-Fei has experienced different levels of disorientation. Her forbidden crossing is associated with finding her desire replacements and induces the danger of objectifying herself. Fei-Fei constantly suffers from her consciousness of the lack of her missing father who abandons the family for another. Her writing diaries and compulsively calling the father imply her desire to be restored to the Symbolic Order. It is at the moment she brings her boyfriend Little Feng to face her father that she finds the man of her own to replace the man she never had.

The accidental encounter between Fei-Fei (flying) and Litte Feng (wind) gradually turns into a love relationship, yet danger creeps in when Fei-Fei's friends cross paths with Little Feng's. In the director's note, Lin Cheng-sheng states, "A couple of youngsters. They meet and they fall in love. In a metropolis like Tai-pei, they spend their youth with no reservations, looking towards a future of huge fortunes, a future in which they can do whatever they want. They have no idea that they're living in an environment that's moving towards danger. And it's often too late when they finally figure it out. Youth that has been spent will not return."[24] Like all newly retired military veterans, Little Feng naively dreams of making big money in the affluent city, becoming famous, returning home in glory. To realize this success, however, Little Feng does not take practical small steps, but hastens into careless chances. Little Feng's crossing, tempted by a friend to raid a cash point and helping the friend to take vengeance on his rival gang-ster, leads his comic yet pointless crossing to a dangerous end. The surprising opportunity that brings Fei-Fei into the entertainment business also casts a shadow on this forbidden crossing. Like Little Feng, who desires to confront the lack and to be someone, the betelnut beauty Fei-Fei now crosses the boundary to become an object of voyeuristic desires for larger audiences. The dangerous crossing suggests a double jeopardy: her love replacement of father may not live through both crossings, and her entering the symbolic realm in different form may result in an ultimate displacement. Fei-Fei and Little Feng (flying in the wind) are the embodiments of postsadness Taiwanese identity. Situated identi-ties on fragile grounds, they are doomed to face crises constantly and to expose themselves to the danger of ultimate displacement.

Lin Cheng-sheng conceptualizes his notion of ordinary Taiwanese of the post-sadness era by playing with the characters' names. Like the repetition of the name Mei-li, Ah-fen, and others, the male character's name, Lin Chun-sheng, appears repeatedly in Lin's films. Chun-sheng or Ah-Sheng, another favorite name of Lin, embodies the director's concept of everyman. In Lin's earlier work *Chun-hua menglu* (A Drifting Life, 1996), Lin Chun-sheng (Ah-sheng) was born up-side down, which caused the death of the mother. His sister, Lin Ru-fen (Ah-fen) was the replacement of the mother and consequently the replacement of the Lin family's despised daughter-in-law. Lin's skillful use of names brings a sense of repetition that links the rural story in *A Drifting Life* to his later film, *Sweet Degeneration*, which is set in the rapidly changing urban society of post-sadness Taiwan. Because the same people appear in both films, it gives the im-pression that the sister-brother in *Sweet Degeneration* may have spent their childhood as the sister-brother in *A Drifting Life*.

That reuse of names such as the sister (Lin Ru-fen or Ah-fen) and brother (Lin Chun-sheng or Ah-sheng) in both *A Drifting Life* and *Sweet Degeneration*, the characters Mei-li in *Murmur of Youth* and Mei-li, the prostitute, in *Sweet De-generation* and Chun-sheng, the baker, in *Murmur of Youth* demonstrates not only a continuity of characters but also the transformation of these characters into

ordinary man and woman. In doing so, Lin address the questions of how the
affluent young Taiwanese man or woman finds meaning in a world full of empty
commodities and how he or she associates his or her incomplete or disoriented
subjectivity with the degenerated family/social structure. In the postsadness era
in which the importance of traditional values has been minimized, it seems that
all communications have been reduced to murmurs. For Lin, the disappearance
of conventional or "normal" family connections generates desire that finds replacements in displaced, degenerate, or forbidden relationships. Therefore, in
all of the films—*Sweet Degeneration, Murmur of Youth,* and *Betelnut Beauty*—
this discursive desire is finally fully expressed, in its most taboo form—a dangerous crossing.

Eat, Drink, Everyman, Everywoman

Both Tsai Ming-liang and Lin Cheng-sheng employ ensemble casts and certain
revisited characters, locations, and themes in their films. By creating a familiarity with these elements, they assert the ordinariness of people and events. In
other words, what has happened to the characters could also happen to anyone,
at any place, in any time. Their shared approach to portraying the man and
woman in the postsadness Taiwan continues the tradition that Fredric Jameson
once called "a linked circle"[25] of Taiwanese new wave films.

Tsai has built all his films around the actor Lee Kang-sheng, who embodies
the disoriented urban youth and represents the man in the affluent but apathetic postsadness society. The characters in other roles, sometimes as protagonists and sometimes as supporting actors or special guests in the films, enact
roles that crisscross their paths with men, women, and each other. In this way
Tsai demonstrates that relationships in the postsadness era occur purely by chance.
As the contemporary relationships of man and woman are triggered accidentally and end unexpectedly (i.e., Little Kang's experience of casual sex and short-
term connections with various male and female characters in different films),
they become each other's replaceable object of desire. Tsai's films that reflect nihilism and overwhelming despair certainly do not intend to reconstruct a social-
political identity like the filmmakers of the previous wave did. For Tsai Ming-
liang, the postsadness Taiwan shares an existence with all displaced metropolitan
cities everywhere.

Like Tsai, Lin Cheng-sheng also casts the same actors. His casting, however,
produces an even stronger sense of repetition. By assigning an actor to play the
same family role in different films (i.e., actor Tseng Jing plays the sister in *A
Drifting Life* and the sister's earlier moment of life in the black and white flashback from *Sweet Degeneration*), Lin evokes a sense of continuity of the past—

the era of sadness while at the same time representing the present—the post-sadness period. Nevertheless, his framing of the uncanny resemblance between generations is not without controversy. The disruption of temporal and spatial continuity (i.e., providing insufficient evidence to identify the Lin family line-age in both *A Drifting Life* and *Sweet Degeneration*) frustrates the viewers who try to imagine a smooth transition between the sadness era and the postsadness. As represented by the insignificant Lin family, which embodies many ordinary families in Taiwan, the conventional family infrastructure, morals, and values are deconstructed and fragmented in one moment. For Lin Cheng-sheng, the postsadness Taiwan constantly faces the danger of forbidden crossing, a line that demarcates the conventional social order.

Tsai Ming-liang and Lin Cheng-sheng also share similar approaches to por-traying men and women. They are neither likeable nor pitiful, neither vicious nor merciful, yet they are rather repulsive. The directors' long shots and static camera positions reveal a sense of reality that is both spatial and temporal; they show viewers familiar urban landscapes, banal daily details, and the odd mo-ments of solitude. Because all the sentimental expressions have been suspended or filtered out, the characters' meaningless daily repetitive actions and routines arouse antipathy from the spectators. Not designed to entertain or provide voy-euristic pleasure, the filmmakers' portrayals of men and women eating, drink-ing, defecating, and having sex are intend to evoke the audiences' consciousness of their own antipathy.

The audience certainly will not find a resolution for the enigma or a resto-ration of order as in a traditional narrative in postsadness films. There is no clo-sure to be achieved. Thus, audiences' reactions to the filmmakers' artistic pre-sentations and narrative styles are quite extreme. Although both Tsai Ming-liang's and Lin Cheng-sheng's films have been well received at international film festi-vals, their attempts to portray postsadness Taiwan are constantly being challenged by their audiences. Both Tsai and Lin intentionally stir up the viewers' sense of frustration by providing them directionless motions and banal routines. Watch-ing films that take a very long time, the audiences expect to have something hap-pen. Yet both directors drive the viewers to realize eventually that almost no de-velopment or drama is offered. The postsadness Taiwan New Cinema does not so much progress in narratives as they do simply last. The stories do not flow into each other, creating a strong sense of forward narrative movement. Instead, they are drifting, fragmented, and nonhistorical. Consequently, feelings of repulsion arouse the unconsciousness of spectators that is common to people in postsad-ness Taiwan. Through the viewing of postsadness films, the audiences experi-ence with the cinematic man and woman the same the feelings of loss, disorien-tation, and displacement.

Through their cinematic representation of eat, drink, man, woman in the post-sadness era, Tsai Ming-liang and Lin Cheng-sheng, the representatives of the current wave, finally make breaks with the concept of representing the sadness past. The Taiwan New Cinema filmmakers of the current wave, who shift their focuses to explore the pain, transgression, and absurdities of contemporary life in Taiwan, direct the postsadness cinema to the reality-conscious representation of the nonhistorical and unsatisfactory realm of the here and the now.

Notes

1. Long Yen Yeh (Ye Longyan), *Chunhua Menglu: zhengzong Taiyu dianying xingshuai lu* (History of the rise and fall of authentic Taiwanese-language cinema) (Taipei: Bo Yang, 1999).

2. Roberto Rosellini called neorealism both a moral and an aesthetic cinema. Like the filmmakers of Italian neorealism who rebelled against Mussolini's fascist restriction, Taiwan New Cinema filmmakers differentiated themselves from the government prescription for cinematic representation of Taiwanese postwar history.

3. According to Mark Nornes Abe and Yueh-yu Yeh, "Narrating National Sadness: Cinematic Mapping and Hypertextual Dispersion" 1994. "This genre featured positive attitudes towards traditional moral values that reflected the attempt to reconcile the inherited ambivalence between the socioeconomic restructuring and moral/ethical values in traditional agricultural society" ("Narrating National Sadness: Cinematic Mapping and Hypertextual Dispersion" [http://cinemaspace.berkeley.edu/Papers/CityOfSadness/table.html], 1994).

4. Abe and Yeh write, "In the late 1970s, a subgenre called "social realism" emerged, featuring sex, violence, and gang subculture. The display and representation of explicit violence, mystified masculinity and misogynous depiction of female sexuality appeared to respond to the long history of the government's repression of sexuality and physicality in cinema through censorship" (ibid.).

5. Abe and Yeh continue, "It is the first Taiwanese film to broach the subject of the most traumatic experience in the nation's history, the February 28 Incident. This was a 1947 massacre by the Nationalist Party (still today's ruling party in Taiwan), which resulted in 18,000 to 28,000 casualties. Using a family as a matrix through which to filter the historical events at the moment of the founding of the nation, Hou represents Taiwanese history in both micro and macro perspectives" (ibid.).

6. Macabe Keliher, "Light, Camera, More Action: Hung Chih-yu and Fellow Young Directors Are Bringing a New Liveliness to Taiwan's Dark Cinema," *Asia Times*. 156.21 (November 27, 2000).

7. Edward Guthmann, "Sad, Lonely 'L'Amour,'" *San Francisco Chronicle* (September 27, 1996): C3.

8. Tsai Ming-liang, *Love, Life, and Lies* [http://www.cse.unsw.edu.au/].

9. Ibid.

10. Review of *He Liu* (The River). *EFC Review*. November 14, 2001 [http://www.efilmcritic.com].

11. Arthur Lazere, film review of *The River* [http://www.culturevulture.net].

12. Jacques Lacan, *Ecrits: A Selection*. Translated by Alan Sheridan (New York: W. W. Norton, 1977).

13. Mark Peranson, "Interview: Cities and Loneliess, Tsai, Ming-liang's 'What Time Is It There?'" *IndiWire*, January 22, 2002 [http://www.indiewire.com/people/int_Tsai_Mingliang_020122.html].

14. Tsai Ming-liang, *Love, Life, and Lies*.

15. Lacan, *Ecrits*.

16. Ibid.

17. Christian Metz, "The Imaginary Signifier," *Screen* 16.3 (1975).

18. Jared Rapfogel, "Tsai Ming-liang: Cinematic Painter," *Senses of Cinema* 20 (May–June 2002) [http://www.sensesofcinema.com/contents/02/20/tsai_painter.html].

19. Fredric Jameson, "Remapping Taipei," in Nick Browne et al., eds., *New Chinese Cinema: Forms Identities, Politics* (New York: Cambridge University Press, 1997).

20. Richard J. Havis, "Interview with Lin Cheng-sheng." *An Interview with the Taiwan Film Centre* [http://www.filmfestivals.com/cannes97/cfilmc21.htm].

21. Teresa De Lauretis, *Alice Doesn't: Feminism, Semiotics, Cinema* (Bloomington: Indiana University Press, 1984).

22. Lacan, *Ecrits*.

23. "Because most users are men, using 'Betelnut Beauties' to sell the product becomes a common practice. These are young women, many of them under 20, who wear very heavy makeup and very little clothes. It therefore becomes connected with the sex trade. This is certainly intolerable to mainstream middle-class values and is the easiest target for a society with such values. But behind such moralistic attacks are efforts to consume these women's sexuality. This is especially true of television, which exploits them by using them to satisfy the voyeuristic desires of society. For the Beauties, the monthly income is high. This is especially attractive to girls with school or family problems. Together, the Beauties and the betelnut trade have created a bizarre subculture" (Interview with Lin Cheng-sheng, "Tales of Cities: Transformation through Camera Eyes," *Chinese Film Showcase* [http://www.amamedia.org/movies/showcase/02showcase/betelnut_beauty.html]).

24. Havis, Interview with Lin Cheng-sheng.

25. In "Remapping Taipei," Jameson writes, "The palpable interweavings of the social, which are both expressed and signified by this system of recurrent imagery and then peculiarly overdetermined by such intertextuality as the casting of Hou Hsiao-hsien himself as the protagonist in Edward Yang's Taipei Story, the material itself moving toward such ambitious historical chronicles as Hou's *City of Sadness* and Edward Yang's *A Brighter Summer Day*, make of Taiwanese new wave films a kind of linked cycle more satisfying for the viewer than any national cinema I know" (123).

CHAPTER FOUR

Working from the Margins

Urban Cinema and Independent Directors in Contemporary China

The emergence of independent film directors and their maverick works in China since the early 1990s has fostered a continuing interest in the politics of naming. Independent filmmaking, according to Chinese critics, refers to experimental practices outside the official production system and its ideological censorship.[1] The independent filmmaker takes responsibility not only for film content and form, but also for raising capital and seeking distribution. Western observers have acknowledged the newly emerged directors as outlaw moviemakers and their films as underground or countercinema.[2]

The tendency to name and categorize film directors reveals a political intent and discursive exhaustion in the trend of defining Chinese cinema. In fact, the term "independent" is fraught with contradictions. On the one hand, the system against which the directors pursue independence remains the hegemonic official apparatus that manipulates production and distribution. On the other, the conditions under which directors experiment with alternative filmmaking show a commercial trend that emphasizes market profit and audience reception. Under the double burden of sociopolitical and commercial imperatives, new film-school graduates entered the film world not as recognizable stars, but as latecomers relegated to the margins. As a matter of necessity, a number of young directors committed themselves to independent filmmaking as a way out. Official intolerance of the films they made and the lack of alternative distribution systems in China compelled these filmmakers to seek recognition through international channels.

As a result, independent film production and its international distribution have stimulated a new current in transnational engagement. Western festival programmers and art-house distributors, for example, welcome Chinese independent films for their "transgressive qualities."[3] These "qualities" depend specifically on a commitment to independent filmmaking and thus to subverting mainstream production and official censorship. Such iconoclastic performances meet the need of international film circles in the desire for a new "other" to succeed the fifth generation and a new vocabulary to define Chinese cinema. For independent directors, the geopolitical transgression of "going abroad" opens up opportunities for the recognition and acclaim that is suppressed within China. They have discovered that official censure at home can enhance their stature overseas, inducing "investors—be they nonmainland critics, film festivals, or producers—to support a director who was conceived of as a quixotic figure in a milieu of cultural repression."[4] In this respect, the group of young film directors embodies a two-sided identity: a shunned minority within mainstream production in China and a valued dissident in the eyes of film critics in the West. Thus, while eagerly sought by international film festivals or art-house distributors, their films remain inaccessible to general Chinese audiences.[5]

Nonetheless, few film directors can depend entirely on foreign acknowledgment. In fact, many of them strive for survival both within and outside the mainstream systems. To this end, independent filmmaking cannot serve as an absolute means of pursuing artistic autonomy; it is a strategic mode of acquiring recognition. Oscillation between the demands of domestic and foreign markets complicates the authenticity of independent cinema. While film critics at home and abroad attempt to theorize it, the concept of independent cinema has already shown transformations, as the following examples illustrate.

Zhang Yuan, a pioneer of independent filmmaking in China, for instance, has become adept at dealing with official restrictions. By writing his own scripts and securing outside financing, Zhang has been able to make a number of indies, such as *Beijing Zazhong* (Beijing Bastard, 1992) and *Donggong xigong* (East Palace, West Palace, 1999). The crucial need for international distribution, however, ironically depends on an official stamp of sanction. The government censor often assures international attention. In a departure from his previous practice, Zhang Yuan sought government permission and financing to finish his recent film *Guonian huijia* (Seventeen Years, 1999). The film, a family melodrama, represents a return to production within the system. Some critics have charged Zhang with "betrayal," claiming that "by collaborating with authorities Zhang sold out and lost the edge that made his other films so powerful."[6] The director denies the charge and explains that he sought permission from the government simply to have his film shown in China. The desire to obtain recognition from international and Chinese audiences, and the difficulty in doing so, indicates just the beginning of the dilemma.

Not as well publicized internationally as Zhang Yuan, Lu Xuechang has struggled to make personal films within the system. His early film *Zhangda chengren* (The Making of Steel, 1995), with production and financial support from Tian Zhuangzhuang's film workshop, won final release only after eleven rounds of heavy editing. The challenge of making a nonmainstream film within the official system, however, confines the director in a "velvet prison," where the authorities promise the artists funding and distribution if the artists agree to "play by the rules." "Few filmmakers would see themselves as collaborators," Paul Pickowicz explains, "but almost all were conscious of the fact that they engaged in self-censorship virtually every day."[7] Gaining financial backing from government-owned studios requires, in addition to a director's political adjustment, the promise of commercial success. The socialist velvet prison and capitalist pressures, therefore, affect the filmmaking mentality in terms of subject selection, form of representation, and market profit. In his recent film *Feichang Xiari* (A Lingering Face, 1999), Lu realizes that the compromise required for official support comes at a high price. The rape scene, the dynamic force of the film, has to be rendered, but the conversation on sexuality between the rape witness and the victim is simply erased.[8]

The entanglement between independent filmmaking and mainstream production raises important questions. The title of this chapter, therefore, raises several questions. Can a truly autonomous and independent cinema exist in China? Will film directors preserve their independent identities if international viewers lose interest in their dissident stance? Can nonmainstream directors, working within the official system, make the films they really want to make? Will the film earn its reputation through artistic qualities rather than political negotiations? If the answers to these questions prove negative or uncertain, the discourse of independent cinema in China will remain problematic and unconvincing. Perhaps the enthusiastic announcement of the emergence of a sixth generation of film directors is premature.

In fact, more attention has been paid to ideological implications than to the cinematic worlds that the young filmmakers have created. Taking their films, especially the early productions, as a point of departure, this chapter investigates how the directors have marked their works as independent and distinguished themselves as experimental artists. Although they differ from each other in significant ways, they share the core quality of wanting to tell one's own story from one's own perspective, free of institutional regulations and ideological manipulation. The worlds that unfold from a personal point of view are no longer traumatic histories and allegorical narratives, but explorations of an urban milieu inhabited by people who live at the fringes of mainstream society.

Urban films are not new to Chinese audiences. Productions in the 1930s and 1940s—such as *Malu Tianshi* (Street Angel, 1937), *Wanjia Denghuo* (Myriad of Lights, 1948), or *Yijiang Chunshui Xiang Dongliu* (The Spring River Flows East, 1947)—used urban space as a cinematic and discursive site to explore national turmoil, urban-rural differences, and family melodramas. Contemporary productions in the 1980s and the 1990s, such as Huang Jianxin's urban series, present the city as a social, cultural, and political setting, against which the films expose a moment of rupture when socialism is winding down yet still a force to be reckoned with. His early works, *Heipao Shijian* (The Black Canon Incident, 1986) and *Cuowei* (The Dislocations, 1987), cast the urban milieu as an absurd confinement the individual is powerless to resist. His recent films, *Lian dui lian, bei kao bei* (Back to Back, Face to Face, 1994) and *Zhanzhi Le, Bie Paxia* (Stand Up, Don't Bend Down, 1992) shift the focus to everyday urban space and how its inhabitants deal with contemporary problems.

Unlike these precedents, however, the city in the young directors' films appears as a personal and subjective space rather than the embodiment of conventional themes, whether from Chinese tradition or national history. The voice and the perspective utter aloud, "I am the protagonist of this urban stage; the city is mine." The setting and tales of urban experience are the signature marks of independent films. Although each director offers a distinct vision, their psychological and cinematic engagements with the city bind them together. The shared urban sensibility often finds rock music as the language of expression, the isolated apartment as a private world, and urban life as a form of youthful self-display.

Melancholy rather than cheerful, their films often envelop the audience within a moody aura of anxiety and loss. Scenes of the city remind them of a past adolescence too minor to claim historical significance. The urban landscape, where young strollers observe the mainstream dramas, denies them space at the center of the social stage. The urban audience, accustomed to historical and melodramatic narratives, finds the voices and images incomprehensible. In the shadow of privileged forerunners and hegemonic discourses, the young and the insignificant see themselves as flaneurs in the urban margins. Personal ties to the city and a professional commitment to filmmaking enable the director to frame the city from an individual perspective and to place the young inhabitants as protagonists. The spatial motif of the city, therefore, acts as a cinematic setting, a metaphor of modernity, and a reflection of the self.

Within the context described above, this approaches three subjects that specifically, but not exclusively, characterize the world and vision of independent film practice: the portrait of the artist-self in film, the nonallegorical depiction of sexuality, and the construction of the coming-of-age narrative.

Portrait of the Artist in Film

Films made by the independent film directors self-consciously show a persistent desire to install the artist in the film. Screening the artist is simultaneously a thematic pursuit and a filming process. The artist becomes an all-embracing figure who blurs the lines between the created image and the creator of the image. Wang Xisoshuai's *Dongchun de Rizi* (The Days, 1994), for instance, reveals a gradually dying relationship between an artist couple. Two avant-garde painters from real life play the roles in the film. Zhang Yuan's *Beijing Bastard* exposes the rock-and-roll world and its performers in Beijing today. The rock pioneer, Cui Jian, simultaneously takes the roles of singer, character, and producer of the film. In addition, rock music provides intertextual interpretation to the film's fragmentary narratives. In Wu Wenguang's documentary *Bumming in Beijing: The Last Dreamers,* the camera tracks a group of artists who struggle to survive "in the margins" and outside the "system."[9] The focus on the artist as the subject, protagonist, and author/director of the film indicates a commitment to bring the marginalized or the excluded into representation. Such focal selection engenders a subjective self-representation, as the film directors themselves share with the characters a marginal position and insignificant status. More important, the mode of the artist as image in and as author of the text allows the film director the freedom to incorporate film narrative and its visual construction into a coherent process.

Frozen (1999), a film by *"wu ming"* (no name), for instance, follows how an artist seeks the meaning of life by performing death and turns his own suicide into his last work of art. The artist engages his body in death experiments related to the four seasons: earth burial in autumn, water burial in winter, fire burial in spring, and ice burial in summer. The film clearly suggests philosophical meanings of death in terms of the seasonal cycle. In addition, the film posits a notion of performativity that sees art production and reception as an open-ended process of engagement between artist and spectator.

Performance art is not completely new in China. A few artists have dedicated themselves to experiments in the process of art making and identity search. Zhang Huan, for instance, has a disturbing fascination with self-torture. Performing the body against unbearable conditions, he experiences how one's physical body endures and enacts social, cultural, and political violations. Ma Liuming, another prominent performance artist, projects the issue of sexual (non)identity

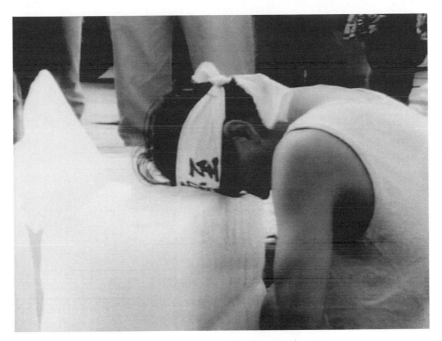

Performance art: ice burial. *Frozen* (dir. "Wu Ming,"1999, China).

directly to the body's nudity. Exposing his male body in feminine masquerade, he demonstrates that neither heterosexual nor homosexual notions can define the body that transgresses sexual difference. In the 1980s, when avant-garde art was subject to official restriction and distanced from mass audiences, performance art remained underground or moved overseas.[10] As performance art involved neither public space nor viewing spectator, the very concept of performativity lost its essential meanings.

Frozen reveals to the audience the cinematic representation of one performative event in China. Taking a particular sequence as an example, an ice burial performance is staged on a street. The artist takes the central role of performer with his peers as assistants and pedestrians as onlookers. The mise-en-scène, penetrated with the sound effect of a beating heart, seizes the moment of a dying process and performative art. The body, melting the ice and performing death, asks both the artist and the viewer to ponder the question of why death as an artwork? The possibility of representation results from the use of flashbacks to rescreen the performance and voice-over narration to reenact the process. In the re-presentation, the artist's body in and as the work of art bears the signs of representation. This enables a cinematic perception and interpretation of the performative event, staged in the past but absent in the present.

Performing death to create art and inspire public perception delivers multiple messages. At a narrative level, the form of public performance exposes the avant-garde subculture in contemporary China. Artists, especially avant-garde ones, excluded from official art museums and working outside traditional conventions, use the body to seek subjective identity and to locate exhibition space. Beyond performance art as an experimental novelty in China and a narrative source in the film, this chapter further explores questions of the politics of performance, representation of the unrepresentable, and gender meanings in relation to performance art.

The politics of performance manifests an encounter between artist-society and body-self. Performing the body as a search for identity indicates the desire and practice of moving from the margin to the center and from the personal to the public. In a society lacking an avant-garde art environment and political tolerance, experimental artists, as well as independent filmmakers, are excluded from the mainstream canon for social and political reasons. For instance, Qi Lei's sister, a physician, loves her brother but is unable to understand his artistic pursuit. "What are they so depressed about?" the sister complains to her colleague. "They are too young to understand life and feel depressed when they get bored," the colleague responds. The conversation indicates an antagonistic social attitude toward the artist and experimental art. The sister's confusion and the colleague's misinterpretation demonstrate a rejection of younger artists who have not yet made a mark in history.

In addition to the problematic reception, performance art faces institutional suppression. Seen as abnormal and outside the mainstream, the artists are considered as mentally aberrant. One sequence in a mental hospital, for instance, stages a metaphorical mise-en-scène to illustrate the confrontation between artist and institution. Qi Lei's girlfriend and another artist take him to the hospital for a checkup. The medical staff cannot distinguish the normal from the abnormal and insist that Qi Lei's friend is the mental patient. During the confrontation between the caretakers and "the patient," the film shows the artist identifying himself repeatedly. His declarations of self-identity, however, are met with deadly ignorance. Any attempt to escape from official authority would receive severe punishment. The sequence shows that self-utterance is unable to establish an individual's identity and that experimental art is seen as mentally abnormal.

If voice and words fail to utter meanings, the body becomes the site of struggle. It is through the body that the institution projects its authoritarian power and the artist seeks resistance. This engagement reflects Peggy Phelan's explanation that "performing oneself necessarily entails cultural visibility, and visibility is necessarily a desirable goal for subjects seeking to reject or transform their position of marginality."[11] The politics of representation generated in this film takes the form of a double subversion: portrait of the artist-self through performing art and through cinematic re-presentation. By using the body in performance, an artist may dramatically unveil the nonnormative subjects conventionally excluded from the mainstream narratives of art history. By screening the body, especially the body of death, the film subject tends to document the artists and their works into history. The significance lies in the fact that the film transforms performance art and the dying body into representation.

The re-presentation gives a cinematic form to the performative that cannot be reproduced. "Performance's only life is in the present," Peggy Phelan observes in her widely cited *Unmarked*. "Performance cannot be saved, recorded, documented, or otherwise participate in the circulation of representations of representations: once it does so, it becomes something other than performance."[12] The cinematic possibility of bringing the performed art into representation suggests dialogical engagement. On the one hand, representing something that is conventionally unrepresentable marks the performance art into history and documentation. The process of visualizing the performative introduces not only performance art, but also independent filmmaking to the audience for interpretation. The intertextual transgression, therefore, mobilizes the artists, performative and cinematic, from margin to center, from personal to public, and from presentation to interpretation. In other words, the filmic form continues to produce meaning at the point where the performative ends.

On the other hand, cinematic representation of the performative raises the question of whether performing art is the authentic medium for truth in art and in life. Ice burial as a staged death performance exposes the most unexpected outcome of the film. In the process of cinematic re-presentation, the film encourages the eye to believe that the artist buried himself in ice and died of hypothermia after emergency treatment failed to bring him back to life. The artist's death is announced, and the exhibition of his art works opened. As the loss of life penetrates perception, the audience is shocked to see the performance artist and the organizer, in hiding, discussing the experimental experience of dying. In exposure or betrayal to the performative, the film projects its cinematic interpretation to the performative. The interpretation sees any art as a different form of representation, even death. There exists hardly any authenticity in art or life. Self-reflexively demonstrating how filmic construction could manipulate the death image, the film exposes the inability to secure a relation between subjectivity and the body.

The search for identity as an artist-self excludes woman, because woman is viewed as an obstacle to male artistic experimentation. Spatial divisions in the film illustrate the point. The spatial mise-en-scène alternates between the artist's private space and public settings such as the street. Qi Lei confines himself in his artistic world to prepare the ice burial and ignores his girlfriend, Shaoyun, when she comes to his door. Moreover, he moves his schedule for the ice burial one day earlier to avoid Shaoyun's possible interruption. The male artist occupies both private and public space where performing art is transformed from personal experiment to public exhibition. In contrast, taking no space in either private or public settings, the female image embodies an ambiguous identity. She is the artist's girlfriend, as the screen image indicates, but remains excluded from his art world. She is a photographer, but we are never told about her pictures. Who is a woman when she has neither space nor identity of her own? The question disturbs any audience concerned about gender issues.

Exclusion from man's art world leaves woman the role of perceiver and signifier of the death experiment. The female protagonist is kept unaware, even as the audience realizes that the entire performative event is staged. While the artist returns to life after his ice burial and shares his "death" experience with the organizer, the woman mourns the "real loss" of her boyfriend. Her emotional grief and psychological response therefore become part of the experimental data collection. The artist considers how the public has responded to his art exhibition and to his "death." Concepts that the artist evaluates involve the meanings of life/death and art/representation. He obtains truth and power from using the woman as a partial experimental instrument. What the audience perceives, therefore, is a narcissistic sense of self through body dichotomy: the male body generates artwork while the female body bears its trial and signifies its power.

Although excluded from the art world, woman retains her sexual identity. Qi Lei, returning home from his "death," observes something unexpected. In one sequence, for instance, his girlfriend and his mentor engage in a conversation about his "death." As the camera projects layered superimposition of the female image onto the window, we see the death project organizer approaching to embrace her. Shaoyun responds by slapping his face. The sexual scene through the male artist's gaze frames the woman as his virtuous mourner and the mentor as an immoral betrayer. Qi Lei committed a real suicidal death after he saw the truth of life. Three months later, we are told, Qi Lei's body was found by a tree with his blood soaked deep into the earth. The question of whether an art form, especially performance art, can illuminate the meaning of truth and life echoes as the artist's body finally disappears from the screen and from reality.

Sexuality beyond Allegories

Sexuality is no longer a nervous or concealed subject in independent films. Along with urban settings, rock music, and fragmented narratives, sexual relations or issues are important markers of urban cinema. Taking sexuality as a subject or a narrative motif, the films share the desire to reveal an arena formerly allegorized and return it to an open form. Sexuality as allegory enabled the fifth-generation film directors to highlight woman as visual images and discursive elements to convey the meanings of nation and history. In Zhang Yimou's films, for example, the close-up view of the female figure magnifies, on the one hand, her discursive role in the narration of sociohistorical traumas, and, on the other hand, offers her exotic image for the fantasies of the international audience. Behind her entrancing visibility, however, lies a gendered desire to inscribe a repressed male subjectivity on the image of the sexualized female body. Sexuality in its open form enables the independent film directors to deal directly with the subject. The camera goes into the households of ordinary people to expose their sexual relations or problems. It also reveals the spaces behind the curtain by making the once-hidden gay image visible. The unrestrained representation of heterosexuality and the counterexposure of homosexuality bring the rhetoric onto center stage and under reinscription.

In *Wushan Yunyu* (Rainclouds over Wushan, 1995), the reevaluation of sexual rhetoric presents the audience with the sexual relationship of ordinary people. A signal operator spends day and night in a lonely lighthouse, guiding ships up and down the Yangtze River. Daily boredom represses as well as arouses his sexual anxiety. A friend who comes to visit offers to share his girlfriend. As the camera frames the man and woman in a locked room, a sexual encounter could occur at any moment. Yet the silence and stillness, while intensifying the tension, seize the man in his moral foundations. In a parallel scene, a widowed hotel clerk has just broken off her relationship with the manager. The "sexual affair," unmentionable in public, bothers her constantly. The narrative transition that breaks the silence is the impending legal investigation that arises from the rejected manager's accusation that the woman has had a sexual affair with the signal worker. The investigator, a young cop, is busy with his wedding preparations. What the audience does not anticipate is the subversion of the conventional definition of a "sexual affair." The signal worker does not deny his sexual encounter with the woman, and the police do not use institutional power to charge him as a rapist. The film allows ordinary people to expose their sexual yearnings in a daily reality and frank form.

Another film, *Zhoumo Quingren* (Weekend Lover, 1994), depicts the sexual triangle of a teenage girl and her two lovers, an old story told from yet different angles. The opening subtitles announce a subjective identification between "we," the filmmakers, and "they," a group of adolescents. The "we" is committed to bringing the true story of "them" to the screen because adolescence is the time and the identity that directors are searching to represent. One of the adolescents, the girl Li Xin, is selected to be the film's protagonist and narrator. Through her voice-over narration, she presents to the audience fragments of her tangled relationship with two boys. The female voice, however, is unable to describe the past from a woman's perspective or from her psychological insight because the two boys' tales, one about rock music and the other about tough personality, interrupt her voice and break the narration into fragments. The true story we are told is a conventional one: two male rivals fight to the death to possess the woman while she oscillates between the two via sexual transactions. A new message is delivered at the end of the film, when the female narrator faces the camera to address the audience directly: we were the naive, arrogant, and impulsive adolescent in the past, but have attained maturity now. Announcing closure to narrative and negation to history indicates an eagerness to end the position in the margins.

Whereas the examples discussed above approach the concept of sexuality in its heterosexual form, Zhang Yuan's recent film, *East Palace, West Palace*, brings the subject of homosexuality out of the closet. The significance of the film lies not so much in the gay image brought to the screen, but in the construction of a gay discourse that the mainstream considers subversive. The narrative focuses on a gay man and a park policeman who arrests and interrogates the supposed criminal. The expected exercise of authority over helpless individuals, however, undergoes a subversive rewriting. The interrogation begins with a display of power but ends with a homosexual encounter between the representative of authority and the prisoner. The possible construction of gay discourse is the result of both the centralization of a gay voice and the cinematic process from a gay perspective. As the voice reveals a personal gay history, images—as flashbacks and in fragments—define the words with illustrations. A gay identity and homosexual life history, because of the film's counterangle, emerge into the culture and into visual representation. In addition to the controversy caused by an openly gay subject in China, the core question that piques one's curiosity is how a cinematic construction subverts hegemonic discourse and brings the gay subculture into cinematic representation and public discussion.

The film selects a public space, a section of the city park where gay men cruise and elude the police, as the locale. The film's title refers to the public toilets on either side of the Forbidden Palace.[13] The spatial connection indicates a discursive engagement between the homosexual and the authoritarian in China. As the establishing shot leads the audience from the park exterior to a men's room, the camera exposes a social scene where police question the gay suspect. In the dark park, gay men cruise around to look for partners and to engage in sexual activities. Park police are also searching for their targeted sexual criminals. Flashlight and nightstick in hand, the police arrest, beat, and humiliate those men whom they see as sexually abnormal and disgusting. Among the criminals, one named A Lan turns himself in to the policeman Shi. In an isolated police station and in the darkened park, an interrogation unfolds. What the audience expects, an authority's interrogation and a prisoner's confession, shifts unexpectedly into an enunciating process through which a gay voice utters homosexual history.

The film operates through an enunciative system that allows a gay voice to address homosexual identity and experience. From the perspective of structuralism, enunciation refers to "the ways in which the speaker or narrator inscribes him or herself in the message, mainly through pronouns such as 'I' or 'me' . . . thus offering a certain mode of address to the spectator."[14] Taking one sequence, for example, the positioning of the police officer as the interrogator and the gay man as the interrogated suggests that an imminent humiliation in the name of state power is about to occur. The gay voice, however, shifts the power order by situating himself as the "I" speaker. The policeman, ambiguous about his own sexual identity, is unable to raise specific questions. His power to force but inability to comprehend the gay confession allows the gay voice to fill the discourse vacuum. "I'm a gay," A Lan addresses himself directly and subjectively to the officer and to the spectator. Forced to continue, A Lan reveals, from a gay person's perspective, how official treatment attempts to "cure" homosexual people with electroconvulsive therapy, heterosexual education, and administrative suppression. "We are forced to participate in the treatment," A Lan utters in his anger of resistance. The "I" speaking position and gay perspective, therefore, opens a subversive force within the authoritarian power.

In addition, the film reveals fragments of hidden gay history in terms of the conjunction between sound and image. "I'm married," A Lan exposes himself further to the cop. "Is that so?" Surprised, the policeman wants to learn whether his wife knows all about his "craziness." A Lan doesn't respond to the question that presumes the value of heterosexuality. Instead, the gay voice subverts the convention by changing the topic to his first gay sexual experience. The film inserts a flashback, uncovering A Lan's engagement with his classmate as lover. The narrating voice continues, but as a voice-over. While the voice dominates the soundtrack and visual images support the utterances, the revelation of a homosexual history "comes out" into discourse: a fatherless childhood, sexual assault in his youth, and homosexual encounters with a number of lovers. As the film narrative alternates between gay memory in flashback and gay narration in voice-over, the audio and visual tracks turn the interrogation into a process of self-representation, the interrogator into the perceiver, and the unspeakable experience into discourse.

As the film cuts between scenes of confession and flashbacks of memory, the

A Lan's flashback: his partner remains unseen. *East Palace, West Palace* (dir. Zhang Yuan, 1996, China/France).

cinematic transgression has the gay subject change to assert the police as his desire. The (dis)placement of the policeman's dual roles is achieved through mise-en-scène.

A two-shot, for instance, frames the characters in the same frame but with the cop in a dominant position, while A Lan reveals his sexual encounter with a sadistic partner. Off screen, the sexual partner remains ambiguous, thereby calling for clarification. To represent the absent, the film (dis)positions the police as a substitute, often turning him into a mirror image. The projected mirror image, with its double identifications, enables the gay man to identify with the cop as both interrogator and lover.

In a different sequence, to give another example, the voice-over and flashback describe a homosexual engagement. A Lan, in close up and with his partner invisible, enjoys the pleasure of being slapped and whipped. As the film brings the gay's memory back to his confession, a jump cut shows the policeman slapping A Lan's cheek in the same manner. The displacement suggests a transformation of identity: the policeman is A Lan's desiring lover. The truth comes at the end when A Lan confesses to Shi, "I have been longing for a powerful policeman since my childhood. Don't you know that I love you as a jail guard loves his female prisoner?" As the gay voice addresses the police and gay memory the audience, we find both spectator and listener caught up in the sequences of homosexual desire. In this respect, *East Palace, West Palace* cinematically releases both fantasy and the concept of homosexuality from concealment behind the curtain.[15]

Restaging the scene with police officer Shi. *East Palace, West Palace.*

East Palace, West Palace frees the gay man from the closet but not, however, from the stereotype of a submissive figure. The film alternates between the revelation of a gay man's homosexual history and enunciation of his homosexual desire for the police. In either situation, the film uses the gay character in the construction of a masochistic identity and role. His personal homosexual history, for instance, revealed through flashbacks, presents sadomasochistic encounters. Each revelation emphasizes his submissive role, willingly taking the invisible partner as dominant and violence as a source of sexual pleasure. His homosexual seduction, foregrounded through interrogation-confession, reinforces the sadomasochistic relation. The film legitimizes the relation by having the gay give himself to the policeman and seduce him with perversion. In addition, the choice of clothing, the cop in his leather jacket and the gay man in soft clothing, further enacts the characters' sadomasochistic roles.

In his study of gay male sexuality, Tim Edwards points out that "sadomasochistic acting potentially perpetuated the oppression of male homosexuality through active-passive dualism."[16] Positioning the gay character as passive not only prevents the film from acknowledging a true gay identity, but also transforms the repressed homosexuality from the oppression of state authority into that of same-sex politics. The interaction between the sadistic master and the masochistic slave confuses the question of whether homosexual acting could bring gay liberation. The sadomasochistic engagement thus premises a fantasy in representation through which the filmmaker and the audience rehearse the possible roles they can play. As the film furthers Zhang Yuan's international recognition, gay identities and homosexual issues in China remain at a rudimentary level in cinematic representation.

Coming-of-Age Narrative

Frequent viewing of the "fifth-generation" films reinforces our perception of their oedipal structure, where rejection of cultural-political father figures drives both narrative construction and psychological reasoning. The presence of fatherly discourse (history and revolution), either on or off screen, serves simultaneously as the subject dominating the narrative and the target subverted by the representation. The desire to rewrite father's history and the inability to free oneself from it trap the film director and the representation in a psychological dilemma. By contrast, films made by the younger directors are concerned with the memory of an adolescent past and the construction of the coming-of-age narrative. What we have observed from the adolescent world is transient youth and the absence of father(s). The lack of a fatherly discourse allows youth and their experience to occupy the center of the representation. The centralization of the coming-of-age narrative also reveals a psychological trajectory, where the loss, search for, and return to the father(s) demonstrate discursive transitions in post-Maoist China.

Zhang Yuan's *Mama* (Mama, 1990), for instance, is a film about a tender relationship between a single mother and her mentally handicapped son. The juxtaposition of the family shot in black and white with interviews videotaped in color divides, as well as links, the worlds of fiction and documentary. The message concerning social ignorance toward the handicapped is unquestionably clear. Yet the absence of the father figure places the narrative in a psychological sphere where the mother-son relationship is framed in a problematic preoedipal complex. Because of his speech disability, Dongdong is constantly denied admission to regular schools. His refusal to speak and rejection by society indicate abandonment by or resistance to the symbolic world. Attachment to his mother, however, secures him a position in the narrative and in the representation. When a series of dissolves shows the mother wrapping the child's entire body with white bandages, the audience watches the return of the boy to his infancy. For a boy to remain attached to the mother and in a preoedipal domain is problematic and forbidden, however, because the son cannot forever possess his loving and caring mother. In refusing to respond to his mother's call and in gazing at his mother's personal, sexual moments, Dongdong announces also his rejection of the mother figure. His dual refusal, to the father and then to the mother, turns the son himself into the *subject* of his own discourse. The transgression, as

Berenice Reynaud explains, becomes a metaphor for young Chinese filmmakers who are "now ready to [make] themselves the *subjects* of their own audiovisual discourse."[17]

In a filmmaking environment where considerations of nationalist ideology and international perception are equally essential, a question lingers: whether independent filmmaking can secure the subjective position of an autonomous discourse. Such an outcome seems improbable. Zhang Yang's *Xizao* (Shower, 2000), for example, a recent film that attracted positive reviews at home and abroad, suggests a return to the "father(s)" and thus to the mainstream. The film is excessively composed with cultural codes and metaphors. Each character, mise-en-scène, and sound serves to elaborate cultural meanings. The father, a public bathhouse manager, embodies all the traditional virtues and values. The actions of his two sons illustrate the consequences of either obeying or betraying the paternal traditions. Daming, the elder son leaves the father for Shenzhen, China's booming economic zone in the south, to pursue material success. Erming, the younger, mentally challenged, son lives with the father and remains within the traditions. Confrontation and conflict between tradition and modernity as well as between father and son unfold through the holy symbol of water.

The concept of modernity is introduced at the beginning of the film, when one of the characters takes an automated shower, a kind of activity we frequently associate with car washes. A quick cut to an old-fashioned public bathhouse, however, compares the modern lifestyle with traditional ways. The bathhouse, as a community center and emotional link, provides its assorted customers with healing social comfort. Through bathing, aging men establish their friendship, a separated couple rebuilds their relationship, and a young man sings. Within the traditional environment and under the father's protection, Erming enjoys a peaceful life. Daming comes back to visit his father and brother. Not a filial son, Daming is situated as the outsider and an observer of the father's world. Witnessing his father's care toward the customers and love for his brother gradually cleanses Daming's confused soul. As the father peacefully passes away, Daming finally recognizes the beauty of tradition and humanity.

The "holy" water, baptizing the soul and purifying human relations, entails even more profound cultural meanings. Two inserted sequences take the audience first to the ancient yellow land and then to a Tibetan holy lake. As the film, in the father's voice-over and cinematic flashback, depicts a prewedding bathing sequence, the mise-en-scène of the yellow plateau shares a cultural code with Chen Kaige's *Yellow Earth*. The allusion reveals a conscious identification with prior film directors and mainstream trends. Such efforts indicate a desire to be acknowledged and accepted by the dominant discourses. The passport to enter the mainstream production system, as *Shower* demonstrates, is the return to the "father." The possibility of returning requires careful consideration of the film's subject issues, institutional censorship, potential audience, and profit margin. The moment the independent film negotiates its way to the mainstream, however, the meaning of independence becomes devalued. As the lines between the independent and the mainstream blur, a final look at Jiang Wen's film debut, *Yangguang Canlan De Rizi* (In the Heat of the Sun, 1995), at least leaves us a brief but bright memory of the adolescent's history.

In the Heat of the Sun subverts China's mainstream film production and fifth-generation allegories with its adolescent subjects and subjective representation. The film restages a revolutionary past that is associated with the protagonist's youth and situated in the capital city of Beijing. Unlike films about the Cultural Revolution, young and privileged youth replace the authoritarian adult figures and occupy center stage in the urban space. The adolescent ferment and idealistic heroism, subordinating history and politics, constitute a coming-of-age narrative. More important, the auteuristic director consciously pursues a subjective directorship and filmic narration through cinematic experiments. The auteurism evident in Jiang Wen's innovation aims for an absolute autonomy of film art that emphasizes film's subject issues and cinematic designation.

Jiang Wen, as author of the screen script, assumes a writerly position, since the process of rewriting Wang Shuo's story into film requires a visual transformation of the written work. The director's persistence in exploring the subject of adolescence and his personal obsession with visual narration drive him to control almost all aspects of production. Every single shot, for instance, is primarily and subjectively framed in the director's imagination. If the screen image turned out not to reflect the director's expectation, Jiang Wen would spend hundreds or thousands of inches of film to reach the desired result. To get the best photo image of the female lead, Milan, for instance, Jiang Wen made the cinematographer shoot 23,040 copies. In addition, the director is unusually stubborn about the selection of actors, music, costumes, and even the color of objects. This subjective position enables him to manipulate the cinematic system to serve his auteuristic imagination: a nostalgic dream of transforming the adolescent past into visual representation.[18]

The audience recognizes subjective authorship in terms of first-person narration. In the title sequence of the film, an off-screen voice-over by the film's teenage protagonist introduces the time and space of the narrative and its potential relation to narration: "Beijing has been transformed into a modern city. The dramatic change has wiped out my memories. I can't tell what's imagined from what's real. My story takes place in a summer. The heat forces people more toward physical restlessness and psychological desire. At that time, the endless summer for us meant splendid sunshine."[19]

What follows—the sounds of revolutionary songs, the icon of Mao's statue, the spectacle of massive crowds—draws our memories back to the era of the Cultural Revolution. The scenes made familiar from numerous works, however —the political humiliations, human disasters, psychological torments, and physical abuses—form a different world in Jiang Wen's film. The difference is announced by the voice-over narrator's declaration that the world full of sunshine belongs to the adolescents after the father(s) have been sent away for revolutionary assignments and the elder siblings sent down for peasants' reeducation. The absence of the father(s) grants the adolescent complete freedom from social institutions and adult authority. A young and privileged group becomes the central protagonist of history and its representation.

The first-person narration, after establishing adolescents as the central characters in history, begins to subvert the writings of the Cultural Revolution, whether official versions or the sent-down youth literature. Where conventional literature recounts traumatic times and the loss of youth, *In the Heat of the Sun* celebrates the good old days of heroic adolescence. The subversion of history arises from the construction of narrative authority. Authority is achieved by an adolescent voice explaining the narrative and by an adult perspective manipulating the narration. The adolescent protagonist and the film director are the same figure, situated in temporal dislocations. The adolescent experience of yesterday and the directorial representation of today create a nostalgic association where the forgotten past and lost memory come to terms with each other.

First, signs of the father's history inspire the adolescent desire to experience the world from one's own perspective. The family, because of the absence of parents, becomes the teenage boy Ma Xiaojun's kingdom. With his ability to pick locks, Xiao Jun opens his father's drawer and discovers badges and a condom. Decorating himself with the badges and blowing the condom into a balloon, Xiao Jun experiences the power of being an adult and the sense of sexuality. Providing the character with such curiosity, the film then engages in gender construction through the adolescent gaze and female image. Bored with school, the restless adolescent seeks adventure by copying keys and entering residential apartments. In one sequence, for instance, Ma Xiaojun finds a telescope in an apartment. The telescope, serving as the camera eye, generates a subjective vision as the boy uses it to examine the world around him. Looking through the window, the telescope frames his male teacher urinating in the corner of the schoolyard. Spinning inside the room, the telescope seizes a girl's photo concealed behind a transparent curtain. Further shot/reverse shots reinforce the connection between the boy's gaze and the photo. The female image in extreme close-up dominates the film screen and excites the boy psychologically and sexually. An internal monologue through off-screen voice-over describes the astonishment of the

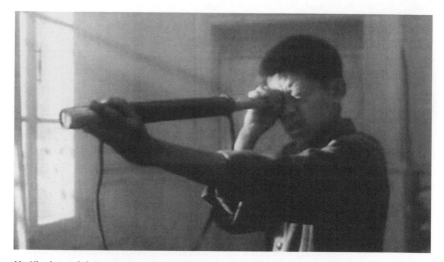

Ma Xiaojun, adolescent gaze. *In the Heat of the Sun* (dir. Jiang Wen, 1995, China).

Milan in extreme close-up: the female image seized by the gaze. *In the Heat of the Sun.*

moment: "The photo that I found made me dizzy. Her image overwhelms my vision and her expression fires my imagination."

The displayed image of an unknown woman, filling the screen and commanding the viewers' gaze, is a forceful, sexual spectacle. Yet, as a voyeur projecting his subjective vision onto the image, the adolescent protagonist has control of the narrative and perspective. The question that the overly cited concept of gaze poses in this film asks what happens when a male adolescent plays the role of voyeur fixated on a female image? The engagement with the female image inspires an adolescent's desire to seek and possess a lover. This intimate romantic or sexual imagination is crucial to defining and confirming the male adolescent's identity, maturity, and masculinity. As DeMarr and Bakerman explain in their study of adolescence in the American novel since 1960, "The possession of a lover who is very attractive, who is won in open competition with another male, or who is generally thought by one's peers to be very desirable obviously enhances a lad's immediate social status, exciting envy among his male associates and enriching his feeling of traditional manliness."[20]

The position of the voyeur and the gendered nature of vision enable the young boy to possess the female body visually. Through the boy's point of view, for instance, the camera leads the viewer toward the young woman undressing, sleeping, and washing herself. The point of view is so subjective that the spectator has no choice but to identify with the adolescent voyeur and join his "pleasure in looking." The reinforcement of a subjective male adolescent gaze, however, leaves no room for a female gaze. It is impossible for female spectators to identify with the voyeur or to "enjoy" the pleasure in looking, because in watching a young woman being watched the female viewer sees a reflection of her own vulnerability. The male adolescent gaze in this gendered construction, therefore, continues a masculinist discourse. The process of looking feeds the male adolescent's self-image and stirs his sexual anxiety. The process of constructing the gaze, however, enables the film director and spectators to look back to their teenage years. Nostalgic memory and filmic representation blur the line between reality and illusion. The process of filming allows director and audience to reexperience adolescence through memory and re-presentation.

The coming-of-age trajectory undergoes different transitions. *In the Heat of the Sun* visually shows the adolescent progression through spatial transitions. The film poses a gender-space issue whereby public places present the rebellious youth with a stage for their displays of masculine heroism, while private places provide the adolescent with an imaginary space to examine the self and act out sexual fantasies. Girls, however, are often caught between male rivals and different spaces. In a number of sequences, for example, escaping from and mocking social institutions such as the school, the family, and the police authorities grant Xiaojun a great sense of freedom. He spends his free time and excess energy invading private spaces, where he discovers the girl he likes. The intimate time and private space he shares with Milan records and reflects the male adolescent's first love experience. Her body, image, and expression inspire the boy's imagination. Through the female other, he experiences subtle, psychological transitions in identity, desire, and the meaning of manhood. In public places, however, Xiaojun introduces Milan to his buddies to announce his ownership of a girlfriend and thereby claim the social status of masculine authority.

As the adolescent protagonist makes his unsteady journey toward manhood, the young woman is seen shifting her body and emotion between the male teenagers. While female sexuality provokes male rivalry, her screen image bears the responsibility of terminating the adolescent's dreams and desires and thus, too, the coming-of-age story and the film narration. She is, in other words, a metaphorical betrayer of the adolescent hero and an interrupter of cinematic narration. In the setting of a swimming pool, for instance, Milan now belongs to another young man and Xiaojun is isolated from the group. The loss of his girlfriend suggests the loss of his adolescent subjectivity. To dramatize the moment of rejection, an extreme low-angle shot is used to over-enlarge Xiaojun's figure on the diving board. As Xiaojun struggles to get out of the pool, one or another of the buddies kicks him into the water again. A series of subjective point-of-view shots taken underwater records how Xiaojun is fatally and symbolically denied by his adolescent peers.

Youth narrative, city setting, and subjective perspective characterize urban cinema and its auteur directors. Nostalgic reconstruction of forgotten memories and the lost experiences of adolescence is a process of finding cinematic ways of capturing that moment of being young. The cinematic journey into lost adolescence makes the film director finally understand that the desire to speak the truth and bring back the memory can never be fully realized. The protagonist's voice-over once again exposes his confusion between reality and illusion, between memory and the moment: "I might have never met Milan, or perhaps nothing happened between her and me. Memory can be altered by emotions." But sounds and images can always seduce the urban stroller into indulging in fantasies of a heroic adolescent past when male heroes took center stage.

Conclusion

In this preliminary study, I have attempted to frame the special features of the urban cinema of independent film directors from three directions. The screening of the artist into the film demonstrates the desire to assert subjective authorship. Such authorship strives for independence from official mainstream production and fifth-generation precedents. In the course of pursuing this ambition, the artist becomes both the author of the representation and the character represented. Empowerment over narrative construction and the filming process enables the experimental director to unfold urban space and experience from a personal, subjective perspective.

As a result, sexual rhetoric undergoes reevaluation. By freeing the notion of sexuality from allegory and treating it openly, the urban films bring sexual relationships or issues directly into perception. The spectator is encouraged to identify not only with heterosexual problems, but also with homosexual identity, a topic previously suppressed. In the process of introducing gay subculture to the screen, the subjective perspective negotiates a discursive confrontation between the authoritarian and the homosexual. The gay character's triumphant seduction of the policeman in Zhang Yuan's *East Palace, West Palace* subverts and sexualizes for the first time the sexless discourse of authority and the allegorical masquerade of the fifth generation.

This subjective perspective and an auteuristic approach also produces the construction of a coming-of-age narrative in which the younger generation records its own understanding of history: with the father(s) absent from view, the street and the city become a stage where adolescents inscribe their own sense of history and experiment with the excitement of youthful impulses. Thus, they rewrite the historiography composed by authority and subverted by the fifth generation's reconstruction.

The extent of independence that film directors might achieve, however, remains highly questionable. In a nation-state undergoing global transition and in a film production system hampered by multifaceted restrictions, independent filmmaking appears to be temporary and fragile. Its moment of emergence and courage to experiment, however, add a page of urban cinema and independent film directors to China's film history. As film critics at home and abroad still wrestle with the problem of how to classify the mavericks and their films, the young filmmakers are moving from the margins toward the center, working both in and outside the system. [21]

Notes

1. References to the younger generation of film directors in China are scattered in film and academic journals. For an insightful overview of the subject, see Jinhua Dai, "*Wuzhong fengjing*" (Preliminary reading of the sixth-generation film directors), *Tianya* 1 (1996): 1–13; see also "*Xinsheng dai dianying yanjiu*" (Film research on the new generation), *Journal of the Beijing Film Academy* 1 (1995): 100–203; Hong Yin, "Memorandum of Chinese Cinema in 1999," *Dangdai Dianying* (Contemporary cinema) 1 (2000): 10–15.

2. The use of terms such as "outlaw," "underground," or "countercinema" indicates more of an ideological perspective than a systematic study of the new film genres. The global market for cinema and the local conditions against which the new films emerge require a multifaceted perspective. See, for example, David Chute, "Beyond the Law: Independent Films from China," *Film Comment* 30 (January–February 1994): 60–63.

3. After reading my draft, Professor Yueh-yu Yeh suggested "transgressive qualities" to describe independent directors and urban cinema. I would like to thank Yueh-yu and Sheldon H. Lu for their editorial comments.

4. In *In the Red: On Contemporary Chinese Culture* (New York: Columbia University Press, 1999), 189–197, Geremie R. Barmé takes the independent film director Zhang Yuan

as a model to illustrate formulas for success. The status of being nonofficial/mainstream privileges a double-trading system in which directors "sell" their cultural products to attract international investment while international dealers "purchase" such works to make ideological profit.

5. Early works by the independent filmmakers are difficult to locate. In the process of writing this chapter, I often tried in vain to find certain titles by phone, fax, or on the Internet. Collected by critics or archives, out of the reach of a general audience, the independent films can seem mysterious in their inaccessibility.

6. Katia Gaskell, "To Get Reality, Forget Reality: China's Bad-Boy Filmmaker Zhang Yuan," *Beijing Scene* 7.5 (February 18–24, 2000) [available from HtmlRes Anchor http://beijingscene .com].

7. Both Barmé and Paul G. Pickowicz have cited Miklos Haraszti's notion of a "velvet prison" in reference to artists in contemporary China. To comment on their (dis)agreement over whether film artists cooperate with the state system, I would add that the velvet prison, under postsocialist conditions, involves not only political negotiations but also market pressures. Paul G. Pickowicz, "Velvet Prisons and the Political Economy of Chinese Filmmaking," in Deborah S. Davis, Richard Kraus, Barry Naughton, and Elizabeth J. Perry, eds., *Urban Spaces in Contemporary China* (Cambridge: Cambridge University Press/Washington, D.C.: Woodrow Wilson Center Press, 1995), 206.

8. For further information, see Wu Guanping, "An Unusual Declaration in an Unusual Summer: Interview with Lu Xuechang," *Dianying Yishu* (Film art) 4 (2000): 61–65.

9. Readers interested in video art, documentaries, or avant-garde films will find interesting arguments in Berenice Reynaud, "New Visions/New Chinas: Video-Art, Documentation, and the Chinese Modernity in Question," in Michael Renov and Erika Suderburg, eds., *Resolutions: Contemporary Video Practices* (Minneapolis: University of Minnesota Press, 1996), 229–257.

10. For publications on performance art and artists in China, see Minglu Gao, ed., *Inside Out: New Chinese Art* (Berkeley: University of California Press, 1999); Zhijian Qian, "Performing Bodies: Zhang Huan, Ma Liuming, and Performance Art in China," *Art Journal* 58.2 (summer 1999): 60–81.

11. The citation draws from the summary by Amelia Jones and Andrew Stephenson in the introduction to their *Performing the Body/Performing the Text* (London: Routledge, 1999), 6.

12. Peggy Phelan, *Unmarked: The Politics of Performance* (London: Routledge, 1993), 147.

13. For further information on this film, see Chris Berry, "Staging Gay Life in China: Zhang Yuan and *East Palace, West Palace*," *Jump Cut* 41 (1998): 84–89; Tony Rayns, "Provoking Desire," *Sight and Sound* (July 1996): 26–29.

14. Robert Stam, Robert Burgoyne, and Sandy Fliterman-Lewis, *New Vocabularies in Film Semiotics* (London: Routledge, 1992), 105.

15. Like the metaphor "out of the closet," common in Western gay cinema critiques, "behind the curtain" is a metaphor for the hidden space where the gay subculture strives to free itself from official suppression.

16. Tim Edwards, *Erotics & Politics: Gay Male Sexuality, Masculinity and Feminism* (London: Routledge, 1994), 77.

17. Reynaud, "New Visions/New Chinas," 236.

18. Information on Jiang Wen's practice of filming is drawn from his book, *Yibu dian-ying de dansheng* (The birth of a film) (Beijing: Huayi chubanshe, 1997).

19. Ibid., 293.

20. Mary Jean DeMarr and Jane S. Bakerman, *The Adolescent in the American Novel since 1960* (New York: Ungar, 1986), 133.

21. Few directors can afford to work entirely "out of the system" now. The desire to win domestic audiences and establish an identity motivates the filmmakers to alternate be-tween in- and outside the system, or move from the margins to the center.

CHAPTER FIVE

Chinese Film Culture at the End of the Twentieth Century

The Case of *Not One Less* by Zhang Yimou

Under the current political system, Zhang Yimou feels that the biggest difference between himself and directors from foreign countries, Hong Kong, and Taiwan lies in that "when I receive a film script, the first thing I think about is not whether there will be an investor for the film, but how I can make the kind of film that I want with the approval of the authorities."[1]

By the end of the twentieth century, it had become increasingly apparent that the 1990s marked a new phase of cultural development distinct from the preceding decade. In the words of one Chinese critic, it was the "era of the hegemony of popular culture" *(dazhong wenhua baquan shidai).*[2] Both elite culture and official ideology were in retreat. The discourses of humanism, enlightenment, and the reconstruction of subjectivity that were fervently advocated by the intelligentsia from the late 1970s through the 1980s had become largely forgotten projects. The government's direct intervention in and subsidy for cultural production also were relatively weakened in the so-called socialist market economy. The general populace had lost interest in high, pure literature (realism, modernism, postmodernism, the avant-garde, etc.), experimental theater (theater of the absurd), avant-garde music, classical music, the ballet, and European philosophy (Freud, Sartre, Heidegger, etc.). "Cultural fast food" *(wenhua kuaican)* became the order of the day: karaoke, television dramas, soap operas, bestsellers, and tabloid journalism. The 1990s were a time of consumerism, commercialization, depoliticization, and deideologization. It was an age without heroes and gods.

In the 1990s, China's domestically made film, as a popular form of art, suffered a tremendous decline in terms of audience numbers and box office sales. Many factors contributed to this reversal: the growing popularity of television programs, widespread piracy of films on videotape and VCD, the importation of foreign films (from Hollywood, Hong Kong, and other places), the lack of government subsidy, and the decline of the quality of film itself. Film workers had to operate under multiple constraints in a socialist market economy: the law of market economy dictates that a film must sell and entertain as a cultural commodity. By contrast, the law of art demands that a film must possess some aesthetic merit and must appeal to the general audience. Moreover, in light of the relative relaxation of state control in film production and consumption in comparison to earlier periods in the history of the People's Republic of China, there remained strict censorship for filmmakers to wrestle with.

Film as an effective form of mass media has had to carry out an ideological mission in postsocialist China. A category of film that the government heavily invests in both ideologically and financially is the so-called mainstream film (*zhuxuan lü*). A major purpose of *zhuxuan lü* was to create role models and rebuild an ethical foundation at a time when people had lost faith in grand ideologies. Put in simple terms, mainstream film has come to be the state's self-legitimation in the cultural realm. Films in the category include biopics of communist leaders such as Mao Zedong, Zhou Enlai, and Liu Shaoqi and model cadres such as Jiao Yulu and Kong Fansen. The new strategy in creating exemplary individuals in filmic discourse is to endear the audience, namely, to bring the audience emotionally closer to the world of the heroes. In contrast to the deification of Mao Zedong and socialist model workers in the past, the approach is de-deification and rehumanization. Filmmakers represent Chinese leaders not as superhumans but as ordinary human beings. In contemporary Chinese film, for instance, Mao and Zhou are portrayed as individuals with common emotions and mundane concerns that all people have (Mao's love for his children, Zhou's love for his colleagues and comrades, etc.). *Zhou Enlai* (dir. Ding Yinnan, 1991) and *Jiao Yulu* (dir. Wang Jixing, 1991) were rather popular films when released to the audience; however, filmmakers working outside the perimeters of mainstream films have to raise their own funds and must be financially accountable to themselves.

Yige dou bu neng shao (Not One Less), directed by Zhang Yimou, was released in mainland China in early 1999. Immediately after its release, the film, the director, and the amateur child actors, became the focus of the Chinese media. The film was packaged and publicized as a popular film, and Zhang Yimou once

Substitute schoolteacher Wei Minzhi, in *Not One Less* (dir. Zhang Yimou).

again became a larger-than-life celebrity figure throughout the country. The film provides a good opportunity to study China's film market and film audience and the values, feelings, and ideas of the populace and to understand the sociological condition of Chinese cinema as a popular art form at the end of the twentieth century.

Not One Less, by Zhang Yimou

Not One Less is a story about children in an elementary school in a poor northern Chinese village—Shuiquan Primary School, Shuiquan Village. The children study in a primitive classroom. There is only one teacher to take care of some thirty students. Teacher Gao's mother is seriously ill, and he has to leave school for some time. To temporarily replace Gao, the village chief is able to find only a teenage girl to act as the teacher until Gao returns. This new teacher, Wei Minzhi, is a thirteen-year-old girl who has just finished elementary school herself. Before leaving, Gao tells Wei that the number of students at the school has been dwindling because of the high dropout rate. He asks her to make sure that the twenty-eight remaining students stay in school, "not one less," until he comes back. He promises that he and the village chief will pay her fifty yuan for doing the job. Thus, Wei becomes the teacher of students who are not much younger than she is.

As events develop, one young boy, Zhang Huike, an especially bright yet naughty student, has to quit school. Because his mother is in debt and can no longer afford to send him to school, Zhang leaves for the city to look for work. When she hears that one of her students has left, Wei is determined to bring him back. After she arrives in the city and learns that Zhang is lost, the film details her tireless efforts to find him. Finally, the city's television station intervenes to help Wei find Zhang and bring him to the village. At the end of the film, the following words appear on the screen: "One million children drop out of school because of poverty in China every year. With the financial assistance from various sources, about fifteen percent of them are able to return to school."

Of all the films Zhang Yimou has made, *Not One Less* most resembles *The Story of Qiu Ju* (1993). Both films are set in a contemporary northern Chinese village, and the heroine in each film is a peasant woman. Wei Minzhi's personality and Qiu Ju's are similar—both are stubborn and single-minded in their pursuits, but they are also comic yet lovable characters. Wei's trek to the city to find her dropout student at all cost parallels Qiu Ju's repeated trips to higher authorities to seek justice for her injured husband. And, in the end, they both win because of their persistence. If *The Story of Qiu Ju* retains a flavor of documentary realism in capturing the sight, sound, scene, and mood of contemporary peasant life, *Not One Less* goes even further. All the characters in the film are played by amateurs, and the real names of the actors and actresses are used for the characters' names. The film is shot at a primary school with the real name of Shuiquan Xiaoxue and at a village with the name of Shuiquan Cun, in Hebei Province. Although a fictional narrative, the film aims to achieve a high degree of realism.

At the textual level, the story of the film elicits sympathy and feelings of love for these indomitable, strong-spirited kids who persevere under adverse circumstances. At the same time, the failure of the country's education system becomes apparent to the audience, which asks, who is to blame? Even as it helps promote the state's project to fund poor children to go to school—"Project Hope" (*xiwang gongcheng*)—the film amounts to an indictment of the sad failure of the country's educational system. At the end of the film, a journalist asks the village chief about how long the students have been using the primitive, dilapidated classroom. His answer is direct and simple: "forty years." The episode, and the entire film, can be easily interpreted by every viewer as a harsh criticism of the state's inability to take care of its children. We see Wei Minzhi, a good girl, sleeping on the streets, and Zhang Huike, an innocent boy, begging for food in the city. On their way back to the village toward the end of the film, when the journalist asks Zhang Huike what his deepest impression of the city is, he hesitates for a moment and then replies, "I was begging for food" (*Wo zai yaofan*). When Wei Minzhi tries to talk her way into meeting the director of the television station, any Chinese film viewer would immediately recognize the type of bureaucratic system—an eerily Kafkaesque situation—sympathize with her, and admire her perseverance.

What Wei Minzhi does to find her lost student is a veritable "divine comedy," an unbelievable journey and undertaking as the viewer watches the series of events in wonder. She first asks the public address announcer at the city's train station, where Zhang Huike first disappeared, to call his name. Failing to get a response from him, she tries something else—she spends every penny she has to buy some ink and white paper to make posters about Zhang's disappearance. When a man advises her that everyone is too busy to read such posters, she approaches the city's television station for help. But the security guard and the receptionist refuse to let her enter the gate because she does not possess proper identification. On learning that the station director is a "middle-aged man with eyeglasses," she accosts—and even runs after—every person fitting that description who comes out of the station, asking him, "Are you the station head" (Ni shi taizhang ma)? These men look at her with either bemusement or annoyance, and all walk away from her. At the end of an unlucky day, the hungry girl grabs and eats a bowl of leftover food in an outdoor restaurant. As night comes, she sleeps on the street. The camera focuses on the sleeping Wei Minzhi at daybreak, while the street cleaners next to her sweep away the garbage and litter, including her posters. The duration of this camera shot is but a fleeting moment, but it creates a lasting effect and freezes in the mind of the viewer. Her activity is finally noticed by a sympathetic staff member of the station, who brings her case to the attention of the station head.

The figure of the single-minded peasant was also performed by none other than film director Zhang Yimou himself. He had previously appeared onscreen as Sun Wangquan, the lead in *Lao jing* (Old Well, 1987) directed by Wu Tianming, and he won the best actor award for that role at the Tokyo Film Festival. *Old Well* is also set in a poor village in Northern China, plagued with severe water shortage. For generations the villagers have tried in vain to discover sources of water. Numerous wells have been dug, to no avail, and much capital and human labor have been wasted in an already financially straitened community. Amid uncertainty and desperation, Sun Wangquan leads his villagers to carry on the search, and they finally find a new source of water—an old well. (Zhang's fans also know something about his career and personality—persistent and hardworking, very much like his own favorite peasant women characters. He came from Shaanxi Province and lived among its peasants for a long time. He fought through various levels of bureaucracy to be admitted to the Beijing Film Academy as an overaged student.)

What we find in common between Wei Minzhi in *Not One Less*, Qiu Ju in *The Story of Qiu Ju*, and Sun Wangquan in *Old Well* is the lovable, almost stupid determination of a humble, honest person trying to do the right thing. That such a stubborn do-gooder appeals to the audience is a sign of strong residual moral seriousness in the Chinese popular consciousness. This seems to be the film's bottom line and Zhang Yimou's moral vision of China. This side of the Chinese mentality runs opposite to the prevalent climate of commercialization, consumerism, money-worship, utilitarianism, and pseudomodernization in the 1990s.

The recurrence of the primitive, the impoverished, the backward, and the miserable in so many of Zhang's films, including *Not One Less*, reveals his trademark approach to representing China. He himself admits that such a heavy, tragic style is his preference. The depiction of suffering, misery, and tragedy is the most thought-provoking, touching, and powerful kind of art.[3] Zhang's point of departure might be characterized as the native-soil, earthbound *(tu)* approach. In the rush toward globalization and modernization, the Chinese film and television industries in the 1990s often projected another image—China as a developed, outward-looking *(yang)* country that has already joined the (post)-modern world. I refer to popular television serials such as *Beijingren zai Niuyue* (Beijingers in New York), *Eluosi guniang zai Harbin* (Russian Girls in Harbin), *Yangniu'er zai Beijing* (Foreign Babes in Beijing), and bestsellers such as *Manhadun de Zhongguo nüren* (A Chinese Woman in Manhattan).[4] These works either describe China as a modern, fashionable, glamorous land whose entrepreneurial men attract and conquer young foreign women or narrate the heroic tales of capable Chinese nationals who lead successful careers overseas and outwit the foreigners at their own games (business, finance, capitalism, etc.) Be it recourse to the native soil, romantic leapfrogging into modernity, or imaginary globalization with a trace of nationalism, these approaches address China's dilemma: backwardness, or the opposite side of the same coin—a wishful progress toward the future. And indeed, images of both the "tu" and "yang" seem to appeal to vast segments of Chinese audiences.

Audience Response to *Not One Less* and Popular Attitudes

The setting of the film is similar to that of many previous films by Zhang—the typically primitive, backward, rural China. This is the mood in many of Zhang's award-winning, "orientalist" masterpieces. His ability to reap numerous awards at international film festivals has earned him nothing less than the title of a modern Chinese myth, the "myth of Zhang Yimou" *(Zhang Yimou shenhua)*.[5] Because of his success abroad, some critics have accused him of catering to the tastes of the Western audience. According to Shi Xiangsheng, scriptwriter of the film and author of the original story, Zhang also wanted to win awards at major international festivals with this film. Zhang predicted that "there is no doubt that Europeans would welcome this film. But it is hard to say about a country like America. The Americans may not like this kind of film."[6]

Zhang Yimou initially sent *Not One Less* and *The Road Home* (*Wo de fuqin muqin*, literally "My Father and Mother") to compete at the 1999 Cannes Film Festival. He had had an amiable relationship with the Cannes festival, but in the comments made by Gilles Jacob, the director of the festival for the year, these two films were seen as vehicles of government propaganda, despite their artistic merit. Such words angered Zhang Yimou, who decided to withdraw the films from the festival. In his letter to Jacob, Zhang criticized what he regarded as a naive and lopsided understanding of Chinese films among many Western viewers. For them, Chinese films must fall under two categories: they are either government propaganda or antigovernment. By this logic, whatever films the Chinese government approves must be bad, and whatever films are banned in China must be good and worth seeing.[7]

Zhang's dream to win international recognition was only temporarily thwarted, however; his fortune turned when he received, for the second time, a Golden Lion Award for the best picture at the Venice Film Festival, in November 1999.[8] (He won a Golden Lion for *The Story of Qiu Ju* in 1993.) His fame grew even greater in his home country because of the film. At the China Obelisk Film Awards (*dianying huabiao jiang*) in 1999, a newly created annual event sponsored by the Chinese government, Zhang Yimou, along with two other directors, received the award for Outstanding Film Director (*youxiu daoyan jiang*) for *Not One Less*, and the film itself, along with nine other films, won the Outstanding Feature Film Award (*youxiu gushi pian jiang*).[9] The awards ceremony was broadcast on Chinese television. While Zhang himself had become a celebrity figure, the film scholars regarded the film as a work of high art.[10] Zhang was frequently invited to talk shows on Chinese television stations. The child actors Wei Minzhi and Zhang Huike also became the darlings of the media. Tours of China's major cities such as Shanghai were organized for them, and they often appeared on television and were featured in newspaper articles.[11]

I saw the film twice, in two different Beijing movie houses, in May 1999. The film had been shown in Beijing for some time, and the first run was over. I was pleasantly surprised to find a few theaters that were still screening the film. I first saw the film on a weekday afternoon, and the audience was small. On another day, a Saturday afternoon, I went to see the film at the Ziguang Theater (Purple Light Theater) in the Chaoyang district of Beijing, which was fifteen minutes away from where I was living. Before I reached the ticket office, I was approached by a number of people who tried to sell their tickets to me at a discount price. Puzzled, I asked them why they did not want to see the film. The would-be scalpers told me that their work units had bought these tickets for them and had given them free. They could make a bit of money by selling the tickets for a film that they had already seen or did not care to see. The question for the researcher is how to measure with accuracy the degree of popularity and the exact box office figure of a film in a "socialist market economy." In light of the multiple factors that come into play in the process (piracy, intervention from social groups, and so forth), the task goes beyond merely adding up statistical figures, which would be only a partial reflection of reality.

On that Saturday, the theater was showing a double feature: *Hong pingguo* (Red Apple) and *Not One Less*. The large theater was filled with viewers, men and women of all ages, unlike the half-empty theater I visited on a weekday. Who are the viewers? I wondered. Did they come here because they wanted to see the two films, or were they given free tickets? *Red Apple* was shown first. During the entire screening, the audience was silent. This Hong Kong–style comedy starring real Hong Kong actors and actresses did not elicit any sort of spontaneous, enthusiastic response. Indeed, a newspaper commentary criticized the over-the-top, typically Hong Kong style of acting in the film. The melodrama lacked a sense of realism and failed to strike a chord among the mainland audience.[12] Next was *Not One Less*. The atmosphere and audience response were completely different. The humor of the film caught on with the audience, and there was continuous laughter throughout the screening. The audience seemed to believe in the authenticity of the situation described or simulated in the film, even though the events often turn out to be rather comic. The lively reaction from the audience is a measure of the film's popularity.

In the art and entertainment columns of China's newspapers, there are sometimes forums devoted to the film. Interested viewers from different social backgrounds talk about the film from their own perspectives. They often marvel at Zhang's vision and art: the skills to fashion fascinating characters out of little children and the ability to add moral weight to otherwise banal details of life. Certain popular attitudes can be gleaned, for instance, from a column appearing in the Chinese newspaper *Nanfang zhoumo* (Southern Weekend), which featured a discussion of the film.[13] Seven viewers from different parts of China voice their opinions about the film. (The views of each commentator are translated, paraphrased, or summarized in the appendix.)

With the exception of the first commentator, all the writers enthusiastically endorsed the artistry and meaning of the film. Although some of them were disappointed by the happy ending of the film, they were impressed by the stubbornness of Wei Minzhi's character. This quality, also seen in Qiu Ju in *The Story of Qiu Ju*, perhaps functions as some sort of deep collective unconscious.[14] In fact, an indigenous (indoctrinated) reader interprets the meaning of the story in the light of the fable *Yugong yishan* (The Old Fool Moves the Mountain), a legend that was taken up by Mao Zedong to describe the efforts of the Chinese people to change their poor country. The acting teacher is hardly heroic, but is rather an all-too-ordinary thirteen-year-old girl. But her silly, single-minded, "foolish" determination is what moves the audience in the theater, the authorities in the film, and the "mountains" in China's social landscape. She becomes the kind of ordinary "hero" in an age when all heroism and idealism are gone in post-1989 China.

Once again, what the film stands for—human beings entrapped in a backward, poor, primitive society, yet with the strong will to change things amid an adverse environment—becomes a national allegory. This collective psyche evoked in the film perhaps explains its popularity, namely, the audience's recognition of and identification with the life-world described in the film. The figure of the teacher has fascinated Zhang Yimou. His next film—*The Road Home,* released in late 1999, is also about schoolteachers. A few years ago, the film *Fenghuang qin,* literally "The Phoenix Zither" (The Country Teachers, dir. He Qun, 1993), starring Li Baotian, was an award-winning film in China because of its realistic depiction of the plight of schoolteachers in a poor village. Hence, the schoolteacher and children in *backward* settings become fitting metaphors for China's *modernization.* The slogan of the cabinet of the state council headed by Premier Zhu Rongji at that time was "build the nation with science and education" *(ke-jiao xingguo).* In the 1990s, massive plans to revamp China's stagnant higher education system began under the leadership of Vice Premier Li Lanqing. Measures were been taken to drastically increase the level of college admission and to modernize China's elite universities, especially Qinghua University and Beijing University. (It is no coincidence that many of China's top leaders as well as administrators at various levels are graduates of Qinghua University, including Zhu Rongji and Li Lanqing). The underdeveloped northwestern part of China (Xibei), the setting for many films by Zhang Yimou and other "fifth-generation" directors, is now the top priority in the state's blueprint for social and economic development at the beginning of the twentieth-first century. This is not to equate the meaning of an artistic product with the hard and dry policies of the government. But the film's concern with China's future—its children living in poverty, as seen in other films by Zhang, has left a deep impression on domestic audiences.

The Film Market in 1999

Statistics about China's film market and box office sales figures are measures of the popularity or notoriety of a given film and therefore can be consulted as indices of the values, feelings, and sentiments of the general population. Yet, because of the nature of China's current "socialist market economy," statistical figures cannot be taken as absolute reliable sources of information. The reception of a given film is conditioned and mediated by many other factors: state censorship, social intervention, the underground film, VCD markets, and so on. Therefore, a brief description of the market mechanism of Chinese film may also help us to determine the exact degree of popularity of a film such as *Not One Less*.

The newly established China Film Corporation *(Zhongguo dianying jituan gongsi)* bought the exclusive rights to screen *Not One Less* for 12 million yuan (or 11.80 million yuan, according to other reports). The company donated the income from the film's first run to Project Candlelight *(Zhuguang gongcheng)*, a program to help China's poorest children go to school. The film began to be shown across the country in mid-February, 1999. Until mid-May, the film grossed nearly 9 million yuan in ticket sales in the Beijing area. At this point, the figure seems unremarkable (if not poor) in comparison to the ticket sales record of 12 million yuan in Beijing for *Bu jian bu san* (Be There Be Square) in the 1999 Chinese New Year season, or even his own earlier film *Youhua haohao shuo* (Keep Cool), which grossed 8 million yuan two years earlier. For the China Film Corporation not to lose its base investment of 12 million yuan, box office sales must reach at least 30 million yuan nationwide, and as of mid-May, sales were only 18 million yuan.[15] According to another report, the film grossed only 3.58 million yuan in box office sales in the Beijing area until May 12, 1999.[16] By November 1999, however, box office sales for the film throughout the country had reached 40 million yuan.[17] This is comparable to the highest box office record for a Chinese-made film in China's domestic market in 1999, which achieved nearly 40 million yuan with *Be There Be Square*.[18]

The Chinese film market suffered further decline in 1999. Through May, there was a 40 percent drop in the Chinese film market. Some statistical figures are alarming. The box office income for *Red Apple*, featuring Hong Kong stars Gu Juji and Shu Qi, received a meager sum of 550,000 yuan in the nine days of its first run after its May 4 release in Beijing. Another May feature did even worse. *Wangluo shidai de aiqing* (Love in the Age of Internet) made a dismal 20,000 yuan on May 13, its first day of screening in more than ten movie theaters in Beijing. Ordinarily, one movie theater alone should make about 10,000 yuan in the first day of screening a new film.[19]

The difficulty in determining the exact condition of reception in the Chinese film market is further complicated by other factors that are not seen in the U.S. film market. First, widespread piracy is a major cause for the decline in film audience. Despite the extreme caution taken by the China Film Corporation, pirated VCDs of *Not One Less* were seen in such places as Shanghai, Jiangsu, Guangxi, Zhejiang, and Guangdong.[20] I myself also saw pirated VCDs of the film being sold for as little as 15 yuan by street peddlers at separate locations in Beijing in May 1999.

There is also direct or indirect intervention from work units and social groups. Many work units have bought tickets of the film for their employees. The motive could be purely for the entertainment and welfare of the employees as it was done in the "workers' state" in the heyday of Maoist, socialist China. It is also possible that the units either feel sympathetic toward the plight of China's poor children or feel pressured to participate in Project Hope/Project Candlelight. Buying the tickets is a way to contribute to the fund for the education of rural children.

The intervention of state agencies in what can be produced and seen in China should not be underestimated. This is part of daily life in China's cultural and political arena. An example is the airing of television programs in China in the wake of NATO's bombing of the Chinese Embassy in Yugoslavia. The incident, whether by accident or intentional, caused widespread indignation across large sectors of the Chinese population. In the days following the event, Chinese television stations canceled many previously scheduled programs in order to air classic Chinese anti-American films and a new documentary about the Chinese-American conflict in the Korean War—*Jiaoliang* (Contest). Chinese films about the Korean War made in the 1950s, 1960s, and 1970s—such as *Shanggan ling* (Heartbreak Ridge), *Qixi* (Surprise Attack), *Daji qinlüezhe* (Punish the Invaders), and *Yingxiong ernü* (Heroic Sons and Daughters)—were broadcast.[21] Intellectuals and cultural critics also seized the opportunity to reexamine popular Hollywood blockbusters that have swept the Chinese film market in recent years. They attempted to uncover the hidden hegemonic agenda beneath the humanism of Hollywood melodramas. In view of NATO's bombing in Yugoslavia and of the Chinese Embassy, they asserted that the humanist elements in films such as *Saving Private Ryan*, which were rather popular in China, were nothing but hypocrisy and were no better than *Red Corner*, a film that demonized China.[22] In their minds, Hollywood's takeover of the international film market was not much different from NATO's military involvement in Kosovo, because both were part of the U.S. strategy of global hegemony. Movie theaters in various Chinese cities also canceled screenings of new American films, but showed instead these anti-American films. According to one report, *Contest* was very popular among Beijing residents. (Interviewees included a railroad worker, four college graduates, a police officer, and two employees at a Sino-foreign joint venture.) It aroused Chinese pride and gave people an outlet to vent their indignation.[23]

It seems that box office figures, sales statistics, and the winning of film awards can be taken only partially as indicators of genuine popular sentiments regarding a film in a society self-styled as "socialism with Chinese characteristics." It is obvious that there is tremendous social support for the kind of film represented by *Not One Less*. The support is expressed in such ways as work units voluntarily or involuntarily purchasing tickets for their employees or the movie houses running and rerunning an unprofitable film. And society is not equivalent to the will of the state (which itself is not a monolithic entity, but consists of individuals and layers of bureaucracies and institutions). Chinese "society" had become far too diverse and heterogeneous. The state's support for a particular educational project or a particular film became much more indirect and invisible. The social support for Zhang's film was a support, in both moral and financial ways, however inadequate, for the rapidly dwindling domestic film industry shattered by Hollywood, pirated VCDs, television programs, and so forth. It is also an affirmation of the conscience of Chinese society: "save the children"—a recurrent theme that goes all the way back to May Fourth literature and appears throughout Zhang's works. The film was packaged, advertised, and promoted as a popular film, a major hit, the best the domestic Chinese film industry could offer. In light of the difficult situation of China's film industry, the film performed moderately well, or "as good as it gets," to use the title of a recent Hollywood film. Its popularity, or the lack thereof, as measured by box office figures, reflects the mechanisms at work in the Chinese film market in general.

Signs of Change in Early Twenty-First Century

The financial and political environment for the Chinese film industry seems to have changed for the better at the beginning of the twenty-first century. This has consequences for all manner of filmmakers: the commercial mainstream and independents, established directors, and new directors.

A new generation of Chinese leaders, headed by President Hu Jintao and Premier Wen Jiabao, has replaced the older generation led by Jiang Zemin. With the fading influence of Jiang Zemin, previous cultural policies have been modified. Although the Chinese Communist Party still upholds Jiang's theory of "Three Represents" *(sange daibiao)*, the new leaders are exploring ways to distinguish themselves from the past and create a fresh image. ("Three Represents" means that the Chinese Communist Party represents the most advanced forces of production, the most developed culture, and the interests of the broadest masses.) Ding Guangen, Jiang's ally and boss of propaganda in the party, retired, and his heavy-handed, conservative, stifling cultural practices were abandoned. The party's new propaganda boss, Li Changchun, advocates a new jingoism: "Three

Closes" *(san tiejin)*. The new cultural doctrine means that literature and arts should be close to life, close to reality, and close to the masses. The new leaders have attempted to portray their style of ruling as low-key, down-to-earth, more lenient, and closer to the concerns of ordinary people. As a result, strict rules of censorship in the film industry have been relaxed to a certain extent and the artists have more freedom to choose what kinds of films to shoot and how to shoot them. This is especially good news for emerging young filmmakers who have yet to establish themselves. Under the new regime, censors approve film projects more quickly and with fewer hindrances than before.

China's entry in the World Trade Organization has also provided a catalyst to the film industry to develop more effective mechanisms of production and distribution. As a sign of China's efforts to open its cultural and film markets, the Warner Brothers and Dalian Wanda Group have signed an agreement to jointly build and manage state-of-the-art multiplex cinemas throughout China. Now foreign capital has not only penetrated the traditional industries, but also infiltrated the guarded spiritual realm of Chinese culture.

Once again, Zhang Yimou is the "hero" who has been able to make the most out of the changing circumstances. Zhang's martial arts film *Hero (Yingxiong)* earned 270 million yuan (about US$30 million) in box office sales throughout China, setting a record.[24] The film rejuvenated China's domestic film market and Zhang became a model for other commercially oriented filmmakers to follow, even in the eyes of Feng Xiaogang, an unabashedly self-avowed commercial filmmaker, whose "new-year pictures" *(hesui pian)* had been widely popular over the years.

From late 2003 to early 2004, Feng Xiaogang's film *Cell Phone (Shouji)* was another extremely successful commercial film. Feng initially invested 16 million yuan for the production of the film.[25] But even before the film was released, much of the production cost was already recouped by fees paid for product placement —advertisements of cell phones within the film. Funny and entertaining in content, fluid and colorful in style, the film touches on the comedies and follies of life unfolding in present China: growing economic prosperity, unequal power relationship between men and women, middle-age crisis, and marital infidelity.

The case of Zhang Yimou is forever instructive. The audience loses the old Zhang Yimou, who had the nerve to probe sensitive untouchable issues of Chinese society and whose films were banned several times. Now he has become the regime's favorite director. While China was bidding for Beijing to be the site of the 2008 Olympic Games, China's Olympic committee chose Zhang to create a short propaganda film to show the new face of the city to the world. The rebel director has transformed into China's "official director." Following the commercial success of *Hero*, Zhang completed another martial arts film set in the past and detached from contemporary politics, *Shimian maifu* (House of Flying Daggers, literally "Ambush from Ten Directions," 2004), using a group of well established bankable film icons from the Greater China area. To keep the production cost low, Zhang did not hesitate to outsource the production, as a good capitalist would do, and he shot some of the scenes in a location in Ukraine, where peasants were paid to plant flowers in a mountain as the setting for action. Zhang's change of heart from the political filmmaker to the commercial filmmaker is a good example of a broad trend in the ever-evolving mechanisms of China's film industry and market.

Appendix: Comments on *Not One Less* in *Nanfang zhoumo*

The film lacks a strong plot, and thus demands superior performance from the cast, but the performance of the female lead is really mediocre. Wei Minzhi has no professional training and lacks performing talents. Throughout the entire film, her facial expression is rather bland except for the ending, when she sheds some tears during the TV interview.

In real life, who is so lucky as she was? She was invited by the TV station as an honored guest, found the lost student, and brought back funds for the difficult primary school. Is this kind of story realistic? In the film, Wei Minzhi only wanted some money; she could not do simple math, nor did she show a thirst for knowledge and a love for education. Could we entrust her with the task of education in a backward area? Is she capable of this? The ending of the film is too idealized and falls in the trap of old convention. Happy laughter covers up heavy reality (Yu Qiong, Beijing Normal University).

Five years ago, I stopped by Shixi Village in Machang Township, Zhenning, Guizhou. That mountain village was not far away from Huangguoshu Falls, and both Miao and Buyi people lived there. The primary school of Shixi Village was even worse than Shuiquan Primary School. The country teacher, Yang Chao, received nineteen yuan for monthly salary, and his food was brought by the students from their home. I lied to him, saying I was a journalist, and we had a long conversation. He told me that he wanted to leave the school many times, but did not have the heart to leave the children behind in the end. Next morning, I saw the kids raise the national flag in the open ground under the direction of the teacher, singing the national anthem. I was never moved by students raising the national flag and singing the national anthem while in the city, but this time I was filled with tears. Before left, I wanted to give the teacher one hundred yuan, but he would not accept them. He urged me to write a report about their situation. It has been my great shame that I never did that as a fake journalist.

Five years later I saw the film *Not One Less* in a movie theater. Deep in my heart I never think this is a film. The truthfulness of the film comes out of not only Zhang Yimou's directorial talent, but also real feelings. Thank you, Zhang Yimou! You allowed me to see the conscience that should be in art (Li Shoutong, Lanzhou).

We see the shadow of Qiu Ju in Wei Minzhi: tough, stubborn, sticking to her belief, and going all the way with no return. This personality, plus the allure of fifty yuan, is what energizes the flow of the film. Being a teenage girl from the countryside, carrying little money with her, Wei goes to the city for the first time. But she is not afraid, does not panic, and does not feel inferior; she keeps her goal in mind and goes all the way to reach it. The director has fallen in love with this personal trait—"if one believes in some dead truth, nine bulls cannot pull her back." But this trait is also a burden for Wei Minzhi. It makes her personality stiff and one-dimensional. In contrast, the little boy Zhang Huike does not suffer from this spiritual burden, and is more natural and spontaneous (Yi Wen, Guangxi University).

The age of hero worship is gone. People don't have the passion to look up to heroes today. We are more and more concerned with the lives and feelings of ordinary people since we are all ordinary people. I cannot forget this little acting teacher [Wei Minzhi]. We are not willing to accept an inflated, unreal hero, but are willing to see and accept some small figures, who are ordinary people, live a real life, with true determination (Zou Penghai, China Textile University [Zhongguo Fangzhi Daxue]).

When Wei Minzhi spoke those heartrending words facing the camera, I thought I understood the meaning that I had been seeking. Just like the old man in [Hemingway's] *Old Man and the Sea*, who has got nothing in eighty-two days and yet still perseveres on the eighty-third day, she possesses the same spirit. Although the film has a conventional happy ending, I have discovered a rare quality in Wei Minzhi. We are used to cowardice, retreat, and giving up on things; and we are used to shying away from responsibility and betraying promises; we are used to "getting used to." Therefore, when we confront single-minded, tough, and persistent Wei Minzhi, she seems to come from a different world. Is she too distant from us, or have we evolutionized too fast? (Old Qing [Lao Qing], Wuhan Midsouth College of Nationalities [Wuhan Zhongnan Minzu Xueyuan]).

Wei Minzhi went to Shuiquan Primary School for fifty yuan. She believed that she would receive fifty yuan from Village Chief if she could keep those twenty-eight students. She stubbornly carried out the instruction of Teacher Gao—"not one less." She thought this was the absolute condition for receiving fifty yuan. After overcoming numerous obstacles, the thirteen year-old girl found Zhang Huike in the city and brought him home. The only weapon she had all along was her unyielding determination. Her determination created a belief—not one must disappear.

In the end, it becomes unclear as to what the goal is between "fifty yuan" and "not one must disappear." The merging of these two ideas is what makes this film moving (anonymous, China News College [Zhongguo Xinwen Xueyuan]).

There is documentary realism in the film on the one hand, and fictional narrative on the other. The audience enters a half-real, and half-illusory world. Wei Minzhi and Zhang Huike are two little weak children in a big city, and they should have encountered many dangers and villains. But Zhang Yimou does not pursue this possibility, and uses instead a conventional, mechanical way of resolving contradictions—the model of the Old Fool Moves Mountains [Yugong yi shan]. As we know, the Old Fool and his children would never be able to remove the mountains. He completed his great project because his spirit moved God, and God helped him fulfill his dream (Deng Guang, Beijing).

Notes

1. Zeng Guang, *"Zhang Yimou duzhong beiju zuopin"* (Zhang Yimou prefers tragic work), *Shijie ribao* (World journal) (Friday, December 17, 1999), C6.

2. Yin Hong, *Jing xiang yuedu: jiushi niandai yingshi wenhua suixiang* (Reading the mirror and the image: thoughts on film and TV culture in the 1990s) (Shenzhen: Haitian chubanshe, 1998), 3–5. For a preliminary demarcation of Chinese popular culture in the 1990s, see my essay, "Postmodernity, Popular Culture, and the Intellectual: A Report on Post-Tiananmen China," *boundary 2*.23 (summer 1996): 139–169.

3. Zeng Guang, *"Zhang Yimou duzhong beiju zuopin."*

4. I discuss these television serials in great length in "Soap Opera in China: The Transnational Politics of Visuality, Sexuality, Masculinity," *Cinema Journal* 40.1 (fall 2000): 25–47.

5. See Wang Yichuan, *Zhang Yimou shenhua de zhongjie* (The end of the myth of Zhang Yimou) (Zhengzhou: Henan renmin chubanshe, 1998). For a book-length study of Zhang's film art, see Chen Mo, *Zhang Yimou dianying lun* (The film art of Zhang Yimou) (Beijing: Zhongguo dianying chubanshe, 1995).

6. Shi Xiangsheng, *Yige dou bu neng shao* (Not one less) (Beijing: Zhongguo dianying chubanshe, 1999), 63.

7. For a report on this episode, see Ge Dawei, *"Kancheng yingzhan Zhang Yimou yige dou bu canjia"* (Zhang Yimou does not participate in the Cannes festival with any film) *Shiji ribao* (World journal) (April 26, 1999): C6. For a French criticism of this film, see Jean-Michel Frodon, "Pas un de moins: un Lion d'or à l'ombre des grandes puissances" (*Not One Less*: a golden lion in the shadows of superpowers), *Le Monde* (November 3, 1999).

8. Zhang Yuan, one of the best-known directors of the so-called sixth generation, won the award for the best director at the Venice Film Festival in 1999 for *Guonian huijia* (Seventeen years). Commonly perceived as the leader of China's independent, underground filmmaking, Zhang sometimes calls Zhang Yimou, his senior schoolmate from the Beijing Film Academy—a representative of the fifth-generation—an "official director" (*guanfang daoyan*). See Zhong Yunlan, *"Liang Zhang shuangying"* (The two Zhangs both win), *Shijie ribao* (World journal) (September 17, 1999): C6. In contrast to Zhang Yuan's stance, Zhang Yimou considers that "underground film" (*dixia dianying*) does not necessarily imply greater artistic freedom; to learn how to survive in the current political system is his advice to the filmmakers of the young generation. See Zeng Guang, *"Zhang Yimou duzhong beiju zuopin."*

9. Chen Bing, *"Zhongguo dianying huabiao jiang, Xia Yan dianying wenxue jiang jinwan banjiang"* (Tonight the ceremony for the China Obelisk Film Awards and Xia Yan Film Literature Awards), *Beijing wanbao* (Beijing evening news) (May 20, 1999): 13.

10. See, for example, the special section devoted to Zhang and the film in *Dangdai dianying* (Contemporary cinema) no. 2 (1999): 4–26. It features an interview with Zhang, an interview with the film's photographer, Hou Yong, and analyses of the screenplay, photography, and sound recording.

11. See *"Wei Minzhi, Zhang Huike, Shanghai gua zhenfeng"* (Wei Minzhi and Zhang Huike's whirlwind tour of Shanghai), *Shijie ribao* (World journal) (July 5, 1999): C6.

12. Peng Li, *"Hong pingguo you di'er suan"* (*Red Apple* tastes a little sour) *Beijing ribao* (Beijing daily) (May 17, 1999): 8.

13. *"Zhongkou pingshuo Yige dou bu neng shao"* (Different perspectives on *Not One Less*) *Nanfang zhoumo* (Southern weekend) (May 21, 1999), 9.

14. Elsewhere, I describe the evolution of Zhang Yimou's film art and assess the characteristics of his individual films in the context of his oeuvre. See "National Cinema, Cultural Critique, Transnational Capital: The Films of Zhang Yimou," in Sheldon H. Lu, ed., *Transnational Chinese Cinemas: Identity, Nationhood, Gender* (Honolulu: University of Hawai`i Press, 1997), 105–136; "Zhang Yimou," in Yvonne Tasker, ed., *Fifty Contemporary Filmmakers* (London: Routledge, 2002), 412–418.

15. These figures are taken from Luo Jingsong, *"Zhang Yimou: wo bu shi jinzi zhaopai"* (Zhang Yimou: I am not a goldmine), *Beijing qingnian bao* (Beijing youth daily) (May 17, 1999), 7. See also Shi Xiangsheng, 64–65.

16. See Peng Li, *"Wuyue dianying: da luo zhilou neng fou da qi"* (Film in May: could there be a great rise after a great decline) *Beijing ribao* (Beijing Daily) (May 17, 1999), 8.

17. Hui Wen, *"Zhang Yimou suipian xuanchuan, Shenzhen tebie pengchang"* (Zhang Yimou promotes and travels with his film, and wins applause especially in Shenzhen) *Shijie ribao* (World Journal) (Friday, November 5, 1999), C6.

18. See Luo Jingsong, *"Beijing penghui sizuo jiangbei: jiuba niandu dianying huabiao*

jiang jiexiao" (Beijing brings home four awards: the results of the 98 obelisk awards for films) *Beijing qingnian bao* (Beijing youth daily) (May 22, 1999), 7.

19. The figures are taken from Peng Li.

20. For a report on the piracy of the film, see Xia Qingjin, *"Jintui zhi jian de Zhang Yimou"* (Zhang Yimou caught in a dilemma) *Dianying shibao* (*Film and TV Times*) no. 704 (April 1999), 1.

21. I myself saw these films on TV while in Beijing in mid-May 1999. For a Chinese newspaper report, see Wang Qing and Chen Xiaoguang, *"Jingcheng yinmu taofa buyi: baixing chongwen kangmei jingdian"* (Beijing's silver screen castigates the unrighteous: people re-watch the classics about resisting America and assisting Korea) *Beijing Guangbo dianshi bao* (Beijing broadcast and TV journal) (May 18, 1999), 1.

22. For a forum on the issue, see *"Killer: chongxin renshi Meiguo dapian"* (Killer: reunderstanding American blockbusters) *Beijing qingnian bao* (Beijing youth daily) (May 19, 1999), 3.

23. See Wang Qing and Chen Xiaoguang

24. Luo Ying, *"Yingxiong piaofang 2.7 yi: Feng Xiaogang xiang Zhang Yimou kanqi"* (*Hero* grossed 270 million yuan at the box office: Feng Xiaogang looks up to Zhang Yimou), *Shiji ribao* (World journal) January 23, 2004, E4.

25. Ibid.

PART TWO

Poetics,
Directors,
Styles

CHAPTER SIX

Transcultural Spaces

Toward a Poetics of Chinese Film

Any phenomenon that grows in strength and renown over twenty years can hardly be dismissed as a fad, so it seems well past time to acknowledge that Chinese-language filmmaking, active in several countries and very different film industries, has become central to world film culture. Artistically speaking, Chinese cinema is more energetic and imaginative than the American studio cinema and most of the work coming out of Europe. Understanding this cinema in all its aspects is thus an urgent task for scholars who wish to stay in touch with the creative work of their time.

But how best to understand the artistic accomplishments of the traditions which make up "Chinese film"? Over the past two decades, many scholars have made great headway in this task, yet we have scarcely begun to appreciate the aesthetic strategies that make these films so remarkable. In what follows, I want to suggest some benefits that could flow from inquiring into how these films elicit particular effects—what I have elsewhere called a "poetics of cinema"— and in pursuing such problems I am following a path marked out by others.[1]

To ask about the poetics governing any filmmaking tradition is to pose at least four broad questions. By what principles are the films created as distinctive wholes—narratives, or other kinds of wholes? Call this domain the "poetics of overarching form." How is the film medium deployed in a film or body of films?

Call this "stylistics." How do form and style shape the uptake of spectators? Call this the "theory of spectatorial activity." How, over time, do form and style exhibit patterns of continuity and change, and how might we best explain these patterns? Call this "historical poetics."

Put this way, inquiry into principles of overall composition, spectatorial activity, and historical traditions would seem to set aside what most concerns many scholars: the ways in which films embody the traces of social and cultural factors. But poetics does not rule out appeal to such factors. Poeticians mount explanations, both functional explanations and causal ones. For example, how do the parts work together to create this distinctive whole, and what circumstances make those principles and wholes emerge at some times rather than others? Thus, the poetician can study how films' form and style bear the traces of the mode of production that has created them and, beyond that, how cultural processes shape film form and style. In seeking causal answers, a film poetics operates "from the bottom up," asking us to start with the principled regularities of form and style we can find in the films and then to ask what real-world activities could plausibly play causal roles in creating them.[2]

A signal advantage offered by poetics is that it makes allowance for artistry. Filmmakers spend an enormous amount of time getting things the way they want them—fiddling with the script, auditioning dozens of actors, trying out different locations and camera angles and cutting patterns. Of course, time and money create pressures, and no filmmaker gets everything she wants; there are always compromises, zones of indecision, lucky accidents, and flat-out mistakes. Still, as an artisan, the filmmaker has resources of knowledge about what works and what does not work. Passed from filmmaker to filmmaker over time, this knowledge coalesces into craft traditions, and they in turn provide schemas, those repeated patterns of shot composition, of lighting, of camera movement or editing that get the job done. The concept of norm-governed schemas seems to me indispensable for appreciating what film artists have accomplished. Who would study Chinese landscape painting without being aware of the different options for representing space (what T. C. Lai translates as "high-distance" composition, "flat-distance" composition, "deep-distance" composition)?[3] Who would study Beijing Opera without recognizing the varieties of face painting *(lianpu)*? We readily admit that artistry in other media can be appreciated only through being aware of the forms that artists have inherited. Yet I am struck by how, in examining Chinese film, so many scholars seem indifferent to the craft traditions that shape the way movies look and sound. An approach through poetics can restore this dimension to our research, while acknowledging the undeniable artistic gifts that filmmakers bring to their activity.

A poetics-based inquiry can also open up a terrain of questions that are not as easy to identify when the research approach is more "top-down"—when, that is, we start with a broad theory of culture, society, or ideology and then find portions of films that fit that theory. This is not an objection to cultural theories, or Theory *tout court*—we shall always need theories, at many levels of generality—but a methodological point. Poetics, as I conceive it, is an inductive, empirical discipline that gives priority to the integrity of the given film, the particularities of the film medium, and the choices made by historical agents working within institutions. The poetician needs to be aware of a range of theories precisely in order to see their relative value for explaining individual cases. A poetics could canvass many cultural theories to explain the regularities and idiosyncrasies we find at the level of the films themselves.[4]

Poetics is inherently a comparative undertaking. To isolate principles of style or narrative, to try to characterize how films engage spectatorial activity, to mount a historical argument about influence or innovation, one can scarcely avoid seeking out differences and similarities across a range of filmmaking practices. It is not just that Hong Kong cinema was influenced by Hollywood cinema; we can, if we are attentive, trace out differences, both large and small, against a background of similarities. More strikingly, by taking a comparative perspective, we are better prepared to give as much weight to convergences as to divergences. As it turns out, this is of particular value in studying Chinese film. For, in film studies today, we often concentrate automatically on the specificities, even the uniqueness, of the culture in which a film is embedded. It is common, for instance, to treat Hong Kong cinema since the early 1980s as addressing the impending 1997 handover or to consider Taiwanese film as part of a complex process of recognizing modernity and contemporary Taiwanese identity. I would not object to these interpretations, which shed light on many aspects of the film. My point is that by looking at the films from the bottom up, we can activate other aspects, and those aspects may lead us to quite another perspective—one I am going to be calling "transcultural." Put another way, culture is as significant in the affinities we find among societies as in the differences that distinguish them. Indeed, those differences often only spring into focus against a background of affinities.

My thesis is this: in the filmmaking strategies and tactics utilized, several traditions of Chinese cinema point up ways in which films can cross boundaries of both nation and culture. One way to study this process would be to consider Chinese culture as a diasporan one and Chinese cinema as a kind of pan-Chinese cultural vehicle. This seems to me a very fruitful approach, but not one I am competent to pursue here. Instead, beginning with some features of the films, I want to consider how it is possible for certain stylistic patterns to be traced to transcultural processes.

Those factors include some international norms of film style, and some wide-ranging—I daresay universal—conditions of filmmaking itself. Chinese films, to put it bluntly, are Chinese. They are, though, also films, and films are a powerful transcultural medium, drawing not only on local knowledge but also on a range of human skills that are shared across many cultures. By mastering several transcultural possibilities of cinema, Chinese films have gained the power to cross national boundaries and be grasped by audiences around the world. It is not that everyone "reads" these films in a uniform way; the commonalities I want to trace operate at a more basic, but still quite powerful and pervasive, level.

If we simply look at films from mainland China, Hong Kong, and Taiwan, we can see, going back quite far, a common stylistic point of departure: the classical continuity system associated with Hollywood since the late 1910s.[5] Several commentators have pointed out the reliance of Chinese cinema upon the basic strategies of this style: establishing and reestablishing shots to inform the audience of spatial layouts; analysis of the space by means of analytical editing, shot/reverse-shot, and eyeline-matching; camera movements to reframe characters, to track with them as they walk, or to move in to isolate a detail. With the coming of sound, takes became longer, camera movements got more complicated, and more filmmakers were drawn to staging in depth. Parallel to these changes, local film industries around the world developed approximate equivalents of Hollywood's division of labor. And this should not surprise us: on the basis of what we know so far, classical continuity became a lingua franca of film style for all the world's mass-market cinemas.

To pose the matter this way is to raise the question of whether such a framework is an imposition of a "Western" conception of cinema, and of human action and identity, on cultures that do not have such conceptions. For some scholars, it is parallel to the question of whether the representational forms known collectively as "Renaissance perspective" is a distinctively Western mode of seeing imposed on alternative representational traditions. I do not see it quite this way, though to explain in detail why would take me afield. So let me simply say that, although the classical continuity framework is definitely a convention, it is a convention that is more quickly learned than alternative ones we might postulate. And it is more quickly learned at least partly because it mobilizes several contingent universals of human experience. This framework exploits, among other things, our ability to identify other members of our species; to "read their minds" in terms of posture, glance, and expression; to situate them in a world of enduring middle-sized objects; to assume as a default value that action unfolds in sequence over time.[6] Just as certain phonological and syntactic rules are theoretically possible but never occur in all the world's languages, we could imagine other representational systems (such as filming every scene upside down, or by framing figures so that we never see facial expressions) but that never occur in the world's popular cinemas. In addition, the continuity system, once mastered, permits the efficient and predictable turning out of films—an advantage for any film industry.

I am not saying that the continuity framework is wired into our brains, or genetically programmed.[7] Nor is it some cinematic essence that enterprising filmmakers have revealed through patient excavation.[8] It constitutes a contingent discovery, through trial and error, of one powerful, quickly learnable vehicle of visual communication. Had history been different, some other formats, perhaps Tom Gunning's "cinema of attractions" or the 1900s tableau cinema, might have endured longer.[9]

So classical conventions for the representation of space and time are constructions, but they are constructed out of human predispositions, and a great many of them—more than we are usually inclined to grant—are shared across cultures. I propose that, for historical reasons, the continuity system has become a transcultural bridgehead. Most Chinese films, like films from India or Argentina, are at this level comprehensible to audiences around the world. Why? Because, after brief exposure and minimal tutoring, this pervasive set of conventions makes a film's fictional world easily accessible to mature perceivers in any culture.

It is not surprising, then, to find that, like most national film industries of the 1920s and 1930s, Shanghai's cinema accepted the continuity framework. Chris Berry, Leo Ou-fan Lee, and other scholars have shown in detail what even a quick sampling of this cinema will confirm: the continuity principles were quickly mastered and frequently utilized by a variety of filmmakers.[10] Thanks to conventions of angle and eyeline-match editing, Yuan Muzhi's *Street Angel* keeps its principal apartment location clear and cogent while almost never showing the room in its entirety. And the gags with the boys putting on a show for the woman across the way depend wholly on the same principles that Hitchcock was later to exploit in *Rear Window*. Similarly, distinctive as Ruan Lingyu's radiant performances are, they are predicated on a standardized system of shooting and cutting that could set off her expressions and postures.

Taking our bearings with reference to this transcultural bridgehead, how might a comparative Chinese film stylistics proceed? I shall look at Hong Kong cinema and Taiwanese cinema in some detail, with mainland cinema, of which my knowledge is spotty, sandwiched in between. Throughout, my interest is to raise some issues in how we might start to understand these traditions' debts to transcultural norms, as well as their particular recastings of those norms.

The study of international film style is really just starting, but it seems clear that once filmmakers in any country adopted classical continuity, they realized that it did not have to be followed slavishly. It could be extended, refined, and explored. Perhaps the best example we have is Japan, where directors recast continuity norms in remarkable ways. A less obvious instance, but one that is of no less interest, is afforded by Hong Kong cinema of the 1980s and 1990s.

Here we have a scaled-down model of a popular cinema operating outside Hollywood. Hong Kong remains a cottage industry with some vertical integration, a fluid labor pool, well-developed technology, a core of controlling distributors, and sources of financing adequate for the low-budget levels of local production. Hong Kong filmmaking also had access to a market beyond its borders — Singapore, Taiwan, Malaysia, Indonesia, Thailand, South Korea, Japan to some extent, and Chinatowns dotted throughout the world. This cinema also gained a purchase in the mainstream theatres of Europe and North America, first in the 1970s with the kung fu boom emblematized by Bruce Lee, and then in the late 1980s and 1990s with fan subcultures, particularly those around the gunplay sagas of John Woo.

Because of its industrial structure, its reliance on stars and genres, and its kinship with American cinema, it is tempting to agree with Peter Chan Ho-sun, who calls Hong Kong film "more Hollywood than Hollywood."[11] At a deeper level, we can acknowledge what the fanboys and fangirls already know: this is a visceral cinema. Pain, bloodletting, farts, runny noses, the greasy fingers and face you get while eating—all these universal human experiences are at the center of these films. Who cannot understand the gag in *Tricky Brains* when Stephen Chow offers his father a piece of toilet paper as a tissue, explaining as the father wipes his face, "It was used, but I cleaned it off?" Who does not writhe in pain when Anthony Wong shrieks during police torture in *The Untold Story?* In a parallel way, through a kind of Lippsian empathy, who cannot feel oneself flinching when a martial artist delivers a powerful blow, or straining to lift one's backside when Jet Li effortlessly hurls himself up to the sky in the kung fu competition in *Fong Sai-yuk?* Here is an obvious way in which cinema can go transcultural: by addressing us at the level of sheer stimulation, recording the torsions of the body in extremis and trusting that it will stir us to what Eisenstein called "reflexively repeating, albeit in weakened form" the original expressive movement.[12]

Yet the perspective of poetics lets us posit more than a cinema of gore, grossout humor, and daredevil stunts. Hong Kong films display some subtle reworkings of classical staging, shooting, and cutting, and these elements contribute to the unique flavor of this popular cinema. For one thing, Hong Kong filmmakers, probably drawing from indigenous Chinese traditions of theatre and martial arts, have developed a rhythmic conception of expressive movement that builds on the sheerly visceral aspect of cinema's appeal. By presenting a cleanly delineated piece of action, framed at beginning and end by a slight pause, Hong Kong filmmakers have created a distinctive staccato rhythm. This, is in turn, amplified by color, music, editing, framing, and other film techniques. And not only fight scenes display this rhythmic tendency. Once it is mastered, filmmakers conceive dramatic and comic scenes that can be subjected to marked rhythmic patterning.[13]

Something else is going on in these films, and we cannot fully understand it without taking a comparative tack. For Hollywood itself changed its stylistic norms somewhat in the 1970s and 1980s—not, as some have argued, by embracing fragmentation and discontinuity, but by narrowing certain stylistic choices and weighting certain others.[14] I call this new approach "intensified continuity."

What constitutes this intensified continuity? Most notably, accelerated cutting rates. U.S. films moved from an average shot length (ASL) of five to eight seconds in the 1970s to around three to six seconds in the mid-1990s. By the end of the 1990s, a great many films had an ASL of two to three seconds. Along with fast cutting, there is an emphasis on a comparatively close shot scale. Of course there are close-ups throughout the history of cinema, but in the 1980s and 1990s, the scale shifted: a filmmaker was likely to work with a range of medium-shots, medium-close-ups, and tight close-ups, rather than the medium-long shot and long shot of the 1950s. Once filmmakers learned how to compose close-ups in widescreen during the 1960s, there appears a greater emphasis on tight facial close-ups, with long shots functioning less as establishing shots and more as accents within a scene. Because of the widescreen ratio, a tight shot can supply enough overall sense of the setting to make traditional establishing shots less obligatory. Because of the concentration on close-ups, there is also more racking focus, as one head goes out of focus and another, in the foreground or background, comes in. Finally, practitioners of intensified continuity exploit a great deal of camera movement—particularly what we might call the "prowling camera." In the 1970s several lightweight camera systems, chiefly Panaflex and Steadicam, were devised to permit versatile tracking shots. Today nearly every American film will include virtuoso following shots through a location, looming track-ins to characters in shot/reverse shot, and a constantly sliding or arcing or circling or swooping camera. I do not have space here to pursue possible historical explanations for the development of intensified continuity, but the answer probably lies partly in filmmakers efforts to adjust classical principles to their conception of what would be suited for a film's ultimate venue: the video monitor.[15]

From the 1970s to the 1990s, as Hollywood was establishing intensified continuity as its major stylistic norm, Hong Kong directors picked up on it and revised it in key ways. The most obvious instance is the work of John Woo, who seems to have mastered all the grace notes of intensified continuity in his films of the mid-1980s. Forget the balletic gunplay for a moment; even in dialogue scenes he displays his indebtedness to this strategy, with constantly arcing and swooping camera movements accompanied by rack focus and abrupt close-up entrances and exits.

Such sequences have counterparts in the work of Tsui Hark, Corey Yuen Kuei, Sammo Hung, Johnnie To, and many others, and they show that filmmakers steeped in a tradition of expressive movement could adapt changing international norms to their own purposes.

Intensified continuity, though developed on American multimillion-dollar pictures, also offers advantages to lower-budget filmmakers. Close-ups are faster and cheaper to light than long shots; relying on editing gives the director flexibility in postproduction. A mobile camera allows filmmakers to switch setups faster, and generally speed up shooting on location (particularly when, as in Hong Kong, sound is dubbed later). With the supply house of Salon Films renting Panaflex cameras for handheld work, and editors working to assemble as many as 1,500 shots, Hong Kong filmmakers could produce work that approximated the production values and visual style of American cinema.

Consider a moment in Benny Chan's *The Big Bullet* (1996), produced when Hong Kong budgets were tightening. Bill and his squadmate Apple need to get into a guarded telephone office, so they fake a robbery attempt in order to distract the guards. Although the overall average shot length for the film is 4.1 seconds, typical for an American film of the same period, this particular scene is handled in a single shot, with tight, fluid close-ups and marked use of racking focus. Apple has just triggered the alarm. Bill blocks the surveillance camera and signals Apple to move toward him. The camera pans right as they duck and flee offscreen left. A guard opens the door, comes toward the camera, followed by another, and halts in tight medium-close-up. As he turns, the camera pans in time to catch Bill and Apple pretending they have just heard the summons. They run to the foreground, with Bill favored and Apple visible in the middle. As Bill argues with the first guard, she pushes the second guard aside in the background, and assumes his position, creating a compact composition. The two cops then rush through the doorway. This sort of scene can be shot quickly and cheaply, thanks to tight framings and simple camera movements that emphasize dialogue and facial reactions.

It seems likely, then, that Hong Kong filmmakers, who had already exploited the dynamic power of editing and close-ups in swordplay and kung fu films, were prepared to extend and refine the canons of intensified continuity. The task was made easier not only by new technologies, but also by Hollywood's favoring of techniques that were fairly easy to replicate on lower budgets. In general, much of what we think of as the "new Hong Kong cinema" within the main-

The Big Bullet (dir. Benny Chan, Hong Kong, 1996).

stream industry was a creative reworking of what were coming to be international norms of mass-market filmmaking—norms often given a precision and kinetic impact not developed much in Western cinema.

The mainstream commercial cinema is not, of course, the only network through which the world's cinema flows. During the 1970s and 1980s, film festivals proliferated, and they acquired a vast appetite for films from all regions. Today, with more than 400 festivals worldwide, film festivals constitute virtually a separate distribution circuit, showcasing films in cities that will never screen those films in commercial theatres. What plays at these festivals? A large part of the programming consists of "art films," those small-scale, often difficult or formally adventurous films that are not judged to be marketable by major international distributors. These films find theatrical venues in "art cinemas."

What is perhaps most evident about this output are certain conventions of branding and packaging. Eroticism is primary: art films since the 1950s have been marketed as daringly sexy. Children are another prominent appeal, from *Bicycle Thieves* and *The 400 Blows* to *Salaam Bombay* and *Life Is Beautiful*. A third factor is exoticism, as Chinese film imports testify. The publicity for *Farewell My Concubine* played it up as a sumptuous costume drama, with a dash of sexual transgressiveness . If we look beyond subject matter, though, we find that many "art films" share a certain approach to storytelling and film style, influenced by modernist movements in various media.[16] In particular, a stylistic tactic that emerged in European art cinema of the 1970s and 1980s becomes quite relevant to understanding another way in which Chinese cinema has gone global. This strategy reacts against the staging practices on which classical continuity norms rely.

Throughout the 1940s and 1950s, many European directors had paralleled Hollywood filmmakers in using the wide-angle, deep image for dramatic scenes. But for a variety of reasons, during the 1960s a different sort of image emerges. In such shots the camera is set up perpendicular to the rear plane, and the human figure is presented in a way so as to avoid the three-quarter view. Instead, we view the characters in frontal or profiled views, and sometimes from directly behind.

We are tempted to call such images "flat." As Godard put it, "This is not a 'just image'; it is just an image." Still, "flat" as they look, these shots still represent depth. We can borrow Heinrich Wölfflin's term, "planimetric," to describe images like these, which present depth as a series of parallel planes. There might be quite a lot of these planes, suggesting many layers of space (and thus depth), but they lack that sense of diagonals plunging into the background we get with more "recessional" compositions. In the 1960s the planimetric composition offered filmmakers an opportunity to create quasi-abstract compositions that stressed the artificiality of the image. In addition, during the period that Hol-

Il Grido (dir. Michelangelo Antonioni, Italy, 1957).

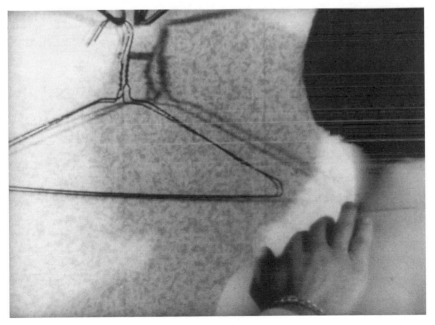

Vivre sa vie (dir. Jean-Luc Godard, France, 1962).

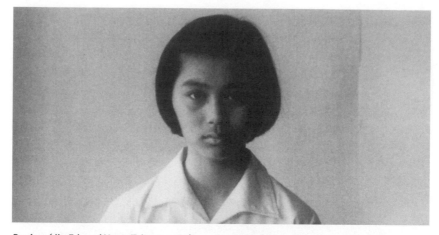

Desires (dir. Edward Yang, Taiwan, 1982).

The Terrorizers (dir. Edward Yang, Taiwan, 1986).

lywood was exploiting pyrotechnics and special effects to reinvigorate cinematic spectacle, the planimetric image invested art cinema with its own, albeit muted, pictorial spectacle. Few directors of the 1980s and 1990s escape the influence of this image, either independent filmmakers in the United States or industry-based ones in Asia. The Japanese director Suo Masayuki used it in his pastiches of Ozu, and it became central to Kitano Takeshi's style. Edward Yang's early films also drew on this aesthetic, from the very first shot of *Desires* to the handling of the Eurasian woman's adventures in *The Terrorizers:* at one point a planimetric shot catches her lifting a john's wallet.

Once this image becomes a major design feature, filmmakers tend to rethink their staging and cutting options in relation to it. Now shots are filmed and cut according to a sort of compass-point principle, with shot-changes organized in multiples of ninety degrees. A fine example comes from Mainland China, He Jianjun's *Postman* (1995). While the young postman is sorting mail with the woman coworker, he is slipping a letter into the batch, and normal continuity editing is adapted to a more stringent pattern of setups suitable to planimetric imagery.

We start with a medium shot of pigeonholes, and the camera tracks right to reveal the doorway and Xiao Dou stamping letters to be delivered. There is a ninety-degree cut to the hero, now very frontal in a classic planimetric image. The scene depends partly on suspense; he is setting aside a particular letter, but does not want her to observe him. So when we get the reverse shot of the woman, handled as a 180-degree cut, with her looking at the camera, he cannot search for the letter. As she resumes her work, cut 180 degrees to reveal the woman in profile in the foreground, in a layered planimetric composition. Another 180-degree cut puts us behind him and sets her in the background as she rises. Cut again 180 degrees. After unpacking a fresh roll of toilet paper, the woman moves to the background and then off left, leaving him alone. He Jianjun has saved this moment for the scene's first close-up, when Xiao Dou pulls the letter from the bag and the camera tilts up to his face. The scene ends with a setup repeating that seen in the bottom right figure on page 154, as he stamps the letter.

The abrupt switches of orientation have activated all sides of the post office's sorting area, which is throughout the film treated as a cluster of boxlike spaces. The location is much more gridlike than that seen elsewhere in the film. Still, He Jianjun also relies on 180-degree cuts to offer contrasting views of the bedrooms at home. He treats the central dining table as a pivot permitting cuts showing one room occupied by his sister's boyfriend, the other to Xiao Dou himself.

In Chen Kaige's *King of the Children* (1988), the planimetric image is put into dialogue, we might say, with quite different ways of representing space. Any film with a schoolroom scene commonly uses a perpendicular shot, for that is the most informative way to show what is on the blackboard. But Chen extends this strategy to filming the schoolhouse itself, turning it into narrow strips of color and texture: windows that compare the teacher to the graffito depicting him, blocks of earth and wood that change color at different times of the day, compositions emphasizing the looming thatch roof and the bare ochre earth stretching up to the school. It seems to me that Chen uses this device expressively, when he wants to isolate Lao Gar or emphasize his solitary mission. Against this is set at least three other visual strategies: a more conventional use of depth staging within the schoolroom when the class is present; a use of light and setting to block key items of information (the unseen Lao Gar when the team leader as-

Above and facing page: *The Postman* (dir. He Jianjun, China, 1995).

signs him to the school in the first scene; the use of the thatched roof edge to conceal faces; and, of course, the expressive, even expressionistic, landscapes rendered in rich depth. Stylistically, Chen has always seemed quite pluralistic, and in *King of the Children* he blends the planimetric image with a wide range of techniques.

I wish I could trace, or even sketch, a causal story showing how the planimet-

ric shot came to be a prime option for ambitious mainland filmmakers. Perhaps Chen and his peers saw European films while studying at the film academy. Or perhaps they were drawn to the image through the concrete demands of production practices. In Europe, the growing prevalence of the long lens, squeezing space into a set of sliced planes and pushing toward a frontality of staging, alerted filmmakers to the possibilities of the planimetric image.[17] The same process may have been at work among mainland filmmakers. Recall, for instance, the centrality of very long lenses in Chen's *The Big Parade* (1985), which stacks faces and bodies in layers that look as thin as cardboard. And there may be still other factors at work. What seems to me undeniable is the fact of convergence, the development in different cultures of a remarkably similar way of constructing space for the viewer, and this convergence may be more than accidental; it may point toward broader areas of transcultural stylistic practice.

Just as important in the festival circuit have been the successive waves of the Taiwanese New Cinema, from the early 1980s to the present. Indeed, here the idea of a festival circuit takes on particular importance, for relatively few of these films receive mainstream theatrical distribution in the West. As if in defiance of Hollywood's "intensified continuity," many Taiwanese films of the 1990s rely on unusually long, often quite static takes. Some researchers have claimed that the long take is a distinctive long-standing tradition of Chinese cinema, but I cannot find evidence for this; the 1930s and 1940s films I have checked yield a range of shot lengths about equal to that we find in other national cinemas of the sound era, including that of the United States.

Certainly, however, what we find in contemporary Taiwanese cinema is sharply different from current mainstream practices. Just to take some instances from the 1990s, Yang's *Confucian Confusion* (1994) has an average shot length of forty-eight seconds, *Vive l'Amour*, thirty-six seconds; *Heartbreak Island* (1995), fifty-two seconds; *Sweet Degeneration* (1997), forty seconds; *Murmur of Youth* (1997), thirty-four seconds; and *The Hole* (1998), fifty-three seconds. For the most part, these films continue to rely on norms of continuity, but in a fairly sparse and selective way. A scene might present only one fairly simple cut-in, or only a pair of shot/reverse-shot cuts, making fairly singular devices of what are normally seen in much more abundance and that usually carry the burden of ongoing spatial construction.

As with the planimetric image, these long takes are not completely without precedent or parallel; in Angelopoulos and several Japanese filmmakers, we find shots of comparable duration. What stands out for the student of international film style, it seems to me, is the way in which the initial decision to use a long take yields particular staging strategies. And these strategies have obliged many Taiwanese filmmakers to exploit cinematic resources that have been all but forgotten in the West. Here there can be no question of the influence of one tradition on another; it is, I will try to show, a matter of two filmmaking traditions, separated by sixty years and half a world, confronting certain constraints built into cinema as a representational technology.

From 1908 to around 1920, while the continuity style was being formed, filmmakers in Germany, France, Italy, and Scandinavia developed rich and subtle patterns of staging within the sustained long shot. Now a student of poetics can-

The Revolutionary (dir. Yevgenii Bauer, Russia, 1917).

not but be struck by the correspondences between this tradition and several films from Taiwan in the 1980s and 1990s. To understand how, we need to examine some fundamental features of cinematic representation. If the playing space of proscenium theatre constitutes a wide but shallow area, the playing space of cinema constitutes a narrowly tapering triangle. This is because of the laws of optics, as light rays focus on a camera lens.

Filmmakers of the 1910s drew a crucial lesson from this trapezoidal playing area. Theatre staging must be broad and lateral, to allow for many sightlines, but film staging had to be narrow and in depth, because the only eye that mattered was that of the camera. Directors learned that one could use this fixed eye creatively. A scene could unfold with precise blocking and revelation of important material—a choreography based not only on figures moving around the frame, but also of figures and objects impeding our view of some things until the precise moment.[18] For example, in Yevgenii Bauer's *The Revolutionary* (1917), our view of a family at the breakfast table changes slightly as different people become important in the scene, and the table's samovar and the foreground uncle block our view of the daughter at strategic moments.

To this day, the visual trapezoid defines the cinematic playing space, but the rise of editing and camera movement in the late 1910s somewhat disguised this fact, because those techniques allowed the filmmaker to create an ever-changing arena for the drama. As a result, staging within the static frame became more and more a lost art. Very few directors today could imagine staging the scene as Bauer did—though, with reflex viewing, it would be much easier today.

One director who could actualize this option, however, is Hou Hsiao-hsien, who makes virtuoso use of precision staging. Again and again, Hou daringly opens up small slices of space and then tucks important story information into them. In *City of Sadness,* the soldiers come to the Lin home looking for Wen-heung, and Grandfather Lin meets them in a dark chiaroscuro frame, soon joined by Mio in frame center. Thereafter, the soldiers' search in the family's quarters takes place in a fractional aperture in the distant middle left, reactivated when Mio leaves the center and goes to the rear—Grandfather having obligingly moved aside to make her exit visible. Grandfather Lin resumes arguing with the official, stepping to the left to bring his silhouette into the aperture and blocking the action in the rear, but then moving aside once more as action develops in the distance. (Hou has even moved the officer from frame right to frame center, making him block the potentially distracting colored glass.) Hou gives us opacity on two levels: the foreground conversation takes place in near-silhouette, with the officer occasionally blocking the father; and in the distance, an important action is so minute as to be barely discernible.

We can get a concise sense of Hou's reactivation of principles of precision staging by considering what has been called the "dinner-table conundrum." Western filmmakers are anxious to avoid shooting scenes involving people arrayed on all sides of a circular or rectangular table. There are problems of continuity, keeping track of eyelines, gestures, and props (partly eaten food and partly empty glasses). But as Bauer's scene in *The Revolutionary* shows, the tradition of precision staging could modulate dinner table encounters through deft deployment of the blocking and revealing yielded by the camera's cyclopean view.

Hou in effect reinvents the strategy. In one scene of *City of Sadness,* as the intellectuals are gathered around the table, slight movements of foreground figures (turned from us) and background figures (facing us) create fluctuating centers of interest, culminating in the opening of the window onto the city as they sing. Another scene, in which Wen-heung meets with the Shanghai gangster family, depends on minimal movement of his foreground figure and slight turning of the gangsters' heads to direct our attention to one face rather than another.

So it seems that the rise of the long-take trend in Taiwanese cinema, combined with an unbudging camera, stimulated filmmakers to cultivate skills that have all but vanished in the West. But what led so many directors to adopt the long-take option in the first place? Probably several factors were at work. Distant long takes permit greater economy in shooting; with careful rehearsal, less

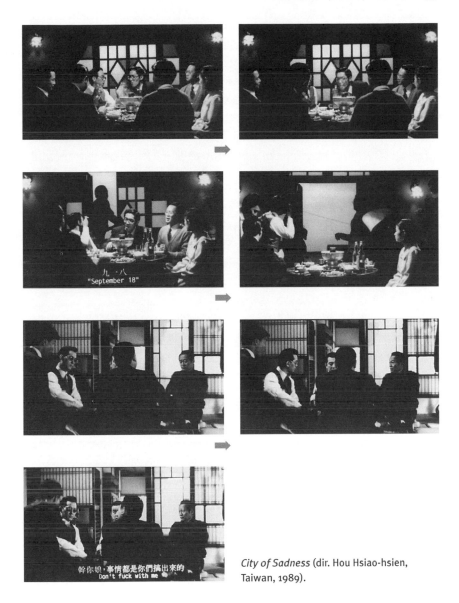

City of Sadness (dir. Hou Hsiao-hsien, Taiwan, 1989).

film is used—a precious commodity for low-budget filmmaking in the 1980s. Distant long takes also minimize the demands placed on nonprofessional actors: Hou has spoken of using long takes and distant shots in *The Boys from Fengkuei* for just this reason.[19] Perhaps, too, this style was embraced as a very evident way of deliberately distinguishing the new Taiwanese cinema from its commercial competition. (A friend of mine likes to say that Taiwanese art films are everything that Hong Kong films are not—slow, subtle, and suggestive.) In sum, the sources of this aesthetic strategy are doubtless local and contingent, but the visual forms it takes work transculturally. Once filmmakers are committed to the long fixed take, the optical constraints of cinematic representation make precision staging a very salient way to develop a scene dramatically, and once the filmmaker sees the rich possibilities of precision staging, it becomes a goal to be pursued for its own sake—no longer a byproduct of a constraint, but a source of delicacy, suspense, surprise, and other artistic effects.

Chinese cinema of the 1980s and 1990s, then, offers a paradigm of three principal ways in which international trends can shape national film traditions. First there are widespread conventions, as in the influence of international continuity norms upon the popular cinema of Hong Kong. The distinctiveness of this cinema handily reminds us that being influenced is not a passive matter; artists seize on what is available to them, transforming it, making it their own, subordinating it to their purposes. Hong Kong's version of intensified continuity is not a simple copy of Hollywood's—indeed, we might consider it an intensification of an intensification, "more Hollywood than Hollywood."

At another level, there may have been some influence of the European art-cinema's planimetric image on mainland filmmakers, perhaps through screenings at the Beijing Film Academy or the circulation of videotapes. But we can entertain another possibility—not influence, but a common stylistic striving, that led Chinese filmmakers independently to explore the possibilities of this sort of image. Once filmmakers have begun using long lenses, the planimetric image may emerge as a likely compositional device. This suggests that there may be a fairly limited number of basic systems of shooting and staging a scene and that they are rediscovered and revised at various points in film history.

Our third example offers yet another way in which we can see transcultural stylistic affinities. Doubtless there was no influence, direct or indirect, of Europe's 1910s depth directors on Hou Hsiao-hsien and his colleagues. Rather, the Taiwanese filmmakers, starting from a similar point of departure—the fixed long take—discovered common features of the medium: the trapezoidal playing space and the opportunities provided by blockage and revelation. They hit on, we might say, similar solutions to a common problem: how to direct attention within the distant, static shot? Of course, their reasons for adopting the fixed long take were different from those of Bauer and his contemporaries, but once that path was taken, the visual trapezoid faced both groups of filmmakers with the same constraints and opportunities.

How may we best understand these acts of historical agents more abstractly? The angle I have pursued has been not to tie them to an abstract theoretical doctrine (hybridity, creolization, globalization) but to work inductively, from the bottom up, generating concepts specific to the regularities we can detect.

The result is perhaps surprising: Not everything of interest about a culture's films is culturally specific, or even specifically cultural! Put less paradoxically, if we attend to the way films are made, we may be led to study transcultural processes, the sharing of craft decisions and stylistic norms, either by influence or through a common point of departure shaped by craft traditions or the particularities of the medium.

This is not to say that culture plays no role in style, nor even in the particular spatial techniques I have fastened on. It is only to say that culture works with givens: the habits and opportunities provided by craft practice, which may have come from national or international sources; the biases and limits of human perception; the propensities and constraints of the very medium with which artists work. These givens are not simply raw material to be wholly absorbed by culture. They leave crucial traces in the very texture of the artwork—like the pebbly comma of ink left by one kind of brush in Chinese painting. It is one task of poetics, as I understand it, to call our attention to these textures, to expose and explore a level of artistry that communicates across local barriers. Culture not only divides us; it unites us. Chinese cinema, by becoming a leader in world filmmaking, owes its energy not only to national and regional traditions, but to the sheer power of film in the hands of creative artists. The triumphs of Chinese filmmaking remind us of the manifold powers of cinema: an art at once deeply tied to local cultural dynamics and yet nonetheless able to move and astonish anyone who has the eyes to see.

Notes

1. Yueh-yu Yeh, "The Poetics of Hou Hsiao-Hsien's Films: Flowers of Shanghai," in *Cinedossier: The 35th Golden Horse Awards-Winning Films* (Taipei: Golden Horse Film Festival, 1999), 94–97; James Udden, "Hou Hsiao-Hsien and the Poetics of History," *CinemaScope* 3 (spring 2000): 48–51.

2. For examples of this approach, see David Bordwell, *Narration in the Fiction Film* (Madison: University of Wisconsin Press, 1985); David Bordwell, Janet Staiger, and Kristin Thompson, *The Classical Hollywood Cinema: Film Style and Mode of Production to 1960* (New York: Columbia University Press, 1985); and Bordwell, *Ozu and the Poetics of Cinema* (Princeton, N.J.: Princeton University Press, 1988), and *The Cinema of Eisenstein* (Cambridge, Mass.: Harvard University Press, 1993). I propose more abstract arguments for a poetics of film in *Making Meaning: Inference and Rhetoric in the Interpretation of Cinema* (Cambridge, Mass.: Harvard University Press, 1989), 263–274.

3. T. C. Lai, *Understanding Chinese Painting* (Hong Kong: Kelly & Walsh, 1980), 91–94.

4. For examples of how cultural processes can be relevant explanations for artistic activities, see Bordwell, *Ozu and the Poetics of Cinema,* chaps. 3 and 8, and *The Cinema of Eisenstein,* 33–39, 164–168, et passim.

5. See Kristin Thompson, "The Formulation of the Classical Style, 1909–1928," in Bordwell, Staiger, and Thompson, *Classical Hollywood Cinema*, 155–240.

6. I elaborate this cross-cultural bridgehead argument in "Convention, Construction, and Cinematic Vision," in David Bordwell and Noel Carroll, eds., *Post-Theory: Reconstructing Film Studies* (Madison: University of Wisconsin Press, 1996), 87–107.

7. It would not occur to me to enter this caveat were this argument not persistently misunderstood. See, for a common misreading, Miriam Bratu Hansen, "The Mass Production of the Senses: Classical Cinema as Vernacular Modernism," in Christine Gledhill and Linda Williams, eds., *Reinventing Film Studies* (New York: Oxford University Press, 2000), 339.

8. I argue against such essentialist accounts in *On the History of Film Style* (Cambridge, Mass.: Harvard University Press, 1997), 149–157.

9. See Tom Gunning, "The Cinema of Attractions: Early Film, Its Spectator, and the Avant-Garde," in Thomas Elsaesser, ed., *Early Cinema: Space, Frame, Narrative* (London: British Film Institute, 1990), 56–60. For a summary of the argument, see Bordwell, *On the History of Film Style*, 125–128.

10. Chris Berry, "Sexual Difference and the Viewing Subject in *Li Shuangshuang* and *The In-Laws*," in Chris Berry, ed., *Perspectives on Chinese Cinema* (London: British Film Institute, 1991), 33–37; Leo Ou- fan Lee, *Shanghai Modern: The Flowering of a New Urban Culture in China, 1930–1945* (Cambridge, Mass.: Harvard University Press, 1999), 96–106.

11. Interview with Peter Chan, November 28, 1996.

12. Sergei Eisenstein and Sergei Tretyakov, "Expressive Movement," *Millennium Film Journal* 3 (winter/spring 1979): 38. The essay is originally from 1923.

13. See Bordwell, "Aesthetics in Action: Kung Fu, Gunplay, and Cinematic Expressivity," in Law Kar, ed., *Fifty Years of Electric Shadows* (Hong Kong: Urban Council/Hong Kong International Film Festival, 1997), 81–89; and Bordwell, *Planet Hong Kong: Popular Cinema and the Art of Entertainment* (Cambridge, Mass.: Harvard University Press, 2000), chap. 8.

14. For example, several essays in Steve Neale and Murray Smith, eds., *Contemporary Hollywood Cinema* (London: Routledge,1998), presuppose narrative fragmentation operates in recent Hollywood films. See in particular James Schamus, "To the Rear of the Back End: The Economics of Independent Cinema," 91–105, and Thomas Elsaesser, "Specularity and Engulfment: Francis Ford Coppola and *Bram Stoker's Dracula*," 191–208. Smith offers some useful clarifications of the issue in "Theses on the Philosophy of Hollywood History," 3–20.

15. I examine this stylistic trend in "Intensified Continuity: Visual Style in Contemporary American Film," *Film Quarterly* 55.3 (spring 2002): 16–28.

16. Bordwell, *Narration in the Fiction Film*, chap. 10.

17. See Bordwell, *On the History of Film Style*, 261–263.

18. For a discussion of precision staging in early film, see ibid., 174–198.

19. Tony Rayns, "The Sandwich Man: Between Taiwan and the Mainland, Between the Real and the Surreal: Tony Rayns Talks to Hou Xiaoxian," *Monthly Film Bulletin* 653 (June 1988): 164.

CHAPTER SEVEN

Poetics and Politics of Hou Hsiao-hsien's Films

The penultimate shot in *City of Sadness:* when the Lin family discovers that one of their own has been struck down in the February 28 massacre, they continue to go about their daily routine. The women are busy in the kitchen, preparing dinner; the sister-in-law who recently lost her husband calls the family to the table. Here, a musical prelude cautiously rises, matching the movement of the characters. On this tentative note, the narrative ends. In the last scene of *Boys from Fengkuei,* we see the soon-to-be-drafted island boys loudly hawking bootleg tapes, accompanied by a background of a popular song singing the passage of time. *The Puppetmaster* ends in a quiet musical eddy, showing in long shot Taiwanese people busy scavenging parts from a crashed American military aircraft.

Hou Hsiao-hsien's films always give us abrupt endings. Such endings are not meant to be upsetting. Instead, they beg for understanding. Like a fascination for puzzles, they invite a reconstruction of the story piece by piece. The ending of *The Puppetmaster* is a confusing long shot in which spectators must recall on-camera interviews with Li Tianlu to realize the scavengers are raising money for a celebration. Here Hou uses his favorite techniques of metonymy and delay to weave a stunningly beautiful memory of Taiwan's colonial history.

Why Hou Hsiao-hsien—Taiwan Cinema at Home and in the World

These moments epitomize Hou Hsiao-hsien's film art—detached, distant, and, at the same time, quotidian, compassionate. This style not only bears Hou's directorial signature, but also encapsulates "Hou Hsiao-hsien" as a discursive object in Taiwan. In Taiwan's film history, no other director has ever been rewarded with as many international awards as Hou; for the past two decades, no other film director has evoked as many polemics as Hou has. From the New Cinema period in the 1980s to the collapse of Taiwan films in the 1990s, Hou was confronted with various interrogations and critiques. Yet, at the same time, his standing as "Taiwan cinema's standard bearer," as one Japanese critic calls him, has grown greater and greater.[1] His name might be very small in the box office list, but his art is substantial enough to attract manufacturers such as Kirin beer, Honda, and Mitsubishi to replicate scenes from his films for their television commercials. He may not survive domestic critics' scrutiny, but he is called "the world's greatest active narrative filmmaker" in the United States.[2] He might still mortgage his house to make films, but his name is catchy enough for the government to use in representing Taiwan cinema abroad.[3]

"Hou Hsiao-hsien" is a magic word signifying a range of contradictory meanings. Hou's critics have suggested different ways of encoding this magic word, from ideological to cultural and literary. Although these methods provide illuminating accounts of Hou's works, most completely pass over the question of film form and fail to satisfy one simple inquiry: why does an unpopular cinema at home become the darling of critics abroad? Is it simply an Orientalist curiosity that bypasses a common aesthetic standard? Is it an aesthetic so culturally bounded that Taiwan audiences' poison becomes Western critics' ambrosia? In the case of Taiwan's film criticism, none of these hypotheses has been proposed and discussed. This is because what Hou Hsiao-hsien signifies at home is never truly about film or film studies. Instead, the contradictory meanings that arise from him and his works represent a cobweb of authenticity, commodity, and discursive power. "Hou Hsiao-hsien" is a key to understanding Taiwan cinema and its form, reception, and politics.

HOU AS A LACK

For me, an audience of 30,000 is just enough. I make films for a small audience.
—Hou Hsiao-hsien[4]

For a typical film producer whose only desire is to see a quick return of his or her investment, Hou Hsiao-hsien is a nightmare because he lacks a commitment to the popular. Beginning with *Boys from Fengkuei* (1983), Hou's second venture in Taiwan's New Cinema movement, his "immobile camera" and the so-called long-take aesthetics[5] have spawned what Peggy Jiao Xiongping (Chiao Hsiung-ping) called, "a polarized" reaction in Taiwan.[6] Critics who were concerned with the survival of the domestic industry questioned whether a style built on oblique narratives was the right path for Taiwan cinema to take. The veteran critic Liang Liang urged Hou to consider that "'oblique' is not the only way out," implying that Taiwan cinema needed more than just art to satisfy a heterogeneous domestic audience.[7] On the other hand, critics who were not as connected to the industry were excited to see Hou's stylistic turn. Film critic Liu Senyao writes, "Banal editing style (rapid cutting in particular) has pushed the image life of our national cinema into a cul-de-sac, away from the scope of realism. Now seeing *Boys from Fengkuei*, I feel that this film rejuvenates our national cinema—a style expressing the image of realism."[8]

To set the record straight, Hou Hsiao-hsien did not decide to make films this way when he first set foot in the trade. He began his film career in 1972 as a continuity keeper ("script girl," in Hollywood parlance) and was soon promoted to assistant director in 1974. Hou assisted studio directors making romantic melodramas in this period.[9] In 1977, Hou wrote his first script, *Good Morning Taipei*, a healthy realist film directed by Taiwan's veteran director Li Xing. "Healthy realism" *(jiankang xieshi zhuyi)* is a term coined to indicate a local style developed in the 1960s based on Italian neorealism. The Central Motion Picture Corporation (CMPC), the country's largest film production company, owned by the ruling National Party, produced a series of "healthy," "realist" films to define a national cinema coded with cultural harmony, agricultural progress, and development. These films are mostly set in rural areas with an emphasis on loyalty, family, and communal life. *The Oyster Girl* (1964), *Beautiful Ducklings* (1964), *Orchids and My Love* (1965), and *The Road* (1967) are famous examples of healthy realism. In Hou's *Son's Big Doll* and *Dust in the Wind*, we see clear citations of *The Oyster Girl* and *Beautiful Ducklings* as references to that period. When Hou directed his first film *Cute Girl* (also known as *Lovable You*), he took his protagonists (played by Taiwan's then top pop singers Feng Feifei and Kenny Bee) to the countryside in the south, where a romantic relationship was more likely to sprout. *Cute Girl* is a romantic comedy with a clear "hangover" from the healthy realist style that favors rural locals and communal life. After this successful debut, Hou made *Cheerful Wind*, yet another romantic comedy set in the Pescadore Islands, the largest offshore chain in the Taiwan Straits (a locale Hou's revisited three years later for his *Boys from Fengkuei*). By this time, Hou's reputation as a popular film director with a noticeable realist sensibility was well recognized.[10] He continued to write scripts for romantic melodrama, remaining part of the film establishment; however, when two young low-ranking producers at CMPC, Wu Nian-

Cute Girl (Jiushi liu liu de ta, 1980), Hou Hsiao-hsien's first film, a romantic comedy featuring pop singer Kenny Bee.

zhen and Xiao Ye, began to change the scene of Taiwan cinema, Hou's career came to a turning point.

In numerous interviews, Hou reminisced about the original "trauma" when he encountered the US-trained repatriates. Hou said that he was "shocked" to discover that there were other ways of making films. He'd never seen a storyboard before, until he saw how Edward Yang prepared his production. This discovery didn't scare Hou away. Instead, he was actively involved in the new project coordinated by Wu Nianzhen and Xiao Ye. First he entered into partnership with Wan Ren and Zeng Zhuangxiang (both had just graduated from American film schools) in making the omnibus *The Sandwich Man* (1983). After the phenomenal success of this first New Cinema film, Hou's tie with these young repatriates grew stronger as the New Cinema was turning into a collective movement.[11] He did the screenplay for Wan Ren's brilliant melodrama *Rapeseed Girl* (1984, also known as *Ah-fei*) and wrote, produced and starred in Edward Yang's *Taipei Story* (1984).

Boys from Fengkuei was considered a landmark in Hou's career. This film contains most of Hou's directorial signatures that he later elaborated. With this film and *Rapeseed Girl, Taipei Story,* and Hou's subsequent *A Summer at Grandpa's* (1984), the New Cinema's detached style with distant camera work, frequent uses of long takes, "natural" acting and oblique storytelling was well established. By the mid-1980s Taiwan films were losing the domestic market to big Hollywood productions and kinetic Hong Kong action films and comedies. The continuous loss of audience for *guopian* (domestic films) prompted the wretched distributors, producers, and their journalist allies to launch attacks on the New Cinema and Hou's "oblique" style in particular. With the release of his 1985 autobiographical film *A Time to Live and a Time to Die,* Hou came to signify the "polarization" of film criticism in Taiwan. These were the so-called pro-Hou faction *(yong hou pai)* and the anti-Hou faction *(fan hou pai).*[12] With Peggy Jiao at its head, the pro-Hou faction used its Western training to establish Hou's artistic standing. To Chen Guofu, Hou's longtime critical support, and film academic Qi Longren, Hou demonstrated an incredible mastery of film language in *A Time to Live and a Time to Die.*[13] To Hou's former collaborator, Wu Nianzhen, *A Time* was Hou's best film so far.[14] But the anti-Hou faction condemned him for his increasingly detached cinematography, immobile camera, and obscure storytelling. They argued that the fact that audiences did not go to his films was the best proof of his failed style. These critics took their conviction into the Golden Horse Awards, Taiwan's annual Oscar hoopla, ensuring Hou's name did not appear on the best director list.

Just as the "anti-Hou" critics had grown tired of Hou's persistent refusal to please the audience and to reengage with a more popular form of filmmaking, Hou brought home the Golden Lion award from Venice in 1990 for *City of Sadness.* This was not simply Hou's personal victory, but also a glorious moment for Hou's supporters at home in Taiwan.

A trophy from Venice meant that *City of Sadness* enjoyed sweeping box office success in Taiwan.[15] Audiences returned to *guopian,* wondering what made an infamously boring director bring home Western recognition. Hou Hsiao-hsien's name appeared, for the first time in ten years (since his *Cute Girl* and *Cheerful Wind*), on the annual box office list. He redeemed himself as a commercially worthy filmmaker and reclaimed his name as a "popular" director. "Popular" in this instance indicated Hou's speedy and timely response to the political changes of 1988.

In winter 1987, the government announced the lift of martial law that had been imposed on Taiwan's civil life for more than four decades. Hou seized this opportunity to exploit the suspension and reworked his original gangster saga into a national epic.[16] *City of Sadness* is set against the historical backdrop of a famous political incident that occurred in modern Taiwan history. On February 28, 1947, civilians rose against the government for its corruption, discrimination against Taiwanese, and unprecedented economic depression. Whenever ordinary people stand up to their rulers, they pay a high price, and this was no exception. As soon as the government took control of the situation, it retaliated. The aftermath of the February 28 Incident spawned massacres, military trials, torture, arrest, forty years of martial rule, and the subsequent suppression of the history of these events in the island.[17]

This buried history, these brutal executions by the ruling party lives vividly in the memory of the older generation. And Hou Hsiao-hsien's *City of Sadness* promised to deliver a re-presentation of, if not an account for, that history for the first time on screen. Critics were sharpening their quills, waiting to see Hou's superb deliverance on this most taboo subject in Taiwan history. The victory at Venice escalated expectations and the audience at home could not wait to see a sensational depiction of the island's worst trauma in image and sound. But all the expectations and excitements became a series of anticlimaxes after the release of the film. Symposiums and articles came out one after another to discuss *City of Sadness* and problems related to historical representation, film censorship, and, most of all, Hou's commitment to exemplifying a liberated cultural scene in the immediate post–martial law period.[18]

The criticism surrounding *City of Sadness* and Hou's politics and style culminated in the 1991 anthology *Xindianying zhi si* (Death of the New Cinema). Writers of the anthology came from various backgrounds—academics, critics, politicians, and historians. Impatient with Hou's distant cinematography, off-balance storytelling and immobile camera, they argued that Hou should have chosen a more direct approach to representing the February 28 Incident.[19] They were irked to see the opportunity for condemning the crime of the ruling Nationalist government slipping away in Hou's diffident handling of history.

But *City of Sadness* was just one count in the book's charges against Hou Hsiao-hsien. A more heinous "crime" was the 1988 promotional music video "Everything for Tomorrow" that he produced for the Ministry of Defense. Directed by one of the pro-Hou critics, Chen Guofu, scripted by Wu Nianzhen and Xiao Ye, this music video was said to appropriate the style of the New Cinema in order to hail its viewers to join the military service.[20] *Death* argued that for a filmmaker who was supposed to be the standard bearer of the New Cinema, who put Taiwan's cinema on the map, who was known for his authentic Taiwaneseness, Hou had no business in working with the most repressive state apparatuses. But he did. This music video was hard evidence of Hou's betrayal of the New Cinema. Hou sold out.[21]

Prior to *City of Sadness,* Hou was seen as a lack because he lacked the commitment—though not the capability—to make popular films. After *City of Sadness,* Hou was seen as another lack for not having "correct" politics. Hou lacked the awareness that art and cultural production in the post–martial law period was supposed to be liberating in the sense that it needed to confront the status quo, not collaborate with it. The victory at the 1989 Venice festival assured the *Death* critics of Hou's co-opted art. As a result, Hou's status at home as a national artist remained unstable and, in fact, became even more problematic.

Here we need to see the harsh criticism against Hou and the pro-Hou faction less as a witch-hunt than as an important exercise of the postrevolutionary cultural critique. In the introduction to *The Death of the New Cinema*, Li Shangren (writing under the pseudonym Mi Zou) and Liang Xinhua state that the work sets out to establish critical paradigms proper to Taiwan's context at the time. One of the several options to achieve this objective, according to the editors, is to examine auteurs and auteur theory of the New Cinema.[22] Hou Hsiao-hsien and his works became the primary targets for these progressive critics of the late 1980s to seize on in order to exemplify the complacent relationship between cultural elites and the status quo. Hou proved once more a useful object of investigation. His film art was judged as a masking of his conservative politics, thus bypassing yet another opportunity for close analysis.[23]

HOU AS *OBJET A*

I want to thank Hou Hsiao-hsien for re-inventing the cinema after it was invented for so many years. —Hasumi Shigehiko[24]

City of Sadness was not just Taiwan film's international triumph; it was also Hou's ticket to his next production, *The Puppetmaster*. Pleased with the outcome of its first collaboration with Hou Hsiao-hsien, ERA International, the company that produced *City of Sadness*, went on to produce the prequel to the film. In this first part of his Taiwan Trilogy, Hou documented the life of Li Tianlu, one of Taiwan's greatest puppeteers, during the Japanese occupation of Taiwan. In this ambitious work, Hou moved his detached style a few steps forward, mixing artifice, memory, family life, and institutions into a semidocumentary of Taiwan's colonial history. During postproduction, Hou and his editor, Liao Qingsong, developed a new narrative strategy (as compared with the editing style in *City of Sadness*) that would distance the spectator even further from an already "cloudy" depiction of the puppet master's drama, dream, and life. His scriptwriter, Zhu Tianwen, called this innovation *yunkuai jianjiefa* (cloud patch editing method), indicating Hou's intention to simulate the concordant movement of clouds. Within this system of cloud patch editing, *The Puppetmaster* is down to 100 shots with running time of 144 minutes. With Li Tianlu's commanding performance/presence and Hou's etiquette editing, *The Puppetmaster* brought home the *Palm d'Or* from Cannes in 1993. Cannes' recognition confirmed Hou's international standing, but audiences at home were not as excited as three years earlier. Distancing, delay, metonymy, or, in Hou's own words, *liubai* (leaving whiteness) were not the Taiwanese audience's cup of tea.[25] Journalists and critics in Taiwan were by now used to Hou's track record but tended to pay little attention, if not outright subject the work to hostile attacks and ridicule.[26]

Before Hou began to receive major awards in Europe, he was already a celebrated director in Japan. If he was regarded by Taiwan critics as co-opted and contaminated, he was seen by Japanese critics and scholars as ingenuous and authentic. In Japan, Hou Hsiao-hsien signifies an inspiration, a link to the origin of cinema, according to Japan's leading film scholar/critic Hasumi Shigehiko. In a talk given in Taiwan, Hasumi elaborated on the opening of *Dust in the Wind* to explain the genius of Hou Hsiao-hsien's art. It is worth quoting at length here:

> A young couple is standing inside the train. Only by looking at the scene, for someone who doesn't know Taiwan, was I aware of its timing—the after school hours. The two people standing next to each other rarely talk; from a bright place the train enters a tunnel and comes out again. The repeated change of lighting and the sound of the moving train track . . . and the two silent people on the train . . . form a situation in which light and shadow, time and sound are delicately and skillfully mixed together. How I wished this moment could extend so that I could feel its beauty and pleasure. At that moment I completely forgot what film history was, only to feel the beauty of cinema. I certainly knew cinema was invented in 1895, but at that moment, I felt that Hou Hsiao-hsien invented the cinema. Cinema lived again at that moment.[27]

For Hasumi, Hou is not only capable of fabricating a desirable Taiwan, but is also able to bring back—or, in Hasumi's words, "invent"—the primordial excitement of cinema. This discovery is most exciting to Hasumi for he is less concerned with Hou Hsiao-hsien as a director than with Hou as the possibility of cinema itself. The way Hou Hsiao-hsien recreates the unity of time and space is as if cinema was never invented at all. Hou Hsiao-hsien, in this regard, is ingenious and exquisite. His film enables Hasumi to ventriloquize Bazin's ontology of cinema—a faithful recreation of movement in time and space.[28]

Japanese critics and journalists had started to notice Hou as early as 1984 and had written extensively on Hou since then. By the time *City of Sadness* came out, Hou was so popular in Japan that he was asked to make a commercial that "used all the iconography of [his] films—trains, train tracks, laundry, long shots and long takes."[29] Entitled "Loving Heaven and Earth," this short film was intended to promote the commitment of a chemical company (Nihon Shokubai) to solving the environmental hazard of acid rain. Because in his early films Hou had shown such sensitivity toward the imagery of rain, he was pursued to undertake this task by the largest advertisement agency in Japan.[30]

Other Japanese critics appear to appreciate Hou for the antiquated, senti-

Sandwich Man (*Erzi de da wan' ou*, 1983) and his antiquated small town

mental charm found in his film world. In 1994, package tours called "journey to the places in Hou Hsiao-hsien's films" were organized by a travel agency, taking people to visit the famous Hou Hsiao-hsien sites. The four-day package tour costs 148,000 yen (around $U.S. 1,200), including visits to the locations of *City of Sadness*, *A Summer at Grandpa's*, and *Dust in the Wind*. Besides a regular guide, the tour includes an on-site lecturer to explain meanings of these locations in Hou's films.[31] In another example, consider the sandwich man in Hou's *Son's Big Doll*. This sandwich man evokes a sense of a familiar antiquity: the oldest commercial campaign for street performances and cinema in this case, when it first arrived at villages and small towns in Asia. But it is in Hou's hands that the sandwich man, with his downtrodden identity, leaves a critical impression. To do so, Hou carefully delineates the verisimilitude of the sandwich man not simply through his professional images: a clown face, a pointed paper hat, the striped baggy costume, and his red, round buffoon nose. In addition, Hou puts him in a quaint environment par excellence: a small town with quiet streets, a tiny train station, and an old blue train somnolently taking its small-minded people in and out on a daily basis.

Whether Japan's love for Hou is rooted in colonial nostalgia remains to be argued, but one cannot deny the fact that, in the eyes of Japanese critics, Hou Hsiao-hsien fulfils various desires. For a society that seems to be desperately seeking a lost history, Hou provides a (better-than-real) replica, as in the case of the package tour and the quaint locale in *Son's Big Doll*. For critics who idealize cinema as pure art, Hou satisfies that consummation with his uncompromisingly self-contained style. For historians who search for residues of Japanese imperialism, Hou answers with his Taiwan Trilogy. Hou Hsiao-hsien, in this context, proves to be another magic wand.

Hou's Japanese supporters led him to Shochiku studio to support the last chapter of the trilogy, *Good Men, Good Women*, as well as his next film, *Goodbye, South, Goodbye*. Unfortunately, these two productions failed to raise Hou's standing in Japan to a higher level. One wonders whether it is the contemporariness of these two films that pushed Hou's Japanese fans away and, if that is the case, whether it is precisely that contemporariness that opened the door for him in Europe? Hou made the following statement when referring to the success of *Flowers of Shanghai* in Paris: "Interestingly after *Good Men, Good Women*, my films were not as popular in Japan. Japanese audiences stay still with my old films; they can't accept new things. But it is the opposite in France; my films sell better and better after *Good Men, Good Women*. France is the world's center of film art after all."[32]

Flowers was shown for more than a month in the famous Paris art theatre Saint-Andre-des-Arts in 1999. As a matter of fact, Hou was never a stranger to French critics. In 1997 Oliver Assayas went to Taiwan to pay tribute to Hou Hsiao-hsien and made the documentary film *HHH: Portrait of Hou Hsiao-hsien*. His interest in Hou began when he was a critic writing for *Cahiers du cinema*. Following the exuberant attention to *Flowers*, the Cinematheque in Paris ran a complete Hou Hsiao-hsien retrospective, including his three early melodramas. Subsequently, *Cahiers du cinema* published the first Western critical appraisal, *Hou Hsiao-hsien*, as we entered the new millennium.[33]

The cover of this essay collection shows Hou holding a long incense stick, standing in front of an altar table, praying to the gods for an auspicious opening of shooting *Goodbye, South, Goodbye*. Roland Barthes's reading of mythology leads one to associate this image with the book's underlying narrative—Hou Hsiao-hsien and his "Chinese-ness." In the lead article, Jean-Michel Frodon describes Hou's oeuvre as "one of the most important contemporary alternative propositions to the mode of gaze and narrative elaborated by the West."[34] Frodon explains that Hou's alternative quality lies in his critique of montage. And montage as a concept, according to Frodon, is never part of Chinese civilization—"Chinese montage does not exist."[35] Hou's films, therefore, constitute a "rupture" in the world of cinema so dominated by "the fragmentation of a Hollywood style showbiz" on the one hand and the romantic tradition inherited in European art and theatre on the other.[36] Frodon goes on to suggest that this rupture

comes from Hou's innate identity as a *Chinese* artist inspired by Chinese painting, literature, and philosophy and a cosmic belief in an "emptiness" that tran-
scends any binary oppositions.[37] Similarly, in the essay that follows, "The Coincidence of Indirectness," Emmanuel Burdeau quotes Sun Zi's *The Art of War* to
attribute Hou's "detour" technique as part of a larger Oriental expression.[38]

"Emptiness," "antimontage," "indirect," "essentially Chinese" define Hou's film
language as a precious option outside the norms of Western cinema. To the *Cahiers* critics, there seems to have no better way than a culturalist hermeneutics
to decipher Hou's art. Hou Hsiao-hsien is great, but this is because he is Chinese.

On the other side of the Atlantic Ocean, following a showcase of Hou Hsiao-
hsien's films in the New York Film Festival in October 1999, *Village Voice* critics
enthroned Hou as the best director of the 1990s. Kent Jones, in *Film Comment,*
uses Hou Hsiao-hsien to argue for a tolerance for "difficult" films.[39] By the end
of the twentieth century, Hou was rewarded with an unprecedented recognition
that no other contemporary Chinese filmmakers ever enjoyed in the West.

The Western reception of Hou Hsiao-hsien appears both distant and familiar. In his report on Hou Hsiao-hsien in the *New York Times,* Phillip Lopate asks,
"Could it be that one of today's most important film artists . . . is a Taiwanese director virtually unknown here?"[40] Indeed, the name "Hou Hsiao-hsien" con-
notes at least two layers of meanings here—being exotic first and extraneous
second. Hou's films, especially since *Good Men, Good Women,* have become in
creasingly elaborate, exquisite, and exotic. The making of *Flowers of Shanghai,*
according to its art director, Huang Wenying, is like an archaeological journey
back to the antiquated, "authentic" China.[41] The reconstruction of life in the opium
dens consumed a major part of the production cost. But the money was not
spent in vain. With its effective Oriental allure, *Flowers of Shanghai* successfully
seduces (Western) critics and cinephiles.

Yet that seduction works because of Hou's extraneous position vis à vis centers of cultural power. In a 1987 review titled "Hou Hsiao-hsien: the Edge of the
World," J. Hoberman wrote, "New French or German directors are taken as a
matter of course; one almost has to apologize for introducing a major talent
from a backwater like Taiwan."[42] Indeed, considering a critic's job is to produce
contexts for readers to make associations, a Taiwanese director is a difficult connection to make for U.S. readers. And for Taiwan, a tiny renegade island still
sought by the mainland Chinese government, to produce such genius seems to
elicit a sense of coincidence. This coincidental sense is also what prompts French
critics to read Hou Hsiao-hsien in such a crude Orientalist fashion. Were he not
Chinese, what remains beneath his creation is a mystery. Is it really so difficult
to come to terms with Hou Hsiao-hsien that a hackneyed East versus West needs

Flowers of Shanghai (Haishang hua, 1998): a patron smoking opium in the pleasure quarters at the turn of the century

to be reenacted? In the search for ways of analyzing Hou effectively, must we always rely on such "mandates" as Marxism in the case of *Death of the New Cinema,* economic logic in the case of Taiwanese producers, cine-archaeology in the case of Hasumi, and Orientalism in the case of *Cahiers du Cinema?*

The Hou Hsiao-hsien corollary has been around for more than a decade, and it remains volatile. For instance, in the summer of 2000, several members in Shelly Kraicer's Chinese Cinema List debated the question whether Hou is elitist or esoteric, or both.[43] The discussion went on for two weeks with pro and con viewpoints regarding various readings of Hou's films. In Taiwan, scholar Qi Longren reopened the issue of politics in Taiwan's first nationwide cultural studies conference in 1999.[44] Like all previous discussions, top-down generalizations reigned while form was rarely discussed in depth to fully express the divided assessment.[45] In the following, I provide an expository discussion, a discussion of what I call the poetics of Hou Hsiao-hsien's films. I propose that by analyzing Hou's film art systematically perhaps we can decipher this magic word, its puzzle, its associated debates, and its effects at home and in the world.

Hou Hsiao-hsien and Poetics

For me, the power of creativity begins with deserting the audience. You can't worry about the problem of communicating with the audience. That's just an excuse.
—Hou Hsiao-hsien[46]

From *Cute Girl* (1980) to *Millennium Mambo* (2001), in a total of more than fourteen films, Hou's command of poetics has become ever more refined. By "poetics" I mean a series of conscious inventions in the means of expression proper to the cinema. David Bordwell's *Ozu and the Poetics of Cinema* provides the main ideas in formulating my discussion on Hou Hsiao-hsien's poetics. Bordwell defines poetics as "the study of how films are put together and how, in determinate contexts, they elicit particular effects."[47] In the case of Ozu, Bordwell urges a historical poetics of cinema, a theoretical frame of reference to answer an individual director's means of expression, his characteristic methods of storytelling and formal organization, as well as the evolution of these through various phases of a career.[48] What is significant here is not identifying or capturing aspects of authorship, attributable to Hou, but instead showing how a corpus impinges on cinema as a narrative art. Hou's corpus expands the range of devices, meanings, and effects available to filmmakers and spectators, thereby bringing poetics, not just authorial or cultural significance, to the screen.

Unlike Ozu's impressive list of fifty-six films, Hou has only made fourteen plus films so far. It might be premature at the current stage to formulate a poetics of Hou's films; however, an inductive and empirical study of Hou is timely and necessary. Film scholars, critics, and students should commit themselves to rigorous viewing of Hou's films to enter a meaningful dialogue with Hou's film language. I tentatively define poetics, in Hou's case, in terms of a consistency in narrative form, fundamental mythos, and a "feedback mechanism" that revises prior experiments and expectations.

Hou Hsiao-hsien is known for the oblique narrative, or, as Emmanuel Burdeau calls it, a "detour" narrative technique. Several factors contribute to this. One is mise-en-scène, which includes setting, scene building, and acting. Consider the contrast between the exteriors and the interiors, for instance. Hou uses landscapes to signify nature and innocence. In *The Puppetmaster* and *Goodbye, South, Goodbye*, the exterior settings connote art, independence, and freedom. Li Tianlu (played by Lin Qiang) finds self-reliance in the itinerant puppet troupe. The young punks enjoy a rare moment of liberty gliding through the mountain roads near southern Taiwan. In contrast to landscapes, Hou favors a domestic architecture typical to the southern Hokkien *(minnan)* style to represent a rigid family life. The interior design of *The Puppetmaster*, for example, is intended to evoke a close, old, and morbid domestic atmosphere. In picturing the family house where death occurs three times, Hou manipulates lighting and color to maximize the morbid aura. In addition, he uses windows, doorframes, and stairways to create multiple spaces. With regard to casting, Hou prefers inexperienced actors so that they appear "natural," "spontaneous," and, as a result, their acting will be closer to a state of "authenticity."

Last shot of the *Puppetmaster*
(*Ximeng rensheng*, 1993)

Mise-en-scène alone does not produce oblique narratives. It relies on a careful composition: it must be framed to give life to the scene. Framing is the second factor in Hou's narrative composition. It determines the size, depth, and off-screen spaces of the shot. Hou's framing in *City of Sadness* emphasizes routine, domesticity, and control as a containment of the political chaos that leaves the family bereft (as in the example discussed above). Yet that loss is manifested precisely by the persistence of the ordinary, indicated through habitual family rituals. Framing defines the boundaries of the shot and the space outside of those boundaries as well. Beyond the doorframes, we realize the existence of the outer space through the characters' movement and off-screen sound.

Chinese-speaking critics like to use "static aesthetic" *(jingtai meixue)* either to attack or show their appreciation of Hou's films. This has to do with the third factor in the oblique style: camera movement plus a relatively long distance between camera and subject, as well as occasional slight movement. This method elongates the distance between spectator and focal point of the narrative. It also delays spectators' identification and recognition of the plot. The final shot of *The Puppetmaster* is confusing because its meaning is not inherent in the shot; what appears to be a postwar pastoral is really a religious and political ritual. In a long shot that opens with a fade-in, accompanied by soothing traditional music, in the far background we see people picking over the downed aircraft. They are preparing to give thanks for answered prayers, if we recall Li's reminiscences about the end of the war.

Finally, the oblique style must rely on the long duration of the shot, that is, the long take. Hou sometimes plays tricks on the spectator in his long take set-ups. A fight scene in *Boys from Fengkuei* shows Hou's mastery of long takes and his brilliant use of location. At the beginning of the shot, we see a man with a kid entering an alleyway, walking toward the island boys, who are gambling with a food hawker. They exchange some words and everyone starts to push each other. As the fight escalates, the action moves away out of frame. After a short while, the fight comes back into frame. This process is repeated twice before there is a cut. Meanwhile, the camera remains still, restricting us to what is happening (or not) on screen: the hawker stays put at his stand, three soldiers pass by, barely curious about the disturbance. Thanks to the long duration of the shot (about thirty seconds), we must wait, observe, and reconstruct the fight based on the limited visual and audio cues granted to us.

These formal choices constitute a narrative style that might appear "boring" and "unintelligible" to audiences who are only used to popular cinema. Nevertheless, they are Hou Hsiao-hsien's way of storytelling, the core of his poetics. But techniques alone cannot produce aesthetic effects. Poetics also involves Hou's fundamental mythos, the themes that occur repeatedly in a director's works. Hou likes to draw inspirations from daily life to build his stories. Nature, cycles, growth, death, disaster, violence, memory, writing, art, and power struggle are aspects of daily life that often appear in Hou's films. He entices us to look at what are apparently ordinary experiences in a new light. Nevertheless, the emphasis on the ordinary and the mundane does not mean his films bear no political or historical weight. In his statement about *Goodbye, South, Goodbye*, Hou says his intention is to depict and preserve the "quotidian space" of Taiwan.[49] These words allow us to interpret the film beyond its nostalgic tone. The film is a coexistence of the local and the global and, as a result, depicts a developing country's resistance to globalization. We can also turn the preservation of Taiwan's "original," "authentic" space toward defining Taiwan as a country without a recognized identity.

Eating occurs in all of Hou's films, not just once, but several times. Again, the meaning of a daily ritual often goes beyond its surface. The last supper in *City of Sadness* is similar to other eating scenes in the film. If we revisit the scene, though, there are differences. The three people around the table are the grandfather, the retarded son (a victim of political brutality), and the young grandson. Who is absent here? The remaining sons, who are lost, killed, or imprisoned. To his depictions of the domestic life of Taiwanese Han culture, Hou also added his critique of the state's brutality. Hou's *Flowers of Shanghai* provides vivid example of his poetics, the fundamental mythos and "feedback mechanism."

The Myopia of *Flowers of Shanghai*

Like all artists who spend their lives repeating, revising, and refining their works, Hou reiterates his themes, recycles his techniques, and searches for new ideas to add to his creations. This leads us to the "feedback mechanism," the last component of Hou's poetics. The "feedback mechanism" allows Hou to examine his early works and provides new inspirations for his next project. *Flowers of Shanghai* is regarded as a departure from Hou's previous works because of the subject matter and the use of fades and more frequent camera movements. In this tribute to the fading of the twentieth century, Hou takes us northward to China's oldest metropolis, away from tropical Taiwan.[50] He shows us Changsan Quarters in late nineteenth-century Shanghai and his reconstruction of the concubine world. In addition to this rare subject matter, *Flowers of Shanghai* employs film language that appears remarkably different from that of his previous films. The first distinction is the consistent use of fades throughout the film. The second obvious change is the closer distance between the camera and characters. The third difference is a frequently moving camera. When we watch the film at first glance, these features appear "new" because they are seldom used in Hou's earlier films. But when we look closely at these features, we find that they still operate according to the principles of Hou's poetics.

Fades function as editing in this film, and, if we watch carefully, nearly 40 percent of the scenes remain unchanged after the fadeout. In addition, each scene is built on just one single shot. For example, there are three shots in the sequence introducing the prostitute Shen Xiaohong and her Huifang quarter. The first shot introduces Shen's customer Master Wang, his friend Tang, and Shen's head maid Chun, who is negotiating on the behalf of her mistress. After a fade-out/-in, in the same setting we see Shen sitting on the other side of the scene, weeping. A fade-out ends the shot, which is immediately superimposed by a fade-in to the following shot. Again, the place remains the same but the story is advancing. We see a man writing a check (issued by Mater Wang to pay off Shen's debt) and a witness sitting to the side who sees the transaction. Then comes another fade to end this sequence in which the first prostitute of the story is introduced.

This editing pattern remains the same throughout the entire film. Between a fade-out and fade-in, Hou uses a pattern of one shot/one scene to tell his story. And each setting is limited to three to four shots. We can conclude that the use of fades maintains spatial unity while executing a temporal ellipsis. This strategy makes it easier for the spectator to recognize the passing of time within the same setting. Spatial unity and temporal ellipsis are precisely the key features of Hou's oblique style. Moreover, the method of dividing a narrative sequence into three to four units indicates the recycling of Hou's systematic, restricted, and economic pattern of storytelling. These observations show that, despite the change in editing method, *Flowers* does not deviate far from Hou's narrative pattern. It remains part of Hou's poetic system.

A closer look at the characters and frequently moving camera are the other two distinctive changes in *Flowers*. In a recent interview, Hou pointed out how and why he made such a style change:

> My idea of cinema before making *Fengkuei* was rather simple: narrative, to tell the story in the script. Later on I met some filmmakers who'd returned to Taiwan from abroad. They had a lot of theories about cinema, which got me all confused. I was puzzled; the script was ready but I didn't know how to give it form. At that time my scriptwriter was Zhu Tianwen. After listening to me she gave me a copy of Shen Congwen's autobiography. After reading the book I discovered that Shen's point of view was somewhat like looking down from above.
>
> Making *Flowers of Shanghai*, I put the camera very close to the characters and watch them, without interference, without judgement, and without emotion. Previously I thought the camera must stay at a distance to present a point of view that overlooks things and is without emotion. With this film I discovered that such a point of view is actually contingent upon how you present the characters. You can be very cool and cold on the set, and still like and love your character[s], you can be with them and at the same time watch over them. You can still achieve the same result even with the camera moving on them. The camera is like a person sitting on the side. He's looking at these people. Sometimes he's looking at this person from this side. Then he hears a voice over there and turns his head. Since the camera cannot turn as fast as a human head, it turns slowly. So maybe by the time he's turned his head that person may have left or stopped talking. But that's okay. In fact it's rather like the narrative in the original novel.[51]

It would seem inevitable that a closer and more intimate relation would bring alive the concubine world of the nineteenth century. Nevertheless, Hou says that he still wants to maintain his "cold," "without emotion" observation of his characters. These are keys to the quiet style that he has established since *Boys from Fengkuei*. Hou says that he wants to move closer to the characters. But does this dictate that the camera actually moves according to the voice and movement of the characters? Is it true that the camera captures the action based on a casual, spontaneous movement? These questions need a careful, close analysis.

Let us choose a sequence with highly elaborate camera movement. This sequence is about conspiracy, one of the main activities in the concubine world. It shows how Zhou Shuangzhu, one of the four major prostitutes featured in the story, and her friend Master Hong conspire to solve the dispute between Zhou's subordinate and her supposed lover-customer. The sequence comprises two scenes. In the first scene, we see a maid carrying opium pipes up a stairway, walking toward the living room of Zhou's quarter. The camera remains in a fixed position when it shows the maid entering the scene, but once the maid starts to approach the living room, the camera begins to move inward in order to make room for the maid. The maid walks directly toward the left side of the frame where she needs to serve the pipes. Accordingly, the camera pans toward the left, on a horizontal line, to follow the maid's movement. Once the maid stops and serves, the camera stops moving. Then Master Hong arrives. He comes in, saying hello to his worried friend, and sits down next to Zhou. To accommodate Hong and his action, we notice that the camera moves slightly to reframe the scene not once, but twice.

Now, does the camera actually follow Master Hong? The answer is no. On the surface, the camera's movement seems subject to character's movement. But it is not the character's movement that is leading the camera but the mise-en-scène, the spatial design of the scene. In other words, the setting of the scene prescribed first and foremost, how the character should move. Second, it prescribes how the camera should move according to its position to the character and its relation with the setting. The earlier observation of the "change of style" should be reversed: when the camera moves around inside those quarters, we see the characters moving according to the position of the camera. Not only that, they move around within the restricted area of the camera movement. In other words, when Hou wants to be more intimate, he still favors a relatively static camera position and a unity with a carefully designed interior.

Hou says that *Flowers of Shanghai* is about women, particularly powerful women who are supposed to be weak and powerless. This paradox is behind the mesmerizing depiction of concubine culture in Shanghai at the turn of the century. But if we put these women back into Hou's mythos, they are variations on Hou's ultimate concern with human survival. To survive, Hou's heroines betray, lie, cheat, fight, maneuver, write, give birth, and eat. These Shanghai flowers are no exceptions. Only this time, the reiteration seems to fall short. The painstaking "restoration" of the nineteenth-century pleasure quarters of Shanghai shows Hou's venture into the world of rococo. The publication of the two picture books associated with the film indicates the production crew's need to share with the audience their meticulous research in rebuilding the old, decadent Shanghai. But in all these admirable efforts, Hou's mythos appears for the first

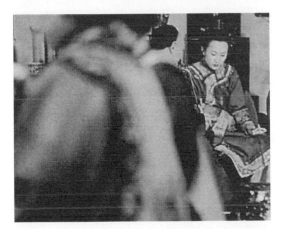

Flowers of Shanghai. Camera movement is restricted by the set design

time as a claustrophobic circularity. These opulent living quarters are in fact, enclaves. They are little kingdoms (ruled by queens) arrested in time. These beautiful mistresses appear to be in full control, but they cannot escape the rules of the concubine world that they themselves perpetuate. Therefore, in this film there is a kind of circular fatality lending a sense of entrapment. This explains why eating and opium smoking as recurring motifs are used to conclude the film. Eating and smoking are repeatedly used in the film to "sublimate" the sexual contract between a prostitute and her patron. Eating and smoking also simulates a marriage relationship between courtesan and customer. At the end, eating and smoking becomes a coded ritual illuminating the circular fate of these Shanghai flowers.

Here, then, is an evocation of an incipient moment, a time whose historical possibilities remain unopened. The world of *Flowers*, however, is aesthetically overdetermined: art, fashion, and ritual dominate these decadent, gaslit chambers. If the world of these "flowers" seems hard to reconcile with the boys from Fengkuei (or with Kenny Bee), it is because the world of Hou's poetics keeps expanding its parameters, renewing its protocols. Kenny Bee, the Fengkuei boys, the puppet master, leftist martyrs, gangsters, and Shanghai prostitutes are all but building blocks of a much larger project, the exact shape of which is still emerging. At this point we are all, including Hou himself, standing too close to what may become an enormous cinematic mural.

Notes

This chapter is an expansion of an early short piece, "The Poetics of Hou Hsiao-hsien's Films: *Flowers of Shanghai*," in *Cinedossier: The 35th Golden Horse Awards-Winning Films* (Taipei: Golden Horse Film Festival, 1999), 94–97. I would like to thank Darrell W. Davis for his comments and Jady Long for helping me trace some of the key sources.

1. K. Ono, *"Tai-wan eiga no Kishu"* (Taiwan cinema's steersman: Hou Hsiao-hsien), *Cho* 347 (June 1990): 358–367.

2. Phillip Lopate, "A Master Everywhere Else Is Ready to Try America" *New York Times*, October 10, 1999, sect, 2, p. 13.

3. In 1999, Hong Kong Arts Centre presented a special program, "Taiwan Film Festival 99: A Tribute to Hou Hsiao-hsien," featuring nine films, including the Hong Kong premiere of *Flowers of Shanghai*. This program was initiated and funded by Kwang Hua Cultural and Information Centre, a representative of Taiwan's government information office in Hong Kong. Hou Hsiao-hsien's service to promote Taiwan's culture and cinema is clear in this event. Hou himself came to the opening event and stayed in Hong Kong for three days, meeting with the press and critics.

4. Hou made this statement in response to a question about the reception of *Flowers of Shanghai* in Taiwan, June 16, 1999, Hong Kong Arts Centre.

5. The terms, "immobile camera" and "long-take aesthetics" are coined by his long-term scriptwriter Zhu Tianwen in her introduction to the published script of *Good Men, Good Women*. See *Hao nan, hao nü* (Good men, good women), Hou Hsiao-hsien's production notes and screenplay (Taipei: Yuan-liou Publishing, 1995), 9.

6. Peggy Jiao, "Great Changes in a Vast Ocean: Neither Tragedy Nor Joy." Interview with Hou Hsiao-hsien, in *Taiwan Films* (Taipei: Variety, 1993), 3–60.

7. Liang Liang, *"Dan bushi weiyi de lu"* (Obscure is not the only way out), in Li Youxin, ed., *Dianying, dianying ren, dianying kanwu* (Film, film people and film magazines) (Taipei: Independent News, 1986), 98–107.

8. Liu Senyao, *"Cong fenggui lai de ren kan dianying de xieshi zhuyi"* (On film's realism: *Boys from Fengkuei*), in Li Youxin, ed., *Gangtai liu da daoyen* (Six directors from Hong Kong and Taiwan) (Taipei: Independent News, 1986), 128.

9. For a relatively complete filmography of Hou Hsiao-hsien up to 1993, see Sachio Yamazaki, *Hou Hsiao-hsien* (Tokyo: Asahi Shimbun, 1993), 208–209.

10. Personal interview with Wu Nianzhen, January 8, 1999, Taipei.

11. For more on Wu Nianzhen and the development of the New Cinema, see Darrell W. Davis, "Borrowing Postcolonial: *Dou-san* and the Memory Mine," in the present volume.

12. Jiao, "Great Changes in a Vast Ocean," 3–10.

13. Chen Guofu made this comment in Olivier Assayas, *HHH: Portrait of Hou Hsiao-hsien* (1998); Qi Longren uses auteur theory to discuss Hou Hsiao-hsien's narrative, in *"Tongnian wangshi: liangzhong yuedu fangshi"* (A time to live and a time to die: two ways of reading), in his *Dianying chensi ji* (A collection of contemplations on cinema) (Taipei: Yuanshen Press, 1987), 89–94.

14. See Assayas' interview with Wu Nianzhen, in *HHH: Portrait of Hou Hsiao-hsien*.

15. *City of Sadness* set a box office record of 30 million Taiwan dollars, next to Jackie Chan's *Mr. Canton and Lady Rose* in 1990.

16. Lee Wu Nianzhen and Zhu Tianwen, *Beiqing chengshi* (City of sadness) (Taipei: Yuan-liou Publishing, 1989), 18–20.

17. For a more detailed account on the February 28 Incident, see the section "Behind *City of Sadness*: the February 28 Incident" of my on-line publication on *City of Sadness* with Abe-Nornes Markus [http://cinemaspace.berkeley.edu/Papers/CityOfSadness].

18. Intellectuals in Taiwan have historically looked at cinema as entertainment and therefore not a worthy object of scholarly attention. This bias changed in the 1960s, when three young directors deftly presented their ethical melodramas, tackling problems of traditional culture. That was also the first time that intellectuals were attracted to domestic films. The second time film attracted talks of similar density took place during the New Cinema Movement in the 1980s. But the third round regarding *City of Sadness* and Hou Hsiao-hsien behaved more like a controversy than an endorsement or compliment.

19. For a brief summary of the articles, see the section "Behind *City of Sadness*: The Controversy" of my on-line publication on *City of Sadness* [http://cinemaspace.berkeley.edu/Papers/CityOfSadness] and *Xindianying zhi si* (Death of the new cinema) (Taipei: Tangshan Press, 1991), 122–168.

20. See *Death of the New Cinema*, 31–52.

21. It is interesting to note that in the Japanese filmography of Hou Hsiao-hsien we cannot find a trace of this music video. See Sachio Yamazaki, *Hou Hsiao-hsien*, 208–209.

22. *Death of the New Cinema,* xi.

23. For response to the Hou criticism in *Death of the New Cinema,* see two Chinese articles, respectively, Yeh Yueh-yu, *"Nüren zhende wufa jinru lishi: zai du Beiqing chengshi"* (Why can't women enter the history: re-viewing *City of Sadness*), *Contemporary Monthly* 101 (September 1994): 64-85, and Shen Shiao-ying, *"Benlai jiu yinggai duokan liangbian: dianying meixue yu Hou hHsiao-Hsien"* (Can't they be vegetables? Film aesthetics and Hou Hsiao-hsien), *Chung-wai Literary Monthly* 26.10 (1998): 27–47.

24. Hasumi Shigehiko, *"Kaoguxue de huanghu: hou hsiao-hsien de* beiqing chengshi" (An oblivion of archaeology: on Hou Hsiao-hsien's *City of Sadness*). Translated by Zhang Changyen, *Film Appreciation* 13.1 (1995): 87.

25. Hou Hsiao-hsien used *liubai,* a technique common in Chinese ink painting, to define the empty shots in *The Puppetmaster.* See Jiao, "Great Changes in a Vast Ocean," 3–47.

26. Peggy Jiao noted that the pro-Hou and anti-Hou "hoopla was silenced after Hou became the darling of international festivals." Jiao, "Great Changes in a Vast Ocean," 3–10.

27. Hasumi, "An Oblivion of Archaeology," 84.

28. Andre Bazin, "The Ontology of the Photographic Image," in *What Is Cinema?* Vol. 1. Translated by Hugh Gray (Berkeley: University of California Press, 1967), 9–16.

29. See Abes-Nores and Yeh, "Ozu and Hou: Nation and Industry."

30. Yokoo Yoshinobu, *"Eiga to komashyaru"* (Film and commercial), in Sachio Yamazaki, *Hou Hsiao-hsien,* 179–180.

31. See the insert of the advertisement in Suzuki Fumiko, *"Eiga de aruku tai-wan"* (Film walks in Taiwan), in Sachio Yamazaki, *Hou Hsiao-hsien,* 135.

32. Li Dayi, *"Hou hsiao-hsien de dianying rensheng"* (Hou Hsiao-hsien's film life), *Film Appreciation* 17.3 (1999): 82.

33. A few months after the release of the French anthology, Taiwan answered with a Chinese anthology edited by academics. See Lin Wenchi, Shen Shiao-ying, and Li Chenya, eds., *Xi lian rensheng: hou hsiao-hsien dianying yenjiu* (Passionate detachment: films of Hou Hsiao-hsien) (Taipei: Rye Field Publishing, 2000).

34. Jean-Michel Frodon, "En haut du mangueire de Fengshan, immerge dans l'espace et le temps," in *Hou Hsiao-hsien* (Paris: Cahiers du cinema, 1999), 11.

35. "Chinese montage does not exist" (Le montage chinois n'existe pas) is one of the subheadings of Frodon's introductory article. Ibid., 22.

36. Ibid., 24.

37. Ibid., 23.

38. Emmanuel Burdeau, *"Les aleas de l'indirect,"* in *Hou Hsiao-hsien* (Paris: Cahiers du cinema, 1999) 29.

39. Kent Jones, "Cinema with a Roof over Its Head," *Film Comment* [http://www.filmlinc.com/fcm/9-10-99/hou.html].

40. Lopate, "A Master Everywhere Else Is Ready to Try America."

41. Yuang Wenying and Cao Zhiwei, *Hai-shang fan-hua lu* (Notes on the making of *Flowers of Shanghai*) (Taipei: Yuan-liou Publishing, 1998).

42. J. Hoberman, "Hou Hsiao-hsien: The Edge of the World," in *Vulgar Modernism: Writing on Movies and Other Media* (Philadelphia: Temple University Press, 1991), 104–105.

43. See Chinese Cinema List, number 367, 383–389.

44. Qi Longren, *"Jiuling niandai taiwan dianying wenhua lunshu: yi beiqing chengshi wei li"* (Discourses of studies in Taiwan film culture of the 90s: using *City of Sadness* as an example), *1999 Wenhua yenjiu de hueigu yu zhanwang yentaohuei lunwen ji* (1999 annual conference proceedings: the practices of cultural studies in Taiwan: retrospects and prospects) (Taipei: Association of Cultural Studies, 1999), 274–282.

45. David Bordwell, "Transcultural Spaces: Toward a Poetics of Chinese Film," in the present volume.

46. Li Dayi, "Hou hsiao-hsien's Film Life," 82.

47. David Bordwell, *Ozu and the Poetics of Cinema* (Princeton, N.J.: Princeton University Press, 1988), 1.

48. Ibid.

49. Hou made this point in a promotional documentary of *Goodbye, South, Goodbye*.

50. *Flowers of Shanghai* is a literary adaptation from Han Ziyun's novel *Hai shang hua*. The work was first released in 1894 in its original Wu dialect. It was then translated into Mandarin by Zhang Ailing (Eileen Chang) in the 1970s.

51. Li, Dayi, "Hou Hsiao-hsien on Interview," *Taiwan Film Festival 99: A Tribute to Hou Hsiao-hsien* (Hong Kong: Hong Kong Arts Centre, 1999), 19.

Jia Zhangke's Cinematic Trilogy

A Journey across the Ruins of Post-Mao China

A gifted young director, Jia Zhangke had by 2000 created three major films of new Chinese cinema of the "Sixth Generation," including *Xiaoshan Huijia* (Xiaoshan Going Home, 1995), *Xiaowu* (Xiao Wu, 1997), and *Zhantai* (Platform, 2000).[1] In these three works, Jia conscientiously explores one man's journey across a ruinous "post-Mao" China.[2] The first shot of *Xiaoshan Going Home* is, strangely, a wood block print that depicts a young man facing up to Mao's portrait on Tiananmen (Gate of Heavenly Peace). In the print the late chairman, appears like a ghostly father figure to the somehow bewildered youth. As Mao's successor Deng Xiaoping has observed, "It isn't only his [Mao's] portrait which remains in Tiananmen Square, it is the memory of a man who guided us to victory and built a country."[3] In an introductory sequence of *Xiao Wu*, however, the itinerant protagonist's theft on a bus is intercut with Mao's portrait hanging at the driver's seat. Here the irony is quite clear: without Mao's guidance, the country has turned pathetically "lawless," especially for a lost young generation that concerns the Sixth-Generation directors dearly. In a similar fashion, *Platform* begins with a stage performance titled *A Train Traveling toward Shaoshan*, a reference to a pilgrimage to Mao's birthplace, which is deemed sacred in the Chinese Revolution. Hence, the opening of Jia's trilogy symbolically initiates a long and tedious journey, only to be accomplished by a male protagonist under the shadow of Mao/Holy Ghost in postmodern terms.

In iconography, this male protagonist/traveler in each film is always played by Wang Hongwei, a talented amateur actor and a new icon of contemporary Chinese cinema. Wang's physical features are typical of an "antihero" in Hollywood classics: he is a small, lanky young man wearing hilariously huge bifocals. In Jia's directing strategy, Wang Hongwei's imagery is persistently used to represent a prodigal son who would challenge the father (be it natural or symbolic) in whatever "unlawful" manner. Spatially, this one man's journey starts from the capital city Beijing in *Xiaoshan Going Home*, continues in a small town called Fenyang in *Xiao Wu*, and finishes in a unknown, barren land in *Platform*.[4] To parallel this passage, I will examine the Wang Hongwei character's journey according to that spatial and temporal order found in Jia Zhangke's cinematic trilogy.

Xiaoshan Going Home: "Who Is Not Afraid of the Big Boss?"

In Jia Zhangke's debut work, the protagonist Xiaoshan is a young man from the countryside, lured to Beijing in search of a better life.[5] In the official Chinese vocabulary, such a character is called *mingong*, meaning "a laborer working on a public project"[6] who belongs with "the 'floating population' (*youmin*) of migrant laborers who travel to and from the cities in search of such temporary work as they can find."[7] The film's storyline is set in Beijing during the eve of Chinese New Year of 1994, and the entire film is shot with a hand-held camera on real locations in the capital city, including famous streets, market places, subways, university buildings, and slum areas. Moreover, all of the characters are played by amateur actors who speak with provincial dialects, and the film surely has a gritty semidocumentary flavor.

As the film opens with Mao's spectral portrait in Tiananmen Square, we simultaneously hear on the soundtrack the rough voice of an invisible woman: "Who is not afraid of the big boss (*da laoban*)?" The symbolism of the imagery combined with the sound is obvious: in a Chinese mind, the late chairman was the "big boss" that nobody dared to challenge while he was *alive*. But, now that the Chairman is dead, a reasonable question should be raised: in post-Mao China, *who* is the new "big boss" whom everyone fears? In *Xiaoshan Going Home*, as it turns out, the enormous vacuum the deceased "big boss" left behind is to be filled not by any *superman*, but by the driving force of a capitalist market economy.

In the first scene, we see a slim and pale Xiaoshan in a cook's white uniform cutting vegetables at a grimy restaurant kitchen. This country boy wears his hair long, as is popular in big cities, although he is one of the "migrant laborers" despised by local residents for their rustic "uncivilized" manners. Naturally, Wang Hongwei has the look of an "antihero," and there is eerily comic-tragic quality to his facial expression and posture. With such feeble and uninviting physique, Wang's imagery presents a striking contrast to that of "revolutionary hero" expressive of male chauvinism and patriarchal authority in Chinese cinema of the Mao era. In this sense, Wang characterizes a "flawed" masculinity felt in Chinese films of the post-Mao reform era, as I will further demonstrate below.

At the moment, Xiaoshan is angry at his "big boss," who gave his employees no day off for the coming Chinese New Year. Sensing Xiaoshan's discontent, the "big boss" fires him on the spot. This episode seems to answer the question of whom to fear in the post-Mao era: the new "big boss" is a capitalist market system that disgraces almost everyone in the film. Now a "free" man, Xiaoshan telephones Wang Xia, a girl from his village, asking her to go home with him for the New Year celebration. When they meet on a bustling street called Chegong-zhuang, located northwest of the capital city, Xiaoshan hurries off without a word, leaving the fashionably dressed Wang Xia behind. A second later, we learn that the girl is a prostitute, whose customers summon her by the pager she carries, which irritates Xiaoshan to no end. When Wang Xia is too "busy" to spend the holidays with Xiaoshan, the angry young man blames the girl for her cheap "occupation." What we hear from Wang Xia is rather shocking, as she hits back at her male accuser: "I sell cunt, *what* do you [men] sell?" (Wang Xia's line is subtitled in Chinese as if being used in a silent movie). And she continues: "If I were you [men], I would steal and rob. My mother is sick in bed, and crying out of pain. Don't you think I'm willing to do this? Who among you [men] *takes care* of me?" Contrary to expectation, Xiaoshan is silent.

Both Xiaoshan and Wang Xia are "migrant laborers" in Beijing, bound to their own "village" communities that are generally isolated from local urban populace.[8] Within this "rural" community situated in a big city, men still exercise power over their women "folks" and care for them by tradition. Because Xiaoshan himself hardly survives the new capitalist market system, his male "authority" is undermined before women. When Xiaoshan imposes his will on an "easy" woman of his kinship, he is crushed badly because he is unable to protect her as required by old agrarian communal "laws." As a result, Xiaoshan no longer has influence over Wang Xia's personal "behavior" or life.

To make up for Wang Xia's grief, Xiaoshan accompanies the girl on a holiday shopping excursion to Xidan, a commercial district in western downtown Beijing. Soon after, we follow them through a gaudy and boisterous marketplace set in Yuetan (Moon Altar), a scenic public park not far from Xidan. This lengthy "shopping" episode is shot with the hand-held camera that efficiently invites us to see "the driving force" of capitalist market economy in mid-1990s China. Time and again, Wang Xia stops to examine some beautiful cloths at a vendor's stand, but she leaves, disappointed after learning the price.[9]

At the end of their shopping trip, Wang Xia and Xiaoshan rest against a ped-dler's stall full of "luxury" woman's fur coats that the call girl craves but cannot afford. Disenchanted, she asks Xiaoshan to "tell" her family that she will not be back home for the holidays because she is busy as a "housemaid" in Beijing. At this moment Wang Xia's pager rings again—another "customer" phones her for service. Thus, in this mise-en-scène of a cheerless farewell, the two "migrant la-borers" are helplessly "locked" in that ruthless free-market system. Wang Xia then vanishes into a dark back alley nearby, which quickly empties. If frantic marketplace activity adds "liveliness" to Beijing, the bare alley compels us to feel a *void* in the capitalistic "prosperity" experienced in Chinese cities during the mid-1990s.

Xiaoshan takes the subway back to his place in the city, and we follow him alone on a long excursion into Beijing's underground. Once more, we stumble across one vender's stall after another, strewn around the dim subway station. Everywhere in the city, above and below, we hear that frenzied market noise on the soundtrack, only this time no subway rider bothers to pause and look at any merchandise. The same gloomy void, it seems, falls upon those tired urban dwell-ers. A medium shot of a sad-faced Xiaoshan holding his "Xidan" shopping bag on the train sarcastically hints at his irrelevance to the city's "prosperity." In the scene that follows, we see Xiaoshan "back home," and that irrelevance is more evident—he lives in a slum of the "thriving" capital. In my view, such a slum rep-resents a ruined "past" socialism, especially in Beijing.[10] And people mostly as-sociated with this "past" and bankrupt socialism are "the victims, not the ben eficiaries, of China's state-sponsored capitalism."[11] Thus, Xiaoshan's and Wang Xia's previous shopping trip paid a tribute to that "state-sponsored capitalism," whereas the young man's lonely homecoming expresses an elegy to the past so-cialism, whose "residual" young citizens, such as Xiaoshan and Wang Xia, hardly survive the new "big boss" of Chinese capitalism.

Xiaoshan makes a second cross-town trip to the Beijing University of Tele-communications, where he visits his fellow villager Wang Dongfang, a student at the school. In a shadowy university dormitory, Xiaoshan asks Wang to pick some college textbooks for his relatives back home, and Wang promises to meet him in a bookstore at Qianmen the next day. Back in his slum, Xiaoshan cele-brates the new year by drinking with several fellow villagers, who talk dirty about Wang Yinhua, a village girl working for the same "big boss" as Xiaoshan's in that shady restaurant in Beijing. The following morning, Wang Yinhua shows up at Xiaoshan's place, but she refuses to go home with him because she wants to enjoy the New Year in the capital. Rejected a second time by a woman from his village, Xiaoshan crossly makes love to the girl in bed without her consent. Afterward, they ride together on a bicycle and pass by Deshengmen (Gate of Victorious Virtue), a most beautiful ancient city gate to have survived both socialist and global capitalist destruction in the past decades. On the street, Xiaoshan eats his breakfast alone at a "tiny open-air restaurant," leaving Wang Yinhua aside. This somehow peculiar scene, however, corresponds to Xiaoshan's compulsory sex with Wang early on. In a sense, Xiaoshan's coarse treatment of Wang is the vengeance of a "poor loser." Because the rustic youth cannot fight against the "big boss" running the capitalist market economy, he picks on Wang Yinhua, who is still working for the most hated "big boss." By abusing the "woman folks" from his village, such as an innocent Wang Yinhua, Xiaoshan believes he "exercises" his "male power" that is crushed by Chinese capitalism in a big city. Here Xiaoshan's "rationale" is certainly pitiful and preposterous, but it is also "customary" within a rural communal system.

Xiaoshan next makes his cross-town trip to Beijing's Nanzhan, or South Railroad Station. During the Chinese New Year, the train ticket is a "hot commodity" in the black market outside the station, especially for "migrant laborers." After a year's toil in the city, they are eager to go home and spend their hard-earned money on the expensive tickets. Xiaoshan finds Qinghua, a fellow-villager specializing in this "underground" business. And Qinghua introduces Xiaoshan to his "woman folks" at the black market, for a "deal" often takes place inside lady's rooms of the station. Yet those ladies have nothing available at the moment, so Qinghua invites Xiaoshan to lunch in a restaurant, adding that "there are two gangs," a hint at the fierceness of the black market. All of sudden, a tall young man enters the restaurant. Having glanced at Qinghua, the man immediately leaves. In the meantime, Qinghua persuades Xiaoshan not to go home this year. Xiaoshan answers: "I *have to go home* for the New Year." Unfortunately, it is *a belief* that none of his fellow-villagers—men and women alike—have so far shared with him. When Qinghua goes out to buy some gifts for Xiaoshan to bring home, he is harshly beaten on the street. The brawl turns out to be a "show of force" by Qinghua's "rival gang" members in the "trade," including the tall young man who "spotted" him at the restaurant. This street violence brings an end to Xiaoshan's "mission" to acquire a train ticket. These events all but shatter his dream of "going home for the New Year *(huijia guonian)*"—a sacred ritual for "the floating population" in Chinese big cities.

Despite these events, Xiaoshan is an unyielding believer in this ritual. He completes his last cross-town trip to Qianmen, where he has made plans to meet Wang Dongfang in a bookstore. The university student, however, has forgotten about this appointment—he went to Tianjin for the holidays. In a close-up, we see Xiaoshan standing in a phone booth on a swarming street of Qianmen, lonely and disheartened. As evinced in the movie, every one of Xiaoshan's trips across Beijing to seek company or help wind up in vain. Nobody from his "village" community in the city is able to abide by that hallowed "Chinese New Year" ritual any longer. In the Deng era of Chinese capitalism, "who is not afraid of the big boss" that has eclipsed Chairman Mao? In fact, Xiaoshan's "journey" does "homage" to the dead Mao/Father that provided the Chinese people with no "capitalist" material goods but a "socialist" sanctuary—which is now in ruins. The last scene of *Xiaoshan Going Home* is astonishingly "otherworldly." Against a tranquil vista of Beijing's high rises, the protagonist is getting a haircut in a sunny street. By shaving off his "Western-style" long hair, Xiaoshan finally admits his irrelevance to this grand Chinese city of a capitalist "boom" and returns to his rural roots placidly.[12]

Xiao Wu: An Unhappy Loner and an "Easy" Woman

Jia Zhangke's second feature, *Xiao Wu*, begins with a bleak scene of China's dusty country road. In it a peasant family of three—father, son and daughter—is waiting at a bus stop. In the next shot, the film's central character Xiao Wu (Wang Hongwei) emerges from a similar, stark landscape of the country's bus line. Dressed in an oversized jacket and baggy trousers, this lean and pale country boy stands alone by the road and edgily smokes a cigarette. In the distance, a smoking tall chimney of a steel factory rises from a barren mountain slope. In my view, the mise-en-scène in this introductory sequence serves to link the youthful protagonist with China's socialist past. Such a steel factory was run by the so-called rural people's commune in the Mao era, producing no usable steel but a great deal of poisonous smoke. It then grows to be a "residue" of the disastrous "Great Leap Forward" campaign launched by Mao almost three decades ago.[13] Allegorically, because Xiao Wu's journey starts from *here*—that is, the ruins of a problematic socialist past—he is doomed to turn into a "residual" figure unfit for China's new reform era.

We find this "residual" trait in Xiao Wu in the first instance soon after he gets on a bus. The conductor asks him to buy a ticket but he refuses, saying: "I'm a policeman." To our surprise, Xiao Wu's phony reply sends the conductor away. (It was in the Mao era that the police ordinarily enjoyed such a "privilege" while on duty, and yet it may continue into Deng's era of economic reforms as another type of "residue.") A moment later, Xiao Wu's true identity is revealed when he successfully snatches a passenger's wallet. As mentioned, Xiao Wu's theft on the bus is intercut with a Mao portrait hanging at the driver's seat. The sarcastic tone of this montage is twofold: Xiao Wu's appropriation of the police "benefit" under Mao's rule, and his lawbreaking penchant while Mao/Father is gone. So, from the very beginning, the protagonist's travel is an ironic "pilgrimage" to the dead father's institutional and moral "legacy" as signified by a catastrophic steel factory and a lawless youngster. Paradoxically, Xiao Wu's "pilgrimage" ends in Fenyang, a small town in northern China, where the local government is resolute to "strike hard *(yanda)*" against various crimes ranging from shoplifting to smuggling to prostitution. In every corner of the city, "strike hard" propaganda is aired through loud speakers, and policemen and television network reporters interview people at random on the street. In this town of a thrilled "mass mobilization," though, Xiao Wu is a loner. The pickpocket and his "crew" —a few boys clothed in the same outsized suits as his—cleverly dodge the police and the media in the crowd. Yet Xiao Wu's evasion is merely indicative of his total isolation from a post-Mao Chinese society.

Even a loner like Xiao Wu has friends beyond his tiny "underclass" circle. Having arrived at Fenyang by that "free" bus, Xiao Wu first runs into his old friend Gengsheng in the street, who gives Xiao Wu a ride on his bicycle. Gengsheng is the owner of a traditional Chinese drug store called *"Huichun"* (Spring Returning), which makes him also a "residual" figure from the Mao era. On their bicycle trip to downtown Fenyang, Gengsheng mentions to Xiao Wu: "Xiao Yong is doing well these days, and I saw him *on TV* yesterday." Xiao Yong is a "sworn brother" of Xiao Wu back in the 1980s (the movie's storyline is set in 1997), and both of them have a Chinese tattoo on their arms that says *"youfu tongxiang"* (share good fortune). Not long before, Xiao Yong was also a pickpocket, but of late the authorities have designated him a *"mofan qiyejia"* (model entrepreneur). Xiao Yong's "success story" and his new marriage are well publicized by the local television station alongside the "strike hard" campaign party line. Unlike Xiao Wu, who stays away from the police and the media, Xiao Yong is a "media savvy" businessman who grants a public relations interview to a television anchor and invites her crew to film his wedding activities. Xiao Yong, however, "neglects" to inform his "sworn brother" Xiao Wu of his wedding because the latter is only a reminder of his own shady past—so it is an embarrassment to his newly acquired social status. (Soon we learn that Xiao Yong's "business" is nothing other than smuggling cigarettes and running karaoke bars—in other words, brothels—in Fenyang, an enterprise as reprehensible as his old trade of picking pockets.

Among those "honorary" guests to attend Xiao Yong's wedding is Hao Youliang, a middle-aged and kind policeman who used to detain the two "sworn brothers" and "educated" them over the past years. At Gengsheng's drug store, Xiao Wu bumps into Hao and respectfully addresses him as "teacher." The policeman then advises Xiao Wu to emulate the good example of Xiao Yong, because the former pickpocket "is now a manager, *a big boss,* and a model worker," and "his new wife is as beautiful as Ni Ping [a movie star and a China Central Television anchor]." In Hao's view, Xiao Yong's fresh identity of "a big boss" accounts for everything in life, no matter how the man attains such a position. Anyhow, throughout the movie we feel a sympathetic relationship between the policeman and the pickpocket, which echoes that of Robert Bresson's masterpiece *Pickpocket* (1959). Similar to the good-natured French inspector in Bresson's classic, Hao serves as a father figure in Xiao Wu's troubled life and would instruct the straying youth on what is "right" to do in a new capitalist economy. In this sense, the benign Chinese policeman personifies the state that labors to carry on the new order and keep everyone in check.

In fact, the nouveau riche Xiao Yong simply acts according to the rules of this new order well guarded by the state, and he rejects anyone who is less viable than him financially and "morally," including those "best friends" from his ambiguous past. By contrast, his "sworn brother" Xiao Wu tries in vain to maintain an "old" fraternal bond. He brings a wedding gift to the bridegroom—the cash wrapped in a red paper, as he "vowed" to give to Xiao Yong years before. In the movie, the mise en-scène of this "gift economy" is a long take of Xiao Yong's home, where the two childhood friends first sit face to face smoking in a sullen silence, then Xiao Yong tries to explain to Xiao Wu why he is not "invited" ("It's just a family gathering," murmurs Xiao Yong apologetically). To some extent, Xiao Wu's "brotherly" ritual to fulfill his pledge is comically noble, for he has lost touch with a new reality of Chinese capitalism. Xiao Yong, however, declines Xiao Wu's "wedding gift," thereafter shattering an "antiquated" male bond that the latter deems as sacred. Sensing this rejection, Xiao Wu stands up and leaves without a word, but he slaps gently on Xiao Yong's left arm that bears the tattoo of "share good fortune." The stern reality of Chinese capitalism is best expressed through this lengthy, stifling shot of an aborted "gift exchange." As the "big boss," Xiao Yong refuses to accept the gift, and the pickpocket Xiao Wu is accordingly not welcome at his wedding to be televised publicly. The "brotherly love" instilled in the two men's "tender years" of the 1980s is hence mercilessly forsaken. (When Xiao Wu first arrives at Xiao Yong's home, a close up shot of the façade of the courtyard house shows a date of "1982" carved on the brick wall; both Xiao Wu and Xiao Yong enter this historical frame of "1982" during the "gift exchange" sequences.)

Under that humiliation Xiao Wu turns reckless. We see him drinking heavily in a restaurant where Xiao Yong's interview with a reporter is being aired on television. Later, Xiao Wu seeks solace in Mei Mei (Hao Hongjian), a prostitute working at a karaoke bar owned by Xiao Yong. Meeting with a tall and volup-

Xiao Wu and Mei Mei, *Xiao Wu* (1997).

tuous Mei Mei, the scraggy Xiao Wu seems incapable of uttering any words of love. In response, the "working" girl invites him to sing along with her as she watches MTV, something the timid young man also fails to accomplish. A few days later, when Xiao Wu visits Mei Mei again in this sleazy karaoke bar, a man dressed in a light yellow suit (director Jia Zhangke in his cameo role) walks into their "private" room—he is sent by Xiao Yong to return the "wedding gift" that Xiao Wu "left" behind in the businessman's home. This brief yet critical scene pronounces a demise of the "gift economy" that used to bind men and women together in a socialist China under Mao.[14] As this "benign" ancient economy is on the wane, so is the "social network" affixed with it. Deserted by his childhood male friend, Xiao Wu attempts to "buy back" his emotions through a woman of "easy virtue" in the friend's employment. When Mei Mei catches a cold and hopelessly stays in bed, Xia Wu comes to visit her and brings a hot water bottle that she needs most. This comforting bottle is also a "gift" from Gengsheng, the drugstore owner and Xiao Wu's only loyal friend in town. When a happier Mei Mei then asks Xiao Wu to sing a song to her, this time the shy young man responds to the girl's love request tenderly—he flips open a golden lighter (which he took from the rich man Xiao Yong by accident as they smoke wordlessly in the "wedding gift" scene) that plays Beethoven's *Für Elise* in tinny electronic tones. Deeply moved, Mei Mei weeps, and burying her face in Xiao Wu's arms. In the next sequence, we observe how a very reticent Xiao Wu grows adept at singing and dancing with Mei Mei in that karaoke bar. Realizing that Mei Mei is fond of him, Xiao Wu buys a "wedding ring" for her, only to be notified that the girl is gone. According to her roommate, Mei Mei was taken away by a few rich men "to a good place." Mei Mei herself never informed the *"duixiang"* (fiancé), Xiao Wu, of her sudden departure, and the desolate lover finds only the hot water bottle in her emptied room—another "returned" gift and another blow to the pitiful youth unprepared for Chinese capitalism. Apparently, Xiao Wu's "purchase power" with a little stolen money counts for nothing if compared with that of the "post-Mao" Chinese bourgeoisie who can "buy off" the prostitute herself. Once again, Xiao Wu is written off by Chinese capitalism even in his personal pursuit of Mei Mei, who in any event must search for a financial security that Xiao Wu is unable to provide with his doubtful "occupation." Thus, under the new order of Chinese capitalism, both the "sworn brother" Xiao Yong and the new girlfriend Mei Mei abandon Xiao Wu without explanation. In Mei Mei's case, the abrupt severance of her "love" relationship with Xiao Wu is rather an "economic" than a "moral" or "emotional" choice, a choice illustrative of new Chinese capitalism that has reduced Xiao Wu to an economic, as well societal, nobody. Here Marx's satiric remark on "the power of money in bourgeois society" still seems most pertinent: "Money, then, appears as this *overturning* power both against the individual and against the bonds of society, etc., which claim to be *essences* in themselves. It transforms fidelity into infidelity, love into hate, hate into love, virtue into vice, vice into virtue."[15]

Barred from such a dwindling "social network" in the city of Fenyang, Xiao Wu has nowhere to go but his home in the country. It is a small, impoverished village where everyone is struggling to survive an economic hardship that has been caused by the government's "free-market" policy. As we soon learn from this "homecoming" sequence, Xiao Wu gives the "wedding ring" to his aging mother, while his cynical father wonders if the ring is "gold" or "copper" ("It is gold," protests Xiao Wu). Although the ring has no more use for an unmarried man, Xiao Wu's "gift giving" is a ritualistic gesture for a filial son in Confucian ethical terms. This Chinese social ritual may as well symbolize what Siegfried Kracauer called "the desire to return to the maternal womb" for an emotionally wounded man in German expressionist cinema.[16] However, sensing the value of the ring, the mother offers it to her daughter-in-law because she has no "betrothal money" to buy any gifts for the bride's family. Insulted by this inordinate "gift giving," Xiao Wu quarrels with his mother, and the old woman chastises her son as *"wuni"* (disobedient). From this sadly ironic Hitchcockian "circulating" ring, we find again an ultimate breakdown of the agrarian "gift economy" and traditional family.[17] In a final shot of the "homecoming" sequence, the angry father wields a rod at Xiao Wu, denouncing his son as *wuni* (the same word his mother used), and Xiao Wu leaves the village for the city. In this way, the young man's peasant parents abandon him, as Xiao Yong and Mei Mei did before.

Within Xiao Wu's family, however, a sibling who still accepts him no matter what he does with his life is his younger sister. In the evening, they go to see a play at a local theater. In my judgment, the performed work is "a play in a play" that sums up new Chinese cinema of the "Sixth Generation." The play tells a heart-wrenching story of a little girl who takes her own life to confront her unfeeling father and mother. After the show Xiao Wu and his sister walk in the dark street on their way home. The sister accidentally steps over a metal object on the ground. Using a flashlight, the girl finds a discarded red can of Coca-Cola, and in blank dismay she kicks it away. From such explicit montage, we discern what is entailed in this young farm girl's symbolic gesture. In her mind, global capitalism—or "socialism with Chinese characteristics"—is to blame for all the tragedies—real or "staged"—that her brother and the family are living through.[18]

In an earlier scene at the bar, Mei Mei asked Xiao Wu to carry a pager, so she could contact him any time. Later in the movie, as it turns out, Xiao Wu is caught in his "trade" in a crowded market place when the pager rings unexpectedly. Afterward, Xiao Wu is arrested by the police and brought to the station, where he meets his "teacher," Hao Youliang. At the station, all of Xiao Wu's possessions are confiscated, including the pager, something that affects him gravely. This time, the pager—now in the possession of the police—buzzes again, and the lenient Hao delivers the received message to Xiao Wu: "A certain Miss Hu [Mei Mei] wishes you that everything goes well." In a close up, we see Xiao Wu's aggrieved face in response to Mei Mei's greetings. A critic vividly portrays this regretful screen persona of the Wang Hongwei character: "This monosyllabic, cheap-suit-wearing, chain-smoking, ill-postured loiterer is perhaps the most hopeless loser ever to darken a movie screen. You can hear the sucking sound produced by two decades of winner-take-all greed, confusion, and despair as it whistles through his soul. His meandering gait echoes the rhythms of someone dragging an overloaded, grimy handbasket to hell. Xiao Wu is so pathetic, you can almost see ducts of downtrodden pathos and meanness welling under his eyes, threatening to explode through his comically large horn-rimmed glasses."[19] To me, this is a most memorable shot, epitomizing the defeatist pessimism of the Sixth-Generation Chinese filmmakers. And among them Jia Zhangke is most likely to be "a thorough pessimist" in a Chinese critic's words.[20] In my judgment, he is a a "fatalist."[21]

The next day, Xiao Wu is taken by Hao to a detention center. On the way, the policeman stops to run errands and handcuffs Xiao Wu to a telephone pole in the street. A mob swarms to watch this "most hopeless" thief in town.

In this closing scene, the wretched Xiao Wu under the public gaze poses a mocking challenge to the party/state, as their leaders proclaim that China is "advancing along the road of 'socialism with Chinese characteristics.'"[22] Perhaps the American historian Maurice Meisner's analysis of China's economic reforms is more relevant here, when he writes that the country's "economic progress has exacted a fearful social price."[23] In my view, this "fearful social price" for China to pay is above all a cruelly impaired human dignity, as we have uncovered in this masterful Jia Zhangke film *Xiao Wu*.

Platform: A Long Frightful Journey Home

In the words of an American film critic, Jia Zhangke's *Platform* is "an allegorical epic that traces China's snarled transition from Maoism to the economic liberalization of the 1980s."[24] Chronologically, Jia's filmic tale is set between 1979 and 1989—the decade of Deng Xiaoping's economic reforms, which have changed the lives of so many Chinese. In the 198-minute epic, musicians and dancers of a provincial performing arts troupe tour the country to "see the outside world." At the beginning, all the young performers of the troupe willingly undertake this journey as "liberation" from their repressive local traditions. In the end, however, almost every one of them is compelled to come back home from "a tortuous trip to nowhere in particular."[25] Thus, on an allegorical level, the troupe sets out on a journey into what I would call "the abyss" of a post-Mao China, that of a mighty and ungoverned "outside world" of Chinese capitalism over the 1980s.

As I mentioned earlier, *Platform* opens with a musical entitled *A Train Traveling Toward Shaoshan,* which pays homage to the bygone Mao era. Shaoshan is well known for being Chairman Mao's birthplace, so it is a sacred site of the Chinese Communist Party that was born in 1927. To me, such an opening before the film's credits sequence suggests a temporally backward movement in Jia Zhangke's cinematic narration. The performers of this musical belong with the Fenyang Peasant Culture Group, a state-run Maoist propaganda troupe that is soon forced to change under Deng Xiaoping's economic reforms. Therefore, from the very start the troupe's "journey" is allegorically a pilgrimage to China's socialist past, not a tribute to the country's capitalist present. This backward movement sets a nostalgic tone for the entire movie of *Platform.*

The key members of this troupe are two pairs of young performers who fall in love with each other: Cui Mingliang (Wang Hongwei) and Yin Ruijuan (Zhao

Tao) and Zhang Jun (Liang Jindong) and Zhong Ping (Yang Tianyi). Further, these men and women share the lovemaking "secrets" that they have learned from Western advertisements, pulp fiction, and popular Hollywood cinema imported to China in the early 1980s. In *Platform,* this impact of the West on a younger generation of the Chinese is ironically linked to the party's call for "ideological liberation" *(sixiang jiefang).* In the movie, following the Chinese title of *zhantai* are the flashy shots of Guangzhou, a big city in southern China, which has been serving as an inspired model for Deng Xiaoping's economic reforms to this day. As Geremie Barmé has pointed out, "As a way station, Guangzhou itself had also risen in prominence. Imitating Hong Kong . . . Guangzhou in the early 1990s was claimed by some to be the second most influential city after Beijing, and it had gone further in its efforts to sweep away feudal remnants and introduce democratic elements into its social life."[26] So, among those swift and ostentatious frames of Guangzhou, we can catch a glimpse of the party's slogan of "ideological liberation." It is written in big, red Chinese characters and takes hold of the "model" city's skyline filled with commercial high-rises. In Barmé's observations, the party's policy of "ideological liberation" is not necessarily oppositional to the West, because, "[d]uring the 1980s, the avowed official ideology —what the authorities presumably out of habit rather than sincere belief still called Marxism-Lennism–Mao Zedong Thought—expanded to embrace a burgeoning realm of market culture."[27] To me, this "market culture" as endorsed by the party is nothing but Western consumerism.

The Guangzhou sequence in *Platform* is followed by a scene that further explicates this party-sponsored "market culture." In a dimly lit courtyard house, Mingliang's mother is altering the blue cotton pants of her "inspired" son, who demands to modify it to look like the "bell-bottom trousers" *(laba ku)* he saw in a local department store. A moment later, Mingliang's father walks in and sees his son trying on that "new" costume. Irritated by the bizarre Western fashion, the father, like the one we saw in *Xiao Wu,* chastises the prodigal son (who is standing somewhat awkwardly in the courtyard under a gray snowy sky), shouting "How can a farmer in such pants go to the field?" The father's condemnation of his son is, however, more rhetorical than real. He himself is never a "farmer" by occupation, but a lowly blue-collar factory worker. And his invocation of "peasantry" is merely a metaphorical speech that compares a diligent Chinese farmer with a lazy and corrupt Western urban dweller that he believes his son is "imitating." (Later in the film, this "protradition" Chinese father deserts his wife and children. He opens a shop and lives with his mistress in the same town of Fenyang.)

In any event, what Barmié calls "feudal remnants" remains strong in Fenyang, a sleepy inland town in northern China. A bitter conflict between the young and the old generation always pivots on those "bad" influences stemming from a capitalist West. If Mingliang's attraction to Western consumerism (namely, going after the fashion of the day) is so appalling in his father's eyes, his pursuit of Ruijuan is deemed as that of "bad influences" in the judgment of the girl's father. Ruijuan's father is a well-respected policeman in Fenyang who is loyal to the party and the state. Yet he does not appreciate the party's motto of "ideological liberation" in connection to Western "market culture" that has deluded the youth in this closely-knit "semirural" community. When the cop sees Ruijuan and Mingliang together in a theater that shows an Indian film from the 1950s, he warns his daughter, "You have seen too many *foreign* movies." Immediately after the admonitions of the worried father to his "liberated" daughter, there is a deep focus shot of the city wall of Fenyang in snow. The overhead camerawork of the extensive wall corridor metaphorically addresses a vital issue: can China's patriarchal authorities protect their children from the impact of the West? The answer to this question is not provided at this moment, but it will be sought throughout this Jia Zhangke epic film.

For me, the same question can also be reversed from the point of view of the young generation, which is to ask, can children break through this solid "wall" of sacred traditions warily guarded by patriarchal authorities? In a consequential long take of the same city wall and its main front gate, we see Mingliang and Ruijuan standing face to face; both of them are framed by the darkened ancient arches.[28] In *Platform*, the old city wall and gate serve as the mise-en-scène for a tortuous romance between Mingliang and Ruijuan. Only in this seclusive corner of the town would they meet to discuss their repressed feelings. So the thick, gloomy, and self-contained city wall is a metaphorical allusion to the oppressive patriarchal authorities. Under the shadow of that omnipresent power, however, the two tender lovers strive for a survival of their relationship. In here the second rendezvous of Mingliang and Ruijuan occurs just before their Maoist propaganda troupe is transformed into a private enterprise. (Later, although the whole crew of performers agrees to go the rounds in the country in order to earn either freedom or money, Ruijuan declines to take this trip because her father falls ill. By contrast, Mingliang is eager to break loose from this walled "prison" of severe repression.) The scene is shot at the top of city gate, where Ruijuan and Mingliang alternate to come in and out of the battlements against a distant, bright sky. In my opinion, this contemplated in-and-out movement effected by the two protagonists can be considered an apt allegory for the young generation today. That is to say, if man must throw off the yoke of traditions, the Woman/Other should stay within it as an "alternative" solution. Tempted by a Western notion of "individual freedom," Mingliang sets himself free of any responsibilities. Yet Ruijuan sacrifices herself to remain inside the soberest tradition of Confucianism; thereby she becomes a "filial" daughter. Unable to reconcile with Ruijuan on this matter, Mingliang takes off from the site of the historic city wall, leaving Ruijuan alone within that "allegorical" wall of weighty patriarchal authorities. (*Platform's* heart-warming ending—the placid marriage of Mingliang and Ruijuan —continually augments this seeming antimodern and antifeminist allegory.)

A year later, on a sunny summer day, Mingliang comes under the city wall to see Ruijuan again, only to be told that her father disapproves their relationship. Afterward, Minliang climbs up the city wall, while Ruijuan stays behind below. Here, in shadow of the Father, the two young lovers cement their subsequent separation. As I have just mentioned above, if Ruijuan is willingly to observe that old Chinese family ritual (that is., being a filial child), Mingliang is earnest to achieve a new goal of "Western individualism." After the break-up an unimpeded Mingliang travels with the private "contracted" troupe gleefully, giving a variety of performances in the countryside, ranging from Chinese revolutionary songs to American break dance. He and Zhang Jun also grow long hair that is not acceptable in their hometown of Fenyang. On this tour, Mingliang had been happy until he meets his cousin Sanming by chance at a small coal mine in remote mountains, where low-wage workers (ten yuan a day), including Sanming, have to sign a so-called life-and-death contract *(shengsi hetong)* that relieves the mine owner of any responsibility for workers' personal safety.[29] At night the troupe performs for those exhausted coal miners. On the next morning, the troupe is on the road again, while Sanming follows them and asks Mingliang to take the money he had just earned to his sister back in Fenyang.

This bitter encounter with his "slave labor" cousin seems to have shaken Mingliang's new faith in capitalist privatization and political liberty. In fact, the coal mine episode portrayed in *Platform* is an enactment of Jia Zhangke's own experience with his own cousin while filming in Shanxi. And Jia's cousin also plays the sad and reserved character in the movie.[30] So this brief "semidocumentary" personal story illuminates another unsolved problem in the film: if Mingliang eagerly undertakes this journey into the faith of new Chinese capitalism, what he has seen on this journey is what I would term as the "ruins" of post-Mao China, as shown by that "private-owned" coal mine where human life has so little value.[31] Ironically, the privatization of the Maoist propaganda troupe indeed allows Mingliang to savor the newly obtained "freedom," but what he discovers on this "exploratory" journey is his cousin's misery in another "privatized" enterprise. So the coal mine episode has become a turning point in Mingliang's journey toward an unknown "outside world" he had been longing for. In the film, as the troupe's truck continues to travel deep into an immense no-man's land, Mingliang plays a tape on a cassette recorder, and, all of sudden, a 1980s rock song hit titled *A Long Platform* is on the soundtrack: "[M]y heart is waiting; there is only a bugle call for departure but no love of return." This theme song of *Platform* felicitously designates the troupe's urgent wish: It is a fearsome journey from which everyone is anxious to return, except for the strong-willed Zhong Ping.

As I have already noted, another pair of young lovers portrayed in the film are Zhang Jun and Zhong Ping from the same troupe, and the couple is also close friends to Mingliang and Ruijuan. In general, Mingliang and Ruijuan still appear as well-behaved children faithful to their family and local traditions, whereas Jun and Zhong Ping turn out to be the avowed "radicals" who succumb to a new "Western" life style without hesitation. Among the troupe performers, Zhang Jun is the only one who takes a trip to see for himself Guangzhou, the city of economic liberation and social democracy, and a perky Zhong Ping is the first girl in town to have her hair done in permanent wave, which in the Mao era was slammed as a "bourgeois world outlook" and which even stuns her timid colleagues at the troupe's business meeting. Moreover, Zhong Ping would share her "new" knowledge of sex with Ruijuan and "practice" it with Zhang Jun. Her sexual liberation results in an abortion, which is performed by a doctor-friend of the troupe owner, in secrecy to avoid a scandal. And the scene is derisively accompanied with a newsreel of Deng Xiaoping inspecting a military parade in Tiananmen Square on October 1 (National Day), 1984, on the soundtrack. In the movie, both Zhong Ping and Ruijuan are trained dancers who give a very different performance. Before an audience of the admiring troupe members, Zhong Ping in a sexy red Spanish costume, revels in a frantic Latin dance. By contrast, Ruijuan, dressed in the dark blue uniform of a tax collector (after she refuses to travel with Mingliang and the troupe, Ruijuan takes a job at the tax bureau in Fenyang), dances serenely alone in her office, a scene that is eerily beautiful.

In *Platform,* such narrative and visual parallels between the two couples can be understood again allegorically in terms of their fate that varies distinctly as the film comes to its end. As we have learned, the sickness of Ruijuan's policeman father has effected an uncertain separation of Mingliang and Ruijuan. The couple reunites after the father dies toward the end of the movie. In the case of Zhang Jun and Zhong Ping, however, their fatal separation springs from an authoritarian stage apparatus and the young man's own lack of faith in their relationship. After that tiring trip through the vast barren land alongside the Yellow River, the troupe stays in a seedy hotel on their way back to Fenyang. Though unmarried, Zhang Jun and Zhong Ping together take a room at the hotel. The local police arrest the amorous couple and interrogate them separately. Zhang Jun is frightened and admits their "unlawful" relationship in that he has no means to produce a "marriage certificate," while the plucky Zhong Ping defends herself and the man she loves until a police officer scorns her by saying that "you are *not* husband and wife at all." This "marriage certificate" fuss is resolved by the troupe owner with the police, as was done before in the event of Zhong Ping's abortion,

Mingliang and Ruijuan, *Plat-form* (*Zhantai*, 2000).

but the benevolent boss fails to save the young couple from their faithless love. A few days later, the troupe arrives in Fenyang, but the owner cannot find Zhong Ping—she has vanished from the scene forever. For me, this sudden disappearance of a female protagonist in *Platform* (which is incomprehensible to a Western audience) is an allegory for a frail and flawed Chinese masculinity that disheartens even so strong a woman as Zhong Ping. In physical appearance, the drastic Zhong Ping is tall and robust, yet her "unadventurous" friend Ruijuan is slender and delicate; and this contrast between the two women is deliberately figurative.

For Zhang Jun, although he had arisen as a most "liberal" person among his peers at the beginning, he now descends into a truly broken man toward the end. In a scene of the baneful backyard of his home in Fenyang, Zhang Jun cuts his "Western"-style long hair with a blade. This "hair cutting" mise-en-scène sullenly echoes that concluding shot of *Xiaoshan Returning Home*. So Jia Zhangke's

Ruijuan and Zhong Ping, *Platform* (*Zhantai*, 2000).

cinematic trilogy is resonant of an almost Buddhist ritual that renounces a male protagonist's shaky faith in Western values. At this moment, Zhang Jun seems determined to return to his rustic Chinese roots, no matter how belated it may sound. He has lost Zhong Ping because of his "impotence" in a spiritual rather than physical sense (the Liang Jindong character is also tall), but he can still seek a safe haven at home. In *Platform*, this long frightful journey home is magnificently portrayed in a scene of a wintry dust storm that bursts over the sterile soil of Inner Mongolia. In it, the troupe in a big truck with a canvas roof is on its way up a hill, leaving a long trail on the ground—and it is just another tiresome performing trip to northern China. When the storm is whipping through the land, the truck stops for safety overnight. On the next morning, under a clear blue sky, the troupe performers emerge from under the roof and all cheer in one single word: "Home! Home!" The truck turns around going downhill and finally completing that extended trail in a U shape on the earth. Therefore, the allegory of Jia Zhangke's cinematic epic is also finalized: For these young people who were once tempted by an impulsive western idealism combined with a brutal Chinese capitalism, home is perhaps the only place where they can revive their lost identity and a common humanity.

Back in the town of Fenyang, Mingliang visits Ruijuan, who remains single and lives quietly at her father's house. Entering a sunny living room, Mingliang glances at some old family photos, especially Ruijuan's deceased parents. After years of that weary journey into the "outside world," Mingliang realizes for the first time that he must settle down with Ruijuan here in this humble parental home. Only in this "inside world" in which he had grown up with Ruijuan can Mingliang find a tranquil happiness again. Earlier, Mingliang went to see his father, who had left his wife and runs a hardware store with his mistress. On that visit, Mingliang was unable to meet his father, but did meet the mistress. He then asked her to tell his father to come home. Now Mingliang, the returned "prodigal son," resolves to become a father in his own right, as we see in a final scene of the film: a dignified yet playful Ruijuan stands by the door holding their newborn baby, while a whimsical Mingliang is "collapsing" into his sofa. Accompanying this heartwarming conclusion of *Platform* is the soundtrack of traditional Chinese music, which is the tune of a song titled *Traveling in Suzhou (Gusu xing)* played on a bamboo flute.[32] And I can think of no other filmic or musical finale that would bring an end to Jia Zhangke's cinematic trilogy that is so ephemerally beautiful.

Epilogue

Like all of his three previous films that I have examined in this study, Jia Zhangke's latest feature, *Unknown Pleasures* (2002), is again "a powerful depiction of the spiritual malaise afflicting Chinese youth as a result of global capitalism" in Howard Schumann's analysis.[33] The story of *Unknown Pleasures* takes place in the city of Datong, Shanxi province, in 2001, where unemployed and disaffected teenagers look for any kind of excitement to enliven their dreary everyday existence. Bin Bin (Zhao Weiwei) dates a female student named Yuan Yuan (Zhou Qingfeng), who is thinking of going to Beijing to attend university. They spend their time together holding hands, watching karaoke and Monkey King videos (from which Bin Bin has derived inspiration for personal freedom). Bin Bin has quit his job at a local market, but he does not tell his mother (Bai Ru). When she finds out, she wants him to join the army. His less-thoughtful friend Xiao Ji (Wu Qiong) stalks a flashy performer, Qiao Qiao (Zhao Tao), who promotes Mongolian King liquor and dates a gangster. The gangster does not appreciate Xiao Ji's attentions and slaps him around. Qiao Qiao seems to like Xiao Ji, but even as a seeming "free-spirited" young woman, she is afraid to defy her violent boyfriend

Qiao Qiao and Xiao Ji, *Unknown Pleasures* (*Ren xiaoyao*, 2002).

(who was also her "coach" at high school). Bin Bin tries to sell bootlegged DVDs on the street to earn a living. One of his customers, a thug named Xiao Wu (Wang Hongwei), complains that Bin Bin does not carry underground titles such as *Xiao Wu* and *Platform*, but he is pleased to find *Pulp Fiction*. Inspired by the American movie, Bin Bin and Xiao Ji plot an ill-fated bank robbery. *Unknown Pleasures* was shown in competition at the 2002 Cannes Film Festival and was also selected for the 2002 New York Film Festival.[34]

More recently, the film critic J. Hoberman of the *Village Voice* wrote admirably of all the three films by Jia Zhangke: "The 1997 *Xiao Wu* (also known, in tribute to Robert Bresson, as *Pickpocket*) was a remarkable, semidocumentary immersion in backwater urban lowlife; his 2000 *Platform*, a movie much promoted by the *Voice*, used the evolution of a panoramic long view of China's transformation from Maoist austerity to free-market confusion. The more overtly pop, impressionistic, and improvisational *Unknown Pleasures*, one of the strongest inclusions in the last New York Film Festival, may be Jia's most concentrated evocation of contemporary China's spiritual malaise."[35] Interestingly, many American reviewers of *Unknown Pleasures* have all noticed the curious final sequence of the film. In it, Bin Bin is arrested by the police after the failed bank robbery, while Xiao Ji flees on his motor bike, which nevertheless breaks down on the road. One reviewer sees no hope for the youth as depicted in Jia's film: "Even with the newly opened superhighway linking them to Beijing and, hopefully, the world at large, it seems no one in Datong is really going anywhere."[36] Another

206 : XIAOPING LIN

reviewer, however, "optimistically" points out, "Rather than head back to town, he hitches a ride from a stranger and perseveres."[37] Schumann's comment on this somewhat ambiguous conclusion of the movie *Unknown Pleasures* is more inspiring: "When Xiao [Ji] finally abandons his sputtering motor bike in the middle of a new superhighway, Jia seems to be suggesting that both he and China itself are at a precarious crossroads in their existence and must discard what isn't working if they are to move on."[38] To me, this is perhaps just another long perilous journey that Jia Zhangke is to embark on in the near future. And I do share the anticipation for the gifted Chinese director's new creation with Kevin Lee, a New York–based filmmaker and writer, as he also remarked on that evasive ending of *Unknown Pleasures:* "Again, we are brought back to the respective fates of Xiao Ji and Bin Bin: one seeks refuge in the anonymity of the impassive crowd, while another sings out defiantly, expressing Jia's unnerved, even virulent need to take a stand against the mounting inequities of the world. This conflict in artistic intent, that confronts the calm observer with the impassioned activist, is to me what makes Jia's next project worth anticipating eagerly. In the meantime, we—those lucky enough to have access to his films either through festival screenings or pirated video—have a small but formidable body of work to interpret, discuss, critique and defend, and in doing so we are reinvigorated with the possibilities of contemporary cinema affect our relationship with the world we live in."[39]

Notes

1. For an analysis of the work of the "sixth-generation" or "urban generation" Chinese filmmakers, see Shuqin Cui, "Working from the Margins: Urban Cinema and Independent Directors in Contemporary China," in the present volume; see also my "New Chinese Cinema of the 'Sixth Generation': A Distant Cry of Forsaken Children," *Third Text*, 60, vol. 16, issue 3 (September 2002): 261–284.

2. For more information, see Maurice Meisner, *Mao's China and After: A History of the People's Republic* (New York: Free Press, 1999).

3. Deng's interview with Orana Fallaci, *Washington Post*, August 31, 1980. Cited in Meisner, *Mao's China and After*, 440.

4. Fenyang is Jia Zhangke's hometown where the director filmed his entire *Xiao Wu* and part of *Platform*.

5. This 1995 film by Jia Zhangke is actually unknown to the Western audience that has admired his *Xiao Wu* (1997), *Platform* (2000), and *Unknown Pleasures* (2002); it is available on pirated VCD in China.

6. See *A Chinese-English Dictionary*, rev. ed. (Beijing: Foreign Language Teaching and Research Press, 1995), 682.

7. See Meisner, *Mao's China and After*, 468.

8. For a detailed discussion of such "villages" (where migrant workers live) in big Chi-

nese cities, see Dorothy Solinger, "China's Floating Population," in Merle Goldman and Roderick MacFarquhar, eds., *The Paradox of China's Post-Mao Reforms* (Cambridge, Mass.: Harvard University Press), 220–240.

9. The market sequence in *Xiaoshan Going Home* echoes fairly what Meisner has vividly described: "The reappearance of petty private enterprise contributed the liveliness of Chinese cities in the early Deng era, which foreigners contrasted to the austere and drab character of urban life in Maoist China. . . . Peddlers, hawkers, and tiny open-air restaurants were soon followed by high-rise hotels, nightclubs, and luxury boutiques—as well as beggars and prostitutes." See his *Mao's China and After*, 455.

10. The capital city of Beijing, to borrow Meisner's words, "began to resemble large cities in most of the world, displaying those stark and painful contrast between ostentatious wealth and grinding poverty that mark most contemporary capitalist society." Ibid., 455.

11. Ibid., 479.

12. According to Meisner, this "boom" in big Chinese cities during the 1990s results from cheap labor provided by the country. As he put it, "Living in shantytowns and working for pitiful wages, they [the "migrant laborers"] supply much of the construction boom that has made Chinese cities appear modern and seemingly prosperous." Ibid., 468.

13. For more information, see Meisner, *Mao's China and After*, part 3, "Utopianism, 1956–1960," sec. 11–13, pp. 191–241.

14. For a discussion of this ancient "gift economy" in modern life as defined by Marcel Mauss, see Michel de Certeau, *The Practice of Everyday Life* (Berkeley: University of California Press, 1984), 26–27.

15. See Karl Marx and Frederick Engels, *Economic and Philosophic Manuscripts of 1844* and *The Communist Manifesto* (New York: Prometheus Books, 1988), 140.

16. As Siegfried Kracauer puts it, "This gesture—recurrent in many German films—is symptomatic of the desire to return to the maternal womb." See his caption for a scene from *The Street* (1923), in *From Caligari to Hitler: A Psychological History of the German Film* (Princeton, N.J.: Princeton University Press, 1947).

17. As Mlader Dolar said of Hitchcock's *Shadow of a Doubt*, "[T]he most important and central to the film is the ring. *Shadow of a Doubt* could be schematically summarized as the journey of a privileged object, the circulation of the ring. It goes back and forth between the two specular protagonists, and their dual relationship can ultimately be seen as the background for this circuit of the object." See his "Hitchcock's Objects," in Slavoj Žižek, ed., *Everything You Always Wanted to Know about Lacan (But Were Afraid to Ask Hitchcock)* (New York: Verso, 1992), 34.

18. As Meisner has pointed out: "The most distressing result of China's 'socialist market system' has been the frighteningly rapid growth of extreme social and economic inequality. In less than two decades, China has been transformed from a relatively egalitarian society to one where the gap between the wealthy and the impoverished is among widest and most visible in the world, a land far more inequitable than such celebrated models of Asian capitalism as Taiwan or South Korea." See *Mao's China and After*, 533. In the movie, the "model entrepreneur" Xiao Yong is awarded a "foreign trip *(chuguo)*" to South Korea by the local government, as Gengsheng the drugstore owner enviously informs Xiao Wu, who, however, in disbelief insists that it must be North Korea—thus we see how he is totally out of touch with current realities!

19. See "Jia Zhangke: Pickpocket Director," in *Beijing Scene*, 5.23 [available at www .beijingscene.com].

20. See Lu Shaoyang, "A Similar Color, a Different Temperature," *Xinwen zhoukan* (News week), June 18, 2001, p. 63.

21. *Xiao Wu* best exemplifies this "fatalism" in Jia Zhangke's work. In this film, Jia Zhangke borrowed a mid-1990s popular Hong Kong rock song titled "My Heart Rains" *(xinyu)* as the "theme song," which, strangely, "predestines" Xiao Wu's doomed love affair with Mei Mei. The song "My Heart Rains" is designed for antiphonal singing (which is perfectly suitable to a karaoke bar "milieu"), so it is a "musical dialogue" between a man and his young female lover who is "to become the bride of the other" (In this emotional context, a more proper English translation for the Chinese title *xinyu* should be "My Heart Bleeds"). In *Xiao Wu*, Jia Zhangke used the melody of "My Heart Rains" on five consecutive occasions, which ultimately seals the tragic fate of the Xiao Wu character. The song is first broadcast on a television when Xiao Wu is drinking in a restaurant, depressed by Xiao Yong's rejection. The second time the song is heard is when Mei Mei asks Xiao Wu to sing along with her, but he fails because, as a busy pickpocket, he has no idea whatever about a song so representative of the Hong Kong pop culture. Later Xiao Wu is able to sing the song alone in a public bathhouse right after lending a sick Mei Mei some help (i.e., the hot water bottle). In the movie, the two lovers sing the song together for one more time just before Mei Mei becomes "the bride of the other" (i.e., she is procured by a handful of "rich men" as a shared sex slave). In this sense, the song "My Heart Rains" is used by Jia Zhangke not to convey Xiao Wu's love, but his ineluctable alienation from the "sworn brother" Xiao Yong and the "fiancé" *(duixiang)* Mei Mei, whose lives are all ruled by the brutal force of the Other—new Chinese capitalism.

22. See Meisner, *Mao's China and After*, 535.

23. Ibid., 532.

24. See Elbert Venture's review of *Platform* [available at www.allmovie.com].

25. Ibid.

26. Geremie Barmé, *In the Red: On Contemporary Chinese Culture* (New York: Columbia University Press, 1999), 125–126.

27. Ibid., 236.

28. In reality, the elegant city wall and gate seen in the film are not from Fenyang, but Pingyao, another town in Shanxi province, which is well known for its classical architectures of the Ming dynasty (1368–1164 B.C.E.).

29. As Meisner cited the Australian scholar Anita Chan by saying that "[t]he abuses suffered by workers in China . . . include: 'forced and bonded labor; control of workers' bodily functions and physical mistreatments; subsistence or below-subsistence wages; and a pervasive climate of violence.'" See his *Mao's China and After*, 533.

30. My interview with Jia Zhangke conducted in the summer of 2001.

31. As Meisner wrote, "[The N]ew Chinese market economy . . . requires the elimination of many of the social welfare and job guarantees of the Mao period. . . . Those who are employed often suffer from physically dangerous conditions of work, especially young men and women workers who labor in hastily constructed private and 'collective' factories, where accidents and fires kill and maim workers in numbers unprecedented in modern industrial history" (*Mao's China and After*, 533).

32. Jia Zhangke told me that he added this piece of music right after hearing a crew-man playing it in the course of final filming of *Platform*.

33. See Howard Schumann's review of *Unknown Pleasures*, "Waves of Longing" [available at www.cinescene.com].

34. Compare the plot synopsis of *Unknown Pleasures* by Josh Ralske, *All Movie Guide* [available at www.allmovie.com].

35. See J. Hoberman, "Film: New Dawn Fades," *Village Voice*, March 26–April 1, 2003 [available at www.villagevoice.com].

36. See Ken Fox, "A Better Tomorrow" [available at www.tvguide.com].

37. See Ed Gonzales's review in *Slant Magazine* [available at www.slantmagazine.com].

38. See Schumann, "Waves of Longing."

39. See Kevin Lee, "Jia Zhangke" [available at www.sensesofcinema.com].

CHAPTER NINE

Novels into Film

Liu Yichang's *Tête-Bêche*
and Wong Kar-wai's
In the Mood for Love

Sitting in a dance hall in Shanghai listening to Wu Yingying singing
"sending my love a thousand miles away on a moonbeam" was entirely different from sitting in a restaurant in Hong Kong listening
to Yao Surong singing "I am not coming home tonight." The mood
was different because the times had changed.
—Liu Yichang, "Intersection"

Novels, short stories, and film have developed a very close and cognate relationship over the years. As the youngest of the arts, film has fed on the techniques
and contents of the other arts, especially of novels, which provide sources of inspiration on plot construction, methods of delineating character, ways of presenting thought processes, and means of dealing with time and space.[1] As George
Bluestone puts it, "The industry's own appraisal of its work shows a strong and
steady preference for films derived from novel, films which persistently rate
among top quality productions. Filmed novels, for example, have made consistently strong bids for Academy Awards."[2] Hence, reciprocity exists in these two
art forms, as evinced by the number of films based on novels, the search for
filmic equivalents in literature, and the effect of adaptation on reading, and so
forth. There has been, of late, a reverse trend of influence of novelizing a film,
much to the chagrin of Woody Allen, but this practice is more commodification
of a marketable cultural product than a full-fledged genre, and the extent of re-
ciprocation is by far less significant. Understandably, the number of novels made

Opposite and upside-down stamps on the front cover of Liu Yichang's novel *Duidao*.

into films in Eastern and Western literary traditions is as staggering and self-evident as to need no further proof of the close relationship between these two arts, or of the indebtedness of the film to literature.

This indebtedness of film to literature in general is no exception in the films in China and Hong Kong. Among others, Zhang Yimou, Chen Kaige, and Wong Kar-wai have turned to Chinese literature—novels in particular—to look for the impulses for their filmic and moral content. The year 2000 saw Hong Kong director Wong Kar-wai virtuosically transform the novel of a local writer, Liu Yichang's *Duidao* (*Tête Bêche*, or *Intersection*), into an award winning masterpiece. Of the telltale signs of the mutation process, there are three quotations from Liu Yichang's (1918–) novels (both short and longer versions), *Tête Bêche*, found in Wong Kar-wai's film *In the Mood for Love* to establish a classic case of *rapport de fait* in the context of filmic adaptation. Liu's novella, initially published in 1972, and later expanded into a full-length novel in 1993, provides inspiration to the film both in form and content.[3]

The exact meaning of the title— *Duidao* (Intersection, literally "opposite and upside down"), or *Tête-Bêche*—describes stamps that are misprinted with the top of the one joining the bottom of the other. In other words, it carries the meaning of a double, or upside-down reflection, used as a trope for contrast or juxtaposition. Liu's story tells of a young girl (Ah Xing) and an old man (Chun Yubai), who go about their lives in a parallel storyline but, until the end of the film, remain strangers. The narrative advances in a paratactic fashion, alternat-

ing from one character to another; however, Wong's film has the two characters—Zhou Muyun, played by Tony Leung, and Su Lizhen, played by Maggie
Cheung—who intersect as neighbors, both betrayed by their spouses, and find
solace in one other as daytime friends and secret lovers, but end up quietly going their separate ways. Their lives have a double existence, as they play out their
own roles as betrayed spouses as well as doubles in an actual-cum-simulated attempt to experience in their own illicit affair how their spouses would have behaved under these circumstances. Borrowing the paratactic plotline, Wong's film
is not as much about adultery and betrayal as it is an evocation of memory, a
"treatise on memory."[4]

Set in the Hong Kong of the 1960s, Liu's story and Wong's film share a common element: a sense of nostalgia. Wong's film as a globalized artistic product
carries with it, by more intent than trend, a no less global epidemic of nostalgia,
the "hypochondria of the heart," as Svetlana Boym describes it in *The Future of
Nostalgia*.[5] The most obvious nostalgic references are of course to the Shanghai
lifestyle of a bygone era in the novel as well as in the film (both Liu and Wong
are of Shanghai extraction). But there is something more, something the writer
and the director have presented, yet differently, an attempt at identifying a quietly melancholic aesthetic, often found in classical Chinese poetry, with regard
to a memory of the past and its concomitant modes of emotion, in their respective invocations of a Hong Kong collective memory.

The structuring of nostalgia in Wong's film and Liu's novel consists of more
than simple homesickness, as a result of incomplete membership of any social
group in the city of Hong Kong, or just a simple remembering of the past. To
analyze the structure of nostalgia in Wong Kar-wai's film, one need not turn to
Freud or Lacan to look for primal sites or to Wordsworthian "trailing clouds of
glory" and postlapserian woes over the loss of "primal sympathy."[6] Whereas Liu's
novel may exude more the kind of nostalgia associated with a specific time or
place, Wong's film suggests something more elusive and delicate that is no longer
treasured in human interactions. To pursue further this vein of analysis, one
may venture to construe that both Liu's novel and Wong's film are about desire
and its repression. To a certain extent, they touch on a kind of subtle emotional
expression, characterized by reserve and delicacy that has since gone out of vogue.
In Liu's story, there is a thematic contrast between old and new values, represented by Chun Yubai and Ah Xing. Given a third-person omniscient point of
view, the readers are able to peep into the youthful Ah Xing's lust-ridden fantasies and their multifarious manifestations—i.e., her interest in the pornographic photo and the T-shirt with "I love you" printed on it, her desire for a
man having the looks of a movie star. Although these secret desires remain private to her, hers are a great contrast to the thoughts of Chun Yubai, who appears

as a pragmatic man living in his own memories of an O'Neillian "what might have been, and no more, farewell." This contrast could be seen in the diffident depiction of Chun's relationship with his former lady friend, Pretty, his estranged wife and son, and Ah Xing's more sex-stoked and lurid fantasies. Against the backdrop of a rapidly changing city, the two paratactic plotlines run their separate courses. The contrast between traditional values of decency and conservatism and a modern desire-ridden mindset seems obvious.

But the contrastive values are not the main focus of the novel. Instead of exploring the theme of desire in a broader cultural context, Liu appears to be more concerned with the personal context of desire. The carefully constructed convergence of the two characters inside the cinema shows that Chun also has suppressed his desire all along. His erotic fantasy about Ah Xing sitting next to him revitalizes his aging metabolism, as he could still respond to an instinctual call even when he was no longer young. Liu's character seems to represent the lamentation of the psychological state of a man aging, a postmodern version of Eliot's J. Alfred Prufrock, weighing all the consequences, but taking no action, only murmuring to himself,

> I grow old . . . I grow old. . . .
> I shall wear the bottoms of my trousers rolled.
> Shall I part my hair behind?
> Do I dare to eat a peach?[7]

To see Chun's emotional state in this psychoanalytic vein, one can perhaps say that his repressed emotions and the retreat to the past are simply defense mechanisms to cope with the problematic present: aging, problems faced by an exilic émigré, and the like. Liu is less concerned with how this retrogression should be equated with an elegant and delicate expression of emotion than telling us more about the repressed nature of reality and the character's grappling with it.

Dramatizing the tension of passion and desire and their repression in a bygone era, director Wong Kar-wai intends to represent a different facet of the desire. The mood of nostalgia in the film highlights an era when people were used to expressing their emotion with a sense of delicacy. It is undeniable that Wong has adopted but transformed the novel's form and content to his own purpose. Liu's lavish but unromantic depiction of desire is replaced by a more poetic portrayal of a forbidden love and its repression. The ebb and flow of desire in the film move forward with the use of cinematic techniques and the director's attention to detail. For example, Lizhen's tight-laced *cheongsam* seems to suggest a body politics about desire and its denial simultaneously. It exudes sensuality and demur. The background music is analogous to abstract steps of dancers. Its

Moods of love in *In the Mood for Love*.

dance rhythm embodies the tension of smoldering passion underneath a façade of social/moral etiquettes, which are in nature constrictive and censor prone.

If nostalgia is connected with time and space, the filmic space is particularly worth investigating, insofar as the manner in which emotion is expressed in a hush-hush manner. Mrs. Sun's apartment and other enclosed spaces are the center of the film. On the one hand, it is a symbol of homey togetherness. On the other hand, the enclosed space intimates a sense of inhibition. For example, the noisiness of the sitting room may remind the audience of the presence of other people's surveillance of Mr. Zhou and Lizhen's illicit feeling for each other. One other instance depicts Lizhen, in tight *cheongsam*, running up and down the staircase, struggling with the desire to see Mr. Zhou. The to-and-fro traffic in an enclosed space suggests a sense of tension, which projects her internal turmoil in the seesawing battle of desire and moral propriety.

The clever use of framing further heightens the effect. In the apartment, walls, windowpanes, or other features of the setting, which serve as objective correlative to their ambivalent relationship and indirectness of their feelings, always obscure the characters. This is a contrast to the scenes filmed in open space—for example, the make-believe parting in the back street, where Lizhen bursts into tears. Only when she leaves the confinement of the apartment can she truly release her emotion. Once again, it highlights the fact to the modern-day audience that their passions are bound by rules of inhibition harking back to a bygone era, one that they could not transgress.

Both Liu and Wong use the mirror to depict the theme of desire and the relationship of gazing and being gazed at. In *Duidao*, Liu mainly focuses on the narcissism of Ah Xing and Chun Yubai's indulgence in their mirror reflections. They seem in love with themselves, that is, Chun's personal sense of reminiscence of the past vigour and emotion is similar in nature to Ah Xing's fantasies about sex and grandeur.

> Staring at the wedding gown, her eyes filled with envy. After she'd been staring for some time, a smile appeared on the manikin's face. A manikin couldn't smile. The smiling woman in the wedding gown was actually herself. The window before her suddenly became opaque and turned into a mirror. Ah Xing saw herself in the "mirror," dressed in a white gauze wedding gown, as beautiful as a goddess.

> She studied the photography closely; she felt so embarrassed that her face grew red hot. She took off her clothes, stood in front of the mirror and stared wide-eyed at herself.[8]

The recurrence of mirrors in the film, however, suggests another function. The characters do not gaze so much into the mirror. Rather, the audience peeps on the behavior of Mr. Zhou and Lizhen through the mirrors hung on the wall. The two characters are being gazed at by the audience, and, similarly, their secret relationship is also under the stealthy scrutiny of a house of decent but conservative people. It is true that the use of mirrors creates an illusion of spaciousness, but the director is interested in showing the contrary effect—the characters are cornered under the pressure of social propriety and mores.

Wong states in the film that he wants to capture that period, a more subtle and delicate time than our own, rather than to offer a critique on a suffocating milieu or culture.[9] The unfulfilled illicit love affair of Mr. Zhou and Lizhen may be more romantic in comparison with the sordid nature of the adultery of their own spouses and the sexual escapade of Mr. Zhou's friend, Ah Bing. To further underscore the sense of delicacy of this illicit love, Wong Kar-wai purposely avoids any sex scene except showing the couple holding hands in a taxi.[10] This intentional brevity again reinforces the nature of concealment of their kind of passion. The director is not only addicted to the romantic melancholy of the doomed love affair, but also obsessed with the subtle delicacy of the period. It is a mood of nostalgia par excellence, yet with not too much poignancy of grief and regret, disappointment and remorse. Zhou and Lizhen might have started their relationship in a revengeful attempt, but theirs never deteriorated into a sordid affair of macabre proportion, unlike the Japanese short story of double suicide/murder by Komatsu Sakyou, *Shinjyu* (To Die for Love), which tells of the suicide of a man and a woman, cuckolded by their spouses, and their revenge on them before their suicide by having them murdered first.[11]

Liu and Wong have a different attitude toward the denial of desire: Wong's homage to the bygone subtlety departs from Liu's focus on the self-indulgent sense of nostalgia. The latter through incorporating or transforming Chun's part into the script presents Mr. Zhou still living in memory of Lizhen. Yet, Mr. Zhou is not an exact parallel to Chun Yubai, as his memories of an unfulfilled romance have more poetry and delicacy. The last scene shows Mr. Zhou whispering his secret love to a hole in Cambodia's Angkor Wat and all his might-have-beens. It is a visual paean to the sense of reserve and decency of a mood long gone. This scene is preceded by the separate visits of Mr. Zhou and Lizhen to the old apartment where they looked in the direction of the camera and asked in a seemingly nonchalant way, eyes wet with tears, the whereabouts of its former occupants.

In an interview, Wong Kar-wai said that his film is about "the end of a period."[12] It is not only about the end of an elegant era when people still behaved in a restrained way and adhered to a decent sense of value; it is also about the disappearing era with its colonial history. Personal desire must then be contextualized with the destiny of a place. The geopolitical and cultural geography is embedded in the last sequence of the film, with the newsreel of Charles de Gaulle's visit to Cambodia in 1966 and Mr. Zhou's leaving his secret in Angkor Wat. Ending the film in the year 1966 has a special meaning, because it marks the end of something and the beginning of something else, said Wong.[13] This political and historical implication is not explicit in the film, perhaps to avoid a facile political overtone. Like the mood permeating the whole film, it can only be evoked or intimated. Antedating the turmoil of 1967 social unrest in Hong Kong, the film's background shows little significance about the uncertainties of the period, except the emigration of Mrs. Sun to America. The hazy presence of history in the film ironically highlights the absence of a presence of a politically apathetic colonized people. After the 1967 social unrest, the social policies of the Hong Kong government turned more liberal, but the underlying nature of a colonial repression was still there, in spite of the fact that some people refer to the British as "benign colonizer." The Hong Kong collective identity was just emerging, still subject to manipulations of the state machine of the colonial government, one of which was to uphold the status-quo imaginary or "Hong Kong is Our Home." The new generation immersed in this embryonic sense of identity was still in need of a proper inculcation of historical consciousness. It is particularly this postwar generation growing up against such a sociopolitical backdrop that feels inclined to regress to a mood of nostalgia in the process of writing their local history. In this sense, Wong's film fits in the genre of nostalgic film as a means of revalorizing a local history about to disappear with the passage of time, as well as demonstrating the links between nostalgia and regressive impulses.

Having said all that, Wong's structuring of nostalgia is not a one-way regression. The audience can sense that Wong not only seems to be interested in holding on to a nostalgic imaginary of old Hong Kong, but also the future of the city. The close-up shot on the plate number of Mr. Zhou's hotel room, 2046, could not be a randomly chosen number; 2046 marks the last year of Hong Kong's "one country, two systems" with a guaranteed high degree of autonomy, stipulated in the 1984 Sino-British Joint Declaration. Besides intimating the mood of the irretrievable, Wong also wants to intimate a sense of inevitable change. One wonders whether this opaque reference may reveal the director's mindset about the city's future. The idea that inevitable changes and wrong timing in the film have led to an unfulfilled love affair may be, after all, a prophecy in anticipation of the uncertainties of the city's future as well, once the timeline of 2046 is reached.[14]

Viewed in this politicized vein, Wong may have chosen to depict the end of a colonial era under the narrative plot of a love story, contrary to the way Liu depicts the images of Hong Kong in both his short stories and novels. In Liu's story, there is a lengthy delineation of the change of the urban landscape of Hong Kong, complemented by Chun's thought of local traffic, mushrooming skyscrapers, and satellite cities. These geographic references serve to reinforce Chun's inability to face rapid changes. Chun has to part with the past, his life in Shanghai, and to adapt to the materialistic and aggressive culture of an émigré city. Liu's political reference is less obvious, as he deals with the end of a period in a more personal note of lamentation of a paradise lost.

Liu's novel into Wong's film brings to the audience the Hong Kong in the 1950s, preceded by a series of political events: the Chinese Civil War, the Korean War, and the mass influx of Chinese refugees into Hong Kong, for example. Chun Yubai's memories, Ah Xing's fantasies, Mr. Zhou and Lizhen's love affair all conspire to conjure up a nostalgic imaginary. Looking back at the past through psychical, as well as temporal, lenses, Wong Kar-wai's film is construed as an evocation of memory. The film ends with a quotation from the novel, which is thought aloud by Chun Yubai: "The past is something he could see but not touch."[15] It seems that both the director and his character, Mr. Zhou, identify with Chun's engrossment with the sense of irretrievability of the past. Wong conveys through images and music his "mood" into something having the esthetic abilities to transform, somewhat unlike the sheer sense of temporality in Liu's novel. The detailed delineation of Chun's memories of the past is a means to reflect how repressive life could force people to escape from reality. Perhaps the dissimilar use of nostalgia by both the film and the novels forms another instance of a *Tête Bêche*, in addition to character, theme, and plot.

With a Chekhovian pattern of coming and going, Wong Kar-wai brings his disjointed film to a sense of closure by successfully extracting the very essence of Liu's novel and transforming it from a personal reminiscence of the past into a visual monument of the grace and elegance of an aestheticized past. Perhaps the quiet and melancholic beauty of the mood in *In the Mood for Love* or the essence of Wong's nostalgia may be best encapsulated by a Tang poem by Cui Hu (ca. the eighth century), "Inscribed on the Door of a House South of the City":

> Last year, today, inside this house,
> Her face glistened in the midst of peach-blossoms.
> Nobody knows whither her face is gone,
> Peach-blossoms remain to smile in the vernal breeze.[16]

This poem represents the epitome of the nostalgic aesthetic, which permeates the whole film of *In the Mood for Love* and has provided invaluable inspirations to either Chinese artists of all types and genres for their enquiry into this area of study or just sheer pleasure to readers in general.

Notes

1. Stuart McDougal, *Made into Movies: From Literature to Film* (New York: Holt, Rinehart, and Winston, 1985), 3.

2. George Bluestone, *Novels into Film* (Berkeley: University of California Press, 1973), 3.

3. The most updated publication of Liu Yichang's *Duidao* is the anthology, bearing the same title, published in December 2000 by Holdery Publishing, Hong Kong, and edited by Wang Dongtao, which carries two prefaces by the novelist, one for the recent anthology, written in September 2000, one for the longer version of the novel in 1992, together with reviews of Liu's two novels. The last appendix in this anthology contains Wong Kar-wai's interpretation of the novels and his utilization of the structural intersecting of the novel in 1972 and his film in 2000 to weave out a story in the 1960's. The three quotations in the film can all be found in the longer version: "That era is over, and everything that belongs to that era no longer exists.... The past is something he could see but not touch" (96). "It was a very unbearable moment. She had her head down all the time, but it was a good time for him to get close to her. He didn't have the courage. She turned away and left" (119–120).

4. Amy Taubin, "In the Mood for Love," *Sight and Sound* 10.11 (November 2000): 55.

5. Svetlana Boym, *The Future of Nostalgia* (New York: Basic Books, 2001), xvii–xviii.

6. Rey Chow—in "Nostalgia of the New Wave: Structure in Wong Kar-wai's *Happy Together*," in Mathew Tinkom and Amy Villarejo, eds., *Keyframes: Popular Cinema and Cultural Studies* (London: Routledge, 2001)—classifies nostalgia in Wong Kar-wai into "nostalgia for a mythic origin," "another sense of home: the banality of everyday life," and "the order and function of images: returning to nature" (228–241).

7. T. S. Eliot, "The Love Song of J. Alfred Prufrock," in *The Waste Land and Other Poems,* with an introduction by Helen Vendler (New York: First Signet Classic, 1998), 11.

8. Liu Yichang, "Intersection," trans. Nancy Li, *Renditions* 29–30 (spring/autumn 1988): 86, 90.

9 .Tony Rayns, "In the Mood for Edinburgh," *Sight and Sound* 10.8 (August 2000): 16.

10. Ibid., 17.

11. Wu Zhi, the editorial consultant of the Hong Kong film magazine *City Entertainment,* first pointed out the similarity in plot between the Japanese novelist Komatsu Sakyo's short story, *Shinjy* (To die for love) and Wong Kar-wai's *In the Mood for Love.* See *City Entertainment* (March 2000): 573. Sakyo's *Shinjyu* has been translated into Chinese as *Xunqing, Taigu shengxiang,* edited and translated by Li Lang (Taipei: Xinyu Publishing, December, 1998).

12. Rayns, "In the Mood for Edinburgh," 16.

13. Ibid.

14. It is therefore no coincidence that *2046* becomes the working title of Wong Kar-wai's next film after *In the Mood for Love.* The year 2046 marks the end of the "one country, two system" autonomous rule of fifty years, as promised in the 1984 Sino-British Joint Declaration, beginning with the handover in 1997.

15. Taubin, "In the Mood for Love," 55.

16. This is the author's own translation. A quietly melancholic legend is associated with this poem about a young man, Cui Hu, and a beautiful maiden. On a spring day, Cui Hu hiked to the south side of the capital, where he saw a house with an exquisite garden. He knocked on the door to ask for some water. After a long wait, a beautiful maiden emerged and offered him a drink. A year later, at about the same time, he revisited the house and, to his disappointment, found it locked and deserted. He wrote the above poem on the door and left. This part of the legend reminds one of the quiet, sad feelings Wong Kar-wai's film evokes. But the association ends here, because the legend has a happy ending on the poet's third visit, when he and his dream lover were reunited.

CHAPTER TEN

Crouching Tiger, Hidden Dragon, Bouncing Angels

Hollywood, Taiwan, Hong Kong, and Transnational Cinema

Questions of Film Paradigms:
The National, the Transnational, the Global

The feature film *Crouching Tiger, Hidden Dragon*, directed by the Chinese-Taiwanese-American filmmaker Ang Lee, was by far the most successful Chinese-language film in the West in terms of box office sales and the amount of awards it was nominated for and received. It won the Golden Globe Award for best motion picture, and Ang Lee was named best director by the American Directors Association in early 2001. Moreover, the film was nominated for ten Oscars in spring 2001, including, paradoxically, both best picture and best foreign picture. Eventually, the film captured four Academy Awards—best foreign picture, best cinematography (Peter Pau from Hong Kong), best artistic direction/costume design (Tim Yip from Hong Kong), and best original music (mainland Chinese-turned American composer Tan Dun). It is the first time that a nondubbed, subtitled Chinese-language film crossed over into the mainstream well beyond the perimeters of art-house cinema in the United States. It also became the top-grossing foreign-language film in many parts of the world.

Because of the unprecedented success of a Chinese-language film in the United States, centers of the Chinese-speaking world basked in a moment of glory. In fact, to be eligible to compete in the category of foreign language picture at the

Crouching Tiger, Hidden Dragon (dir. Ang Lee).

Academy Awards, the film was entered as a Taiwanese film. Taiwan was Lee's birthplace after all. At the same time, the film was nominated for sixteen awards and won eight at the Twentieth Hong Kong Film Awards in spring 2001. Because Hollywood, Hong Kong, and Taiwan all claim the nationality of the film, the paradigm of *national cinema* is further contested and questioned in this instance. The politics of labeling, naming, and categorizing becomes messy and murky.

The logo of Columbia Pictures appears at the very beginning of the film, making it clear to the audience that this is a Hollywood production. Yet, the film also lists many coproducers, including Good Machine International and China Film Co-Production Corporation. (Moreover, it is a Sony Classics film, a Japanese company!) As evidenced by the phenomenal box-office sales, large audience numbers, and worldwide distribution, this Hollywood blockbuster makes a classic example of *global cinema* in the age of globalization. As an American-made/ Chinese-language film, *Crouching Tiger, Hidden Dragon* intensifies a pattern of transnational film coproduction and distribution around the world on an unprecedented scale. Hence, it also constitutes a clear expression and a major case of *transnational cinema*. Yet, at the same time, as a *Chinese-language film (huayu dianying)*, *Crouching Tiger, Hidden Dragon* allows us to reexamine the nature of a new type of film culture from the Third World, and prompts us to reconsider existing (outdated) models of film studies in regard to Third World production such as "Third Cinema," "national cinema," "diaspora cinema," and so forth.

The phenomenon of transnational cinema has had its unique manifestations in the history of Chinese-language cinemas. Because of the long-standing, historical, geopolitical fragmentation of the Chinese nation-state into the mainland, Taiwan, and Hong Kong, three separate cinematic traditions have flourished. From the 1980s to the present, there has been increasing coproduction and collaboration across national and regional borders among these three Chinese cinemas and between them and other film industries.[1] In the case of Hong Kong cinema, collaboration between film industries and the trafficking of film artists, ideas, and motifs across regional and national borders is the most obvious. Indeed, transnationalism, "flexible production," and "flexible citizenship" have of late become the mode of operation among Hong Kong film artists.[2] Interestingly enough, the flow of personnel and ideas and the crossing over of genres are also evident in a kind of transnational, joint, U.S.–Hong Kong television drama *Martial Law*. All of these factors and trends culminate in *Crouching Tiger* rightfully at the beginning of a new century and millennium.

Transnational cinema as an emergent mode of filmmaking implies the trespassing of national borders in the processes of investment, production, circulation, and consumption. Although such films have existed all along in world film history, I want to highlight the specific historical moment for such cinema, namely, the post–cold war period. The intensity and scale of this new wave of joint film production are unseen in earlier history. *Crouching Tiger* points to the prospects and possibilities of commercial transnational cinema for global entertainment.

The sense of flexible filmmaking in such transnational cinema overlaps with, and yet is to be distinguished from other categories of border-crossing filmmaking such as "exilic cinema," "diasporic cinema," and "postcolonial ethnic cinema." These various cinemas imply a spatial or psychological distance between current place of residence and original homeland in the lives of filmmakers. As Hamid Naficy aptly writes, "Diaspora, like exile, often begins with trauma, rupture, and coercion, and it involves the scattering of populations to places outside the homeland."[3] Yet, no matter how "accented" such a foreign language might be, a transnational film like *Crouching Tiger* has none of the pathos of displacement, alienation, homelessness, and quest. Although the setting is another country (ancient China), the story is about the quest for a lost object (a mighty sword) and the theme might be the nostalgia for a bygone era of chivalry, the film evokes no feelings of modernist angst, political alienation, or cultural displacement, but provides enormous thrills and pleasures to worldwide audiences of all classes and races.

Nor does such transnational cinema about or from the Third World contain a revolutionary, liberational, oppositional, and anticapitalist impulse as in types of so-called Third World cinema, Third Cinema, or countercinema, vis-à-vis mainstream Hollywood and European film. In fact, it partakes of the mechanisms of Hollywood filmmaking and is thoroughly at peace with the economic principles of transnational capitalism. It takes advantage of the fluid and multiple channels of funding, investment, and distribution afforded by post–cold war capitalism. The filmmakers and distributors intend to pursue handsome returns and profits from the capital they have invested in the making of these films on a grand global scale that was impossible during the cold war years, when national cinemas were often drawn along both geographic and ideological lines between East and West.

The production of *Crouching Tiger* involves artists from the mainland, Hong Kong, and China and turns into a trans Chinese talent show. It has the biggest pan Asian stars on the silver screen: Chow Yun-Fat, from Hong Kong (Li Mu Bai); Michelle Yeoh, from Hong Kong/Malaysia (Yu Shu Lien); mainland actress Zhang Ziyi (Jen); Taiwanese actor Chang Chen (Lo); Taiwanese actor Lung Si-hung (Sir Te); and veteran Hong Kong female martial arts star Cheng Pei Pei (Jade Fox). Coco Lee sings the theme song while Yo-Yo Ma performs the music on his cello. Despite the geographic and political divisions, a sense of "cultural China" (Tu Wei-ming's term) emerges from the film. And this image of a disappearing "good old China" is precisely what Ang Lee intends to construct in this film.

It seems that a new chapter in world film history and theory yet to be written is to describe the varieties and characteristics of transnational film adequately. Several categories of the transnational have already emerged. To judge from the patterns of production and circulation, blockbusters such as *Crouching Tiger, Hidden Dragon* and certain action and martial arts films by Jackie Chan and his like clearly demarcate the domain of the *commercial transnational cinema,* or even the terrain of *global cinema*. Independent directors from countries troubled with heavy censorship make up another category of the transnational. Certain directors living inside the Chinese state bypass domestic censorship by funding, producing, and exhibiting their films outside China. Such "international festival films" constitute the category of the *independent art-house transnational cinema*. A latent political critique of the totalitarian state sometimes underlines these films. Numerous examples exist, for instance, *East Palace West Palace* (dir. Zhang Yuan, 1997) and, more recently *Beijing Bicycle* (dir. Wang Xiaoshuai, 2001) and *Platform* (dir. Jia Zhangke, 2000). Moreover, independent directors, estranged from the nation-state—e.g., the Islamic state—and living in exile and diaspora, produce *exilic transnational cinema* for expatriate and foreign audiences.

Ang Lee's Invention of China and the Globalization of the Wuxia Genre

The globalization of Chinese-language films from the mainland, Taiwan, and Hong Kong has taken several paths over the past fifteen years or so. First, there is the art-house paradigm. Films such *Raise the Red Lantern* by Zhang Yimou and *Farewell My Concubine* by Chen Kaige have been screened in art-house movie theaters in the West. Second, Jackie Chan's martial arts films, or more precisely kung fu (*gongfu*, fistfight) films such as *Rumble in the Bronx* and *Supercop* have had far more appeal in the United States than the art films. Sometimes these films are dubbed into English for release to U.S. audiences. *Crouching Tiger, Hidden Dragon* represents a new wave in the globalization of Chinese-language films. In terms of Chinese/Hong Kong film genres, the film belongs to a long-standing tradition of *wuxia* films (swordfight, knight-errantry) that includes distinguished directors such as Chang Che, King Hu, Tsui Hark, and Ching Siu-tung. As one critic puts it, "From a historical perspective, *Crouching Tiger, Hidden Dragon* becomes a millennial synthesis of the *wuxia* tradition."[4] The film carries the influences from earlier films. Unlike the usual *wuxia* films, however, this one is not about a deadly war between good and evil or about some single-minded revenge story. Instead, *Crouching Tiger* builds a romantic, sentimental, and philosophical dimension to martial arts and the characters. As the film's screenplay writer James Schamus writes, "*Crouching Tiger, Hidden Dragon* is not a kung fu movie that we associate with street fighting. This movie is more about inner strength and centeredness. That is where the floating comes in, more romantic choreography and dance." "The people are expressing where they are, their ambiguities and ambivalences, the conflicts they feel. In most of the fights in this movie, they can't fully fight, because emotionally they are torn. So, the fighting is a way of thinking and feeling and relating."[5] The film becomes a quest for China, or a representation of an imaginary ancient China. In Ang Lee's own words, "The film is a kind of dream of China, a China that probably never existed, except in my boyhood fantasies in Taiwan. Of course, my childhood imagination was fired by the martial arts movies I grew up with and by the novels of romance and derring-do I read instead of doing my homework. That these two kinds of dreaming should come together now, in a film I was able to make in China, is a happy irony for me."[6]

There exists a combination of martial arts and a lyrical romantic sensibility. Rapid-fire action is united with sentimentality (strongly felt yet suppressed feelings on the part of Li Mu Bai and Shu Lien). The film is "an attempt to blend the two dominant genres of Chinese filmmaking, the feminine operatic melodrama, like 'Love Eternal,' and the masculine martial-arts adventure, and to do it in a way that also integrates Western notions of psychoanalytical character development."[7] This is an idealization of the old China. Beijing was home to Lee's mother, and mainland Chinese culture is part of Lee's cultural upbringing. But when he finally visited Beijing, the China he had in mind was no more. Lee has repeatedly stated his nostalgia for classical China, an imaginary China that probably did not exist in reality.

> I didn't see what I was looking for—it felt as if I were in a big Taipei. I had no thrill because that China does not exist anymore, either in Taiwan or America or here: it's a history. It is a dream that all the Chinese people in the world have, an impression. Gone with the wind.
>
> But you can't remove China from the boy's head. So I'm finding China now. That's why I am making this movie with these people, to talk about things we know and that practically don't exist. Good old China.[8]

The film amounts to a rewriting of the martial arts genre by way of a Taoist sensibility. Wudang Mountain, a holy Taoist center—rather than the holy Buddhist center, Shaolin Temple, also the setting of many martial arts films—represents a cultural origin and a brand of philosophy. Green Destiny, the legendary sword itself, sets the tone and generic boundary for the film's actions. The film embodies the Taoist ideal/idea of personal and spiritual liberation. Yet the veteran fighters Li Mu Bai (Chow Yun-fat) and Yu Shu Lien (Michelle Yeoh) are not entirely free from human responsibilities and emotional restraints. Li Mu Bai and Shu Lien love each other deeply, and yet they hide their emotions. Green Destiny, in the guardianship of Li Mu Bai, is a symbol of both phallic strength and impotence. Li asks Shu Lien to safeguard it for him, but it is stolen by a young upstart. It is the novice Jen (Zhang Ziyi) who achieves freedom from emotional, familial, and social inhibitions. She steals the sword, and indeed steals the show from her senior Chinese stars Chow and Yeoh because she is the only one who obtains total freedom. Zhang Ziyi is a young and upcoming actress, who just established her stardom in Zhang Yimou's art-house film *Wode fuqin muqin* (The Road Home, 2000). The magic final scene of the film shows her flight to freedom, an airy lightness of being, a total physical and mental liberation from human bondage. Together with Yeoh's character, Zhang's performance gives weight to the importance of women warriors and builds up the overall elegance of the film.

As a filmmaker, Lee trained in the United States and perfectly understands Hollywood conventions of filmmaking. In his previous films, he has shown a superb ability to render the smooth and plausible flow of narrative. His mastery of the formal procedures of the classical continuity principle of Hollywood has allowed the audience to appreciate the realism of emotions, sense, and sensibility that he describes in his films. In this respect, Lee belongs to an international, Hollywood-originated, "transcultural poetics" of cinema observed by American, Chinese and other film artists from around the world. Yet *Crouching Tiger, Hidden Dragon* also looks to another source of film art and represents a new departure for him not only in term of genre, but also in terms of film aesthetics. Lee had established himself as a virtuoso craftsman of family drama and period drama (*The Wedding Banquet, Eat Drink Man Woman, Sense and Sensibility, The Ice Storm*). *Crouching Tiger* is his first martial arts film. As opposed to the Chinese appropriation of the Hollywood realist narrative convention, theatricality, spectacle, performance, and expressionism constitute another enduring legacy of genres and aesthetics from the beginning of Chinese film history to the present. Martial arts, kung fu, *wuxia,* ghosts and spirits, vampires, and opera films are all subgenres of this "cinema of attractions." And this time, Lee combines the two strains of the poetics of Chinese cinema and puts his own signature on the genre of martial arts film in *Crouching Tiger.*

The aestheticization of the *wuxia* film accounts for part of the strong appeal of the movie to international audiences. The narrative of the film moves from the lush exquisite landscape of southern China (houses, architecture, courtyard, streets, rivers, bridges) to the harsh, barren, vast, awe-inspiring Gobi Desert in northwestern China (Xinjiang). The characters and actions are packaged in ancient Chinese costumes and traditional Eastern music. Perfectly framed shots remind the viewer of the best of Chinese art-house films. Yuen Woo-ping's elegant choreography, balletic fighting sequences, and dancelike actions add to the wonder of the film. But does it all work? If yes, for whom?

Reception Gap in Transnational Cinema between East and West; or, the Question of Realism

The reception of transnational films has proven to be uneven and asymmetrical from region to region, continent to continent. This is due to different degrees of cultural proximity among the spectators, namely, discrepancy in levels of audiences' familiarization with Chinese film genres, artistic conventions, and film history. *Crouching Tiger* is in Mandarin Chinese (rather than Cantonese or Fukienese dialect), the official "mother tongue" of China and Taiwan, and Ang Lee states that the film is the projection of his vision of the old Chinese tradition. This particular vision of China, or the packaging of old China in Lee's film art, elicits drastically different reactions from world audiences. In the West, especially in the United States and the United Kingdom, the film attained an unprecedented level of box-office success for foreign-language films and was highly rated by critics and viewers alike. The showering of awards testifies to Lee's popularity. Yet, in mainland China and Hong Kong, the film appears to be unspectacular, bland, a cliché, deja vu.[9] The Chinese audiences have seen enough of martial arts films—including improbable stunts such as characters flying on rooftops and fighting on bamboo trees. The fighting scene in the bamboo forest at the end of the film appears extraordinary and refreshing to non-Chinese viewers only because they are not familiar with what has already been done in the past—for example, the famous scene of fighting in a bamboo grove in King Hu's masterpiece *A Touch of Zen* (1971). The episode of tavern fighting is a traditional set piece in the genre and harkens back to moments in earlier *wuxia* films such as King Hu's *Dragon Gate Inn* (1966). Although Zhang Ziyi performed remarkably well in the episode, the theatrical spectacle appears all too ordinary to Chinese viewers. The lyricism of the film and the oriental/Taoist philosophy of the characters again appear contrived. A very funny, yet jarring, aspect of the film is the phenomenon of real accent in cinema. ("Accented cinema"!) Hong Kong superstars Chow Yun-fat and Michelle Yeoh's Cantonese-accented Mandarin, as well as Chang Chen's Taiwanese-accented Mandarin, obviously deviate from the dialectal standard of the regions of China that they are supposed to represent in the film (Jiangnan, Beijing, Xinjiang). (It is like having actors with heavy Southern accents performing the roles of Yankees in an American film.) Their accents broach the rule of plausibility and verisimilitude and indeed elicited giggles from Chinese audiences watching the film. The box-office figures are below average during the first round of screening in mainland China. With the news of the film receiving unexpected high honors from Hollywood for a Chinese-language film, theaters in China begin to screen the film again in the hope of attracting more viewers. The usual question about successful Chinese-language films has been raised again in regard to Lee's film this time: who is his target audience? Did he make a Chinese-language film for the Chinese or for the global market? Is he susceptible to the accusation of orientalist self-fantasy?

It is helpful to compare the two fighting scenes in the bamboo forest in King Hu's *A Touch of Zen* and Ang Lee's *Crouching Tiger, Hidden Dragon*. In the former, the pace of fighting is much slower, without fast motion. The viewer sees clear shots of how and where the swords hit and hears the clanging of swords as they clash together. The warriors' fighting style is much more plausible, realistic, and "authentic." But Ang Lee comes after the technical innovations of martial arts film in the Hong Kong New Wave from the mid-1980s onward. Directors such as Tsui Hark and Ching Siu-tung have thoroughly revamped and changed the martial arts genre. The excessive use of special effects, new technologies of computer graphics, the accelerated tempo of action, and the shortened average shot length have completely transformed what martial arts look like in a film. The fighting sequence of Li Mubai (Chow Yun-fat) and Jen (Zhang Ziyi) in the bamboo forest, as they freely fly on top of trees, defies the law of gravity. The unbelievable sequences of characters jumping over rooftops and walls throughout the film create a film bordering on the "fantastic."

A Heroic Trio of Women Warriors: *Charlie's Angels*

The Hong Kongization, Sinification, and Asianization of Hollywood style at the beginning of the new century are also manifested in the new *Charlie's Angels* (Columbia Pictures, 2000), a filmic update of the 1970s television series. This film is far less notable and taken much less seriously than *Crouching Tiger,* but it is significant enough for our analysis of transnational motifs and styles. In featuring three women warriors/beauties/martial arts experts—played by Drew Barrymore, Cameron Diaz, and Lucy Liu—the film enters into an intricate network of intertextuality surrounding Hong Kong martial arts films.

Charlie Angels is to some extent a Hollywood version of the Hong Kong film of *Dongfang sanxia* (The Heroic Trio, 1992) and its sequel *The Executioners* (also known as *The Heroic Trio II*, 1993, both directed by Johnny To and Ching Siu-tung).[10] Like the heroines in the Hong Kong movies—Michelle Yeoh, Maggie Cheung, Anita Mui—these American women detectives become kung fu masters showing off their hand-to-hand combat skills. For instance, while Barrymore defeats her captors toward the end of the film, she calls out the styles of Chinese martial arts she is using, paying self-referential homage to a long tradition of kung fu films. The film also feels like an American feminine version of a Jackie Chan film. Episodes in this film copy and allude to the daring feats of Jackie Chan films. For instance, the heroines fighting in and dangling down from a helicopter in the last combat scene reminds the viewers of Jackie Chan's extraordinary performance in *Supercop* (1992). The new version feels more like a Hong Kongized action film than a repeat of an old American television series. The action choreography of both *Crouching Tiger, Hidden Dragon* and *Charlie's Angels* is none other than veteran Hong Kong martial arts film director Yuen Woo-ping, who is also the action choreographer of the film *Matrix.* The weight-

Charlie's old angels.

less flight of action and soaring imagination in this Hollywood production derive in part from the ingenuities of Hong Kong action film.

The casting of Lucy Liu as an Asian American "woman warrior," to appropriate the title of Maxine Hong Kingston's famous novel, evokes an established tradition of Hong Kong action heroines. Michelle Yeoh has been the premier action actress as exemplified in such films as *Wing Chun* (1993, dir. Yuen Woo-ping), *Supercop*, and *Tomorrow Never Dies* (1997). Yeoh's American counterpart would be Cynthia Rothrock, who furiously played and kicked ass in many Hong Kong martial arts films such as *Righting Wrongs*.[11] A former Miss Hawaii, Kelly Hu was groomed to be a new Asian action heroine in the television drama *Martial Law,* in which she performed marvelous feats of combat alongside veteran Hong Kong martial arts film superstar Sammo Hung. Prior to *Charlie's Angels,* Lucy Liu appeared in the Jackie Chan vehicle *Shanghai Noon.* In addition to appearing in the popular television program *Ally McBeal,* Liu stars in Quentin Tarentino's swordplay film *Kill Bill* (2003), where she fights Uma Thurman.

A light film about bouncing, sexy babes and smart airheads nevertheless conveys a serious message. With the inclusion of Lucy Liu as a minority, Asian American actress in an otherwise all-white-female cast, *Charlie's Angels* is transformed.

Charlie's new angels.

"Identity politics," "gender politics," and multiculturalism find their way in this new version of the story. The ostensible, unmistakably Chinese flavor in this American-made English-language film bespeaks the hybridization and transnationalization of film genres and conventions. It is becoming more difficult to establish and maintain borders between national film industries with the borrowing and crossing over of motifs, styles, ideas, and artists. The hyphenated state of joint film production and mixed film styles in these cases call for more attention to aspects of film culture beyond the national in the study of both Hollywood and Chinese-language film.

Conclusion

It should be emphasized that, in the cases of recent Hollywood films such as *Charlie's Angels* and *Rush Hour 2* (starring Jackie Chan and Chris Tucker), ethnicity is ultimately detached from nationality despite the ostensive surface flirtations with foreign cultures. Ethnicity-*cum*-culture becomes a portable object that travels and is carried across national borders. Ethnic identity (Chineseness) is dissociated and "disembedded," to borrow a term from Anthony Giddens, from the contexts of the original home country, from the deep pathos of the nation-state.[12] Although nationality and the nation-state are often perceived as a menacing, demonic entity—as seen in films such as *Red Corner, Kundun, Seven Years in Tibet,* and *Xiu Xiu: The Sent-Down Girl*—culture/ethnicity, in the forms of Chinese cuisine, martial arts, and so on, is harmless, nonthreatening, and benign. For instance, the Jackie Chan and Chris Tucker characters could enjoy "Chinese soul food" in America in *Rush Hour 2*, just as Jackie Chan films and Chinese food are consumed daily by customers around the world, whether in Hong Kong, Vancouver, New York, or Seoul. Asian culture becomes a depthless postmodern pastiche of ethnic cuisines and martial arts styles. All this is obviously different from the nationalist longings in old martial arts films produced before the 1990s, where the national tradition is necessarily tied to Chinese identity. One recalls certain Bruce Lee films, or early Jackie Chan films, or Tsui Hark films where the Chinese heroes (performed by Bruce Lee, Jackie Chan, Jet Li, etc.) encounter and fight imperialists (Japan, the United Kingdom, and so forth) to defend the honor and sovereignty of the Chinese nation. Yet, as *Charlie's Angels,* Chris Tucker, and a suave globe-trotting Jackie Chan toy with Chinese martial arts in these new movies, ethnicity has turned into a transnational, moveable, deterritorialized, and humorous practice detached from any sense of serious grounding in history and national(ist) politics in an increasingly borderless world.[13]

Crouching Tiger, Hidden Dragon, as a quintessential example of global cinema, embodies the most basic inner contradiction of globalization, namely, the push and pull between the local and the global. On the one hand, the film artist feels compelled to hold onto some uncontaminated authentic national culture, to search for the wellsprings of local tradition, that is, the legacies of Chinese martial arts film and melodrama as shaped by previous masters such as King Hu and Li Hanxiang. On the other hand, the logic of global entertainment forces the artist to produce homogeneous, prepackaged cultural fast food to be effortlessly consumed by audiences from all over the world. Paradoxically, the nonexistent imaginary old China as admittedly invented by Lee is a dehistoricized, disembedded entity in the global commercial film market. If Chinese history—say, the Ming Dynasty—with all the attendant emotional depths and political specificity, matters in an old martial arts film such as *A Touch of Zen*, China in Lee's film has become a shallow fantasy world, a wishful thinking, a stage for global entertainment. The seeming return to history and resort to national culture is a décor, a show, a contemporary spectacle.

The ending of the film is as uncertain and provocative as it can be: Jen, the Zhang Ziyi character, jumps off a bridge and flutters in the sky. The "unbearable lightness of being," this airy defiance of the laws of gravity and plausibility, creates a suspension of belief. The ending makes a good film example of the "fantastic" as Tzvetan Todorov defines the genre.[14] The viewer wonders whether the final scene is real or unreal. The woman warrior/romantic lover flies away from all earthly, social, emotional attachments toward the realm of nothingness. She hovers above the earth just as the film as a transnational commodity travels and circulates freely from place to place, country to country to be consumed. Could this truly happen? What to believe? The enigmatic ending is as incredible, ephemeral, insubstantial, and lightheaded as the processes of globalization.

Notes

Early versions of this chapter were presented at the conference "Global Hollywood: Re-thinking the National, Transnationality, and Globalization," organized by the German Historical Institute and the University of Victoria, in Victoria, British Columbia, Canada, November 29–December 1, 2001, and at the symposium "Island of Light: Taiwan Cinema and Culture," held at the University of Wisconsin—Madison, March 2002. I thank the organizers of the conference (Christof Mauch, Heide Fehrenbach, and Thomas Sauders) and the symposium (Nicole Huang, David Bordwell, and Jim Udden) for inviting me and giving me opportunities to present my ideas. Christof Mauch offers a report on the "Global Hollywood" conference in the *Bulletin of the German Historical Institute* no. 30 (spring 2002): 193–199.

1. See Sheldon H. Lu, "Historical Introduction: Chinese Cinemas (1896–1996) and Transnational Film Studies," in Sheldon H. Lu, ed., *Transnational Chinese Cinemas: Identity, Nationhood, Gender* (Honolulu: University of Hawai`i Press, 1997), 1–31.

2. Sheldon H. Lu, "Filming Diaspora and Identity: Hong Kong and 1997," in Poshek Fu and David Desser, eds, *The Cinema of Hong Kong: History, Arts, Identity* (Cambridge: Cambridge University Press, 2000), 273–288.

3. Hamid Naficy, *An Accented Cinema: Exilic and Diasporic Filmmaking* (Princeton, N.J.: Princeton University Press, 2001), 14.

4. David Bordwell, "Hong Kong Martial Arts Cinema," in Linda Sunshine, ed., *Crouching Tiger, Hidden Dragon: A Portrait of the Ang Lee Film* (New York: New Market Press, 2000), 20.

5. James Schamus, quoted in Sunshine, ed., *Crouching Tiger, Hidden Dragon,* 42.

6. Ang Lee, quoted in Sunshine, ed., *Crouching Tiger, Hidden Dragon,* 7.

7. Rick Lyman, "Crouching Memory, Hidden Heart: Watching Movies with Ang Lee," *New York Times* (March 9, 2001).

8. Ang Lee, quoted in Sunshine, ed., *Crouching Tiger, Hidden Dragon,* 40.

9. Derek Elley, "Asia to 'Tiger': Kung-Fooey—Asia's Slouching Tiger: 'Hidden' Drag-gin'," *Variety* (February 5–11, 2001), 1, 85; Mark Landler, "Lee's 'Tiger,' Celebrated Every-where But at Home," *New York Times* (February 27, 2001): B1, B2. James Schamus, Ang Lee's longtime collaborator and screenwriter of this film, defended it as the top-grossing Chinese-language film in many parts of the world. See Stephen Teo, "We Kicked Jackie Chan's Ass! An Interview with James Schamus," *Senses of Cinema* (spring 2001) [www .sensesofcinema.com/contents/01/13/schamus.html]. For other reviews, ranging from praise to reservation, see William Rothman, "New Life for an Old Genre: Ang Lee's

Crouching Tiger, Hidden Dragon," *Persimmon* 2.3 (winter 2002): 80–83; Pauline Chen, film review of *Crouching Tiger, Hidden Dragon* in *Cineaste*, 26.4 (fall 2001): 71–72.

10. See Anne T. Ciecko and Sheldon H. Lu, "The Heroic Trio: Anita Mui, Maggie Cheung, Michelle Yeoh—Self-Reflexivity and the Globalization of the Hong Kong Action Heroine," *Post Script* 19.1 (fall 1999): 70–86. (This article appears in a special issue on Hong Kong cinema.)

11. For a frame-by-frame analysis of Rothrock's performance in action films, see David Bordwell's discussion in *Planet Hong Kong: Popular Cinema and the Art of Entertainment* (Cambridge, Mass.: Harvard University Press, 2000), 238–243.

12. Anthony Giddens, *The Consequences of Modernity* (Stanford, Calif.: Stanford University Press, 1990).

13. The indestructible link between Chinese martial arts and the Chinese nation is evident, for instance, in Tsui Hark's Huang Feihong series. Tony Williams offers a rereading of the Huang Feihong films in light of cultural and geographic diaspora in "Under 'Western Eyes': The Personal Odyssey of Huang Fei-hong in *Once Upon a Time in China*," *Cinema Journal* 40.1 (fall 2000): 3–24.

14. Tzvetan Todorov, *The Fantastic: A Structural Approach to a Literary Genre*, translated by Richard Howard (Cleveland: Press of Case Western Reserve University, 1973).

PART THREE

Politics,
Nationhood,
Globalization

CHAPTER ELEVEN

Borrowing Postcolonial

Wu Nianzhen's *Dou-san* and the Memory Mine

The empires of our time were short-lived, but they have altered the world forever; their passing away is their least significant feature.
—V. S. Naipaul, The Mimic Men

Yifen, a fashionable Taiwanese coed, sat in a Taipei movie theater, puzzled. She had just watched Wu Nianzhen's *Dou-san: A Borrowed Life* (1994) and the closing credits were rolling. An older man sat a few rows ahead, sobbing, his face in his hands. The house staff gingerly swept up around him. He was about the age of Yifen's father. It had been a long film, a little depressing, but nothing to get *that* upset about. The film was about the relationship between a father and son, which got complicated because of the father's loyalty to Japan. Yifen liked Japanese things, especially clothes and style magazines, but the old guy in the film had been a fanatic, upsetting everybody—including that man still sitting up there—with his Japanese obsessions. Maybe, she thought, he was mental; maybe they *both* were mental. Hurriedly Yifen picked up her bag and left.

This is a model postcolonial situation, repeated many times across Taiwan with the release of Wu's film. A young woman witnesses a catharsis. She sees someone from the older generation moved to tears by a narrative of postcolonial intransigence and desire. In spite of Japan's defeat, many older Taiwanese cling to colonial-era thinking and even continue to admire Japan. After the war, they must have experienced wrenching anxiety, inevitably to be passed down to their children. The man Yifen watched would be the age of those children, the

postwar, postcolonial generation. All over Taiwan, people responded emotionally to Wu's film. At its outdoor premiere in Ruifang, Wu's hometown, many
people's recognition was so great they could not bear to stay to the end.[1] One
man wrote that he broke down in tears when he saw *Dou-san,* and numerous
Taiwanese friends have told me variations of the Yifen story. Wu himself describes the film as a collective memory unlocked by the scripting and filming of
his personal experience.[2] He says it was excruciating to make.

But who is Wu? Wu Nianzhen is a novelist and screenwriter for Hou Hsiao-
hsien's most important films, including *City of Sadness* (1989), *The Puppetmaster* (1993), and *Dust in the Wind* (1987); the latter is based on Wu's own story. Together with Hou and the noted writer Zhu Tianwen, Wu is responsible for many
of the most acclaimed films of the Taiwan New Cinema. With *City of Sadness,*
there was considerable friction in the approach to the material and writing. Wu,
as a native Taiwanese, had differences with Zhu and Hou, both of whom are
mainland transplants.[3] With such inflammatory historical material as the Two
Two Eight Incident (February 28) and a complex chorale of languages, including Japanese, Shanghainese, Fukienese, Hakka, and Mandarin, it is not surprising that scripting *City* was a delicate undertaking.

Wu's other scripts include *The Sandwich Man* (1983), an omnibus picture
based on stories by Huang Chunming, with segments directed by Hou Hsiao-
hsien, Zeng Zhuangxiang, and Wan Ren; *Hill of No Return* (dir. Wang Tong,
1992); *People between Two Chinas* (dir. Yu Kanping, 1988); and *Woman of Wrath*
(dir., Zeng Zhuangxiang, 1984). As of 1992, a total of sixty-four of Wu's scripts
had been produced, including three for Ann Hui (*Song of the Exile* [1989], *Zodiac Killers* [1991], and *My American Grandson* [1991]) and at least two with Edward Yang (*Mah-jong* [1996] and *That Day on the Beach* [1983]).[4] He has directed
two of his own pictures, *Dou-san* and *Buddha Bless America* (1996). Until September 1999, he was host of *Wu Nianzhen's Taiwan,* a television show that explored
Taiwan's heritage. This show ran weekly on Taiwan's biggest cable network, TVBS.
The popularity of Wu's program and its strong nativist appeal made him the
object of KMT courtship (Guomingdang, the Nationalist Party) during the 1998
mayoral election for Taipei. Instead, Wu supported the DPP (Democratic Progressive Party) incumbent, Chen Shui-bian (Chen Shuibian). Wu then became
the object of a KMT smear campaign, though Chen lost the election.

Back in the 1980s, Wu's motivation for scripting the biographical *Dou-san*
was not merely personal, but also political. He had noticed how journalists used
to ridicule Lee Teng-hui (Li Denghui) for his halting Mandarin Chinese.[5] Lee
was the first native Taiwanese to become head of the KMT and president of the
Republic of China. As a native, Lee's mother tongue is Taiwanese Hokkien, not
Mandarin. He was raised in an adoptive Hakka family, and as a teenager during

the occupation he was educated in Japanese. His higher education was in Kyoto and later the United States. People joke that the former president is fluent in everything but Mandarin. As president, Lee also was adept in the international language of political provocation.[6]

Wu's film *Dou-san* is testament to a connection between the mixed pedigree of President Lee and that of Wu's own father, a coal miner. Though personal, the film is also an argument about the maturation of Taiwan's civil society. It sounds a call to two generations of islanders: aging "historical/cultural orphans" who grew up under the Japanese and then were abandoned by the Americans to the KMT.[7] For younger, postwar Taiwanese, Wu's film unpacks baggage long stored away by their parents, yet handed down to them in oblique, often twisted ways. The film acknowledges Taiwan's mixed background, particularly its time as a Japanese colony. Though *Dou-san* is not the first film to grapple with Japanese postcolonial issues (Hou Hsiao-hsien's *City of Sadness,* scripted by Wu, is the most famous), it probably is the most heartfelt and thus elicited powerful reactions.

Keeping this in mind, the purpose of this chapter is to unpack aspects of postcolonial experience in the Taiwan New Cinema context.[8] I mean this as a supplement, within the Taiwanese context, to the formidable theoretical elaborations of Western postcolonial theory.[9] Wu's film released a barrage of postcolonial feeling among Taiwanese people. It is an index of Taiwan postcoloniality because it intervened at a moment when democratic pluralism was overtaking KMT enforcement but memories of underdevelopment and regimentation still had force. To understand the link between discredited authority figures and colonial power, past and present, it is crucial to grasp both the establishment and forsaking of the Japanese colonial legacy. Wu's work represents this with great force.

Three Senses of Postcolonial

At the risk of oversimplifying, we may distinguish between historical, political and psychological senses of the term "postcolonial."[10] The historical sense is the chronological period after the loss of colonial authority, dominance, or hegemony.[11] This period may already have started during the colonial regime because of resistance movements, or it could begin well after the physical departure of colonizers because of perpetuation of neocolonial structures. Taiwan is an unusual, perhaps unique, case because, although the colonizers were expelled, the country never got its independence.[12] In August 1945, Japanese colonial machinery was being dismantled as Chinese troops and officials arrived from the mainland.[13] This process took some time. Japan formally surrendered Taiwan to General Chen Yi on October 25, though "[in November] the Japanese forces were still masters of the island," according to one British eyewitness.[14] There were nonetheless high expectations of democratic self-determination among the Taiwanese civilian population.[15]

Taiwan, however, did not then achieve democracy or independence. Instead, it became a spoil to be handed back to the Chinese Nationalists, parallel to its handover to Japan after the first Sino-Japanese war in 1895. Taiwan therefore shouldered a second colonial yoke at almost precisely the time its Japanese colonial burden was lifted: Taiwan's postwar phase was not postcolonial, nor even neocolonial, but rather a recolonization under the KMT. By February 28, 1947, the KMT's brutality was apparent, making Japanese colonial domination seem comparatively benign. February 28 saw KMT troops throughout Taiwan beating and killing civilians on a pretext of quelling (Communist) revolt. An anticipated historical period of postcolonialism soon reverted to recolonization under a guise of Chinese reunification.

A second, political sense of postcolonial is the transitional condition characterized by struggles for legitimacy and power. Inextricably linked with the historical, there is nevertheless an important distinction to be made between questions of periodization, political economy, and government control. Although the immediate postwar period in Taiwan was provisional, the Nationalists behaved otherwise: "In its present form [February 1946] the Government more closely resembles an Occupational Government than a Government of the people."[16]

A third, psychological sense of postcolonial concerns liminal spaces in which the ego seeks new objects of identification following breakdowns—and compensatory continuities—in colonial structures of thought.[17] The psychological sense is most useful in discussing *Dou-san*, because the film is a remarkable character study of colonial subjectivity in an emerging postcolonial age. The eponymous character, the film's style and narrative, and Wu's efforts in Taiwan's media all express a vivid, complex sense of postcolonial psychology. This historical, biographical character is a specimen of contemporary Taiwanese ambivalence toward colonial legacies, Japanese and KMT. In addition, Wu's position in contemporary Taiwan media, including his commercial and political activities, is important in situating Dou-san—the person and the film—as a bellwether for Taiwanese who recognized him in their own experiences.

To conclude, I will introduce a fourth sense of postcolonial, one that involves space and place. This is an effort to read history through space, the mediated spaces of cinema, television, and the digital web, rather than seeing space through history. In other words, screens are spatialized; they take on depth when they mediate historical layers normally regarded as foundational to social memory. The selective, emotional prospecting of Wu's film reveals a lode of postcolonial memory that, judging from the strong reaction to the film in Taiwan, somehow had been overlooked.

Mine and Identity

Who, or what, is Dou-san? The very name evokes the Japanese occupation. "Dou-san" means "papa" in Japanese. The term is a bastardized Japanese name for the writer/director's father, whose proper name in the film is Seiga, powerfully acted by Cai Zhennan, a noted musician. Wu Nianzhen gives his film the familiar name of the father, adding the subtitle "A Borrowed Life." The life is borrowed, along with the name. Taiwan's main language, Fukienese, is partly distinguished from its mainland sibling by an abundance of Japanese loanwords, like *Dou-san* or *Kaa-san* (mother), and words for certain foods, machines, and slang. Remnants of Japanese are even more pronounced in Taiwan's aboriginal languages. Dou-san (Seiga) embodies a pronounced indigenous identity in his preference for the old ways, which happen to be Japanese ways.

Seiga worked the gold mines of Jiufen in the 1950s and raised his family in the squalid company shanties provided for workers. When the gold ran out, the digging continued, only for coal, which promptly lodged itself in the recesses of the miners' lungs or collapsed on them while they worked in the inky blackness. The peril and terrible darkness of the mineshafts is underlined when accidents happen and Dou-san runs into the mine to rescue his friends. Pulling a heavy boxcar, he brings their battered bodies out of the shaft, to deliver them to weeping wives and families.

In 1946, Lieutenant Commander Max Berman, a British officer inspecting what was then called the Itahashi coal mine, wrote, "Although the Coal Industry is one of Formosa's oldest industries, it is one of the least developed, by modern standards, and the conditions of labour in the mines is Formosa's prime example of Japanese exploitation. It is difficult to understand the Japanese mentality and attitude in this particular case, in view of the great strides made in other directions, on this Island."[18] Berman describes the long descent into the pit on a narrow-gauge track, followed by "miles of back-breaking trudging along water-logged tracks," then a cable that lowered miners down an incline. Finally, the last sixty yards to the coalface was reached through a tunnel so small one had to crawl on one's belly.[19] The Japanese also exploited aboriginal labor in the mines, though this does not figure in Wu's or Hou's films. In Hou's *Dust in the Wind*, the young autobiographical hero watches a television documentary on coal miners, spellbound by the claustrophobic spaces.

As a boy Wu, in voice-over, imagines the mine as a monster, its black maw devouring his father every day. But every night, it somehow relinquishes him to his wife and children. Dou-san quarrels with his wife and ignores his daughter, but he dotes on his son. He tries to teach him Japanese and cultivate in him an affinity for Japanese things—pleasures such as gambling, teahouses, and Japa-

Dousan, his son, and cohorts at the mouth of a mine.

nese movies. Dou-san never explains his Japanese infatuations, which is something of a mystery in this film. But there are hints.

Seiga is what the Japanese call *yo-shi*: a man adopted by marriage into his wife's family, taking her name, status, registry, and forfeiting his own. The *yo-shi* system is a way for heirless families to carry on the family name; it amounts to "purchasing" a son for the sake of family continuity, but it also means he cancels out his identity in favor of his spouse. It reverses the usual patrilineal pattern of marrying off daughters to pass the family estate through sons and grandsons. A contradictory affair, the adopted husband is not really master of his own family but rather a father-manqué; his firstborn son cannot take the father's name, but instead he is named after the mother. Dou-san is a hired gun, as it were, but in practice most *yo-shi* are embraced as full-fledged father figures, despite their ambiguous pedigree. Li Tianlu, Hou Hsiao-hsien's eponymous *The Puppetmaster* —also written by Wu—was a *yo-shi*, too, though he commanded more respect than Dou-san. This can be connected to Lee Teng-hui, who was adopted into a foster Hakka family. His true origins are obscure, but some (including PRC officials, no doubt) assume he is Japanese, at least in part. The notion that Taiwanese identity is a borrowed affair involving questions of paternity finds an effective allegory in the figure of the *yo-shi*.

Exchanges of kinship, patriarchal authority, and the maintenance of appearances show the ways Dou-san's life is borrowed. His connections with his own family are strained. Seiga's people, from Jiayi, in south-central Taiwan, dissoci-

In a downpour, the young Wu will hear his father explain why they carry different names.

ate from him because of his sympathy for victims of the Two Two Eight Incident. In public, he burns joss sticks for the repose of their souls, a dangerous gesture in the police-state tensions of 1947. Because of this, he is fired from his job. In response, Seiga flees to the north and is lucky to make a deal that gives him a bride. But in exchange, his firstborn son must take the bride's name. The family is desperately poor and relies on the generosity of their neighbors in the mining village. Dou-san also proves himself a spendthrift and womanizer. When the family visits relatives, they must borrow clothes, shoes, and even a watch to save face. One key scene shows Dou-san explaining to his son why he carries his mother's name and why he should never forget his (officially disavowed) patrilineal name.

During the colonial occupation Japan relentlessly suppressed indigenous languages and names. Taiwanese and Korean subjects not only had to learn, and school their children in the colonizers' language, they also had to take Japanese names and register under the *koseki* (registration) system.[20] The registration of family births, marriages, deaths, and adoptions, used in Japan since 1872 for civil transactions, was expanded and adapted to the colonial purpose of overall police surveillance. One's given name, as a legal identity, was outlawed. The Japanese language was foisted heavily on Taiwan and Korea and was bitterly resented, but it was useful to divide and stratify colonials. The greater one's proficiency in Japanese, the better one's prospects for employment, education, and preferential treatment. Language was the path to civilization, as offered by Japan. But

Japanese colonials had no choice, their native languages being outlawed, unlike Indochinese under the French or Indians under the British.[21]

Another sense in which Dou-san's life is borrowed is that he has given it up to the mining company, which eventually closes and leaves him a diseased wreck. He gets a small settlement but in the end, the mine claims his life. Dou-san seems to have little bitterness, however, except to urge his son to get out of the mineshafts, up from the laboring class. After his death Dou-san's widow says, "Not long after you were born, your Dou-san said that the greatest wish in his life was that his children should never have to work underground again. He was half buried even when he was young. His children should be free from that."[22] The occasion for Dou-san's wish is the death of the Japanese Showa emperor, in 1989, and his succession by his son. Somehow, a connection has been forged between Dou-san's colonial yoke and Showa imperialism.

Why then does Dou-san idolize Japan? Like an immigrant in his own country, he wants his children to rise from the submerged half-life of labor into a brighter day of educated prosperity. His idolization is very far from any aestheticized, Orientalist Japanophilia. Dou-san's identification is a kind of escape; something freely chosen despite the constraints he faces in the 1950s. Unlike Lee, he was not of elite colonial stock, confident of successful assimilation, studying and working alongside their Japanese masters. As an uneducated laborer, Dou-san was beneath notice of the Japanese colonial machine, except as conscript labor. Perhaps Japan signifies, for Dou-san, an "imagined community" of order, stability, and fairness, the postcolonial yearning of a man who never directly benefited from colonialism.

Dou-san's Japanese identifications, in other words, are less about Japan as a signifier of plenty than about exercising choice—even when there are no options available. There was no more "Ah-I-Ooh-Eh-Oh," the Japanese alphabet, the language of Seiga's meager schooling and the road to employment and prosperity. All of a sudden, that road was closed, replaced by the Mandarin "Buh-Puh-Muh-Fuh," an alien language Dou-san never learned and many Taiwanese still do not speak. In Hou's *Dust in the Wind*, based on Wu's autobiographical script, an old shopkeeper explains this blockage to the boy about to go into national service. In a 1945 interview, General Chen Yi expressed his hope that the important task of teaching Mandarin to the Formosans could successfully be accomplished within four years.[23] Fond hope indeed from the general who had to take responsibility for the February 28, 1947, massacre of Formosans.

During the occupation, Japan tried to kindle desires for modernization and Japanization under an imperial assimilation policy called *ko-minka (huangmin hua).*[24] Ironically, *ko-minka* was a variation of the ancient Chinese method of civilizing barbarians. But among modern colonial powers in Asia, this policy of

Poring over a Japanese newspaper.

absorption of a colonial people by a "master race and culture" was unprecedented.[25] Taiwanese subjects were not only to mimic and come to resemble, but to *become* Japanese: to "dress, eat, and live as Japanese do, speak the Japanese tongue as their own and guard our national spirit in the same way as do Japanese born in Japan," according to Governor Kawamura Takeji in 1929.[26] "Assimilation is the opposite of colonization," writes Albert Memmi, and if the governor was aware that an erasure of *all* difference would mean the end of Japanese colonial privilege, it did not faze him.[27]

Wu Nianzhen, a postwar baby (born in 1952), did not carry the Japanese baggage of his father, except vicariously and unconsciously. But for Dou-san's generation, raised in an environment of Japanese assimilation, the abrupt cancellation of Japanese language and its Mandarin replacement was traumatic.[28] For them it was an enforced infantilization, and at the same time it opened a chasm between them and their children, who were growing and learning under a new, unfamiliar system. How could Dou-san be a father when the circumstances of his upbringing were completely different? How could the father's aspirations be translated to postcolonial progeny? What could he possibly teach his children?[29]

The liminal, twilight spaces of psychological confusion one would expect from the postwar postcolonial period are handed down to the family in the 1950s and 1960s. In this time of hard-core KMT consolidation, Dou-san clings to borrowed, inherited forms of culture in language, kinship, livelihood, and personal preferences. He refuses to "trade in" his colonial identity formations. His connections with the Japanese occupation, though imaginary, are relational, intimate, and inherited, and, as such, he tries to will them to his son. In the displacement of a father's colonial complex onto his son, in a time of neocolonial martial law, there is a fateful logic. In homage to his father's willful embrace of a foreign patrimony, Wu illuminates a link between the Japanese and KMT as imposition, inheritance, and imposter. In this light, the jumbled disarray between historical, political, and psychological senses of postcoloniality seems less baffling. The affective, filial power of colonialism lingers on down, through regret and nostalgia.

There is a metaphor that evokes the colonial and cinematic imagery equally well. Borrowed from Deleuze, Robert J. C. Young's metaphor combines the mechanical, factory-like operations of colonialism with the power of affect and desire: "Colonialism was a machine: a machine of war, of bureaucracy and administration, and above all, of power. . . . [But] it was also a machine of fantasy, and of desire—desire that was constituted socially, collectively, as the many analyses of Western colonialism have shown us. Colonialism, in short, was not only a machine of war and administration, it was also a desiring machine. This desiring machine . . . was itself the instrument that produced its own darkest fantasy—the unlimited and ungovernable fertility of 'unnatural' unions."[30]

This desiring machine is tenacious. Dou-san obsessively harbors a desire constituted in an earlier age. But his desire does not keep pace with a political-historical change. The colonial subject is marooned in his desire, confused. He dies in 1991, Wu tells us in voice-over. One imagines, by this time, father might be used to the prosperity of his now-educated, successful son and has abandoned his Japanese fantasies. But, instead, his last days find him cajoling the family to get things ready for a trip to Japan, to see Mt. Fuji! Watching the Asian Games with his daughter, he quarrels with her about the superiority of Japanese athletes over Taiwan's. Disgusted, she accuses him of being an "unreasonable maniac,"[31] a traitor and collaborator. He grumbles to his son about skin magazines with Caucasian girls, insisting that Japanese porn is sexier. In the end, he wrests control over his miner's lung disease and refuses to show himself in his final, broken state. In all this Dou-san shows his endurance and intransigence.

From Fetishism to Theodicy

Dou-san sticks with his anachronistic object-choices to the end. He embraces a vestigial, imaginary colonial object and stubbornly maintains an "incorrect" postcolonial posture. One thinks of the Japanese soldier discovered surviving in the jungles of Guam in the 1970s, waiting for orders. Unlike his son, Dou-san

Bags packed, Seiga waits to go to Japan.

In hospital, Seiga faces death alone.

A Japanese cinema, ca. 1958; Seiga's refuge.

never emerges into social relations of a more open, comfortable sort—a national bourgeoisie, in other words. He struggles, spits, and fights, even when he does not need to, claiming for himself a life always precarious, provisional, borrowed. His last months at home and in hospital reveal him to be more than just cantankerous; his wheezing outbursts are grotesque and at the end, monstrous. He is a throwback living in a private colonial world. His grandchildren cannot talk to him because they were raised in educated, middle-class Mandarin. In hospital, Dou-san still refuses to let anyone see him. Wu (as director and as son) leaves his father not as a cancerous bag of bones; instead, at the moment of death, we see a crisp, smiling Dou-san, rakishly combing his hair and swaggering down a bright hallway, as if on his way to a Japanese teahouse. This tunnel image, besides referring to the birth canal, also recalls many shots of Dou-san moving slowly in and out of the mouth of the coal mine. In voice-over, Wu takes us back to what Chaoyang Liao calls the "traumatic scene" in the Japanese movie house: "All of a sudden, I recalled the time when I was a little kid and was abandoned by Dou-san, left alone in the movie theater. In a trance, I imagined that Dou-san has played his trick again and stood me up. I was again thrown into a void filled with subdued sobbing, and he went away to a place that was strange, mysterious, and beyond my understanding, to have a good time with his old buddies."[32]

The liminal spaces of psychological postcoloniality find other visual outlets in the film. The characteristic image of Dou-san is of a slight, out-of-focus figure sitting in the light, seen obliquely through a doorway or curtain. This provides a clear frame within the shot for both object and point-of-view, which in turn lurks—tentatively, surreptitiously—in darkness. This is the introductory shot of Dou-san, repeated many times as a touchstone image. It shows Wu's mixture of admiration and bafflement toward his father. Chaoyang Liao uses the term "divisive focalization" to describe this splitting of subjectivity. This is clear in the division between Mandarin Chinese voice-over, the grown-up son recalling his early life with father, and the diegetic dialect spoken by Dou-san and his family. Liao, however, neglects the ways that Wu builds this divisiveness —or what I call "liminality"—into the structure of his images.

The bright, swaggering shot of Dou-san combing his hair is a picture with which one would *want* to remember one's father. Is it a memory or a fantasy? Is a willed memory no different from fantasy? "Caught in between reality and fantasy, rationality and delirium," Dou-san projects himself onto his son's reconstructed memories, pushing aside the emaciated, wheezing figure in hospital.[33] It seems to be imaged from both memory and imagination, a displacement of the dark, claustrophobic reality of Dou-san's final days. Wu's combination of memory, will, and desire produces an otherworldly, but still historical space for Dou-san to inhabit.

Finally, there is Dou-san's "unreasonable" fetishism of Japan. This seems less political than psychological. The question is *why* does Dou-san think so highly of Japan—a defeated, former colonial power? Despite its defeat, despite its half-century occupation of Taiwan, Japan still provides structures of thought to which Dou-san remains subject. He, and thousands of Taiwanese like him, deliberately inclines himself toward these structures and away from structures of the postwar KMT-American alliance. Is this an unconscious form of resistance? A denial of Japanese imperialism and its defeat? The strangeness and irony of a subject people that looks up to their colonial rulers—even after they were defeated and expelled—may be partly explained by the profound disappointment people felt toward KMT betrayal. But it also has to do with the respect many Taiwanese had, and still have, toward Japan and Japanese people. The abuses of Chen and Chiang's regime did not create that respect, even though they helped cement it, retroactively, more firmly in place.

Granted, in 1945 there was a political sea change in Taiwan, but what about the cultural, social, and economic ties, what Edward Said calls "a legacy of connection," the intricate networks of personal and business loyalties built up over fifty years?[34] These did not just stop cold when the war ended. What has to be accounted for is the continuity of people's everyday allegiances, the durability of habit, even though awareness of the Japanese defeat was palpably there—the defeat of an intimate, if also imperialist, power.

The collision of people's personal allegiances and habits with global political forces creates peculiar psychological complexes.[35] Freud and Marx both analyzed fetishism as a way for the mind to cope, in psychosexual and socioeconomic relations, with unacceptable, but undeniable propositions. Dou-san fetishizes Japan as a way to mask his self-abnegation—he literally has no existence outside his role as husband and "Dou-san"—as well as his economic impotence. For Japan to work as a fetish, its defeat and disappearance is a necessary condition: "Colonialism returns at the moment of its disappearance," writes Anne McClintock.[36] For Dou-san, Japanese colonialism is a basic framework of his outlook, a structure of feeling he cannot do without.[37] Mind over matter: the Japanese empire as external historical matter is not necessary; in fact it works better in mind alone.

Going beyond the vocabulary of psychoanalysis to religion, one could also invoke "theodicy": a rupture in faith caused by the collision of belief in an omnipotent God with the undeniable existence of evil. The "rational" thing, it would seem in the face of such contradiction, is to give up the faith. But that is not what people always do. Instead, they often rationalize evil as an instrument of divine goodness.

In Europe, civilization processes *(mission civililatrice)* were matters of religious mission, the Christianizing of heathen barbarians.[38] Conversion of pagans to Christianity was bedrock of colonial policy. Education, health, hygiene, morality, law, economic, and technological progress were all linked to primitives' need for salvation.[39] Japan, too, embarked on a late Meiji "ministry of modernization" (Marius Jansen) and linked its national cosmologies of Shinto animism with Confucian notions of hierarchy and filial piety.[40]

But compared to Christian missions, this was little more than window dressing for the crucible of civilization: nationality. Japanese national identity itself took on religious overtones, especially in those overheated periods following war victories.[41] Japanese notions of civilization *(bunmei)* had less to do with proselytizing heathens than a destiny of divine right, a conviction of invincible fate. Japan was fated to lead, not convert, Asia. That was its mission.[42] Shinto was not primary, but secondary; the emphasis in state Shinto fell on the state. Nevertheless "as part of the Kominka program the Taipei bureaucrats required every household in Formosa to maintain a proper Shinto altar *(kamidana)* upon which to display emblems of the Sun Goddess and his latest descendant, the Emperor Hirohito."[43] Like Christian evangelism, the *ko-minka* policy was antiessentialist; it depended on the mutability of people, in Taiwan and Korea, as a basis for conversion.[44] Furthermore, Japanese colonialism, coopting anticolonial activism, was offered all over Asia as an agent of liberation from European domination.[45] Dou-san's theodicy is his continued recognition of imperial authority in spite of, or maybe because of, its disappearance. There is no evidence of any rationalization or reconciliation with the manifest historical reality.

Wu's portrait of Dou-san is not that of a rationalizer; he is not a man whose ideology or creed is tested (like the Old Testament Job), but whose faith in the Japanese is emotional, a form of "blind worship."[46] Dou-san scorns rationalizations, not understanding his daughter's charge that his blind faith amounts to a betrayal of his own country. Dou-san's notion of his own country does not admit any distinction, despite the war's outcome, between Taiwan and the "Home Islands."

In contrast to this, Wu's notion of Taiwan incorporates Dou-san's fetishism, in all its irrationality. He feels little compunction to explain this tangle of postcolonial desires, only to present and accept it as a fait accompli, a fact of Taiwanese life and part of his own personal heritage.

Wu Nianzhen, Taiwan New Cinema, and Nativism

Wu's activities in the media go beyond scriptwriting to include pushing for more challenging projects within Taiwan film culture. As a key figure in the writing department at Central Motion Picture Company (CMPC), Wu was behind *In Our Time* (1982), an omnibus production with segments by Edward Yang, Ke Yizheng, Zhang Yi, and Tao Dechen. He also worked on Wang Tong's *Portrait of a Fanatic* (1982) and *Strawman* (1987). Wang's "Native Regional Trilogy" (*Strawman, Banana Paradise* [1989], and *Hill of No Return* [1992]) was made with encouragement and advice from Wu, who considers himself less a creator than a facilitator, a promoter, a person who enjoys knocking ideas around with his friends.[47] The Wu-scripted *Hill of No Return*, like *Dust in the Wind*, was set in Wu's hometown and closely observes life in a mining community under the Japanese. Like *Dou-san*, it features a mining accident, but director Wang handles it with great suspense and drama. One critic has likened Wang's work to that of the Japanese director Imamura Shohei.[48]

Inspired by the "nativist literature" *(xiangtu wenhue)* of the 1970s, Wu, Wang, Hou and like-minded filmmakers sought to develop a style that expressed "real life" (as opposed to government exhortation) in Taiwan in the 1980s.[49] One reality was the sad state of film culture, and Wu's position within the CMPC meant that his ideas would find a hearing from the funding powers. Wu had in mind a distinctive Taiwanese style, focusing on the rhythms and predicaments of ordinary lives, especially such islanders as fishermen, farmers, and shopkeepers who watched the procession of so many outsiders. This included the backwash of such powers as the Japanese, the Americans, the KMT, and triads within the already complex divisions in Taiwanese society.[50] The New Cinema was political, but as a by-product of its primary concern with plausible storytelling about Taiwanese experiences. There is also a sly sense of humor that depends on an apparent recognition of power differences, often aligned on an axis of "advanced, modern" vs. "backward, traditional" only to switch their positions in deft, satirical reversals. This is exemplified in *The Sandwich Man,* a trio of stories by nativist writer Huang Chunming, adapted by Wu for the screen.

Another example is a scene in one of Hou's first commercial works (*Cute Girl,* 1980) that drew Wu's attention to Hou and prompted the two to start collaborating. An old man argues with government surveyors sent to a neighborhood marked for redevelopment. The man protests that the new highway runs straight through his yard, and how is he supposed to get to the outhouse, especially at night? He is told not to worry. "We'll paint a crosswalk for you when you need to use the loo." The humor lies in the ambiguity: who is fooling whom? It is based on a real incident, according to Wu. Such humorous situations abound in the New Cinema, where apparently sharp outsiders proposition apparently gullible natives. A good literary example is Wang Zhenhe's satirical *Rose, Rose, I Love You.*[51]

Wu's *Buddha Bless America* (*Taiping tianguo,* 1996) is a fine black comedy. It is full of Taiwan-style humor. In the 1960s, a peasant village is victimized by an American army garrison exercising jointly with KMT troops. The Americans unintentionally crush their ancestral graves and cabbage patches with their tanks. In response, the villagers sneak out at night to pilfer American rations. Browbeaten by his wife, the ex-schoolteacher Sen-eh finally goes to steal the biggest, heaviest, most American thing he can find. He returns with a huge metal box, which contains—corpses, the bodies of two young victims of friendly fire. Frightened, the villagers burn joss sticks and pray for the Americans' souls. When the soldiers pack up and leave, the villagers pick through the rubble and reflect on their encounter. They are well compensated and well fed, but their lives have been uprooted and they are no closer to comprehending their oversized visitors.

Compared to the austere, challenging films of Hou and Edward Yang, *Buddha* is accessible. Its tone is lighter than *Dou-san,* which looks a bit like a Hou Hsiao-hsien film. Yet its raffish humor enfolds postcolonial experiences and ideas. It gently sends up the godlike view of Americans many Taiwanese held during the 1960s. This is not a problem for peasants, Wu says, but rather an American "colonization of mind" among the intellectual and professional classes.[52] Sen-eh, the ex-schoolteacher who should know better, succumbs to the plunder mentality of his fellow villagers and is brought up short.

Allegories aside, the film is a practical critique of the Taiwan New Cinema. Despite his role in getting the movement started, Wu claims it soon became homogenized. He likens the New Cinema films to 7-11 convenience stores: they all sell the same things; their only difference is the size of their neon signs.[33] He objects to the institutionalization of the New Cinema as a formula; Wu believes this has given filmmakers the idea that reaching an audience is not important.[54] The suppression of drama, humor, and entertainment in the New Cinema has led to arid films that may be acceptable to Western film festivals, and to Japanese audiences, who were conspicuous in their support of the New Cinema. But no one wants to see them in Taiwan.

Wu therefore welcomed the chance to host his own television program in 1997 called *Wu Nianzhen's Taiwan (Taiwan Nianzhen qing)*. This was an opportunity for Wu to work against the "colonization of mind" he sees among intellectuals and artists while also developing his vision of Taiwan. He dislikes the term "host," instead calling himself a mediator or facilitator *(chuan chang ren)*. The show uses the native dialect almost exclusively and it is appropriate to call the program populist. It is also very popular, commanding a weekly prime-time slot and numerous A-list sponsors such as Kirin and Nissan. Wu himself sometimes appears in these commercials, which often have an organic connection with the show itself.

Its substance ranges wide, from ecology, marine life, agriculture, food, crafts, architecture, folk performances, music, education, rural practices, aboriginal life, and so forth. Each show has a "road segment," with Wu or a proxy enjoying backroad travel, landscapes, food, and discussions with locals. This is followed by an in-depth studio interview with one guest and concludes with a short coda in which Wu reflects on the conversation. Virtually all the programs on *Wu Nianzhen's Taiwan* are historical, connecting in some vital way to practices originating in Taiwan during the Japanese, Manchu (the Qing Dynasty), Dutch, or even Portuguese periods. So, without being overtly political, the show is still profoundly political in its cultural, regional, and historical commitments. Because of this program, Wu has emerged as a courageous public figure that epitomizes a Taiwanese cultural identity.

Another layer of meaning can be seen in the program's commercial sponsorship. A number of Kirin beer spots, starring the teetotaler Wu, features a historic railway, playtime in a mountain stream, a walk in an old-growth forest. The director of these was Hou Hsiao-hsien, and it is intriguing to think of these sandwiched between segments of *Wu Nianzhen's Taiwan*. The link here between Taiwan New Cinema, nativism, and commodity fetishism is very stark. Because of his recognition value, Wu sells all kinds of products, from beer to sausages to politicians, anything that might benefit from a nativist cachet. One pauses at the thought that the man who explores Taiwan's heritage also lends his image to a Japanese beer. One could just as well reverse that thought, and assume that it is Kirin attaching itself to Taiwan's heritage through its most visible figures. Does

健康的滿漢
肉品的專家

平保呷信用

Wu's commercial activities: the taste of heritage.

the commercialization of heritage necessarily dilute it? Or do the commercials enable it by giving it greater visibility and range?

A Fourth Dimension

We have discussed Taiwan's postcolonial history, politics and psychology in relation to *Dou-san*. We have reinserted this into Wu Nianzhen's media activities as a nativist spokesman. To conclude, we should consider how all of this changes the land of Taiwan, its physical space and experiences of place.

An archetype of colonization is the discovery-gesture, the claim made on a certain space on behalf of some authority, like a king or emperor. A flag, for instance, is used as a marker, and in this way some space is transformed into someplace. A spatial transformation takes place in the minds of desirous colonizers, but it is also a rupture. What happens when the original inhabitants do not recognize the colonial transformation? They are usually displaced, and often exterminated, if they fail to make way for settlers.[55]

In postcolonial or decolonizing situations, too, places change: their names, their connotations, and their reconstitution into different kinds of places and spaces.[56] "'Place' in postcolonial societies is a complex interaction of language, history and environment," writes Bill Ashcroft. "[There is a] widespread sense of displacement from the imported language, of a gap between the 'experienced' environment and descriptions the language provides, and secondly, by a sense of the immense investment of culture in the construction of place."[57] So in addition to our preliminary distinction between postcolonial history, politics, and psychology, we can understand postcolonial as a form of fractured, conflicted space.

In Wu's film, the main conflict is a generational one: Dou-san identifies with Japan, the former colonial power, but his son does not. The conflict and identification plays out to some extent in language: Dou-san speaks Japanese, which his son cannot. But it also emerges in the places Dou-san likes to go. He frequents Japanese teahouses for drinking, gambling, and female companionship, and he also enjoys Japanese movie theaters, complete with live *benshi* narration. These entertainments conjure an artificial, nostalgic environment built on Japanese references, allusions, and pleasures. His son tags along but does not really comprehend his father's activities: the opting out of his familial responsibilities, his escape from an identity as "Dou san" into a Japanese floating world. In Ashcroft's terms, Dou-san's experienced environment *is* the imported, colonial environment; the Mandarin-speaking Chinese chauvinism of his son's generation is the alien, unwelcome interloper. Much writing about postcoloniality laments the destruction of precolonial cultures and identities; Dou-san represents the loss of a *colonial* identity, and because this was due to Japan's and later the Nationalists' defeat, rather than Taiwan's victory, Wu's film is a kind of elegy, if not exactly a lament. The gradual acculturation of Dou-san's children in the new postwar Chinese environment explains his increasing recalcitrance as the colonial environment recedes.

Dou-san brings his young son along in his illicit adventures. He appears to forget about the boy, leaving him in an empty movie theater while he goes to a teahouse to enjoy himself. A maternal, sensuous woman comes to the boy's rescue, takes him to the teahouse and there gives him a sweet. The boy's understanding of these places is limited, but his senses are keen: the distress of being left alone in a dark theater. His enjoyment of sweets and coddling by geisha are mixed with tears of abandonment. The names of these places and activities— movie theater, teahouse, *benshi, geisha*—are unknown to him at the time, so they do not yet "register." "For by the act of place-naming," writes Paul Carter, "space is transformed symbolically into a place, that is, a space with a history."[58]

What happens when a place ("a space with a history") is saddled with a new, and different history? There is pressure, fracturing, and to some extent, amalgamation. This is what happened to Dou-san's Taiwan. Dou-san's artificial, nostalgic colonial Taiwan has given way to a different kind of nostalgic artifice: "The question of time is always about space and place. And vice versa, of course."[59] Leigh Gilmore specifies this in terms of inheritance: "The imagined geography

Maternal Taiwanese geisha in a Japanese-style teahouse.

that links land to body also links parents to child."[60] But that geography changes radically with a different generation, and with a "divisive focalization." Wu's Taiwan is not Dou-san's Taiwan. His vision of Taiwan is inclusive, incorporating the father's Japanese colonial fantasies, but it also is divisive, because it is at home in a new, alien world where colonial fantasies can be 'incorporated' as products: "Colonial Inc." The sybaritic fantasies for sale in global tourism, especially in places like Taiwan, Korea, and the Philippines, is one form of this, but it can be as harmlessly educational as colonial Williamsburg.

In particular, consider the space of Jiufen, the former mining town where Dou-san worked his whole life. If you go to this little town today, you will find a pleasant, upscale village with winding streets, cafes, and galleries. There are restored red brick buildings and up on the hillside you can see ruins of the old mines. It is very picturesque.

For more than a decade, Jiufen has been a favorite location for film and television crews. It featured mainly in ghost stories. Then, directors of the New Cinema, supported by CMPC, arrived and shot their personal stories of ordinary people in old Taiwan. Most famous of the films shot there were *City of Sadness, Dust in the Wind, The Puppetmaster,* Wang Tong's *Hill of No Return,* and so on. Wu scripted all these, and Jiufen started to accumulate "aura."[61] Over the past few years, this space of backbreaking labor has been transformed into a fashionable place for shopping and strolling. Because of its beautiful views and cool air, and because of the international success of the New Cinema, speculators eager to serve Taipei's "nostalgia-consuming professionals" besieged the town.[62] A group of academics and progressive preservationists devised a plan to preserve and restore Jiufen, which won a prestigious award at the Pratt Institute in New York—the 1993 "What Is Socially Responsible Design?" exhibit.[63] Although the plan was conceived as an antidote to the global architectural proliferation of "nostalgic simulation," Jiufen became gentrified. It has been cleaned up, thematized, and made attractive to couples and families. Hou Hsiao-hsien even proposed to turn Jiufen into a historical theme park, a living museum.

Jiufen was never a pleasure quarter originally, but a rough mining community, so its transformation into a cool retreat for rich young people from Taipei is incongruous. Not everybody appreciates what has happened to Jiufen. A Taipei restaurateur from Jiufen thinks it has gotten slightly stuffy and much too expensive. As a kind of living monument to old Taiwan, Jiufen, he thinks, is self-conscious and precious.

Dou-san too was shot on location in Jiufen, based more directly than Wu's other scripts on his own life. This location, the scene of the writer's earliest memories, works as both evocation and displacement of Dou-san's postcolonial cartography. The film is an overwriting of an earlier, simpler map. The original terrain can be made out underneath the new schema, but just barely. Wu has written about his sense of miners' relation to the land, a relation of "no fate" or lack of karma because miners gouge their harvest from deep inside the earth, then move on to the next dark pit. Their destiny, with respect to the land, is to be truncated, uprooted, and displaced.[64] Mining and miners really have no "place." They are doomed to be "half buried," as his mother put it, deep underground.

Dou-san's inchoate political sentiments are undone by his son's education and success as a writer, an artist secure in his profession and his *national* identity. Yet Wu is anxious to respect, to understand and above all to remember his father. Thus, the film doesn't dwell on the son's success, or the father's reaction to it. The psychology of Dou-san's quixotic loyalty to the Japanese is eventually replaced by Wu's filial loyalty to his dependent father. Finally, the historical upheaval of the postwar period, in which a foreign colonial power was replaced by an equally foreign regime that soon declared martial law, is resolved into a democratic prosperity. Taiwan's postwar struggles were prolonged by KMT's presence, but an unintended consequence was the mellowing of Taiwanese recollections of the colonial period. Nationalist rewriting of Taiwan space made the Japanese colonial place seem sweeter than it really was. Until 1987 KMT orthodoxy prescribed a nationalist narrative of anti-Japanese and anti-Communist salvation, a rewritten (not overwritten) narrative in which positive cultural specificities of the colonial era have no part. This is exactly the stuff of Dou-san's tastes, his memories of teahouses, *geisha,* and *chambara-eiga,* the very material rubbed out by the KMT.[65] This material, and Dou-san's refusal to give it up, is what makes him so interesting and (daftness notwithstanding) courageous.

Dou-san articulates the colonial space of the father and gives it a name: "Wu Nianzhen's Taiwan." Unlike the erasures of the KMT, this version restores to the island its aboriginal, Dutch, Japanese, and regional Chinese dimensions, seeking a more complete, inclusive view of Taiwan/Formosa's heritage. But in giving it a heritage, Wu also gives it something new: a national identity, as opposed to a Nationalist one.

This is not only highly contested within and outside Taiwan, it may not ring true to Dou-san's borrowed life, which was in thrall to Japan until its end. Wu unshackled his father's life and times by committing it to film, but such an active work of memory cannot but alter its object. Dou-san never wanted his Japanese bonds dissolved, and he got his lifelong wish when Wu "repatriated" his father's remains to Tokyo. In a postmortem pilgrimage, Wu took his (photographic) Dou-san around to all the places he had wanted to see in Japan. There is no doubting Wu Nianzhen's sincerity. There seems a karmic bond between Wu's filial piety toward his father's Japanese allegiance, his success in the Japanese market, and his encouragement of an online "family" of fans in which he takes the role of "Ojisan" (Uncle) and his production manager "Obasan" (Auntie). What will become of this little "imagined community" now that *Wu Nianzhen's Taiwan* is off the air? What will happen to Taiwan's native heritage?

The remote, abject mining village of Jiufen has been transformed into a space of tourism and nostalgia, suitable for yuppies and truncated from the real community that originally gave the place life. The mines are defunct, but they have become mines for memory, a monument to something—backbreaking, exploited labor, environmental depredation, and community solidarity—long gone. The tourist-trap simulacrum of Jiufen is the remaining link with the historical place where Dou-san once eked out his existence. What was it that launched Jiufen the place into the rarefied space of postcolonial nostalgia? Well, film and television and the marketing of heritage.[66] Moreover, the circle is completed by the availability of location tours that, for a small fee, take visitors around to all the shot setups in Jiufen and Jilong where Hou and Wu made their celebrated films and gave these places renewed, perhaps borrowed, life.

Making History, Imaginary Maps

With Chen Shui-bian's election in March 2000, Taiwan's postcolonial development has entered a "properly" political phase. Is this the end of Taiwan's "unique triple colonization"?[67] Certainly the defeat of the KMT means a truncation of the ruling power and also a traumatization for Beijing, now bereft of its favorite bête noir. Real decolonization depends, therefore, on Beijing's restraint as well as dismantling the vast business networks of KMT influence. Credit is due to Lee Teng-hui for extending this process in the 1990s, sometimes inadvertently, and for effectively splitting the party between the Lian Zhan and James Soong (Song Chuyu) factions; however, the real meaning of Chen's victory is not the fracturing of KMT or cold war with PRC. It is the addition of a new voice to the social chorus, members of the XY generation, in their twenties, who took seriously the candidacy of Chen/Lu and shrugged off the old power-money axes. This is the generation of young consumers, like our hypothetical teenager Yifen, who came of age amid informational and economic plenitude.

Above all, Taiwan can count on continued coexistence of various shifting coalitions, factions, and voices in the wilderness. The point to be stressed is not the supercession of KMT-era politics by a new generation, but a continuing jumbled concatenation of different commitments, regions, and interests. Just as the 1999 earthquake exposed structural weaknesses in Taiwan's development practices, so did postcolonial initiatives in the Lee era encourage the rise of unheard voices. It is not difficult to imagine aging KMT sympathizers sharing a household with their thoroughly democratic, progressive children. Dou-san admitted no distinction in his mind between Taiwan and the "Home Islands," and others his age, despite Chen's election, will recognize no sovereign other than China. But it is Taiwan, not Japan or China, that tolerates and even encourages this sort of dislocated nostalgia and sedimentation, as the work of Wu Nianzhen shows.

What else is a mine, after all, whether gold, coal, or memory, but a sustained sedimentation of foreign elements through extreme pressure and time? A privileged tool for colonial and postcolonial studies, as well as a rich metaphor, is the map. William Boelhower writes, "Caribbean sites are layered over with many such colonial reflections. So that for the postcolonial writer, it is always a question of which scale and which level of consciousness we are talking about."[68] In this discussion, metaphors proliferate: geography is a hermeneutic; geography/cartography as *autopsie*; the world as network or web of lines. All of these metaphors and images can be submerged, as it were, into the figure of the "treasure island" (coincidentally, the English title of a 1993 film by Chen Guofu).[69] Treasure maps show locations of buried treasure. They are memory aids to show the way to deliberately hidden loot. Treasure hunters solve puzzles devised by mapmakers, while miners must read the codes of the earth itself. The gestures of layering, peeling away, cutting into, and networking of colonial maps, as analyzed by Boelhower, may work better in metaphors of mining. Colonial and postcolonial codes of meaning are so tightly imbricated, so petrified by centuries of both use and neglect, that geology may be more apposite than geography.

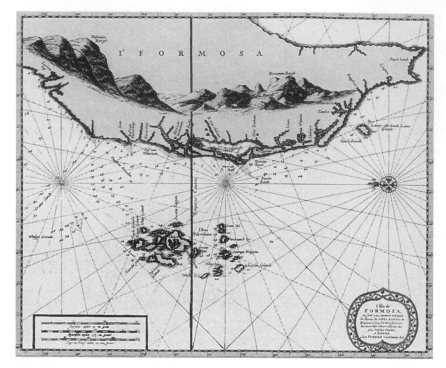

Colonial articulations: a work of Dutch mapmaker Pieter Van der Aa, ca. 1719.

Taiwan itself works as a metaphor, sometimes. Regarding U.S.–Cuba relations, an American columnist refers to the "semi-autonomous province of South Florida, a kind of upside-down Taiwan."[70] Here it appears Taiwan's political predicaments approach caricature, but it also shows Taiwan signifying something that carries across time and space. What appears to be intransigence to the outside world, the intractable throwback of the colonial fathers, can also be respect and fidelity to ancestral beliefs. The beauty of Isla Formosa is that it contains, preserves, and widely disseminates these tutelary rites.[71] They can even be found on television.

Notes

I wish to thank Wu Nianzhen, Jady Long, and Emilie Yueh-yu Yeh for their assistance and encouragement.

1. Interview with Wu Nianzhen, Taipei, January 8, 1999. For a published version of this interview, see Darrell William Davis, "A New Taiwan Person: Questions for Wu Nienchen," published in *positions: east asia cultures critique* 11.3 (fall 2003). Wu Nianzhen's Web site is located at the following address: www.tvbs.com.tw/code/e-bank/wu/review.asp.

2. Interview with Wu.

3. Interview with Wu.

4. Huang Zhiming, ed., *Directors' Dossier: Wu Nianzhen* (Taipei: Golden Horse Film Festival, 1992). Recently, Wu appeared in Edward Yang's *Yi Yi* (A One and a Two). There is some discrepancy between the filmographies of Wu and Yang, reflecting, perhaps, a "Confucian confusion" over proper distribution of script credits. But Ann Hui gives credit to Wu for the success of *Song of the Exile*: "The film's best part is the script, it is the script that delivers the film," a statement which compromises autobiographical interpretations of Hui's film. *Xu Anhua shuo Xu Anhua* (Ann Hui on Ann Hui), edited by Kuang Powei (Hong Kong: Hongye Press, 1998), 47.

5. Interview with Wu.

6. *Taiwan Statement* (1999), where Lee elaborates his notorious "state-to-state" argument for the adjustment of relations with the mainland.

7. Interview with Wu.

8. For a summary of colonial stages in Taiwan, see Ping-hui Liao, "Rewriting Taiwanese National History: The February 28 Incident as Spectacle," *Public Culture* 5.2 (1993): 281–296.

9. The literature on postcolonial issues is enormous. See, for starters, Patrick Williams and Laura Chrisman, *Colonial Discourse and Post-Colonial Theory* (New York: Columbia University Press, 1994); Bill Ashcroft, Gareth Griffiths, and Helen Tiffins, eds., *The Postcolonial Studies Reader* (London: Routledge, 1995); and Padmini Mongia, ed., *Contemporary Postcolonial Theory: A Reader* (London: Edward Arnold, 1996). I also intend this chapter as a critical supplement to the framing of postcolonial issues nearly always in relation to European colonialism. It is clear that questions of hybridity and mimicry, legitimacy and bastardization, the violence of historical revisionism, cultural fetishism, and metropolitan supremacism all find concrete and personal expression in Wu Nianzhen's work. It is his work and its revelations about emerging forms of Taiwanese identity, however, that is my primary interest.

10. These distinctions are pragmatic and pedagogical, the result of my failure to find texts on postcolonial theory suitable for undergraduates. Several recent efforts to fill this niche are Robert J. C. Young, *Introducing Postcolonial Theory* (Oxford: Blackwell, 1999); Leela Gandhi, *Postcolonial Theory: A Critical Introduction* (New York: Columbia University Press, 1998); Peter Childs and Patrick Williams, *An Introduction to Post-Colonial Theory* (New York: Prentice Hall, 1997). My schematic distinctions are not offered as adequate to postcoloniality itself, even within Taiwan only; they are heuristic devices to open up Wu's films, broadcasts, and writings, which are (it seems to me) adequate to this task. These preliminary distinctions merely point out aspects in which his work functions as postcolonial texts.

11. Taking care to distinguish between a contingent postcolonial history and postcolonial history, vividly described by Gyan Prakash as "the prison-house of historicism." See Gyan Prakash, ed. *After Colonialism: Imperial Histories and Post-Colonial Displacements* (Princeton, N.J.: Princeton University Press, 1995), 4–5.

12. Taiwan's "unique triple colonization" under the Dutch, the Japanese, and the Nationalist Chinese represents this phenomenon. Thanks to an anonymous reader of an earlier draft of this chapter for pointing this out.

13. Robert L. Jarman, ed., *Taiwan: Political and Economic Reports, 1861–1960* (Slough, U.K.: Archive Editions), 125.

14. Jarman, ed., *Taiwan,* 129.

15. Liao, "Rewriting Taiwanese National History," 290.

16. Lieutenant Commandor Max Berman, R.N.V.R., February 5, 1946, in Jarman, ed., *Taiwan,* 201. In contrast to this, many mainland officials really believed that they were more generous than the Japanese in their distribution of government positions to Taiwanese, according to the official history written by Tse-han Lai, Ramon H. Myers, and Wou Wei, A Tragic Beginning: The Taiwan Uprising of February 28, 1947 (Stanford, Calif.: Stanford University Press, 1991). Years before, Japanese wartime administration in (British) Malaya had divided the population by promoting Malays to senior posts at the expense of Chinese. See Lynn Pan, *Sons of the Yellow Emperor* (Boston: Little, Brown, 1990), 207. See also Paul Kratoska, *The Japanese Occupation of Malaya* (London: Hurst, 1998).

17. Anne McClintock, "The Angel of Progress: Pitfalls of the Term 'Post-Colonialism'" *Social Text* 31/32 (spring 1992): 89. Reprinted in Patrick Williams and Lauren Chrisman, eds., *Colonial Discourse and Post-Colonial Theory: A Reader* (New York: Columbia University Press, 1994), 291–304. This piece has stimulated many criticisms and rejoinders.

18. Berman, in Jarman, ed., *Taiwan,* 148.

19. Ibid., 149.

20. Tessa Morris-Suzuki, "The Frontiers of Japanese Identity" in S. Tonesson and H. Antelov, eds., *Asian Forms of the Nation* (Surrey: Curzon, 1996), 57–58. Here we find Fukuzawa Yukichi's idea of *bunmei* (civilization) as a Meiji-era neologism "laden with overtones of progress." See also George Kerr, *Formosa: Licensed Revolution and the Home Rule Movement, 1898–1945* (Honolulu: University Press of Hawai'i, 1974), 58.

21. The African critic and filmmaker Manthia Diawara, who is from Mali, summarized the French colonial message to Africans as follows: "Learn French and you will become a black Frenchman. Learn French and you will be emancipated. Learn French and you will become an economic and cultural partner with France." (Documentary film, *Rouch in Reverse,* 1996). V. S. Naipaul has a more jaundiced view: "In the French territories [the West Indian] aimed at Frenchness, in the Dutch territories at Dutchness; in the English territories he aimed at simple whiteness and modernity, Englishness being impossible (quoted in Pan, *Sons of the Yellow Emperor,* 294). See also Lewis H. Gann, "Western and Japanese Colonialism: Some Preliminary Comparisons" in R. Myers and M. Peattie, eds., *The Japanese Colonial Empire, 1895–1945* (Princeton, N.J.: Princeton University Press, 1984), 516–517.

22. Chaoyang Liao, "Borrowed Modernity: History and the Subject in *A Borrowed Life*," *boundary 2* 24.3 (1997): 238.

23. Memo to British embassy, in Jarman, ed., *Taiwan,* 121.

24. In *Japan's Total Empire* (Berkeley: University of California Press, 1998), Louise Young calls it an "imperialization" policy (365).

25. Kerr, *Formosa,* 162–168. See also Wan-yao Chou, "The Kominka Movement in Taiwan and Korea: Comparisons and Intepretations" in Peter Duus et al., eds., *The Japanese Wartime Empire, 1931–1945* (Princeton, N.J.: Princeton University Press, 1996), 40–68.

26. E. Patricia Tsurumi, *Japanese Colonial Education in Taiwan* (Cambridge, Mass.: Harvard University Press, 1977) 109.

27. Albert Memmi, *The Colonizer and the Colonized* (Boston: Beacon Press, 1967), 149–150. Prakash discusses how linguistic transference upset the hierarchy between civilized colonizer and native in need of civilization. See Prakash, ed., *After Colonialism*, 1.

28. Chaoyang Liao calls this "traumatic time" (Hal Foster, *The Return of the Real; The Avant-Garde at the End of the Century* [Cambridge, Mass.: MIT Press, 1996) a pattern of truncations and interruptions initiated by Seiga and passed on to his son—the boy's abandonment in a Japanese movie house being the earliest and Dou-san's suicide being the final trauma. Liao also invokes a Buddhist sense of emptiness (Nishitani Keiji, *Religion and Nothingness* [1982]) to account for this trauma of the real (Liao, "Borrowed Identity," 228).

29. The younger child, a daughter, is pointedly ignored by Dou-san, a harsh lesson to her in its own right.

30. Robert J. C. Young, *Colonial Desire: Hybridity in Theory, Culture, and Race* (London: Routledge, 1995) 98.

31. Liao, "Borrowed Identity," 234.

32. Ibid., 236.

33. Prakash, commenting on Frantz Fanon's *Black Skin, White Masks*: "Caught in between reality and fantasy, rationality and delirium, originary colonial identities take shape in the uncertain moment of the fearful gaze." Prakash also quotes Homi Bhabha's foreword to Fanon's book: "It is through image and fantasy—those orders that figure transgressively on the borders of history and the unconscious—that Fanon evokes the colonial condition." See Prakash, *After Colonialism*, 8.

34. Edward Said, *Culture and Imperialism* (New York: Knopf, 1993), 282.

35. According to Aime Cesaire, Fanon's early writings (*Black Skin, White Masks*) are the most penetrating diagnosis of colonial psychology, especially the alienation, self-division, and "colonialist subjugation." See Cesaire, *Discourse on Colonialism*, translated by Joan Pinkham (New York: Monthly Review Press, 1972).

36. McClintock, "The Angel of Progress," 86. In this passage McClintock is discussing the conceptual vortex of "postcolonialism," a flattening of difference, multiplicity, and concreteness under an overvaluation—or fetishism—of an abstract theoretical paradigm.

37. For a topographical interpretation of Williams's notion "structures of feeling," see Said, "Secular Interpretation, the Geographical Element, and the Methodology of Imperialism," in Prakash, ed., *After Colonialism*, 30.

38. Walter Mignolo, "Globalization, Civilization Processes, and the Relocation of Languages and Cultures," in Frederic Jameson and Masao Miyoshi, eds., *The Cultures of Globalization* (Durham, N.C.: Duke University Press, 1998), 32.

39. Cesaire (*Discourse on Colonialism*) bitterly contradicted this, declaring the putative evangelical basis of colonialism to be rank hypocrisy. There is an "infinite distance" between civilization and colonialism, the latter inevitably leading to savagery (13). The equation "Christianity = civilization, paganism = savagery" was, for him, a rationalization that came *after* the naked aggression of Cortez, Pizarro, and Marco Polo (10–11).

40. See Marius B. Jansen, "Japanese Imperialism: Late Meiji Perspectives" in Myers and Peattie, eds., *The Japanese Colonial Empire*, 72–73, and Stefan Tanaka, *Japan's Orient: Rendering Pasts into History* (Berkeley: University of California Press, 1993), 176–178. The "sacred texts" of the Imperial Rescript on Education (1890) and the Meiji Constitution

(1889) enshrined the notion of *kokutai,* national essence. See Bob Tadashi Wakabayashi, ed. *Modern Japanese Thought* (Cambridge: Cambridge University Press, 1998), 11.

41. See Darrell Wm. Davis, *Picturing Japaneseness: Monumental Style, National Identity, Japanese Film* (New York: Columbia University Press, 1996), for a discussion of this in relation to cinema and urban culture, especially in the 1930s.

42. Tanaka, *Japan's Orient,* 201. See Thomas W. Burkman, "Nitobe Inazo: From World Order to Regional Order," in J. Thomas Rimer, ed., *Culture and Identity: Japanese Intellectuals During the Interwar Years* (Princeton, N.J.: Princeton University Press, 1990), 200. Nitobe: "Japan's advance, . . . in search of a life-line, is as irresistible an economic force as the westward march of the Anglo-Saxon empires." (See also n. 20.)

43. Kerr, *Formosa,* 168.

44. Nicholas Thomas, *Colonialism's Culture: Anthropology, Travel, and Government* (Cambridge: Polity Press, 1994), 190.

45. Young, *Japan's Total Empire,* 50.

46. Leo Ching, "Imaginings in the Empire of the Sun," in Rob Wilson and Arif Dirlik, eds., *Asia/Pacific as Space of Cultural Production* (Durham, N.C.: Duke Unversity Press, 1995), 282.

47. Interview with Wu.

48. Zhang Changyan in *Taiwan Films* (Taipei: Variety Publishing, 1993), 4–5.

49. See Sung-sheng Yvonne Chang, *Modernism and the Nativist Resistance* (Durham, N.C.: Duke University Press, 1993), chap. 5: "Nativist literature as a creative genre—the main features of which are use of the Taiwanese dialect, depiction of the plight of country folks or small-town dwellers in economic difficulty and resistance of [*sic*] the imperialist presence in Taiwan—can be traced back to a patriotic literary trend under the Japanese occupation" (149).

50. Having dealt with the Japanese and the Americans already, Wu says he may direct a film about the role of triads in the postwar period. Triads and informal bands of "security," Wu says, were a stabilizing force in those chaotic times.

51. Wang Chen-ho, *Rose, Rose, I Love You,* translated by Howard Goldblatt (New York: Columbia University Press, 1998). Wu's film *Buddha Bless America* has a premise almost identical to this novel.

52. Interview with Wu. Recall the title of Kenyan essayist Nguni wa Thiong'o's collection, *Decolonizing the Mind: The Politics of Language in African Literature* (London: James Currey, 1986).

53. Interview with Wu. 7–11 stores in Taiwan are also a Japanese franchise.

54. For a discussion of formula and Orientalism in the international marketing of Chinese cinema, see Yeh Yueh-yu, "A Life of Its Own: Musical Discourses in Wong Kar-wai's Films," *Post Script* 19.1 (fall 1999): 115–136.

55. This echoes the incommensurability of the Northwest waterways as seen by Indians and European explorers: "White invaders from the Age of Reason burst into an Indian world of primitive, animist, sensory navigation. Naval ships and cedar canoes, though afloat in the same water, were sailing on two different seas. . . . The animist sea of the Indians was reinvented by the Europeans in the image of their own age" (Jonathan Raban, *Passage to Juneau: A Sea and its Meanings* [New York: Pantheon, 1999]). In an interview, the author remarks, "The more I sailed, and sopped up the lore of our tricky

local sea, the more I saw that the water here was a 'place,' as full of intricacy and character as any sweep of land."

56. In Hong Kong, the use of the prefix "Royal" for place names almost disappeared at the time of the handover, but it is making a quiet return. In Jiayi, Taiwan, a reservoir built by the Dutch called "Red Hair Bay" was renamed "Orchid Lake" in the 1950s. People continued to use the old name until the 1980s and 1990s, when their children, with no attachment to the old name, grew up.

57. Bill Ashcroft, Gareth Griffiths, and Helen Tiffin, eds. *The Post-Colonial Studies Reader* (London: Routledge, 1995) 391.

58. Paul Carter, "The Road to Botany Bay," excerpt in ibid., 377.

59. W. J. T. Mitchell, "Geopoetics: Space, Place and Landscape," *Critical Inquiry* 26.2 (winter 2000): 173.

60. Leigh Gilmore, *Autobiographics: A Feminist Theory of Women's Self-Representation* (Ithaca, N.Y.: Cornell University Press, 1994), 29. See also Chiao Hsiung-Ping, "Autobiographical Masterpiece," *Free China Review* (February 1988): 33–35.

61. Ironically, Jiufen's aura is conferred precisely by the reproductive technologies Benjamin identified as iconoclastic to the aura of traditional culture. Do the temporal disjunctions analyzed by Benjamin (traditional aura yielding to mechanical reproduction) work on colonial subjects such as Dou-san in a postcolonial Sinocization? Dou-san's incorrigible anachronism is too easily capitalized (on) in the age of electronic reproduction. As Benjamin once said, an "appreciation of heritage" is tantamount to "catastrophe." See Barbara Kirshenblatt-Gimblett, *Destination Culture: Tourism, Museums, and Heritage* (Berkeley: University of California Press, 1998), 1.

62. Marshall Johnson, "Making Time: Historic Preservation and the Space of Nationality," *positions: east asia cultures critique* 2.2 (1999): 233.

63. Ibid., 235.

64. Wu Nianzhen, *Xunzhao taiping tianguo* (Taipei: Mai-tian, 1996).

65. *Chambara-eiga* is the term for old-fashioned samurai films.

66. See Kirshenblatt-Gimblett, *Destination Culture*, especially the section "Destination Museum." Another postmodern account of heritage is Priscilla Boniface and Peter J. Fowler, *Heritage and Tourism in the Global Village* (London: Routledge, 1993). Asia-Pacific heritage tourism is analyzed in Michel Picard and Robert E. Wood, eds., *Tourism, Ethnicity, and the State in Asian and Pacific Societies* (Honolulu: University of Hawai'i Press, 1997), and an essay on Taiwan aboriginal tourism is Hsieh Shih-chung, "Tourism, Formulation of Cultural Tradition, and Ethnicity: A Study of the *Daiyan* Identity of the Wulai Atayal" in S. Harrell and Huang Chun-chieh, eds., *Cultural Change in Postwar Taiwan* (Taipei: SMC Publishing, 1994), 184–202.

67. See note 12.

68. William Boelhower, "Enchanted Sites," in A. Hornung and E. Ruhe, eds., *Postcolonialism and Autobiography: Michelle Cliff, David Dabydeen, Opal Palmer Adisa* (Amsterdam: Rodopi, 1998) 119.

69. The original title in Chinese is *Zhiyao weini huo yitian*, "I just want to live one day with you."

70. Hendrik Hertzberg, "A Tale of Two Cubas," *New Yorker*, April 17, 2000, 33.

71. The famous folklorist Yanagita Kunio on tutelary shrines: "The space of the deities

was really the place of the village. . . . When referring to the *kamisama*, the gods, which is the language of our commoners, and speaking of temples and shrines, what these mean are our villages and households. They are the same words for father and mothers." Quoted in H.D. Harootunian, "Disciplining Native Knowledge and Producing Place: Yanagita Kunio, Origuchi Shinobu, Takata Yasuma" in *Culture and Identity* (see n. 42), 112.

Locating Feminine Writing in Taiwan Cinema

A Study of Yang Hui-shan's Body and Sylvia Chang's *Siao Yu*

Since the arrival of motion pictures, women filmmakers have never been absent. Whether it is the innovative Germaine Dulac from France, with her impressionistic *The Smiling Mme. Beudet* (1923), or Dorothy Arzner, who managed to survive well into the heyday of Hollywood with her numerous star-studded movies, women have left their mark in the world of filmmaking.

It is only in the 1970s, however, that feminist film theory met up with women's filmmaking—in 1972, a women's event was held in conjunction with the Edinburgh Film Festival, and in 1973, a season of women's cinema was organized by Claire Johnston at the National Film Theater. Claire Johnston, with her "Women's Cinema as Counter-Cinema" (1973), heightened the awareness of how sexuality operates in filmic representation and called for a cinema that would challenge representations imbued with dominant patriarchal values.[1] In 1975, Laura Mulvey, in "Visual Pleasure and Narrative Cinema," used psychoanalytical theories to further establish the point that the pleasure of looking in the world of cinema is a male pleasure—that is to say, "the look" in cinema is directed at the male.[2] These seminal articles expose the patriarchal ideology in mainstream cinema and reveal the importance of creating and supporting alternative visual languages.

The history of women filmmakers and feminist film theory most certainly has attracted and still deserves more attention in today's film studies. My interest, however, lies more in the realm of film criticism. I hope, with knowledge of the history of women in film and sensitivity to feminist film theories, through careful analysis of film texts by women film workers to arrive at some understanding of what can be imagined as a cinematic *écriture féminine* (feminine writing).

Écriture féminine is a term put forward by the French thinker Hélène Cixous, exploring ways in which women's sexuality and unconscious shape their imaginary, their language, and their writing. And through this exploration, one hopes to find what is repressed in culture, revealing the unconscious of history. By borrowing this term, I wish to initiate such an exploration in my readings of film texts, on works from Taiwan cinema. Through this exploration, I hope to reveal the faces of female film aesthetics, the voices that are embodied in them, and analyze what they might tell and mean.

Feminine writing in Taiwan cinema is dealt with in this chapter first by means of studying the performance of actress Yang Hui-shan in her films done in the 1980s, and then by an extended examination of Sylvia Chang's *Siao Yu* (1995). My study of Yang Hui-shan explores how the body of a powerful actress interacts with its era and exposes a culture's notion of womanhood. My focus on *Siao Yu* is an attempt to show that what is sometimes unutterable, beyond language, or unspeakable in female sensibilities can often be forcefully unleashed by way of creative use of film language—the design of film form and style, the tension set up between image and sound. This focus on the female is as yet an unmined area in Taiwan film scholarship. I hope with the following study to open up a site in the field that would invite continued interest and better work to come.

Yang Hui-shan: Performing Chinese Womanhood

In film studies, serious work on Hollywood female stars and spectatorship has already been attempted and proven its validity with efforts by scholars such as Judith Mayne and Jackie Stacey.[3] In Taiwan cinema, there is an actress whose work has consistently and forcefully spoken for different forms of female desire, and a study on her performances and their effects is long overdue. Yang Hui-shan has collaborated with filmmaker Chang Yi in *Yu-ch'ing sao* (Jade Love, 1984), *Wo che-yang kuo le yi-sheng* (Kuei-mei, A Woman, 1985), and *Wo te ai* (This Love of Mine, 1986)—three films centered on three women of different periods. Chang Yi has been considered to be one of the more classical stylists of the 1980s' Taiwan New Cinema group of directors; his classical style gives presence to the commanding acting of Yang rather than call attention to itself, making an analysis of Yang's physical language, rather than Chang Yi's cinematic language, a more interesting task.[4]

In *Jade Love*, Yang Hui-shan portrays the sexually autonomous widow, Nanny Jade, in China during the time of the Sino-Japanese War. Yang, on the one hand, presents well the delicate, tender, and genteel qualities of a traditionally approved Chinese woman. On the other hand, she manages, through her naked body, to highlight the strong sexual desires that can be underneath that genteel appearance. Aside from baring her body and raising her legs in *Jade Love*'s crucial love scene, Yang/Jade, at the end of the film, after she has killed her young lover and before she stabs herself, unflinchingly stares at the camera, jolting the audience into realizing its own complicit position of gazing at the female body. In other words, Yang's body, in the film's final sex scene, paradoxically functions simultaneously as provider of visual pleasure for the audience and—through the ultimate maiming of her sexual body—as challenger to that pleasure, defiant against the shackling morals repressing female desires.

Revealing the female body as an object of desire was by no means an alien task for Yang Hui-shan. Before *Jade Love*, during the seventies, Yang was *the* actress for "female revenge" movies, often appearing scantily clad, menacingly toting a handgun, an Uzi, or a samurai sword on film posters. Yang accrued the reputation as "the star with a thousand faces" and as an actress with "the face of an angel and the body of the devil."[5] In other words, during the early 1980s, Yang's shapely body was a familiar entity for both the film going public and for the people in the industry. In fact, one of the sure selling points of *Jade Love* was the presence of Yang and the implicit promise of what she could deliver in the love scene. Before *Jade Love*, in the female revenge pictures, Yang's body was taken as a very marketable commodity, but with the serious *Jade Love*—an adaptation of the work of Pai Hsien-yung, one of Taiwan's premier fiction writers—it suddenly came to be burdened with representing much more than that.

Yang's body in *Jade Love* first distracted the GIO (Government Information Office) censors, leading to a cut that shortened the love scene. It then offended some of the judges of the Golden Horse Award, resulting in Yang's portrayal of Jade being excluded from nomination for best actress; instead, the judges nominated and awarded her best actress for her performance as the mother in *Hsiao t'ao-fan* (Teenage Fugitive). Critics Hsiao Yeh and Peggy Chiao mention in their books that what the Golden Horse judges objected to was how Yang's presentation of Jade deviates from what they perceived as the proper image of Chinese women.[6] There was even disapproval of "how high Yang's legs were positioned" in the sex scene.[7]

The female body has long been an object of desire and a site of contention in the history of cinema. In *Jade Love*'s case, the film does frame the female body as an object of desire, as an exploitable and marketable commodity. But, at the same time, it also positions Jade's body as the emblem of a woman's refusal to play the expected role of the chaste widow and as a sign of a woman's rejection of returning to and being again contained in yet another marital arrangement. The censors and the judges were not merely unsettled by the baring of the female body in *Jade Love* (after all, Yang only showed her bare back and legs in the film), but were more, perhaps unwittingly, threatened by what the female body signified in the film. The commercially familiar body of Yang had suddenly become foreign, necessitating at least two institutions to neutralize it. Ironically for Yang, these actions against her body meant that her acting and her filmic body were now taken seriously.

After exercising her bodily and maternal performative powers in *Jade Love* and *Teenage Fugitive*, Yang combined the two skills in 1985 with *Kuei-mei, A Woman*, a film about the life of Kuei-mei in Taiwan during the two decades after the 1960s. With this film, Yang brought filmic interpretation of Chinese motherhood to new heights. For her role of Kuei-mei, Yang gained twenty kilos (about forty-four pounds), stressing with her rounded torso that the ideal Chinese woman needs to be maternal, with a Mother Earth–like body. By disfiguring her shapely frame, Yang dissipates the sexual edge of Kuei-mei. Instead, with her spectacular physical transformation, with her maternal body, Yang demonstrates such virtues as self-reliance, self-sacrifice, care for the family, and industriousness— all traits that facilitated the economic transformation of Taiwan. Yang's maternal body is not only a powerful nurturing and reproductive vehicle (Kuei-mei gives birth to twins in the film), but also represents the force that fosters the growth of the family and, in a larger sense, the development of a society. By the end of the film, however, Yang shows us the toll such a life-long process of nurturing takes on the female body: the exhaustion and collapse of the nurturing organ as Kuei-mei struggles with uterine cancer.[8]

Yang Hui-shan's physically spectacular representation of the sacrificing woman/ mother was met with general approval: critics lauded Yang for her physical commitment to her role, the public paid to satisfy their curiosity to see her sensational transformation (*Kuei-mei, A Woman*'s box-office gains placed tenth among the Chinese films shown that year), and the Golden Horse Awards responded by according Yang with its 1985 best actress award. Whereas the institutional repressing of Yang's shapely body in *Jade Love* points to a general fear of a woman's assertion of her self through her sexual body, the celebration of the disfiguring of the overly sexually coded body of Yang in *Kuei-mei, A Woman* manifests a system's desire to neutralize and tame the female body by shaping and coding it into a figure of feminine and maternal virtues of selflessness and sacrifice.

Before Yang Hui-shan retired from Taiwan cinema in the late 1980s, after shedding her extra weight, she used her by then pliant body to translate the afflictions of the urbanized woman in *This Love of Mine*. The toll of fast-paced socioeconomic change on women was already suggested in *Kuei-mei, A Woman* in its ending with Kuei-mei's invisible uterine cancer. With *This Love of Mine*, the symptoms of urban malaise are more externally represented. Yang chose to assume an extremely tense body to show the effects of the constant struggle against the various kinds of urban pollution. The sensitive female body, confronted with the pressures and gnawing of the city, twitches uncontrollably; it attempts to gain some control of the environment by compulsively cleaning it—washing and peeling all fruits, aversion to using detergents, repeated cleansing of toilets and bathrooms. The female body further contends with her loss of orientation in the metropolis by way of transforming herself. We see Yang cutting her long hair into a crew cut midway through the film, as if shedding her outward femaleness could help her gain some potency against the city. Faced with the looming metropolis, the harsh haircut becomes a form of self-mutilation, and the resulting sculpted masculine hairstyle becomes a parody of the female protagonist's disintegrating self. The tenseness and constant twitching that Yang Hui-shan portrays in *This Love of Mine* displays a woman's struggle against, and her final defeat by the encroaching forces of, the urban, a woman on the verge of a breakdown who finally opts to find solace in an eerie ritual of death.

With *This Love of Mine*, Yang's body became a cipher that exposed the underside of Taiwan's urbanization, a process that was lauded by Yang's fertile body in *Kuei-mei, A Woman*. Such an exposure was met with total denial in the 1986 Golden Horse awards. By giving many of the major prizes to Hong Kong productions, the Golden Horse diverted its eyes from the ugly pictures of urban malaise painted by films such as *This Love of Mine*, at the same time also erasing and silencing Yang Hui-shan from the screens of Taiwan cinema.[9]

After accumulating acting experience from the many "femploitation" movies of the seventies, Yang Hui-shan in the eighties, like a phoenix, transformed her body performances into definitive portrayals of Chinese womanhood. Yang Hui-shan can be identified as the actress who has mastered the power of the filmic female body in Taiwan cinema. She has, in her mature work, always managed to find, to retain, an indelible feminine space in her roles. Her performances in the 1980s fashioned some of the most notable women's pictures of the decade, and in these films Yang's body provided an ineffaceable cinematic feminine writing yet unsurpassed by any other actress as Taiwan cinema moves into the twenty-first century.

Sylvia Chang: Refining Melodrama

By the 1990s, with the collapse of the market for domestic movies, Taiwan cinema was unable to produce any star who came close to Yang Hui-shan's stature.

Yang Kuei-mei has given noteworthy performances in works by Tsai Ming-liang
—Ai-ch'ing wan-sui (Vive l'amour, 1994), Tung (The Hole, 1998)—and in Ang
Lee's Yin-shih nan-nü (Eat Drink Man Woman, 1994). Another actress who was
quite visible in Taiwan cinema of the 1990s is Liu Jo-ying. She can be seen in the
works of Chen Kuo-fu—Wo te mei-li yu ai-ch'ou (The Peony Pavilion, 1995),
Cheng-hun ch'i-shih (The Personals, 1999)—and in Lin Cheng-sheng's, Mei-li
tsai ch'ang-ke (The Murmur of Youth, 1997). Liu has also appeared in the works
of Sylvia Chang, Shao-nu Hsiao-yu (Siao Yu, 1995) and Chin-t'ien pu hui-chia
(Tonight Nobody Goes Home, 1996). Neither Yang Kuei-mei nor Liu Jo-ying
has accumulated a body of work that can be considered to be of the same weight
as that of Yang Hui-shan's. Taiwan cinema during the 1990s might not have had
exceptional filmic feminine writing in the form of screen performance; however, with Siao Yu—a film based on a story by Yen Ke-ling, directed by Sylvia
Chang, and acted by Liu Jo-ying and having quite a high feminine quotient—
perhaps another kind of cinematic feminine writing can be identified.

In the 1990s, with Ang Lee's emergence, the Central Motion Picture Corporation (CMPC) found a formula that proved to be profitable for not only the domestic market, but even more so internationally. Siao Yu, a CMPC production,
has many similar elements to Ang Lee's Hsi-yen (Wedding Banquet, 1993): it deals
with the life of overseas Chinese in New York, marital machinations, issues of
cultural difference, and negotiations in gender sensibilities. The film tells of how
Siao Yu, an illegal migrant from China, in order to stay with her Chinese student
boyfriend in New York, tries to acquire legal residency in the United States by
buying and arranging a marriage with Mario, an aging, over-the-hill writer.

With these similarities to the Wedding Banquet, Siao Yu seemingly should
have been another hit for CMPC. In fact, the film's performance at the box office proved to be quite dismal (in Taipei, Wedding Banquet made more than 22
million NT, Siao Yu only 1.2). The unpopularity of Siao Yu in Taiwan might be
due to its audience's alienation toward the story's mainland protagonists; however, another way of comprehending it is to look into the kind of sensibility Siao
Yu embodies, a sensibility quite different from that of Ang Lee's work, a sensibility that can be analyzed by examining Sylvia Chang and Ang Lee's treatment of
the setting, food scenes, and the notion of family in their films.

In his Wedding Banquet, Lee, when trying to highlight the Chinese background
of the male protagonist, quickly rolls out easily identifiable cultural items such
as scrolls of Chinese calligraphy throughout the male protagonist's apartment.
In Eat Drink Man Woman, Lee identifies Taipei with its most easily recognizable
traditional-looking landmarks, such as the Grand Hotel. To add to these Chinese-
looking landmarks, Lee even makes the father in the film consecutively run in
both the Botanical Garden and the Chiang Kai-shek Memorial (sites in two dif-

ferent parts of Taipei, quite a distance from each other). Distinct from Ang Lee's touristy spatial presentation, Sylvia Chang, when introducing the New York setting of *Siao Yu*, gives us a long shot of the Loyal Martyr Gate that frames the entrance of Chinatown. This master shot, though denoting Chineseness, also embodies that which the film wants to expose and undermine — the set values of the past and the segregated state of cultures in the metropolis, things the female protagonist, Siao Yu, shall by the end of the film break away from. The gate's English commemoration states its remembrance of those who have given themselves in defense of freedom; *Siao Yu* will also show us its protagonist's distinct notion of freedom. Thus, *Siao Yu*'s seemingly quiet introductory shot of the setting speaks more than the spectacular sights that Ang Lee likes to deploy.

The food scenes in *Eat Drink Man Woman* are perhaps some of the most spectacular ones in film history. The spectacular food, at the same time, functions as an alienating force within the film — these sensational foods absolutely feast the eyes, but nobody seems to really enjoy consuming them. In contrast to Lee, Sylvia Chang, in many of her film's dining scenes, chooses not to present us with any food close-ups. Food in *Siao Yu*, instead of alienating, functions as a medium of communication and cultural contact. One scene in the film shows Siao Yu buying Ta-cha crab (hairy crab).[10] The crab not only announces the coming of fall, but also subtly conveys a sharing of a nostalgia for home when Siao Yu intimately consumes it with her boyfriend. Gingerly eating Ta-cha crab then becomes a way they share their common Chineseness.

Another meal scene is set up to indicate a different connection Siao Yu establishes with Mario, her husband on paper. While the boyfriend consumes pizza and cheats on her, Siao Yu has a sit-down dinner with Mario. And through food, Siao Yu manages to ironically communicate her background to him: "Chinese eat everything.... Somebody was asking whether Chinese people are too poor, so they have to eat everything, or they are too rich, so they know how to make everything into a great dish." It is through the sharing of this meal that Siao Yu and Mario come to better understand and find commonness between each other: to realize that Chinese food can be like Italian food, that eggplants are welcomed in both cuisines.

The film also includes a hotpot dinner scene appropriately set up for the reunion of the boyfriend's housemate's family. Ironically, this very traditional reunion meal points to the beginning of the unraveling of Siao Yu and her boyfriend's relationship.

In his father trilogy, Ang Lee is well known for his safeguarding of the vestiges of patriarchal powers. Although Lee cannot but admit today's diminishing authority of the father, he does still, through many means, try to reinvigorate the role of the father. Recall the end of *Eat Drink Man Woman*. The potency of the father is regained as we surprisingly witness Lang Hsiung impregnating his new-lywed wife, who used to be a college classmate of his daughter's, played by none other than Sylvia Chang. While Ang Lee struggles between the emaciation and resuscitation of family and patriarchy, Sylvia Chang's *Siao Yu* seems to have no intention of reestablishing the traditional family. The character Siao Yu is made to be an orphan; she has no ties to any father. Her move to the new world then gives her the opportunity to establish a different form of familial relationship.

With this kind of subtle setting, subdued treatment of food scenes, and un-traditional notion of family, perhaps it is no surprise that *Siao Yu* failed to grab a large audience. When we look even more closely into the film text, we also no-tice the film's ambition in exploring not only a sensibility that is different from that of a classical film, but also a cinematic language that opens up a unique fem-inine space.

Siao Yu can be seen as a film that deals with the transformation and growth of a woman. The film, however, does not stress female economic autonomy or sex-ual realization. It is concerned with a more subtle form of female transforma-tion and affirmation. The female protagonist Siao Yu illegally works in a New York sweatshop, making a meager income, but this does not trouble Siao Yu at all—the film does not situate Siao Yu's strivings at the site of economic improve-ment. Siao Yu illegally stays in the United States to be with her boyfriend, who came to the States to study and work. That is to say, Siao Yu is not further seek-ing romance and love. Also, the sex scenes between Siao Yu and her boyfriend testify that sexual enlightenment is not an issue for her either. This film does not concern itself with matters related to middle-class females—economic indepen-dence, emotional and sexual autonomy—like the ones treated by Edward Yang in *Hai-t'an te yi-t'ien* (That Day on the Beach, 1983) during the eighties (whose leading role was also played by Sylvia Chang). *Siao Yu* tackles a more intangible female need.

This female desire is not easily transmittable through language, through di-alogue. What is exceptional with *Siao Yu* is that Sylvia Chang, through cinematic language, has managed to convey that sentiment. Liu Jo-ying, the actress who plays Siao Yu, is not known for high-energy, exuberant, external acting; Liu's more quiet style seems to be what the film wants. Still, to help communicate the more inward nature of the character, Sylvia Chang would, for example, use highly feminine material—gossamer-textured fabric—to *show* Siao Yu's soft and sup-ple strength. For instance, at the beginning of the film, Siao Yu quickly runs out from the sweatshop to escape a raid from the immigration office; the camera follows the officers to the roof of the building, and Siao Yu's presence is shown through the slight intrusion into the frame of part of her light red skirt. Again, Mario, knowing a bit about Siao Yu after agreeing to the fake marriage, intuitively senses her strength, and comments, "She's a fighter, just not in a style we recognize." And when Siao Yu is absent from the apartment, Mario tries to capture her presence by smelling Siao Yu's pink blouse.

Of course, fabric only does not necessarily convey a certain feminine sensibility (although we have also seen Jane Campion use textile for similar purposes in *The Portrait of a Lady*, 1996), and inner strength alone does not make up for Siao Yu's transformation. In contrast to Mario's proximity to language—him being a writer—the film relates its women to music. The film not only makes Mario's girlfriend, Rita, a singer, it also, out of the blue, inserts a song sung by Hsia T'ai-feng, who plays one of the female sweatshop workers. The song occurs in the sweatshop, in the second half of the film, after Siao Yu has realized that her boyfriend might be cheating on her. While Siao Yu and other female workers labor at their sewing machines, the radio announces the rising temperature and the passing of winter. The song *"Chüeh-ting"* (Decision), by Hsin Hsiao-ch'i, then streams out. Hsia then sings out. Siao Yu and others raise their heads from their work and look toward Hsia; Siao Yu appears quite pensive. Beside Hsia and on her lap are her sleeping children; the song then becomes like a lullaby of sorts. As the song ends, we see in the next scene a shot of Siao Yu alone in her room in Mario's apartment, a ray of light shoots through the window; Siao Yu, with a pot of flowers in front, takes off her pink cardigan and looks out the window. The shot is accompanied by the piano tune of "Decision."

When we think of narrative progression, the Hsia T'ai feng song scene can be quite redundant, even out of place; however, should we think of transmission of feminine sensibility, the scene then becomes quite potent. In this scene, the women are engaged in the female labor of sewing. The director lets Hsia's more mature and full voice cover Hsin Hsiao ch'i's more delicate interpretation of the song, and by adding sleeping children to the frame—female workers, female voice, maternity—a nonverbal feminine space is created. In the scene that follows, with Siao Yu by herself, there are sunlight, flowers, and music, affirming the quiet existence of a springlike feminine presence.

Should we insist on looking for the verbal in this two-minute-long nondialogue sequence, it can be found in the lyrics of Hsia's song:

I've come here without ever suspecting
Gave you all of my heart
Can anything be made perfectly clear
Do you really know what is true and dear

You may not be my one and only love
Though your support was once much needed
Knowing what you have given me was true affection

I won't I didn't and I can't forget
I hope you no longer will hold me tightly in your hands
How I long to breathe freely
You know how beautiful the skies are here
So let me decide for myself

The actress Liu Jo-ying is also a singer. The film chose not to have her sing the song, thus, giving Siao Yu more space for solitary reflection. After the song scene, Siao Yu looks out the window to the arrival of spring and ponders alone in her room. What is Siao Yu considering? What is she deciding? Siao Yu does not negate her love and relationship with the boyfriend even after knowing he has strayed. Once getting residency, Siao Yu is not eager to seek better employment, either. Siao Yu's growth and transformation occur in her insistence on her inherent capacity to care, to love, to give, and her reflective final affirmation of these qualities.

When Mario struggles with his heart attack, he begs Siao Yu not to send him to an impersonal hospital to die by himself. Siao Yu decides to promise him that. Even when the boyfriend objects to her decision and threatens to break their relationship, Siao Yu still decides to stay and be with Mario for a while. Female caring has always been confined to the realm of the family, or sublimated to the professional realm of nursing. Should loving care traverse these domains, it might be considered to be socially unacceptable. Siao Yu's decision and insistence on staying with Mario expand the space of female giving and caring. Siao Yu's action stresses her desire for the coexistence and acceptance of her true and earnest emotions for her boyfriend and her tender care for Mario. Siao Yu desires, appeals for, and insists on a space—the beautiful skies—to freely decide on such matters.

Sylvia Chang conveys Siao Yu's quiet presence through very tactile and sensual red and pink fabrics. Moreover, music and song are used to help reveal the touching inner struggle and to explicate the reflection and the decision that Siao Yu goes through and comes to at the end. With these subtle and yet powerful arrangements, with the keen combination of melody and drama, with adroit interaction of image and sound, Sylvia Chang has managed to communicate elusive feminine sentiments and desires. Chang has contributed to finely extend the very feminine genre of melodrama and insert delicate feminine writing to a conventional film genre.

Finally, I will turn to something written by the brother of Ang Lee, Lee Kang, who has been interested in exploring a film career ever since Ang Lee established himself in the industry. Lee Kang wrote the screenplay of Sylvia Chang's second directorial collaboration with CMPC, *Today Nobody Goes Home*. In his book *A Bit of Sensibility, Yet Not Insensible*, Lee Kang talks of his experience in writing *Today*; he ends his essay with a jab at Sylvia Chang, noting that her alterations to his story were done with an eye toward the market and commercial considerations and stating that Chang's film has diminished his story's devotion to women's consciousness.[11]

One of the curious cinematic devices Chang employs in *Today* is this seemingly random insertion of drawings that appear unrelated to the action. When one studies them more closely, however, one realizes that they are in fact the film's very conscious way of commenting on itself. It is no accident that the male characters are all associated with animal drawings—frog, tropical fish, hound dog—and the female characters with domestic settings—window cleaning, wedding picture. In other words, Chang has consciously left an imprint of her feminine writing in *Today*, making ironic the actions of the male characters and sympathizing with the world of the female.[12]

Another mention of Chang by Lee Kang occurs when he expresses his puzzlement over Chang's changing his original title to *Today Nobody Goes Home*.[13] With a little knowledge of film history, one would recognize Chang's title as the same with the 1969 film directed by Pai Ching-jui, a major Taiwan filmmaker of the 1960s and 1970s. A look back into Pai's urban family comedy, and one would note the structural similarity between Pai and Chang's films: both develop a plot in which family members leave home in droves and by the end of the film all return home. Both films probe the challenge modern urban life poses on the family unit. Chang makes her acknowledgement of Pai's film (and perhaps her tribute to Pai himself) even more explicit by incorporating the theme song Pai used in 1969 into her own *Today*, giving it a 1990s disco beat.

Whereas Lee Kang might be somewhat unfamiliar with film history, Sylvia Chang is herself very much part of Chinese film history. Chang entered the world of entertainment in 1969 as a teenager and since then has established her presence in Taiwan and Hong Kong as actress (she has won two best actress awards from the Golden Horse), producer, writer, and director.[14] A study of her three-decade film career is in itself a concise history of Taiwan and Hong Kong cinema. Others might retire after such a long and illustrious career, but with Sylvia Chang, with her recent *Hsin-tung* (Tempting Heart) turning out to be the most celebrated Chinese film in both Hong Kong and Taiwan in 1999, it seems her best is yet to come. And it is the task of film studies to recognize the treasure trove that is Sylvia Chang and analyze the unique blend of filmic feminine writing she has registered in the world of cinema.

Notes

Because this essay deals with Taiwanese materials, I have not used pinyin, but instead keep the way certain names and film titles have been romanized by habit and choice.

1. Claire Johnston, "Women's Cinema as Counter Cinema," *Notes on Women's Cinema*, British Film Institute pamphlet, 1973.

2. Laura Mulvey, "Visual Pleasure and Narrative Cinema," *Screen* 16.3 (autumn 1975): 6–18.

3. See "Star Gazing" in Judith Mayne's *Cinema and Spectatorship* (New York: Routledge, 1993), 123–141. Also, Jackie Stacey, *Star Gazing: Hollywood Cinema and Female Spectatorship* (New York: Routledge, 1994). For a more popular, but nevertheless insightful, look into the place of women in film, see the collection in the "Icons" part of Pam Cook and Philip Dodd, eds., *Women and Film: A* Sight and Sound *Reader* (Philadelphia: Temple University Press, 1993), 1–75.

4. For an in-depth study in English of Chang Yi's direction of *Jade Love, Kuei-mei, A Woman,* and *This Love of Mine,* see Shiao-ying Shen, *Permutations of the Foreign/er: A Study of the Works of Edward Yang, Stan Lai, Chang Yi, and Hou Hsiao-hsien* (Ann Arbor, Mich.: UMI, 1995), 122–160. For a Chinese study on the collaboration between Yang Hui-shan, Chang Yi, and Hsiao Sa (novelist and screenwriter), see Shiao-ying Shen, "The Body vs. the Pen: Permutation of the Female Body in the Chang-Yang Trilogy," *Chung-Wai Literary Monthly* 302 (1997): 98–114.

5. Most reports on Yang Hui-shan during the 1980s never fail to mention her chameleon-like acting and her shapely figure. For an example, see Lin Yi-lin's article *Yang Hui-shan hsing-k'ung mi-hang* (Yang Hui-shan, lost amongst the stars), *United Daily,* October 23, 1986: 9.

6. See Hsiao Yeh, *Yi-ke yun-tung te k'ai-shih* (The beginning of a movement) (Taipei: Shih-pao, 1986), 192. Also see Chiao Peggy Hsiung-p'ing, "*Yu-ch'ing sao: hsing te chi-tien*" (*Jade Love:* rite of sex), in Chiao Hsiung-p'ing, ed., *Taiwan hsin-tien-ying* (Taiwan New Cinema) (Taipei: Shih-pao, 1988), 172–175.

7. See Chan Hung-chih, "*Hsing-tien-ying te chieh-kou hsing wei-chi*" (The structural crisis of New Cinema), in Chiao Hsiung-p'ing, ed., *Taiwan New Cinema,* 89–96.

8. Before the 1980s, illness of female protagonists in Taiwan cinema often functions as a metaphor for the repression of romantic desires—often in the form of schizophrenia—or as melodramatic impossibility of the fulfillment of a certain romantic relationship—often in the form of leukemia. The tagging of Kuei-mei with the rather unromantic illness of uterine cancer shifts the signification of woman's illness to a more social sphere. Kuei-mei's uterine cancer becomes the mark of the toll of maternal sacrifice and the cipher for the consuming effects of the nurturing of the collective economic well-being.

9. Although the 1986 Golden Horse award for best picture was given to Edward Yang's *K'ung-pu fen-tzu* (Terrorizer), the other major prizes were given to Hong Kong's John Woo, *Ying-hsiung pen-se* (A Better Tomorrow), and Sylvia Chang, *Chui-ai* (Passion). The scandal of the affair between Yang Hui-shan and Chang Yi (married at the time to novelist and screenwriter Hsiao Sa) exploded before the screening of *This Love of Mine.* By

the time of the Golden Horse, the scandal wiped out the film's chances of winning any award, also driving Chang and Yang out of the industry.

10. In many Chinese communities in different parts of the world, Ta-cha crab comes into the market during autumn, and it is the fad for those who can afford them to consume them during the season.

11. See Lee Kang, *Yu-tien kan-hsing, yu pu-shih li-hsing* (A bit of sensibility, yet not insensible) (Taipei: Yuan-liu, 1996): 234–236.

12. For a further understanding of the difference between Lee Kang's idea of *Today Nobody Goes Home* and Sylvia Chang's film version, see Lee Kang, *Chang Ai-chia tien-ying: chin-t'ien pu hui-chia* (A Sylvia Chang movie: today nobody goes home) (Taipei: Yuan-liu, 1996); this is the novel form of Lee Kang's original screenplay.

13. See Lee Kang, *A Bit of Sensibility,* 184.

14. Sylvia Chang has also acted in films from the West; one more notable recent involvement can be found in *The Red Violin* (1999).

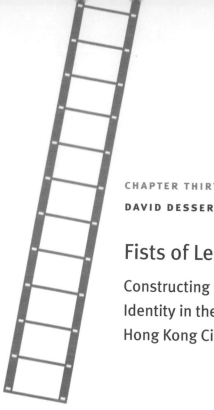

Fists of Legend

Constructing Chinese
Identity in the
Hong Kong Cinema

It has been clear for some time now in the English-language criticism of Hong Kong cinema, that something like a "Chinese nationalism" may be detected in a number of films emanating from the former British colony. For Stephen Teo, for instance: Bruce Lee stood for something that in the 1990s is hardly deemed politically correct: "Chinese nationalism as a way of feeling pride in one's identity. . . . Lee's nationalism cannot be easily dismissed if one wishes to appreciate fully his appeal to Chinese audiences. . . . Kung fu films were particularly conducive to nationalism of the abstract kind. . . . Lee is literally putting his bravest face (and body) forward in order to show that the Chinese need no longer be weaklings."[1]

Similarly, for Teo, Jackie Chan's movies of the 1980s "were practically alone in preserving Bruce Lee's tradition of kung fu as an instinctive but disciplined art linked to a cultural and national identity."[2] Steve Fore also relies on a kind of cultural nationalism to account for Chan's appeal in Asia: "In East Asia, where Chan is already a major star, the "Chineseness" of his persona is, of course, more closely aligned with the cultural heritage and life experiences of the average moviegoer, whether at the primary level of cultural proximity (for audiences in Hong Kong, Taiwan, and the PRC), or at a secondary level (for non-Chinese audiences in Asian countries where Hong Kong movies are widely distributed)."[3]

And it is certainly no stretch of the imagination to see how Tsui Hark's "Once Upon a Time in China" series, especially parts 1, 2, and 6, play into nationalistic sentiments.[4]

But just when, exactly, do these nationalistic sentiments begin to occur and how? I would like to suggest that this nationalism, this "Chineseness," comes to be literally *embodied* on the *male body* of stars like Bruce Lee, Jackie Chan, and Jet Li; on a *body of knowledge* that we may call "Chinese learning," more specifically, the Chinese martial arts; on a *displaced body* in diaspora or in exile from a homeland, Hong Kong; on a *body of work*, specifically, the Hong Kong Mandarin-language cinema and the return to Cantonese language productions thereafter. These bodies come to fruition in a particular historical moment that both enables and encourages this symbolic nationalistic body to appear, grow, develop, and stabilize.

It is clear that we can date this new Chinese symbolic nationalism to the middle-late 1960s. This was a period in which Hong Kong had achieved an economic strength while undergoing much internal turmoil and self-examination. In terms of cinematic culture, Hong Kong film could assume a new international space while asserting its own economic force: The cinema of the PRC was virtually inactive, thus removing much sense of a "Chinese cinema"; there was increasing competition from Taiwanese cinema, forcing both cinemas into a competitive mode, but also into transnational cooperation; and there was within Hong Kong an internal struggle between an almost strictly local cinema, a cinema of and for Cantonese speakers, and an emerging transnational cinema utilizing Mandarin dialect. Within this Mandarin cinema, most productively understood as the films of the Shaw Brothers Studio, comes a new attitude not only in terms of global outreach but also within Hong Kong film genres, especially the martial arts film. Once the special province of Cantonese cinema, martial arts films made in Mandarin revolutionized the local cinema, created a global audience and, in so doing, highlighted an emerging (transnational) Chinese nationalism and identity. Through this body of work (the Mandarin-language cinema of Hong Kong) emerges the heroic male body, the nationalistic Chinese body of knowledge, which helps create this male body while displacing it across space and time.

There are a number of ways to demonstrate the emergence of the heroic, Chinese, masculinized male body and the interconnections this masculinized body has with the Chinese martial arts, with exilic or diasporic culture, and the body of work, the Mandarin cinema, in which these all occur. Space does not permit a full investigation of all the interconnections that feed into a resurgent cultural nationalism at the site of the male, Chinese body. Nevertheless, it behooves us to see how Mandarin-language cinema has come to be associated with a new form of masculinity, that this new masculinity is built on the body of a specifically Chinese knowledge, and that these male figures are displaced from Hong Kong, the site of the films' production, but that the very site of this production creates a body of work that recontains the exilic body. We will see that there is a cluster of images and motifs around which these bodies—male bodies, a body of knowledge, the body in diaspora—coalesce. Here I have in mind the image and significance of Japan and the Japanese and how the bodies of Chinese male stars, forged by a body of Chinese knowledge, interact with, defeat or otherwise highlight the ability of China to compete with Japan and, perhaps, with the West. I specifically have in mind the stardom of Bruce Lee, Jackie Chan, and Jet Li and the concept of the *jingwu men,* the martial arts school as nationalist site. Lee, Chan and Li all made variations of the film *Jingwu men,* as a means not only to assert their stardom, but also to claim a kind of Chinese identity, an identity that comes to fruition in juxtaposition with the Japanese: Bruce Lee, *Jingwu men* (*Fist of Fury,* also known as *The Chinese Connection,* 1972); Jackie Chan, *New Fist of Fury/Xin jingwu men* (1976); Jet Li, *Fist of Legend/Jingwu yingxiong* (1994).

Muscular Mandarin

If Bruce Lee was the biggest star in the history of Hong Kong cinema, is it ironic that in his films he is alienated from Hong Kong by both geographic locale and dialect? That is, it has not been sufficiently theorized or even noted why all of Bruce Lee's Hong Kong films have been set outside of Hong Kong: *The Big Boss* in Thailand, *Fist of Fury* in prewar Shanghai, and *Way of the Dragon* in Italy, all of which were released in the Mandarin dialect. Lee is, then, never in Hong Kong, never speaking Hong Kong Cantonese. He, as much as anyone, helped establish the reputation of Hong Kong cinema as a vital, action-oriented, masculine cinema without ever actually being in Hong Kong on screen, interacting with Hong Kong. A minor star of sorts in the Cantonese Hong Kong cinema of the early 1950s, Lee established another minor stardom in the United States in the 1960s. Fierce negotiations were undertaken upon his return to the territory in the early 1970s, as if recognizing that he would be something new and special in the Hong Kong cinema. But Lee's cinema becomes less a "Hong Kong cinema" than a new symbol of "Chinese cinema" precisely by its diasporic relationship to Hong Kong and by its rejection of previous "Chinese cinema." The only way to understand Lee's image and its significance is to see how he brings to fruition a number of motifs bubbling up in the Hong Kong cinema immediately before his arrival.

The Hong Kong cinema achieved its international economic viability, along with a new aesthetic maturity, via the Mandarin-language martial arts films produced beginning in the middle of the 1960s. Now-familiar directorial names like King Hu and Zhang Che have become synonymous with the rise to prominence of the Hong Kong cinema, along with a roster of movie stars that only Hollywood in its heyday could match. But why exactly did Mandarin-dialect films virtually displace Cantonese films in Cantonese-speaking Hong Kong by 1970? For the moment, let us equate the emerging dominance of Mandarin-language films with the output of the Shaw Brothers Studio. And let us recall that the vast majority of these films were martial arts films, *wuxia pian*. But even here we need recall that martial arts films were a commonality, indeed a staple, of Cantonese films and thus martial arts alone cannot explain the drastic, even shocking, decline of Cantonese cinema, the special and unique province of the Hong Kong cinema since the 1930s.

At the time of this Mandarin-emergence in the Hong Kong cinema, there was a vital Cantonese language output, with first-class directors such as Chor Yuen and Lung Kong, and an impressive roster of stars, such as Josephine Siao and Chan Po-chu. But as Sek Kei notes, "In the Cantonese cinema, a group of young female stars predominated, while in the Mandarin cinema, male action stars ruled the screens." Sek notes that both the Cantonese and Mandarin stars were young—a new generation of stars for a new generation of Hong Kong filmgoers. But the female stars of the Cantonese cinema were, it seems, "comparatively gentle and conservative," whereas the male stars of the Mandarin cinema manifested "strong emotions more suited to the restlessness of the times." Sek goes on to claim that the new Mandarin cinema of Hong Kong marked a break from the Chinese tradition of the "weak male," a tradition taken up, with some exceptions, in the postwar Cantonese cinema with its emphasis on the female star.[5] This recognition of a female-centered Chinese cinema tradition is further seen in the recent Stanley Kwan film *Yin and Yang,* where the director claims that the figure of Bruce Lee brought a masculinist nationalist pride new to Chinese cinema. Tony Rayns also notes the particularly "masculinist" dimension of Lee's films, claiming that Lee became synonymous with "a very particular set of (male) dreams, concerning consummate physical prowess, Chinese racial identity, the status of the immigrant (especially the Chinese immigrant) and the relationship between China and other countries (especially western countries)."[6] But Lee was not alone in this "masculinization" of Hong Kong films. Critic Tian Yan notes the contributions of director Zhang Che, whose so-called new *wuxia pian* films were so popular that they "catalyzed the rise of the Mandarin cinema, which ultimately replaced Cantonese cinema." And central to Zhang's films was a "male-oriented/dominated ideology."[7] For Teo there is indeed a distinctly masculinist dimension to the Mandarin martial arts hero, one revolving around a newly economically assertive Hong Kong: "The *wuxia* or martial hero emerged in the mid-1960s, when China was asserting its newly acquired superpower status and Hong Kong was becoming 'an Asian tiger' while the Japanese economic expansion into East and Southeast Asia was at its most aggressive."[8] I am not sure whether Teo is implying that Japan's aggressive assertion in the Asian market led Hong Kong to a feeling of competition with their former colonizer and enemy, but Hong Kong's economic success unquestionably affected its self-image as a tiger, a fighter, a warrior, which was reflected in the newly emergent Mandarin-language cinema.

The masculinist dimension, then, seems to be the major factor behind the triumph of the Mandarin cinema, in conjunction with the economically assertive power of the Shaw Brothers Studio. I will set that dimension aside and recommend, for instance, Poshek Fu's essay "Going Global: The Transnational Cinema of the Shaw Brothers Studio, 1960–1970," for some of how the Shaws achieved an economic dominance of the Asian market.[9] Here I will simply note the total dominance of Mandarin martial arts films in the Hong Kong market beginning in 1970. From 1970 to 1972, for instance, as far as I can tell, virtually every film in the top-ten highest grossing films list was a martial arts movie; in 1971 Bruce Lee's first Hong Kong film, *The Big Boss,* was number one and in 1972 *The Way of the Dragon* and *Fist of Fury* were first and second, respectively. The "new-style" martial arts films, especially those of Zhang Che and his favorite star (later to turn director) Wang Yu, are the major presences and influences in this early period. But this masculinist dimension of the Hong Kong cinema is not confined merely to the triumph of Mandarin cinema in the Zhang Che-King Hu-Wang Yu-Bruce Lee era, but returns later in the 1970s. If martial arts films were no longer so thoroughly to dominate the top-ten highest-grossing lists in the middle of the decade—which marks the return to Cantonese production—they would do so again later in the decade with the emergence of Jackie Chan and the triumphs of director Lau Ka-leung (Liu Jialiang) and star Gordon Liu Chia-hui: films like *Drunken Master* and *Snake in the Eagle's Shadow,* along with *The 36th Chamber of Shaolin* and *Challenge of the Ninja* (also known as *Heroes of the East*). That is to say, the emergence of new male stars later in the 1970s is very much in the tradition of Bruce Lee, and they would return both martial arts and a resurgent nationalism to the fore. Though in the case of Jackie Chan and, later, Jet Li, it would be a Cantonese-inflected Chinese nationalism.

The Japanese Connection

The masculinist dimension to the Mandarin cinema, which involved something of a rejection of earlier Chinese cinema, including the Cantonese cinema, also involved an embrace of Japan. And I mean this in two ways: an embrace of certain

Japanese genres and modes of production and an embrace of Japan as on-screen foil for this newly masculinized Chinese male.

"The rise of Hong Kong's martial arts genre was also inspired by the popularity of imported Japanese samurai movies. The Zatoichi 'Blind Swordsman' series had been a particularly big hit. The ... major studios ... seized the opportunity to produce their own brand of samurai movies in the form of the sword fighting *wuxia* picture."[10] The genre came to dominate the popular imagination of overseas Chinese audiences from the middle of the 1960s, when the Chinese genre began with films such as *The Jade Bow, Tiger Boy*, and *Come Drink With Me* (King Hu) until the early 1970s, when sword fighting *wuxia* was replaced by kung fu fighting.

The influence of Japanese cinema on the Hong Kong cinema was quite direct. While employed by the Shaw Brothers, Xu Zhenghong (who directed the Chinese version of *Zatoichi Meets His Equal,* a joint venture between Katsu Productions and Golden Harvest, in 1971) led a delegation to Japan in 1966–1967, at the suggestion—it is interesting to note—of Raymond Chow, then an executive at Shaw. They toured the Shochiku studios and watched location filming as well. The Shaw Brothers would rely almost exclusively on studio productions, and what they learned about set construction from Shochiku, the masters of the home drama, would stand them in good stead, even in their preferred mode of the action film. Xu specifically notes that the new-style *wuxia* was indebted to Kurosawa's films and to the Zatoichi series. Similarly, screenwriter Qiu Gangjian notes that *Yojimbo* and *Sanjuro* were particularly influential for the way the films achieved their dramatic effects. It should be noted that by 1966, when the new-style *wuxia* appeared, several Japanese directors and cinematographers were employed at the Shaw studio. Most, however, would be unrecognizable by the credits, adapting their names to Chinese pronunciations according to screenwriter Qiu. One notable Japanese director who worked for the Shaws was Nakahiro Ko, under the name Yang Shuxi. Chinese directors, cinematographers, and screenwriters actually saw a number of Japanese films at the Shaw studio, including and especially the Zatoichi series, which was distributed in Hong Kong and Southeast Asia by the Shaw Brothers chain. Oftentimes the Shaw Brothers would acquire distribution rights to Japanese films, screen them for their production personnel, but not release them publicly so as to take away from the Hong Kong variations.[11]

As Japan provided personnel, production models and the opportunity for one of the great coproductions in film history, *Zatoichi Meets His Equal,* it also provided a kind of countermodel, the Japanese as enemy, which itself contributed to the continued growth and development of the Hong Kong cinema and the assertion of a pan-Chinese or transnational Chinese identity. Teo notes, as have many others, the significance of the war with Japan on Chinese cinema (though I would, along with many others, go further and state the significance of the war with Japan on Chinese identity). According to Teo, "Historians have usually pointed to the outbreak of war on the Mainland as a turning point in Hong Kong's film history. It led to the growth of the local film industry as Hong Kong absorbed migrants fleeing Shanghai."[12] Space does not permit a discussion of the Shanghai connection in Hong Kong cinema, though the Hong Kong International Film Festival has devoted one of its invaluable catalogues to this very subject. For our purposes, we need note that, "As China dug in to fight a war with Japan, film-makers on the Mainland were forced to make films on the move," including in Hong Kong, and that "[a] new genre appeared in Chinese cinema: the 'national defence' movie. These were patriotic war films that recreated images of the Japanese overrunning Chinese villages, committing atrocities, and the heroic resistance of the Chinese against the foreign invaders. National defense movies were made not least in Hong Kong where many film-makers from Shanghai had fled after the Japanese had occupied the Chinese sections of the city in 1937."[13] The national defense movie and the war with Japan would form one of the predominate tropes in the cinema of the Peoples' Republic, and thus it is no surprise to find the centrality of this theme in the early films of the Fifth Generation, such as *Yellow Earth* and *Red Sorghum*.

For the Hong Kong cinema and the new generation of *wuxia* films in the late 1960s through the early 1970s, the Japanese on screen would be no less significant than they had been off screen. If *The One-Armed Swordsman* is the key text in the aesthetic maturity and hence economic triumph of the Mandarin-language *wuxia* sword film, star Wang Yu, directing himself, produced the key text in the *wuxia* kung fu genre: *The Chinese Boxer* (also known as *Hammer of God*, 1970). Here he plays a kung fu student whose teacher is killed by Japanese karate fighters. After losing a battle with them, he vows to train even harder and masters the "iron palm" technique. Eventually, he must combat a team of samurai swordsmen and karate fighters, defeating them all in climactic combat.[14] I want to claim that the very title, "The Chinese Boxer" — which is what kung fu is best called in English, that is, "Chinese boxing" — indicates how the film sets off its Chinese-ness and does so in opposition to Japanese-ness, China/Japan, kung fu/karate. That *The Chinese Boxer* would set the tone for an entire genre is captured by a writer for the Hong Kong Movie List on the Internet Hong Kong Movie database: "It has all the elements you would expect in a Wang Yu film — brutality, evil Japanese, training and secret styles."

Secret styles put to the service to defeat the Japanese appear again in *King Boxer*, (also known as *Five Fingers of Death*, 1972), a fairly typical Shaw Brothers movie starring Lo Lieh, who had costarred with Wang Yu in *The Chinese Boxer*.

Five Fingers of Death is the film that started the whole kung fu craze of 1973 in the United States, along with Bruce Lee's first two Hong Kong films. In its vague outlines, *Five Fingers of Death* is quite similar to *Chinese Boxer*—a young kung fu fighter's mentor and friends are killed by the members of an evil kung fu school who have hired three Japanese fighters to do their evil bidding—a samurai swordsman, a judo fighter, and a karate expert. This time the hero learns the "iron fist" technique (though it looks like the iron palm technique when his hands glow to the accompaniment of the theme of the old *Ironside* television series).

But it was Bruce Lee who truly internationalized Hong Kong cinema, and it was Bruce Lee's second film, *Jingwu men* (*Fist of Fury*, or *The Chinese Connection*, 1972), that set the tone for the cultural nationalism of the Hong Kong kung fu film. Here, Lee plays Chen Zhen, whose master is betrayed by a Chinese lackey of the Japanese in prewar Shanghai. The Japanese taunt him and his fellow classmates at their master's funeral, calling China, "the sick man of East Asia." Early in the film, Chen expresses his displeasure at anti-Chinese sentiments and at the racism of the Japanese, leaping into the air and tearing down a sign at the entrance to a public park that reads "No Dogs or Chinese."

Throughout the rest of the film, Lee goes out of his way to antagonize and fight with the Japanese, using unarmed combat and also the kung fu weapon, the nunchuks, or *nunchaku*, which was to become a particular specialty of Lee's in his later films, especially *Enter the Dragon*. For critic Cheng Yu, it is kung fu that is of prime import to Lee and not simply or necessarily anti-Western or anti-Japanese sentiments.

Instead, Lee's films are an attempt to "demote" karate and other foreign martial arts. . . . In the United States, the major obstacle to Lee's rise to stardom was Japanese karate, and he was determined to prove that Chinese martial arts . . . were deadlier than the Japanese style. This concern resurfaces in various ways in Lee's films and when he later became an international legend, his name also became synonymous with Chinese kung fu.[15]

Lee's early demise had a great impact on the Hong Kong cinema in Hong Kong. Although stars like Wang Yu, Lo Lieh, along with Ti Lung and David Chiang, among others continued to produce, direct and star in films at a healthy rate, no one could quite replace Bruce Lee, especially and including the likes of Bruce Li and Bruce Le. But for those who know their Hong Kong film history, a new star would indeed arise to the kind of acclaim and love that even, perhaps, Lee never achieved: Jackie Chan.

I want to claim that Hong Kong filmmakers were well aware of the connection between anti-Japanese sentiments and the assertion of a pan-Chinese nationalism when it came to the star-making early roles of Chan. Though he had appeared in a handful of films by 1976, including an uncredited bit part in *Enter the Dragon* (1973), it was *New Fist of Fury/Xin jingwu men* (1976), directed by Luo Wei, who had directed Bruce Lee in *The Big Boss* and *Fist of Fury*, that helped make him a star. The film is something of a sequel to the Lee film. This time, the students of the kung fu school in Shanghai in which Lee was a student have already been killed off by film's start and the surviving remnants leave for Taiwan, which we will remember was under direct Japanese occupation before World War II. The direct link between the two films, besides director Luo Wei, is costar Nora Miao, involved with Lee's character in the first film and then with Chan's in the sequel. (Miao, by the way, starred in all three of Lee's Hong Kong films—*The Big Boss, Fist of Fury,* and *Way/Return of the Dragon;* thus she is herself an icon connecting Lee and Chan.)

We note that in this film Chan is not yet skilled in kung fu, but at the start is instead a petty thief who steals from his fellow Chinese. As he says shortly after his introductory scene, it is all the same to him whether the Japanese or the Chinese hit him. Soon, however, he learns the difference between the Chinese and the Japanese and becomes more Chinese precisely when he becomes anti-Japanese and when, at the same time, he learns kung fu. Like Lee, in his embracing of the Chinese *Jingwu men,* Chan, too, dies at the end of the film, though the same could not be said of his career, which was just beginning.

Chan's star would ascend permanently just two years later with *Snake in the Eagle's Claw* and *Drunken Master.* Both are period films revolving around the protagonist's mastery of kung fu, that paradigmatic sign of Chinese nationalism of the abstract kind. In the latter film, Chan plays the young Wong Fei-hung. And here is where the anti-Japanese competition intersects with the idea I have been developing of "a body of Chinese knowledge" that enables the hero to the defeat the Japanese—Lee's kung fu and all those earlier iron palm/fist techniques and, by the end of *New Fist of Fury,* Chan's kung fu. For it is exactly "kung fu" or Chinese boxing, that enables all those Japanese villains to bite the dust.

Wong Fei-hung and/as Chinese Knowledge

Jackie Chan carried on the nationalistic, masculinist legacy of Bruce Lee through the on-screen mastery of kung fu put to service in the anti-Japanese cause. Chan also extended the legacy of Bruce Lee's kung fu through his spectacular stunt work, while connecting kung fu itself back to the earlier Cantonese cinema by his incarnation of Wong Fei-hung. In a perhaps tangential sense, Bruce Lee acknowledged his own debt to Wong Fei-hung as a marker of Chineseness in the use of actor Shi Jian in *Enter the Dragon.* As Rayns notes, "Shi, the perennial villain of the Huang Feihong series, evokes the vanished Cantonese cinema of the

1950s [while] linking the conservative traditions of *wuxia pian* of the 1950s with the world-conquering ambitions of the *wuxia pian* of the 1970s."[16] Chan's Wong Fei-hung becomes an even clearer marker of a new, globalized Hong Kong, which is the transmitter of this new (since the late 1960s) transnational Chinese nationalism. Though made in Cantonese, the filmic resurrection of Wong Fei-hung by Jackie Chan in *Drunken Master*, and the later apotheosis of the character by Jet Li in Tsui Hark's internationally popular "Once Upon a Time in China" films, are a far cry from the localized Wong Fei-hung of Kwan Tak-hing, the Cantonese cinema's most durable and popular star of the 1950s. Chan's stardom of the late 1970s and Li's of the early 1990s allowed Hong Kong and diasporic Chinese audiences to revel in their greatest stars since Bruce Lee. But even on the local level, Wong Fei-hung's Chinese kung fu and its ability to defeat Japanese enemies filtered through the local industry. Coincident with the rise to stardom of Jackie Chan, we may also find Lau Ka-leung (Liu Jialiang) directing Gordon Liu Chia-hui in *Challenge of the Masters* (1976), in which Gordon Liu plays Wong Fei-hung, and *Challenge of the Ninja* (1979), in which Liu stars opposite Japanese actor Kurata Yasuaki in a film revolving around the superiority of kung fu over ninjitsu. One might claim that the combination of Bruce Lee tributes revolving around on-screen anti-Japanese combat and an incarnation of Wong Fei-hung seems a particular strategy in the star-making machinery revolving around Jackie Chan, Gordon Liu, and Jet Li. This is to say that the muscular masculinity they all incarnated (Gordon Liu had the best physique since Bruce Lee, but both Chan and Jet Li are clearly skilled, like Lee, in martial arts) was expressed through anti-Japanese violence abetted by the mastery of the body of Chinese knowledge revolving around kung fu.

In this respect we must note Jet Li's version of the *jingwu men* archetype: *Fist of Legend/Jingwu ying xiong*. Though *Fist of Legend/Jingwu ying xiong*, a close variation on the Chinese title as well as the English title of the Lee and Chan films, was certainly not Li's star-making role, as it had been for Lee and to a lesser extent for Chan, it solidified his status as Hong Kong's successor to both Lee and Chan. Of course, there are differences in the status and image of Japan by the time of Li's film. Closer in spirit to Liu's *Challenge of the Ninja* (including the recurrence of Japanese actor Kurata Yasuaki) there is much less overt anti-Japanese rhetoric and, most interesting, Li speaks Japanese and, like Liu in the earlier film, has a Japanese girlfriend. This lessening of anti-Japanese rhetoric stems, no doubt, from the solid place the Hong Kong cinema occupies in the world film market, Hong Kong's success in the arena of global capitalism and a few more decades worth of direct interchange between Hong Kong and Japan. By this time, for instance, two major stars of the Hong Kong cinema are Japanese: Takeshi Kaneshiro (a favorite of director Wong Kar-wei) and Yukari

Oshima, action heroine extraordinaire. Japanese comic books, called *manga,* are as ubiquitous (though in Chinese translation) in Hong Kong as they are in Tokyo. *Anime* fills the TV and home video screens there as elsewhere. And a number of direct adaptations from Japanese *anime* and *manga* (not to mention literature) have made their way to Hong Kong screens, including Jackie Chan's *City Hunter* and Tsui Hark/Peter Mak's *Wicked City.* Japan and the Japanese, then, are much more normalized by this time. The anti-Japanese element of *Fist of Legend* helps solidify Li's participation in a stream of masculinist Chinese imagery that connects him to Bruce Lee and Jackie Chan, even if that anti-Japanese dimension is toned down. For, in fact, it may have been less *Fist of Legend* that made Li a star and more his legacy of kung fu that more clearly situates Li within the masculinist Chinese nationalist imaginary.

If it wasn't *Fist of Legend* that made Jet Li a star, it surely was *Once Upon a Time in China,* known in Chinese as *Wong Fei-hung.* And in Tsui's brilliant epic *Wong Fei-hung* takes on a specifically nationalistic character, a far cry from Kwan Tak-hing's days where Wong was the marker of "Cantonese Chinese" (e.g., his Southern style kung fu and his Canton locale). For Tsui it is precisely Wong's kung fu and another body of Chinese knowledge, Chinese herbal medicine, that makes the character a model of anti-Western anti-imperialism, a model of Chinese masculinity created by a body of Chinese knowledge.

Of course, this idea of a body of Chinese knowledge has other expressions in the Hong Kong cinema. Another important manner in which Chinese knowledge is acknowledged is through the recurring use of the motif of secret scrolls, on which are written a body of secret learning or knowledge. Iron palm or iron fist techniques are often passed on from teacher to student via a scroll or a manual, as in *Five Fingers of Death.* Wang Yu's one-armed swordsman learns his craft from a manual of one-armed swordsmanship. Perhaps this is related to the traditional Chinese valuation of scholarship and the recurring figure of the scholar in Hong Kong cinema. In this manner, two Chinese traditions—martial arts and scholarship—come together to create the newly masculinized Chinese hero. Thus, there is something quite wicked in Tsui Hark's *Swordsman* trilogy, which begins with the theft of a secret scroll, the object of attention throughout the remaining entries in the series. Mastery of the learning contained within the scroll necessitates castration, the demasculinization of the hero who is thus transformed into a woman, specifically Brigitte Lin Ching-hsia who, by part 3, becomes Invincible Asia!

The Chinese respect for learning not only translates into the recurring figure of the scholar and the recurring use of secret scrolls, but, even more important, into the figure of the priest, specifically the Shaolin priest. As much as Wong Fei-hung or Fong Sai Yuk or other folk heroes of the Chinese past, it is the Shaolin temple that stands in as the ultimate repository of Chinese learning and, thus, of a specifically Chinese identity. The number of recurrences of the Shaolin temple would be almost impossible to figure, but the Shaolin temple is no less central to the masculinization of the Chinese cinematic hero than Wong Fei-hung himself. The films of Lau Ka-leung—for instance, *Executioners of Shaolin, The 36th Chamber of Shaolin, Shaolin Mantis, Shaolin Challenges Ninja, Shaolin and Wu-Tang*, and *Martial Arts of Shaolin*—indicate the centrality of the Shaolin temple to the new-style masculinized martial arts hero. Similarly, the association of Jet Li with the Shaolin temple—as in *Abbot Hai Teng of Shaolin, Shaolin Kung Fu, New Legend of Shaolin*, and *Tai Chi Master*—conflates Li's image of master of Chinese martial arts with the image that he carries over from his Wong Fei-hung and Fong Sai Yuk films.

The clear association of Lee, Chan, and Li with Chinese martial arts and anti-Japanese or other anti-imperialist causes is a major reason, I suggest, for their stardom, but clearly not the only reason. Nor would I suggest that lacking muscular masculinity or a particular association with Chinese knowledge prevents stardom: Chow Yun-fat, Andy Lau, Gordon Chan, Lau Ching-wan, and so forth may have no such associations. Alternately, I would say that in the 1970s such associations were crucial to the star images not only of Bruce Lee and Jackie Chan, but also of Wang Yu, Ti Lung, Alexander Fu Sheng, and Gordon Liu. I would also insist that on the body of stars on which Chinese knowledge has left its mark rests a major reason for the global impact of Hong Kong cinema and the manner in which Hong Kong cinema stands in for "Chineseness" in the Chinese diaspora.

Exile or Diaspora?

I pointed out above the irony of Bruce Lee's exilic or diasporic locations in all three of his Hong Kong films, the geographic distance of Thailand for *The Big Boss*, the spatiotemporal shift to prewar Shanghai in *Fist of Fury*, and the setting in Italy in *Way of the Dragon*. One might even mention the Hollywood setting of *Game of Death*. This may mirror both the situation of those in Hong Kong who feel alienated from "China" and a large portion of the audience, which is, precisely, Chinese in the diaspora. Though Western audiences have been able to experience the significant pleasures of the Bruce Lee (and, later Jackie Chan and Jet Li) films, we must recall that these films were consumed by Chinese audiences in specialized, ethnic-oriented theatres, for many years exactly in "Chinatown." Watching Bruce Lee portray the immigrant, the innocent, in *The Big Boss* and *Way of the Dragon* clearly mirrored an immigrant's experience in the diaspora, while Lee's triumph, precisely through Chinese knowledge and culture (kung fu) is a happy wish-fulfillment of the immigrant's dream of acceptance and success. Moreover, Lee's substantial physical beauty and martial prowess themselves provide a source of pan-Chinese pride: Kwai-cheung Lo notes that "the characters Lee played were . . . generically 'Chinese.' . . . He was broadly held as a 'Chinese hero' who used the power and philosophy of kung fu to defeat the Westerner and the Japanese, arousing a Chinese nationalistic fantasy in the Hong Kong audience more strongly than any particular local identification."[17]

Whereas Lee's *Big Boss* and *Way of the Dragon* mirrored the contemporary diaspora of Hong Kong Chinese throughout the world—Southeast Asia, Europe, North America—the Shaw Brothers' Mandarin-language films mirrored the notion of exile that reflected the situation of all Hong Kong Chinese, in Hong Kong and across the globe: all were alienated from the mainland. The lack of Cantonese dialect in the Hong Kong cinema of the early 1970s, in Hong Kong and certainly across the diaspora, is among the most striking features of the era. But equally striking is the manner in which virtually every Shaw Brothers *wuxia* film is set in the past. Censorship laws in the territory made the production of politicized films problematic, while a continued focus on local social problems (a feature of 1960s Cantonese cinema) might itself have worked against the solidification of the transnational Chinese audience that the Shaw Brothers achieved through their domination of the Mandarin-language movie circuit. But the setting in the past and the use of Mandarin dialect situates the films, geographically and linguistically, in China and while the Shaw Brothers films use only the vague outlines of Chinese history for their settings, they specifically use Chinese knowledge for their themes. Ming versus Qing conflicts, Manchu versus Han, corrupt emperors versus the Shaolin temple, all only vaguely relate to the political history of China but clearly relate to the formation of a modern pan-Chinese identity, especially at a time when the Chinese cinema (in the Peoples' Republic) is moribund.

The return of Cantonese dialect to the Hong Kong cinema in the 1970s marked an increased focus on contemporary settings within Hong Kong itself. Certainly this was the major feature of the Hong Kong New Wave. Hong Kong cinema through the films of Michael Hui and, later, the New Wave, could create for itself a local focus, a local identity. Pride in Hong Kong's accomplishments as a global economic power, including the Hong Kong cinema itself, certainly lent pride to a specifically Hong Kong identity. Yet this very specificity—of dialect, of issues—may be one reason that the global impact of Hong Kong cinema, achieved through the release of dubbed Mandarin-language films in the early and middle 1970s, declined. But in the 1980s we see something like the globalization of Hong Kong itself, not only as an established economic power, but also as a globalized cinema, seen by a marked increase in the use of overseas locales in contemporary settings, where Cantonese language and culture comes to occupy the space within the frame; where Cantonese is spoken by all the characters, much the way that Hollywood cinema uses global locales while forcing every screen character to speak English. No other cinema save the Hollywood cinema, has so colonized global space for its own use. Jackie Chan broke the boundaries of Hong Kong filmmaking not only by becoming an international star—as, after all, Bruce Lee before him had—but also by situating his films globally: mainland China in *Police Story 3: Supercop;* Russia and Australia in *First Strike; Mr. Nice Guy,* set entirely in Australia; *Armor of God* in Europe and *Armor of God II: Operation Condor,* set in Europe and Africa; and *Who Am I?* with its lengthy African sequence; finally reaching an apotheosis in *Rumble in the Bronx,* set in New York but shot in Vancouver. Not coincidentally, then, the final installment of the *Once Upon a Time in China* series takes place in the United States, the endpoint, as it were, of Hong Kong's globalized cinema and culture, Jet Li following Chan as an international star and an up-and-coming Hollywood icon.

It would be the work of stars like Chow Yun-fat, Danny Lee, Simon Yam, Gordon Chan, Lau Ching-wan, to create a local Hong Kong masculinized imaginary. Jet Li, too, could participate in the contemporary action drama *(Bodyguard from Beijing, High Risk, Hit Man)* and recoup for contemporary Hong Kong some of the masculinized nationalism typically and previously displaced onto the past or onto the global. But even here it is worth noting that only Chow Yun-fat has achieved an international stardom while being strictly associated with Hong Kong's contemporary era and setting (and mostly through the films of John Woo and Ringo Lam, who work in the globalized genre of the action film). This is to say that to assert a national identity on the part of the Hong Kong Chinese it still behooves them to work in the international arena, to create a transnational image, to become global sometimes at the expense of the local.

Export/Import/China

It is well known by now that the Hong Kong cinema attained its first international presence in the early 1970s through the importation by U.S. and European distributors of Shaw Brothers and Golden Harvest films in dubbed versions. Prior to what was termed the "kung fu craze," Shaw Brothers had a profitable, if modest, circuit of overseas theatres which they owned and operated including a handful in the United States: in New York, San Francisco, Los Angeles, and Honolulu. Their bread and butter was their Southeast Asian circuit, and they benefited, also, from Taiwan. This initial importation of martial arts films in the United States has been the subject of my previous research, and there I noted that a substantial box-office impact was realized by these Hong Kong imports. Moreover, this marked the first time that Hong Kong cinema influenced U.S. genres, intersecting with Blacksploitation, for instance, and eventually leading to the creation of U.S. martial arts films and film stars.[18] Yet Hong Kong had been producing martial arts films for more than twenty years before *Five Fingers of Death* and *Fist of Fury* punched their way to the top of the U.S. box-office charts in 1973. What accounts not for the successful importation of these films, but, rather, their successful exportation? That is, it is easy to see why these films were popular in the United States. But why those films and not earlier ones? Most previous scholarship has focused on how Hong Kong films were received (and co-opted) by overseas film industries, but few have noted the manner in which this overseas importation coincides with the assertion of a Hong Kong/Chinese identity. Specifically, the beginnings of Hong Kong's assertion of its export potential is realized via the masculinization of the newly emergent domination of the male star through the imaging of Japan and the Japanese and the forceful foregrounding of Chinese martial arts in the Mandarin-language film productions of the Shaw Brothers. Once, that is, the Hong Kong cinema had joined in what was essentially a masculinist domination of the world-wide action cinema (including spaghetti westerns, Black action films, British horror movies, and so forth), it created a space for itself not only at the box office at home, but also abroad.

By avoiding contemporary political issues, by rarely setting their films in Hong Kong itself, by utilizing muscular masculinity within specifically Chinese cultural dimensions (martial arts especially), the Shaw Brothers created and exported an image of China that came to replace earlier cinematic constructions, especially in an era (1966–1976) when Chinese (i.e., mainland) cinema itself had disappeared. And although it is the case that Taiwanese cinema had a powerful industrial impact on Hong Kong and throughout Southeast Asia (also through martial arts films, to be sure), it did not have the clout of the Shaw Brothers both in the European and American "Chinatown circuit" and in the international arena of coproductions and sales to Euro-American distributors. Thus, it was that the Shaw Brothers, and, later, Golden Harvest, came to be associated with Hong Kong cinema, which, in turn, became the premier creator and distributor of "China."

For the later generation of Hong Kong cinema, the ascension of Jackie Chan to superstardom amid the routine production of Cantonese-dialect films, Hong Kong came to mean not just "China" but "Asia," enabling Chinese nationalism to become pan-Asian cultural nationalism.

> Hong Kong movies were characterized by "vertical integration" during the 1950s and 1960s. However, after the 1970s, Hong Kong movies experienced a reduction in vertical integration [which led to] the so-called "pre-sale" practice, meaning a system that

requires distributors to pay before a movie is actually made . . . The availability of financial investment from overseas distributors by the "pre-sale" practice has boosted film production in Hong Kong. More importantly, the function performed by the distributors increasingly exerts pressure on the production strategies of Hong Kong movies. Thus important decisions in terms of genres, casting and storylines can be influenced by overseas distributors. This accounts for why so many international elements can be found in Hong Kong films.[19]

There is thus a kind of imperialism taking place, but also a kind of pan-Asian identification. Jackie Chan's films, noted above, which take place outside of Hong Kong, represent a kind of "Asianization" — "a fusion or synthesis of different Asian cultures into one Asian culture. . . . In other words, what Jackie Chan stands for is Asia, not Hong Kong. This creation of an Asian identity is the most important message that Chan's works have conveyed."[20] Thus, if Bruce Lee's and the Shaw Brothers' films substituted Hong Kong for China, Chan's substitute Asia for Hong Kong. In the attempts to make Jackie Chan, Chow Yun-fat, and Jet Li stars in the United States (as was the case with Bruce Lee earlier), we might even see the Asianization of Hollywood, an interesting and significant outcome of the masculinization of the Chinese man.

This newly (or recently) masculinized Chinese man accounts for the manner in which "the Asianization of Hollywood" as I have just termed it, precisely comes about. Certainly, it was an influx of Chinese directors who began this process, directors such as John Woo, Tsui Hark, and Ringo Lam who had been associated with New Wave martial arts and gangster (hero) films that reintroduced Hong Kong cinema to world audiences in the late 1980s. Surely there is no need to rehearse the impact of John Woo on the action cinema, of Ringo Lam on the enormously influential Quentin Tarantino, and so forth. The point is that these Hong Kong directors came to Hollywood precisely to continue the masculinist practices that gave them their international fame, each director, perhaps oddly enough, making his U.S. film debut by directing Jean-Claude van Damme, himself a direct descendent of the Bruce Lee–influenced American martial arts film. But following the legacy of Bruce Lee and the action-oriented cinema of the Hong Kong directors, Hong Kong action stars could be slotted into the sorts of roles previously reserved for Caucasian or black actors.

Though Chow Yun-fat was relatively chaste with Mira Sorvino in *The Replacement Killers* (1998), by the time of the nonaction-oriented *Anna and the King* (1999), he could at least maintain a sexual presence. This is a far cry from the original film version of *Anna and the King of Siam* (1946) and the more famous musical remake, *The King and I* (1956), when non-Asian actors had to play the role despite the chaste relationship between the eponymous leads. That there has been a particularly interesting pairing with black stars, male and female (Jackie Chan and Chris Tucker in *Rush Hour* [1998], Samo Hung and Arsenio Hall in the now-canceled American television show *Martial Law,* Jet Li and Aaliyah in *Romeo Must Die* [2000], and so forth) should not disguise the significant fact of the Asian male action star in Hollywood cinema today. Strangely enough, in another phenomenon little noted, it is often the case that, for instance, the characters portrayed by Samo Hung and Jet Li are associated not with Hong Kong, but with the mainland. Although it is the case that these stars, are, in fact, mainlanders by birth, their cinematic association is with Hong Kong, yet their on-screen characters belie their Hong Kong associations. This disavowal of Hong Kong and the substitution of "China" continues the deja disparu identified so memorably by Ackbar Abbas—here not the disappearance of Hong Kong's culture within Hong Kong, but the disappearance of Hong Kong itself via the very directors and stars who called attention to Hong Kong in the first place.

Notes

1. Stephen Teo, *Hong Kong Cinema: The Extra Dimension* (London: British Film Institute, 1997), 110–111.

2. Ibid., 122.

3. Steve Fore, "Jackie Chan and the Cultural Dynamics of Global Entertainment," in Sheldon Hsiao-peung, ed., *Transnational Chinese Cinemas: Identity, Nationhood, Gender* (Honolulu: University of Hawai`i Press, 1997), 247.

4. Teo, *Hong Kong Cinema,* 169.

5. Sek Kei, "The War between the Cantonese and the Mandarin Cinemas in the Sixties; or, How the Beautiful Women Lost to the Action Men," in *The Restless Breed: Cantonese Stars of the Sixties.* The Twentieth Hong Kong International Film Festival Catalogue (Hong Kong: Urban Council, 1996), 30.

6. Tony Rayns, "Bruce Lee and Other Stories," in *A Study of Hong Kong Cinema in the Seventies.* The Eighth Hong Kong International Film Festival Catalogue (Hong Kong: Urban Council, 1984), 26.

7. Tian Yan, "The Fallen Idol: Zhang Che in Retrospect," in *A Study of Hong Kong Cinema in the Seventies,* 45.

8. Teo, *Hong Kong Cinema,* 97–98.

9. Poshek Fu, "Going Global: The Transnational Cinema of the Shaw Brothers Studio, 1960–1970," in *Border Crossings in Hong Kong Cinema.* The Twenty-Fourth Hong Kong International Film Festival (Hong Kong: Urban Council, 2000), 43–51.

10. Teo, *Hong Kong Cinema,* 98.

11. Lau Shing-hon, "Three Interviews," in *A Study of the Hong Kong Swordplay Film (1945–1980).* The Fifth Hong Kong International Film Festival (Hong Kong: Urban Council, 1981), 208.

12. Teo, *Hong Kong Cinema,* 7.

13. Ibid., 5

14. Ibid, 103–104.

15. Cheng Yu, "Anatomy of a Legend," in *A Study of Hong Kong Cinema in the Seventies,* 24.

16. Rayns, "Bruce Lee and Other Stories," 29.

17. Kwai-cheung Lo, "Muscles and Subjectivity: A Short History of the Masculine Body in Hong Kong Popular Culture," *Camera Obscura* 39 (September 1996): 110.

18. David Desser, "The Kung Fu Craze," in Poshek Fu and David Desser, eds., *The Cinema of Hong Kong: History, Arts, Identity* (New York: Cambridge University Press, 2000), 19–43.

19. Tzann Lii, "A Colonized Empire: Reflections on the Expansion of Hong Kong Films in Asian Countries," in Kuan-Hsing Chen, ed., *Trajectories: Inter-Asia Cultural Studies* (London: Routledge, 1998), 129.

20. Ibid., 134.

CHAPTER FOURTEEN

Hong Kong Diaspora Film and Transnational Television Drama

From Homecoming to Exile to Flexible Citizenship

Hong Kong Diaspora Film

It is common knowledge that three important historical moments have greatly influenced the construction of place, self, and nationality in Hong Kong's filmic discourse: the Joint Sino-British Declaration in 1984, the Tiananmen incident in 1989, and Hong Kong's return to China in 1997. I want to suggest that there seems to be a significant paradigm change in the representation of issues related to nationality, identity, and citizenship in Hong Kong films depicting the Chinese diaspora. In a nutshell, the change may be characterized as a shift from a "China syndrome" in the mid-1980s to an "exile complex" or "persecution complex" shortly after 1989 and finally to a discourse of flexible citizenship and transnationalism around 1997.[1]

The signing of the Joint Sino-British Declaration in 1984 made it certain to Hong Kong residents that the island would eventually return to Chinese sovereignty. Hong Kong films began a process of searching for Hong Kong's identity, often resulting in an identification with its ultimate "homeland"—mainland China. Critics have noticed a fascination with the mainland, a "China syndrome," in some films produced in this period. Such films portray an emotional attachment to mainland China as ancestral home and motherland. "The directors of the new wave mooted questions of identity, nationality and ethnicity in their works. These were sensitive questions never asked before."[2] A good example in this regard is Yim Ho's film *Sishui liunian* (Homecoming). Li Cheuk-to and Esther Yau singled out two 1984 films—*Homecoming* and *Shenggang qibing* (Long Arm of the Law)—as perfect examples that deal with the relationship between Hong Kong and China. Whereas *Homecoming* offers a benign, idyllic vision of China at one end of the spectrum of filmic representation of the mainland, *Long Arm of the Law* occupies the other end of the spectrum, presenting a dark, negative picture of China.[3]

Hong Kong's fascination with and nostalgia for the mainland, however, was shattered within a few years by the Tiananmen incident in 1989. The change of mood is seen in a number of films, for example, Clara Law's *Ai zai biexiang de jijie* (Farewell China, 1990), Ann Hui's *Ketu qiuhen* (Song of Exile, 1990), Evans Chan's *Fushi lianqu* (To Liv[e], 1992) and *Cuo ai* (Crossings, also known as Wrong Love, 1994), and Stanley Kwan's *Ren zai Niuyue* (Full Moon in New York, 1990). China is now seen as source of oppression and brutality, and its children were forced to suffer untold hardships. Ethnic Chinese in diaspora become homeless, uprooted, unwelcome travelers of the world, and they constantly experience alienation and displacement in daily life. Their emotional attachment to the motherland is "wrong love," to use the title of a film by Evans Chan.

Commenting on an interrelated group of love stories, family melodramas, and diaspora films, Gina Marchetti attempts to describe the phenomenon with more precision. She outlines "three related subgenres that have become quite popular in Hong Kong after Thatcher's visit to Beijing. The trend picked up even more after June 4, 1989."[4] One subgenre has to do with romantic entanglements and family problems in regard to the issue of emigration. Examples include Shu Kei's *Hu du men* (Stage Door, 1996) and Evans Chan's *To Liv(e)*. A second subgenre concerns the trials and tribulations faced by new immigrants to America, Canada, and Australia. Stanley Kwan's *Full Moon in New York*, Peter Chow's *Yimin shijie* (Pickles Make Me Cry, 1987), and Clara Law's *Fusheng* (Floating Life, 1996) are such examples. Evans Chan's *Crossings* and Allen Fong's *Meiguo xin* (Just Like Weather, 1986) blend both subgenres. A third subgenre involves mainland Chinese in Hong Kong. Mabel Cheung's *Feifa yimin* (Illegal Immigrants, 1985) and Peter Chan's *Tian mimi* (Comrades, Almost a Love Story, 1996) are examples.

The discourse of exile underlines the mood of diaspora film at one point, and it is well articulated in Ann Hui's classic film *Song of the Exile* (1990). The idea of "exile" conjures up its opposite meaning: "home," a sense of belonging, which could be Hong Kong, Macau, China, or Japan in the context of the film. Tony Williams reads the film as a "subdued melodramatic treatment of an allegory of reunification, which in the film is depicted through the protagonist Hueyin's relationship to her mother and grandparents."[5] Commenting on the "politics of home" in the film, Chua Siew Keng writes, "The exiled subject, then, not only feels a sense of exclusion and marginality in this space-other-than-home, but she also perceives and constructs the otherness of this space where s/he is presently located."[6] In short, estrangement and exclusion define the exile's sense of home or the lack thereof. A more literal translation of the original Chinese title of the film would also convey the sense of homelessness—*Ketu qiuhen* (Autumn Sorrows of a Traveler on the Road). Mobility, travel, and deterritorialization are thought to be causes of physical dislocation as well as psychological disorientation.

The habit of approaching Hong Kong films through some notion of original home, homeland, or mainland China-as-fatherland, has been a standard procedure in film criticism. Such a strategy has its moments of both insight and blindness. The homogenizing tendency in this critical maneuver is acutely pointed out by Emile Yueh-yu Yeh. Reflecting on the pitfall of constructing a Hong Kong cinema solely upon an "identity crisis" and a child-parent relationship between Hong Kong and the mainland, Yeh cautions us against the danger that "teleological determination overruns actual history. The critics write as if Hong Kong cinema is so haunted by 1997's ghost that immediate, current factors have no power to speak and be seen in the films."[7] To overstate the "China syndrome" is to neglect the local condition of Hong Kong and the evolution of Hong Kong film genres themselves. "Border crossing" between Hong Kong and the mainland in the mid-1980s is not border crossing at all; it is the return to "roots" and "origins," rather than the trespassing of geographic boundaries.

In the 1990s, Hong Kong was the biggest foreign investor in the Chinese economy. Hong Kong's investment in the mainland fueled the growth of the Chinese economy, created new sources of wealth for both Hong Kong people and the mainlanders, and made the business tycoons richer and richer. As the memory of Tiananmen receded in people's minds, attracting transnational capital became the top priority in the calculations of political leaders and entrepreneurs in China, Hong Kong, and the rest of the world. In response to the blurring of borderlines between nation-states in the post-Cold War, post-1989 era, and in anticipation of the 1997 handover of Hong Kong to China, Hong Kong cinema began a new description of identity, ethnicity, and location about people in diasporic conditions. In both critical and filmic discourse, diaspora does not necessarily result in displacement, dislocation, disorientation, and impotence, but rather entails reorientation and repositioning. Flexible citizenship and transnationalism become ways of empowerment and agency. Identity is no longer defined in terms of some original nation-state, but implies local participation and global imagination. Chinese-ness still matters, but does not mean fixed geographic origin and strict affiliation with some nation-state. Identity-formation is a fluid, deterritorialized, flexible mechanism. Deterritorialization is not equivalent to displacement or exile, but it is a new mode of spatial engagement with the real, a new strategy of reterritorialization outside the homeland.

In light of the potential for both domination and liberation in an era of global border crossing of people, capital, information, goods, and images, contemporary film studies demands, in the words of Marchetti, a truly "dialectical thinking" and a "radical critique."[8] We must be attentive to new configurations of the nation, ethnicity, citizenship, and gender in world cinema. There seems to be the beginning of a paradigm change in Hong Kong cinema as well as Hong Kong film criticism. I refer to recent films by Wong Kar-wai and Peter Chan such as *Chunguang zhaxie* (Happy Together, 1997), *Comrades, Almost a Love Story*, and so on. In terms of film scholarship, there is a strong interest in re-examining the archaeology of the transnational roots of Hong Kong cinema. For instance, the *Hong Kong Cinema Retrospective Catalogue* for the Twenty-Fourth Hong Kong International Film Festival (April 2000) is such a collective undertaking, and it is appropriately titled *Border Crossings in Hong Kong Cinema*.[9] To the delight of the researcher, the catalogue also contains a selective list of "border-crossing films in Hong Kong (1946–1984)," chronicling several decades of Hong Kong films that involve transnational and transregional flows and collaborations between Hong Kong and China, Taiwan, Japan, Korea, Southeast Asia, Europe, America, and other places, from the end of World War II to the year of the signing of the Joint Sino-British Declaration.[10]

Diaspora has been a recurrent theme of Wong Kar-wai's films. Diaspora is not necessarily the condition of homelessness, exile, and dislocation. It builds new relationships, finds new homes, and empowers the migrants. Yeh notices that many of Wong's films center on the motifs of "leaving," "arriving," "moving ahead," and "waiting.""These abstract motifs nonetheless constitute traveling in the most practical and mundane sense. Each time the character leaves his or her lover, it also marks a new hope, the beginning of a new relationship, or at least the beginning of something else."[11] The 1997 film *Happy Together* has perhaps the happiest ending in all of Wong's films. As a film about Hong Kong citizens traveling the world, it has an open ending and gives different possibilities for the future. Lisa Stokes and Michael Hoover write, "*Happy Together* offers several possible scenarios for the reunion of Hong Kong and China: escape, lament, embrace, acceptance, and choice. Rather than provide simple commentary, the movie maps out complications, contradictions, and conflicts, reflecting the preoccupations and concerns of Hong Kong people on the brink of the handover."[12]

The upbeat tone and the fast-moving images at the close of the film (to the beat of Frank Zappa's song "Happy Together") offer hope, reconciliation, energy, and new beginning. Likewise, the ending of Wong's earlier film *Chongqing senlin* (Chungking Express, 1994) also expresses the exhilaration of traveling to faraway places (as a flight attendant) and the flight of imagination in the tune of "California Dreamin."

We may take Peter Chan's film *Comrades, Almost a Love Story* as another example of such as a discursive shift. The film is about two mainlanders-turned-Hong Kongers-turned-New Yorkers: Li Qiao (Maggie Cheung) and Xiaojun (Leon Lai). Although the immigrants endure many hardships throughout the film, the pathos of "exile" is no longer present. While their fortunes rise and fall in the pursuit of the "Hong Kong dream," "American dream," or for that matter "Chinese dream," mobility, border crossing, and transnationality are sources of change and empowerment for Li Qiao and Xiaojun. All this does not mean that identity and cultural affiliation do not matter. In an early scene in the film, Xiaojun as a restaurant delivery boy rides a bicycle happily in the streets of Hong Kong while the soundtrack plays the music of the Chinese national anthem. But this facile construction of nationality is short-lived as Xiaojun learns more about the life of an immigrant and renegotiates his relationships to Hong Kong, China, and even his former fiancée from the mainland. Deng Lijun's (Teresa Tang) songs, not the Chinese national anthem, serve as the unifying element in the inner lives of the two main characters. They finally reunite in New York, under the soundtrack of Deng Lijun's song *"Tian mimi"* (Sweetie). The ending is again a moment of hope, union, new beginning. The pan-Chinese songs of Deng Lijun are a defining marker of the transnational identity of ethnic Chinese scattered at various locales of the globe regardless of their specific origins.

Hong Kong films as such are much more mature and level-headed than the obsessively paranoid vision of Hong Kong on the eve of the handover in Wayne Wang's *Chinese Box. Comrades* is also very different from earlier films such as *Farewell China* in the treatment of issues of diaspora and national identity. Both films are rather similar in detailing the difficult odyssey of Chinese citizens from the mainland to America/New York, but the tone and the ending have changed. In *Farewell,* the image of China lapses into either a mythical farmland of childhood and innocence or a terrifying body politic that drives its people to tragedy. One hears refrains of an old Chinese ballad at the end of the film; one also hears the patriotic Chinese song *"Wo de zuguo"* (My Motherland), familiar to any Chinese who grows up in the mainland, at the cathartic, climactic moment of Yahong and Nansheng's tearful reunion in New York. The song expressing the love for the motherland is turned against itself into an indictment of the Chinese state's inability to take care of its citizens. The pursuit of the American dream becomes a nightmare as the narrative unravels. As *Farewell* is firmly grounded

Li Qiao (Maggie Cheung) and Xiaojun (Leon Lai), two immigrants from the mainland, fall in and out of love in the streets of Hong Kong, in *Comrades Almost a Love Story* (Peter Chan, 1996, Hong Kong).

in the paradigm of the nation-state (the protagonists' love for or disillusion with it), "Sweetie," both the song by Deng Lijun and the original Chinese title of *Comrades*, offers an alternative way of envisioning nationality and diaspora.

In the final scene of *Farewell*, Yahong, suffering from schizophrenia, stabs her husband Nansheng to death in front of a replica of the Statue of Liberty, or "Goddess of Democracy" *(minzhu nüshen)*, on a rainy day in New York. The flag of the United States flutters above the Goddess of Democracy. The episode with all its symbolism is a reminder of what happened in Tiananmen Square in 1989, an event that has the proportion of a national tragedy. The film ends with shots of the Chinese countryside: trees, roads, rivers, alleys, chimneys, a farmer tilling the land, and finally a child while the soundtrack plays an old Chinese ballad. Although the subject matter is about going abroad, the film is a sad allegory of the Chinese nation-state. *Comrades*, however, does not repeat the same narrative strategy. Toward the end of the film, Li Qiao (also portrayed by Maggie Cheung!) works as a tour guide in New York. She leads a group of mainland Chinese tourists to the Statue of Liberty. The wealthy Chinese ladies are impatient with staying at the site for too long. They are eager to go shopping, to buy "Gucci bags." They inform Li Qiao, who has not gone back once after leaving

Schizophrenic Yahong (Maggie Cheung) looks at their old picture after she has stabbed her husband Nansheng to death (*Farewell China*, dir. Clara Law, 1990, Hong Kong).

China many years ago, that the country has changed, that now Hong Kong people go to China to make money. Li Qiao has just received her green card at this point. With the safety of a green card, she can travel to China now. A green card means to Li Qiao primarily mobility, freedom in travel, work, and residence on an individual base. This Statue of Liberty episode has no trace of the agony associated with a national struggle. The political implications of the Statue of Liberty are attenuated while the opportunities for work, travel, and money making are emphasized.

It is interesting to note that Maggie Cheung portrays the female protagonist in both films. She also stars in Olivier Assayas's film *Irma Vep* (1996), which rehearses a Hong Kong actress' involvement in a remake of a film classic in France. This metafilm charts out the trajectory of the career of a contemporary Hong Kong actress—her past glory in Hong Kong cinema, present participation in European cinema, and a future appointment with the American film director Ridley Scott as hinted at the end of the film. The transnational adventure of the film character is followed up by the real life story of Maggie Cheung—her education and upbringing in Hong Kong and Great Britain and marriage to a European director—Olivier Assayas.

Flexible Citizenship, Multiculturalism, and Transnational Television Drama

The emergent transnationalism and flexible citizenship are not only evident in filmic discourse, but are also manifested in new patterns of international collaboration and coproduction between film industries, between Hong Kong and Hollywood. The exodus of Hong Kong film talents is a force of renewal for both Hollywood and international film culture in large. As Steve Fore noted, Hollywood, by absorbing the ingenuities of the traveling Hong Kong film artists, "has accelerated its appropriation of visual motifs, performance idiosyncrasies, and even styles of attire associated with Hong Kong movies. This phenomenon has moved well beyond the homages-cum-ripoffs of Tarantino and his wannabes."[13] The list of Hong Kong directors, actors, and actresses participating in Hollywood and foreign projects grows: John Woo (*Hard Target, Broken Arrow, Face/Off, Mission Impossible 2, John Woo's Once a Thief* [a television drama]), *Tsui Hark* (Double Team), Ringo Lam *(Maximum Risk)*, Jackie Chan *(Rush Hour)*, Sammo Hung *(Martial Law)*, Chow Yun-fat *(The Replacement Killers, Corruptor, Anna and the King)*, Michelle Yeoh *(Tomorrow Never Dies)*, Maggie Cheung *(Irma Vep)*, Stanley Tong *(Martial Law)*, Yuen Woo-ping *(Matrix, Charlie's Angels)*, Jet Li *(Lethal Weapon 4, Romeo Must Die)*, and Peter Chan *(The Love Letter)*. As a result of their "flexible citizenship" and participation in joint film productions, the hybridization of genres, motifs, and styles with a Hong Kong flavor is changing the shape of global film culture and revamping preexisting conventions of filmmaking.[14]

The globalization of Hong Kong cinema is most literally personified by Jackie Chan and the evolution of his martial arts films. The old Hong Kong martial arts film genre is now turned into a Chinese diaspora film set at various locales of the world, and Jackie Chan has become a Hong Kong version of James Bond. For example, consider the transformation of the setting in the *Police Story* series from China and Hong Kong in *Police Story I* and *II*, to Asia (Malaysia) in *Police Story III: Supercop*, to Europe and Oceania (Ukraine and Australia) in *Police Story IV: First Strike*. His films *Rumble in the Bronx* and *Rush Hour* topped box-office sales when released in the United States. The persona of Jackie Chan, in the role of a Hong Kong cop, is the new quintessential Hong Kong traveler and citizen with a fluid, transnational, cross-cultural identity.

Capitalizing on the success of Jackie Chan in America, CBS launched a Saturday night television drama series *Martial Law*. It consisted of a multiethnic cast: Sammo Hung as Sammo Law, Arsenio Hall as Terrell Parker, Kelly Hu as Grace Chen, and Gretchen Egolf as Amy Dylan. Stanley Tong was codirector and co-producer of the series. Hong Kong martial arts film superstar Sammo Hung portrayed a Shanghai "supercop" working in the Los Angeles Police Department (LAPD). He collaborated with his American colleagues to solve both local and international crimes. Kelly Hu, a Chinese American actress, former Miss Teen USA and Miss Hawaii, was groomed to be a new television version of Michelle Yeoh. Her martial arts skills and sex appeal have earned her the status of a new action heroine as well as a "femme fatale."[15]

Normally *Martial Law* aired at 9 P.M. Eastern time, followed by *Walker, Texas Ranger*, starring Chuck Norris, immediately after, at 10 P.M. on Saturdays. On Saturday, February 19, 2000, *Martial Law* and *Walker, Texas Ranger* aired a two-hour, crossover, double presentation: Chuck Norris appeared in *Martial Law,* and Sammo Hung appeared in *Walker, Texas Ranger.* The two episodes, *Honor Among Strangers* and *The Day of Cleansing,* made up one continuous story. The two martial arts superstars traveled back and forth between Los Angeles, California, and Dallas, Texas, to fight against domestic terrorism. A group of white supremacists, headed by the character Cliff Eagleton, was intent on a cleansing of "genetically inferior races" in America. Eagleton and his followers believed that ethnic minorities were threatening the American way of life and that the country was under invasion by foreign-owned businesses. According to Eagleton, the U.S. government was impotent, and it was up to his group to effect a change, a "revolution," an ethnic cleansing, to create a new order in the new millennium. They planned to blow up various foreign businesses such as Tanaka Plaza in Los Angeles, and to pull off an explosion at the plaza more powerful and devastating than the Oklahoma City bombing. They also resented gender equality and mocked "political correctness," as seen in the army officer Monroe's mistreatment of undercover soldier Grace Chen (Kelly Hu). This ultraright-wing group murdered people and stole and smuggled weapons—guns, ammunition, and hi-tech missiles. In response, Sammo, Walker, and their comrades set out to crush the criminal organization and maintain peace. At the end of the double episode, Walker and Sammo risked their lives by driving away a truck full of high explosives to safe ground and thus averting the destruction of the city. Their heroic acts successfully protected America and what it stands for—justice, multiculturalism, racial equality, gender equality, and, no less important, free trade and transnational capital. Their actions demonstrated that xenophobia, racism, sexism, discrimination, and terrorism have no place in America.

The traditional themes of camaraderie, loyalty, and honor in Asian martial arts films are ostensibly present in the multiracial setting of the American television drama. Predictably, there are abundant spectacular fighting scenes, exhibiting the snappy martial arts skills of the actors and actresses. There are sprinklings of Sammo's characteristic earthy Chinese wisdom. In the series, Sammo, no longer a young man, proves to be an agile, seasoned fighter and a dedicated officer. He is also a warm, caring, compassionate person. (For instance, he gives fatherly advice and encouragement to an inexperienced junior woman officer— lieutenant P. J., who dies in line of duty later in the story.) The old martial arts genre now serves a new American agenda and sends out a progressive message. (These elements are already present in the Jackie Chan films *Rumble in the Bronx* and *Rush Hour.*)

With the guest appearance of Sammo Hung in *Walker, Texas Ranger,* the martial arts genre has come full circle. It originates from Hong Kong (with Bruce Lee, and so forth), and now returns and reappears in mainstream American entertainment. Chuck Norris has obtained the status of a martial arts superstar in part because he appeared and fought in Hong Kong films such as Bruce Lee films. In the episode *The Day of Cleansing,* Walker reminds his doubtful Texan colleagues that Sammo is a "Chinese martial arts specialist" and that "he has a unique style of fighting." The LAPD/Shanghai cop comes to their turf at his invitation. Initially, in the prior episode *Honor Among Strangers,* Sammo was wary of Walker's cowboy hat, thinking that it is a big target that attracts attack; however, at the end of the double episode, Sammo has come to love the Texas way of life and even dresses up like a cowboy, complete with a big hat. Cross dressing, crossover television dramas and genres (martial arts and Western), and the crossing of borders between Shanghai and Los Angeles indicate a phase of increasing exchange of artists, ideas, capital, technologies, and industries between nations and cultures. *Martial Law* is an example of a new kind of transnational TV culture-in-the-making between the East and the West. Gone are the stereotypes and orientalism as cast in the Charlie Chan detective film series; also gone are the hang-ups with exile, persecution, or mythical homeland. The traveling Hong Kong or Shanghai cop by way of Jackie Chan and Sammo Hung epitomizes a new breed of globe-trotting Chinese who can operate anywhere in the world without anguish or apology. At the same time, what might be called "transnational visuality" in this type of crossover television drama series is appropriated to serve a domestic American agenda: multiculturalism and global capitalism.

If decentralized, "flexible accumulation" is a dominant characteristic of the post-Fordist, postmodern mode of production and capital accumulation in late capitalism, according to David Harvey, "flexible citizenship" is the corresponding mode of subject-formation and human agency among an elite group of global citizens.[16] According to Aihwa Ong, " 'Flexible citizenship' refers to the cultural logics of capitalist accumulation, travel, and displacement that induce subjects to respond fluidly and opportunistically to changing political-economic conditions. In their quest to accumulate capital and social prestige in the global arena, subjects emphasize, and are regulated by, practices favoring flexibility,

Chinese martial arts transformed into American multiculturalism in the CBS TV series
Martial Law. Sammo Hung
and Kelly Hu are the stars
of the show.

mobility, and repositioning in relation to markets, governments, and cultural regimes."[17]

Ong's original model of analysis is based on successful ethnic Chinese businessmen in the greater China region and Southeast Asia. This group may be expanded to include all Chinese in the diaspora with flexible citizenship: businessmen, professionals, cultural workers, academics, and others. Even more broadly, small-time entrepreneurs, migrants, immigrants, travelers, guest workers, all those people caught in cross-cultural, transnational traffic, such as the fictional characters in the films *Happy Together* and *Comrades* or the television drama *Martial Law*, are flexible citizens in real or metaphoric terms. Filmic representations of the Chinese diaspora as well as the changing patterns in Hong Kong and international film and television industries bespeak such a fluid mechanism of residence and national affiliation. Furthermore, Hong Kong residents as a whole have always had a much more flexible national and cultural identity in comparison to those subjects living in mainland China, Taiwan, and the United Kingdom. In fact, many Hong Kong people have dual or multiple identity and citizenship: they are often citizens or permanent residents of China, Taiwan, Great Britain, Canada, Australia, the United States, and other countries. Hong Kong cinema and film artists exemplify an emergent mode of constructing and making sense of nationality, place, and self from the mid-1990s into the twenty-first century by continuing a tradition of transnational film discourse.[18]

A few cautionary words are needed here as I conclude my observations. The emphasis on the emergent transnational film discourse does not entail the reification of transnationalism as a concept or social process, for the matter at hand requires a more dialectical grasp from us. It is evident that "opportunism" is inevitably a function of "flexible identity." In the relentless, opportunistic pursuit of money and the market, the flexible citizens—be they businessmen, filmmakers, or immigrants—could easily fall prey to the reign of capital, often resulting in an even wider gap between the rich and the poor, the have and the have-not. The unequal distribution of wealth and resources could be further exacerbated by the division between the mobile and the earthbound. (Witness the down side of the global trafficking of human beings in the international market—the smuggling of Chinese peasants from Fukien/Fujian Province to Europe and America by the "snake-heads"; the selling of women from Asia and Eastern Europe into prostitution in the rich countries; and the horrendous stories of death and degradation among the migrants in their desperate attempt to cross borders by hiding in boats, cargos, freighters, and trucks.) Even in the Hong Kong films that I have mentioned (*Farewell China* and *Comrades, Almost a Love Story*), it is tragically clear that the freedom of travel and residence for the Chinese migrant comes at a high price, sometimes at the cost of life itself. At the level of cultural production and reception, artistic uniformity under the guise of transnationalism threatens to erase creativity if the artists try all too eagerly to pander to the taste of particular segments of audiences to win favors or awards. Hence, the utopian yearnings unleashed from the notions of the transnational and the postnational must be critically reflected upon in the first place.[19]

There is also, however, no denying that globalization has created liberating effects on the processes of identity formation and cultural production. Flexible citizens could escape restrictive government policies, the oppressive social structures of a given nation-state, and the lofty yet paranoid rhetoric of nationalism. Film artists could exploit, opportunistically yet fruitfully, the new freedom and mobility afforded to them and could accomplish things that were impossible prior to the postnational blurring of borderlines between regions, countries, and industries. In the realm of political economy, transnational capitalism can work both as a democratizing force in breaking down the barriers of the secluded body politic and as a reactionary force in neglecting the conditions and rights of workers in the quest for maximum profit. One of the main sites that transcribe and translate such complexities of the contemporary world is the film text and the film industry. Transnational film and television studies, then, is never a single-minded, unthinking one-way street to facile solutions of real problems; to the contrary, it must come to terms with the multifarious configurations of resistance, liberation, agency, deprivation, and complicity embedded in social life and the artistic product.

Notes

An early version of this chapter was presented at the Conference on Media and Culture Production in Taiwan, Hong Kong, and the Greater Chinese Region, Taipei, Taiwan, April 12–14, 2000, and the Second International Conference on Chinese Cinema organized by Hong Kong Baptist University—Year 2000 and Beyond: History, Technology and the Future of Transnational Chinese Film and Television, Hong Kong, April 19–21, 2000. I thank Lee Tain-dow and Emile Yueh-yu Yeh, the organizers of each conference, for their invitation, and the audiences for helping me think through the issues.

1. I first outlined a possible paradigm change in Hong Kong filmic discourse in my chapter "Filming Diaspora and Identity: Hong Kong and 1997," in Poshek Fu and David Desser, eds., *The Cinema of Hong Kong: History, Arts, Identity* (New York: Cambridge University Press, 2000), 273–288, especially 285–286. Also see my chapter "Representing the Chinese Nation-State in Filmic Discourse," Claire Sponsler and Xiaomei Chen, eds., *East of West: Cross-Cultural Performance and the Staging of Difference* (New York: Palgrave, 2000), 111–123.

2. Stephen Teo, *Hong Kong Cinema: The Extra Dimensions* (London: British Film Institute, 1997), 207.

3. Li Cheuk-to, "The Return of the Father: Hong Kong New Wave and Its Chinese Context in the 1980s," in Nick Browne, Paul G. Pickowicz, Vivian Sobchack, and Esther Yau, eds., *New Chinese Cinemas: Forms, Identities, Politics* (Cambridge: Cambridge University Press, 1994), 160–179, especially 169–174; Esther Yau, "Border Crossing: Mainland China's Presence in Hong Kong Cinema," in *New Chinese Cinemas*, 180–201.

4. Gina Marchetti, "Transnational Cinema, Hybrid Identities and the Films of Evans Chan," *Postmodern Culture: An Electronic Journal of Interdisciplinary Criticism* 8.2 (January 1998), a special issue on film.

5. Tony Williams, "*Song of the Exile*: Border-Crossing Melodrama," *Jump Cut* 42 (1998): 95. For further reflections on Hong Kong diaspora film in this respect, see Williams, "Hong Kong Cinema, the Boat People, and To Liv(e)," *Asian Cinema* 11.1 (spring/summer 2000): 131–142.

6. Chua Siew Keng, "*Song of the Exile*: The Politics of 'Home,'" *Jump Cut* 42 (1998): 90. For a study of Ann Hui's oeuvre, see Patricia Brett Erens, "The Film Work of Ann Hui," in Fu and Desser, eds., *The Cinema of Hong Kong*, 176–195.

7. Emile Yueh-yu Yeh, "Defining 'Chinese,'" *Jump Cut* 42 (1998): 75.

8. Marchetti, "Introduction: Plural and Transnational," *Jump Cut* 42 (1998): 68.

9. *Hong Kong Cinema Retrospective Catalogue—Border Crossings in Hong Kong Cinema* (Hong Kong: Leisure and Cultural Services Department, 2000).

10. Ibid., 178–182.

11. Yeh, "A Life of Its Own: Musical Discourses in Wong Kar-Wai's Films," *Post Script*

19.1 (fall 1999): 133. Tony Rayns offers a brief review of Wong Kar-wai's diaspora films in "Charisma Express," *Sight and Sound* 10.1 (January 2000): 34–36. Also see Marchetti, "Buying America, Consuming Hong Kong: Cultural Commerce, Fantasies of Identity, and the Cinema," in Fu and Desser, eds., *The Cinema of Hong Kong*, 289–313.

12. Lisa Odham Stokes and Michael Hoover, *City on Fire: Hong Kong Cinema* (London: Verso, 1999), 278.

13. Steve Fore, "Introduction: Hong Kong Movies, Critical Time Warps, and Shapes of Things to Come," *Post Script* 19.1 (fall 1999): 5–6.

14. Anne T. Ciecko and I discussed aspects of the globalization of Hong Kong cinema in "The Heroic Trio—Anita Mui, Maggie Cheung, Michelle Yeoh: Self-Reflexivity and the Globalization of the Hong Kong Action Heroine," *Post Script* 19.1 (fall 1999): 70–86.

15. A sexy picture of Kelly Hu graces the cover of an issue of the magazine *Femme Fatales*. See Craig Reid, "Kelly Hu: 'Martial Law' Mistress," *Femme Fatales* 7.15 (May 7, 1999): 8–17. The issue contains many revealing photos of Hu.

16. David Harvey, *The Condition of Postmodernity: An Inquiry into the Origins of Cultural Change* (Cambridge: Basil Blackwell, 1990).

17. Aihwa Ong, *Flexible Citizenship: The Cultural Logics of Transnationality* (Durham, N.C.: Duke University Press, 1999), 6.

18. I attempted to review the history of Chinese cinemas from the beginning up to the eve of Hong Kong's handover to China from a transnational perspective, in "Historical Introduction: Chinese Cinemas (1896–1996) and Transnational Film Studies," in Sheldon H. Lu, ed., *Transnational Chinese Cinemas: Identity, Nationhood, Gender* (Honolulu: University of Hawai`i Press, 1997), 1–31.

19. Intimations of potentially liberating effects of the "postnational" world order are given in Arjun Appadurai, *Modernity at Large: Cultural Dimensions of Globalization* (Minneapolis: University of Minnesota Press, 1996).

CHAPTER FIFTEEN

CHU YIU WAI

Hybridity and (G)local Identity in Postcolonial Hong Kong Cinema

During the late transitional period before Hong Kong's 1997 reversion to main-land China, Hong Kong identity was one of the most contested issues in the field of Hong Kong cultural studies. The China factor, in this context, is almost indispensable in any Hong Kong imaginary since the 1980s. For instance, there has been a burgeoning interest in the "father" image of China in Hong Kong films since the 1980s.[1] Although the China factor remains the top agenda of Hong Kong cultural discourse in the 1990s, another trend of negotiating Hong Kong identity emerged in Hong Kong cinema. After John Woo, Jackie Chan, Chow Yun Fat, and others had successfully established themselves in the Hollywood film industry, the question of local identity in a global film industry and its relation to criti-cal issues such as Orientalism and postcolonialism came to the forefront in Hong Kong film studies. Since then, the role of "Chineseness" in Hong Kong cultural imaginary and its different transformations in the global era have been widely discussed. Yet a significant aspect of post-1997 Hong Kong local imaginary has been left unexamined.

The negotiation of Hong Kong cultural identity in the context of globaliza-tion is one of the major topics in the study of postcolonial Hong Kong cinema. On one hand, the success of Hong Kong film directors and actors in Hollywood has generated a new discursive space for the remaking of Hong Kong identity in a transnational context. On the other hand, there are also various efforts to represent Hong Kong history and/or identity in "local" Hong Kong films. While the former has attracted more attention, this study proposes to examine the latter aspect in the light of the global/local dialectic. Recently there have been quite a number of Hong Kong films that try to rethink Hong Kong history and/or identity since the handover. Some important examples include Mabel Cheung's *Boli Zhicheng* (City of Glass, 1998), Ann Hui's *Qianyan Wanyu* (Ordinary Heroes, 1999), and Fruit Chan's trilogy *Xianggang Zhizao* (Made in Hong Kong, 1997), *Qunian Yanhua Tebieduo* (The Longest Summer, 1999) and *Xilu Xiang* (Little Cheung, 2000). If John Woo, Chow Yun Fat and Jackie Chan's success in Hollywood brings forth the problem of Orientalism and global/local dialectic, then Fruit Chan's trilogy stirs up reflections on Hong Kong identity before and after 1997 from different indigenous perspectives. Woo, Chow and Jackie Chan's success stories are now too famous to need retelling here. Unlike these global stars, Fruit Chan is well known for using "realistic" characters and local locations (from the public housing estate in *Made in Hong Kong,* the street scenes in *The Longest Summer,* the Portland Street in *Little Cheung* and its sequel *Liulian Piaopiao* [Durian Durian, 2000] to the Tai Hom shantytown in *Xianggang Youge Helihuo* [Hollywood Hong Kong, 2001]), giving the strong impression that his productions represent "local" Hong Kong films in the age of globalization.

Besides these two ways of envisaging Hong Kong, a strangely hybridized local imaginary of Hong Kong emerged in films such as *City of Glass, Ordinary Heroes,* and Sylvia Chang's *Xin Dong* (Tempting Heart, 1999), evoking a middle-way Hong Kong identity. This dimension of Hong Kong imaginary has received far less, if any, attention. As I shall show, such imaginary might shake the dichotomy of the global as economic (as exemplified by Chow Yun Fat and Jackie Chan's success in Hollywood) and the local as cultural (as exemplified by indigenous productions such as Fruit Chan's trilogy). Instead of arguing for an "authentic" portrayal of "local" Hong Kong, I would rather try to demonstrate that the strange "inauthentic" local imaginary in these films poses important questions to the concept of Chineseness in the global age. A consideration of these recent local hybridized imaginaries reshaped by a new transnational Chineseness will in turn allow us to modify our conception of Hong Kong and envision alternative Chinesenesses.

Inauthentic Local Identity?

In *City of Glass, Ordinary Heroes,* and *Tempting Heart,* the seemingly local imaginary is unabashedly "impure." One just has to take a look at the cast to be convinced. In *City of Glass,* the leading actress, Shu Qi, comes from Taiwan and speaks Cantonese with a typical Mandarin accent. In *Tempting Heart,* the leading actor, Takeshi Kaneshiro, is of Japanese-Taiwanese extraction and speaks "impure" Cantonese in the film. In *Ordinary Heroes*, one of the leading actors, Li Kang-sheng, comes from Taiwan, and in the film his Cantonese dialogue is being dubbed. Although these actors are not local in origin, they are acting as if they are native to Hong Kong in these films. Of course it is not unprecedented for foreign actors/actresses to play an important role in Hong Kong films.[2] The important point is that Shu Qi, Takeshi Kaneshiro, and Li Kang-sheng are acting as "authentic" Hong Kong characters in films that place heavy emphasis on cinematic verisimilitude in the representation of Hong Kong history.

Before moving onto the implication of the Hong Kong imaginary on the representation of Chineseness in this global era, a brief analysis of the implications of the castings of the three films is in order. First, in *City of Glass*, the death of Leon Lai and Shu Qi in a car accident in London in 1997, a highly symbolic venue and time, implies that the love story is actually also allegorical. Through Daniel Wu and Nicola Cheung's exploration of the old story of their parents (Leon Lai is Wu's father, and Shu Qi Cheung's mother), the film uncovers memories of romance as well as the story of Hong Kong from the late 1960s to 1997. The Alex Law and Mabel Cheung combo tries to represent Hong Kong history in a love story that is also, in a sense, a metaphor for Hong Kong's reunification with China. As the director, Mabel Cheung, asserts, "I suddenly realize that lots of beautiful things we took for granted to be everlasting will in fact vanish in a short while. We are living in a glamorous city of glass, and the brilliant glory and hallucination will evaporate all at once."[3] The scriptwriter, Alex Law, claims in a similar vein that he wants to "write a story on the city as an image in the glass, about its harbour, buildings, flags, scenery, people, belief and sorrow, having them frozen once and for all."[4] Taking into consideration the director's and scriptwriter's ambition of representing Hong Kong history, one must find the casting of *City of Glass* rather striking. The leading actor and actress in the film, Leon Lai and Shu Qi, are not native to Hong Kong. In spite of his origin in Beijing, Leon Lai has generally been accepted by the people of Hong Kong as one of them. But in a similar film that uses Hong Kong history as the period setting of a love story, Peter Chan's *Tian Mimi* (Comrades, Almost a Love Story, 1996), Lai plays the role of an immigrant newly arrived from the mainland. He is not an authentic native, so to speak. By contrast, in *City of Glass* he plays a local student of the University of the Hong Kong in the 1960s. The case of Shu Qi causes offers even more problems. As an elite university student in the 1960s, Shu Qi speaks Cantonese with a typical Mandarin accent throughout the film (set from the 1960s until the 1990s). Her accent almost incessantly reminds the audience of her Taiwan origin. (Supporting actor Daniel Wu also speaks with a strange accent, but because the character he plays has grown up in England, it is reasonable for him to speak this way.) In a film that tries hard to represent Hong Kong history in an authentic way, such a casting choice cannot but be acutely foregrounded.

Compared to *City of Glass, Ordinary Heroes* puts even more emphasis on the representation of Hong Kong history. Along with the dramatic representation of Hong Kong political activism in the 1970s and 1980s via true events surrounding an Italian priest (Anthony Wong), there is also the fictional story of a girl (Rachel Lee, also known as Loretta Lee) who is suffering from amnesia after an accident. Through flashbacks of real and fictional characters not only the girl's story, but also the historical incidents of Hong Kong political activism are being reconstructed in the film. As the director Ann Hui claims, "Many of the events of the film are therefore based on real historical events in the eighties and most of the main characters are based on real people or composites of real people."[5] Hui also mentions on another occasion that the shooting of the film is "between stylish and documentary" in nature.[6] In fact, there are actors playing themselves in the film (such as Mok Chiu Yu); however, the casting of two of the leading actors, Li Kang-sheng and Anthony Wong, seems to somewhat deviate from the director's emphasis on cinematic verisimilitude. Although it is debatable whether Anthony Wong, a Chinese-British actor, can be seen as an expedient choice to play the role of the Italian father (Father Kam) who speaks fluent Cantonese, there is little doubt that Li Kang-sheng seems something like a square peg in a round hole. In this "semidocumentary" film, Li is the only character whose dialogue had to be dubbed, but in the film he plays a Hong Kong native, no different from other characters played by Rachel Lee and Tse Kwan Ho. (Recently there were other similar cases, such as the dubbing of dialogue of Ren Xianqi in Jingle Ma's *Xing Yuan* [Flying to Polaris, 1999].)

The case of *Tempting Heart* is different but related. In the film, a romance story between Takeshi Kaneshiro and Gigi Leung, Sylvia Chang's emphasis on the epic representation of Hong Kong's past is not as heavy as Mabel Cheung's or Ann Hui's. In order to highlight the different stages of the relationship between the two protagonists, she chooses to handle the film in a way that gives the audience a sense of "real" Hong Kong history. According to Chang, "There are three main characters in the film [Takeshi Kaneshiro, Gigi Leung, and Karen Mok], but I think the fourth character is the atmosphere, which was created by our art director, Man Lim-chung, and cinematographer, Lee Ping-bing. They did a wonderful job in forming the 'reality' of the different times and places in which the film is set."[7] It is apparent that Sylvia Chang thinks the "reality" of different settings do matter in the film. If we consider the plot of the film alone, it seems reasonable to choose Takeshi Kaneshiro to be the leading actor, since his Japanese extraction matches well with the character in the film (who later moves to Japan). In light of the director's desire for verisimilitude, however, the strange Cantonese accent of Kaneshiro, who plays a native of Hong Kong in the film, must strike the audience as strange. (His Japanese and Mandarin are presumably far more fluent than his Cantonese.) Along this line of thought, the problem of hybridized local identity in *City of Glass* and *Ordinary Heroes* also appears in *Tempting Heart*, giving rise to an "inauthentic" local imaginary.[8] An anecdote can be added here. In the Nineteenth Hong Kong Film Awards (2000), Gigi Leung, Cecilia Cheung (the leading actress of *Tempting Heart* and *Flying to Polaris* respectively) and Rachel Lee were all nominated for the best leading actress. By contrast, only Anthony Wong was nominated for the best leading actor. In addition, Ann Hui and Sylvia Chang were both nominated for the best director, *Tempting Heart* and *Ordinary Heroes* for the best film. Evidently the two films have been well received by film critics, but Takeshi Kaneshiro, Li Kang-sheng, and Ren Xianqi are not on the list. This seems to speak volumes about their awkward positions in these "local" productions.

When Hong Kong film stars go to Hollywood, they almost always have to play the role of the Other, such as new immigrants or Chinese police officers handling a case in the United States, so that the problem of their English accents can be downplayed. In *Anna and the King* (1999), Chow Yun Fat, albeit highly praised for his much-improved English, plays a Siamese King, and thus there is not any problem with his impure English accent. This situation does not phase out even after Jackie Chan and Chow Yun Fat successfully found the road map to Hollywood. In *Shanghai Knights* (2003) and *Bulletproof Monk* (2003), they still play the role of foreigners. In sharp contrast to these examples are the characters mentioned earlier who speak "impure" Cantonese accent—or cannot even speak Cantonese, so the dialogue has to be dubbed—in films that put different emphasis on the representation of the history of Hong Kong. Interestingly enough, they do not have to mask their impure accent with a "foreign" identity. They *are* authentic indigenous Hong Kong people in the films. Readily observable from these examples is a "local" imaginary that is actually "impure" or "hybridized."

Postmodern Cultural Logic and Postcolonial Identity Politics

The foregoing discussion gives the impression that the issue at stake is the "impure" and "inauthentic" local Hong Kong identity as represented by not-quite-local actors such as Shu Qi, Takeshi Kaneshiro, and Li Kang-sheng. It seems to conveniently lead to the conclusion that a "pure" local Hong Kong identity should be advocated, or at best a more theoretical conclusion as such: the "local" has actually been globalized. Although I support the latter argument in part, I would like to take the issue one step further in this chapter. If we try looking at the issue from a different perspective, we might arrive at a different conclusion leading to a new idea of Chineseness and local identity in the age of global capitalism. As I have mentioned earlier, a China syndrome has profoundly influenced Hong Kong cinema from the late 1970s until the early 1990s. Almost all reflections on local Hong Kong identity have to deal with the question of Chineseness. "Reverence and fear,"[9] among others, have been the key sentiments of the people of Hong Kong toward mainland Chinese. In Hong Kong films, these sentiments were often dismissed by the use of stereotyped mainland Chinese figures such as "Ah Chan" (new Chinese immigrants), "Big Circle Gangs" (gangsters from the mainland), and the later "Biaojie" (women officials from the mainland). These stereotyped figures function as a kind of "mimicry"[10] or demonization of mainland Chinese, letting Hong Kong people laugh away the "fear" of Communist sovereignty over Hong Kong after 1997. The situation then underwent a significant transformation in the early 1990s. To borrow the terms of Stephen Teo, "Hong Kong-as-home" and the later "new optimism" ("the easiest way Hong Kong can identify itself with China is through a booming economy") came onto the scene.[11] The "new optimism," as Teo convincingly notes, has led Hong Kong films into a "postmodern" stage. (The "postmodern" here is apparently used to depict the cultural logic that holds consumerism in esteem. It does not have anything to do with other possible "space-clearing gestures" that the term might imply.) To take Teo's analysis of the transformation of Hong Kong cinema from the 1980s to the 1990s one step further, we can argue that post-1997 Hong Kong cinema has evolved into a stage that mixes postmodern cultural logic with postcolonial identity politics. The reconstruction of local Hong Kong identity must be interwoven with postmodern consumerism in the context of global capitalism.

To put the following discussion of (in)authentic local identity in context, it is necessary to sidetrack and briefly trace the development of local consciousness in Hong Kong films. According to Matthew Turner, "civil identity," "society," and other similar concepts were first widely disseminated in Hong Kong after the 1967 riot.[12] In the aftermath of the riot, the Hong Kong government designed a series of programs, such as the Hong Kong Festival, to develop a kind of local consciousness in order to curb the anticolonial/national sentiment of post-1967 Hong Kong society. Before then, the people of Hong Kong had never been conscious of their own identity. This lack of local consciousness can partly be attributable to the fact that Hong Kong was traditionally seen as a transient shelter but not a true home. The radical transformation of the sociopolitical background and the swift development of the mass media in the 1970s provided a historical juncture at which "Hong Kong" consciousness came into being at long last. It was in the early 1970s that local consciousness developed swiftly in Hong Kong culture. In the 1970s, as suggested by Li Cheuk-to, Hong Kong films tried to "articulate reality by rehabilitating the indigenous dialect and culture."[13] In the 1980s, the China factor became the frame of reference for Hong Kong imaginary after the Sino-British Joint Declaration, and this extended well into the 1990s. In light of this sweeping summary, it is possible to conclude that the "Hong Kong" consciousness sprang not so much intrinsically from the people of Hong Kong, as extrinsically from political and economic factors. Most significant is not the lack of identity, but rather the appearance of a kind of "fictive identity."[14] This "fictive identity" was first driven by post-1967 political considerations (using a so-called Hong Kong identity to displace national sentiments), and thus the prerequisite of its appearance was paradoxically its disappearance (the "Hong Kong" identity created is *not* Hong Kong in the sense that it was actually contrived by political concerns). In other words, it is defined more by the conformity to some political and economic factors than by the shared positive characteristics of the people of Hong Kong. Such a collective identity is in a sense importantly negative. In the past twenty years or so, Hong Kong people have been innocently searching for local identity within the limited space afforded by political and economic conditions. An entire massive chapter of "Hong Kong" identity across three decades has grown out of this limited space.

When the discourse on globalization flourished swiftly in the 1990s, the global/local dialectic and its relation to critical issues such as Orientalism came onto the scene. The "fictive" or "negative" identity of Hong Kong was then reshaped in this new context. As I have pointed out elsewhere, works such as *Wo Shi Shui* (Who Am I? 1998), *Gu Huo Zai V* (Young and Dangerous V, 1998), and *Xingyun Yitiaolong* (The Lucky Guy, 1998) are related in one way or another to the issue of postcolonial Hong Kong local identity, presenting a mixture of postmodern consumerism and postcolonial identity politics in the context of global capitalism.[15] In these films, in short, the negotiation of postcolonial Hong Kong identity tends to point toward a pure local identity that has been lost in the past. It gives the impression that Hong Kong people have to reclaim their long lost pure local identity after 1997. Such an imaginary fails to admit that Hong Kong identity has been transformed since the rise of global capitalism. From the 1980s onward, postmodern consumerism has merged with postcolonial identity politics in Hong Kong, giving rise to a more complicated "local" imaginary. As previously mentioned, this "local" imaginary is in a sense tainted by global capitalism. If we merely try to see the "impure" local characters in the light of consumerism, the casting of Li Kang-sheng, Shu Qi, and Takeshi Kaneshiro in local productions is definitely, at least in part, targeted on the foreign markets of Taiwan and Japan, respectively. Along this line of argument, the "impure" representation of Hong Kong identity can be expounded in terms of market considerations —Teo's notion of "postmodern" that mainly suggests commercialism. Needless to say, the film industry must be commercial by nature. But it would be a gross simplification if we considered postmodern consumerism to be the only reason for the "hybridized" local identity seen in the films mentioned above.

In the age of global capitalism, the "local" has been successfully (re-)appropriated by transnational capital to become part of the globalizing process. In giant shopping malls, for instance, one can often find shops selling various "local" commodities. Take the example of the food courts present in almost all shopping malls. Chinese, American, Continental, Vietnamese, Thai, French, Italian, and many other cuisines are being sold in one food court. Most of these "authentic" local food shops (such as Shanghai's Delight or Delifrance) are actually being run by transnational corporations. Meanwhile, in mainland China there are more and more theme parks (such as ethnic minority villages) selling indigenous culture. As Liu Kang notes, they are "transforming local spaces into global sites for tourism."[16] The "multilocal" outlook is actually operating in the manner of global capitalism. To put it in another way, it is "globalism's localisms."[17] I have diverted from my previous discussion of Hong Kong cinema to bring up an important question. If consumer culture takes great pains to "simulate" a sense of locality, what prevents the aforementioned "Hong Kong" films from manipulating similar strategies? It has been argued that when Hong Kong actors go to Hollywood, they have to play the role of mainland Chinese (such as Chow Yun Fat in *The Replacement Killers* (1997), Michelle Yeoh in *Tomorrow Never Dies* (1997), and Samo Hung in the television series *Martial Law*) or even "Siamese" (Chow Yun Fat in *Anna and the King*). The problems of their imperfect English can easily be discounted in these cases. One is then compelled to ask the following questions: In similar situations, why do characters like those played by Li Kang-sheng, Shu Qi, and Takeshi Kaneshiro not have to assume such a "foreign" identity? Why are they allowed to play Hong Kong natives in films that place so much emphasis on authentic representation of Hong Kong history?

To answer these questions, it is necessary to further examine the case of Li Kang-sheng. Although Li is different from Shu Qi or Takeshi Kaneshiro in the sense that his dialogue is completely dubbed, his representation of Hong Kong locality is not without problems. As mentioned above, Li is the only character whose dialogue has to be dubbed. In a film that is designed to be a semidocumentary of the social protests in Hong Kong, such a "foreign" character inevitably begs questions about authenticity. There must be strong reasons to make the director sacrifice her desire for cinematic verisimilitude. The first and foremost reason for the director's choice can be related to the dawning of a new transnational Chinese film culture. In the 1990s, filmmaking in Hong Kong and some other Asian countries has evolved into a transregional/transnational industry. Within Greater China, for example, there are more and more collaborations (Chen Kaige's *Farewell My Concubine* is a good example in the early 1990s) that lead to a new dynamics of transregional/transnational film culture unfolding in Greater China.[18] Cross-fertilization among these regions and countries can be seen as a way to facilitate the development of Asian film industries. Because of the new developments in transregional/transnational film culture, the representation of local Hong Kong history in *Ordinary Heroes* involves the operational logic of transregional/transnational Chinese cinemas. The casting of Li Kang-sheng can thus be understood in industrial terms in the global era. In other words, his position in the film represents a kind of cross-fertilization between Hong Kong and Taiwan cinemas. Besides bringing mutual benefits such as the development of new markets, this kind of collaboration also embodies the global/local dialectic. If the casting of Takeshi Kaneshiro and Shu Qi was influenced by commercial market concerns, that of Li Kang-sheng underlines the influence of the transregional/transnational Chinese film industry.[19] Both show signs of global in the local.

Had industrial elements been the only factors behind the casting of Li Kang-sheng, the issue would be less complicated—but it was not. The director's view of local Hong Kong offers another significant way to interpret the casting of Li Kang-sheng. When asked about the casting of the film, Ann Hui explained why she chose Li Kang-sheng: she wanted someone who looks like a "foreigner."[20] The character of Li Siu Tung (played by Li Kang-sheng) is actually based on a real person who is native to Hong Kong. According to Hui, he has special traits that are not quite common in people native to Hong Kong: he was educated on the mainland and later joined in Hong Kong prodemocracy activities. Although Hui does not go into the details of why she wanted someone who looks foreign, her explanation is in a sense cryptic. As reflected from the real person on whom Li Kang-sheng's character is based, Hui wants to have someone who is almost but not quite local. Why is this so? Perhaps it is his education on the mainland and his ideal of democracy that make him appear "foreign." In other words, Hui already had in mind an idea of "local Hong Kong" identity in the 1990s. Although Hui is willing to take an active part in the new transregional/transnational Chinese film industry, she seems not to be content with the new social atmosphere of Hong Kong in the 1990s. It is apparent in the film that Hui's impression of Hong Kong in the 1990s is characterized by commercialism and indifference to social injustice. The message is that the commercialism in Hong Kong has gradually transformed the aura of social movements in the 1970s and spawned a myth of global capitalism in the 1990s, which can also be read in *City of Glass*. The director seems not to have a taste for this new typical "Hong Kong," and those "not-quite–Hong Kong" characters in the film are exactly those considered to be "ordinary" heroes. All in all, no matter that the casting of Li Kangsheng is orientated toward overseas markets, film awards (such as the Golden Horse best director award, which Hui later won), or the sense of being not quite local, we can detect a strange hybridized local Hong Kong imaginary in this character. All things considered, it can be concluded that this character represents a mixture of the global concern about transregional/transnational film industry and a local concern about "Hong Kong" (or the subsequent "not-quite–Hong Kong") identity.

Local Identity and Hybridized Imaginary

In the above examples, Hong Kong local identity has been importantly hybridized. But does it mean that the notion of "hybridity" can be used as the focus of discussions on Hong Kong identity? In postcolonial discourse, the notion of cultural hybridity is generally considered to be able to subvert the narratives of dominant cultures and point toward new cosmopolitanism.[21] Because hybrid cosmopolitanism "ignores the necessity of the nation-state precisely because they regard cultural agency as unmoored from, or relatively independent of, the field of material forces that engenders culture,"[22] it seems to be highly applicable to Hong Kong culture; however, as Pheng Cheah points out, "although the meaning and symbols of neocolonial culture are unmotivated, their materialization via economic and political institutional structures in an unequal global order means that they cannot be translated, reinscribed, and read anew in the ways suggested by theories of hybridity."[23] Therefore, "nation" still plays an important part in cultural formations in the global economy, and "[t]he postcolonial nation must be seen as a specter of global capital (double genitive—both objective and subjective genitive)."[24] This notion of "spectral nationality" allows us to examine local Hong Kong imaginary in a different light. Similar to other postcolonial national imaginaries, the Hong Kong imaginary has been enthralled by a kind of "spectral nationality"—the China factor in this case. As reflected in the local imaginary in Hong Kong films of the 1980s, the China factor remains as a specter despite Hong Kong's effort to develop its own local character. Even in the post-1997 Hong Kong film industry, the most widely discussed topic is the role of these émigrés to Hollywood. One wonders whether Hong Kong film stars actually export "Chineseness" as a commodity to the West on the one hand and facilitate the globalization of Hollywood films to Asia on the other. Unlike other national imaginaries in the postcolonial stage, Hong Kong has to deemphasize the national dimension so as to retain its autonomy (even though it is merely fictive). To develop an autonomous imaginary free from the domination of the China factor, the Hong Kong imaginary tends to place heavy emphasis on a particular past—a time and space in which Hong Kong seemed to be outside the influence of 1997 and global capitalism. Paradoxically, Hong Kong has to claim its own local imaginary by referring to theories of "hybridity" —a culture of translation instead of tradition—while remaining to search for an authentic and pure local identity. I would term this complex imaginary a "hybridized" nostalgia for a pure local past. This is to say, the Hong Kong cultural imaginary tries to invoke "hybridized" cosmopolitanism, as well as reinscribe a local narrative that subverts *this* cosmopolitanism at once. The important consideration is that the "local" here has already been transformed into a more complex cultural space.[25]

Edward Said writes, "Memory and its representations touch very significantly upon questions of identity, of nationalism, of power and authority."[26] The use of the past as a basis for constructing locality spontaneously gives rise to a sense of nostalgia that is directly related to the issue of identity formation. As I have mentioned elsewhere, *City of Glass* exhibits a kind of nostalgia for the lost good old days of the 1960s.[27] In short, everything seems to be better in those days. The affair between Leon Lai and Shu Qi can be interpreted as a symbolic supplement to the past that has been lost once and forever. Such nostalgia for a romantic ideal past is actually not uncommon in Hong Kong films. For instance, the works of the United Filmmakers Organization, such as Peter Chan and Lee Chi Ngai's *Xin Nanxiong Nandi* (He Ain't Heavy, He's My Father, 1993), frequently use the past as a source of inspiration. When compared to these films, the nostalgic dimension in *City of Glass, Ordinary Heroes,* and *Tempting Heart* that mix global concern with local imaginary is even more intricate. In what follows, I focus on *Ordinary Heroes* in order to describe the special form of nostalgia that overdetermines identity formation in the local imaginary.

First of all, we can easily read a nostalgic dimension in the titles of the three episodes in the film: "To Forget," "Ten Years of Revolution," and "Not to Forget." The subtext embedded in the structure of the three episodes reminds the audience that the ideal can only be realized by "Not to Forget" (which is nostalgic in nature) the good old days, the "red-hot" period of the 1970s. In fact, *Ordinary Heroes* is a film about memory and the loss of memory. The film focuses on the recollection of the past through the character of Rachel Lee, who loses her memory after an accident. In addition, the red-hot period of social movements in Hong Kong in the 1970s is reconstructed in the film through the experience of several activists. The backdrop of this red-hot period serves to accentuate the days of being "ordinary" but uncorrupted. It can be deduced from the title of the film that the director wants to define heroes by the "ordinary" characteristics that are rooted in the commonality of everyday life. In the film, the character played by

Tse Kwan Ho later turns sour when he begins to actively involve himself in politics. When "ordinary" things go out of the course, it is no longer heroic. According to Hui, "[M]any of them [the activists in the film] impressed me deeply because, just as they were nowhere near the political mainstream, they were also a minority in the money-grabbing and materialist society of Hong Kong."[28] Because Hui seems not to be content with the new developments in Hong Kong in the 1990s, she tries to romanticize the past by demonizing the present. A Hong Kong film critic has rightly noted, "Tse Kwan-ho's dismay after the June 4th incident and his rape of Rachel Lee were very awkward. Such developments are not plausible and it is here that the film's overly simplistic polarization of good and bad is obvious."[29] This overly simplistic polarization can be attributed to the director's attempt to contrast "the ordinary" with "the no-longer-ordinary." Such a polarization gives one the feeling that one should aspire to a pure local past when things were uncorrupted (in a sense not yet hybridized).

The polarization of the good and the bad is not completely sustained. Through the representation of the past of Hong Kong, the film implies a wish to begin from the origin. Unfortunately, this wish is contaminated by the fear of experiencing everything once again. (For instance, when Lee remembers the past at the end of the film, both she and Li Kang sheng suffer a great deal.) Since "the desire to begin from the origin—from 'the first' as it were"—is "a wish to repeat, to revisit something familiar, something that has already been lived through before," it is "haunted by the inherent duplicity of its own articulation."[30] The wish to begin from the origin comes with the fear of experiencing once more the corruption of the ideal past in the 1990s. To put it another way, the reconstruction of the local red-hot ideal past is hopelessly intertwined with the global indifferent corrupted present in the film. When "tens of thousands of words and utterances" (the Chinese title of the film) cannot sum up the feelings toward the rapid transformation of Hong Kong society, amnesia seems a better way out. Perhaps this is the reason why amnesia becomes a major theme in *The Longest Summer* as well.

As mentioned already, *Ordinary Heroes* was produced amid the new dynamics of transregional/transnational Chinese film culture. The memory of the "ordinary" local past constructed in the global context of *Ordinary Heroes* should also articulate a global inherent in the duplicity of the local. Moreover, as Long Tin, a Hong Kong film critic, points out, Hui "tells us that to capture the mood of an era, she can totally ignore its political sensibilities." But, unfortunately, "[p]olitics never leave us alone."[31] The "ordinary" local ideal past must be rooted in the "no-longer-ordinary" power structure of the present. It is in this sense that I think the dichotomy of the global as economic and the local as cultural collapses in the nostalgia that cannot but be hybridized in the film. Neither "local" nor "hybridized" alone can adequately account for the emergent characteristics of Hong Kong cinema in the global economy. The films analyzed above suggest a hybridized imaginary that spans across Greater China and refuses to see the future of the local without that of the global. This may also hint at a flexible imaginary of identity in the age of transnationalism.

Concluding Remarks

To summarize the previous discussion, I would like to propose that the "local" Hong Kong portrayed in Hong Kong cinema has to be problematized before any formation of identity can be negotiated in the age of transnationalism. Besides the seemingly pure local identity of Hong Kong as seen in works like Fruit Chan's trilogy and the transnational or global imaginary in Hollywood—Hong Kong stars such as Chow Yun Fat and Jackie Chan, the "glocal" dimension may also shed light on further discussions of the nature of Hong Kong identity.[32] When we wonder whether Chow Yun Fat, Jackie Chan, and John Woo are "exporting" Chineseness to Hollywood for the consumption of Western audience, we also have to remember that Hong Kong cinema is "importing" Chineseness from neighboring regions in Greater China. When we argue that Jackie Chan, Chow Yun Fat, and John Woo are not Hong Kong and have to be understood in the framework of the transnational imaginary of Chineseness, we should not forget that the "local" imaginaries of Hong Kong could also be impure. Fruit Chan's attempt to cross the mainland—Hong Kong border in *Durian Durian* and *Hollywood Hong Kong* can also be a proof of this. He claims in an interview that, ever since *Made in Hong Kong*, going away from Hong Kong has already been an implied theme in his works, but it does not become apparent until *Durian Durian* and *Hollywood Hong Kong*.[33] In *Renmin Gongce* (Public Toilet, 2002) the motif of going beyond Hong Kong is further developed. Although the setting goes global to the mainland, Indian, Korea, and the United States, the characters are also rather hybridized (the foreign student in Beijing speaks *putonghua,* and the young Indians in Hong Kong speak Cantonese). This shows that the director generally agreed to be a "local" representative of Hong Kong cinema that has already gone beyond local.

In the age of transnational Chinese film industry, an analysis of the global, the local, and the glocal tells us that it is important to transcend the issue of (in)authenticity to a discussion on the level of *not not* Hong Kong. The "local" should be problematized, so to speak. In much recent writing, the "local" and the diasporic are often conceived as the site that might resist the globalizing machine. But actually they are not unproblematic. Recognizing that the local is not an innocent power-free site without disciplinary and hegemonic exploitation,[34] we should also not take for granted that "what is diasporic, fluid, border-crossing, or hybrid is intrinsically subversive of power structures."[35] Even native people's claims about their own culture have to be problematized since, as Aihwa Ong puts it, "apprehension, ownership, and representation are practices embedded in strategies of positioning, control, and maneuver."[36] The concept of identity needs to be flexible. "As a *homo economicus* in the age of transnational capitalism, mobile investment, flexible accumulation, and global postmodernity," Sheldon Lu claims, "the Chinese in diaspora renegotiates a flexible set of spatial, geographic, economic, and cultural considerations in the identity formation process."[37] The flexibility of Hong Kong identity in postcolonial Hong Kong cinema can perhaps be seen as a precursory imaginary of future Chinese identity formation that transgresses the stable signified of authentic Chineseness.

It should now be apparent that this chapter has no intention of arguing for a pure local Hong Kong identity. Rather, it tries to offer an account of the global dimension in the contrived local identity portrayed in post-1997 transnational Chinese cinema, insinuating a self-critique of any stable notion of Hong Kong identity. The imagined local identity portrayed in the film analyzed above has proved that "postcolonial national identity-formation is in part a response to neocolonial economic globalization."[38] Furthermore, in the age of global capitalism, while Chineseness has been suggested to have to be plural,[39] Hong Kongness has since the beginning exemplified how identity formation cannot but be plural (both Chinese and diasporic, but at the same time neither Chinese nor diasporic). In this sense, one must refuse to believe that identity is a kind of determinate "being." It is a kind of "becoming," and Chineseness should be seen as an "open signifier."[40] In addition to the emphasis on the plurality of the term "Chinesenesses," it is also important to bear in mind that each component of Chinesenesses (such as Hong Kong, Taiwan, Singapore and so on) is also plural in nature. This is the sense of "(g)local" identity with emphasis on the flexibility of identity in the age of global capitalism that I want to stress. In sum, the search for local identity in Hong Kong cinema in the 1980s has been transformed in the 1990s into a self-revelation of a glocal hybrid in the age of transnational Chinese cinema. The authentic Hong Kong local imaginary paradoxically evinces its inauthentic locality. It still remains to be seen what it will become.

Notes

This chapter was first presented at Year 2000 and Beyond: History, Technology and Future of Transnational Chinese Moving Image Media, the Second International Conference on Chinese Cinema, hosted by the Department of Cinema-TV, Hong Kong Baptist University, April 19–21, 2000. The valuable comments of Sheldon Lu and Emile Yueh-yu

Yeh are gratefully acknowledged. Throughout the chapter, I refer to the original Cantonese version of the films discussed. The transliteration of directors and actors follows the names as they appear in the English subtitles of the films (including *pinyin,* Wade-Giles, and "Hong Kongese" forms of romanization).

1. See for instance Li Cheuk-to, *"Fuqin di yinying: bashiniandai Xianggang xindianying di Zhongguo mailuo"* (The father's shadow: the China factor in Hong Kong cinema in the 1980s), in Hong Kong Urban Council, ed., *The China Factor in Hong Kong Cinema* (Hong Kong: Hong Kong Urban Council, 1990), 77–85. For another comprehensive analysis of the China factor in the Hong Kong cinema in the 1990s, refer to Esther Yau, "Border Crossing: Mainland China's Presence in Hong Kong Cinema," in Nick Browne, Paul G. Pickowicz, Vivian Sobchack, and Esther Yau eds., *New Chinese Cinemas: Forms, Identities, Politics* (Cambridge: Cambridge University Press, 1994), 180–201.

2. "Border Crossings in Hong Kong Cinema" is the main theme of "Hong Kong Cinema Retrospective" of the Twenty-Fourth Hong Kong International Film Festival (April 2000). As stated in the introduction of the retrospective, "Hong Kong cinema had been border-crossing since the 1940s." See Hong Kong Provisional Urban Council ed., *The 24th Hong Kong International Film Festival Programme* (Hong Kong: Hong Kong Provisional Urban Council, 2000), 82. It is apparent, however, that none of the "border-crossing" works presented in the retrospective places emphasis on local Hong Kong history.

3. Cited from an interview with Mabel Cheung and Alex Law, *City Entertainment* 510 (October 1998), 38.

4. Ibid.

5. Hong Kong Provisional Urban Council ed., *The 23rd Hong Kong International Film Festival Main Catalogue* (Hong Kong: Hong Kong Provisional Urban Council, 1999), 15.

6. Kwong Po Wai ed., *Xu anhua suo xu anhua* (Ann Hui talking about Ann Hui) (Hong Kong: Kwong Po Wai, 1998), 95.

7. Cited from the page of "Director's Note" on the homepage of *Tempting Heart* [http://wanita.net/temptingheart].

8. By the way, the rise of "hybridized" moving image production is not limited to the hybridized stars in the film industry. In the television media, recently there have been lots of similar cases. A good recent example is Michael Wong (from the United States) and Nicky Wu (from Taiwan) in Hong Kong Television Broadcasting Company's soap opera *The Making of a New Century.* Meanwhile, there have also been lots of imported programs in the television media, such as *Huanzhu Gege* (Princess Huanzhu), since the late 1990s. Some of them are in fact transregional (Hong Kong, Taiwan, and the mainland) productions (such as *Fang Shiyu*). All of the above examples amount to a strange hybridized local imaginary in Hong Kong moving image media after 1997.

9. Stephen Teo, *Hong Kong Cinema: The Extra Dimensions* (London: British Film Institute: 1997), 207–218.

10. The "mimicry" here does not exhibit the double articulation and intervention power as desired by postcolonial discourse. For a detailed account of mimicry, refer to Homi Bhabha, *The Location of Culture* (London: Routledge, 1994). In short, Bhabha's notion of mimicry embodies a double vision: "in disclosing the ambivalence of colonial discourse also disrupts its authority" (88). There are Hong Kong films that utilize mimicry qua sly civility to subvert the hegemonic signifier of China. For instance, Stanley Kwan's

works can be categorized as using such mimicry as a kind of tactics of intervention. Refer to Lin Wenchi, *"Houxiandai di fengge, houjimin di Xianggang"* (Postmodern style, postcolonial Hong Kong), in Jian Yingying ed., *Yingtong, chayi, zhutixing: cong nuxingzhuyi dao houjimin wenhua xiangxiang* (Identity, difference and subjectivity: from feminism to postcolonial cultural imagination) (Taipei: Lixu, 1997), 175–216.

11. Teo, *Hong Kong Cinema*, 189, 245.

12. Matthew Turner, "Hong Kong Sixties/Nineties: Dissolving the People," in Matthew Turner and Irene Ngan, eds., *Hong Kong Sixties: Designing Identities* (Hong Kong: Hong Kong Art Center, 1994), 13–19.

13. Li Cheuk To, "Postscript," in Hong Kong Urban Council, ed., *A Study of Hong Kong Cinema in the Seventies* (Hong Kong: Hong Kong Urban Council, 1984), 127–131.

14. This term is derived from Etienne Balibar's notion of "fictive ethnicity," in Immanuel Wallerstein and Etienne Balibar, eds., *Race, Nation, Class: Ambiguous Identities* (London: Verso, 1991), 96.

15. Chu Yiu Wai, "Who Am I? Postcolonial Hong Kong Cinema in the Age of Global Capitalism," in Esther Cheung and Chu Yiu Wai, eds., *Between Home and World: A Reader in Hong Kong Cinema* (Hong Kong: Oxford University Press, 2004), 39–58.

16. Liu Kang, "Is There an Alternative to (Capitalist) Globalization? The Debate about Modernity in China," *boundary 2* 23 (fall 1996): 196.

17. This term is borrowed from Dana Polan, "Globalism's Localisms," in Wimal Dissanayake and Rob Wilson, eds., *Global/Local: Cultural Production and the Transnational Imaginary* (Durham, N.C.: Duke University Press, 1996), 255–283. What Polan means by "globalism's localisms" is that "each and every local case is readable, in Jamesonian terms, 'symbolic response' to the global" (259).

18. For a detailed discussion of the transnationalism in the cinemas of Hong Kong and Taiwan, refer to Sheldon Hsiao-peng Lu, "Historical Introduction: Chinese Cinema (1896–1996) and Transnational Film Studies," in Sheldon H. Lu, ed., *Transnational Chinese Cinemas: Identity, Nationhood, Gender* (Honolulu: University of Hawai'i Press, 1997), 12–19. See also Yeh Yueh-yu, "A Life of Its Own: Musical Discourses in Wong Kar-Wai's Films," *Post Script* 19.1 (fall 1999): 135.

19. I owe the idea for this interpretation to Emile Yueh-yu Yeh.

20. Cited from an interview with Ann Hui, *City Entertainment* 521 (April 1999): 29.

21. See, for instance, Bhabha, *The Location of Culture*.

22. Pheng Cheah, "Given Culture: Rethinking Cosmopolitical Freedom in Transnationalism," *boundary 2* 24 (summer 1997): 173.

23. Ibid.

24. Pheng Cheah, "Spectral Nationality: The Living On [*sur-vie*] of the Postcolonial Nation in Neocolonial Globalization," *boundary 2* 26 (fall 1999): 252.

25. As pointed out by John Tomlinson, the deterritorialization brought about by globalization "cannot mean the end of locality" since "the ties of culture to location can never be completely severed and the locality continues to exercise its claim upon us as the physical situation of our lifeworld." See Tomlinson, *Globalization and Culture* (Cambridge: Polity, 1999), 149. But the "locality" in such a context has transformed into a more complex cultural space. It is in this sense that I believe the Hong Kong imaginary cannot be merely oriented toward the global.

26. Edward Said, "Invention, Memory, and Place," *Critical Inquiry* 26 (winter 2000): 176.

27. Chu Yiu Wai, *"Quanqiuhua dushi di bentu shenhua: Bolijicheng di Xianggang tuxiang"* (A local myth in a global city: the "Hong Kong" in City of Glass), *Chung-wai Literary Monthly* 28 (April 2000): 40–53.

28. Cited from the *23rd Hong Kong International Film Festival Main Catalogue*, 15.

29. Po Sharp, "Reviewing *Ordinary Heroes*," cited from the web page of Hong Kong Film Critics Society [http://filmcritics.org.hk/ordinaryheroes/review.html].

30. Rey Chow, "Nostalgia of the New Wave: Structure in Wong Kar-wai's *Happy Together*," *Camera Obscura* 42 (September 1999): 36. In this article, Chow offers a suggestive reading of the nostalgia in Wong Kar-wai's *Happy Together* (1997), which may shed light on the postcolonial Hong Kong imaginary. Approaching the special kind of nostalgia inherent in the structure of *Happy Together*, Chow uses the poststructuralist "epistemological rupture," $1 = 1+$, to argue that "1 is always already a *reiteration*, which makes sense only in the supplementarity of 1+" (34). The "nostalgia" as expounded by the formula "$1 = 1+$" here can be twisted a bit to account for the special kind of nostalgia in *Ordinary Heroes*—"ordinary = ordinary +."

31. Long Tin, "Reviewing *Ordinary Heroes*," cited from the web page of Hong Kong Film Critics Society [http://filmcritics.org.hk/ordinaryheroes/review.html].

32. "Glocal," translation of the Japanese word *dochakuka*, meaning the tailoring of global goods and services to local markets, is made popular by Roland Robertson when he uses it to describe the intimate and complex relationship between the global and the local. See Roland Robertson, "Glocalization: Time-Space and Homogeneity-Heterogeneity," in Mike Featherstone, Scott Lash, and Roland Robertson eds., *Global Modernities* (London: Sage, 1995), 25–44.

33. Thomas Shin and Keeto Lam, "Fruit Chan: Life and Death in Global Cesspool" [an interview with Fruit Chan], *Hong Kong Panorama, 2002–2003* (Hong Kong: Hong Kong International Film Festival, 2003), 90.

34. Arif Dirlik, *The Postcolonial Aura: Third World Criticism in the Age of Global Capitalism* (Boulder, Colo.: Westview, 1997).

35. Aihwa Ong and Donald M. Nonini, "Toward a Cultural Politics of Diaspora and Transnationalism," in Aihwa Ong and Donald M. Nonini, eds., *Ungrounded Empires: The Cultural Politics of Modern Chinese Transnationalism* (New York: Routledge, 1997), 326.

36. Aihwa Ong, *Flexible Citizenship: The Cultural Logics of Transnationality* (Durham, N.C.: Duke University Press, 1999), 243.

37. Sheldon H. Lu, "Filming Diaspora and Identity: Hong Kong and 1997," in Poshek Fu and David Deeser, eds., *The Cinema of Hong Kong: History, Arts, Identity* (New York: Cambridge University Press, 2000), 285.

38. Cheah, "Given Culture," 181.

39. Chow, "Introduction: On Chineseness as Theoretical Problem," *boundary 2* 25 (fall 1998): 1–24.

40. Stuart Hall, "Cultural Identity and Cinematic Representation," *Framework* 36 (1989): 68–81; Ien Ang, "To Be or Not To Be Chinese: Diaspora, Culture, and Postmodern Ethnicity," *Southeast Asian Journal of Social Science* 21 (1993): 1–19, "On Not Speaking Chinese," *New Formations* 24 (winter 1994): 1–18, and "Can One Say No to Chineseness? Pushing the Limits of the Diasporic Paradigm," *boundary 2* 25 (fall 1998): 223–242.

Global Modernity, Postmodern Singapore, and the Cinema of Eric Khoo

A fundamental tension at the heart of Singapore as a place spills over into any understanding of film culture there. Singapore balances the process of nation building it has undertaken since becoming an autonomous state in 1965 with the important transnational role the port plays in global flows of capital, commodities, and labor. Chua Beng-Huat succinctly summarizes Singapore's situation as follows: "If cultural hybridization and syncretism is a mark of postcoloniality, then the cultural sphere in Singapore may be said to be 'postcolonial.' Yet, with slightly more than three decades of political independence, its political sphere is still firmly placed in the modernist trajectory of nation formation; whereas postcoloniality requires for its politics the deconstruction of the nation-state as a move to escape from Eurocentrism of the colonial masters."[1]

Thus, Singapore must be staunchly anti-imperialist and chauvinistically "pan-Asian" in some circles and still open to Westernized consumer culture within the global marketplace in which it has been, until the regional crash in 1997, enormously successful. The government officially calls for adherence to "Asian values," principally based on a Chinese understanding of Confucian morals that reinvents bourgeois ideology in a postcolonial context.[2] The city-state officially decries the decadence, materialism, individualism, and moral bankruptcy of Western consumer culture, a conception primarily drawn from an American model based on Hollywood movies, Disneyland, and McDonald's fast food restaurants; however, competition is encouraged, material success lauded, and participation in the international marketplace celebrated.

Singapore and its cinema must negotiate the complexities of the global/local divide. The Singapore film industry, for example, builds itself up on the foundation of what had been a thriving colonial business[3] to situate itself in the global arena of the international art film and Chinese transnational cinema culture,[4] while still appealing to a domestic market hungry for local images of the country's unique cultural mélange. As a global cinema with a local flavor, it competes with Hollywood and Hong Kong for the domination of Singapore's screens.

Eric Khoo has been credited with single-handedly reviving Singapore's long-dormant film industry in the mid-1990s with two internationally recognized features, *Mee Pok Man* (1995) and *Twelve Storeys* (*Shi Er Lou*, 1997).[5] Khoo shot films as a child and went on to study film production in Australia. An award-winning short filmmaker, Khoo has also worked in music videos, television commercials, and series television in Singapore. With keen observational skills and a very dark sense of humor, Khoo paints a portrait of the city-state of Singapore as a global society wrestling with the postmodern condition.[6] To this end, Khoo juxtaposes the public, global "face" of Singapore as an ultramodern, hygienic, orderly, rational, Confucian nation-state with the underbelly of Singapore's colonial past, transnational sex trade, urban blight, racism, political oppression, and economic inequities. This chapter looks at Khoo's two critically acclaimed features, *Mee Pok Man* and *Twelve Storeys,* in relation to the malleability and uncertainty of Singapore's identity within global postmodernity.

Exposing Contradictions

Khoo has a succinct way of exposing and concretizing the contradictions at the root of contemporary Singaporean society. Toward the end of *Twelve Storeys,* for example, Khoo introduces the character of Eddy (Ronald Toh Chee Kong), who comes to pick up his teenage, GenerAsian X girlfriend Trixie (Lum May Yee).[7] Before he may go off on his date, Eddy must first win the approval of Trixie's older brother Meng (Koh Bon Pin). Eddy and Meng, of course, are polar opposites, each symbolizing extremes within Singaporean society. The bespectacled Meng is the poster boy for Singapore—that is, a schoolteacher, proud of his academic accomplishments and compulsory military service. He wears the casual, but sober short shirtsleeves characteristic of the ruling People's Action Party (PAP) or T-shirts with government slogans.[8] He does calisthenics in accordance with government directives, can spout statistics on health, education, and social welfare in Singapore, believes in the campaign to increase "graciousness" in the society, and takes his role as elder brother seriously as well as his filial obligation to keep his younger siblings in order while their parents are away. Eddy, on the other hand, has difficulty remembering how he scored on his school exams. He deals in industrial parts and prides himself on his ability to get his international clientele what they want—namely, attractive women. He speaks Singlish, as opposed to Meng's more proper English.[9] Eddy drives a flashy car; Meng has no car. Unlike Meng, Eddy wears gaudy, tasteless, plaid trousers and buckskin loafers. Meng looks on uncomfortably as the uncouth Eddy uses a manicured pinky nail to dig wax out of his ear canal.[10]

Meng epitomizes what Singapore struggles to represent to the world—filial piety, Confucian virtue, cleanliness, orderliness, good manners, academic achievement, and sexual reserve. Eddy embodies the other side of Singapore—mercantilism, business savvy over academic acuity, the ability to play the middleman, sexual license, earthiness, and the flamboyant display of the "good life" through women, dress, leisure activities, and mode of transportation. Meng attempts to be modern Singapore, confident that an upgraded government flat, a good education, and the possibility of buying a car will make him and his family happy. Eddy represents Singapore's actual postmodern condition. His ability to thrive in an international market for spare parts puts him within the old order of Singapore's legacy as a colonial port, within an economy that does not produce but repackages and recirculates and that is very much at ease with the transnational flow of people and goods. Positioning him somewhere between a traditional Chinese and a postcolonial Singaporean identity, Eddy's Singlish enables him to do business in the transnational marketplace with Americans as easily as the Japanese or Koreans he recognizes as wanting the "same thing." His relaxed attitude toward sex permits him to take advantage of postfeminist women like Trixie, who are freed from commitment to traditional marriage and family and able to survive independently in newly available careers or within the ever-expanding service sector without challenging male domination in more fundamental ways. Moreover, Eddy can also luxuriate in the port's historical institution of prostitution. Meng berates Eddy for being a pimp; however, Eddy claims he is simply a good capitalist, just giving the customer "what he wants."

It is important to keep in mind that Eddy and Meng do not represent simple binary oppositions like past/future, modern/traditional, global/local, Chinese/Singaporean, national/transnational, or conservative/progressive. Each contains aspects of the other. Eddy's ability to make cash out of trash puts him at the forefront of the postindustrial economy as well as links him to Singapore's colonial past. Meng's ardent patriotism allows him to deplore British colonialism and celebrate the benefits of proper English diction and traditional British reserve and etiquette. The sex trade is as much a part of the old society as the contemporary global economy.

Meng and Eddy seem at odds, but, when taken together as two sides of a single Singaporean coin, they present a picture of how Singapore functions as the embodiment of the dream of modern rationality linked to capitalism, consumerism, the legacies of colonialism, nationalism, sexism, and class stratification. Within the narrative structure of *Twelve Storeys,* all these interests coalesce within the figure of Trixie, whom Eddy calls a "hot babe." Eddy and the repressed, incestuous Meng both desire Trixie. Just as Singapore needs women's labor in the official sectors of the offices and shops as well as the unofficial sector of the sex trade, Eddy needs Trixie on his arm as a symbol of the achievements of capitalism. Similarly, Meng needs Trixie to be a "good girl," a virgin before marriage, a filial contributor to the patriarchal household, and eventually "pear-shaped" after marriage and childbearing like "all Chinese women." The nubile Trixie, like Singapore itself, has difficulty being both the virgin and the whore within the national and transnational economies. Trixie's own desires seem far less grandiose than either Eddy's or Meng's. Trixie wants to quit school, enjoy going to the trendy nightclub Zouk's, work at the mainstream department store Metro, read international glamour magazines, have sex when she likes, and go to the movies with her boyfriend. She seems to have genuine affection for her square older brother and her trendy younger one. Speaking Singlish and wearing mini-skirts and go-go boots, she functions less as a marker of national identity, economic mobility, or patriarchal power and more as an emblem of a hybridized, transnational, GenerAsian X, youth culture, taking Singapore with her out of a patriarchal past and into a postmodern present. She literally embodies the contradictions of Singaporean capitalism that measure success in material terms while condemning Western consumerism. As Chua Beng-Huat notes, "[T]he body has become the locus of consumption, particularly for the young where the need to own a house is still far on the horizon of possessions. The visibility of consumption on the body only leads to further condemnation of 'excess' by the guardians of thrift. Against the background of an unceasing exhortation to save, such behaviour is political without necessarily having subjective intentions."[11] Trixie's body represents this contradiction through her youth, style, and interest in fashion. Her existence and destruction mark moments of crisis in the film and, perhaps, in the society. Trixie represents a youthful, female desire not beholden to traditional notions of national, class, ethnic, or gender identity, and this desire takes on an existence beyond her generation and gender as a symbol of a Singaporean identity somehow out of control and in crisis.

The triangular relationship, established by Eddy, Meng, and Trixie, repeats itself in several permutations in both *Mee Pok Man* and *Twelve Storeys,* exposing contradictions that stand unresolved even as the narratives reach their own conclusions. In *Mee Pok Man,* the unnamed, simple-minded *mee pok* (noodle seller) man (Joe Ng) wins possession of the prostitute Bunny (Michelle Goh) from her pimp Mike Kor (Kay Tong Lim) and her British boyfriend Jonathan Reese (David Brazil), even though the *mee pok* man ends up with only her decaying corpse for company. In *Twelve Storeys,* in addition to Meng and Eddy's tussle over Trixie, Ah Gu (Jack Neo) struggles for possession of his mainland Chinese bride, Lili (Chuan Yi Fong), with a string of off-screen suitors. San San (Lucilla Teoh) must endure her mother (Lok Yee Loy), who harangues her about her inability to attract a suitable mate and throws up her old charge Rachel (Neo Swee Lin) as the ideal woman who has found an overseas husband and gone to live in America. Like Lili and Trixie, San San does not fit in with traditional, patriarchal expectations, and the patriarchy in crisis is also blamed for the unnamed suicide's (Ritz Lim) demise, since a woman is assumed to have "driven him to it."[12] In each case, sexual and familial relations indicate a more general social malaise, and, in light of the Confucian link between the health of the family and the well-being of the kingdom, the fact that these dysfunctional interpersonal relationships point to larger problems within the nation and beyond seems logical.[13]

Postmodern Spaces

Visually, Khoo's postmodern critique of Singapore's modernist project of nation building can be seen clearly in the way in which he uses space, particularly Singapore's distinctive architectural spaces, in *Mee Pok Man* and *Twelve Storeys.* In *The Condition of Postmodernity,* David Harvey distinguishes between modernist and postmodernist architecture:

> In the field of architecture and urban design, I take postmodernism broadly to signify a break with the modernist idea that planning and development should focus on large-scale, metropolitan-wide, technologically rational and efficient urban *plans,* backed by absolutely no-frills architecture (the austere "functionalist" surfaces of "international style" modernism). Postmodernism cultivates, instead, a conception of the urban fabric as necessarily fragmented, a "palimpsest" of past forms superimposed upon each other, and a "collage" of current uses, many of which may be ephemeral. Since the metropolis is impossible to command except in bits and pieces, urban *design* (and note postmodernists design rather than plan) simply aims to be sensitive to vernacular traditions, local histories, particular wants, needs, and fancies, thus generating specialized, even highly customized architectural forms that may range from intimate, personalized spaces, through traditional monumentality, to the gaiety of spectacle.[14]

Khoo most commonly sets his narratives in the two urban spaces that most typ-
ify Singapore—the HDB (Housing and Development Board) block and the
hawkers' stalls of the open-air food courts that often line the bases of the HDB
apartments. The outdoor food stalls hark back to the colonial period and the
lines of shop houses that can still be found in some of the shrinking older quarters of Singapore. The shop houses consist of three basic parts: a downstairs
shop, upstairs living quarters, and an overhang that forms an arcade-like shelter
for those walking from shop to shop and protects customers from intense tropical sun and frequent rain. Crowded together, the shops and food stalls form a
marketplace and public forum for shopping, eating, chatting, and general so-
cializing. As Khoo depicts these spaces, they exist somewhere between the colonial marketplace and postmodern shopping malls.

The HDB apartment blocks are strictly within the modernist tradition of
urban planning. The buildings, which look like high-rise public housing found
in any metropolitan setting, give the Singaporean skyline its distinctively mo-
notonous and uniform quality. The majority of those living in these housing
projects, however, own their apartments, and most Singaporeans live in these
buildings and, thus, enjoy a common standard of housing determined by the
government. Indeed, simply by depicting housing in a particular way, Khoo implicitly critiques the Singapore government (dominated since independence in
1965 by the People's Action Party [PAP] headed by Senior Minister Lee Kuan
Yew). In "Considering the 'Singapore Film,'" Audrey Wong describes Khoo's
"HDB Filmscape" as follows:

> The minute, hidden tragedies of daily life in the orderly blocks of HDB flats are
> fleshed out in Khoo's feature films. Within the cramped flats where the majority of
> Singapore's population lives, stories of thwarted desire, love, hate, and conflict are
> played out. In *Mee Pok Man*, the climax, horror and sadness of the love story takes
> place within the dull confines of the *mee pok* man's small, plainly furnished flat as he
> props the decaying body of Bunny the prostitute at the dining table in the kitchen.
>
> The claustrophobic spaces of HDB flats also intensify the hate and heartache. In
> *Twelve Storeys*, San San is tormented by her mother's constant nagging—and brow-
> beaten into silent submission because she is unable to escape from her mother in such
> a small living space. The close proximity in which Trixie and Meng live throws into
> sharp relief Meng's hidden desire for his sister. He wakes her up in the mornings when
> he is given a good view of her in bed, and her underwear hangs openly up to dry in the
> kitchen. These things give those of us who are familiar with such living spaces a shock
> of recognition. We realize that there may be small dramas in our lives that may be-
> come volcanic as well.[15]

In *Twelve Storeys,* Khoo begins his depiction of these housing estates with a series of abstracted views of the buildings' exteriors. Florescent lights illuminate empty hallways. A long shot shows three illuminated apartments making a pattern that looks like a Piet Mondrian painting. The orange incandescent lights of the interior cells mark a sharp contrast to the cool bluish exterior illumination. The soulful string music that plays over this opening sequence underscores the sense of isolation of the individuals boxed in by the walls of their apartments. The camera maintains its distance, and a sense that these apartments are organized to invite surveillance comes to mind. The spaces unfold for the camera like the prisoners' cells on view in the panoptican Michel Foucault describes in *Discipline and Punish.*[16] A montage gives rapid glimpses of the people who inhabit these apartments. Khoo offers a glance at the range of ethnicities (Chinese, Malay, Indian), generations (infants to grandparents), and family arrangements (singles to extended families) that inhabit these spaces.

Most of the people introduced in this opening montage do not reappear in the film; however, this slice of life in the HDB block shows that the organization of the architectural space defines these people's lives in important ways. They live in close proximity, but they do not operate as a cohesive community. The concrete walls of the apartments separate people. The cramped spaces within the apartments further isolation and atomization. Most of the shots isolate individuals in the frame, show the lack of communication among family members involved in the electronically mediated spaces of the television or computer screen, or show the separation of ethnic/racial communities within housing that must meet various racial/ethnic quotas to ensure against the ghettoization of any given group and the possibility of race riots and/or political uprisings based on race or ethnicity.[17] Within the collective, modernist monolith of the public housing block, the montage emphasizes the postmodern condition of fragmentation, disassociation, and disaffection.

The architectural design of the HDB flats defines key aspects of the narrative in many other important ways. For example, to be more efficient, the elevators in HDB buildings do not stop on every floor. In the case of the housing estate in *Twelve Storeys,* the elevators stop at one, six, and eleven. Inhabitants of the twelfth floor are those just unlucky enough to miss the convenience of an elevator stop by one floor, so they have to trudge up one extra flight to their homes. Thus, the film's title points to those within the society who seem to just miss the Singaporean ideal. They are off a floor, and out of pace, and unable to conform to the rest of the society.[18]

The building also provides fuel for Beijing-born Lili's fiery temper as she verbally assaults HDB housing standards as an indirect attack upon the Singaporean husband she despises. In one of her heated tirades, she complains about the filthy conditions in the HDB block by noting the infestation of mosquitoes in the building as well as the necessity for urine detectors in the elevators that simply moved the miscreants to the building's corridors to relieve themselves. She admits that the public toilets in her hometown of Beijing are filthy, but claims never to have heard of elevators being used for urinals.

In *Mee Pok Man* and *Twelve Storeys,* the HDB flats serve as more than just in-dicators of a local setting; they become the concrete emblems of the nation and society. Just as government propaganda celebrates the virtues of privately owned, publicly funded, rationally designed, modern housing, Khoo's camera reveals the dirt behind the façade and the urine in the overly efficient elevators.

In *Mee Pok Man,* parallel editing links the spaces inhabited by the prostitute Bunny and the *mee pok* man together as shots show both showering and prepar-ing for bed simultaneously. The striking similarity of the design and decoration of the two apartments brings these two different people together in essentially the same space. The HDB flats visually cue them as coming from the same so-cial milieu, class background, and, by extension, sharing the same fate.

Like *Twelve Storeys, Mee Pok Man* begins with a montage that presents a range of people within a characteristically Singaporean space. The focus here, how-ever, is on the hawkers' open-air food court rather than the HDB apartments. As in *Twelve Storeys,* the preponderance of the people introduced in the opening montage play no role in the narrative that follows. Just as *Twelve Storeys* con-nects the ultramodern HDB estates with the base bodily functions, *Mee Pok Man* links the hawker stalls with food and sex. The rapid montage, set to a driv-ing hardcore punk beat,[19] intercuts shots of men and women eating noodles lustily, close-up fragments of nude women's breasts, buttocks, and pubic areas, noodles being cooked in a wok, mounds of food on display, hanging meat, close-ups of flies alighting on piles of refuse, and more noodles and ribs devoured by Asian and white clientele. The neon light of the streets and the harsh fluores-cents in the stalls give the scene a distinctly unappealing quality. Seedy hotels and a Shell station frame the hawkers' food court between the official economy of transnational capitalism (e.g., Singapore's position as one of the leading cen-ters for oil refining situated on the shipping lanes between the Persian Gulf and East Asia) and the other, unofficial, transnational economy of the sex trade. The proximity of the Shell station to the world of the food hawkers and prostitutes inexorably ties these Singaporean businesses together, tacitly commenting on the links between the official face and hidden realities of the nation.

The tables at the hawkers' stalls in both *Mee Pok Man* and *Twelve Storeys* pro-vide rare public spaces in which customers can indulge in their vices (e.g., pick up prostitutes, gamble on the lottery, drink liquor), and also speak their minds (e.g., talk about recent news items like the Flor Contemplacion execution and the Michael Fay caning). Part of the street culture and service economy like prostitution and an official part of the legitimate economy of business owners and entrepreneurs, hawkers, like the eponymous *mee pok* man and the tofu vendor Ah Gu in *Twelve Storeys,* eke out an existence that embodies the contradictions of Singapore's economy. The hawker courts are both marginal to the operation of the country and central to an understanding of its culture. Unlike the atomized HDB flats, the food courts open up spaces for a potential mixing of languages, foods, ethnicities, and classes; however, this space also allows for pimps, hooligans, and the detritus of society to operate in the open air.

In both films, Khoo works well with the global/local spaces that characterize Singapore. Although the urban flats, food courts, office buildings, public mass transit, and shopping districts decorated for Christmas can be found in most of the world's large, metropolitan cities,[20] Khoo maintains a very local understanding of the way in which these transnational spaces take on a peculiarly Singaporean form. Ironically, the global force of modernity allowed for the circulation of capital and people that makes the local so important for Singaporean industries like tourism. As Mike Featherstone points out in *Undoing Culture: Globalization, Postmodernism and Identity,* the local takes on a new significance in the global postmodern environment: "With postmodernism, there is a re-emergence of the vernacular, of representational forms, with the use of pastiche and playful collaging of styles and traditions. In short, there is a return to local cultures in the plural, the fact that they can be placed alongside each other without hierarchal distinction."[21]

Khoo visualizes the "messiness" of postmodern spaces set against the imposed order and belief in rationality epitomized by high modernist architecture. The irrational, chaotic, and uncontrollable lies at the foundation of the hygienic orderliness of the Orchard Road shopping district, the downtown financial center, the efficient MRT rapid transit, and the HDB flats. In Khoo's oeuvre, the pick-up bars, hawkers' stalls, and vomit-strewn toilets in the Singaporean cityscape get more than equal exposure.

The Politics of Language

One of the most strikingly hybridized characteristics of *Mee Pok Man* and *Twelve Storeys* is the use of language. Since splitting from Malaysia in 1965 to establish itself as an autonomous nation, Singapore's government has tried to create a national culture that would maintain multiculturalism as orthodoxy. In "Contending with Primordialism: The 'Modern' Construction of Postcolonial Singapore," C. J. W.-L. Wee points out that nationalism, multiculturalism, and modernity formed the strategy for Singapore's creation under Lee Kuan Yew:

> Since there was no one racial identity—and thus no single "nation"—upon which safely to erect a national identity, Lee and his colleagues aimed to make industrial modernity the metanarrative which would frame Singapore's national identity, and to create a remarkable "Global City" which, because of its trading links, would escape the restraints placed upon it by history and geography. The "national" as a category was not to be jettisoned but to be renovated so that Singapore's racial and cultural difference would be contained and to some extent homogenized for the leap into modernity. The people of Singapore would have to adapt their ways of life to fit the new state.[22]

Rather than choosing a single language that might alienate the majority Han Chinese; the Malays, who make up the majority of the neighboring populations of Malaysia and Indonesia; the South Asians, who have been an important economic force as merchants, laborers, and government officials since the British colonial administration; or the very marginal "Eurasians" (a rather malleable classification that seems to include biracial individuals as well as people of various racial and national groups who do not fit in the other three categories), who maintain important economic and cultural ties to the West and the rest of Asia, Singapore chose a limited form of multiculturalism. Thus, Singapore has four official languages (English, Mandarin, Malay/Bahasa, and Tamil). Although English is the primary medium of commerce and instruction, the three other "mother" tongues can also be used to conduct "official" business and must be included in the curriculum at government schools. Although this may seem like a logical path to multiculturalism, the irony of the situation lies in the fact that the preponderance of the majority Chinese population does not consider Mandarin its native dialect. Hokkein (spoken by the majority population on Taiwan and by Mainlanders across the Taiwan Straits), Cantonese (spoken by the majority in Hong Kong and by most in Guangdong Province in the Peoples' Republic of China), and the Shanghai dialect, among others, are very much in use "unofficially" in Singapore. Although, as the official language of both Taiwan and the People's Republic, Mandarin makes sense as a medium of education and commerce, the concomitant drive to eliminate the other dialects has also inhibited free expression in Singapore. For a time, Cantonese opera, Hokkein puppet shows, and other entertainments were banned, and most Cantonese films from Hong Kong still must be dubbed in Mandarin before exhibition in Singapore.[23] A similar irony exists for the Indian community. Although the majority in Singapore comes from Tamil-speaking southern India, Hindi, the Indian nation's "official" language may seem more attractive to some as a medium of commerce and education.

In *Mee Pok Man* and *Twelve Storeys,* Khoo concentrates on the Chinese majority. Khoo marginalizes the Malays and South Asians within his films. The non-Chinese Singaporeans provide a backdrop, much as they do in the nation at large. Meng, for example, has a brief exchange with a neighbor in Bahasa that only reinforces Meng's privileged position as an educator in the community.

Khoo, however, does not attempt to forward the Chinese as the unified "face" of Singapore. Mandarin divides as much as it unifies the Chinese community within Singapore as well as Singaporean Chinese within the rest of the "Greater China" global sphere. Although Singapore's government (among other forces in "Greater China") has attempted to forward Mandarin as a unifying force among the Chinese globally and Confucianism as an orthodoxy so that "Chinese" values (e.g., filial piety, patriarchy, and authoritarian hierarchical order) could stand for Asia and against the West, Khoo remains suspicious of the role Singapore has fashioned for itself in Asia.

For Khoo, Singapore, as represented by the Chinese community in his films, is fragmented, without a coherent sense of self, or unambiguous means of self-articulation. Mandarin competes with Singlish, Hokkein, and Cantonese as the favored means of expression. In fact, narrative points are often made through changes in dialect. When Hokkein is spoken freely in the hawker stalls, the mood relaxes, plot development slows, and social commentary can be inserted; however, Trixie and her younger brother's Singlish sets up a wall between them and their elder brother Meng who sticks with "proper" English. Bunny, too, sets herself apart by speaking the transnational languages of Mandarin and English, hoping to escape the constraints of Singaporean society, ironically through mastery of two of its "official" tongues. The switch from the strident Cantonese of San San's mother to San San's halting Mandarin to communicate with Rachel speaks volumes about the social gulf between the two women. In his analysis of *Twelve Storeys,* Michael Lee points out the implications of the use of Cantonese as follows: "It appears ... that repressed dialects have found a way of returning ... in the form of a nagging Cantonese-spurting mother. The audience sees and hears an old woman nag, yet may enjoy the language in which she does it, immersing in moments that are at once painful, yet pleasurable."[24] Like many of the plays and other public performances that have become increasingly prominent since the relaxation of censorship in 1991, the polyglot nature of Khoo's films has a political significance. As Chua Beng-Huat notes, "A hybridity of tongues protests the eraser [*sic*] of collective memories effected by the elimination of Chinese dialects from the public sphere; the prevalent use of dialects inverts the primacy of English in the political hierarchy of languages."[25]

Khoo's self-conscious use of dialects situates his features within a uniquely local culture in Singapore. Unlike the Shaw Brothers' use of Mandarin to establish a transnational Chinese audience for their films throughout the Chinese diaspora by celebrating a golden age of the Han Chinese by creating an imaginatively unified audience through the modern, mass medium of the motion picture, Khoo creates a very different, hybrid, transnational, postmodern, postcolonial discourse. The address may still be primarily to a global Chinese audience, but it does not disguise its cosmopolitan, Singaporean origins. Khoo uses language much the same way that Wong Kar-Wai uses Mandarin, Japanese, Cantonese, and English in *Chunking Express* to depict a very particular, local environment marked by its cosmopolitan hybridity. Rather than use English or Mandarin to appeal to broad segments of the audience, or use Cantonese or Hokkein exclusively to make a statement against U.S. cultural imperialism experienced through the use of English or the pressing political hegemony of the "official" Mandarin speaking governments of the People's Republic or Singapore, Khoo and Wong prefer creating films that cross linguistic boundaries more fluidly, but, also, more self-consciously. Language becomes opaque, and it presents an implicit critique of the unified nation and the cohesive self within the transnational, postmodern city.

Postmodern Style

Postmodern texts tend to favor allegory. Gregory L. Ulmer,[26] Craig Owens,[27] Fredric Jameson,[28] among many others, have commented on the parallels between the slippery signifiers of allegory in which the sign always stands in for something else and the uncertainty and contingency that characterizes postmodernism. The relationship between allegory and postmodern style finds a particularly welcome meeting ground in the work of Eric Khoo. Like Wong Kar-wai, Ang Lee, Tsai Ming-Liang, Edward Yang, Evans Chan, Clara Law, Ann Hui, Stanley Kwan, Tsui Hark, Huang Jian-Xin, Tian Zhuang-Zhuang, and many other directors working in the People's Republic, Hong Kong, Taiwan, and throughout the Chinese diaspora, Khoo draws on a tradition of allegory within Chinese discourse to circumvent political restrictions and weds it to a contemporary taste for displacement and slippage within texts.[29] Although visual style, dramatic interest, and narrative pleasures may overwhelm figurative readings, these allegorical interpretations are still available. In fact, within postmodern aesthetics, the surface takes precedence over depth, and these texts are enjoyed, from this perspective, as stylish, exotic, playful and superficial.

Like many postmodern texts, *Mee Pok Man* and *Twelve Storeys* slide between being part of the circulation of images characteristic of postmodern consumerism and critiquing that image market. Both films travel as commodities while also being self-consciously critical of the marketplace. Resuscitating the idea of a "national" cinema by presenting a vision unique to Singapore, Khoo frustrates any fantasy of nation building by systematically underscoring the mistakes and excesses of Singapore's government from education and housing to law enforcement.

Mee Pok Man and *Twelve Storeys* situate themselves within the spectacle of everyday life. Radio and television broadcasts, cartoon characters, internationally recognized brand names, and other images of global consumer culture saturate the mise-en-scène and soundtrack. *Twelve Storeys*, and *Mee Pok Man*, to a lesser degree, rely on a televisual aesthetic that privileges the surface of images over meaning. As in postmodern texts generally, the signifier has become unhitched from the signified, and signification, as a consequence, becomes problematic. Channel surfing, particularly in *Twelve Storeys*, dominates the film's aesthetic, as it cuts among its various plotlines, often paralleled by characters clicking through the available images from Hong Kong films to television commercials. Moreover, *Twelve Storeys'* televisual style makes it "look" like Singapore, with the HDB flats illuminated from within to look like television monitors and images of HDB interiors abound on Singaporean television in popular comedy series like *Under One Roof*.[30] Shot on Super 16 in the academy ratio that replicates the shape of the television box, *Twelve Storeys'* reliance on talking heads places it squarely within a televisual sense of space. San San's mother's direct address to the camera mirrors the parade of talking heads that cross international television broadcasts of everything from news stories to soap operas. *Twelve Storeys* replicates that immediacy and intimacy of the television screen for viewers in the theater as well as those who wait to see the film on video. In many respects, this method of filming fits perfectly with the confined spaces of the HDB apartments. The confined frame, the camera's close proximity to its subjects, and intense scrutiny of the close-up bring to the fore the film's critique of the claustrophobia and insularity of the HDB flat and, by extension, Singaporean society.

The mass media pervade this cloistered world, but fail to offer any outlet. Rather, mass (mis)communication is revealed to be woefully inadequate to provide a forum for public discourse for its audience. *Twelve Storeys*, for example, includes an upbeat radio deejay who comments on the weather (which is usually monotonously hot and humid) as Meng gleefully goes through his morning calisthenics and San San rather gloomily looks on. The public "face" of the radio broadcast is greatly at odds with the lives of the characters in the film. Similarly, in *Mee Pok Man*, the pleas of Xiao Ming, a suicidal student in the midst of the viciously competitive "examination hell," which sweeps the country every year and can determine the future educational level and job prospects of many at a very young age, contrast with the flippancy of the female deejay to whom he confides.

As direct interpersonal communication shuts down, mediated communication attempts to fill the gap. In the opening montage of *Twelve Storeys,* a teenager pulls away from a grandparent in order to pursue a conversation with a stranger on the Internet. Playing with his Sony Game Boy and listening to punk music, Bunny's younger brother begins to hear her voice through her diaries only after she is dead. Meng serves as a ventriloquist's dummy for government propaganda on topics as wide ranging as eating breakfast to boost productivity, the AIDS crisis, and improving the quality of life by being "gracious." Ah Gu tries to fashion a sense of Asian masculinity by watching soap operas, happy family television commercials, and Bruce Lee movies. Jonathan criticizes Bunny for casting herself in the Julia Roberts role in *Pretty Woman,* and *Twelve Storeys'* unnamed ghost positions himself in relation to GI Joe dolls and Japanese *anime.* As in other postmodern texts, the range of affect associated with these popular culture references runs the gamut from pathos and nostalgia to grotesque repulsion.

Khoo's films exist on the borders between the high art world of the international art film and the low pop cultural environment of the B-grade exploitation film, the television soap opera, and the cartoon. As such, the films contain enormous contradictions, narrative gaps, and inconsistencies of tone. Khoo does not assume a unified viewership, and he attempts to communicate with local teenagers in Singapore, art film aficionados internationally, and with the mixed audience for Chinese films globally.

To this end, Khoo draws broadly from an international lexicon of film style. The voyeuristic aspects of *Mee Pok Man* and *Twelve Storeys* refer to Hitchcock's films. *Twelve Storeys'* setting in an apartment block conjures up *Rear Window* in particular. The corpse at the center of *Mee Pok Man* links it to *Psycho,* while the plot mirrors any number of films dealing with the attempted rescue of fallen women, most notably John Ford's *The Searchers* and Martin Scorsese's *Taxi Driver,*[31] as well as lighter fare like *Pretty Woman.* The specifically Asian setting of *Mee Pok Man* links it to films like *The World of Suzie Wong, Saint Jack,* and a host of others that have exploited Asian street life to both profit from and condemn white men's lascivious interests in the "Orient." Khoo connects with Asian popular culture as well through Hello Kitty, Bruce Lee, and references to Hong Kong romances like Stanley Kwan's *Rouge.*

Khoo also alludes to Ozu through his inclusion of cutaway shots of empty corridors, still lives of bric-a-brac, and consistent breaking of the rules surrounding continuity editing (particularly the eye-line match). Khoo uses a film language dramatically out of step with classical conventions, creating a sense of image-sound disjuncture (particularly in his use of voice-over narration), non-linearity, lack of causality, and disregard for classical conventions that places his work close to the European New Wave. This also connects Khoo to other Asian New Wave directors who have drawn on Ozu, as well as Godard and Antonioni, to craft a portrait of the contemporary Asian metropolis. In many respects, Khoo's Singapore is a lot like Edward Yang's or Tsai Ming-Liang's Taipei, Wong Kar-wai's Hong Kong, or Lino Brocka's Manila. Khoo takes up New Wave counter-cinema stylistics to create a sense of alienation, disaffection, and angst, placing his work in conversation with contemporary international art cinema.

Like his New Wave cohorts, Khoo reflects on his own place in the image mar-ket. Not only does GI Joe pop up throughout his oeuvre, but animated cartoons and popular music become reoccurring motifs. More directly, Mike Kor reap-pears in *Twelve Storeys* to comment on the loss of Bunny to the *mee pok* man in the earlier feature, forming a bridge across his works to reward the cognoscenti, much the same way that *Jurassic Park* or *The Untouchables* (1987) reward cine-astes who can recognize King Kong's gate or Eisenstein's Odessa steps.

Although the hybridity and "double consciousness" of the postmodern con-dition may be a novelty for the white European male whose unified Cartesian ego dominated the globe for so many years, the pastiche and schizophrenia that characterizes postmodern consumer culture for Fredric Jameson has long been a part of the colonial and postcolonial condition.[32] Indeed, postmodern schizo-phrenia resonates with Singapore's split identity as former British colony, Third World nation, transnational entrepot, and bastion of traditional Confucian val-ues, as well as with the city-state's visual pastiche that incongruously juxtaposes Asian noodle dishes, hanging ducks, Shell Oil signs, Hello Kitty, imported beer, birth control pills, and jade bracelets.

The malleability, heterodoxy, hybridity, and playfulness that characterize post-modern stylistics serve Khoo, and many other filmmakers in similar circum-stances, well. Postmodernism maximizes viewer pleasure by structuring various shifting points of identification within its ironic, ambiguous, contradictory, and, generally, mysterious texts. For commercial Hollywood, postmodernism canni-balizes film history, rewards intertextual knowledge, plays with political critique, and promises both resistance to and nostalgia for the status quo. For Khoo, and other filmmakers within and outside of the Chinese diaspora who often work under the weight of official censorship, pressure to excel in international film competitions, and the economic constraints of the cinematic marketplace, post-modernism satisfies an even wider range of needs. For example, the loose con-struction of the narratives, the lack of linearity and causality, the fragmentation of space and the uncertainty of time all lend themselves to working with censors while still offering audiences sex, violence, and topical commentary on current events.

In *Twelve Storeys*, for example, Khoo alludes to two of the most sensitive topics involving Singapore in the international press in recent years; however, he mentions these events playfully and in passing, during a conversation among friends in the hawkers' food court. Without mentioning the condemned Filipina maid Flor Contemplacion by name, the friends agree that being a Filipino is great because the Philippine people treat murderers as heroes, referring to the throngs that gathered when Contemplacion's executed body was repatriated for burial. The conversation continues with a reference to "My Café." At first, the other fellows cannot understand what their friend may be talking about, until they realize he means "Michael Fay," the American boy who confessed to vandalism and was sentenced to a caning in 1994. After Clinton asked for clemency, the number of strokes was reduced, but the international press still had a field day with accusations of Singaporean barbarism. All agree that being an American is also wonderful because the American president comes to the aid of even hooligans. The playfulness of the scene hides the more subversive ways in which it can be read. While it can be interpreted as satirizing the international press for making two isolated incidents stand for the excesses of an entire nation, the scene can also be seen as a knowing critique of what the Singaporean media cannot say because of censorship (e.g., that innocent people may be executed and teenagers beaten under draconian laws that are out of step with international standards for human rights). Further, it indirectly critiques a system in which the "average" Singaporean is so out of touch with international sentiment as to fail to question Contemplacion's guilt or the excessiveness of Fay's sentence. Beyond the ambiguity at the heart of the scene, however, the scene itself is expendable. Like many of the scenes in *Mee Pok Man* and *Twelve Storeys*, this scene does nothing to further the plot or provide insight into the character of one of the film's protagonists. Rather, only loosely motivated by the narrative, the scene allows for a potential moment of resistance or critical observation that can be easily dismissed as mere play or eliminated altogether if the censors demand it.

Like most postmodern texts, *Mee Pok Man* and *Twelve Storeys* offer fragmented, localized, and isolated points of resistance rather than call for any revolutionary change. Belief in universal emancipation gives way to poking fun at the PAP's campaign to get Singaporeans to smile or critiquing the obviously excessive aspects of capitalist consumerism in the institution of prostitution.

In fact, Khoo tries very hard to work within a system that had recently changed to broaden what was permissible on Singaporean screens. Certainly, *Mee Pok Man* could not have been made before 1991, when a ratings system was introduced to allow for the exhibition of films restricted to adult audiences. Modeled on Hong Kong's category III films, *Mee Pok Man* addresses an adult audience interested in lurid sexuality and a violent underworld, while obliquely critiquing the status quo and offering an "artistry" that gives it what the American courts have termed "redeeming social value." With *Twelve Storeys,* Khoo wanted to break out of this R(A) ghetto in order to converse with his preferred audience of GenerAsian X Singaporeans, and the film's multiple plots, unrelated incidents, and mercurial characterizations are made to order for a film in which violent incidents (e.g., Meng's likely rape and murder of his sister Trixie) or sensitive issues (e.g., relations between the Chinese and their Malay and Indian neighbors) would need to be reworked throughout the course of the project.[33] Khoo won the battle for his young, local audience with its hip mix of angst, punk music, *anime,* and sexy young performers. It did not, however, fit as easily into the international art film market as *Mee Pok Man* did, with its affinities to Asian softcore porn and titillating exposés of the Asian sex industry. Still, the more local flavor of *Twelve Storeys* positioned it to travel well outside of Singapore, and the film competed at Cannes and was picked up for distribution by Hong Kong's EDKO Film Limited and the local Golden Village Entertainment Company.[34] Thus, Khoo has managed to find a domestic, regional, and international market with a postmodern style that travels easily within global film culture.

The Traffic in Women

The narrative movement in both *Mee Pok Man* and *Twelve Storeys* parallels the passage of the films internationally. Both narratives rely on the circulation of images of women within a libidinal economy linked to the global sex trade as well as the transnational market for female domestic workers. Desire fuels this economy, and the women travel to fulfill the dreams of men who expect the sensual, but submissive Asian prostitute or the equally docile, loyal domestic servant. In *Twelve Storeys,* the opening montage introduces the image of the Singapore Airlines stewardess, an emblem of Singaporean national industry, dressed in distinctive batik, who travels the globe to promote the nation as a sensual servant.[35] Just as oil passes through the centrally located port of Singapore, women circulate within the marginal service economies as prostitutes, brides, and maids; however, this libidinal economy intersects with and stands in for the broader Singaporean economy in Khoo's films. Prostitution becomes a metaphor for the dubious underpinnings of capitalism, and it seems appropriate that Meng should label Eddy a pimp in *Twelve Storeys.* Women, like goods, circulate to enrich men, and Singapore's economy enriches some at the expense of others.

   Mee Pok Man, for example, offers both a detailed account of the sex trade and a more general appraisal of the effects of capitalism and the legacy of colonialism.[36] The film begins in a public lavatory. One of Bunny's fellow prostitutes has presumably just finished shooting up drugs as she slowly gets up from the floor next to the toilet. Khoo immediately links the sex and drug trades together. Because the penalty for drug trafficking in Singapore is death, Khoo soberly places the sex trade in the same category as the violently suppressed narcotics business. Defining itself against Peter Bogdanovich's *Saint Jack* (1979) that romanticized Singapore's sex trade and Yang Fan's *Bugis Street* (1994) that looked at the world of transvestite and transsexual prostitution in Singapore from a gentler perspective, *Mee Pok Man* does not shy away from showing the toll prostitution takes on the women involved in Singapore's sex industry.[37] Throughout the film, the pimps, taxi drivers, and clients talk casually about their whores. Nationality is often used as a marker of sexual desirability as men talk about the relative merits of prostitutes from Indonesia, Thailand, the Philippines, and Russia, in relation to the Chinese, Malay, and Indian women native to Singapore. Bunny and her fellow prostitutes sit at the *mee pok* man's stall and talk about coping with or escaping from their profession. Bunny, for example, romanticizes her clients (e.g., her friends remind her of a string of foreign boyfriends before Jonathan who also did not deliver on promises to take her back to Japan or Indonesia), and she sees herself as able to manipulate men to free herself from prostitution.

Ironically, within the transnational sex industry, Bunny finds herself inextricably rooted in Singapore. Jonathan, a photographer and "professional" voyeur, enjoys his base in Singapore and has no plans to take Bunny away. He is one of those transnational professionals who benefits enormously from his expatriate position in Singapore. He can come and go as he pleases, enjoy his penchant for Asian women, and be free from any stigma, competition, or expectation for a more settled, married existence he may find in London.

Despite Jonathan's refusal, Bunny insists on living out the fantasy that he is her "white knight" who will take her away from the world of prostitution. Bunny, though, does not enjoy the same fate as Suzie (Nancy Kwan) in *The World of Suzie Wong* (1960) or any of the number of other Asian prostitutes saved by white men in Hollywood films.[38] When Bunny gets up enough courage to leave Mike Kor, she does not fall into the arms of her white savior, but, instead, ends up near death in the gutter from a hit and run.

As soon as Bunny is knocked unconscious and, thereby, silenced, her subjective voice is finally heard. Her younger brother has found, along with birth control pills, the pager she carries to communicate with her pimp, a well-marked map of Europe, and Bunny's diaries. As he reads the diaries, Bunny's voice-over and inserts of the written text reveal her perspective on her profession. The diaries follow a reverse chronology so that Bunny's immediate past gives way to a change in her voice that indicates the transition to her childhood. Ironically, as her brother learns more about what led Bunny to prostitution and as her voice becomes more childlike and innocent, her body decays in the *mee pok* man's apartment. The gulf between Bunny's diaries and the plot events shown in conjunction with their presentation is startling.

The segment devoted to Jonathan picking up a prostitute to succeed Bunny is particularly telling. While Bunny's diary talks of meeting "Mr. Right" (likely her future pimp Mike Kor), Jonathan walks down an arcade with a display of photographs of Asian women. Jonathan enters a disco and tells the hostess he is from England, wants a girl who speaks English, and prefers to look around on his own. Jonathan seems to know the routine well, and this sequence, reminiscent of Godard's *Vivre sa Vie* (1962), takes the viewer through a step-by-step explication of the procedure involved in procuring a whore in Singapore.

Jonathan sits down and begins to chat with one of the women. He uses his photography as a means to pick up the woman. When he tells the young woman that she is photogenic and has unusual looks, she replies that her mother was Eurasian (adding that she never knew her father), but she cannot be a model because she is too short; however, she readily agrees to pose for Jonathan on the condition he buys her a drink first.

All of the basic elements of the global sex trade are found in this sequence: the use of Asian women's images as enticements, the sale of the exoticism of the women to white men intent on continuing a fantasy of colonial domination in a postcolonial situation, the importance of a postcolonial hybridity to these transactions that need to take place in English with women who are "Western" enough to understand how to fulfill Eurocentric male fantasies, the promise of a return to absolute male sovereignty in a land where feminism does not exist, the bar as a marketplace for Asian women, the meeting of the legitimate and "unofficial" economies in the bar that uses the women to push the sale of liquor, the symbiotic relationship between bar owners, hostesses, and pimps in exploiting the women at several points in the transaction, the emphasis on the marketability of the image in this exchange between photographer and potential model, the importance of capturing and using these women and their images in transnational exchanges that bring capital into related industries ranging from pornography to travel and tourism.

In addition to circulating as prostitutes, women also circulate as domestic laborers in Khoo's features. Although not treated in detail like prostitution, the maid trade does appear and parallels the transnational trafficking in prostitution. Even though space is severely limited in the preponderance of Singaporean homes, the maid (almost always a foreign national, typically a Filipina) is a common fixture in many households. A holdover from colonialism when an Asian maid (usually a Chinese *amah*) indicated a standard of living above what could be expected in England for many in the middle ranks of the colonial administration, the maid also indicated a higher class standing for wealthier Asian families. Although small apartments require little maintenance, the increase in households with two working parents, lack of day care, and the expectation that the elderly be cared for in the home, all make the added expense of a maid seem like less of a burden. Many larger flats have small separate rooms off the kitchen expressly for the maid, and some even have separate maid entrances.

Although in the past, maids generally came from poorer areas of China, or, occasionally, were poorer or unmarriageable female relations,[39] most maids in Singapore (and, for similar reasons, in Hong Kong) are from the Philippines.[40] Because of the close control Singapore's government exercises on the ethnic balance of the nation, maids are chosen for their inability to assimilate easily into Singaporean society. Nevertheless, maids must be able to communicate with employers and must come from a country close enough to make travel relatively inexpensive and poor enough to make the wages offered seem attractive. In all cases, the Filipinas fit the bill. As Tagalog-speaking Catholics, the Filipinas are different enough to make them less attractive as potential wives; however, they speak English, because of the American colonial legacy in the Philippines, and, therefore, can communicate in the common language of commerce and public transactions. Also, because their culture and language is closely linked to Malaysia and Indonesia, they tend to be able to cook food palatable to most Singaporeans. As the dialogue between the two Filipina maids in *Twelve Storeys* indicates, maids often have children back home and are, thus, even less likely to plan on taking up long-term residence in Singapore. Large numbers of Indian, Malaysian, Indonesian, or Chinese maids, by contrast, would threaten the ethnic balance of the country and potentially lead to racial unrest.

The existence of a maid of any national origin in cramped quarters, however, carries its own set of social problems. Although Flor Contemplacion is only mentioned in passing in *Twelve Storeys,* her tragedy resonates throughout the film. Convicted of killing a fellow Filipina maid and a young boy in her care, Contemplacion was executed in 1995, after Philippine president Fidel Ramos failed to persuade the Singaporean government to grant a stay of execution. Only mentioned in passing as a joke at an outdoor gathering of the local men, the story still shades the way in which Rachel's Philippine maid is viewed as well as the way in which San San and her mother are depicted.

All of these women seem to be trapped by the same dynamic. Like Flor Contemplacion, Rachel's maid must leave her family behind in the Philippines while she raises another woman's son. The warmth and affection of the relationship between the boy and the maid is indicated as they hold hands in the backseat while Rachel drives the car on their visit to San San; however, the alienation of the maid's mother from her own child is illustrated by San San's strained relationship with her mother who favored her charge Rachel over San San while in service. Although how the sharp-tongued Cantonese maid found her way into Rachel's family's service is not explained, it seems to represent an earlier moment of the transnational circulation of labor, when, during the colonial period, Chinese coolie/"*ku li*" (bitter labor) workers poured into Singapore to satisfy the demand for cheap labor.[41] In their essay, "Contemporary Singapore Filmmaking: History, Policies and Eric Khoo," Tan See-Kam, Michael Lee, and Annette Aw make a compelling case that San San's adoptive amah mother may, indeed, be part of a lesbian sisterhood of domestic workers who fled China to escape not only poverty but also the constraints of arranged, forced, heterosexual unions.[42]

Rachel herself represents another aspect of diasporic displacement, since she endured an unhappy marriage to an overseas Chinese in the United States. Like the Philippine maids and the Southeast Asian prostitutes, she went abroad hoping to better herself financially or escape the confines of a closed society and encountered instead a man who, as she confides to San San, tried to treat her like a "servant" because of a mother that spoiled him when he was young. Like Bunny, Rachel unrealistically expects comfort, wealth, security, and liberation in the West through a liaison with a foreign man, whereas the men abroad expect Asian women to be happy in domestic bondage. The fact that Rachel ends up back in Singapore after the divorce provides a tacit commentary on fantasies of life in the West. In "Sex Machine: Global Hypermasculinity and Images of the Asian Woman in Modernity," L. H. M. Ling summarizes the conundrum for women in postcolonial Asia: "Within this saga of colonial relations, the image of the Asian female Other takes on a particularly interesting twist. To the white master, she is a potential ally as well as a handy maid. To the Asian male Other, she vacillates from sublime mother to the white man's profane whore. Yet, the Asian female also fulfills a common function for both. Her image embodies profits and fantasy, markets and sovereignty, globalism and colonialism, East and West."[43]

The China Bride

As a bride, Rachel joins the ranks of women who have left Asia through marriage. In Taiwan, Hong Kong, as well as Singapore and throughout the Chinese diaspora, mainland Chinese women have filled the gap in potential brides. With the exponential increase in travel to and from the People's Republic of China since the end of the Cultural Revolution and institution of economic reforms under Deng Xiaoping, marriages between Chinese women and so-called overseas, or diasporan, Chinese have been on the increase. The "China bride," in fact, has become a fixture in a range of comedies and romantic melodramas from Taiwan,[44] Hong Kong, and other parts of the Greater China cultural sphere.

Twelve Storeys, along with films like *The Wedding Banquet* (1993), produces a portrait of this new cinematic type.

In certain respects, Ah Gu's desire for mainland women parallels Jonathan's lust for Asian women. Like Jonathan, Ah Gu looks for the "perfect woman" (i.e., conventionally attractive, feminine, submissive, domestic, but undemanding) in a location that is supposedly economically, socially, and culturally inferior. As the "stronger," more "modern," (i.e., more masculine and potent) West sees itself as naturally superior to a feminized Asia, the nation of Singapore (represented by Ah Gu) sees itself as superior to the more rural, traditional, and "backward" mainland. The China bride (much like Bunny), however, usually has a very different appreciation of her relationship to the Western or overseas Chinese male. Lili, for example, sees herself in control of the relationship because of her sexual desirability. In this respect, Lili fares better than Bunny, and Ah Gu feels he has a real treasure in the physically attractive Lili. Much like Meng, Ah Gu has a genuine belief in the Confucian patriarchy, and he takes his obligation to have children quite seriously. Although he may fraternize with the other hawkers, he spends the preponderance of his time in his flat trying to convince Lili to have sex with him. He longingly watches television commercials of the ideal Singaporean family and bolsters his own sense of a failed masculinity by watching old Bruce Lee movies.

Lili, on the other hand, has no illusions about her relationship with Ah Gu, which she sums up as economic and gender inequality in action: "Because we people from China are poor, you think you can push us around. . . . You married me because you needed a toy, and I happen to be a pretty and cheap toy." Lili compares herself to other commodities made in China, and she clearly articulates the disadvantage she experiences as coming from the mainland; however, she also attempts to take advantage of that unequal relationship as best she can. She married to better herself socially and economically. When she met Ah Gu in Beijing, she expected a thriving businessman with a good home and car, not a struggling hawker with a cramped flat and nearly defunct auto. After decades of anti-Confucian campaigns, integration into the labor force, and governmentally sanctioned women's liberation, Lili, and her mainland sisters, have little commitment to Confucian values beyond the desire for the material prosperity and security promised by a strong, economically prosperous patriarch. Though the liberated Lili with her string of male admirers and penchant for the latest couture may have little in common with the "traditional" Chinese bride, Ah Gu also falls short as an icon of Singapore's prosperity and modernity. Actually, Ah Gu, with his buck teeth (that can be read as "poor," since he does not have the money for orthodontics) and T-shirt (that can be read as "uncouth" and "working class"), has more in common with the vision of the mainland held by the Chinese abroad, and Lili appears as the Westernized, independent, untrustworthy, liberated woman that has soured the pool of available mates for overseas Chinese men and for whom a mainland bride should provide a cure.

Twelve Storeys devotes considerable screen time to establishing Lili as a self-ish, materialistic, shrew and Ah Gu as the ridiculous, masochistic, hen-pecked cuckold. Even when the couple appears in public holding hands to present the proper "face" to their relationship, Ah Gu's cronies intuitively know the real situation and comment that Lili will divorce as soon as she acquires permanent residence status and, thus, no longer needs Ah Gu to live and work in Singapore legally.

Twelve Storeys, however, does not permit a simple, one-dimensional interpretation of the mainland gold digger to go uncontested. Rather, the film presents its final view of Lili at the edge of her bed with Ah Gu loudly snoring in the background. She takes out a photograph of herself in Tian'anmen Square in Beijing next to a young man, wearing a red star on his cap, under the portrait of Chairman Mao. Lili weeps. Like many of the unexplained images and narrative fissures in *Twelve Storeys* and *Mee Pok Man*, this image resonates far beyond anything even remotely hinted at in the narrative. Although a romantic interest may be assumed between Lili and the young man, nothing is stated. The sunny day and dispositions of the couple in the photograph point to happier times; however, the sheer volume in the composition devoted to Mao and the gate may conjure up the carefully censored news items involving Tian'anmen in 1989.[45] Questions surrounding why Lili needed to leave Beijing become more complicated, and affairs of the heart and pocketbook take on an implicitly political dimension.

This image may conjure up a range of emotions and thoughts in Singapore. Very simply, it could be read as a direct confirmation that Lili's "true love" is not Ah Gu and her heart is miles away. Another interpretation could take the allegorical significance of that a step further by confirming the suspicion that mainland émigrés really do not owe allegiance to Singapore, but continue to picture themselves in the mainland.

However, in light of *Twelve Storeys'* critique of Singaporean society generally, other possibilities also seem likely. Lee Kuan Yew, throughout his political career, has had a love-hate relationship with the People's Republic and with communism. Stan Stesser, for example, notes that Singapore's "authoritarian government functions in many ways like that of a communist state yet is dedicated wholeheartedly to the pursuit of capitalism."[46] When Lee's PAP, came to power on a vehemently anticolonial platform, the government modeled itself on many aspects of socialism while viciously suppressing the Communist Party out of a dual fear of losing Western capital pouring in from the multinationals and of coming too closely under the control of the mainland.[47] Lee carefully positioned newly independent Singapore between capitalism and communism by reviving a Confucian trust in authority and obligation. After the end of the Cultural Revolution and the death of Mao, Singapore, along with Japan and most of the West, warmed toward the reformers in the People's Republic, coveting the gigantic market potential and cheap labor of the mainland. The relationship, like Ah Gu and Lili's marriage, however, has not been entirely blissful. The image of Mao and the Tian'anmen gate conjures up, particularly after 1989, feelings of loss, terror, and confusion, that link Mao, Deng Xiaoping (a close personal and political ally of Lee), and Lee Kuan Yew. The photo seems to be nostalgic, alluding to both the romance of halcyon youth and the stability of a potent political authority. This double loss of love and political certainty, however, also seems tainted by Singapore's own record of political oppression indirectly linked to the bloody events of May–June in Beijing. Personal sentiments and political events become intertwined, and political uncertainty is associated with the decay of the patriarchy, the unhappy consequences of women's independence, and a postmodern deterioration of the Confucian order.

Within the postfeminist universe of *Mee Pok Man* and *Twelve Storeys*, the economic liberation of women, their increasing ability to move away from the familial sphere of father, elder brother, and husband, and their expression of personal desire does not equal freedom from patriarchal restraint. Meng and Bunny fall victim to the last desperate gasps of the sexual excesses of the patriarchy. Lili suffocates in a marriage of convenience, and San San does not stand a chance in a system in which physical appearance means everything. While a feminist modernity may have promised equality within the public and domestic spheres, Khoo's films underscore the dissipation of the opposing promises of the Confucian patriarchy and the international women's movement. Both fail the films' struggling female characters, just as the promise of modernity is revealed as a sham for the nation as a whole.

Chinese Ghost Stories

Ghosts, apparitions, and visions of various sorts are commonplace in the Khoo universe, as they are in many other postmodernist fictions (e.g., David Lynch's *Twin Peaks*). Although most Western filmgoers are more familiar with the cinematic ghosts found in Hong Kong popular films like the Tsui Hark–produced *A Chinese Ghost Story* series (1987–1991; animated version, 1997) and Stanley Kwan's *Rouge* (1987, a clip of which is included in *Twelve Storeys*), Khoo's ghosts operate somewhat differently as part of the quotidian lives of the characters in *Mee Pok Man* and *Twelve Storeys*. The ghost is a familiar figure (e.g., a loved one) who becomes transformed by death into something ghastly (e.g., a corpse). After Bunny's death, for example, the *mee pok* man transforms her from a flashy prostitute by replacing her scanty black evening dress with a housedress he has fashioned from the apartment's curtains. Domesticated, Bunny is relegated to the kitchen, permanently immobile, and totally under a man's tutelage; however, because Bunny is a corpse, the *mee pok* man's necrophilia takes his desire to possess Bunny into the realm of the grotesque. The patriarchal impulse to rescue the fallen woman and reinsert her into an idealized, male-dominated domestic sphere becomes a monstrous vision of desire out of control.

As the interior and the exterior psyche dissolve in what Jameson has labeled the schizophrenia characteristic of postmodern existence, ghosts, and other liminal figures, insinuate themselves into the quotidian lives of the characters inhabiting an otherwise conventionally realist diegetic universe. As the generic breakdown of postmodern texts enables the merger of horror, science fiction, comedy, romance, soft-core pornography, gore, and the domestic melodrama in Khoo's fiction, the psychic fragmentation of the postmodern subject makes the appearance of ghosts and other supernatural and/or delusional visions unremarkable.

These visions make any feeling of a common reality problematic. Who sees what and when becomes questionable, and Khoo casts the viewer adrift in a world in which vision veers far from truth or certainty. Eye-line matches are unreliable, and characters glance off-screen to see or, perhaps, not to see what comes up in the next shot. In *Mee Pok Man*, for example, Bunny looks off screen in close-up as an unidentifiable john pumps her. A shot of an empty chair in the corner of the seedy hotel room matches her eye-line. When the same set-up appears later in the scene, the *mee pok* man sits in the chair. Although this seems to be Bunny's vision and the rules of classical Hollywood editing would favor this interpretation, the connection is far from absolute. Does this shot indicate Bunny's psychic connection to the *mee pok* man? Does the entire scene reflect the *mee pok* man's obsession with Bunny? Does the shot merely prefigure the narrative twist that will bring the *mee pok* man and Bunny together in their own fated or fateful sexual encounter? As in most postmodernist fiction, the tie between signifier and signified ruptures, and the meaning of any given shot becomes difficult to grasp.

This is particularly striking in the case of San San and her mother in *Twelve Storeys*. *Twelve Storeys* takes place during the course of a single day within the immediate vicinity of a single apartment block. As the narrative enfolds, San San calls her mother's old charge, Rachel, to give her a package her mother willed to her. Although the mother has been sitting in the flat up to this point, San San's call to Rachel breaks the spell, and it becomes clear that San San's mother has been dead the entire time. What had been taken for granted about the abusive relationship between mother and daughter now comes into question. Is San San's mother's harangue really San San's own voice of inadequacy and regret? Was the mother really this bad or is San San exaggerating her abuse? Does Rachel have a point when she says that San San's mother was a *"hao ren"* (a "good person")?

The appearance of ghosts and spirits makes the porous quality of these narratives more palpable. Some of these narrative lacunae can be explained by referring to Chinese ghost stories and lore surrounding the dead, whereas other aspects remain unexplained idiosyncrasies of these two films. For example, from a Western perspective, the ghost of the young man who committed suicide, the ghost of the *mee pok* man's father, and the ghost of San San's mother would all operate on the same supernatural plane, and they would be assumed to be malevolent until proven conclusively otherwise. Within Chinese mythology, however, the spirits of ancestors (e.g., San San's mother, *mee pok* man's father) would be perceived of as qualitatively different from the ghost of the young suicide victim. In fact, the English word "ghost" really is not appropriate to the position these spirits occupy as "ancestors," though the distance implied by the word "ancestor" in English does not really fit the intimate link these spirits have to their progeny.[48] According to Chinese cosmology, dead or alive, ancestors are ancestors and should be accorded filial respect. They can still take an active interest in their descendents' lives and must be given the same attention granted to them while they were still among the living. Although it may seem peculiar from a Western perspective and a little old-fashioned in Chinese thinking, the *mee pok* man's daily breakfast ritual of offering an egg and a lit cigarette to the photographic portrait of his stern father exists within the realm of proper filial obeisance. When the *mee pok* man's father's ghost pays a visit and sits in the kitchen chair recently occupied by Bunny's corpse, he seems to be taking account of what is going on under his roof, since the *mee pok* man's affair with a corpse will produce no progeny. Similarly, San San's mother's spirit seems out of line with her continuous harangues; however, she does seem to have a point when her own inability to raise a daughter suitable for marriage is taken into account. This is a black mark against any spirit given the task of producing sons to carry on a family name and, if that proves impossible, at least seeing to it that a daughter will be dutiful and fit to move into another household. When looked at from this perspective, any sympathy for the *mee pok* man or San San must be linked to their potential rebellion against Confucian authority. The possibility emerges that the *mee pok* man may be perfectly happy with an unproductive corpse and that San San may be the "fat sow" her dead mother accuses her of being to escape the confines of the patriarchy. The *mee pok* man, however, may simply be a tragic victim of fate and star-crossed romance, and San San may be suicidal because she cannot live up to her mother's expectations. The narrative provides both options, and, in postmodern fashion, it is impossible to determine whether the conservative or the transgressive reading is favored.

This becomes even more apparent when San San's mother and *mee pok* man's father are contrasted with the young suicide. Of all the supernatural entities that people these two films, this suicide is the only one that would be considered a genuine ghost within Chinese cosmology. Because he died without progeny and visits living beings with whom he has no blood relationship, he must be classified differently from the others who have the parental authority to haunt their children. The young man represents the type of spirit that can cause the most trouble. Always hungry because they do not have progeny to "feed" them as the *mee pok* man dutifully offers food to his dead father, these rogue ghosts can bother the living if they are not occasionally appeased by the odd offering at the roadside or during the annual Hungry Ghost Festival.

In *Twelve Storeys*, however, this unnamed ghost brings with his unmotivated suicide a number of issues that resonate within Chinese cosmology in ways that differ dramatically from Western traditions. Historically, suicides in Chinese culture have been identified less with personal angst and more with public acts of defiance and protest. Women forced into unwanted, arranged marriages or victims of domestic abuse saw suicide as not only a personal way out of an impossible situation, but as a public statement against the excesses of the patriarchal system. Certainly, the best-known suicide in Chinese history involves the patriot Qu Yuan, who threw himself into a lake because he was so frustrated with the poor government of his ruler. The annual Dragon Boat festival celebrates this act as dragon boats symbolically race to save his body from hungry fish, and *zong zi*, wrapped packages of glutinous rice thrown into the river, appease sea creatures that would otherwise nibble on his corpse. Like Qu Yuan, Khoo's unnamed suicide seems to be generally fed up with Singaporean society. The young man's mother and Meng speculate that romantic difficulties are behind his drastic act. However, the film remains silent on the exact motivation, allowing the suicide to be caused by everything generally and/or nothing at all in particular. It can be interpreted as a nihilistic act of self-destruction or as the ultimate critique of a corrupt society. Like the hardcore punk music the young man listens to before he dies, the roots of his malaise may be a very personal self-destructive impulse or a very political, public rebellion against a society that gave him few options.

Extratextually, the ghost is linked to Khoo himself. Like Khoo, the ghost surrounds himself with GI Joe dolls (alluding to Khoo's early short *Barbie Digs Joe*, 1990) and the shots of comic books and cartoon characters like Mickey Mouse seem to allude to Khoo's own penchant for animation. Like Khoo, who comes from a privileged family of well-to-do hoteliers, the young man is an "outsider" in the building, a new arrival, whose wealthy family purchased the flat to appease their son's desire for his own apartment. The suicide, however, is also the consummate "insider," able to penetrate into every crevasse, just as Khoo's camera voyeuristically exposes the lives of his characters for the audience. Also, like Khoo, the ghost remains a mute presence that simply uses his eyes, as Khoo uses his camera, to point to and point out what must be assumed to be most abominable. The ghost, like the filmmaker, is the ultimate voyeur, privy to the private lives of the characters he scrutinizes. In light of the censorship regulations governing filmmaking in Singapore, Khoo and his suicidal avatar must remain mute. Critique lies in what is only glimpsed, the liminal, the proper realm of the ghost.

Just as the viewer may speculate on the symbolic significance of the suicide in relation to Qu Yuan or Eric Khoo, the young man becomes an object of intense speculation in the narrative. Following the folk superstition that sees a link between sudden death and the ability to predict the future, a taxi driver quickly jots down all the numbers associated with the fresh corpse. As he chats with his cronies at an outdoor food stall, he decides to play the number of the floor from which the young man jumped and his age. They all agree to exorcise his ghost after they hit the lottery jackpot. The folk behaviors surrounding the young man's death may seem odd to those outside Chinese society; however, stories of taxi drivers and truckers winning big with numbers based on the license plates of cars involved in fatal crashes are the stuff of urban legends throughout the Chinese diaspora.

It is important to note, too, that speculation on the suicide brings diverse characters together as a community. The fact that so many of the characters in the film find the suicide fascinating and, beyond that, somehow identify with the young man's desire to die seems to move this speculation beyond the narrative exigency, which attempts to link three separate plotlines into a single narrative and into the realm of social critique. For example, Meng discusses the suicide with Trixie and their younger brother Tee (Roderick Lim) by referring to government statistics, but Tee identifies silently with the young suicide to the point of lying down in the bloodstain left after the corpse is removed. Ah Gu literally speculates on the death by arranging with the taxi driver and his cronies to purchase the lottery ticket. The young man's parents are left to speculate as to the reasons behind the suicide as his father insists he was a good son who "knew how to make money"—in other words, with no reason to feel out of step within Singapore's booming and often cut-throat economy. The viewer, too, can join this fictional community and be drawn into that mechanism of the discourse that invites speculation and critical thought beyond that which is actually directly expressed within the narrative. The fictional world of ghosts, however, also safely distances the viewer from any danger that too sharp a critique may evoke.

The extreme close-up of San San's eye intercut with the abstract pattern of the HDB building and the blank screen with the child Bunny's voice's promise to listen to teacher and do better in school that end *Twelve Storeys* and *Mee Pok Man* say more by eerie implication than by actual articulation. San San merges with the HDB flat as the stricken soul of Singapore, still on the verge of suicide, and the child Bunny pathetically places her faith in the educational system that tragically failed her. The housing project and the school represent two of the principal institutions of governmental control over the lives of Singaporeans, and these films' implicit critique of the failure of the promise of modernity embodied by those institutions haunts the final moments of these films like a ghost.

Conclusion

Like Singapore itself, Khoo's films seem positioned on the crossroads of global traffic in people, images, cultures, and capital. They thrive on the indeterminacy of the postmodern condition and the hybridity of postcolonialism. Khoo's films are local favorites and the emblem of an emerging national cinema, while they vigorously critique the very foundations of that national identity. Though laying claim to a peculiar local Singaporean flavor, they are also transnational products able to appeal to Western tastes for the exotic and a Chinese diasporic sense of connection through language, ethnicity, and a common history. They acknowledge resistance, embodied by hip representatives of GenerAsian X, but playfully pull back from any direct commitment to social or political change. By delving into the depths of Singapore's postmodern condition, Khoo's features find themselves in the thick of a global film culture that thrives on instantaneous images, ephemeral style, indeterminate meanings, dark humor, impenetrable surfaces, self-referentiality, and intertextuality where Singapore's marginal, postcolonial position becomes part of the central concerns of current cinematic practice.

Notes

I would like to thank Philip Cheah of the Singapore International Film Festival, Audrey Wong of the Substation, and my colleagues and students in the School of Communication at Nanyang Technological University, where I was a senior fellow in 1997 and 1998. I am also grateful to Eric Khoo for his generosity in granting me an interview. For more information on *Mee Pok Man* and *Twelve Storeys*, as well as Khoo's complete oeuvre, visit the Zhao Wei Company web site at www.zhaowei.com.

1. Chua Beng-Huat, "Culture, Multiracialism, and National Identity in Singapore," in Chen Kuan-Hsing, ed. *Trajectories: Inter-Asia Cultural Studies* (London: Routledge, 1998), 186. Although the author does not include a discussion of the formation of modern Singapore as a nation-state, it is useful to look at Benedict Anderson, *Imagined Communities* (New York: Verso, 1991), for a discussion of the relationship between colonialism and modernity in the formation of nations in Southeast Asia, including the colonial history of Singapore.

2. For an incisive commentary on Asian values in the Singaporean context, see Chua Beng-Huat, "'Asian Values' Discourse and the Resurrection of the Social," *positions* 7:2 (1999): 573–592.

3. It must be remembered that the Cathay Organization and the Shaw Brothers have strong roots in Singapore, which date back to the British colonial era, as film exhibitors, regional distributors, and producers. For more on the history of film in Singapore, see Jan Uhde and Yvonne Ng Uhde, *Latent Images: Film in Singapore* (New York: Oxford University Press, 2000).

4. For more on Chinese transnational cinema, see Sheldon H. Lu, ed., *Transnational Chinese Cinemas: Identity, Nationhood, Gender* (Honolulu: University of Hawai`i Press, 1997). For a detailed discussion of Singapore's role in current formations of transnational Chinese cinema, see Tan See Kam, Michael Lee, and Annette Aw, "Contemporary Singapore Filmmaking: History, Policies, and Eric Khoo," *Jump Cut* 46 (summer 2003).

5. See Uhde and Uhde, *Latent Images;* and, Audrey Wong, "Considering the 'Singapore Film,'" *The Arts Issue* 7, National University of Singapore's Centre for the Arts [www.nus.edu.sg/NUSinfo/CFA/artsmag/arts7-4sfilm1.htm]. For more information on film in relationship to other mass media in Singapore (including information on censorship), see David Birch, *Singapore Media: Communication Strategies and Practices* (Melbourne: Longman Cheshire, 1993), and Tan Yew Soon and Soh Yew Peng, *The Development of Singapore's Modern Media Industry* (Singapore: Times Academic Press, 1994). For information on Singapore's film industry in relation to other Asian cinema industries, see John Lent, *The Asian Film Industry* (Austin: University of Texas Press, 1990). For information on the short film culture that Khoo helped to shape, see Cheah, Philip, "Singapore Shorts," *Cinemaya* 28–29 (1995): 30–31.

6. Scholars working in a range of disciplines have taken up the subject of postmodernism and "Greater China." For example, see Arif Dirlik and Zhang Xudong, eds., "Postmodernism and China: A Special Issue," *boundary 2* 24.3 (fall 1997).

7. For more on GenerAsian X, see Gina Marchetti, "The Gender of GenerAsian X in Clara Law's Migration Trilogy," in Murray Pomerance, ed., *Ladies and Gentlemen, Boys and Girls: Gender in Film at the End of the Twentieth Century* (Albany: State University of New York Press, 2001), 71–87.

8. In fact, it is difficult not to see Meng as an imitation Lee Kuan Yew, with his combination of British colonial roots, evidenced by his command of English, and "Asian values," as he mouths neo-Confucian government propaganda. It must be kept in mind that Lee was British educated and came from an ethnic Chinese family that favored English. Lee learned Mandarin as an adult to break from his own as well as Singapore's colonial status. For more on Lee Kuan Yew and his successor Goh Chok Tong, see Greg Sheridan, *Tigers: Leaders of the New Asia-Pacific* (St. Leonards, Australia: Allen and Unwin, 1997).

9. "Singlish" is English laced with Malay and Chinese words from various dialects, strongly accented, with grammatical formations frequently closer to Chinese than English.

10. The fingernail may also point to cocaine use or the affectation of "cool" based on the assumption that he snorts cocaine from the nail.

11. Chua, "Culture, Multiracialism, and National Identity in Singapore," 201.

12. In light of the taboos surrounding homosexuality in Singapore and the increasingly frank treatment of this issue in Chinese language cinema transnationally, it is not unreasonable to conjecture that this unnamed suicide may be gay and, thus, as distressed by the heterosexist patriarchy as the other characters. San San's sexual orientation could also be an unstated factor, as well as her mother's possible lesbianism.

13. See Jerome Silbergeld, *China Into Film: Frames of Reference in Contemporary Chinese Cinema* (London: Reaktion Books, 1999).

14. David Harvey, *The Condition of Postmodernity* (Oxford: Basil Blackwell, 1989), 66.

15. Wong, "Considering the 'Singapore Film.'" The importance of the HDB flat in *Twelve Storeys* is also discussed in Nazir Keshvani's review of the film, *Cinemaya* 35 (1997): 26–28.

16. Michel Foucault, *Discipline and Punish: The Birth of the Prison*, translated by Alan Sheridan (New York: Vintage, 1979). For a somewhat different reading of Foucault in relation to Khoo, see Michael Lee, "Dead Man Gazing: Posthumous Voyeurism in *12 Storeys*, or 'Splacing' Singapore's Official and Unofficial Discourses?" *Asian Cinema* (fall/winter 2000): 99–131.

17. Stan Sesser, *The Lands of Charm and Cruelty: Travels in Southeast Asia* (New York: Vintage, 1994). The riots between the Chinese and Malays in July 1964, in particular, had lasting ramifications not only internally, but with Singapore's relationship to Malaysia.

18. The seedy hotel in *Mee Pok Man* is called the "7th Storey," again missing the elevator cutoff by a single floor.

19. Khoo's films not only feature punk music, but also take on a punk sensibility inflected by a contradictory mix of youthful exuberance, anger, rebelliousness, and nihilism. Joe Ng, who plays the *mee pok* man, is a member of a band, The Padres, for example, and his stage persona carries over into his performance. See Philip Cheah's review of *Mee Pok Man, Cinemaya* 30 (1995): 25. For the definitive study of music in Chinese-language films, see Yeh Yueh-Yu, *Phantom of the Music: Song Narration and Chinese-language Cinema* (in Chinese) (Taipei: Yuan Liu, 2000).

20. Interestingly, the Chinese American architect I. M. Pei has been responsible for some of the architectural similarities between Western cities like New York and Asian cities like Hong Kong, a point brought out by C. J. W.-L. Wee, "Contending with Primordialism: The 'Modern' Construction of Postcolonial Singapore," *positions* 1.3 (1993): 715–743.

21. Mike Featherstone, *Undoing Culture: Globalization, Postmodernism and Identity* (London: Sage, 1995), 96.

22. Wee, "Contending with Primordialism," 717.

23. Recently, there has been some relaxation of this rule. In 1998, for example, *Mad Phoenix* was allowed to be exhibited in Cantonese, since it dealt with Cantonese opera and would be very difficult to dub. Given that its homosexual subject matter further restricted it to adult audiences made the issue of language less urgent. A further historical

note needs to be added as well. The Mandarin campaign as an antidote for Westernization displaces an earlier distrust of Mandarin as the language of communism.

24. Lee, "Dead Man Gazing," 114.

25. Chua, "Culture, Multiracialism, and National Identity in Singapore," 199.

26. Gregory L. Ullmer, "The Object of Post-Criticism," in Hal Foster, ed., *The Anti-Aesthetic: Essays on Postmodern Culture* (Port Townsend, Wash.: Bay Press, 1993).

27. Craig Owens, "The Allegorical Impulse: Toward a Theory of Postmodernism," *October* 12 (1980) and *October* 13 (1980).

28. Fredric Jameson, *Postmodernism; or, The Cultural Logic of Late Capitalism* (Durham, N.C.: Duke University Press, 1991).

29. For more on allegory in films from the People's Republic, see Silbergeld, *China Into Film*.

30. A top-rated situation comedy produced by the Television Corporation of Singapore in the mid-1990s.

31. Although the taxi driver is a marginal figure in *Mee Pok Man* and *Twelve Storeys*, Khoo did go on to produce a television series called *Drive* that more prominently featured taxis.

32. Fredric Jameson, "Postmodernism and Consumer Society," in Foster, ed., *The Anti-Aesthetic*.

33. Khoo discussed this issue with me in an interview I conducted with him at his Zhao Wei production offices in the Goodwood Hotel (a Khoo family-owned enterprise) on July 3, 1997.

34. Internet Movie Databank [http://us.imdb.com/Title?0120116].

35. Singapore Airlines is probably Singapore's most globally visible government-run enterprise. The stewardess, like the presence of Shell Oil, in Khoo's films tacitly signals the importance of Singapore's geographic location to its success as a transportation center.

36. There are many excellent studies of the sex trade/sex tourism in Southeast Asia, including Thanh-Dam Truong, *Sex, Money, and Morality: Prostitution and Tourism in Southeast Asia* (London: Zed Books, 1990), and Eliza Noh, " 'Amazing Grace, Come Sit on My Face,' or Christian Ecumenical Representations of the Asian Sex Tour Industry," *positions* 5:2 (1997): 439–465, among others. For more on the Asian sex industry in a global perspective, see Cynthia Enloe, *Bananas, Beaches and Bases: Making Feminist Sense of International Politics* (Berkeley: University of California Press, 1990).

37. Although Bogdanovich was welcome to film in Singapore, the finished film offended the censors and was banned from exhibition for almost two decades. The film was eventually shown at the Singapore International Film Festival in 1997.

38. See Gina Marchetti, *Romance and the "Yellow Peril": Race, Sex, and Discursive Strategies in Hollywood Fiction* (Berkeley: University of California Press, 1993).

39. Likely San San's mother falls into one of these categories.

40. For a broader perspective, see Roland B. Tolentino, "Bodies, Letters, Catalogs: Filipinas in Transnational Space," *Social Text* 14.3 (fall 1996): 49–76.

41. The presence of Chinese merchants in the area goes back centuries. It was, however, Sir Stamford Raffles' settlement of Singapore in 1819 that brought it into the larger economy of imperial England. With that came laborers from China and India. The influx of the Chinese during the colonial period was particularly dramatic and created complex

social stratification. Perhaps the most striking division involved the Peranakans—established descendents of Chinese and Malay marriages who kept certain Chinese customs, did not convert to Islam, and spoke Malay—who saw themselves as distinct from the overseas Chinese born in China and who were often vastly better off in terms of both cultural and actual capital. For example, the traditionally patrilocal Chinese adopted the matrilocal Malay custom of the newlyweds living with the wife's family to solidify their roots in the local community to considerable economic advantage. For the definitive account of the relationship of the British Empire to the Chinese diaspora, as well as Chinese emigration in other parts of the world, see Lynn Pan, *Sons of the Yellow Emperor: A History of the Chinese Diaspora* (New York: Kodansha International, 1990).

42. Tan, Lee, and Aw, "Contemporary Singapore Filmmaking."

43. L. H. M. Ling, "Sex Machine: Global Hypermasculinity and Images of the Asian Woman in Modernity," *positions* 7.2 (1999): 296.

44. Shu-mei Shih, "Gender and a Geopolitics of Desire: The Seduction of Mainland Women in Taiwan and Hong Kong Media," in Mayfair Mei-Hui Yang, ed. *Spaces of Their Own: Women's Public Sphere in Transnational China* (Minneapolis: University of Minnesota Press, 1999), 278–307.

45. Around the time of the release of *Twelve Storeys,* there was a minor controversy surrounding the screening of Carma Hinton's *Gate of Heavenly Peace* at the Singapore International Film Festival. Even in 1997, the events of 1989 in Tian'anmen remained a touchy subject for the censors.

46. Sesser, *The Lands of Charm and Cruelty,* 5.

47. The PAP has been in power in Singapore since 1959, before it became a sovereign entity after its split from Malaysia in 1965.

48. See the distinction drawn between *"gui"* and *"shen"* in the entry on ghosts in Wolfram Eberhard, *A Dictionary of Chinese Symbols: Hidden Symbols in Chinese Life and Thought,* translated by G. L. Campbell (London: Routledge, 1986), 128–129.

Filmography
Selected Chinese-Language Films

COMPILED BY JING NIE

All the Corners of the World (Haijiao tianya) 海角天涯 (Tsai Ming-liang, Taiwan, 1989)

Azalea Mountain (Dujuan shan) 杜鹃山 (Xie Tieli, People's Republic of China, 1974)

Back to Back, Face to Face (Bei kao bei, lian dui lian) 背靠背，脸对脸 (Huang Jianxin, People's Republic of China, 1994)

Banana Paradise (Xiangjiao tiantang) 香蕉天堂 (Wang Tong, Taiwan, 1989)

Barbie Digs Joe (Wa wa zhi lian) 娃娃之恋 (Eric Khoo, Singapore, 1990)

Be There Be Square (Bujian busan) 不见不散 (Feng Xiaogang, People's Republic of China, 1998)

Beautiful Ducklings (Yangya renjia) 养鸭人家 (Li Xing, Taiwan, 1964)

Beijing Bastard (Beijing zazhong) 北京杂种 (Zhang Yuan, Hong Kong/China, 1993)

Beijing Bicycle (Shiqishi de danche) 十七岁的单车 (Wang Xiaoshuai, Taiwan/France, 2001)

Beijing'ers in New York (Beijingren zai Niuyue) 北京人在纽约 (Zheng Xiaolong, Feng Xiaogang, People's Republic of China, 1993; television drama)

Betelnut Beauty (Aini aiwo) 爱你爱我 (Lin Cheng-sheng, France/Taiwan, 2001)

Better Tomorrow, A (Yingxiong bense) 英雄本色 (John Woo, Hong Kong, 1986)

Big Shot's Funeral (Daiwan) 大腕 (Feng Xiaogang, People's Republic of China, 2001)

Birth of Ne Zha, The (Ne Zha chushi) 哪吒出世 (Li Zeyuan, China, 1928)

Black Canon Incident, The (Heipao shijian) 黑炮事件 (Huang Jianxin, People's Republic of China, 1986; documentary)

Buddha Bless America (Taiping tianguo) 太平天国 (Wu Nianzhen, Taiwan, 1996)

Bumming in Beijing: The Last Dreamers (Liulang Beijing) 流浪北京：最后的梦想者 (Wu Wenguang, People's Republic of China, 1990)

Burning of the Red Lotus Temple (Huoshao Hongliansi) 火烧红莲寺 (Zhang Shichuan, China, 1928)

Cell Phone (Shouji) 手機 (Feng Xiaogang, People's Republic of China, 2003)

Changban Slope (Chang Ban Po) 长板坡 (Ron Qingtai, China, 1905)

Cheerful Wind (Fenger ti ta cai) 风儿踢踏踩 (Hou Hsiao-hsien, Taiwan, 1981)

Chinese Ghost Story, A (Qiannü youhun) 倩女幽魂 (Ching Siu-tung, Hong Kong, 1987)

Chinese Odyssey, A (Dahua xiyou) 大话西游 (Jeffrey Lau, Hong Kong/China, 1997)

Chungking Express (Chongqing senlin) 重庆森林 (Wong Kar-wai, Hong Kong, 1994)

City of Glass (Boli zhi cheng) 玻璃之城 (Mabel Cheung, Hong Kong, 1999)

City of Sadness, A (Beiqing chengshi) 悲情城市 (Hou Hsiao-hsien, Taiwan, 1989)

Comrades, Almost a Love Story (Tian mimi) 甜蜜蜜 (Peter Chan, Hong Kong, 1997)

Country Teachers (Fenghuang qin) 凤凰琴 (He Qun, People's Republic of China, 1993)

Crossings, also known as *Wrong Love (Cuo ai)* 错爱 (Evans Chan, Hong Kong, 1994)

Crouching Tiger, Hidden Dragon (Wohu canglong) 卧虎藏龙 (Ang Lee, United States/ Taiwan/China, 2000)

Cute Girl, also known as *Lovable You (Jiushi liuliu de Ta)* 就是溜溜的她 (Hou Hsiao-hsien, Taiwan, 1980)

Days, The (Dongchun de rizi) 冬春的日子 (Wang Xiaoshuai, People's Republic of China, 1993)

Dingjun Mountain (Dinjun shan) 定军山 (Ren Qingtai, China, 1905)

Dislocations, The (Cuowei) 错位 (Huang Jianxin, People's Republic of China, 1987)

Dou-san: A Borrowed Life (Dou-sang) 多桑 (Wu Nien-chen/Wu Nianzhen, Taiwan, 1994)

Dragon Gate Inn (Longmen kezhan) 龙门客栈 (Hu Jinquan/King Hu, Taiwan, 1967)

Drifting Life, A (Chunhua menglu) 春花梦露 (Lin Cheng-sheng, Taiwan, 1996)

Durian Durian (Liulian Piaopiao) 榴梿飘飘 (Fruit Chan, France/Hong Kong, 2000)

Dust in the Wind (Lianlian fengchen) 恋恋风尘 (Hou Hsiao-hsien, Taiwan/United States, 1987)

East Palace, West Palace (Donggong xigong) 东宫西宫 (Zhang Yuan, France/China, 1997)

Eat Drink Man Woman (Yinshi nannü) 饮食男女 (Ang Lee, Taiwan, 1994)

Executioners, The, also known as *The Heroic Trio II (Xiandai haoxia zhuan)* 现代豪侠传 (Ching Siu-tung, Hong Kong, 1993)

Fang Shiyu (Fang Shiyu) 方世玉 (Yuan Kui, Hong Kong, 1993)

Farewell China (Ai zai biexiang de jijie) 爱在别乡的季节 (Clara Law, Hong Kong, 1990)

Female Knight-errant Black Peony, The (Nüxia Heimudan) 女侠黑牡丹 (Ren Pengnian, China, 1931)

Female Knight-errant Li Feifei, The (Nüxia Li Feifei) 女侠李飞飞 (Shao Zuiweng, China, 1925)

Female Knight-errant Rescues the Lady, The (Xianü jiu furen) 侠女救夫人 (Zheng Zhengqiu, China, 1928)

Female Pirate, The (Nü haidao) 女海盗 (Zheng Jiduo, China, 1929)

Five Vengeful Girls (Wunü fuchou) 五女复仇 (Gao Xiping, China, 1928)

Floating Life (Fusheng) 浮生 (Clara Law, Australia, 1996)

Flowers of Shanghai (Haishang hua) 海上花 (Hou Hsiao-hsien, Taiwan/Japan, 1998)

Flying Shoes, The (Feixing xie) 飞行鞋 (Pan Chuitong, China, 1928)

Foreign Babes in Beijing (Yangniu'er zai Beijing) 洋妞儿在北京 (Wang Binglin, Li Jianxin, People's Republic of China, 1996; television drama)

Frozen (Jidu hanleng) 极度寒冷 (Wang Xiaoshuai, Hong Kong/Netherlands/People's Republic of China, 1997)

Full Moon in New York (Ren zai Niuyue) 人在纽约 (Stanley Kwan, Hong Kong, 1989)

Girl Bandit, A (Lan guniang) 兰姑娘 (Zhang Huimin, China, 1930)

Good Men, Good Women (Haonan, haonü) 好男好女 (Hou Hsiao-hsien, Taiwan/Japan, 1995)

Good Morning Taipei (Zao'an Taibei) 早安台北 (Li Xing, Taiwan, 1980)

Goodbye South, Goodbye (Nanguo zaijian, nanguo) 南国再见，南国 (Hou Hsiao-hsien, Taiwan, 1996)

Great Flying Bandit, The, also known as *Little Sister, I Love You (Feixing dadao)* 飞行大盗 (Dan Duyu, China, 1929)

Great Knight-Errant of Aviation, The (Hangkong daxia) 航空大侠 (Chen Tian, China, 1928)

Happy Together (Chunguang zhaxie) 春光乍泄 (Wong Kar-wai, Hong Kong, 1997)

He Ain't Heavy, He's My Father (Xin nanxiong nandi) 新难兄难弟 (Peter Chan, Hong Kong, 1993)

He and She (Jianghu qingxia) 江湖情侠 (Wen Yimin, China, 1928)

Heartbreak Ridge (Shanggan ling) 上甘岭 (Shan Lin, Meng Sha, People's Republic of China, 1956)

Hero (Yingxiong) 英雄 (Zhang Yimou, People's Republic of China, 2002)

Hero and Heroine (Ernü yingxiong) 儿女英雄 (Wen Yimin, China, four series, 1927–1930)

Heroic Sons and Daughters (Yingxiong ernü) 英雄儿女 (Wu Zhaodi, People's Republic of China, 1964)

Heroic Trio, The (Dongfang sanxia) 东方三侠 (Johnni To, Hong Kong, 1992)

Hill of No Return (Wuyande shanqiu) 无言的山丘 (Wang Tong, Taiwan, 1993)

Hole, The (Dong) 洞 (Tsai Ming-liang, France/Taiwan, 1998)

Hollywood Hong Kong (Xianggang youge helihuo) 香港有个荷里活 (Fruit Chan, Hong Kong/France/United Kingdom/Japan, 2001)

Homecoming (Sishui liunian) 似水流年 (Yim Ho, Hong Kong, 1984)

House of Flying Daggers (Shimian maifu) 十面埋伏 (Zhang Yimou, People's Republic of China, 2004)

Illegal Immigrants (Feifa yimin) 非法移民 (Mabel Cheung, Hong Kong, 1985)

In Expectation, also known as *Rainclouds over Wushan (Wushan yunyu)* 巫山云雨 (Zhang Ming, People's Republic of China, 1996)

In Our Time (Guangyin de gushi) 光阴的故事 (Edward Yang, Zhang Yi, Ko Yi-cheng, T'ao Te-ch'en, 1982)

In the Heat of the Sun (Yangguang canlan de rizi) 阳光灿烂的日子 (Jiang Wen, People's Republic of China/Taiwan/Hong Kong, 1994)

In the Mood for Love (Huayang nianhua) 花样年华 (Wong Kar-wai, Hong Kong, 2000)

Jade Love (Yuqing sao) 玉卿嫂 (Zhang Yi, Taiwan, 1986)

Jiao Yulu (Jiao Yulu) 焦裕禄 (Wang Jixing, People's Republic of China, 1990)

Just Like Weather (Meiguo xin) 美国心 (Allen Fong, Hong Kong, 1986)

Keep Cool (Youhua haohao shuo) 有话好好说 (Zhang Yimou, People's Republic of China, 1997)

King of Comedy Tours Shanghai, The (Huaji dawang you hu ji) 滑稽大王游沪记 (Zhang Shichuan, China, 1922)

Kuei-mei, A Woman (Wo zheyang guole yisheng) 我这样过了一生 (Zhang Yi, Taiwan, 1986)

Laborer's Love (Laogong zhi aiqing) 劳工之爱情 (Zhang Shichuan, China, 1922)

Leopard (Jinqianbao) 金钱豹 (Beijing Fengtai Photography, China, 1906)

Life of Wu Xun, The, also known as *The Biography of Wuxun (Wuxunzhuan)* 武训传 (Sun Yu, People's Republic of China, 1950)

Lingering Face, A (Feichang Xiari) 非常夏日 (Lu Xuechang, People's Republic of China, 2000)

Little Cheung (Xilu Xiang) 细路祥 (Fruit Chan, Japan/Hong Kong, 1999)

Little Chinese Seamstress (Xiao cainfeng) 小裁缝 (Dai Sijie, France/People's Republic of China, 2003)

Long Arm of the Law (Shenggang qibing) 省港骑兵 (Johnny Mak, Hong Kong, 1984)

Longest Summer, The (Qunian yanhua tebieduo) 去年烟花特别多 (Fruit Chan, Hong Kong, 1999)

Love Eterne (Liang Shanbo yu Zhu Yingtai) 梁山伯与祝英台 (Li Hanxiang, Hong Kong, 1963)

Love in the Age of Internet (Wangluo shidai de aiqing) 网络时代的爱情 (Jin Chen, People's Republic of China, 1998)

Made in Hong Kong (Xianggang zhizao) 香港制造 (Fruit Chan, Hong Kong, 1997)

Mahjong (Majiang) 麻将 (Edward Yang, Taiwan, 1996)

Making of Steel, The (Zhangda Chengren) 长大成人 (Lu Xuechang, People's Republic of China, 1995)

Mama (Mama) 妈妈 (Zhang Yuan, People's Republic of China, 1992)

March of Happiness (Xingfu jinxingqu) 幸福进行曲 (Lin Cheng-sheng, Taiwan, 1999)

Mee Pok Man (Bo mian) 薄面佬 (Eric Khoo, Singapore, 1995)

Millennium Mambo (Qianxi manbo) 千禧曼波 (Hou Hsiao-hsien, France/Taiwan, 2001)

Mr. Canton and Lady Rose, also known as *Miracles (Qiji)* 奇迹 (Jackie Chan, Hong Kong, 1989)

Mulan Joins the Army (Mulan congjun) 木兰从军 (Pu Wancang, China, 1939)

Murmur of Youth, The (Meili zai changge) 美丽在唱歌 (Lin Cheng-sheng, Taiwan, 1997)

My American Grandson (Shanghai jiaqi) 上海假期 (Ann Hui, Taiwan, 1991)

My New Friends (Wo xin renshi de pengyou) 我新认识的朋友 (Tsai Ming-liang, Taiwan, 1995)

Not One Less (Yige dou bu neng shao) 一个都不能少 (Zhang Yimou, People's Republic of China, 1999)

Old Well (Lao jing) 老井 (Wu Tianming, People's Republic of China, 1986)

Once a Thief (Zongheng sihai) 纵横四海 (John Woo, Hong Kong, 1991)

Orchids and My Love (Wo nü Ruolan) 我女若兰 (Li Jia, Taiwan, 1965)

Ordinary Heroes (Qianyan wanyu) 千言万语 (Ann Hui, Hong Kong, 1998)

Oyster Girl, The (Ke nü) 蚵女 (Li Xing, Taiwan, 1964)

Passion (Zui ai) 最爱 (Sylvia Chang, Hong Kong, 1986)

Peony Pavilion, The (Wo de meili yu aichou) 我的美丽与哀愁 (Chen Kuo-fu, Taiwan, 1995)

People Between Two Chinas (Haixia liangan) 海峡两岸 (Yu Kanping, Taiwan, 1988)

Personals, The (Zhenghun qishi) 征婚启示 (Chen Kuo-fu, Taiwan, 1998)

Pickles Make Me Cry (Yimin shijie) 移民世界 (Peter Chow, United States/Hong Kong/People's Republic of China, 1988)

Platform (Zhantai) 站台 (Jia Zhangke, France/Japan/Hong Kong, 2000)

Police Story (Jingcha gushi) 警察故事 (Jackie Chan, Hong Kong, 1985)

Portrait of a Fanatic (Kulian) 苦恋 (Wang Tong, Taiwan, 1982)

Princess Huanzhu (Huanzhu Gege) 还珠格格 (Li Ping, Ding Yangguo, People's Republic of China/Taiwan/Hong Kong, 1999; television drama)

Public Toilet (Renmin gongce) 人民公厕 (Fruit Chan, South Korea/Hong Kong, 2002)

Punish the Invaders (Daji qinlüezhe) 打击侵略者 (Hua Chun, People's Republic of China, 1965)

Puppetmaster, The (Xi meng rensheng) 戏梦人生 (Hou Hsiao-hsien, Taiwan, 1993)

Raise the Red Lantern (Dahong denglong gaogao gua) 大红灯笼高高挂 (Zhang Yimou, China/Taiwan/Hong Kong, 1991)

Rapeseed Girl, also known as *Ah Fei (Youma caizi)* 油麻菜籽 (Wan Ren, Taiwan, 1983)

Rebels of the Neon God (Qingshaonian ne zha) 青少年哪吒 (Tsai Ming-liang, Taiwan, 1992)

Red Apple (Hong pingguo) 红苹果 (Chen Jiashang, People's Republic of China, 1998)

Red Heroine (Hong xia) 红侠 (Yao Shiquan, Wen Yimin, China, 1929)

Red Skeleton (Hongfen kulou) 红粉骷髅 (Guan Haifeng, China, 1921)

Remorse at Death (Shengsi hen) 生死恨 (Fei Mu, China, 1948)

Retribution for Killing One's Own Son (Shazibao) 傻子堡 (China, 1908)

Right a Wrong with Earthware Dish (Wapen shenyuan) 瓦盆申冤 (China, 1909)

Righting Wrongs (Zhifa xianfeng) 执法先锋 (Ma Wu, Hong Kong, 1986)

River, The (Heliu) 河流 (Tsai Ming-liang, Taiwan, 1997)

Road Home, The (Wo de fuqin muqin) 我的父亲母亲 (Zhang Yimou, People's Republic of China, 2000)

Road, The (Lu) 路 (Li Xing, Taiwan, 1993)

Romantic Heroine, A (Langman nü yingxiong) 浪漫女英雄 (China, 1929)

Rouge (Yanzhikou) 胭脂扣 (Stanley Kwan, Hong Kong, 1987)

Rounding Up the Draftees (Zhua zhuangding) 抓壮丁 (Chen Ge, Shen Yan, People's Republic of China, 1963)

Rumble in the Bronx (Hongfanqu) 红番区 (Stanley Tong, Hong Kong, 1995)

Russian Girls in Harbin (Eluosi guniang zai Harbin) 俄罗斯姑娘在哈尔滨 (Sun Sha, People's Republic of China, 1994; television drama)

Sandwich Man (Erzi de da wan'ou) 儿子的大玩偶 (Hou Hsiao-hsien, Zeng Zhuangxiang, Wan Ren, Taiwan, 1983)

Seventeen Years (Guonian huijia) 过年回家 (Zhang Yuan, Italy/China, 1999)

Shower (Xizao) 洗澡 (Zhang Yang, People's Republic of China, 1999)

Siao Yu (Shaonü Xiao Yu) 少女小渔 (Sylvia Chang, Taiwan, 1995)

Sing-Song Girl Red Peony (Genü Hongmudan) 歌女红牡丹 (Zhang Shichuan, China, 1931)

Song of the Exile (Ketu qiuhen) 客途秋恨 (Ann Hui, Taiwan/Hong Kong, 1990)

Spring River Flows East, The (Yijiang chunshui xiangdong liu) 一江春水向东流 (Cai Chusheng, Zheng Junli, China, 1947)

Stage Door (Hu du men) 虎度门 (Shu Kei, Hong Kong, 1996)

Stand Up, Don't Bend Down (Zhanzhi le, bie paxia) 站直了，别趴下 (Huang Jianxin, People's Republic of China, 1993)

Stealing a Roasted Duck (Tou shaoya) 偷烧鸭 (Liang Shaobo, Hong Kong, 1909)

Story of Qiu Ju, The (Qiuju da guansi) 秋菊打官司 (Zhang Yimou, People's Republic of China/Hong Kong, 1992)

Strawman (Daocaoren) 稻草人 (Wang Tong, Taiwan, 1989)

Street Angel (Malu tianshi) 马路天使 (Yuan Muzhi, China, 1937)

Summer at Grandpa's, A (Dongdong de jiaqi) 冬冬的假期 (Hou Hsiao-hsien, Taiwan, 1984)

Supercop (Chaoji jingcha) 超级警察 (Stanley Tong, Hong Kong, 1992)

Surprise Attack (Qixi) 奇袭 (Xu Youxin, People's Republic of China, 1960)

Sweet Degeneration (Fanglang) 放浪 (Lin Cheng-sheng, Japan/Taiwan, 1997)

Sword versus Sword (Duidao) 对刀 (China, 1906)

Swordswoman from the Huangjiang River (Huangjiang nüxia) 黄江女侠 (Chen Qiangran, China, 1930–1932)

Taipei Story (Qingmei zhuma) 青梅竹马 (Edward Yang, Taiwan, 1985)

Teenage Fugitive (Xiao taofan) 小逃犯 (Zhang Peicheng, Taiwan, 1986)

Tempting Heart (Xin dong) 心动 (Sylvia Chang, Hong Kong/Japan, 1999)

Terrorizers, The (Kongbu fenzi) 恐怖份子 (Edward Yang, Taiwan, 1987)

That Day on the Beach (Haitan de yitian) 海滩的一天 (Edward Yang, Hong Kong/Taiwan, 1983)

The Flying Knight-Errant Lü Sanniang (Feixia Lü Sanniang) 飞侠吕三娘 (Yang Xiaozhong, China, 1929)

This Love of Mine (Wo de ai) 我的爱 (Zhang Yi, Taiwan, 1988)

Thugs, The (Da chushou) 大出手 (China, 1906)

Time to Live and a Time to Die, A (Tongnian wangshi) 童年往事 (Hou Hsiao-hsien, Taiwan, 1985)

To Liv(e) (Fushi lianqu) 浮世恋曲 (Evans Chan, Hong Kong, 1992)

To Live (Huozhe) 活着 (Zhang Yimou, People's Republic of China, 1994)

Tonight Nobody Goes Home (Jintian bu huijia) 今天不回家 (Sylvia Chang, Taiwan, 1996)

Touch of Zen, A (Xia nü) 侠女 (King Hu, Taiwan, 1970)

Twelve Storeys (Shi'er lou) 十二楼 (Eric Khoo, Singapore, 1997)

Two Stage Sisters (Wutai jiemei) 舞台姐妹 (Xie Jin, People's Republic of China, 1964)

Unknown Pleasures (Ren xiaoyao) 任逍遥 (Jia Zhangke, People's Republic of China/
Japan, 2002)

Uproar at the Baolin Temple (Danao Baolin si) 大闹宝林寺 (Ling Yun, People's
Republic of China, 1963)

Valiant Girl White Rose, The (Nüxia Bai meigui) 女侠白玫瑰 (Zhang Huimin, China,
1929)

Vive L'Amour (Aiqing wansui) 爱情万岁 (Tsai Ming-liang, Taiwan, 1994)

Wedding Banquet, The (Xiyan) 喜宴 (Ang Lee, Taiwan, 1993)

Weekend Lover (Zhoumo qingren) 周末情人 (Lou Ye, People's Republic of China,
1995)

What Time Is It There? (Ni neibian jidian) 你那边几点? (Tsai Ming-liang, Taiwan/
France, 2001)

White Gold Dragon (Baijinlong) 白金龙 (China, 1933)

White-Haired Girl, The (Baimao nü) 白毛女 (Wang Bin, Shui Hua, People's Republic
of China, 1950)

White-Water Beach (Baishuitan) 白水潭 (Beijing Fengtai Photography, China, 1907)

Who Am I? (Wo shi shui) 我是谁? (Jackie Chan, Benny Chan, Hong Kong, 1998)

Wing Chun (Yong Chun) 咏春 (Yuen Woo-ping, Hong Kong, 1994)

Woman Bodyguard, A (Guangdong nüxia, also known as Nü Biaoshi) 广东女侠（女
镖师）(Ren Pengnian, China, 1931)

Woman of Wrath (Sha fu) 杀夫 (Zeng Zhuangxiang, Taiwan, 1984)

Wu Nien-chen's Taiwan (Taiwan Nianzhen qing) 台湾念真情 (Wu Nianzhen,
Taiwan, TVBS television series, 1996–1998)

Xiao Wu (Xiao Wu) 小武 (Jia Zhangke, People's Republic of China/Hong Kong,
1998)

Xiaoshan Going Home (Xiaoshan huijia) 小山回家 (Jia Zhangke, People's Republic of
China, 1995)

Xue Pinggui and Wang Baochuan (Xue Pinggui yu Wang Baochuan) 薛平贵与王宝川
(He Jiming, Taiwan, 1954)

Yellow Earth (Huang tu di) 黄土地 (Chen Kaige, People's Republic of China, 1984)

Zhou Enlai (Zhou Enlai) 周恩来 (Ding Yinnan, People's Republic of China, 1992)

Zodiac Killers (Jidao zhuizong) 极道追踪 (Ann Hui, Hong Kong, 1991)

Chinese Glossary

COMPILED BY JING NIE

Selected Names and Terms

Chan Hung-chih (Zhan Hongzhi)
　詹宏志
Chan, Benny　陈木勝
Chan, Evans　陈耀成
Chan, Fruit　陈果
Chan, Gordon (Chen Jiashang)　陈嘉上
Chan, Jackie　成龙
Chan, Peter　陈可辛
Chang Che (Zhang Che)　张彻
Chang Chen (Zhang Zhen)　张震
Chang Yi (Zhang Yi)　张毅
Chang, Eileen (Zhang Ailing)　张爱玲
Chang, Sylvia (Zhang Aijia)　张艾嘉
Chen Kuo-fu (Chen Guofu)　陈国富
Cheng Jihua　程季华
Cheng Peipei　郑佩佩
Cheung, Cecilia　张柏芝
Cheung, Mabel　张婉婷
Cheung, Maggie　张曼玉
Chiao Hsiung-p'ing (Peggy Chiao/
　Jiao)　焦雄屏
Ching Siu-tung　程小东
Chow Yun-fat　周润发
Chow, Stephen　周星驰
Chu T'ien-wen (Zhu Tianwen)　朱天文
Dai Jinhua　戴锦华
Dai Sijie　戴思杰
Deng Lijun (Teresa Tang)　邓丽君
Ding Yinnan　丁荫楠

Fei Mu　费穆
Feng Feifei　凤飞飞
Feng Xiaogang　馮小剛
Gong Li　巩俐
Guan Dexing (Kwan Tak-hing)　关德兴
Han Ziyun　韩子云
He Qun　何群
Hou Hsiao-hsien (Hou Xiaoxian)　侯孝
　贤
Hou Yong　侯咏
Hsiao Sa (Xiao Sa)　萧飒
Hsin Hsiao-ch'i (Xin Xiaoqi)　辛晓琪
Hu Die　胡蝶
Hu Jinquan (King Hu)　胡金铨
Hu Jubin　胡菊彬
Hu Ke　胡克
Hu Peng　胡鹏
Huang Ch'un-ming (Huang
　Chunming)　黄春明
Huang Feihong (Wong Fei-hung)　黄飞
　鸿
Huang Jianxin　黄建新
Huang Shiren　黄世仁
Huang Wenying　黄文英
Huang Zuolin　黄佐临
Hui, Ann (Xu Anhua)　许鞍华
Hung, Sammo (Hong Jinbao)　洪金宝
Jia Lielei　贾磊磊
Jia Zhangke　贾章柯
Jiang Wen　姜文
Jiao Yulu　焦裕禄

Kaneshiro, Takeshi　金城武

Khoo, Eric　邱金海

Ko Yi-cheng (Ke Yizheng)　柯一正

Kong Fansen　孔繁森

Kwan, Stanley　关锦鹏

Lai, Leon　黎明

Lam, Ringo　林岭东

Lau Ka-leung　刘家良

Lau, Andy　刘德华

Law, Clara　罗卓瑶

Lee Chi Ngai　李志毅

Lee Kang (Li Gang)　李岗

Lee Kuan Yew　李光耀

Lee Ping-bing　李屏宾

Lee Teng-hui　李登辉

Lee, Ang　李安

Lee, Coco　李玟

Lei Gang　雷刚

Leung, Gigi　梁咏琪

Leung, Tony Chiu-wai　梁朝伟

Li Baotian　李保田

Li Cheuk-to　李焯桃

Li Hanxiang　李翰祥

Li Kang-sheng (Li Kangsheng)　李康生

Li T'ien-lu (Li Tianlu)　李天禄

Li Xing　李行

Li Xun　李迅

Li Yiming　李亦明

Li Youxin　李幼新

Li, Jet　李连杰

Liang Liang　梁良

Liao Qingsong　廖庆松

Lin Cheng-sheng　林正盛

Lin Daiyu　林黛玉

Lin Nien-tung (Lin Niantong)　林年同

Lin, Brigitte Ching-hsia (Lin Qingxia)　林青霞

Liu Sanjie　刘三姐

Liu Shaoqi　刘少奇

Liu Yichang　刘以鬯

Liu, Lucy　刘玉玲

Lu Hongshi　陆宏石

Lu Xuechang　陆学长

Lu Xun (Lu Hsun)　鲁迅

Lung Sihung　郎雄

Luo Yijun　罗艺军

Ma Liuming　马六明

Ma Xiaojun　马晓军

Mao Dun (Shen Yanbing)　茅盾　（沈雁冰）

Mei Lanfang　梅兰芳

Mei Shaowu　梅少武

Mok, Karen　莫文蔚

Mui, Anita　梅艳芳

Pai Ching-jui (Bai Jingrui)　白景瑞

Pai Hsien-yung (Bai Xianyong)　白先勇

Pau, Peter (Bao Dexi)　鲍德禧

Qi Lei　齐磊

Qi Longren　齐隆壬

Qiong Yao　琼瑶

Ren Fengtai　任丰泰

Ren Xianqi　任贤奇

Sek, Kei (Shi Qi)　石琪

Shen Congwen　沈从文

Shi Xiangsheng　施祥生

Shu Kei　舒琪

Shu Qi　舒淇

Shui Hua　水华

Sun Shiyi　孙师毅

Sun Yu　孙瑜

T'ao Te-ch'en (Tao Dechen)　陶德辰

Tan Dun　谭盾

Tan Xinpei　谭鑫培

Teo, Stephen　张建德

Tian Zhuangzhuang　田壮壮

To, Johnnie　杜琪峰

Ts'ai Chen-nan (Cai Zhennan)　蔡振南

Tsai Ming-liang　蔡明亮

Tseng Chuang-hsiang (Zeng Zhuangxiang)　曾壮祥

Tsui Hark　徐克

Wan Ren　万仁

Wang Chen-ho (Wang Zhenhe)　王祯和

Wang Hongwei　王宏伟

Wang Jixing　王冀邢

Wang Shuo　王朔

Wang T'ung (Wang Tong)　王童

Wang Xiaoshuai　王小帅
Wong Kar-wai　王家卫
Wong, Michael　王敏德
Woo, John　吴宇森
Wu Nien-chen (Wu Nianzhen)　吴念真
Wu Wenguang　吴文光
Wu Zuguang　吴祖光
Wu, Daniel　吴彦祖
Xi'er　喜儿
Xia Yan　夏衍
Xiao Ye　小野
Xie Jin　谢晋
Xie Tieli　谢铁骊
Yang Fan　杨凡
Yang Hui-shan (Yang Huishan)　杨惠珊
Yang, Edward　杨德昌
Yeoh, Michelle　杨紫琼
Yi Wen　易文
Yim, Ho　严浩
Yip, Tim　叶锦添
Yu K'an-p'ing (Yu Kanping)　虞戡平
Yuen Woo-ping　袁和平
Yuen, Corey (Yuen Kuei)　元奎
Yungu　云姑
Zhang Changyan　张昌彦
Zhang Shichuan　张石川
Zhang Yimou　张艺谋
Zhang Yuan　张元
Zhang Ziyi　章子怡
Zheng Zhengqiu　郑正秋
Zhong Dafeng　钟大丰

Selected Terms

baxi　把戏
chuanchang ren (ch'uan-ch'ang jen)　串场人
chujian chubao, jiuliang jipin　除奸除暴，就良济贫
Daguanlou　大观楼
dan　旦
Dangdai dianying　《当代电影》
datong　大同
dazhong wenhua baquan shidai　大众文化霸权时代

Deshengmen　得胜门
dianguang yingxi　电光影戏
Dianshizhai huabao　《点石斋画报》
dianxing　典型
dianying　电影
Dianying huabiao jiang　电影华表奖
Dianying yishu　《电影艺术》
Dianying yuebao　《电影月报》
dixia dianying　地下电影
dongzuo　动作
Duidao　《对倒》
duixiang　对象
fan hou pai　反候派
feikexuede　非科学的
feilü feima　非驴非马
feixia　飞侠
Fengshen bang　《封神榜》
Fenyang　汾阳
gongfupian　功夫片
guaixia　怪侠
guanfang daoyan　官方导演
guopian　国片
Gusu xing　姑苏行
guzhuangpian　古装片
guzhuangxi　古装戏
Honglou meng　《红楼梦》
hsiang-tu wen-hsueh (xiangtu wenxue)　乡土文学
huangmeidiao　黄梅调
huangminhua　皇民化
huanyuan wutai, gaoyu wutai　还原舞台，高于舞台
huayu dianying　华语电影
huichun　回春
huodong yinghua　活动影画
huodong yingxi　活动影戏
huoshao　火烧
Jiang Qing　江青
jiankang xieshi zhuyi　健康写实主义
jieding　接顶
jin, da, ming　近，大，明
Jinggang Shan　井冈山
jingjuhua　京剧化
jingtai meixue　静态美学

jinguo yingxiong　巾国英雄

ju　剧

kanke　看客

kejiao xingguo　科教兴国

kunqu　昆曲

Kuomingtang (Guomingdang)　国民党

la yangpian　拉洋片

laba ku　喇叭裤

laodong renmin　劳动人民

liangxiang　亮相

lianpu　脸谱

liubai　留白

maxi　马戏

Mingxing Company　明星公司

mingxing　明星

mingzi　名字

minzu xingshi　民族形式

minzhu nüshen　民主女神

mofan qiyejia　模范企业家

Nanfang zhoumo　《南方周末》

Nanyang　南洋

Nanzhan　南站

Ne Zha　哪吒

niezhong　孽种

nü　女

nüxia　女侠

Pingyao　平窑

pinyin　拼音

qi　气

qiguan　奇观

qing　情

renxia haoyi　仁侠好义

san tiejin　三贴近

san tuchu　三突出

shengsi hetong　生死合同

shenguai　神怪

Shijie ribao　《世界日报》

shijue yundong　视觉运动

sixiang jiefang　思想解放

Taiwan hsin-tien-ying (Taiwan xindianying)　台湾新电影

Tang Sanzang　唐三藏

Tianyi　天一

tongsuhua　通俗化

tu　土

wanyi'er　玩意儿

weixinde　唯心的

wenmingxi　文明戏

Wo de zuguo　《我的祖国》

wu　武

wudao　舞蹈

wudapian　武打片

wushengxi　武生戏

wushu　武术

wuxia pian　武侠片

wuxia shenguai pian　武侠神怪片

xi　戏

xia　侠

Xia Yan dianying wenxue jiang　夏衍电影文学奖

xiahun　侠魂

xiake　侠客

Xibei　西北

Xidan　西单

xieyi　写意

xifa　戏法

Xijubao　《戏剧报》

xindianying zhi si　新电影之死

xingfen ji　兴奋剂

xingxia　行侠

Xinjiang　新疆

xinqi　新奇

xinyu　心雨

xiqu fengwei dianying　戏曲风味电影

xiqupian　戏曲片

xiwang gongcheng　希望工程

xiyang yingxi　西洋影戏

Xiyou ji　《西游记》

xuanji　玄机

xuechang yangbanxi　学唱样板戏

Xunqing (hsün-ching)　殉情

yanda　严打

yang　洋

yangbanxi　样板戏

yangge　秧歌

ying　影

Yingshi wenhua　《影视文化》

yingxi 影戏
Yingxi shenghuo 《影戏生活》
Yingxi zazhi 《影戏杂志》
yingxizhe, xi ye 影戏者，戏也
yong hou pai 拥侯派
youfu tongxiang 有福同享
Youmin 游民
youxiu daoyan jiang 优秀导演奖
Yuan Shikai 袁世凯
yuan, xiao, hei 远，小，黑
Yu-ch'ing sao (Yuqing sao) 玉卿嫂
Yuetan 月坛

Yugong yi shan 愚公移山
yunkuai jianjiefa 云块剪接法
zaji 杂技
Zhang Yimou shenhua 张艺谋神话
Zhongguo dianying huabiao jiang 中国
    电影华表奖
Zhuguang gongcheng 烛光工程
zhuren 主人
zhuzhong jiu daode, jiu lunli 注重旧道
    德，旧伦理
Zouchu Beiqing 走出悲情

Bibliography

COMPILED BY JING NIE

Most references cited in the volume are listed below. Pinyin is used for most Chinese material.

Abe, Mark Nornes, and Yeh Yueh-yu. "Narrating National Sadness: Cinematic Mapping and Hypertextual Dispersion." 1998 [http://cinemaspace.berkeley.edu/Papers/CityOfSadness/table.html].

Altman, Rick. "An Introduction to the Theory of Genre Analysis." *American Film Musical,* 1–9. Bloomington: Indiana University Press, 1987.

Anderson, Benedict. *Imagined Communities.* New York: Verso, 1991.

Andrew, Dudley. "The 'Three Ages' of Cinema Studies and the Age to Come." *PMLA* 115.3 (May 2000): 341–351.

Ang, Ien. "Can One Say No to Chineseness? Pushing the Limits of the Diasporic Paradigm." *boundary 2* 25 (fall 1998): 223–242.

———. "On Not Speaking Chinese," *New Formations* 24 (winter 1994): 1–18.

———. "To Be or Not to Be Chinese: Diaspora, Culture, and Postmodern Ethnicity." *Southeast Asian Journal of Social Science* 21 (1993): 1–19.

Appadurai, Arjun. *Modernity at Large: Cultural Dimensions of Globalization.* Minneapolis: University of Minnesota Press, 1996

Ashcroft, Bill, Gareth Griffiths, and Helen Tiffin, eds. *The Post-Colonial Studies Reader.* London: Routledge, 1995.

Bai, Jingshen. "Throw Away the Walking Stick of Drama." In *Chinese Film Theory: A Guide to a New Era,* edited by George S. Semsel, Xia Hong, and Hou Jianping. Translated by Hou Jianping, Li Xiaohong, and Fan Yuan, 5–9. New York: Praeger, 1990.

Barmé, Geremie R. *In the Red: On Contemporary Chinese Culture.* New York: Columbia University Press, 1999.

———. "Persistence de la tradition au 'royaume des ombres,' Quelques notes visant à contribuer à une approche nouvelle du cinéma chinoise." In *Le Cinéma Chinois,* 113. Paris: Catalogue of Centre Georges Pompidou, Chinese Film Retrospective, 1985.

Bausinger, Hermann. *Folk Culture in a World of Technology.* Translated by Elke Dettmer. Bloomington: Indiana University Press, 1990.

Bazin, Andre. "The Ontology of the Photographic Image." In *What is Cinema?* Vol. 1. Translated by Hugh Gray, 9–16. Berkeley: University of California Press, 1967.

Beijing qingnian bao. "Killer: *chongxin renshi Meiguo dapian*" (Killer: re-understanding American blockbusters). *Beijing qingnian bao* (Beijing youth daily). May 19, 1999.

Belden, Jack. *China Shakes the World.* New York: Monthly Review Press, 1970.

Benjamin, Walter. "Theses on the Philosophy of History." In *Illuminations,* edited by Hannah Arendt, 261–262. New York: Harcourt, Brace & World, 1968.

Berry, Chris. "Staging Gay Life in China: Zhang Yuan and *East Palace, West Palace.*" *Jump Cut* 41 (1998): 84–89.

———. "Sexual Difference and the Viewing Subject in *Li Shuangshuang* and *The In-Laws.*" In *Perspectives on Chinese Cinema,* edited by Chris Berry, 33–37. London: British Film Institute, 1991.

Berry, Chris, ed. *Perspectives on Chinese Cinema.* London: British Film Institute, 1991.

Berry, Chris, and Mary Farquhar. "From National Cinemas to Cinema and the National: Rethinking the National in Transnational Chinese Cinemas." *Journal of Modern Literature in Chinese* 4.2 (January 2001): 109–122.

Bhabha, Homi. *The Location of Culture.* London: Routledge, 1994.

Bhaskar, Roy. *Reclaiming Reality: A Critical Introduction to Contemporary Philosophy.* London: Verso, 1989.

Birch, David. *Singapore Media: Communication Strategies and Practices.* Melbourne: Longman Cheshire, 1993.

Bluestone, George. *Novels into Film.* Berkeley: University of California Press. 1973.

Boelhower, William. "Enchanted Sites." In *Postcolonialism and Autobiography: Michelle Cliff, David Dabydeen, Opal Palmer Adisa,* edited by A. Hornung and E. Ruhe, 115–134.Amsterdam: Rodopi, 1998.

Boniface, Priscilla, and Peter J. Fowler. *Heritage and Tourism in the Global Village.* London: Routledge, 1993.

Bordwell, David. "Intensified Continuity: Visual Style in Contemporary American Film," *Film Quarterly* 55.3 (spring 2002): 16–28.

———. "Hong Kong Martial Arts Cinema." In *Crouching Tiger, Hidden Dragon: A Portrait of the Ang Lee Film,* edited by Linda Sunshine, 14–21. New York: New Market Press, 2000.

———. *Planet Hong Kong: Popular Cinema and the Art of Entertainment.* Cambridge, Mass.: Harvard University Press, 2000.

———. "Aesthetics in Action: Kung Fu, Gunplay, and Cinematic Expressivity." In *Fifty Years of Electric Shadows,* edited by Law Kar, 81–89. Hong Kong: Urban Council/ Hong Kong International Film Festival, 1997.

———. *On the History of Film Style.* Cambridge, Mass.: Harvard University Press, 1997.

———. *The Cinema of Eisenstein.* Cambridge, Mass.: Harvard University Press, 1993.

———. *Making Meaning: Inference and Rhetoric in the Interpretation of Cinema.* Cambridge, Mass.: Harvard University Press, 1989.

———. *Ozu and the Poetics of Cinema.* Princeton, N.J.: Princeton University Press, 1988.

———. *Narration in the Fiction Film.* Madison: University of Wisconsin Press, 1985.

Bordwell, David, Janet Staiger, and Kristin Thompson. *The Classical Hollywood Cin-*

ema: Film Style and Mode of Production to 1960. New York: Columbia University Press, 1985.

Bordwell, David, and Noel Carroll, eds. *Post-Theory: Reconstructing Film Studies.* Madison: University of Wisconsin Press, 1996.

Boym, Svetlana. *The Future of Nostalgia.* New York: Basic Books, 2001.

Browne, Nick, Paul G. Pickowicz, Vivian Sobchack, and Esther Yau, eds. *New Chinese Cinemas: Forms, Identities, Politics.* Cambridge: Cambridge University Press, 1994.

Burdeau, Emmanuel. *"Les aleas de l'indirect": Hou Hsiao-hsien.* Paris: Cahiers du cinema, 1999.

Burkman, Thomas W. "Nitobe Inazo: From World Order to Regional Order." In *Culture and Identity: Japanese Intellectuals During the Interwar Years,* edited by J. Thomas Rimer, 191–216. Princeton, N.J.: Princeton University Press, 1990.

Calinescu, Matei. *Five Faces of Modernity: Modernism, Avant-Garde, Decadence, Kitsch, Postmodernism.* Durham, N.C.: Duke University Press, 1987.

Carter, Paul. "The Road to Botany Bay." Reprinted in Bill Ashcroft, Gareth Griffiths, and Helen Tiffin, eds. *The Post-Colonial Studies Reader.* London: Routledge, 1995.

Césaire, Aimé. *Discourse on Colonialis.* Translated by Joan Pinkham. New York: Monthly Review Press, 1972.

Chang, Sung-sheng Yvonne. *Modernism and the Nativist Resistance.* Durham, N.C.: Duke University Press, 1993.

Cheah, Pheng. "Spectral Nationality: The Living On [*sur-vie*] of the Postcolonial Nation in Neocolonial Globalization." *boundary 2* 26 (fall 1999): 252.

———. "Given Culture: Rethinking Cosmopolitical Freedom in Transnationalism." *boundary 2* 24 (summer 1997): 173.

Cheah, Philip. "Singapore Shorts." *Cinemaya.* 28–29 (1995): 30–31.

———. *Cinemaya* 30 (1995): 25.

Chen, Bing. *"Zhongguo dianying huahiao jiang, Xia Yan dianying wenxue jiang jinwan banjiang"* (Tonight: the ceremony for the China Obelisk Film Awards and Xia Yan Film Literature Awards). *Beijing wanbao* (Beijing evening news) May 20, 1999.

Chen, Mo. *Zhang Yimou dianying lun* (The film art of Zhang Yimou). Beijing: Zhongguo dianying chubanshe. 1995.

Chen, Xihe. "Shadowplay: Chinese Film Aesthetics and Their Philosophical and Cultural Fundamentals." In *Chinese Film Theory: A Guide to the New Era,* edited by George S. Semsel, Xia Hong and Hou Jianping. Translated by Hou Jianping, Li Xiaohong and Fan Yuan, 192–204. New York: Praeger, 1990.

Chen, Zhiqing. *"Duiyu shizhi guzhuang yingpianzhi yijian"* (My views on making costume films). In *Zhongguo wusheng dianying* (Chinese silent film), edited by Zhongguo Dianying Ziliaoguan (Chinese Film Archives), 639–642. Beijing: Zhongguo dianying chubanshe, 1996.

Chen, Pauline. "*Crouching Tiger, Hidden Dragon*" (film review). *Cineaste* 26.4 (fall 2001): 71–72.

Cheng, Jihua, ed. *Zhongguo dianying fazhanshi, shang* (A history of the development of Chinese cinema). Vol. 1. Beijing: Zhongguo dianying chubanshe, 1981.

Chiao, Hsiung-ping (Peggy Chiao) (Jiao Xiongping). "Autobiographical Masterpiece." *Free China Review* (February 1988): 33–35.

———. "*Yuqing sao*: xing de jidian" (*Jade Love*: rite of sex). In *Taiwan xin dianying* (Taiwan New Cinema), edited by Chiao Hsiung-ping, 172–175. Taipei: Shibao chuban gongsi, 1988.

———. "Great Changes in a Vast Ocean: Neither Tragedy nor Joy." Interview with Hou Hsiao-hsien in *Taiwan Films*, edited by Zhang Changyan, 3–60. Taipei: Variety, 1993.

Childs, Peter, and Patrick Williams. *An Introduction to Post-Colonial Theory.* Upper Saddle River, N.J.: Prentice Hall, 1997.

Ching, Leo. "Imaginings in the Empire of the Sun." In *Asia/Pacific as Space of Cultural Production,* edited by Rob Wilson and Arif Dirlik. Durham, N.C.: Duke Unversity Press, 1995.

Chou, Wan-yao. "The Kominka Movement in Taiwan and Korea: Comparisons and Intepretations." In *The Japanese Wartime Empire, 1931–1945,* edited by Peter Duus et al., 40–68. Princeton, N.J.: Princeton University Press, 1996.

Chow, Rey. "Nostalgia of the New Wave: Structure in Wong Kar-wai's *Happy Together.*" *Camera Obscura* 42 (September 1999). Reprinted in *Keyframes: Popular Cinema and Cultural Studies,* edited by Mathew Tinkcom and Amy Villarejo, 228–240. London: Routledge, 2001.

———. "Introduction: On Chineseness as Theoretical Problem." *boundary 2* 25 (fall 1998): 1–24.

Chu, Yiu Wai. "Who Am I? Postcolonial Hong Kong Cinema in the Age of Global Capitalism." In *Between Home and World: A Reader in Hong Kong Cinema,* edited by Esther Cheung and Chu Yiu Wai, 39–58. Hong Kong: Oxford University Press, 2003.

———. "*Quanqiuhua dushi di bentu shenhua: Bolijicheng di Xianggang tuxiang*" (A local myth in a global city: the "Hong Kong" in *City of Glass*). *Chung-wai Literary Monthly* 28 (April 2000): 40–53.

Chua, Beng-Huat. "'Asian Values' Discourse and the Resurrection of the Social." *positions* 7.2 (1999): 573–592.

———. "Culture, Multiracialism, and National Identity in Singapore." In *Trajectories: Inter-Asia Cultural Studies,* edited by Chen Kuan-Hsing, 186. London: Routledge, 1998.

Chua, Siew Keng. "*Song of the Exile*: The Politics of 'Home.'" *Jump Cut* 42 (1998): 90–93.

Chute, David. "Beyond the Law: Independent Films from China." *Film Comment* 30 (January –February 1994): 60–63.

Ciecko, Anne T., and Sheldon H. Lu. "The Heroic Trio: Anita Mui, Maggie Cheung, Michelle Yeoh—Self-Reflexivity and the Globalization of the Hong Kong Action Heroine." *Post Script* 19.1 (fall 1999): 70–86.

Cook, Pam, and Philip Dodd, eds. *Women and Film: A Sight and Sound Reader.* Philadelphia: Temple University Press, 1993.

Dai, Jinhua. "*Wuzhong fengjing*" (Preliminary reading of the sixth-generation film directors). *Tianya* 1 (1996): 1–13.

———. "*Xinsheng dai dianying yanjiu*" (Film research on the new generation). *Beijing dianying xueyuan xuebao* (Journal of the Beijing Film Academy) 1 (1995): 100–203.

————. "On Reading Xia Yan's *Problems of Screenwriting.*" In *Film in Contemporary China, Critical Debates, 1979–1989,* edited by George S. Semsel, Chen Xihe, and Xia Hong, 75–84. Westport, Conn.: Praeger, 1993.

Davis, Darrell W. "A New Taiwan Person: Questions for Wu Nien-chen." *positions: east asia cultures critique* 11.3 (winter 2003): 717–734.

————. *Picturing Japaneseness: Monumental Style, National Identity, Japanese Film.* New York: Columbia University Press, 1996.

De Certeau, Michel. *The Practice of Everyday Life.* Berkeley: University of California Press, 1984.

De Lauretis, Teresa. *Alice Doesn't: Feminism, Semiotics, Cinema.* Bloomington: Indiana University Press, 1984.

DeMarr, Mary Jean, and Jane S. Bakerman. *The Adolescent in the American Novel since 1960.* New York: Ungar, 1986.

Desser, David. "The Kung Fu Craze." In *The Cinema of Hong Kong: History, Arts, Identity,* edited by Poshek Fu and David Desser, 19–43. New York: Cambridge Univeristy Press, 2000.

Directors' Dossier: Wu Nianzhen. Taipei: Golden Horse Film Festival, 1992.

Dirlik, Arif. *The Postcolonial Aura: Third World Criticism in the Age of Global Capitalism.* Boulder, Col.: Westview, 1997.

Dirlik, Arif, and Xudong Zhang, eds. *Postmodernism and China. boundary 2* 24.3 (fall 1997).

Ditmer, Lowell. "Radical Ideology and Chinese Political Culture: An Analysis of the Revolutionary *yangbanxi.*" In *Moral Behaviour in Chinese Society,* edited by Richard Wilson, Sidney Greenblatt, and Amy Wilson, 126–151. New York: Praeger, 1981.

Dolar, Mlader. "Hitchcock's Objects." In *Everything You Always Wanted to Know about Lacan (But Were Afraid to Ask Hitchcock),* edited by Slavoj Žižck, 31–46. New York: Verso, 1992.

Dou, Ying. "*Shenguai ju zhi wo jian*" (My opinion on the magic-spirit film) [1927]. In *Zhongguo wusheng dianying* (Chinese silent film), edited by Zhongguo Dianying Ziliaoguan (Chinese Film Archives), 662–665. Beijing: Zhongguo dianying chubanshe, 1996.

E, Chang. "*Guzhuangpian zhong zhi yin zhuyi zhe*" (Things to consider in the classical costume drama). In *Zhongguo wusheng dianying,* 653–654. Beijing: Zhongguo dianying chubanshe, [1927] 1996.

Eberhard, Wolfram. *A Dictionary of Chinese Symbols: Hidden Symbols in Chinese Life and Thought.* Translated by G. L. Campbell. London: Routledge, 1986.

Edwards, Tim. *Erotics & Politics: Gay Male Sexuality, Masculinity and Feminism.* London: Routledge, 1994.

Eisenstein, Sergei, and Sergei Tretyakov. "Expressive Movement." *Millennium Film Journal* 3 (winter/spring 1979) [originally published 1923].

Eliot, T. S. *The Waste Land and Other Poems.* New York: First Signet Classic, 1998.

Elley, Derek. "Asia to 'Tiger': kung-fooey—Asia's slouching tiger: 'Hidden' draggin.'" *Variety* (February 5–11, 2001): 1, 85.

Elsaesser, Thomas. "Cinema Futures: Convergence, Divergence, Difference." In *Cinema Futures: Cain, Abel or Cable?* edited by Thomas Elsaesser and Kay Hoffman, 9–26. Amsterdam: Amsterdam University Press, 1998.

———. "Specularity and Engulfment: Francis Ford Coppola and *Bram Stoker's Dracula*." In *Contemporary Hollywood Cinema*, edited by Steve Neale and Murray Smith, 191–208. London: Routledge, 1998.

———. "General Introduction, Early Cinema: From Linear History to Mass Media Archaeology." In *Early Cinema*, edited by Thomas Elsaesser with Adam Barker, 1–8. London: British Film Institute, 1990.

———. "The Institution Cinema: Introduction." In *Early Cinema*, edited by Thomas Elsaesser, with Adam Barker, 153–173. London: British Film Institute, 1990.

Elsaesser, Thomas, with Adam Barker, eds. *Early Cinema: Space Frame Narrative.* London: British Film Institute, 1990.

Enloe, Cynthia. *Bananas, Beaches, and Bases: Making Feminist Sense of International Politics.* Berkeley: University of California Press, 1990.

Erens, Patricia Brett. "The Film Work of Ann Hui." In *The Cinema of Hong Kong: History, Arts, Identity,* edited by Poshek Fu and David Desser, 176–195. Cambridge: Cambridge University Press.

Fallaci, Orana. Interview with Deng Xiaoping. *Washington Post* (August 31, 1980).

Fan, Dainian. *"Dui 'Wusi' Xinwenhua yundongde zhexue fansi—ji ershi niandai chu de kexue yu renshenguan da lunzhan"* (A philosophical reflection on the May Fourth New Culture movement—on the great debate on science and the view of life in early twentieth century). In *Kexue shi lunji* (An anthology on the history of science), edited by Fang Lizhi, 255–276. Hefei: Zhongguo kexue jishu daxue chubanshe, 1987.

Fan, Xuepeng. *"Wo de yinmu shenghuo de huiyi"* (Remembering my life on the silver screen) [1956]. In *Zhongguo wusheng dianying,* edited by Zhongguo Dianying Ziliaoguan (Chinese Film Archives), 1475–1483. Beijing: Zhongguo dianying chubanshe, 1996.

Featherstone, Mike. *Undoing Culture: Globalization, Postmodernism and Identity.* London: Sage, 1995.

Fei, Faye Chunfang. "Huang Zuolin: China's Man of the Theater." Ph.D diss., City University of New York, 1991.

Fore, Steve. "Introduction: Hong Kong Movies, Critical Time Warps, and Shapes of Things to Come." *Post Script* 19.1 (fall 1999): 2–9.

———. "Jackie Chan and the Cultural Dynamics of Global Entertainment." In *Transnational Chinese Cinemas: Identity, Nationhood, Gender,* edited by Sheldon H. Lu, 239–262. Honolulu: University of Hawai`i Press, 1997.

Foster, Hal. *The Return of the Real: The Avant-Garde at the End of the Century.* Cambridge, Mass.: MIT Press, 1996.

Foucault, Michel. *Discipline and Punish: The Birth of the Prison.* Translated by Alan Sheridan. New York: Vintage, 1979.

Frodon, Jean-Michel. "En haut du mangueire de Fengshan, immerge dans l'espace et le temps." *Hou Hsiao-hsien.* Paris: Cahiers du cinema, 1999.

———. "Pas un de moins: un Lion d'or à l'ombre des grandes puissances" (*Not One Less*: a Golden Lion in the shadows of superpowers). *Le Monde*, November 3, 1999.

Fu, Poshek. "Going Global: The Transnational Cinema of the Shaw Brothers Studio, 1960–1970." In *Border Crossings in Hong Kong Cinema*, Twenty-Fourth Hong Kong International Film Festival, 43–51. Hong Kong: Leisure and Cultural Services Department, 2000.

Fumiko, Suzuki. *"Eiga de aruku tai-wan"* (Film walks in Taiwan). In *Hou Hsiao-hsien*. Tokyo: Asahi Shimbun, 1993.

Gandhi, Leela. *Postcolonial Theory: A Critical Introduction.* New York: Columbia University Press, 1998.

Gann, Lewis H. "Western and Japanese Colonialism: Some Preliminary Comparisons." In *The Japanese Colonial Empire, 1895–1945*, edited by R. Myers and Mark Peattie, 497–525. Princeton, N.J.: Princeton University Press, 1984.

Gao, Minglu, ed. *Inside Out: New Chinese Art.* Berkeley: University of California Press, 1999.

Gaskell, Katia. "To Get Reality, Forget Reality: China's Bad-Boy Filmmaker Zhang Yuan." *Beijing Scene* 7.5 (February 18–24, 2000). [Available at http://beijingscene.com.]

Ge, Dawei. *"Kancheng yingzhan Zhang Yimou yige dou bu canjia"* (Zhang Yimou does not participate in the Cannes festival with any film). *Shijieribao* (World journal), April 26, 1999, C6.

Giddens, Anthony. *The Consequences of Modernity.* Stanford, Calif.: Stanford University Press, 1990.

Gilmore, Leigh. *Autobiographics: A Feminist Theory of Women's Self-Representation.* Ithaca, N.Y.: Cornell University Press, 1994.

Gledhill, Christine, and Linda Williams, eds. *Reinventing Film Studies.* London: Arnold; New York: Oxford University Press, 2000.

Gong, Tong. *"Wuhu huoshao"* (Apropos burning). *Yingxi shenghuo* (Movie Weekly) 1.7 (1931).

Gunning, Tom. "The Cinema of Attraction: Early Film, Its Spectator and the Avant-Garde." In *Early Cinema: Space Frame Narrative*, edited by Thomas Elsaesser and Adam Barker, 56–62. London: British Film Institute, 1990.

———. "Early American Cinema." In *The Oxford Guide to Film Studies*, edited by John Hill and Pamela Church Gibson, 255–258. Oxford: Oxford University Press: 1998.

Guojia dianying ziliaoguan koushi dianyingshi xiaozu (Oral Cinema History Unit, Taipei Film Archive). *Taiyupian shidai, 1* (The era of Taiwanese-language films, vol. 1). Taiwan Cinema History Series No. 3. Taipei: Guojia dianying ziliaoguan, 1994.

Hall, Stuart. "Cultural Identity and Cinematic Representation." *Framework* 36 (1989): 68–81.

Hansen, Miriam Bratu. "Fallen Women, Rising Stars, New Horizons: Shanghai Silent Film as Vernacular Modernism." *Film Quarterly* 54.1 (2000): 10–22.

———. "The Mass Production of the Senses: Classical Cinema as Vernacular Modernism." In *Reinventing Film Studies*, edited by Christine Gledhill and Linda Williams, 332–350. New York: Oxford University Press, 2000.

Haraway, Donna. "A Cyborg Manifesto: Science, Technology, and Socialist-Feminism in the Late Twentieth Century." In Donna Haraway, *Simians, Cyborgs, and Women: The Reinvention of Nature*, 149–182. London: Free Association Books, 1991.

Harootunian, H. D. "Disciplining Native Knowledge and Producing Place: Yanagita

Kunio, Origuchi Shinobu, Takata Yasuma." In *Culture and Identity*, edited by J. Thomas Rimer, 99–127. Princeton, N.J.: Princeton University Press, 1990.

Harvey, David. *The Condition of Postmodernity: An Inquiry into the Origins of Cultural Change*. Cambridge, Mass.: Blackwell, 1990.

Hasumi Shigehiko. *"Kaoguxue de huanghu: hou hsiao-hsien de beiqing chengshi"* (An oblivion of archaeology: on Hou Hsiao-hsien's *City of Sadness*). Translated by Zhang Changyan. *Film Appreciation* 13.1 (1995): 80–87.

Havis, Richard J. Interview with Lin, Cheng-sheng. *An Interview with the Taiwan Film Centre* [http://www.filmfestivals.com/cannes97/cfilmc21.htm].

He, Xiujun. *"Zhang Shichuan he Mingxing yingpian gongsi"* (Zhang Shichuan and the Mingxing film company). *Wenshi ziliao xuanji* (An anthology of research material on cultural history). Beijing: Zhonghua shuju, 1980.

Hertzberg, Hendrik. "A Tale of Two Cubas." *New Yorker* 17 (April 2000): 33.

Hill, John, and Pamela Church Gibson, eds. *World Cinema: Critical Approaches*. Oxford University Press, 2000.

———. *The Oxford Guide to Film Studies*. London: Arnold; New York: Oxford University Press, 1998.

Hjort, Mette, and Scott MacKenzie, eds. *Cinema and Nation*. London: Routledge, 2000.

Hoberman, J. "Film: New Dawn Fades." *Village Voice* (March 26–April 1, 2003) [http://www.villagevoice.com].

———. "Hou Hsiao-hsien: The Edge of the World." In J. Hoberman, *Vulgar Modernism: Writing on Movies and Other Media*, 104–107. Philadelphia: Temple University Press, 1991.

Holm, David. *Art and Ideology in Revolutionary China*. Oxford: Clarendon Press, 1991.

Hong Kong Cinema Retrospective Catalogue: Border Crossings in Hong Kong Cinema. Hong Kong: Leisure and Cultural Services Department, 2000.

Hong Kong Provisional Urban Council, ed. *Twenty-Third Hong Kong International Film Festival Main Catalogue*. Hong Kong: Hong Kong Provisional Urban Council, 1999.

———, ed. *Twenty-Fourth Hong Kong International Film Festival Programme*. Hong Kong: Hong Kong Provisional Urban Council, 2000.

Hsieh, Shih-chung. "Tourism, Formulation of Cultural Tradition, and Ethnicity: A Study of the *Daiyan* Identity of the Wulai Atayal." In *Cultural Change in Postwar Taiwan*, edited by S. Harrell and Huang Chun-chieh, 184–202. Taipei: SMC Publishing, 1994.

Hu, Ke. "Hong Kong Cinema in the Chinese Mainland (1949–1979)." *Hong Kong Cinema Retrospective—Border Crossings in Hong Kong Cinema (Xianggang dianying huigu zhuanti—kuajiede Xianggang dianying)*. Twenty-Fourth Hong Kong International Film Festival. Hong Kong: Leisure and Culture Services Department, 2000.

Huang, Wenying, and Cao Zhiwei. *Haishang fanhua lu* (Notes on the making of *Flowers of Shanghai*). Taipei: Yuan-liou, 1998.

Huang, Zhiming, ed. "Director's Note." Homepage of *Tempting Heart* http://wanita.net/temptingheart.

Huang, Zuolin. "Mei Lanfang, Stanislavsky, Brecht—A Study in Contrasts." In *Peking*

Opera and Mei Lanfang, edited by Wu Zuguang, Huang Zuolin and Mei Shaowu, 14–29. Beijing: New World Press, 1981.

Hui, Wen. *"Zhang Yimou suipian xuanchuan, Shenzhen tebie pengchang"* (Zhang Yimou promotes and travels with his film, and wins special applause in Shenzhen). *Shijie ribao.* November 5, 1999: C6.

Interview with Ann Hui. *City Entertainment* 521 (April 1999).

Interview with Lin Cheng-sheng. *Tales of Cities: Transformation through Camera Eyes.* Chinese Film showcase [www.amamedia.org/movies/showcase/02showcase/betelnut_beauty.html].

Interview with Mabel Cheung and Alex Law. *City Entertainment* 510 (October 1998).

Jameson, Fredric. *Postmodernism, or, The Cultural Logic of Late Capitalism.* Durham, N.C.: Duke University Press, 1991.

———. "Postmodernism and Consumer Society." In *The Anti-Aesthetic: Essays on Postmodern Culture,* edited by Hal Foster, 111–125. Port Townsend, Wash.: Bay Press, 1993.

———. "Remapping Taipei." In *New Chinese Cinemas: Forms, Identities, Politics,* edited by Nick Browne, Paul G. Pickowicz, Vivian Sobchack, and Esther Yau, 117–150. Cambridge: Cambridge University Press, 1994.

Jansen, Marius B. "Japanese Imperialism: Late Meiji Perspectives." In *The Japanese Colonial Empire,* edited by R. Myers and Mark Peattie, 61–79. Princeton, N.J.: Princeton University Press, 1984.

Jarman, Robert L. ed. *Taiwan: Political and Economic Reports, 1861–1960.* Vol. 1. Slough, U.K.: Archive Editions, 1997.

"Jia Zhangke: Pickpocket Director." In *Beijing Scene* 5.23 (1999) [www.beijingscene.com].

Jiang, Wen. *Yibu dianying de dansheng* (The birth of a film). Beijing: Huayi chubanshe, 1997.

Jin, Taipu. *"Shenguaipian chajin hou: jinhou de dianyingjie xiang nali zou?"* (After the censoring of the magic-spirit film: where is the film world heading?) *Yingxi shenghuo* 1.32 (1931): 1–4.

Johnson, Marshall. "Making Time: Historic Preservation and the Space of Nationality." *positions: east asia cultures critique* 2.2 (1994).

Johnston, Claire. "Women's Cinema as Counter Cinema." *Notes on Women's Cinema.* British Film Institute pamphlet, 1973.

Jones, Amelia, and Andrew Stephenson. *Performing the Body/Performing the Text.* London: Routledge, 1999.

Jones, Kent. "Cinema with a Roof over Its Head." *Film Comment* (September/October 1999) [www.filmlinc.com/archive/fcm/9-10-99/hou.html].

Kaminsky, Stuart, and Jeffrey Mahan. *American Television Genres.* Chicago: Nelson-Hall, 1986.

Keiji, Nishitani. *Religion and Nothingness.* Translated by Jan van Bragt. Berkeley: University of California Press, 1982.

Kerr, George. *Formosa: Licensed Revolution and the Home Rule Movement, 1898–1945.* Honolulu: University Press of Hawai`i, 1974.

Keshvani, Nazir. *Twelve Storeys* [film review]. *Cinemaya* 35 (1997): 26–28.

Kirshenblatt-Gimblett, Barbara. *Destination Culture: Tourism, Museums, and Heritage.* Berkeley: University of California Press, 1998.

Kracauer, Siegfried. *From Caligari to Hitler: A Psychological History of the German Film.* Princeton, N.J.: Princeton University Press, 1947.

Kratoska, Paul. *The Japanese Occupation of Malaya.* London: Hurst, 1998.

Kraus, Richard Curt. *Pianos and Politics in China: Middle-Class Ambitions and the Struggle over Western Music.* New York: Oxford University Press, 1989.

Kwong, Po-wai, ed. *Xu anhua shuo xu anhua* (Ann Hui on Ann Hui). Hong Kong: Hongye chubanshe, 1998.

Lai, T. C. *Understanding Chinese Painting.* Hong Kong: Kelly & Walsh, 1980.

Lacan, Jacques. *Ecrits: A Selection.* Translated by Alan Sheridan. New York: W. W. Norton, 1977.

Landler, Mark. "Lee's 'Tiger,' Celebrated Everywhere But at Home." *New York Times* (February 27, 2001): B1, B2.

Lau, Shing-hon. "Three Interviews." *A Study of the Hong Kong Swordplay Film (1945–1980).* The Fifth Hong Kong International Film Festival. Hong Kong: Urban Council, 1981.

Lau, Jenny Kwok Wah. "Globalization and Youthful Subculture: The Chinese Sixth-Generation Films at the Dawn of the New Century." In *Multiple Modernities: Cinemas and Popular Media in Transcultural East Asia,* edited by Jenny Kwok Wah Lau, 13–27. Philadelphia: Temple University Press, 2002.

Lazere, Arthur. *The River* [film review] [www.culturevulture.net].

Lee, Kang. *Youdian ganxing yu bushi lixing* (A bit of sensibility, yet not insensible). Taipei: Yuanliu, 1996.

———. *Zhang Aijia dianying: jintian bu huijia* (A Sylvia Chang movie: today nobody goes home). Taipei: Yuanliu, 1996.

Lee, Kevin. "Jia Zhangke" [www.sensesofcinema.com].

Lee, Tain-Dow, ed. *Dangdai huayu dianying lunshu* (Studies in contemporary Chinese-language film). Taipei: Shibao wenhua chuban gongsi, 1996.

Lee, Leo Ou-fan. *Shanghai Modern: The Flowering of a New Urban Culture in China, 1930–1945.* Cambridge, Mass.: Harvard University Press, 1999.

Lee, Michael. "Dead Man Gazing: Posthumous Voyeurism in *12 Storeys,* or 'Splacing' Singapore's Official and Unofficial Discourses?" *Asian Cinema* (fall/winter 2000): 99–131.

Lent, John. *The Asian Film Industry.* Austin: University of Texas Press, 1990.

Li, Cheuk-to. "The Return of the Father: Hong Kong New Wave and Its Chinese Context in the 1980s." In *New Chinese Cinemas: Forms, Identities, Politics,* edited by Nick Browne, Paul G. Pickowicz, Vivian Sobchack, and Esther Yau, 160–179. Cambridge: Cambridge University Press, 1994.

———. *"Fuqin di yinying: bashi niandai Xianggang xindianying di Zhongguo mailuo"* (The father's shadow: the China factor in Hong Kong cinema in the 1980s). In *The China Factor in Hong Kong Cinema,* edited by Hong Kong Urban Council, 77–85. Hong Kong: Hong Kong Urban Council, 1990.

———. "Postscript." In *A Study of Hong Kong Cinema in the Seventies,* edited by Hong Kong Urban Council, 127–131. Hong Kong: Hong Kong Urban Council, 1984.

Li, Dayi. *"Hou hsiao-hsien de dianying rensheng"* (Hou Hsiao-hsien's film life). *Film Appreciation* 17.3 (1999): 76–83.

———. "Hou Hsiao-hsien on Interview." In *Taiwan Film Festival 99: A Tribute to Hou Hsiao-hsien.* Hong Kong: Hong Kong Arts Centre, 1999.

Li, Haiyan. *"Huashuo Baimaonü—minzu xuzhizhongde jieji yu xingbie zhengzhi"* (On *The White-Haired Girl*: class and sexual politics in national narrative). *Ershiyi shiji* 52 (1999): 110–118.

Li, Suyuan. *"Guanyu Zhongguo zaoqi dianying lilun"* (About film theories in early China). *Dangdai dianying*, 61. 4 (1994): 21–34.

Li, Suyuan and Jubin Hu. *Zhongguo wusheng dianying shi* (Chinese silent film history). Zhongguo dianying chubanshe, 1996. [English edition: *Chinese Silent Film*. Translated by Wang Rui, Huang Wei, Hu Jubin, Wang Jingjing, Zhen Zhong, Shan Wanli, and Li Xun. Beijing: China Film Press, 1997.]

Li, Yiming. *"'Shiqi Nian' Shaoshu Minzu Ticai Dianying Zhong de wenhua Shidian yu Zhuti"* (The cultural perspective and themes of minority nationality films after the "Seventeen Years"). *Lun Zhongguo shaoshu minzu dianying* (A discussion of Chinese minority films), edited by Zhongguo dianying xiehui (Chinese Filmmakers Association). Beijing: Zhongguo dianying chubanshe, 1997.

Liang, Liang. *"Dan bushi weiyi de lu"* (Obscure is not the only way out). In *Dianying, dianying ren, dianying kanwu* (Film, film people and film magazines), edited by Li Youxin, 98–107. Taipei: Independent News, 1986.

Liao, Chaoyang. "Borrowed Modernity: History and the Subject in *A Borrowed Life.*" *boundary 2* 24.3 (1997): 225–245.

Liao, Ping-hui. "Rewriting Taiwanese National History: The February 28 Incident as Spectacle." *Public Culture* 5.2 (1993): 281–296.

Lii, Tin-zann. "A Colonized Empire: Reflections on the Expansion of Hong Kong Films in Asian Countries." In *Trajectories: Inter-Asia Cultural Studies*, edited by Kuan-Hsing Chen, 122–141. London: Routledge, 1998.

Lin, Nien-tung. "Foreword, Some Notes on the Post-war Hong Kong Cinema Survey 1946–1968." *Hong Kong Cinema Survey (1946–1968)*. Hong Kong: Urban Council, 1979.

———. "Some Problems in the Study of Cantonese Films of the 1950s." In *Cantonese Cinema Retrospective (1950–1959) (Wushi niandai, Yueyu dianying huiguzhan)*, 11–16 Second International Film Festival of Hong Kong. Hong Kong: Provisional Urban Council, 1978.

Lin, Wenchi. *"Houxiandai di fengge, houjimin di Xianggang"* (Postmodern style, post-colonial Hong Kong). In *Rentong, chayi, zhutixing: cong nüxingzhuyi dao houzhimin wenhua xiangxiang* (Identity, difference and subjectivity: from feminism to postcolonial cultural imagination), edited by Jian Yingying, 175–216. Taipei: Lixu, 1997.

Lin, Wenchi, Shiao-ying Shen, and Chenya Li, eds. *Xi lian rensheng: hou hsiao-hsien dianying yenjiu* (Passionate detachment: films of Hou Hsiao-hsien). Taipei: Rye Field Publishing, 2000.

Lin, Yilin. *"Yang Huishan xingkong mihang"* (Yang Hui-shan, lost amongst the stars). *United Daily* 23 (October 1986): 9.

Lin, Xiaoping. "New Chinese Cinema of the 'Sixth Generation': A Distant Cry of Forsaken Children." *Third Text* 60.16.3 (September 2002): 261–284.

Ling , L. H. M. "Sex Machine: Global Hypermasculinity and Images of the Asian Woman in Modernity." *positions* 7:2 (1999): 227–306.

Liu, Kang. "Is There an Alternative to (Capitalist) Globalization? The Debate about Modernity in China." *boundary 2* 23 (fall 1996): 193–218.

Liu, Senyao. *"Cong fengkuei lei de ren kan dianying te xieshi zhuyi"* (On film's realism: Boys from Fengkuei). In *Gangtai liu da daoyen* (Six directors from Hong Kong and Taiwan), edited by Li Youxin, 128–134. Taipei: Independent News, 1986.

Liu, Yichang. "Intersection." Translated by Nancy Li. *Renditions* 29–30 (spring/autumn 1988): 84–101.

————. *Duidao*. Edited by Wang Dong Tao. Hong Kong: Holdery Publishing, 2000.

Lo, Kwai-cheung: "Muscles and Subjectivity: A Short History of the Masculine Body in Hong Kong Popular Culture." *Camera Obscura* 39 (September 1996): 105–125.

Loh, Wai-fong. "From Romantic Love to Class Struggle: Reflections on the Film *Liu Sanjie*." In *Popular Chinese Literature and Performing Arts in People's Republic of China, 1949–1979*, edited by Bonnie McDougall, 165–176. Berkeley: University of California Press, 1984.

Lopate, Phillip. "A Master Everywhere Else Is Ready to Try America." *New York Times* (October 10, 1999): 2: 13.

Lu, Hongshi. *"Ren Qingtai yu shoupi guochanpian kaoping"* (Evaluations of Ren Qingtai and first Chinese films). *Dianying yishu* 2 (1992): 82–86.

Lu, Shaoyang. "A Similar Color, a Different Temperature." *Xinwen zhoukan* (News week) (June 18, 2001)

Lu, Sheldon H. "Zhang Yimou." In *Fifty Contemporary Filmmakers*, edited by Yvonne Tasker, 412–418. London: Routledge, 2002.

————. *China, Transnational Visuality, Global Postmodernity*. Stanford, Calif.: Stanford University Press, 2001.

————. "Filming Diaspora and Identity: Hong Kong and 1997." In *The Cinema of Hong Kong: History, Arts, Identity*, edited by Poshek Fu and David Deeser, 273–288. Cambridge: Cambridge University Press, 2000.

————. "Representing the Chinese Nation-State in Filmic Discourse." In *East of West: Cross-Cultural Performance and the Staging of Difference*, edited by Claire Sponsler and Xiaomei Chen, 111–123. New York: Palgrave, 2000.

————. "Soap Opera in China: The Transnational Politics of Visuality, Sexuality, Masculinity." *Cinema Journal* 40.1 (fall 2000): 25–47.

————. "Historical Introduction: Chinese Cinemas (1896–1996) and Transnational Film Studies." In *Transnational Chinese Cinemas: Identity, Nationhood, Gender*, edited by Sheldon H. Lu, 1–31. Honolulu: University of Hawai`i Press, 1997.

————. "National Cinema, Cultural Critique, Transnational Capital: The Films of Zhang Yimou." In *Transnational Chinese Cinemas: Identity, Nationhood, Gender*, edited by Sheldon H. Lu, 105–136. Honolulu: University of Hawai`i Press, 1997.

————. "Postmodernity, Popular Culture, and the Intellectual: A Report on Post-Tiananmen China." *boundary 2* 23.2 (summer 1996): 139–169.

Lu, Sheldon H., ed. *Transnational Chinese Cinemas: Identity, Nationhood, Gender*. Honolulu: University of Hawai`i Press, 1997.

Lu, Xun (Lu Hsun). *"Mingzi"* (Names). *Lu Xun quanji* (Collected works of Lu Xun). Vol. 8: 99–100. Beijing: Renmin wenxue chubanshe, 1982.

———. *A Brief History of Chinese Fiction*. Translated by Yang Hsien-I and Gladys Yang. Peking: Foreign Languages Press, 1976.

Luo, Jingsong. *"Beijing penghui sizuo jiangbei: jiuba niandu dianying huabiao jiang jiexiao"* (Beijing brings home four awards: the results of the 1998 Obelisk Film Awards). *Beijing qingnian bao* (Beijing youth daily) (May 22, 1999), 7.

———. *"Zhang Yimou: wo bu shi jinzi zhaopai"* (Zhang Yimou: I am not a goldmine). *Beijing qingnian bao (Beijing qingnian daily)* (May 17, 1999), 7.

Luo, Yijun. *"Dianyingde minzu fengge chutan"* (A Preliminary Discussion of National Style in Film). *Zhongguo dianying lilun wenxuan, 20–80 niandai* (An anthology of Chinese film theory). Vol. 2. Edited by Li Pusheng, Xu Hong, and Luo Yijun. Beijing: Wenhua yishu chubanshe. [Originally published in *Dianying yishu*, 11 (1981).]

Luo, Zhixi. *Kexue yu xuanxue* (Science and metaphysics). Shanghai: Commercial Press, 1927.

Lyman, Rick. "Crouching Memory, Hidden Heart: Watching Movies with Ang Lee." *New York Times* (March 9, 2001).

Mackerras, Colin. *Peking Opera*. Hong Kong: Oxford University Press, 1997.

———. *Chinese Drama, A Historical Survey*. Beijing: New World Press, 1990.

———. *The Chinese Theatre in Modern Times, from 1840 to the Present Day*. London: Thames and Hudson, 1975.

———. *The Rise of Peking Opera, 1770–1870*. Oxford: Clarendon Press, 1972.

Mao, Tse-tung (Mao Zedong). "Yenan Forum on Literature and Art." In *Selected Works of Mao Tse-tung*. Vol. 3. Peking: Foreign Languages Press, 1975.

Marchetti, Gina. "The Gender of GenerAsian X in Clara Law's Migration Trilogy." In *Ladies and Gentlemen, Boys and Girls: Gender in Film at the End of the Twentieth Century*, edited by Murray Pomerance, 71–87. Albany: SUNY Press, 2001.

———. "Buying America, Consuming Hong Kong: Cultural Commerce, Fantasies of Identity, and the Cinema." In *The Cinema of Hong Kong*, edited by Poshek Fu and David Desser, 289–313. New York. Cambridge University Press, 2000.

———. "Introduction: Plural and Transnational." A special section on "Chinese and Chinese Diaspora Cinema." *Jump Cut* 42 (1998): 68–72.

———. "Transnational Cinema, Hybrid Identities and the Films of Evans Chan." *Postmodern Culture: An Electronic Journal of Interdisciplinary Criticism* 8.2 (January 1998) [a special issue on film, http:// muse.jhu.edu/journals/pmc/voo8/8.2marchetti.html].

———. *Romance and the "Yellow Peril": Race, Sex, and Discursive Strategies in Hollywood Fiction*. Berkeley: University of California Press, 1993.

———. "*Two Stage Sisters*: The Blossoming of a Revolutionary Aesthetic." *Jump Cut* 34 (1989) [revised version reprinted in *Transnational Chinese Cinemas: Identity, Nationhood, Gender*, edited by Sheldon H. Lu, 59–80. Honolulu: University of Hawai`i Press, 1997].

Marx, Karl, and Frederick Engels. *Economic and Philosophic Manuscripts of 1844 and the Communist Manifesto*. New York: Prometheus Books, 1988.

Mauss, Marcel. "Techniques of the Body." *Economy and Society* 2.1 (February 1973): 73–75.

Mayne, Judith. *Cinema and Spectatorship*. London: Routledge, 1993.

McClintock, Anne. "The Angel of Progress: Pitfalls of the Term 'Post-colonialism.'" *Social Text* 31/32 (spring 1992): 84–98 [reprinted in *Colonial Discourse and Post-colonial Theory: A Reader*, eds. Patrick Williams, and Lauren Chrisman, 291–304. New York: Columbia University Press, 1994].

McDougal, Stuart. *Made into Movies: From Literature to Film*. New York: Holt, Rinhart and Winston, 1985.

Meisner, Maurice. *Mao's China and After: A History of the People's Republic*. New York: Free Press, 1999.

Metz, Christian. *Language and Cinema*. Translated by Donna Jean. The Hague: Mouton, 1974.

Mignolo, Walter. "Globalization, Civilization Processes, and the Relocation of Languages and Cultures." In *The Cultures of Globalization*, edited by Frederic Jameson and Masao Miyoshi, 32–53. Durham, N.C.: Duke University Press, 1998.

Mitchell, W. J. T. "Geopoetics: Space, Place and Landscape," *Critical Inquiry* 26.2 (winter 2000): 173–174.

Mongia, Padmini, ed. *Contemporary Postcolonial Theory: A Reader*. London: Edward Arnold, 1996.

Morris-Suzuki, Tessa. "The Frontiers of Japanese Identity." In *Asian Forms of the Nation*, edited by Stein Tonnesson and Hans Antlov, 41–66. Surrey: Curzon, 1996.

Mulvey, Laura. "Visual Pleasure and Narrative Cinema." *Screen* 16.3 (autumn 1975): 6–18.

Musser, Charles. "The Nickelodeon Era Begins: Establishing the Framework for Hollywood's Mode of Representation." In *Early Cinema*, edited by Thomas Elsaesser, with Adam Barker, 256–273. London: British Film Institute, 1990.

Naficy, Hamid. *An Accented Cinema: Exilic and Diasporic Filmmaking*. Princeton, N.J.: Princeton University Press, 2001.

Nanfang zhoumo. "*Zhongkou pingshuo Yige dou bu neng shao*" (Different perspectives on *Not One Less*). *Nanfang zhoumo* (Southern weekend) (May 21, 1999): 9.

Ng, Ho (Wu Hao). "The Legend and Films of Huang Fei-hong." *Cantonese Cinema Retrospective (1950–1959) (Wushi niandai, Yueyu dianying huiguzhan)*. Second International Film Festival of Hong Kong. Hong Kong: Hong Kong Provisional Urban Council, 1978.

Ngugi wa Thiong'o. *Decolonizing the Mind: The Politics of Language in African Literature*. London: James Currey, 1986.

Noh, Eliza. "'Amazing Grace, Come Sit on My Face,' or Christian Ecumenical Representations of the Asian Sex Tour Industry." *positions* 5:2 (1997): 439–465.

Ong, Aihwa. *Flexible Citizenship: The Cultural Logics of Transnationality*. Durham, N.C.: Duke University Press, 1999.

Ong, Aihwa, and Donald M. Nonini. "Toward a Cultural Politics of Diaspora and Transnationalism." In *Ungrounded Empires: The Cultural Politics of Modern Chinese Transnationalism*, edited by Aihwa Ong and Donald M. Nonini, 323–332. New York: Routledge, 1997.

Ono, K. "*Tai-wan eiga no: hou hsiao-hsien*" (Taiwan cinema's steersman: Hou Hsiao-hsien). *Cho* 347 (June 1990): 358–367.

Owens, Craig. "The Allegorical Impulse: Toward a Theory of Postmodernism." *October* 12 (1980): 67–86 and *October* 13 (1980): 59–80.

Pan, Lynn. *Sons of the Yellow Emperor: A History of the Chinese Diaspora*. New York: Kodansha International, 1990.

Peng, Li. "Hong pingguo *you di'er suan*" (*Red Apple* tastes a little sour). *Beijing ribao* (Beijing daily), May 17, 1999, 8.

———. "*Wuyue dianying: da luo zhilou neng fou da qi*" (Film in May: great rise after great decline?). *Beijing ribao*, May 17, 1999, p. 8.

Peranson, Mark. "Interview: Cities and Loneliness, Tsai, Ming-liang's 'What Time Is It There?'" *IndiWire*, January 22, 2002 [www.indiewire.com/people/int_Tsai_Mingliang_020122.html].

Phelan, Peggy. *Unmarked: The Politics of Performance*. London: Routledge, 1993.

Picard, Michel, and Robert Everett Wood, eds. *Tourism, Ethnicity and the State in Asian and Pacific Societies*. Honolulu: University of Hawai`i Press, 1997.

Pickowicz, Paul G. "Velvet Prisons and the Political Economy of Chinese Filmmaking." In *Urban Spaces in Contemporary China*, edited by Deborah S. Davis, Richard Kraus, Barry Naughton, and Elizabeth J. Perry, 193–220. Cambridge: Cambridge University Press and Washington, D.C.: Woodrow Wilson Center Press, 1995.

———. *Marxist Literary Thought in China: The Influence of Chú Ch'iu-pai*. Berkeley: University of California Press, 1981.

Po, Sharp. Review of *Ordinary Heroes*. Web page of Hong Kong Film Critics Society, 2000 [http://filmcritics.org.hk/ordinaryheroes/review.html].

Polan, Dana. "Globalism's Localisms." In *Global/Local: Cultural Production and the Transnational Imaginary*, edited by Wimal Dissanayake and Rob Wilson, 255–283. Durham, N.C.: Duke University Press, 1996.

Prakash, Gyan. *The Colonizer and the Colonized*. Boston: Beacon Press, 1967.

Prakash, Gyan, ed. *After Colonialism: Imperial Histories and Post-Colonial Displacements*. Princeton, N.J.: Princeton University Press, 1995.

Prasenjit, Duara. "Knowledge and Power in the Discourse of Modernity: The Campaign against Popular Religion in Early Twentieth-Century China." *Journal of Asian Studies* 50.1 (February 1991): 67–83.

Pu, Feng, and Zhaoxing Li, eds. *Jingdian liangbai: zunjia huayu dianying liangbaibu* (Two hundred classics: two hundred best Chinese-language films). Hong Kong: Hong Kong Film Critics Society, 2002.

Qi, Longren. "*Jiuling niandai taiwan dianying wenhua lunshu: yi beiqing chengshi wei li*" (Discourses of studies in Taiwan film culture of the 90s: using *City of Sadness* as an example). In *1999 Wenhua yenjiu de hueigu yu zhanwang yentaohuei lunwen ji* (1999 annual conference proceedings: the practices of cultural studies in Taiwan: retrospects and prospects), 274–282. Taipei: Association of Cultural Studies, 1999.

———. "*Tongnian wangshi*: liangzhong yuedu fangshi" (*A Time to Live and a Time to Die*: two ways of reading). In *Dianying chensi ji* (A collection of contemplations on cinema), 89–94. Taipei: Yuanshen Press, 1987.

Qian, Zhijian. "Performing Bodies: Zhang Huan, Ma Liuming, and Performance Art in China." *Art Journal* 58.2 (summer 1999): 60–81.

Qu, Qiubai. *Qu Qiubai wenji* (Selected literary works of Qu Qiubai). Vol. 2. Beijing: Renmin wenxue chubanshe, 1953–1954.

Raban, Jonathan. *Passage to Juneau: A Sea and Its Meanings.* New York: Pantheon, 1999.

Ralske, Josh. Plot synopsis of *Unknown Pleasures. All Movie Guide* [www.allmovie.com].

Rapfogel, Jared. "Tsai Ming-liang: Cinematic Painter." *Senses of Cinema* 20 (May–June 2002) [www.sensesofcinema.com/contents/02/20/tsai_painter.html].

Rayns, Tony. "In the Mood for Edinburgh," *Sight and Sound* 10.8 (August 2000): 14–17.

———. "Charisma Express." *Sight and Sound* 10.1 (January 2000): 34–36.

———. "Provoking Desire." *Sight and Sound* 6.7 (July 1996): 26–29.

——— "Bruce Lee and Other Stories." In *A Study of Hong Kong Cinema in the Seventies*, 26–29. The Eighth Hong Kong International Film Festival Catalogue. Hong Kong: Urban Council, 1984.

Review of *HeLiu* (*River*). The EFC Review. November 14, 2001 [www.efilmcritic.com].

Reid, Craig. "Kelly Hu: 'Martial Law' Mistress." *Femme Fatales* 7.15 (May 7, 1999): 8–17.

Reynaud, Berenice. "New Visions/New Chinas: Video-Art, Documentation, and the Chinese Modernity in Question." *Resolutions: Contemporary Video Practices*, edited by Michael Renov and Erika Suderburg, 229–257. Minneapolis: University of Minnesota Press, 1996.

Robertson, Roland. "Glocalization: Time-Space and Homogeneity-Heterogeneity." In *Global Modernities*, edited by Mike Featherstone, Scott Lash and Roland Robertson, 25–44. London: Sage, 1995.

Rothman, William. "New Life for an Old Genre: Ang Lee's *Crouching Tiger, Hidden Dragon.*" *Persimmon* 2.3 (winter 2002): 80–83.

Said, Edward. "Invention, Memory, and Place." *Critical Inquiry* 26 (winter 2000): 175–192.

———. "Secular Interpretation, the Geographical Element, and the Methodology of Imperialism." In *After Colonialism: Imperial Histories and Post-Colonial Displacements*, edited by Gyan Prakash, 21–39. Princeton, N.J.: Princeton University Press, 1995.

———. *Culture and Imperialism.* New York: Knopf: Random House, 1993.

"The Sandwich Man." *Monthly Film Bulletin* 653 (June 1988): 164.

Schamus, James. "To the Rear of the Back End: The Economics of Independent Cinema." In *Contemporary Hollywood Cinema*, edited by Steve Neale and Murray Smith, 91–105. London: Routledge, 1998.

Sek Kei. "The War Between the Cantonese and the Mandarin Cinemas in the Sixties; or, How the Beautiful Women Lost to the Action Men." In *The Restless Breed: Cantonese Stars of the Sixties.* Twentieth Hong Kong International Film Festival Catalogue. Hong Kong: Urban Council, 1996.

———. "Thoughts on Chinese Opera and the Cantonese Opera Film." *Yueyu xiqupian huigu* (Cantonese opera film retrospective). Eleventh International Film Festival of Hong Kong. Hong Kong: Urban Council, 1987.

———. "Li Hanxiang." *Hong Kong Cinema Survey (1946–1968).* Third Hong Kong International Film Festival Catalogue. Hong Kong: Provisional Urban Council, 1979.

Shao, Zhou. *"Sun Yu yu dianying Wu Xun Zhuan"* (Sun Yu and the film *The Life of Wu Xun*). Dianying yishu 215.6 (1990): 91–101.

Schumann, Howard. "Waves of Longing" [www.cinescene.com].

Sesser, Stan. *The Lands of Charm and Cruelty: Travels in Southeast Asia.* New York: Vintage, 1994.

Shen, Shiao-Ying. *"Benlai jiu yinggai duokan liangbian: dianying meixue yu hou hsiao-hsien"* (Can't they be vegetables? Film aesthetics and Hou Hsiao-hsien). *Chung-wai Literary Monthly* 26.10 (1998): 27–47.

———. "The Body vs. the Pen: Permutation of the Female Body in the Chang-Yang Trilogy." *Chung-Wai Literary Monthly* 302 (1997): 98–114.

———. *Permutations of the Foreigner: A Study of the Works of Edward Yang, Stan Lai, Chang Yi, and Hou Hsiao-Hsien.* Ann Arbor, Mich.: UMI, 1995.

Shen, Yanbing. *"Fengjiande xiaoshimin wenyi"* (The feudal arts of the petty urban dwellers). In *Yuanyang hudie pai yanjiu ziliao* (Research material on the Mandarin Ducks and Butterflies literature). Vol. 1. Edited by Wei Shaochang, 47–52. Shanghai: Wenyi chubanshe, 1984.

Sheridan, Greg. *Tigers: Leaders of the New Asia-Pacific.* St. Leonards, Australia: Allen and Unwin, 1997.

Shi, Xiangsheng. *Yige dou bu neng shao* (Not one less). Beijing: Zhongguo dianying chubanshe, 1999.

Shi, Hong. *"Diyici langchao: Mopianqi Zhongguo shangye dianying xianxiang shuping"* (The first tide of movies: on the phenomenon of Chinese commercial movies in the period of silent film). *Dangdai dianying* 65.2 (1995): 5–12.

Shih, Shu-mei. "Gender and a Geopolitics of Desire: The Seduction of Mainland Women in Taiwan and Hong Kong Media." In *Spaces of Their Own: Women's Public Sphere in Transnational China,* edited by Mayfair Mei-Hui Yang, 278–307. Minneapolis: University of Minnesota Press, 1999.

Shijie Ribao. *"Wei Minzhi, Zhang Huike, Shanghai gua zhenfeng"* (Wei Minzhi and Zhang Huike's whirlwind tour of Shanghai). *Shijie ribao.* July 5, 1999: C6.

Shin, Thomas, and Keeto Lam. "Fruit Chan: Life and Death in Global Cesspool" (Interview with Fruit Chan). In *Hong Kong Panorama 2002–2003.* Hong Kong: Leisure and Cultural Services Department, 2003.

Silbergeld, Jerome. *China Into Film: Frames of Reference in Contemporary Chinese Cinema.* London: Reaktion Books, 1999.

Smith, Murray. "Theses on the Philosophy of Hollywood History." In *Contemporary Hollywood Cinema,* edited by Steve Neale and Murray Smith, 3–20. London: Routledge, 1998.

Snow, Lois Wheeler. *China on Stage: An American Actress in the People's Republic.* New York: Random House, 1972.

Solinger, Dorothy. "China's Floating Population." In *The Paradox of China's Post-Mao Reforms,* edited by Merle Goldman and Roderick MacFarquhar, 220–240. Cambridge, Mass.: Harvard University Press, 1999.

Stacey, Jackie. *Star Gazing: Hollywood Cinema and Female Spectatorship.* London: Routledge, 1994.

Stam, Robert, Robert Burgoyne, and Sandy Fliterman-Lewis. *New Vocabularies in Film Semiotics.* London: Routledge, 1992.

Stokes, Lisa Odham, and Michael Hoover. *City on Fire: Hong Kong Cinema.* London: Verso, 1999.

Sunshine, Linda, ed. *Crouching Tiger, Hidden Dragon: A Portrait of the Ang Lee Film.* New York: New Market Press, 2000.

Sun, Shiyi. *"Dianyingjie de guju fengkuangzheng"* (The craze for the old drama in the film world). In *Zhongguo wusheng dianying,* 643–645. Beijing: Zhongguo dianying chubanshe, 1926.

Tan, See Kam, Michael Lee, and Annette Aw. "Contemporary Singapore Filmmaking: History, Policies, and Eric Khoo." *Jump Cut* 46 (summer 2003) [www.ejumpcut .org/currentissue/12Storeys/index.html].

Tan, Yew Soon, and Soh Yew Peng. *The Development of Singapore's Modern Media Industry.* Singapore: Times Academic Press, 1994.

Tanaka, Stefan. *Japan's Orient: Rendering Pasts into History.* Berkeley: University of California Press, 1993.

Taubin, Amy. "In the Mood for Love." *Sight and Sound* 10.11 (November 2000): 55–56.

Teo, Stephen. "We Kicked Jackie Chan's Ass! An Interview with James Schamus." *Senses of Cinema* (spring 2001) [www.sensesofcinema.com/contents/01/13/schamus.html].
———. "Only the Valiant: King Hu and His *Cinema Opera.*" In *Transcending the Times: King Hu and Eileen Chang.* Twenty-Second Hong Kong International Film Festival Catalogue. Hong Kong: Provisional Urban Council, 1998.
———. *Hong Kong Cinema: The Extra Dimensions.* London: British Film Institute, 1997.

Thomas, Nicholas. *Colonialism's Culture: Anthropology, Travel and Government.* Cambridge: Polity Press, 1994.

Thompson, Kristin. "The Formulation of the Classical Style, 1909–1928." In *Classical Hollywood Cinema,* David Bordwell, Janet Staiger, and Kristin Thompson, 155–240. New York: Columbia University Press, 1985.

Tin, Long. "Reviewing *Ordinary Heroes.*" Web page of Hong Kong Film Critics Society, 2000 [http://filmcritics.org.hk/ordinaryheroes/review.html].

Todorov, Tzvetan. *The Fantastic: A Structural Approach to a Literary Genre.* Translated by Richard Howard. Cleveland: Press of Case Western Reserve University, 1973.

Tolentino, Roland B. "Bodies, Letters, Catalogs: Filipinas in Transnational Space." *Social Text* (fall 1996): 49–76.

Tomlinson, John. *Globalization and Culture.* Cambridge: Polity Press, 1999.

Truong, Thanh-Dam. *Sex, Money, and Morality: Prostitution and Tourism in Southeast Asia.* London: Zed Books, 1990.

Tsurumi, E. Patricia. *Japanese Colonial Education in Taiwan.* Cambridge, Mass.: Harvard University Press, 1977.

Turner, Matthew. "Hong Kong Sixties/Nineties: Dissolving the People." In *Hong Kong Sixties: Designing Identities,* edited by Matthew Turner and Irene Ngan, 13–19. Hong Kong: Hong Kong Art Center, 1994.

Udden, James. "Hou Hsiao-Hsien and the Poetics of History." *CinemaScope* 3 (spring 2000): 48–51.

Uhde, Jan, and Yvonne Ng Uhde. *Latent Images: Film in Singapore*. New York: Oxford University Press, 2000.

Ullmer, Gregory, L. "The Object of Post-Criticism." In *The Anti-Aesthetic: Essays on Postmodern Culture*, edited by Hal Foster, 83–110. Port Townsend, Wash.: Bay Press, 1993.

Venture, Elbert. *Platform* [film review] [www.allmovie.com].

Wakabayashi, Bob Tadashi, ed. *Modern Japanese Thought*. Cambridge: Cambridge University Press, 1998.

Wallerstein, Immanuel, and Etienne Balibar eds. *Race, Nation, Class: Ambiguous Identities*. London: Verso, 1991.

Wang, Chen-ho. *Rose, Rose, I Love You*. Translated by Howard Goldblatt. New York: Columbia University Press, 1998.

Wang, Gangshen. *Kexue lun ABC* (The ABC of science studies). Shanghai: Shanghai shuju, 1928.

Wang, Qing, and Xiaoguang Chen. *"Jingcheng yinmu taofa buyi: baixing chongwen kang Mei jingdian"* (Beijing's silver screen castigates the unrighteous: people re-watch the classics about Resisting America). *Beijing guangbo dianshi bao* (Beijing broadcast and TV journal). May 18, 1999, p. 1.

Wang, Yichuan. *Zhang Yimou shenhua de zhongjie* (The end of the myth of Zhang Yimou). Zhengzhou: Henan renmin chubanshe, 1998.

Wang, Zhaoguang. "The film censorship system of the Nationalist Party in the early 1930s." [The original source of this information is from NFCC, ed., *"Dianying jiancha gongzuo zong baogao"* (A general report on the work on film censorship), and Luo Gang, *"Zhongyang dianjianhui gongzuo gaikuang"* (An overview of the work of the NFCC), both in *Zhongguo dianying nianjian*, in China Education Film Association, ed., 1934.]

Wang, Zhaoguang. *"Sanshi niandai chuqi de Guomingdang dianying jiancha zhidu"* (The film censorship system of the Nationalist Party in the early 1930s), *Dianying yishu* (Film art) 3 (1997): 60–66.

Wee, C. J. W.-L. "Contending with Primordialism: The 'Modern' Construction of Postcolonial Singapore." *positions* 1: 3 (1993): 715–743.

Wei, Betty Peh-T'i. *Crucible of Modern China*. Hong Kong: Oxford University Press, 1987.

Williams, Alan, ed. *Film and Nationalism*. New Brunswick, N.J.: Rutgers University Press, 2002.

Williams, Tony. "Hong Kong Cinema, the Boat People, and To Liv(e)." *Asian Cinema* 11.1 (spring/summer 2000): 131–142.

———. "Under 'Western Eyes': The Personal Odyssey of Huang Fei-hong in *Once Upon a Time in China*." *Cinema Journal* 40.1 (fall 2000): 3–24.

———. "*Song of the Exile*: Border-Crossing Melodrama." *Jump Cut* 42 (1998): 94–100.

Williams, Patrick, and Laura Chrisman, eds. *Colonial Discourse and Post-Colonial Theory*. New York: Columbia University Press, 1994.

Wong, Audrey. "Considering the 'Singapore Film.'" *Arts* 7 (1997) [www.nus.edu.sg/NUSinfo/CFA/artsmag/arts7-4sfilm1.htm].

Wu, Guanping. "An Unusual Declaration in an Unusual Summer: Interview with Lu Xuechang." *Dianying yishu* (Film art) 4 (2000): 61–65.

Wu, Nianzhen (Wu Nien-chen). *Xunzhao taiping tianguo* (In search of a peaceful heavenly state). Taipei: Rye Field Publishing, 1996.

Wu, Nianzhen website [www.tvbs.com.tw/code/e-bank/wu/review.asp].

Wu, Nianzhen, and Tianwen Zhu. *Beiqing chengshi* (City of sadness). Taipei: Yuan-liou, 1989.

Wu, Zuguang, Zuolin Huang, and Shaowu Mei. *Peking Opera and Mei Lanfang*. Beijing: New World Press, 1981.

Xia, Qingjin. *"Jintui zhi jian de Zhang Yimou"* (Zhang Yimou caught in a dilemma). *Dianying shibao* (Film and TV times) (April 1999): 1.

Xiao Ye. *Yige yundong de kaishi* (The beginning of a movement). Taipei: Shibao chubangongsi, 1986.

Xiao, Zhiwei. "Anti-Imperialism and Film Censorship During the Nanjing Decade, 1927–1937." In *Transnational Chinese Cinemas: Identity, Nationhood, Gender,* edited by Sheldon H. Lu, 35–57. Honolulu: University of Hawai'i Press, 1997.

———. "Constructing a New National Culture: Film Censorship and Issues of Cantonese Dialect, Superstition, and Sex in the Nanjing Decade." In *Cinema and Urban Culture in Shanghai: 1922–1943,* edited by Yingjin Zhang. Stanford: Stanford University Press, 1999.

Xu, Ben. "*Farewell My Concubine* and its Nativist Critics." *Quarterly Review of Film and Video* 16.2 (1997): 155–170.

Yamasaki, Sachio. *Hou Hsiao-hsien.* Tokyo: Asahi Shimbun, 1993.

Yan, Tian. "The Fallen Idol—Zhang Che in Retrospect." In *A Study of Hong Kong Cinema in the Seventies,* edited by Hong Kong Urban Council, 44–46. Hong Kong: Hong Kong Urban Council, 1984.

Yao, Gengchen. *"Tan wuxia pian"* (On the martial arts film). *Zhongguo wusheng dianying.* Beijing: Zhongguo dianying chubanshe, 1927.

Yau, Esther. "Border Crossing: Mainland China's Presence in Hong Kong Cinema." In *New Chinese Cinemas: Forms, Identities, Politics,* edited by Nick Browne, Paul G. Pickowicz, Vivian Sobchack, and Esther Yau, 180–201. Cambridge: Cambridge University Press, 1994.

Yeh, Yueh-yu. *Phantom of the Music: Song Narration and Chinese-language Cinema* (in Chinese). Taipei: Yuan-liou, 2000.

———. "A Life of Its Own: Musical Discourses in Wong Kar-Wai's Films." *Post Script* 19:1 (fall 1999): 120–136.

———. "The Poetics of Hou Hsiao-hsien's Films: *Flowers of Shanghai.*" *Cinedossier: The 35th Golden Horse Awards-Winning Films,* 94–97. Taipei: Golden Horse Film Festival, 1999.

———. "Defining 'Chinese.'" *Jump Cut* 42 (1998): 73–76.

———. *"Nüren zhende wufa jinru lishi: zai du Beiqing chengshi"* (Why can't women enter the history: re-viewing *City of Sadness). Contemporary Monthly* 101 (September 1994): 64–85.

Yeh, Yueh-yu, Pak-tong Cheuk and Ho Ng, eds. *Sandi chuanqi: huayu dianying ershi nian* (Romance of three places: twenty years of Chinese-language cinemas). Taipei: Caituan faren guojia dianying ziliaoguan, 1999.

Yeh, Long Yen (Ye Longyan). *Chunhua menglu: zhengzong Taiyu dianying xingshuai lu* (A drifting life: history of the rise and fall of authentic Taiwanese-language cinema). Taipei: Bo Yang, 1999.

Yin, Hong. "Memorandum of Chinese Cinema in 1999." *Contemporary Cinema (dangdai dianying)* 1 (2000): 10–15.

———. *Jing xiang yuedu: jiushi niandai yingshi wenhua suixiang* (Reading the mirror and the image: thoughts on film and TV culture in the 90s). Shenzhen: Haitian chubanshe. 1998.

Young, Louise. *Japan's Total Empire: Manchuria and the Culture of Wartime Imperialism. Twentieth-Century Japan: The Emergence of a World Power,* Vol. 8. Berkeley: University of California Press, 1998.

Young, Robert J. C. *Introducing Postcolonial Theory.* Oxford: Blackwell, 1999.

———. *Colonial Desire: Hybridity in Theory, Culture and Race.* London: Routledge, 1995.

Yu, Cheng. "Anatomy of a Legend." In *A Study of Hong Kong Cinema in the Seventies,* edited by Lao Shing-hon, 23–25. Hong Kong: Urban Council, 1981.

Zeng, Guang. *"Zhang Yimou duzhong beiju zuopin"* (Zhang Yimou prefers tragic work). *Shijie ribao* (December 1999): C6.

Zhai, Jiannong. *Yangbanxi dianyingde xingshua: wenge dianying: 20 shiji teshude wenhua xianxiang* (Ups and downs of the films of "model Beijing opera": the films of the Cultural Revolution period: the special cultural phenomenon of the twentieth century. Part 1) *Dangdai dianying,* 65.2 (1995): 37–43.

Zhan, Hongzhi. *Xindianying de jiegou weiji* (The structural crisis of New Cinema). In *Taiwan xindianying* (Taiwan New Cinema), edited by Chiao Hsiung-ping, 89–96. Taibei: Shibao chuban gongsi, 1988.

Zhang, Changyan. *Taiwan Films.* Taipei: Variety, 1993.

Zhang, Gansheng. *Minguo tongsu xiaoshuo lungao* (Studies on popular fiction of the Republican period). Chongqin: Chongqin chubanshe, 1991.

Zhang, Geng. *"Huiyi Yan'an wenyi zuotanhui qianhou 'liuyi'de xiju huodong"* (Reminiscences of the drama movement in "Luyi" before and after the Yan'an Forum on Literature and Art). *Xijubao* 5 5 (1962): 11.

Zhang, Zhen. "Zhang Yuan." In *Fifty Contemporary Filmmakers,* edited by Yvonne Tasker, 418–429. London: Routledge, 2002.

———. "Teahouse, Shadowplay, Bricolage: *Laborer's Love* and the Question of Early Chinese Cinema." In *Cinema and Urban Culture in Shanghai, 1922–1943,* edited by Zhang Yingjin, 27–50. Stanford, Calif.: Stanford Univeristy Press, 1999.

———. "An Amorous History of the Silver Screen: Film Culture, Urban Modernity, and the Vernacular Experience in China, 1896–1937." Ph.D diss., University of Chicago, 1998.

———. "The 'Shanghai Factor' in Hong Kong Cinema: A Tale of Two Cities in Historical Perspectives." *Asian Cinema* 10.1 (fall 1998): 146–159.

Zhang, Yingjin. *Screening China.* Ann Arbor: University of Michigan Center for Chinese Studies, 2002.

Zhang, Yingjin, ed. *Cinema and Urban Culture in Shanghai, 1922–1943.* Stanford, Calif.: Stanford University Press, 1999.

Zhang, Yingjin, and Zhiwei Xiao. *Encyclopaedia of Chinese Film*. London: Routledge, 1999.

Zhao Wei Company web site [www.zhaowei.com/].

Zheng, Shusen (William Tay), ed. *Wenhua piping yu huayu dianying* (Cultural criticism and Chinese-language cinemas). Taipei: Maitian, 1995.

Zhong, Yunlan. *"Liang Zhang shuangying"* (The two Zhangs both win). *Shijie ribao*, September 17, 1999, C6.

Zhong, Dafeng, Zhen Zhang, and Yingjin Zhang. "From *Wenmingxi* (Civilized Play) to *Yingxi* (Shadowplay): The Foundations of Shanghai Film Industry in the 1920s." *Asian Cinema* 9.1 (fall 1997): 46–64.

Zhongguo dianying nianjian (Yearbook of Chinese cinema). Beijing: Zhongguo dianying chubanshe, 1996.

Zhongguo Dianying Ziliaoguan (Chinese Film Archives), ed. *Zhongguo wusheng dianying* (Chinese silent film). Beijing: Zhongguo dianying chubanshe, 1996.

Zhongguo dianying zongmulu (A comprehensive catalogue of Chinese films). Beijing: Zhongguo dianying ziliaoguan, 1960.

Zhongguo wusheng dianying shi (Chinese silent film history). Beijing: Zhongguo dianying chubanshe, 1996.

Zhou, Weizhi. *"Ping Baimaonü yingpian"* (On the film *The White-haired Girl*). In *Dangdai Zhongguo dianying pinglunxuan, shang* (Anthology of contemporary Chinese film criticism, vol. 1), edited by Wang Baishi and Wang Wenhe. Beijing: Zhongguo guangbo dianshe chubanshe, 1987.

Zhu, Tianwen (Chu Tien-wen). Introduction to the published script and production notes of *Good Men Good Women* (*Haonan haonü*) by Hou Hsiao-hsien. Taipei: Yuan-liou, 1995.

Zielinski, Siegfried. *Audiovisions, Cinema, and Television as Entr'actes in History*. Translated by Gloria Custance. Amsterdam: Amsterdam University Press, 1999.

Notes on Contributors

Chris Berry teaches film studies at the University of California, Berkeley. He is coauthor of *China On Screen: Cinema and the National* (forthcoming), editor of *Chinese Films in Focus: 25 New Takes* (British Film Institute), coeditor of *Island on the Edge: Taiwan New Cinema and After* (Hong Kong University Press), *Mobile Cultures: New Media and Queer Asia* (Duke University Press), and *The Filmmaker and the Prostitute: Dennis O'Rourke's "The Good Woman of Bangkok"* (Sydney: Power Institute Press), translator of Ni Zhen's *Memoirs from the Beijing Film Academy: The Origins of China's Fifth Generation Filmmakers* (Duke University Press), and cotranslator of Ding Xiaoqi's *Maidenhome* (San Francisco: Aunt Lute).

David Bordwell is Jacques Ledoux Professor of Film Studies and Hilldale Professor of Humanities at the University of Wisconsin–Madison. His most recent books are *On the History of Film Style* and *Planet Hong Kong: Popular Cinema and the Art of Entertainment*. *Figures Traced in Light: On Cinematic Staging*, which contains a chapter on Hou Hsiao-hsien, will be published in 2004 by the University of California Press.

Chu Yiu Wai is associate professor of Chinese and humanities at Hong Kong Baptist University. His most recent publications include *In the Name of Law: Postcolonial Hong Kong Legal Culture*, *Hong Kong Literature @ Cultural Studies*, and *The Local Myth: Discursive Production in the Age of Globalization* (all in Chinese). He is coeditor of a reader in Hong Kong cinema entitled *Between Home and World* (Oxford University Press).

Cui Shuqin is associate professor of Asian studies at Bowdoin College. She is the author of *Women Through the Lens: Gender and Nation in a Century of Chinese Cinema*. She is currently working on her next book, which has the working title *Body and Text: Women and Writing in Modern China*.

Darrell W. Davis teaches film history and Asian cinema at the University of New South Wales, Sydney. He is the author of *Picturing Japaneseness: Monumental Style, National Identity, Japanese Film* (Columbia University Press) and coauthor of *Taiwan Film Directors: A Treasure Island* (Columbia University Press, 2005).

David Desser is professor of cinema studies and comparative literature at the University of Illinois. He is the author or editor of numerous books on Asian cinema, including *Ozu's*

Tokyo Story and *The Cinema of Hong Kong: History, Arts, Identity*. Most recently, he spent three semesters as a visiting scholar at Hong Kong Baptist University.

Mary Farquhar is director of the Asia Pacific Research Institute at Griffith University in Australia. She specializes in China studies. Her publications include *Children's Literature in China: From Lu Xun to Mao Zedong* (M. E. Sharpe), which won the annual International Children's Literature Association Award for the "most distinguished, scholarly book" published in the field in 1999. She is presently completing a book on Chinese cinemas with Chris Berry. She is also a qualified lawyer and publishes on law and media.

Xiaoping Lin received his Ph.D. in art history from Yale University and is associate professor of Asian art and cinema in the Department of Art at Queens College, City University of New York.

Sheldon H. Lu is professor of comparative literature and founding codirector of film studies (2002–2004) at the University of California, Davis. He is author of *From Historicity to Fictionality: The Chinese Poetics of Narrative* (Stanford University Press, 1994; Korean edition, 2001); *China, Transnational Visuality, Global Postmodernity* (Stanford University Press); *Culture, Mirror-Image, Poetics* (in Chinese; Tianjin People's Press); and editor of *Transnational Chinese Cinemas: Identity, Nationhood, Gender* (University of Hawai`i Press). His critical essays have appeared in numerous journals and anthologies.

Thomas Y. T. Luk is a professor in the Department of Modern Languages and Intercultural Studies, the Chinese University of Hong Kong, specializing in film and literature, comparative drama, theater studies and adaptations, Romanticism and cultural studies, and so on. He is the writer and editor of *Before and after Suzie: Hong Kong in Western Film and Literature*, with James P. Rice.

Gina Marchetti is an associate professor in the Department of Cinema and Photography at Ithaca College. In 1995, her book *Romance and the "Yellow Peril": Race, Sex and Discursive Strategies in Hollywood Fiction* was named best book in the area of cultural studies by the Association of Asian American Studies. She has published essays in several anthologies, including *Classic Hollywood, Classic Whiteness; Keyframes: Popular Cinema and Cultural Studies; At Full Speed: Hong Kong Cinema in a Borderless World; Ladies and Gentlemen, Boys and Girls: Gender in Film at the End of the Twentieth Century; Out of the Shadows: Asians in American Cinema; Countervisions: Asian American Film Criticism; The Cinema of Hong Kong: History, Arts, Identity; Transnational Chinese Cinemas: Identity, Nationhood, Gender; The Birth of Whiteness: Race and the Emergence of United States Cinema; Unspeakable Images: Ethnicity and the American Cinema*, and other collections. She has published articles in *Journal of Film and Video, Genders, Journal of Communication Inquiry, positions: east asia cultures critique, Postmodern Culture, Post Script*, and others, as well as *Jump Cut* (where she serves on the editorial board). She is also a member of the editorial board of *Popular Communication*. Her current book, *From Tian'anmen to Times Square: China on Global Screens*, will be published by Temple University Press. She is also coeditor, with Peter X. Feng and Tan See-Kam, of *Chinese Connections: Critical Perspectives on Film, Identity and Diaspora* (Temple University Press, forthcoming).

Jing Nie received her master's degree in film studies from the School of Film at Ohio University. She is currently a doctoral student in the comparative literature program at the University of California, Davis.

Shiao-ying Shen is an associate professor in the Department of Foreign Languages and Literature at National Taiwan University. Her articles on Western and Chinese-language cinema have been published in *Chung-wai Literary Monthly* and *Film Appreciation*. She is also coeditor of *Passionate Detachment: Films of Hou Hsiao-hsien* (in Chinese) and is currently working on studies of works of a series of female filmmakers.

Meiling Wu is assistant professor of modern languages and literatures at California State University, Hayward. Her research interests include postmodern and postcolonial theories, twentieth-century Chinese literature and film, Sino-Asian/American literature, and women's study. She has the honor of being the recipient of the First Prize of *Taiwanese Central Daily News* short story award in 1995, and her creative works have been published ever since. She has given papers at conferences throughout the United States and in Asia and Europe. She is author of numerous articles and book projects, such as "Women, Herstory and Taiwanese Cinema" and "Other, Native, and/or Alter-Native: Nobel Writings of Chinese Women."

Emilie Yueh-yu Yeh is associate professor of film studies and associate director of David C. Lam Institute for East-West Studies at Hong Kong Baptist University. She is the author of *Phantom of the Music: Song Narration and Chinese-language Cinema* (in Chinese) and coauthor of *Taiwan Film Directors: A Treasure Island* (Columbia University Press, 2005).

Zhang Zhen teaches film studies at New York University. Her scholarly and creative writings have appeared in numerous journals and anthologies. She is currently completing a book manuscript on early Chinese film culture and also editing a volume, *The Urban Generation: Chinese Cinema and Society at the Turn of the Twenty-First Century*, to be published by Duke University Press.

Index

HAWAI

Production Notes for Lu and Yeh / CHINESE-LANGUAGE FILM

Cover and interior design by April Leidig-Higgins

Text in Minion with display type in Meta

Composition by Copperline Book Services, Inc.; bilingual composition
by ASCO Typesetters

Printing and binding by The Maple-Vail Book Manufacturing Group

Printed on 60# Sebago Eggshell, 420 ppi